THE FORMATION OF CANDOMBLÉ

A BOOK IN THE SERIES

Latin America in Translation/en Traducción/em Tradução

Sponsored by the Consortium in Latin American Studies at the
University of North Carolina at Chapel Hill and Duke University

THE FORMATION OF
CANDOMBLÉ

Vodun History and Ritual in Brazil

LUIS NICOLAU PARÉS

Translated by Richard Vernon in collaboration with the author

THE UNIVERSITY OF NORTH CAROLINA PRESS Chapel Hill

Translation of the books in the series Latin America in Translation / en Traducción / em Tradução, a collaboration between the Consortium in Latin American Studies at the University of North Carolina at Chapel Hill and Duke University and the university presses of the University of North Carolina and Duke, is supported by a grant from the Andrew W. Mellon Foundation.

Designed by and set in Arno Pro and Calluna Sans types by Rebecca Evans

Originally published in Portuguese as *A formação do Candomblé: História e ritual da nação jeje na Bahia* (Campinas: Editora da Unicamp, 2006), © 2006 Luis Nicolau Parés and 2006 by Editora da Unicamp.

The paper in this book meets the guidelines for permanence and durability of the Committee on Production Guidelines for Book Longevity of the Council on Library Resources. The University of North Carolina Press has been a member of the Green Press Initiative since 2003.

Library of Congress Cataloging-in-Publication Data
Parés, Luis Nicolau, author.
[Formação do Candomblé. English]
The formation of Candomblé : Vodun history and ritual in Brazil / Luis Nicolau Parés; translated by Richard Vernon in collaboration with the author.
pages cm.—(Latin America in translation / en traducción / em tradução)
Originally published in Portuguese in Campinas by Editora da Unicamp as A formação do Candomblé: História e ritual da nação jeje na Bahia, 2006.
Includes bibliographical references and index.
ISBN 978-0-8078-3311-7 (cloth : alk. paper)
ISBN 978-1-4696-1092-4 (pbk. : alk. paper)
ISBN 978-1-4696-1093-1 (ebook)
1. Candomblé (Religion)—Brazil—Bahia (State) 2. Blacks—Brazil—Bahia (State)—Ethnic identity. 3. Blacks—Brazil—Bahia (State)—History. 4. Blacks—Brazil—Bahia (State)—Religion. 5. Bahia (Brazil : State)—Religious life and customs.
I. Title. II. Series: Latin America in translation/en traducción/em tradução.
BL2592.C35P3713 2013   299.673098142—dc23   2013020448

IN MEMORIAM

VICENTE PAULO DOS SANTOS

CONTENTS

FIGURES, ILLUSTRATIONS, MAPS, AND TABLES

PREFACE

The result of more than seven years of research, this book aims to recover the historical memory of a group that is largely forgotten, both within Afro-Brazilian studies and among Candomblé practitioners. The prestige of the Jeje nation within Candomblé[1] is still recognized among religious experts, and scholars do refer occasionally to certain aspects of its ritual practice. However, no book to date has been dedicated to an in-depth and detailed study of this "root" of Afro-Brazilian culture.

This work also encompasses both the history and the anthropology of Afro-Brazilian religion. This interdisciplinary approach embraces, therefore, a number of diverse yet internally intertwined themes, including among others the construction of Jeje ethnicity in colonial Brazil, the contribution of the vodun* cults to the formative process of Candomblé, the microhistory of two Jeje terreiros,* and a selective ethnography of the vodun pantheon and ritual practice in contemporary Bahia.

Another significant aspect of this study is its complementary use of both oral and written sources, in combination with an analysis of ritual behavior. Although this is not an entirely new methodology, the interface between history and ethnography has been little used in Afro-Brazilian studies. The critical intersection of these varied sources proved to be quite fertile and opened interpretative paths that would have been impossible if I had worked with only one kind of source. This exercise was especially relevant in the reconstruction of the histories of the Bogum terreiro in Salvador and Seja Hundé in Cachoeira, in the Bahian Recôncavo,* both founded by Jeje Africans during the time of slavery.

The framework of this study's subject responds to linguistic criteria. One could say that the book deals with the historiography of two words: *Jeje* and *vodun*—the first having primarily an ethnic meaning and the second a religious one. These two words guided and determined the documentary research, as well as the selection of the two terreiros where the field research was conducted, given that these congregations define themselves as belonging to the "Jeje nation" and are distinguished from other nations through their worship of certain deities called voduns.

To define the African geographic area where the ethnic groups known in Brazil as Jeje originated (the topic of chapter 1), I also employed essentially linguistic criteria. Here I followed the suggestion of Hounkpati B. C. Capo and adopted the expression "Gbe-speaking area," or simply "Gbe area," to designate the southern region of present-day Togo, Republic of Benin, and southwest Nigeria, where live the peoples traditionally labeled as Adja, Ewe, Fon, or a combination of these terms such as Adja-Ewe. For all these groups, the word *gbe* means language, and, although it is not a term used for autochthonous self-identification, it has the advantage of not being an "ethnocentric" term that privileges the name of one subgroup to designate the whole.[2] It is precisely among these peoples sharing linguistic roots since ancient times that the term *vodun* is used to designate the deities or invisible forces of the spirit world.

The demarcation of a geographic area based on linguistic criteria results from a descriptive and analytic need, but it is important to point out that the Gbe-speaking area was always a multicultural and polyethnic society, in which the mercantile system, wars, and the slave trade contributed to populations' movements from one area to another, which in turn contributed to this diversity.[3] Cities such as Ouidah and Abomey were relatively cosmopolitan centers, in some ways comparable to the urban centers of colonial Brazil, where the same encounters of culturally diverse human groups occurred, again with economic motives connected to the slave trade. This structural similarity suggests that the collective identity dynamics of minority groups, as well as strategies of assimilation and resistance in relation to dominant groups, could have been reproduced in a similar manner both in Bahia and in the Gbe-speaking area.

Fredrik Barth speaks of an "encompassing social system" in reference to the social structure or the set of social relations shared by all members of a plural society (macrosocial consensus) and also of the borders between *ethnic groups* as the "maintenance of cultural diversity" (microsocial difference). He also insists on the importance of not confusing culture for ethnicity, as the latter is a dynamic developed from the valorization of just a few cultural elements—the diacritical signs that express difference.

The persistence of ethnic groups, however, requires a "systematic set of rules governing interethnic social encounters"; in other words, there must exist "a congruence of codes and values," which ultimately requires and creates a "similarity or community of culture."[4] Therefore, multiethnic social systems involve a relative cultural symbiosis, a basic consensus from which difference is articulated. As I will show, Candomblé is a clear example of this dynamic of progressive institutional homogenization, accompanied by a parallel dynamic of "ethnic" differentiation based on a discrete series of ritual elements.

One of the central goals of this work is to understand the genesis and maintenance of African ethnic identities in Brazil. To deal with this question I have

opted to use the "relational" theories of ethnicity proposed by Barth, as opposed to those characterized as "primordial" and maintained by authors such
as Max Weber or Clifford Geertz.[5] The "situational" theory put forth by Barth
sees ethnic identity as a relational, or dialogic, dynamic according to which
"the we is constructed in relation to them." Ethnic identity is not, therefore,
simply a conglomerate of fixed diacritical signs (origin, biological kinship, language, religion, etc.) but rather a historic and dynamic process in which the
signs are selected and (re)elaborated in a contrastive relation to the "other."[6] As
Maria Carneiro da Cunha suggests, "the original culture of an ethnic group, in
the diaspora or in situations of intense contact, is not lost or simply dissolved,
but acquires a new function, one that is essential to and adds to others, as it
becomes *a culture of contrast*."[7]

Abner Cohen, however, conceives of ethnic groups as interest groups that
manipulate elements of their "traditional" culture as a means of motivating
group unity in their quest for power.[8] Thus, chapter 2's analysis of the construction of a Jeje identity in Bahia during the eighteenth and nineteenth
centuries suggests that Africans developed "identity strategies" in which the
social actors, through assessing their situation, used their identity resources
in a strategic manner, generally for the purpose of achieving some objective.
For example, a slave or freed person could identify him- or herself, depending
on the context and the interlocutor, as Savalu, Jeje, Mina, or African, moving
from the most specific to the most general. The various categories of identity
functioned one overlapping the other, so to speak, or as Russian dolls—one
contained with another.

From this perspective, there is not a fixed and rigid identity but rather
many and intersecting *identification processes* generated by different contexts
and interlocutors. In these social interactions certain fluid and flexible diacritical signs are valued by virtue of their utility to a particular identification
and according to the preferences and interests of the moment. But this in-
strumentalization of identity has its limits in that identity is also the result of
an identification imposed from without by others, and groups or individuals
must consider these limits in formulating their strategy.[9] The "situational" nature of identification processes, together with the existence of a repertoire of
referential categories, allows one to postulate the notion of a *multidimensional
identity*. The Jeje case suggests that the plasticity and multiplicity of identity,
which is typically attributed to late modernity, was a phenomenon occurring
at least as early as the eighteenth century.

Furthermore, chapter 2 highlights the critical importance of the associative dynamics and the formation of social institutions, such as the Catholic

lay brotherhoods, work groups, and candomblés as spaces for sociability in which the contrastive identification processes of ethnic identity found fertile ground for expression. In fact, the domain of religious practices and values was one of the richest cultural spaces for the articulation of ethnic differences. Thus—intimately connected to the problem of ethnic identity of Africans in Brazil—chapters 3 and 4 deal with Candomblé's process of institutionalization and its contribution to the formation of an "Afro-Brazilian culture."

One of the central themes of comparative studies on Afro-American religion is the relative degree of either continuity or transformation undergone by African religious cultures in the New World. While authors such as Melville Herskovits or Roger Bastide give particular emphasis to the continuity of African cultural forms and to the "tenaciousness of tradition," more recently other authors have noted the "dramatic" transformations that occurred in the transfer process, concluding that the experience of the New World essentially diluted the African legacy. The dilemma is in knowing if black culture or, in the more specific situation dealt with here, Afro-Brazilian religion, should be understood as a retention or survival of Africanisms, or as a creative adaptation to the hardships of slavery and racism.

The first interpretative tendency values the concept of *cultural survival*, introduced by Herskovits to designate those elements of ancient culture preserved "intact" in the new "syncretic" culture and seeks to prove the continuity of culture at any price despite apparent modifications. This interpretation, also assumed by the "traditionalist" groups of Candomblé practitioners, has promoted the idea of the institution's ethnic and ritual "purity" and, legitimized by historic "myths," supports the concept of tradition as invariable repetition. In Afro-American studies this posture is typically aligned with an Afrocentric ideology.[10]

The second interpretative current views tradition as a stimulant for innovation and change; it highlights the hybridity, or creolization, of Afro-Brazilian religion and the need to study it, not in relation to its African origins but rather within the specificity of the Brazilian historic process and sociocultural context. This model criticizes the obsessive search for "Africanisms" or cultural survivals undertaken by researchers, which is seen in certain cases as a form of "exoticizing" religion. It is important to point out that this "creolist" view does not preclude continuity with Africa but emphasizes the cultural processes that, in the new colonial context, considerably modified certain ritual practices while maintaining others and seeking parallels among different religious traditions.[11]

Within this theoretical field, Sidney Mintz and Richard Price, influenced by American symbolic anthropology, suggest a new focus for studies on continuity and change. More than compare the forms and functions of religious elements, they call attention to the necessity of comparing the *meaning* of "Africanisms" and the persistence of certain cognitive orientations and worldviews; in essence, they suggest comparing not the structural aspects of African and diasporic cultural representations but what these representations mean, intend, and express.[12]

The problem of permanence and change, or of the interaction between structure and action, is a recurring theme in anthropological studies. With certain specificities, this problematic is also applicable to Afro-Brazilian religion. Throughout the history of Candomblé, one finds the persistence of certain values and practices together with the resignification or creation of others. There is, therefore, something that is permanent alongside something else that changes. I argue for the need to understand the simultaneity or synchronicity of continuity and discontinuity processes, as well as for the importance of understanding the proportion between these dynamics. The problem is a question of emphasis, and my own stress does not fall on "Africanisms" or "inventions" but on the complex interaction between the two.

Herskovits defines the notion of *reinterpretation* (or, in its updated version, *resignification*) as "the process by which old meanings are ascribed to new elements or by which new values change the cultural significance of old forms."[13] The interest of culturists in demonstrating the continuity of meanings (even with changes) led them to emphasize the first part of the definition. In contrast, those who defend the creolist position tend to highlight the second part of the definition, privileging the concept of agency, of the participants' active and transforming involvement. Marshall Sahlins speaks of the continuous "functional re-evaluation" of cultural categories and of how "culture is historically altered in action."[14]

Of course not all cultural legacies are continuous, and none are primordial. One might ask nonetheless whether Candomblé would be the same if the African groups imported to Brazil had been others. There is no way to answer this question with any certainty, but it is probable that without the contribution of certain groups from West Africa, it would have been very difficult for Candomblé to achieve the forms of conventual organization by which it is known today. In other words, the specificity of certain African religious traditions was as important as the slave system in determining the formation of this religious institution.

One of the main arguments of this book, developed in chapters 3 and 4, is that it was the religious traditions of the Mina Coast, and especially those from the Gbe-speaking area, that is, the vodun cults, that provided eighteenth-century Brazil with the first referents necessary for the organization of the religious group into an ecclesial or conventual structure. The devotional activity resulting from the devotees' consecration to deities through initiation processes, and the establishment of fixed shrines in stable sacred spaces, contrasted with the more individualized and itinerant therapeutic and oracular practices of the majority of colonial *calundus*.*

The chronological analysis of the documentation on the religious practices of Africans in eighteenth- and nineteenth-century Brazil reveals a gradual increase in complexity, at both the ritual and organizational levels. As I suggested, Jeje religious experts, with their experience and memory of the vodun cult traditions of the Gbe-speaking area, provided important referents for the institutionalization of Candomblé, particularly in regard to the organization of extradomestic congregations of an ecclesiastical nature.

This thesis is complemented by the argument, developed in chapter 7, that the juxtaposition of various deities in the same temple and the organization of serial forms of ritual performance, characteristics of contemporary Candomblé, has a clear antecedent in the vodun traditions of the Gbe-speaking area, since from at least the eighteenth century, principally in the royal cults or those of the socially dominant lineages in cities such as Ouidah and Abomey. Therefore, the establishment of multideity cults would not be, as studies have claimed,[15] merely a local "invention" resulting from the new sociocultural conditions found in Brazil, specifically in Bahia, but would take the vodun cults in Africa as its *organizational model*, being replicated by varied ethnic groups with their particular deities.

What I am emphasizing, then, are certain continuities, despite there being transformations, in the structural lines of the cults, and the importance of certain African religious traditions in this process. It should be clear, however, that I am not defending a single "primordial model" of Candomblé, nor do I wish to reduce its formation to a mere conglomeration of direct continuities. It is known, for instance, that the charisma of a religious leader can be critical in the legitimization of a new ritual behavior and in its subsequent replication by others. Thus the individual, as a transmitter of culture, becomes an agent for change, and for this reason historians of Candomblé must study the subjects who were its protagonists.

With this perspective in mind, chapters 5 and 6 endeavor to present a *longue durée* historical reconstitution, from the second half of the nineteenth century to contemporary times, of two Jeje-Mahi Candomblé congregations—Bogum and Seja Hundé. The main objectives were to organize, with the greatest possible rigor, the scarce documentary data and the multiple and contradictory oral testimonies regarding the history of these two Jeje communities. This is a provisional attempt that, undoubtedly, can be expanded and refined through future research. Based on this comparative analysis between written and oral sources, the effort to recover the historical memory of the Jeje people is in line with the New History trend of studying the cultural history of minority groups, subaltern groups, the excluded, and those "without history."

These chapters also supply interesting material for the study of the dynamic of cooperation, conflict, and complementarity among the Candomblé leadership. The articulation of networks of solidarity and strategic alliances combines with the struggle for power during times of succession, the rivalries between competing factions, accusations of witchcraft, and the decrees of the gods in settling conflicts. The micropolitics of Candomblé, and among the Jeje in particular, is extremely dynamic and complex. Using Victor Turner's concepts, one could say that conflict develops within "social dramas" (with the four phases of breach, crisis, redress, and reintegration or schism) and is resolved through ritual, itself understood as a regenerative and creative force.[16]

In chapter 7 and especially in chapter 8, my intention is to interpret the differential factor of Jeje religious identity within Candomblé, retaking some of the ideas already presented in relation to processes of ethnic identification. The principal aim is to identify what makes the Jeje nation different from others. This interest originates primarily from the fact that this is a common preoccupation among the Candomblé community and is expressed by its practitioners through a variety of forms. This differential factor can be conceived of as having two main simultaneous features: (1) certain specific elements from the Gbe-speaking area that, whether or not resignified, still persist; and (2) a relational contrastive process with competing groups (that is, Jeje versus Nagô). I have privileged the second feature, in which relations of contrast mark the boundaries between Candomblé nations, in the same way they do among ethnic groups. Religious identity is, then, relational and is expressed in the context of an institutionalized consensus.

Chapter 7 examines the Jeje pantheon in relation to its African antecedents, focusing on the vodun deities who, undoubtedly, make up one of the diacritical signs of the Jeje liturgy. The final chapter contains a more ethnographic and descriptive approximation of Jeje ritual. It should be made clear that this ethnography—the result of a positioned observer at a given time in a specific place—is only an approximation and is far from exhaustive. The Jeje are known to be quite reserved and do not speak easily about their religion, which itself perhaps constitutes another of their diacritical signs. At times my condition as an uninitiated, white foreigner caused somewhat explicit resistance on the part of some individuals, and it was only through great patience and persistence that I gained the confidence of others. Innumerable internal liturgical aspects of the Jeje houses remain hidden, and others that I may have learned were censored in the text in deference to the practitioners' explicit request. Thus it was through the assiduous participant observation of successive annual festival cycles that, gradually, I came to understand ritual behaviors and practices of intricate complexity and to identify the singularities of the Jeje nation.

To conclude, it is important to point out that this work, because of its focus and framing, tends to valorize the Jeje. This valorization does not stem from any intent to "purify" or reify this tradition, as some inattentive readers might think, but it is the result of an interest in justly recognizing and calibrating its contribution (though clearly not the only one) to the formative process of Candomblé. The value given in this study to the Jeje tradition does not presuppose any notion of "cultural superiority" but is rather the result of prolonged research and conclusions based on relatively reliable empirical data and on proof that the vodun cults played a critical role in the formation of Candomblé. Historical perspective is important inasmuch as it aids in the understanding or the assessment of the play between continuities and change. It has not been my intention to use "History" ideologically, highlighting origins and defending direct continuities between Africa and Brazil in order to justify or legitimize a given cultural hierarchy, as certain other studies and oral traditions have tended to suggest in relation to other nations.

ACKNOWLEDGMENTS

This book is the result of a long research process that would have been impossible without the help of a great many people and institutions to whom I would like to express my gratitude. First, I would like to give my thanks to those more elderly individuals who very patiently shared their time and wisdom with me: the late *Humbono* Vicente Paulo dos Santos, the late *Gaiaku* Luiza Franquelina da Rocha, and her brother the late Eugenio Rodrigues da Rocha, the late *Ogã Kuto* Ambrosio Bispo Conceição, the late *Ogã Impe* Bernardino Ferreira, and *Agbagigan* Everaldo Conceição Duarte. I would also like to thank the members of the Jeje congregations and those of other candomblés who accepted my presence in their ceremonies, as well as all of those members of the *povo-de-santo** who, at some time or another, helped with my research, and whom it would not be possible to list individually here.

Among scholars, I would like the thank the invaluable help and support of Professors João José Reis and Vivaldo da Costa Lima, Ambassador Alberto da Costa e Silva, Maria Inês Cortes de Oliveira, Renato da Silveira, Luiz Mott, Mariza de Carvalho Soares, Silvia Hunold Lara, and the members of the research group Escravidão e Invenção da Liberdade (Slavery and the Invention of Liberty) of the Postgraduate Program in History at the Universidade Federal da Bahia (Federal University of Bahia), where I presented preliminary versions of chapters 1–3. I am equally grateful to my colleagues in the Postgraduate Program in Social Sciences at the Federal University of Bahia, particularly Maria Rosário de Carvalho, Graça Druck, and Miriam Rabello, who consistently provided a stimulating academic environment for my research.

I am also grateful for the help of other scholars and friends, such as Hypolite Brice Sogbossi, Roger Sansi, Lisa Earl Castillo, Luiz Cláudio Nascimento, Fernando Araújo, and Peter Cohen. I would also like to thank the staff members at the Arquivo Regional de Cachoeira (Cachoeira Regional Archive), Arquivo Público do Estado da Bahia (State of Bahia Public Archive), and the Instituto Geográfico Histórico da Bahia (Historical and Geographic Institute of Bahia) for their help with my documentary research. My thanks also to Sheila Cavalcante dos Santos for her patient revision of my Portuguese, and to Bete Capinan for her efforts in finding resources for the publication of my original Portuguese manuscript.

The research behind this book would not have been possible without the Visiting Researcher Grant I received from the CNPq (Conselho Nacional de Desenvolvimento Científico e Tecnologia [Brazilian National Center for Scientific and Technological Development]) from 1999 to 2002 and a previous Visiting Professor Grant bestowed by CAPES (Coordenação de Aperfeiçoamento de Pessoal de Nível Superior [a Brazilian federal agency for the support and evaluation of graduate education]) from 1998 to 1999. Also, in 2003, the FAPESB (Fundação de Amparo à Pesquisa do Estado da Bahia [Research Support Foundation of the State of Bahia]) granted me funds toward the publication of this work. I am grateful to these Brazilian institutions for sponsoring my research.

As for the English edition, I am particularly thankful to James Sweet and João José Reis for their initial support of the proposal and to Elaine Maisner, senior executive editor at the University of North Carolina Press, for accepting it. I am also grateful to Professor Paulo Franchetti, head of Editora da Unicamp, for granting the rights for the English publication. Also, my sincere thanks to Richard Vernon for the translation and his commitment through these years to bringing the project to a good port despite its many challenges. Michael Iyanaga also read two chapters and made valuable suggestions. Finally, I would like to acknowledge the support of the National Humanities Center in North Carolina, where I spent the 2010–11 academic year, for allowing me to devote some of my time to the revision of the English manuscript.

NOTE ON NAMES AND ABBREVIATIONS

The names of places, cities, and ethnic groups related to the history of the Gulf of Benin follow English spellings (e.g., Ouidah, Abomey) but will follow the Portuguese spelling when used in the Brazilian context (e.g., Nagô nation). The names of African deities (orixás and voduns) follow the Portuguese spelling (e.g., Xangô for Shango or orixá for orisha), even when used in the African context. Vernacular terms are put in italics (except vodun, orixá, candomblé, and terreiro) and those followed by an asterisk at their first appearance are found in the glossary at the end of the book (e.g., *povo-de-santo,* * *egun**).

ABBREVIATIONS

AAPBa   Anais do Arquivo Público da Bahia

ACMS   Arquivo da Cúria Metropolitana de Salvador

AHU   Arquivo Histórico Ultramarino

ANTT   Arquivo Nacional da Torre do Tombo—Lisbon

APEBa   Arquivo Público do Estado da Bahia—Salvador, Bahia

ARC   Arquivo Regional de Cachoeira—Cachoeira, Bahia

ASMPAC   Arquivo da Sociedade Montepio dos Artistas Cachoeiranos—
         Cachoeira, Bahia

CEAO   Centro de Estudos Afro-Orientais

ED   *Études Dahomeénnes*

FTFC   Fórum Texeira de Freitas—Cachoeira, Bahia

IHGBa   Instituto Histórico e Geográfico da Bahia—Salvador, Bahia

UFBa   Universidade Federal da Bahia

THE FORMATION OF CANDOMBLÉ

1 Between Two Coasts

Nations, Ethnicities, Ports, and the Slave Trade

"African" Nations and "Metaethnic" Denominations

This chapter reflects on the so-called Jeje nation based on an analysis of the context of West Africa and the historiography of this ethnonym in relation to the slave trade. Before evaluating who the Jeje were, however, it is important to understand what the term *nation* meant in the seventeenth and eighteenth centuries.

Along with other terms such as *country* or *kingdom*, *nation* was used at that time by slave traders, missionaries, and administrative officials from the European factories along the Mina Coast to designate diverse autochthonous populations. The initial use of *nation* in the context of West Africa by the English, French, Dutch, and Portuguese resulted from a sense of collective identity then prevalent in the European monarchic states, an identity projected on their commercial and administrative enterprises along the Mina Coast.

These sovereign European states found a strong and parallel sense of collective identity among West African societies. This identity was based, above all, on kinship relationships to certain chieftaincies normally organized around monarchical institutions. Additionally, the collective identity of West African societies was multidimensional and articulated on various levels (ethnic, religious, territorial, linguistic, and political). First and foremost, group identity derived from kinship ties among associations of families recognizing a common ancestry. Religious activity related to the cult of certain ancestors or other spiritual entities was thus the vehicle par excellence of ethnic or communal identity.[1] Belonging to such a group was normally signified by a series of physical marks or scarring on the face or other parts of the body.

Language and city or territory of residence were also important factors and denominations of group identities: in West Africa there exists a nomenclature by which cities share the name of their inhabitants.[2] Finally, political alliances and tributary dependencies of certain monarchies also formed new and more inclusive "national" identities.

These diverse collective identities were subject to historic transformation resulting from factors such as alliances through marriage, wars, migrations, aggregation of slave lineages, appropriation of foreign religious cults, and political changes. In many cases, groups adopted names used for them by neighboring peoples or external powers. These external names often encompassed multiple, originally heterogeneous groups.

It is from this perspective that one should view the formation of a group of African "nations" in the context of colonial Brazil. In the sixteenth century the expressions "gentio da Guiné" (gentile or heathen from Guinea) or "Negro da Guiné" (black from Guinea) were used to refer generically to all Africans. But even by the first half of the seventeenth century distinctions emerge between the various nations. In Recife, in 1647, during the war with the Dutch, Henrique Dias, head of the Regiment of Black Men, wrote in a letter, "The regiment is comprised of men from four nations: Minas, Ardas, Angolas, and Creoles."[3] The mention of Creoles (*crioulos*,* referring to descendants of Africans born in Brazil) as a "nation" suggests that as early as the seventeenth century this concept corresponded not to political or ethnic criteria prevalent in Africa but to distinctions elaborated by the dominant classes in the colony, which served the slave-based society.

André João Antonil, a Jesuit priest who lived in the seventeenth century and published *Cultura e opulência do Brasil* (Culture and Opulence of Brazil) in 1706, wrote: "And because often [the slaves] are from different *nations.* . . . Those who come to Brazil are Arda, Mina, Congo from S. Tomé, from Angola, from Cape Verde, and some from Mozambique, who come on ships from India."[4] In the eighteenth century the expression "gentio da Guiné" gradually disappears, although "gentio da Costa" (gentile from the Coast) was still common in Salvador, and the classification of Africans according to nation seems to become more common, coinciding with the increase and diversification of slave trading, which came to include a wider variety of routes and ports of origin.

The names of the nations are not homogenous, as seen in the Antonil quotation, and can refer to ports of embarkation, kingdoms, ethnicities, islands, or cities. Slave traders and owners used these names to serve their own interests of administrative classification and control. In many cases, the port or geographic area of embarkation appears to have been one of the principal criteria in the development of these categories (Mina, Angola, Cape Verde, São Tomé, etc.). These denominations, therefore, did not necessarily correspond to the ethnic self-denominations used by Africans themselves in their regions of origin. As Maria Inês Cortes de Oliveira points out, the African nations, "as they came to be known in the New World, did not preserve in their names, nor in their social compositions, a correlation with the forms of self-ascription then in use in Africa."[5] It should be emphasized that this process may not have been quite so unilateral or so radical, for in some cases the names used by the slave traders actually corresponded to those of ethnic or collective identities in use in Africa, but they gradually expanded their semantic reach to designate a plurality of groups previously differentiated. This seems to have been the case with denominations such as *Jeje* and *Nagô*, among others.

I will analyze the case of the Jeje further on, but in the case of the Nagô, for example, we know that *Nagô*, *Anagô*, or *Anagonu* was the ethnonym or self-denomination of a group of Yoruba-speaking people who inhabited the region of Egbado in present-day Nigeria, but who eventually emigrated and disseminated through various parts of present-day Republic of Benin. At the same time, the inhabitants of Dahomey, a kingdom that existed from the middle of the seventeenth century until the end of the nineteenth, began to use the term *Nagô*, which in the Fon language was probably derogatory, to designate a number of Yoruba-speaking peoples under the influence of the kingdom of Oyo, their neighbor and feared enemy. Thus, an ethnic self-denomination, restricted to a particular group, came to be used by a group outside this community to designate a more extensive collection of peoples.[6]

The logic of this generalization lies in the fact that these peoples shared many cultural commonalities, such as language, habits, and customs. With time, this group of Yoruba-speaking peoples came to assimilate the external designation imposed by the Dahomeans and, once the name lost its pejorative association, began using it as a self-denomination. For their part, the European slave traders appropriated the local Dahomean use of the term *Nagô*, which was thus transferred to Brazil, preserving the generic and inclusive dimension established by the Dahomeans.

In order to analyze this type of process, it is useful to distinguish between "internal" denominations, used by members of a given group to identify themselves, and "external" denominations used, whether by Africans or European slavocrats, to designate a *plurality* of initially heterogeneous groups. In the first case, one could use the term *ethnonym* or simply "ethnic denomination"; in the second case, one could use *meta-ethnic denomination*, which, according to Cuban scholar Jesús Guanche Pérez, would be the external denomination used to refer to a number of neighboring groups that shared some linguistic and cultural features, had a degree of territorial stability, and, in the context of slavery, were embarked from the same ports.[7]

It should be noted that metaethnic (external) denominations, imposed on relatively heterogeneous groups can with time, become ethnic (internal) denominations when appropriated by these groups and used as a means of self-identification. The concept of metaethnic denomination is only useful when describing the process by which originally discrete and differentiated identities are included under a broad-reaching denomination to generate new collective identities. Using this terminology, one could claim that a series of metaethnic denominations were elaborated by the slave traders and owners of colonial Brazil (based either on the place of purchase or the port of slave embarkation), while other denominations, such as *Nagô*, that were already operative in Africa were appropriated and gradually modified in Brazil.

Thus the Africans who came to Brazil encountered a plurality of nation names—some internal and others metaethnic denominations—that allowed them multiple forms of self-identification. Once in Brazil, Africans who were previously unaccustomed to the metaethnic denominations quickly assimilated them and came to employ them because of their utility within the slavocratic society. However, within the more private social context of the black-mestizo community, the Africans generally continued to use the ethnic denominations prevalent in their regions of provenience.

Mariza de Carvalho Soares uses the concept of *provenience group* (*grupo de procedência*) to refer to the collection of peoples encompassed under the same metaethnic denomination. She distinguishes between the use of the term *nation* as an emblem of identity based on geographical *provenience* (Angola or Mina nation) and the use of *nation* to refer to an identity based on *ethnicity* (Ketu or Makii nation).[8] Essentially Soares employs a different terminology from mine to analyze the same problem. In this study I avoid speaking of *provenience groups* or *provenience identities* because it seems to me that the identifying processes constructed around metaethnic denominations (*Mina, Angola, Nagô*) were not restricted exclusively or primarily to an awareness of a common geographic origin. The place of provenience as a determining factor in the construction of the idea of nation is connected to the so-called primordial theories of ethnicity that privilege origins, while my perspective is closer to relational theories of ethnicity. The formation of African nations in Brazil is understood in this case as an especially dialogic process of cultural contrasts made among the diverse groups encapsulated under the various metaethnic denominations.

The result of this dynamic is that names of nations acquired distinct contents depending on the period and Brazilian region. The case of the term *Mina*, is illustrative. Like the expression "gentio da Guiné" utilized in the sixteenth century, *Mina* was a denomination that, over time, amplified its semantic domain until it became nearly synonymous with *African*. But it was not always so. Initially *Mina* had a more concise meaning and referred to slaves embarked from Elmina Castle. The Portuguese Crown built this fort on the Gold Coast, in present-day Ghana, between 1482 and 1484 and, until 1637, when it was occupied by the Dutch, Elmina was the most important Portuguese enclave for the commerce of gold and slaves.

Elmina Castle was a center to which slaves from various zones of the West African coast were taken. The correspondence of Duarte Pacheco Pereira, captain of the fort from 1520 to 1522, mentions the presence of slaves from the distant kingdom of Benin, located in present-day Nigeria, in the area that the English were already calling the Slave Coast. Slaves from Congo also passed through the fort before embarking for the Americas. As early as the 1660s, Wilhelm Johann Muller, a clergyman of the Danish African Company, alludes, for example, to the presence of slaves from Allada on the Gold Coast. It is evident, then, that from the beginning "Mina" referred to a port of embarkation and that the slaves bought there came from very diverse areas.[9]

From 1680 the Ga of Accra and the Fante-Ané from Elmina began to arrive in the area of Petit-Popo and Glidji, on the coast of present-day Togo, in order to escape the wars with the Akwamu. Since the fugitive Ga came from the Gold Coast, they were called "Mina" by the Europeans as early as the seventeenth century.[10] This group mixed with the local inhabitants, such as the Hula and Uatchi, and from this confluence emerged the Gen or Genyi kingdom in the eighteenth century. The Gen kingdom, whose largest port was in Petit-Popo (Ané ho), was involved in the slave trade, meaning that the denomination *Mina*, principally in the final decades of the eighteenth century and the first decades of the nineteenth, could also designate slaves embarked in Ané ho and in other ports of the western zone of the Mono River.

As Pierre Verger noted, the expression "Mina Coast" gradually came to indicate, not the Gold Coast but, more precisely, the Slave Coast, that is, the leeward coast of Elmina Castle, extending from the Volta River delta in Ghana to the mouth of the Niger River (Lagos River), in Nigeria. Consequently, as Nina Rodrigues accurately observed, "Mina" or "Mina black" could refer not only to Africans from the Gold Coast but also to those from the Ivory Coast and the Slave Coast, the latter including Togoland, Benin, and western Nigeria.[11] In this way, the term *Mina* came to include all the peoples from the Gulf of Benin, from an Ashanti to a Nagô.

This process of semantic change explains why the term meant something different in Rio de Janeiro, Minas Gerais, Bahia, and in Maranhão. In Rio, references to slaves from the Mina Coast appear from the beginning of the seventeenth century and, as the *compromissos*, or statutes, of eighteenth-century black Catholic brotherhoods show, *Mina* seems to correspond to the peoples from the present-day Republic of Benin, called Jeje in Bahia, being as the latter denomination was then unknown in Rio. By the nineteenth century, French artist and traveler Jean Debret mentions the Mina, Mina-*Callava*, Mina-*Maí*, and Mina-*Nejós*. The denomination *Mina-Callava*, which Rodrigues transcribes as "Mina-Cavalos," probably refers to slaves embarked in the port of Calabar, although Oliveira believes that they could also be slaves from Abomey-Calavi, along the banks of Lake Nokué. The "Néjo" would probably be the Nagô, or maybe the Mina from Aného (Petit-Popo), while the Maí or Mahij people would be the Mahi. All of these peoples inhabited the eastern area of the Gulf of Benin, which would confirm the expansion of *Mina*'s semantic inclusiveness and geographic domain.[12]

In the eighteenth century, in Minas Gerais as in Rio, *Mina* seems to designate those peoples who in Bahia were called Jeje. When in 1741 António da Costa Peixoto wrote *Obra nova da língua geral de mina* (*New Book of the Common Language of Mina*), the language identified as such corresponds to that spoken in the south of the present-day Republic of Benin. In fact, the expression "gente mina" (Mina people) is identified with the term *Guno*, referring specifically to the Gun inhabitants of Porto-Novo.[13] In Maranhão, in contrast, twentieth-century authors such as Nunes Pereira mention the "Mina-Achanti, Mina-Nagô, Mina-Cavalo, Minas Santé, Minas Mahys," and the Mina-Jeje. Otavio da Costa Eduardo documents denominations such as *Mina-Nagô, Mina-Jeje, Mina-Popo, Mina-Fulupa*, and even *Mina-Angola* and *Mina-Cambinda*.[14] This means that, in certain places, including Maranhão, *Mina* came to designate simply African, regardless of place of origin.

This case demonstrates how the metaethnic denominations varied in content according to changing times and regions. We should make a second observation. As the metaethnic denominations grow in generality, they are qualified with a second, more restricted, term (*Cavalo, Maí, Nagô, Jeje*, etc.). This second denomination can be yet another metaethnic denomination, though of more limited scope. In any case, what we should keep in mind is that the term *Mina*, from the eighteenth century onward, included the African population from the Slave Coast or Gulf of Benin, most especially that from the kingdom of Dahomey and its environs, a population that in Bahia was known as Jeje.

Though the metaethnic denominations used and imposed by the slave-owning elite were for the most part strongly associated with certain ports or geographic areas of embarkation, they could also underscore a certain homogeneity of cultural and linguistic features shared by the people thus designated.

It is precisely the recognition of that community of cultural elements that will favor the adoption of these external denominations and the subsequent configuration of a collective identity (nation) assumed by the Africans themselves.

These cultural elements were not necessarily or exclusively of African origin. As I have already mentioned, in the eighteenth century the Mina slaves of Minas Gerais were those who spoke the "common language of Mina." Therefore, at the foundation of the meaning of the term *Mina* was not only the place of embarkation, but also a linguistic factor and, implicitly, other cultural similarities. However, the "common language of Mina," though it corresponds most closely to Gun, a language itself derived from Aizo—the original language of Allada—seems to have been a kind of lingua franca evolved in Brazil through a process of inclusion of lexical items from other languages from the Gbe-speaking group, such as Fon, and even Nagô.[15] A similar situation occurs with the Nagô spoken in nineteenth-century Bahia. This language did not correspond entirely to that spoken by the Nagô or Anagô of Egbado, but it seems to have developed, in the Brazilian context, into a type of "patois" from various Yoruba dialects along with lexical contributions from other African languages and even from Portuguese.

Thus, peoples included under the same national denomination are defined by a number of intimately related factors: the areas or ports where the slaves were purchased or embarked, a relatively stable and common geographic area of residence, and a similarity of cultural-linguistic components. Still, it was language—the ability of Africans to communicate with and understand one another—that in Brazil led to the absorption of these denominations as forms of self-identification and to the consequent creation of new communities or feelings of collective belonging.

The Peoples from the Gulf of Benin and the Vodun Area

The term *Jeje* appears in Bahian documents for the first time in the early 1700s, designating a group of peoples originating from the Mina Coast. But who were these Jeje peoples? The Jeje have been usually identified, at least from the nineteenth century and subsequently in Afro-Brazilian scholarship, as Dahomeans, that is, groups originating from the former kingdom of Dahomey. But in fact the term *Jeje* seems to have originally designated an ethnic minority, probably localized in the area of the present-day city of Porto-Novo. As a result of the slave trade, the term gradually came to include a plurality of locally differentiated ethnic groups. It is, therefore, another metaethnic denomination.

So why were the Jeje designated as such? Might this term refer to these

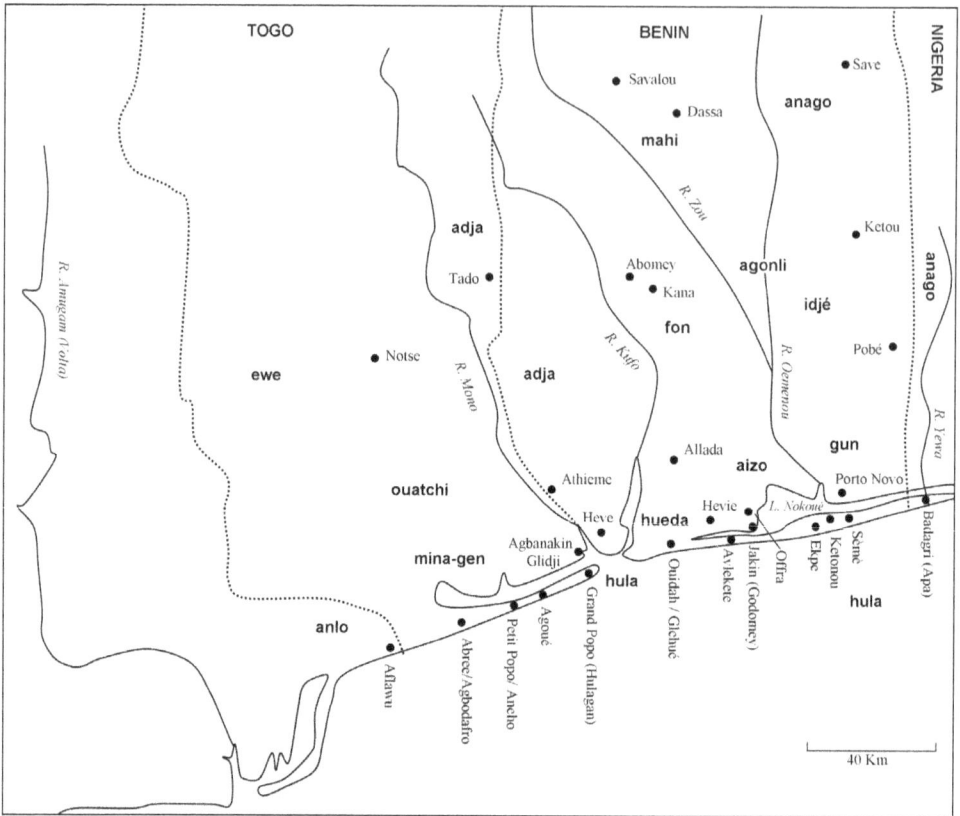

MAP 1 The Gbe-speaking area and its principal ethnic groups

peoples living in a specific geographic area? What might this area be? Might *Jeje* refer to groups sharing certain linguistic and cultural features? Or is this word related to factors intrinsically connected to slavery, such as the ports of embarkation or a group of merchants responsible for their sale? In order to answer these questions, we should first briefly survey the history and ethnic composition of the Gulf of Benin.

As Claude Lepine points out, the entire area of the Gulf of Benin, from the Volta River to the Niger River, "constituted a large cultural area, where one can observe marked similarities among social and political institutions, customs, practices, and religious beliefs. The cultural unity of the region is explained by the history of its settlement and by its history of migrations and contacts."[16]

Contemporary historians of this area of West Africa speak of a series of successive migrations by the so-called proto-Yoruba groups who, having arrived from the east, settled in the Gulf of Benin beginning in the seventh century. A later migration led by Oduduwa settled in Ilê Ifé around the year 1000. From then on, the grandchildren of Oduduwa, in additional migrations, came to occupy the coast and the interior of the region that later would become the kingdom of Dahomey. Some authors suggest that the first inhabitants of the coast, the Hula or Popo, are descendants of Olupopo or Olukpokpo, sixth son of Okambi and grandson of Oduduwa. Other proto-Yoruba groups, such as the Guedevi, whose ethnonym derives from the name of their king Iguede, and the Fon would have occupied the Abomey plateau at that time.[17]

There is another migratory wave spoken of, probably contemporary to that of Oduduwa. It involved the ancestral group of the Adja, under the leadership of Togbin-Anyi. Originating from the Nupe or Kwara River (Niger) region, this group came to settle in the area of what would become Oyo. Through rivalry with another proto-Yoruba group from Ilê Ifé, Togbin-Anyi's people initiated a long migration path to the west. After establishing themselves temporarily in Ké (later Kétou) and in Savè, this group came to Tado, a city on the west bank of the Mono River, in present-day Togo, some 100 kilometers from the coast. There, the descendants of Togbin-Anyi came into contact with the Azanu, whose ancestors are the Za, originating from the cultural area of Sonrai, at the source of the Niger River. It is possible, however, that in Tado there were other inhabitants, such as the Alu ironworkers.[18]

From this confluence in Tado among the descendants of Togbin-Anyi, from the east, and the Azanu from the northwest, groups subsequently known as Adja, though probably including a plurality of peoples, began new migrations. The oldest is considered to be that of a group known as Huisi, which sometime in the thirteenth century established itself on the plain between the Koufo and Ouemé Rivers, founding there the kingdom of Davie, which preceded that of Allada. These groups were later known as Aizā, or by the modern name Aizo.[19] The oral traditions of the Hula and Hueda groups indicate that they also would have come from Tado. However, as I have pointed out, these groups that occupied the coastal lagoon would have come from the east with the earlier proto-Yoruba migrations. Thus, the myth of Tado origin might be based in memories left by later invasions or alliances that involved Ajda groups that had come from Tado.[20]

In the sixteenth century, new Adja migrations from Tado occupied the territory of the Aizo, encouraging the founding of the city of Togudo, capital of the Allada kingdom, which at that time became the hegemonic power in the region, as suggested by the appearance of its name ("Arida" and "Ardra") in Portuguese navigational maps beginning in 1570. According to oral tradition, a group of the so-called Agasuvi departed from Allada in the first half of the seventeenth century and headed north. After subjugating the local populations

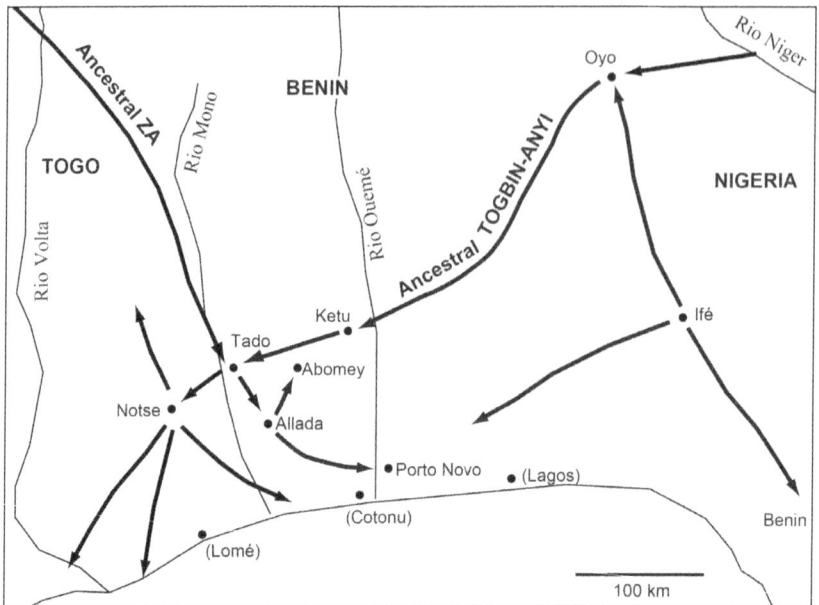

MAP 2 Migrations of the Adja. Source: F. Medeiros, ed., *Peuples du Golfe du Bénin* (Paris: Karthala, 1984), 12.

such as the Guedevi and the Fon, this group founded the Dahomey kingdom, establishing Abomey (Agbome) as their capital. The population of this kingdom was subsequently known by the ethnic denomination *Fon,* that is, the name of one of the indigenous groups subjugated by the Agasuvi.

When the Fon or Dahomeans conquered Allada in 1724, the royal family of this kingdom and its followers fled to the east and came to settle in the eastern region of Lake Nokué, where they founded the Adjaché or Adjasé kingdom, known among Europeans as Porto-Novo. The Adja who settled there were called *Gun* or *Gunnu.* It is worth noting that this historic narrative regarding the foundation of the kingdom of Porto-Novo in the eighteenth century, maintained by Isaac Akinjogbin, contradicts the oral traditions of Allada, Dahomey, and Porto-Novo.[21]

Subject to multiple variations that I synthesize here, the foundational myths of these kingdoms all affirm that the royal dynasty of Allada was matrilineally connected with that of Tado, and that its founder was a foreigner who married, or procreated with, a Tado princess, who according to Abomey tradition, was called Aligbonon. Following a conflict over the succession of the Tado throne, the Agasuvi—descendants of this princess and the foreigner Agasu, usually identified as a mythical panther—had to flee the city, under the leadership of

Ajahuto, a name generally translated as "the killer of the Adja." Ajahuto was the founder of the kingdom of Allada. Some generations later, a new succession dispute resulted in the parting of three brother princes. One of them is said to have stayed in Allada, another went north to found Dahomey, and the third went east to found Porto-Novo. According to these traditions, the founding of the Porto-Novo kingdom would have been contemporaneous to the founding of Dahomey.[22]

Recent historical studies show that these foundational myths could be relatively late constructions, probably from the eighteenth century but only documented in the nineteenth and originally elaborated by the Dahomean royal family in order to legitimize its royal power, basing it upon ascendency in Tado. These myths could subsequently have been appropriated and reelaborated by the royal dynasties of Porto-Novo and Allada, the latter already under Dahomean domination.[23] In any case, these narratives suggest that sometime in the sixteenth century Adja groups originating in Tado migrated east and, dominating and absorbing preexisting autochthonous peoples, founded the kingdom of Allada, from where the authority of Dahomey and Porto-Novo was subsequently legitimized.

These migrations from Tado to the east were followed by others in the early part of the seventeenth century, but this time in a westerly direction. At some undetermined point, probably around 1610 according to Jacob Spieth, groups coming from Tado founded the city of Notsé, the center of additional migrations that in the following decades resulted in the occupation of the northern region of present-day Togo and Ghana. These groups were known by the meta-ethnic denomination *Ewe*, which originates from one of their ethnonyms.[24]

It was Colonel Alfred Ellis, with his book *The Ewe-Speaking Peoples of the Slave Coast of West Africa* (1890), who popularized the term *Ewe* to designate all linguistically related peoples who occupied the region of the Volta River in Ghana and the southerly areas of Togo and Benin. Thus the term *Ewe* would come to designate not only those who had left Notsé but all those who had come from Tado. Subsequently, the German linguist Diedrich Westermann, working in Togo, came to consolidate the term *Ewe*. In francophone studies, terms such as *Adja*, *Aja*, or *Aja-Tado* have been more frequently used to designate these groups. More recently, one sees the use of terms such as *Fon-Ewe*, or *Ewe-Fon*, *Adja-Ewe*, or *Ewe-Aja*, *Foja* (*Fon-Adja*), and *EGAF* (*Ewe-Gen-Aja-Fon*).[25]

Throughout this study, I will generally use the *Adja* denomination in a restricted sense to designate those peoples who assert Tado origin and emigrated to the east, settling in the area of the present-day Republic of Benin and in southwest Nigeria. Among them, the Fon were the dominant group from the time of Dahomey expansion. In contrast, I will use the term *Ewe* to designate those peoples who left Notsé and expanded in a westerly direction, through Togo and Ghana. In 1980, in a conference held in Cotonou, Hounkpati B. C. Capo proposed the use of the expression "Gbe-speaking area" to designate the region occupied by these linguistically related groups, as *Gbe* is a common term meaning "language" in most of the fifty-one registered "dialects." The hope with this more neutral and generic expression is that one might avoid the ethnocentrism of designating a plurality of peoples with the name of only one of them. As I stated in the preface, I use the expression "Gbe-speaking area" to designate the geographic zone occupied by those peoples previously called Adja-Ewe (or variants of this term).

However, this region was not inhabited exclusively by Gbe-speaking peoples. As I stated earlier, the cultural substratum of the proto-Yoruba remained strong, principally in the eastern area of the region. Since the Ilê Ifé migrations at the turn of the millennium, many of these groups traveled west, founding several city-states that eventually became kingdoms. The Nagô, Anagô, or Anagonu, originating in the Egbado area (Nigeria), settled in the area of what would become Porto-Novo (Adjaché), and in the areas of Sakété and Pobé eventually constituting one of the largest Yoruba populations in Dahomey. Other proto-Yoruba groups established the city of Ké, from which later would emerge the kingdom of Kétou. The Savè founded their kingdom (which they call Tchabè) on both banks of the Okpara River, but the border between Nigeria and Dahomey established by the colonial powers divided their territory, the groups on the west bank (in Dahomey) remaining within the Savè district, currently the *sous-préfecture* of Savè. The Dassa founded their kingdom (which they also call Idatcha) in the Mahi area, north of the Zou River. To the northwest of Dassa, the Ife, the Itsha, and the Manigri constituted additional groups of proto-Yoruba peoples. The Ohori (also known as the Idjè or Holli) settled in the Hollidjè region, between Pobé and Kétou.[26]

The cultural influence of these peoples is confirmed by the frequent use of some of the many Yoruba dialects among the Gbe-speaking peoples, a fact documented from the mid-seventeenth century. In 1668, Olfert Dapper commented: "It is curious that these negroes [from Allada and Jakin] do not value their mother tongue, which they use rarely, while learning another of more current usage that they call Ulkumy [Anagô]."[27] Allada was initially a tributary of the Benin kingdom, a fact documented in 1670,[28] but in the late seventeenth century the hegemonic power in the region was the Oyo kingdom. In 1698, Allada was invaded by the Oyo as a result of the Allada's killing the king of Oyo's

ADELE Amlamé •Alakpame
AKPELEN
AXLON
DAYIN
AKPAFU GBIN
KPANDO •Kpandu
ANFOIN
AVATÍME AGU
HÓ
PECÍ Hó Tavégan
AKWAMU AVÉDAKPÁ •Djolo Laguna de Togo
TƆWUN AVÉNO AWLAN LOMÉ
DANGME

WANCÉ STÁDÓ HWE
HWE
DOGBÓ SIKPI
TSÁPHE GBÉSI •Allada
Loc •Bopa
SE Ahémo
Comé PHELÁ
WACÍ
ADÁNGBE VO Vo-Koutímé WACÍ
PHLA Grand Popo
BE GEN Anecho
Kéta Lagoon Keta

MAXÍ
Zagnanado
Abomey AGBÓME YORUBA
•Adjohan YORUBA
WÉME
AYIZƆ̀ TƆFIN GUN
PORTO-NOVO
Loc Nokoué ALADA
KPASE COTONOU

N

Note: Except for glossonyms (given in the uniform standard Gbe orthography) all other names are in the "official" (French or English based) orthography.

0 10 20Km.

The Gbe dialect cluster
▲ ....Vhe lects
⇧ ....Gen lects
▼ ....Ajá lects
■ ....Fon lects
● ....Phla-Pherá lects
YORUBA ....non-Gbe lect

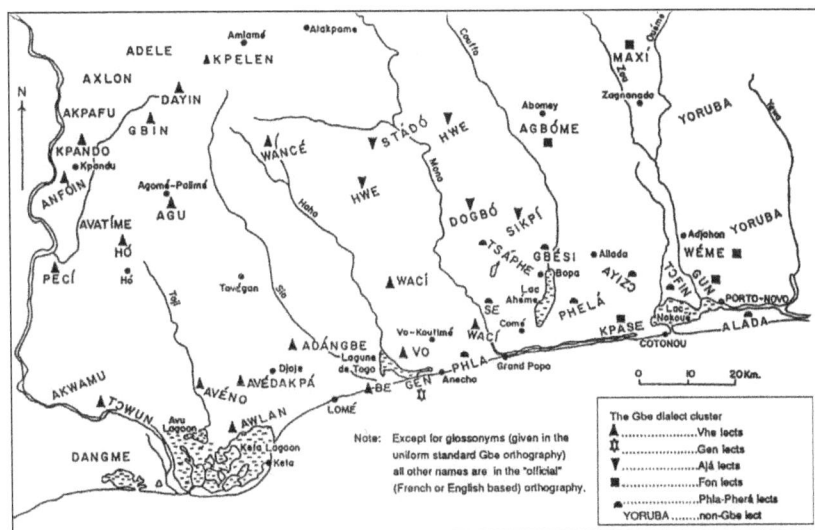

MAP 3 The Gbe-speaking area and its glossonyms. Source: H. B. C. Capo, *Comparative Phonology of Gbe* (New York: Foris, 1991).

messengers who had been sent there.[29] The Oyo incursions into Adja territory continued during the eighteenth century. As a result, Dahomey continued to be a tributary kingdom of Oyo from 1712 until the beginning of the nineteenth century, when King Ghezo succeeded in liberating his people from this subjugation. In contrast, following the conquest of the coast by King Agaja in 1724–27, groups of Gbe-speaking Hueda, Ouemenu, Hula, and Aizo were displaced into areas inhabited by the Nagô, in Porto-Novo, Badagri, and Lagos.[30]

We have, therefore, an area in which political dependencies, diplomacy, commerce, wars, slavery, and crisscrossing migrations all contributed to create a situation of intense Nagô-Adja cultural contact. It is a border area where values and practices, traditions and languages intermingle and influence one another in mutual appropriation and reelaboration. This culturally heterogeneous and multilingual area, in which Gbe speakers mixed with Yoruba speakers, became a propitious space for processes of ethnic differentiation, as well as for complementarity and cultural assimilation brought about by their continued comingling.

Despite important politico-cultural similarities, the Adja and the Yoruba, living together in this polyethnic society, can be distinguished by certain significant differences, which demonstrate, as Honorat Aguessy points out, that "even populations from a common stock come to differentiate themselves through centuries of living apart."[31] Roberto Pazzi notes some of these differences. The Yoruba traditionally drink palm wine (*deha*), while the traditional drink of the Adja is corn beer (*liha*). The Yoruba royal throne has three legs, while that of the Adja has five, as does that of the Blu found to the north and west of the Gbe-speaking area. Among the Yoruba, the weekly cycle has four days, while among the Adja, this cycle, despite being maintained for ancestral rites and fallowing land, is combined with the seven-day cycle characteristic of the Blu, which is applied to the celebration of birthdays. Pazzi suggests that these similarities with the practices of the Blu (particularly those of the Ashante of Kumasi) and of other populations from the source of the Niger River (formerly related to the Mali empire) are the result of the Azanu influence over the Adja in Tado, which would further justify the claim that the Azanu originated in the Songhai area. Also, the Yoruba and the Adja practice circumcision, and in both cases kinship is established by patrilineal descendancy, with the exception of the Ewe, who practice a mixed system. Perhaps the origin of this difference with the Ewe can also be explained by the influence of the Blu, among whom kinship is organized along matrilineal lines.[32]

In the religious domain one also finds differences and similarities between the Yoruba and the Adja. One of the most significant differences is linguistic. While the Yoruba groups use the term *orixá*** to refer to their deities, all of the Gbe-speaking groups, not only the Adja, use the term *vodun*. This word is first recorded in the translation of *Doctrina christiana* into Arda (Allada) completed by the Spanish Capuchins in 1658.[33] The word's etymology is uncertain but, generally, the term evokes an idea of mystery, the ineffable that cannot be known.[34] Another word used in the Gbe-speaking area to designate the voduns is *hùn*, a polysemous term also meaning blood. In the extreme western part of the Gbe-speaking area, primarily in Togo, the voduns are designated by the term *yehwe*. Among the Gen, *yehwe* seems to be applied to deities of the sea and thunder pantheon of Hula and Aizo origin.[35]

In those parts of the Gbe-speaking area where Yoruba-speaking groups live, it is possible to find orixá cults. The orixás are not deities of Adja origin as occurs with the *yehwe*. On the contrary, it is probable that certain voduns are of Yoruba origin. For example, the expression "Lisa" ("Toi Lisa," "Elisa") appears in *Doctrina christiana* translation as the name of Jesus Christ. Given that *Lissá* is a vodun associated with the color white, it is not strange that the Allada translators chose this referent to designate the god of the whites. The term *Lissá* derives from the Nagô *orisa*, for when appropriated by Gbe-speakers Nagô words lose the initial vowel and transform the *r* into *l*.[36] This evidence indicates that by the middle of the seventeenth century the Nagô religious system had already penetrated deeply into the vodun religious system. Aguessy affirms that, "in addition to a structural homology of their pantheons[,] . . . there is also a word-for-word correspondence between numerous deities."[37] What is important to remember is that the processes of cultural interpenetration that occurred in Brazil between the Jeje and the Nagô already had a long tradition in Africa.

Despite the commonality of conceptual and ritual elements forming the religious system of the majority of the Gulf of Benin societies, the linguistic boundary allows one to trace the borders of a hypothetical area of vodun cults between the Mina-Gen *yehwe* cults and the Nagô orixá cults. These borders, established through the words used to designate the deities, are reinforced by the names given to the oracular practices that normally accompany these cults: *Ifa* in the orixá cults, *Fa* in the vodun cults, and *Afa* in the Ewe area.[38] Although precise geographic borders are not possible to determine, the differences in religious terminology convey an idea of a "vodun area," inserted within the broader religious and cultural system that stretches from Ghana to Nigeria.

The interest in circumscribing a vodun area that practically coincides with the linguistic area of the Gbe-speaking peoples derives from the fact that Jeje Candomblé in Brazil can be defined as a religious institution characterized by the worship of spiritual entities called voduns. Thus, defining a vodun area can aid in identifying the Jeje area of origin. Taking into account the Jeje deities worshiped in contemporary candomblés (Hevioso, Sakpata, Dan) and the various Jeje "subnations" still remembered today (Mahi, Savalu, Mundubi, Dagomé, Mina-Popo), one is led to conclude that the area of Jeje provenience must have been the regions stretching from Aného to Badagri, between the Hoho and Yewa Rivers, including the inland area of the Mahi and the coastal area of the Mina-Gen, perhaps leaving aside the Ewe peoples of the north, whom Capo identifies as the "Vhe lects" (Kplen, Dayin, Gbin, Agu, Ho, Pecí). Therefore, the vodun area would be that of the Gen, Uatchi, Adja, Fon, Hueda, Hula, Aizo, Gun, Ouemenu, Mahi, and other peoples connected to them.

These ethnic groups correspond principally to the Gbe-speaking peoples who, since the eighteenth century, were submitted to, or under the influence and control of, the kingdom of Dahomey. The ethnic composition of this kingdom and its environs is rather complex and lends itself to various typologies or classifications. Paul Hazoumé mentions at least fourteen peoples among the ethnic groups of the kingdom of Dahomey: Adja, Hula (Pla), Uatchi, Kotafon, Hueda (Peda), Aizo, Tofinu, Fon, Gun, Ouemenu, besides the Yoruba, Nagô and Holli, who came from the east. The most important ethnicity of lower Dahomey is the Adja-Aizo-Fon and Mina (Gen) group, according to A. Serpos Tidjani, who points out that to speak of Dahomeans is essentially to refer to this group.[39] It should be noted that what has been designated as the vodun area comprises an area somewhat larger than Dahomey and includes peoples who, although subject to Dahomean slave raids, did not necessarily fall within Dahomey's political borders.

The Mahi people, one of the groups with the strongest presence in Bahia, serve to illustrate this point. Akinjogbin calls the Mahi country a "slave hunting ground."[40] Effectively, all the kings of Dahomey from Agaja to Glele, executed military campaigns in this area with varying degrees of success. The term *Mahi* seems to have emerged in the eighteenth century as a denomination used by the Dahomeans to refer to a number of peoples dwelling north of the Zou River. Although questionable, J. A. M. A. R. Bergé and Robert Cornevin give, as the etymology for *Mahi*, the expression "ma-hi-nou," which means "the victims of fury" or "the destruction of fury," perhaps an allusion to this slave-hunting past.[41]

The first known written reference to the Mahi appears in a letter to the viceroy of Bahia from João Basílio, the director of the Portuguese fort in Ouidah, dated September 8, 1732: "As the King Daomé was fortunate to have overpowered the country of the Mauis (Mahis). . . ."[42] Another reference appears later in Robert Norris's report, written in 1773: "The Mahees . . . are a powerful confederation of many united and independent states; whose form of government seems to be of the feudal kind. Their leading men possess vassals or slaves, but do not treat them with the Dahomean asperity. Nevertheless, they sell slaves in considerable numbers to the Dahomean factors."[43] Therefore, even while maintaining relative independence, the Mahi "confederation" was in constant contact with its neighbors. The Mahi frequently established alliances with the Oyo in order to defend themselves from Dahomean aggression, but as early as the eighteenth century, certain Mahi groups also formed an important part of the Dahomean army.[44]

Bergé collected the oral traditions of the kingdoms of Fitta (or the Fellattah country), Dassa, and of other peoples from the Mahi area, as well as those of the neighboring kingdom of Savalou, which, despite being located to the north of the Zou River, is not considered part of the Mahi country by Bergé. Describing in detail the multiple migrations of these peoples, Bergé concludes that the Mahi constitute "a true racial cocktail," resulting from a slow intermixing and cultural symbiosis of the original Nagô-Yoruba populations with successive groups of Adja and Fon originating from the south.[45] For example, the kingdom of Dassa (Idassa), with its most important center in Dassa Zoumé, and whose royal dynasty goes back as far as 1700, was founded by the Nagô-Egba who had come from the area of present-day Abeokuta.[46] The Fitta and the

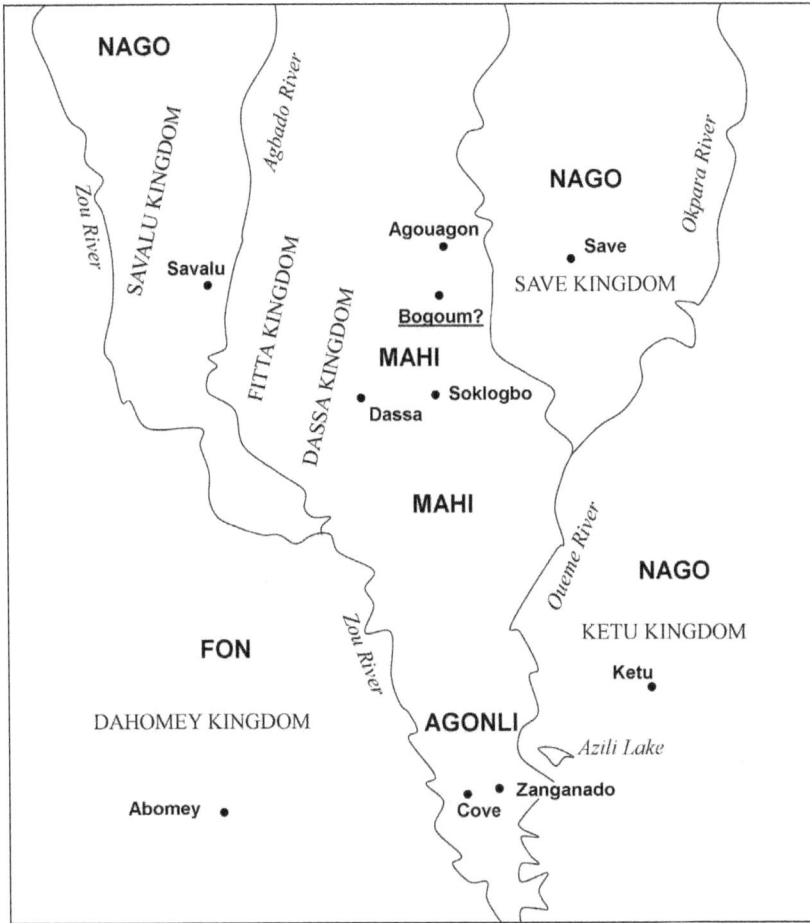

MAP·4 The Mahi country

Savalou (Tchevelou) were also of Nagô-Yoruba origin. Others might have had Ajda (Guedevi, Gbanli, Dovi) ancestry and fled to the mountainous region of the Mahi country with the surge of the Dahomey kingdom into the Abomey plateau in the first half of the seventeenth century.

The case of the Savalou deserves special attention, as this ethnonym appears in Brazil (as *Savalu*) beginning in the eighteenth century and even today designates one of the "subnations" of Jeje Candomblé. Savalou is currently the most important city in the Mahi region, and the Gbaguidi family has been the ruling clan from probably as early as the end of the seventeenth century. According to local tradition, the ancestors of Gbaguidi had originally come from Lake Ahémé, from the island of Mitogbodji, inhabited by Dovi fishermen (their ethnonym means "sons of the net"), who were themselves of Hueda origin. Following a fratricidal dispute, Ahossu Soha emigrated to the north, passing through the Ouemé River region and the Abomey plateau until arriving finally at Savalou, or Tchebelou, "originally a Nagô city" inhabited by the Ifé. This migration would have occurred in the time of the Dahomean kings Hwegbaja (ca. 1650–80) or Akaba (ca. 1680–1708).[47]

Savalou, along with other regions of the Mahi country, was attacked on various occasions by the Dahomean kings in their search for slaves, and maintained a relationship as much of conflict as of cooperation with this kingdom, alternating between periods of independence and tributary submission. It was only during the reign of Ghezo (1818–58) that Savalou and a large portion of the Mahi country (with the exceptions of the kingdoms of Dassa and Fitta) were occupied by Dahomey. In that time, Savalou was considered Anagô land, but its rulers—the Gbaguidis who were of Hueda origin and aided King Ghezo in dominating the Mahi—retained great privileges. In 1845, John Duncan claims that, after the caboceer of Ouidah, Gbaguidi was the second most powerful person in Dahomey and maintained a relative independence in terms of political control, not only of the Savalou region, but also of the neighboring Mahi cities.[48]

Because of these privileged relations with the Fon, the members of the Gbaguidi family today consider themselves Fon: "Although our ancestry is Peda [Hueda] from Mitogbodji, we, his descendants, consider ourselves Fon. Our passage through Wavè, in the Fon territory, caused us to take on the habits of the Fon. We are not Mahi. On the contrary, we command this entire people."[49] Therefore, despite being established among the Anagô, the Savalou (or at least their rulers), who speak a language similar to Fon and preserve Fon customs, seem to have constructed an ethnic identity distinct from the Mahi. The comments of the Gbaguidi clearly show how ethnic identities can be the result of an ideological orientation that answers to the political interests of the group; in this case, identifying with the Fon serves to legitimize their hegemony over neighboring Mahi and Nagô. Although theses peoples belong to the same geographic area, the ethnic differentiation between the Savalou and the Mahi would explain the differentiation maintained in Bahian Candomblé between the Jeje-Mahi and the Jeje-Savalu nations.

Another group whose presence in Brazil was rather significant was the "Agolin," who correspond to the Agonli or Agonlinu, established to the east of Abomey, in the environs of cities such as Zagnanado and Cové. Although Bergé does not recognize this area as part of the Mahi country, it is probable that, because it is located to the north of the Zou River, the Dahomeans did.

It was through contact with peoples from this region next to Lake Azili that the Dahomeans appropriated the religious practices associated with the river spirits that they identify as Mahi. The cult of the *Tohosu* and the *Tobosi* deities, which constitute an important ritual base in the royal ancestral cults of Abomey (Nesuhue), come from the Agonli.[50]

Moreover, another ritual modality among the Jeje Candomblé is the Jeje-Mundubi. *Mundubi* (and its variants "Mudubi," "Mandubi," "Mondubi," "Mondobi," "Mendobi," and "Modobê") is an ethnic denomination recorded in Bahia beginning in 1812, infrequently at first; it seems to be more common after 1830.[51] In any case, I did not find the term documented in the Gbe-speaking area. Some authors have erroneously identified Mundubi as a Bantu group,[52] but the ethnonym certainly designates groups from the Gbe-speaking area because, in the Brazilian religious context, this term applies specifically to the family of thunder and sea voduns (Hevioso, Sogbo, Averekete, etc.) that come from this area. Verger identifies the Mundubi with the Hueda and Hula,[53] which is probably correct since these ethnicities are two of the groups that originally worshipped these gods. But other groups from the coast who, in the beginning of the nineteenth century, also worshipped them (i.e., the Aizo, Fon, Tori, Dovi, Gen, Anlo) should not be dismissed (see chapter 7). The etymology of *Mundubi* is confusing, and the possibility that the ethnonym is a Brazilian creation should not be discarded.[54]

Having demarcated the approximate geographic area of the Adja-Ewe peoples, outlined in broad terms their complex ethnic composition, and pointed out their linguistic unity (referred to as the Gbe-speaking area) and their cultural unity (here essentially defined in religious terms as the vodun area), we can identify and locate the principal groups that lent their names to the "subnations" or "ritual modalities" of Jeje Candomblé. These are namely the Jeje-Marrin or Marrino (Mahi), the Jeje-Savalu, the Jeje-Dagomé (Dahomey), the Jeje-Mundubi, and the Jeje-Mina-Popo.[55] Just as the slave trade metaethnic denominations were qualified with a secondary, more restrictive term (e.g., *Mina-Nagô, Mina-Jeje*), so too was this denominational dynamic perpetuated within the nations of Candomblé and ethnic names from "provinces" or territories of the vodun area added to the generic *Jeje* denomination.

The Portuguese Slave Trade in the Vodun Area prior to the Eighteenth Century

The history of the slave trade is beyond the scope of this study. However, a brief overview of this process is needed to show when and from which ports of embarkation the peoples of the vodun area were shipped to Bahia. Preceding Verger, Luiz Viana Filho established a chronological division of the Portuguese slave trade in three major cycles: the Guinea cycle, during the second half of the sixteenth century; the Congo-Angola cycle, in the seventeenth century; and the Mina Coast cycle, during the first three quarters of the eighteenth century. To this Verger adds the Bight of Benin cycle, between 1770 and 1850, including therein the period of the illegal slave trade.[56] Of greatest interest to this study are the third and fourth cycles, which occur throughout the eighteenth century and during the first half of the nineteenth century. It was during this time that the greatest number of the slaves from the vodun area arrived in Bahia. We will therefore analyze the previous period only briefly.

Commerce in gold and slaves carried out by the Portuguese on the Mina Coast began around 1470, but not until 1553 is there news of Portuguese contact with the coastal peoples of the Gbe-speaking area, the *Papouès*, or Popo, probably in present-day Grand-Popo.[57] One can assume that a short time later the Portuguese established contact with the kingdom of Allada (Ardra), which maintained a hegemonic power in that region. Documents indicate the presence of slaves called Aradas or Araras in Peru as early as the middle of the 1560s. The Dutch merchant Pieter de Marees, describing the conditions of the slave trade in 1601 (or earlier), notes that the Portuguese were buying "many slaves" from Allada for the sugar plantations in São Tomé and Brazil. Other references show that in Allada the Portuguese commerce in slaves as well as in other products remained active at least until the late 1620s, when the Dutch came to control the region.[58]

In 1580, the United Provinces of the Low Countries, at war for independence from the king of Castile since 1568, took advantage of Portugal's forced submission to the Spanish Empire as a pretext to attack its overseas territories in the Americas and in Africa. Important to the Dutch was not only the fact that the Portuguese competed with them in the slave trade, but also that the Portuguese had now joined with their enemy, the Spanish Empire. This led to a frustrated attempt to invade Bahia (1624–25), and in the 1630s the Brazilian Northeast was invaded (Pernambuco in 1630, Rio Grande do Norte and Paraíba in 1634). The necessity of providing slaves for the Brazilian sugar mills led the Dutch to invade the Portuguese trading posts on the African coasts. Elmina Castle was conquered in 1637. In 1641, despite the peace treaty King João IV signed with the Dutch, the islands of São Tomé and Principe were occupied. The same would happen to Angola (Luanda was occupied until 1648). Thus, the Dutch West India Company (WIC) dominated the trade on the Mina Coast, coming occasionally to establish itself in the ports of Offra

(Offer for the Dutch) and Apa. Between 1636 and 1647 the WIC purchased an annual average of 800 slaves from Allada, taken principally to Brazil, but also to São Tomé.[59]

The first shipments of slaves from the Gbe-speaking area to Brazil date, therefore, from this period of 1570 to 1647. These are the slaves that, coming from Allada, were recruited into paramilitary regiments during the war of independence against the Dutch in Pernambuco. In his previously mentioned letter of 1647, Henrique Dias makes the first reference to the Arda, "so fiery that they wish to cut down everything in one blow." Also in 1647, Gaspar Barléus mentions the *Ardrenses*, "who are very ignorant, stubborn, and stupid; they detest work, with the exception of a very few, who are very patient workers, and this raises their price." Antonil mentions the *Arda*, but already among a plurality of denominations of origin, which demonstrates the gradual growth of the intercontinental trade. His comments indicate that "the Arda and Mina are robust."[60]

Arda was used to designate the commercial center where the slaves had been sold to the Portuguese. Like *Mina*, *Arda* and *Arada* were metaethnic names developed from the name of the place of "commercial" origin. As Jean-Baptiste Labat points out in *Voyage du Chevalier des Marchais en Guinée*, published in 1730, *Arada* did not necessarily refer to an indigenous population of that kingdom. "The Arada are the best slaves that can be bought in the kingdoms of Juda [Ouidah] and Ardres [Allada]; but they are not to be confused with those actually from Ardre, they do not come from that kingdom. They are brought to Juda from a country some 150 leagues to the northeast."[61]

During the second half of the seventeenth century, the commercial competition between the Dutch, English, and French, centered on the slave trade, caused an unprecedented politico-economic transformation on the coast of the Gbe-speaking area that threatened and undermined the hegemonic power of Allada. Favored by their coastal location, commercial opportunities, and by arms from the Europeans, lesser kingdoms grew in power, such as Popo and, above all, the Hueda kingdom, with its capital in Savi and its port in Ouidah. These kingdoms lived in constant dispute with Offra and later with Jakin, the ports of embarkation for the merchants of Allada. From 1680 onward, with the arrival of the Gan and the Fante-Ané, and the subsequent foundation of the Gen kingdom with its port in Petit-Popo (Aného), these interethnic disputes increased. It was a time of great social instability, with constant wars among Coto, Aného, Popo, Ouidah, Allada, Offra, and Jakin. The aim of these wars was both to capture slaves as well as to destabilize and consequently control the neighboring trade.

The primary conflict between the kingdoms of Allada and Hueda was further complicated by Offra, which, motivated by trade profits, frequently rebelled against its sovereign. As a counteroffensive strategy, Allada blockaded the routes from the interior, diverting the trade at times to Ouidah, other times to Offra, depending on the needs of the moment. The rebellious attitude of the lord of Offra—who in 1690 had assassinated the Dutch factor van Hoolwerff—led the king of Allada to summon the army of Petit-Popo, with which he would resolve the problem. In 1692, Offra was totally destroyed. From this point on, the Dutch, French, and English centered their trade in Ouidah, to the detriment of Allada. In 1703, indicating their growing strength, the Hueda refused to pay the traditional tribute to Allada. After 1714, when the commercial conditions in Ouidah became more difficult because of new pressures applied by Allada, the trading factories were again transferred to Allada's ports, this time to Jakin, never to return to Offra.[62]

Meanwhile, as has been well explained by Verger, the Portuguese and Bahian commerce on the Mina Coast was subject to Dutch economic and military control. The ten-year truce, signed in 1641 between Portugal and the Low Countries, recognized Dutch sovereignty on the Guinea coast. The 1648 Treaty of Münster (Westphalia) required the Portuguese to buy all African slaves directly from the WIC, except in the area of Luanda (Angola). This accord would remain in effect until the treaty of 1661, which recognized Portuguese free trade in Africa but specifically prohibited it on the Mina Coast.

As a result, any Portuguese ship wishing to trade leeward of Elmina Castle was required to pay the Dutch in that port the equivalent of 10 percent of its merchandise. Additionally (following the Treaty of Münster, according to Pazzi), each ship was required to apply for a passport in order to do business in Elmina. The 10 percent duty is documented as early as 1717 but is rumored to have actually begun in 1654 when the Dutch left Pernambuco. This seems improbable, since the Dutch departure from Pernambuco was actually the result of an expulsion by the Portuguese and therefore is unlikely to have led to any such tax. In any case, whenever possible, the Brazilian merchants sought to avoid its payment.

On June 15, 1733, the viceroy of Bahia wrote to the secretary of state, explaining that "the vessels from Brazil normally do business only in the ports of Jaquin, Ajudá [Ouidah], and Apa and others they call Lower Ports, in which the Dutch do not have authority nor do they presently have factories [. . .] without going to the Castle [Elmina] to pay them the 10 percent of the tobacco they carry." Precisely when the Dutch restricted the right of Portuguese vessels to conduct trade on the Mina Coast to the four ports of Popo, Ouidah, Jakin, and Apa is uncertain, but the measure remained in effect until at least 1770.[63]

Despite the restrictions and the naval vigilance of the Dutch, in the final decades of the seventeenth century the Portuguese and Bahian ships, brigs, and smacks carried on a clandestine but constant trade in other minor ports, such as that of the kingdom of Coto, to the east of the Volta River, or Petit-Popo (Aného).[64] Moreover, in 1711, as evidenced by WIC correspondence, "the Portuguese have in fact free trade there [along the coast] the more as they are able to escape the Company's ships, just by sailing under the protection of the guns of any fort of foreign nations."[65]

The 10 percent charge was necessarily paid in tobacco, as trade in other European products was prohibited to the Portuguese. As Antonil points out, the planting of tobacco in Bahia began toward the end of the sixteenth century. In 1644, Dom João IV "had authorized his vassals to go to Guinea in order to take third-quality tobacco and bring slaves to the ports of Brazil." The Dutch acquired this third-quality Bahian tobacco, the so-called *refugo* (waste, refuse) tobacco from the Recôncavo, in order to trade with the Africans, who valued this product above all others.

As Verger explained in detail, this preference had important repercussions that especially favored the Bahian merchants who stocked this tobacco, to the detriment of Portuguese merchants and those from other parts of Brazil who, without it, saw their trade opportunities in this part of the coast greatly diminished. Portugal encouraged its merchants, in Lisbon and in the colonies, to buy slaves in Angola, Congo, or Guinea, where the power of the Dutch was less evident, but the Bahians were not authorized to sell their tobacco in these ports. During the second half of the seventeenth century and for all of the eighteenth, the slave owners of Salvador and the tobacco-growing areas of the Recôncavo continued to develop the tobacco trade in the Gbe-speaking area, and to a lesser extent, the sugar and *cachaça* trade, importing, systematically and in great quantity, Gbe-speaking slaves to the sugar mills and tobacco plantations of the Recôncavo.[66]

From 1698 onward, with the discovery of gold in Minas Gerais, the demand for slaves increased. As Braz do Amaral observed, despite the fact that the opinions of the colonial powers did not always agree, there was a growing preference for the Mina slaves over those from Angola. On November 17, 1718, the viceroy of Bahia, Dom Sancho Faro, wrote to Lisbon: "The Negroes of the Mina Coast are more sought after for the mines and the sugar mills than the Angola because of the facility with which the latter die and commit suicide."[67] In 1726, referring to a slave revolt in Minas Gerais, which had failed because of an internal dispute between the Mina and Angola, the governor of Rio wrote, "The Mina blacks have a greater reputation for that type of work. The miners say they are stronger and more vigorous, but I believe that they have acquired that reputation through being known as sorcerers and they have brought in the devil that only they discover gold and for the same reason there is no miner who can live without his Mina negress, claiming that only they bring good luck."[68]

While the mixing with Angola captives continued to be recommended as a means of avoiding subversive unions among slaves, the demand for Mina blacks increased. Thus begins the Mina Coast cycle, which traditionally corresponds to the first three quarters of the eighteenth century. This period also gives rise to trade in smuggled gold with the Mina Coast, which alongside trade in tobacco and liquor constituted the foundation of Bahian commerce. It is precisely in the first decade of the 1700s that the term *Jeje* comes into use in the Bahian Recôncavo.

Hypothesis Regarding the Geographic Origin and Etymologies of the "Jeje" Name

"Luiza Geige," valued at eighty mil-reis, appears registered in the inventory of Antonio Sardinha, on September 3, 1711, in the parish of Muritiba in the Recôn-cavo.[69] This is the first known record of the *Jeje* ethnonym in Brazil. I found a second reference, from 1714, in the parish of São Gonçalo dos Campos, to a "Joanna Gege sick and having a swollen leg and with a wound, valued at thirty mil-reis"; and a third in 1717, also in Muritiba, to a slave "Catherina Gege."[70] After 1719, the records of Jeje slaves in the inventories of the Recôncavo begin to increase progressively (see below). As the inventories are only drafted upon the death of the proprietor of the goods, one can infer that the term *Gege* was already known and used some years prior to 1711, when the purchase of "Luiza Geige" took place, probably in the first decade of the eighteenth century.

The first fact worth pointing out is that the use of *Jeje* is restricted to Brazil and does not appear documented in Haiti, Cuba, Trinidad, or in other parts of the Americas, while other ethnonyms from the Gbe-speaking region such as *Alada* ("Lada," "Arada," "Rada," "Ardra") or *Mahi* ("Mai," "Makii") have been preserved in various parts of the New World (Cuba, Haiti, Trinidad). Furthermore, in eighteenth-century Brazil the use of the ethnonym appears to be limited to the Captaincy of Bahia and, to a lesser extent, to the state of Maranhão (district of Piauí), where a first and only reference to Jeje slaves is found in 1758.[71] Even in *Obra nova da língua geral de mina*, a vocabulary of the language of the Gbe-speaking slaves in Minas Gerais, written by Peixoto in 1741, there is no mention of the term *Jeje*. In Rio it is only in 1835 that the first reference to the ethnonym *Gege* appears, which significantly is in relation to slaves imported from Bahia.[72] It may also be during this late period that the term was "exported" from Bahia to Pernambuco as a consequence of the internal slave trade. This implies that the use of the ethnonym was originally related to the Bahian slave trade and maybe, more specifically, the Recôncavo, and from there it would have spread to other regions.

In West Africa, the term *Jeje* only appears documented as *djédji* beginning in the second half of the nineteenth century, principally in the writings of the priests of the Missions Africaines de Lyon. It was used normally to designate the Gun, the Adja inhabitants of Porto-Novo, or to refer to their language and, more rarely, as in the writings of A. L. d'Albeca, to refer generically to the Gbe-speaking area, when speaking of the "Djedji coast." Additionally, on an 1892 map "based on the most recent expeditions," the term *djedjis* designates the peoples along the shores of Lake Aheme, the majority of whom are Hula and Hueda.[73] Cornevin concludes that *Jeje*, written as "djedje," was the name given to the Gun in Porto-Novo by the French colonial administration.[74] Today, the term is no longer in use but is still remembered as relating to the Gun. However, it is worth noting that when the term *Jeje* appeared in the Recôncavo, Porto-Novo did not yet exist.

Lorand Matory suggests that the historiography of the written term showing precedence in Brazil could indicate that the word developed there and was possibly brought to Benin by African ex-slaves who returned there in the nineteenth century.[75] Given that the use of the ethnonym was common among slave traders and owners, as well as among Africans themselves, it is more likely that, despite the lack of documentation, the term *Jeje* originated in Africa, as happens with almost all other denominations of African ethnic nations in Brazil. More precisely, one could hypothesize that it resulted from a Portuguese adaption of some African term by Bahian slave traders.

Because the term *Jeje* appeared in the Recôncavo in the first decade of the 1700s and came into general use by the second, one ought to consider what was happening then along the coast of the Gbe-speaking area and which of the ports of embarkation used by the Portuguese (Popo, Ouidah, Jakin, Apa) might have been the term's geographical origin. This analysis might help identify which peoples were denominated as Jeje.

As I have mentioned, after 1692, with the destruction of Offra, the European factories and commerce were concentrated in Ouidah. The Dutch established themselves there in 1703, and an estimated 30,000 slaves embarked there annually. In 1704 the French built Fort St. Louis de Grégoy. With the increase in demand, the price of slaves in Ouidah doubled between 1700 and 1701.[76] Despite the constant Dutch threat and lacking Lisbon's support, the Bahian merchants were active in Ouidah. Between 1698 and 1702 they intended to build a fort there (or alternatively in Popo) and establish a company to monopolize the trade in that part of the coast to the detriment of the Portuguese merchants, but the project failed.[77]

However, the slave trade continued to grow, and between 1701 and 1710, 216 Bahian ships anchored on the Mina Coast.[78] The independent and unregulated activity of the Bahian merchants, who, in their eagerness to fill their ships quickly, sometimes paid more than market prices, brought about a certain degree of commercial chaos and generally led other Europeans to oppose their presence in Ouidah. In 1714, du Colombier, director of the French fort, wrote of "the confusion and disorder of the Portuguese," saying they had "spoiled everything" in this area.[79]

Thus, between approximately 1700 and 1714, the trade in the Gbe-speaking area was centralized in Ouidah, to the detriment of Allada and Jakin, Allada's port at the time. The fact that the term *Jeje* began to appear in the Recôncavo precisely at this time, when significantly the term *Arda* began slowly to recede from use, suggests an initial hypothesis that the term *Jeje* occurred in direct relation to the emergent commercial hegemony of Ouidah.

However, when Labat, in his report of the Chevalier de Marchais's voyage in 1725, lists the various denominations attributed to the slaves in Ouidah and Allada—*Arada, Nagô, Foin (Fon), Tebou (Ijebu), Guiamba, Mallais (Malês), Ayois (Oyo), Minois (Mina),* and *Aquera*[80]—he does not mention the term *Jeje*. Given that the slave traders distinguished very well between the diverse groups of slaves they were buying and that, as Labat points out, "the American colonies learned to know them through long experience," the absence of the term *Jeje* from his list suggests that its use was restricted to Bahian or Lusophone traders and was not used by traders from France or other nations. Alternatively, the term's appearance should be sought among other ports outside of Ouidah.[81]

Nina Rodrigues, in his classic *Os africanos no Brasil* (*The Africans in Brazil*), identifies the "Jeje" with the Dahomeans. Influenced by his reading of Ellis's *The Ewe-Speaking People*, Rodrigues suggests that *Jeje* derives from the ethnonym *Gen*. "The Gêge denomination comes from the zone or territory of the Slave Coast that goes from Bageida [in Togo, to the west of Agbodrafo (Porto Seguro)] to Akraku [between Petit- and Grand-Popo] and that the English spell Geng, but that the blacks pronounce 'egége.'"[82]

For Rodrigues, *Jeje* designates primarily the Gen peoples located on the coast to the west of the Mono River, in the area of Mina-Popo, whose largest ports were Ané́ho and Agoué́, "from whence came a large number of slaves to Brazil." However, the laws of phonetic transformation do not corroborate the hypothesis, given that the term *Gen* is pronounced as "guen" (as the "gue" in "guest") even—contrary to Rodrigues's opinion—by the very natives, and its repetition in the form of "guenguen" could not easily become Jeje.[83] The occurrence of "egége" in that region could result from the late diffusion of the term by those returning from Brazil who settled on that part of the coast beginning in 1835.

Vivaldo da Costa Lima suggests that *Jeje* derives from the word *âjèjì*, which in the Yoruba language means foreigner or stranger. He explains that the Nagô from the area of Porto-Novo called the Adja invaders, who came from the west, *ajeji*, or, in abbreviated form, *jeji*. Subsequently, the Adja who settled in Porto-Novo, that is the Gun, appropriated the term to refer to themselves and, as I have mentioned, the term was finally appropriated by the French administrators and missionaries.[84] This etymological hypothesis attributing a Yoruba origin to the term *Jeje* is persuasive. There is, however, a noteworthy historical objection: The migrations of the Ajda "foreigners" into the area of Porto-Novo came about only after 1724, after the conquest of Allada by Agadja and, therefore, subsequent to the appearance of the term *Jeje* in Brazil.

The same etymological hypothesis might work better in the context of Apa, which, in the seventeenth century, was the easternmost port of the Allada kingdom on its border with the kingdom of Benin, in the area of present-day Badagri. In 1682, traders there bought slaves from Allada, Offra, Ouidah, and Popo and sold cloth brought from Benin, indicating the presence of Yoruba- and Edo-speaking merchants.[85] When the Dutch in Ouidah considered moving to Apa in 1707, the king of Allada promised them exclusive trade rights "excepting the Portuguese," suggesting that the Bahian merchants were trading in Apa at that time.[86] By 1715, Apa had obtained a certain degree of independence from Allada, and both Fon merchants from the emergent kingdom of Dahomey as well as Yoruba- and Edo-speakers from the kingdom of Benin sold their slaves there.[87] It is therefore possible that the denomination *ájèji*—applied perhaps to slaves brought by the Dahomeans—was popularized by the Yoruba-speaking merchants in the port of Apa and appropriated afterward by the Portuguese slave traders.

Verger further suggests that the term *Jeje* derives from the ethnonym *Adja*, but once again, phonetic laws have no easy explanation for the evolution of *Adja* to *Jeje*.[88] It is clear that the term *Jeje* came to designate a plurality of Adja peoples; however, I am inclined to think that at its origin the denomination was restricted to a more specific group or geography. Along these lines Hypolite Brice Sogbossi suggests another etymology related to a proto-Yoruba group called the Idjè, localized in the area between Pobé and Kétou, to the north of Porto-Novo.

Idjè is this group's ethnic self-denomination, while the Yoruba called them Ohori or Ahori, which the Fon pronounced "Holli." The French colonial administration came to call the group by the compound term *Hollidjé* (*Hollidjè*), which, besides being an ethnonym, became a toponym and glossonym. Sogbossi argues that *Jeje* could be a reduplication of this ethno-glossonym (Idjè > Djè or Idjè > Djèidjè > Djèdjè). The onomatopoeic reduplication of monosyllabic indigenous terms seems to have been a common practice among the Portuguese to designate native peoples. Pazzi gives various examples such as *Popo*, which could be a reduplication of *Kpo* or, on the Ivory Coast, *Quaqua*, which would be a reduplication of the local greeting *kwa*.[89]

The Idjè are known for their independence and resistance against French colonial power, but if their ethnonym is at the origin of the term *Jeje*, it would imply that they occupied the Hollidjè area before the eighteenth century. An oral tradition of their neighbors, the Ajda-Wéré, explains that the Idjè were descendants of a group of Nagô hunters who had come from Méko, in what is now Nigeria, and that they occupied the area between Pobé and Kétou only after the arrival of the Adja after 1730. However, the Idjè themselves declared that they were the first inhabitants of this region, a view that would be corroborated by their alleged distinct phenotypic traits that some say differ from those of the Nagô. Christian Merlo and Pierre Vidaud also speak of the existence of Idjè hunters farther to the south, in the area of Akron and Adjaché (later Porto-Novo), before the fourteenth century. Based on ethnographic similarities, these authors suggest that the Hula and the Hueda, peoples today considered as being from Tado, actually came from this proto-Yoruba group, which would confirm the Idjè's long presence in the region. Though Tidjani identifies their language as a "modified Yoruba dialect," this might be the result of a long process of acculturation between the Idjè and their Nagô neighbors. Furthermore, the French missionary Laffitte, at the end of the nineteenth century, seems to refer to the Idjè when, in his account of the traditions pertaining to the founding of the kingdom of Porto-Novo, he mentions "the Djedgi, a ferocious people from the interior," who would have expelled the Nagô founders of that kingdom from their territory in the seventeenth century.[90]

To contribute to this etymological debate, I presented in a previous study another possible interpretation according to which Jeje comes from the toponym *Adjaché*.[91] Adjaché (written by different authors as "Ajâcé," "Adjatchè," "Adjarchè," "Ajase," or "Jasin") was the capital of a region that the Oyo called Adjaché Ipo, an area to which the Adja of Allada fled following the conquest of their kingdom by the armies of Agaja in 1724. According to Pazzi, "Ajâcé" means "the Adja settled here," and according to Adolphe Akindélé and Cyrille Aguessy, "Adjatchè" means "conquered by the Adja." According to another version, Adjaché and Akron were the original villages from which later emerged Xògbónú, capital of the kingdom of Porto-Novo, which the Nagô continued to call Adjaché.[92] It is known that the Yoruba words lose the initial vowel when appropriated by Gbe-speaking peoples. Thus, one possible phonetic transformation would be: Adjaché > Djaché > Djedjé > Jeje. This hypothesis would only be valid if, as Merlo and Vidaud and Akindélé and Aguessy maintain, this toponym emerged before the founding of the kingdom of Porto-Novo.[93] This would also explain why in the nineteenth century the term *Djedje* was applied to the Gun of Porto-Novo.

The etymological debate, though not conclusive, therefore seems to relate the origin of the *Jeje* denomination with peoples captured along the west bank of the Oueme River, whether in the area of Adjaché (Porto-Novo) or, more probably, in the Idjè area between Pobé and Kétou. In the first decade of the eighteenth century these slaves could have been sold to the Portuguese in the neighboring port of Apa, either by Fon or Yoruba and Edo traders from the kingdom of Benin or by other groups who traded there. From Apa or from other ports such as Ouidah, Jakin, or Popo the slaves could then have been shipped to Brazil. With time, the ethnonym *Idjè*, or the toponym *Adjaché*, appropriated and transformed by the Bahian tradesmen into *Jeje*, came to denominate a plurality of Adja peoples in Bahia, while in West Africa it remained restricted to the Gun of the kingdom of Porto-Novo. The other possibility would be that the term was used by Bahian traders to designate slaves embarked in the port of Ouidah. In this case, the etymological origin of the term would remain nebulous and future studies would be necessary to resolve the question.

The Bahian Slave Trade in the Vodun Area following Agaja's Conquest of the Coast (1724–1850)

To continue with the history of the Bahian slave trade on the Mina Coast, in 1721, one year following the arrival of Vasco Fernandez César de Menezes as governor of Bahia and viceroy of Brazil, navy captain Joseph de Torres finally obtained the resources necessary to build the fort of Ajuda in Ouidah, despite opposition from other European nations. Soon after, in June 1723, Bahian merchants created the Corisco Company in order to monopolize and solidify the slave-trade bases along the Mina Coast. However, these Bahian efforts did not come to fruition until years later, after the conquest of the coast by the Dahomeans.[94] In 1724, during the reign of Agaja, the Dahomean army, continuing the expansion begun by Hwegbaja, invaded Allada. In 1727, the Dahomeans attacked Savi, the capital of the Hueda kingdom, and Ouidah (Glehue), its port, fell shortly thereafter.[95]

These military campaigns triggered important migrations of Hueda and Hula toward the west, into the Popo area, where the Hueda, in addition to making various attempts to reconquer their own kingdom, became involved in a long civil war. Other Hula groups, as well as Aizo and Ouemenu, escaped to the east, into the area of Porto-Novo, Apa, and Badagri. The devastation caused by the wars and periodic invasions of Oyo caused a decline in trade in Ouidah until at least 1733. Jakin, the coastal slave center of Allada, succeeded initially in maintaining a certain degree of commercial activity, while declaring its submission to the Fon. In 1731, against the interests of the Ajuda fort, then controlled by João Basílio, Joseph Torres constructed a new factory flying the Portuguese flag in Jakin. However, Jakin was invaded and completely destroyed by the army of Agaja on April 2, 1732, following the conspiracy of the Dutch factor Hertog who, allied with the local population and promising the future support of the Hueda and Oyo, intended to end Dahomean domination of the slave trade. The Dahomeans thus came to control the major ports of the Gbe-speaking area—Ouidah and Jakin—while Grand-Popo and Apa, lesser ports, declined in importance. The slave trade became the principal economic activity in the kingdom of Dahomey.[96]

Between 1727 and 1740, the Dahomean wars for coastal domination, despite the damage inflicted on commerce during the initial years, generated a great number of prisoners: according to some estimates 11,000 taken during the conquest of Ouidah in 1727 and 4,538 in Jakin in 1732.[97] Historians of slavery have noted that the exportation of Africans from the Mina Coast to Bahia increased greatly between 1700 and 1730, then declined substantially after 1730 with the sugar economic crisis.[98] One might suppose that during this period a great number of those enslaved and shipped in Bahian vessels belonged to coastal groups, such as the Hula, Hueda, and Aizo. At the same time, when the cessation of Oyo attacks allowed it, the Dahomean incursions into Mahi country and the Ouemé River region continued to provide important contingents of slaves from the hinterland. This continuous influx of Gbe-speaking people into Bahia during the first half of the eighteenth century gradually created a stratum of slave population so demographically significant as to develop a new collective identity that in the second half of the century would become the "Jeje nation."

Besides the traditional ports of Grand-Popo, Ouidah, Jakin, and Apa, the Bahian merchants would occasionally trade in other enclaves outside the area of Fon influence, such as Aného or the new port of Epe (Ekpe), located near Porto-Novo. As Verger documented well, the slave trade on the Mina Coast was gradually displaced from the above-mentioned ports to Porto-Novo, Badagri, and Onim (Lagos) after the 1750s. In the first year of that decade, the Dahomean king Tegbesu, perhaps foreseeing this move, sent an ambassador to Portugal, by way of Bahia, asking for exclusive commercial rights in his ports. The Marquis de Pombal did not agree to this monopoly, fearing a progressive increase in the price of slaves, which, since the conquest of Ouidah by Agaja, had been highly inflated. Thus, Pombal can be considered the political mentor of the displacement of Portuguese trade to the eastern ports.

The Porto-Novo slave trade was controlled by the kingdom of Oyo, while that of Onin was controlled by the kingdom of Benin. In 1758, Theodozio Rodrigues da Costa, in charge of the fort of Ajuda, writing to the viceroy of Portugal, mentioned the "new port" (Porto-Novo) for the first time, noting that there slaves could be traded for eight to twelve rolls of tobacco, whereas in Ajuda the price was between thirteen and sixteen rolls. In 1776, the governor of the French fort in Ouidah wrote to the minister of the colonies reporting on the economic advantages of Porto-Novo and Badagri, "where business has been profitable for some years." João de Oliveira, a former Yoruba slave in Recife who resided and served as caboceer in West Africa between 1733 and 1770, was instrumental in opening the slave trade in the eastern ports.

Around 1775, the commerce in Ouidah entered into serious decline. In 1777, the new Dahomean monarch, Kpengla, unsuccessfully attempted to re-vitalize the port of Jakin to attract European interests. In the same year, the director of the French fort, Olivier Montanguère, notes that "the Dahomeans are in a weakened state that does not allow them to obtain prisoners of war." The eastern ports could not be attacked with impunity by Dahomey, for they were under the protection of Oyo, but Kpengla used subterfuge and combined strategies in order to obtain his ends. For example, in 1781, he attacked Epe, Ketonou (not to be confused with Cotonou), and other places within the influence of Porto-Novo, "under the pretext that they had participated in the depredations committed by the people of Badagri in Porto-Novo." Then in 1783, he allied himself with Oyo and Porto-Novo to attack Badagri. Despite, or perhaps because of, this destabilizing policy, commerce in Ouidah declined throughout the 1780s. The result was a significant drop in the importation of Jeje slaves to Bahia (see chapter 2, table 1).[99]

The rivalry between the ports controlled by Dahomey and the eastern ports of the Gulf of Benin lasted until the end of the slave trade. In 1795, the Dahomean king Agongolo sent two ambassadors to Bahia with a new proposal to grant the slave trade monopoly in the port of Ouidah. The idea was rejected, among other reasons, out of fear of an excessive concentration of "slaves from a single nation, from which pernicious consequences could easily result."[100] The Dahomean king Adandozan also insisted on this monopoly with the Portuguese, as shown in his letter to the Portuguese king Dom João VI of November 1804.[101]

It is worth noting that in this year the Fulani began a jihad against the Hausa, which resulted in many prisoners from both sides being sold in the ports of the gulf by slavers from Oyo. Likewise, the Oyo kingdom, because of various internal conflicts beginning with Afonja's revolt (c. 1797), came progressively to lose its power, and successive civil wars also resulted in a great number of captives. Consequently, many Hausa and Nagô slaves were shipped from Porto-Novo to Bahia—primarily by Portuguese, Brazilian, and even Afro-Brazilian merchants—contributing significantly to the African revolts that occurred between 1807 and 1835.[102]

In 1807 the Portuguese abandoned the fort at Ouidah, and the English unilaterally abolished the slave trade. Between 1807 and 1809, the slave trade in Ouidah all but ceased. Adandozan sought alternative forms of commerce in agriculture, but the Anglo-Portuguese treaty of 1810 allowed the continuation of the slave trade in Ouidah while prohibiting it in Aného, Porto-Novo, Badagri, and Lagos. This revitalized Dahomean slave interests. It was precisely in 1810 that the Bahian Francisco Felix de Souza returned to Ouidah, becoming from that point on the most important slave trader in the area.[103] An estimated forty-five Bahian vessels traded in Ouidah in 1812.[104] Thus, the importation of Jeje slaves to Bahia, which had declined since 1780, experienced a second and final resurgence between 1810 and 1820 (see chapter 2, table 1).

The slow disintegration of Oyo caused general economic and political destabilization in the region, accompanied, after 1830, by the rise of refugee cities such as New Oyo, Ibadan, and Abeokuta. This was the period of significant numbers of clandestine shipments of Nagô slaves to Bahia through the eastern ports of Porto-Novo, Badagri, and Lagos, but also from Ouidah, where the Chacha Felix de Souza, under the protection of King Ghezo, exercised near absolute control over the slave trade until the beginning of the 1840s.[105] Similarly, since 1835 there had existed a constant reflux of freed Africans from Brazil to the Mina Coast, which lasted until the end of the century. Some of them moved periodically between the two Atlantic coasts, establishing trade relations and regular contacts that kept the African population of Bahia informed as to the happenings of the African coast. The colonies of the freed *retornados* (returnees) (Nagô, Hausa, and Jeje) in Aného, Agoué, Ouidah, Porto-Novo, and Lagos contributed to both the continuation of the illegal slave trade until its extinction and the development of an alternative agricultural economy based on the production of palm oil.[106] Brazil declared the end of the slave trade in 1850, though there are reports of the seizure of frigates and brigs with illegal human cargo in 1851 and as late as 1856.[107]

As a result of the expansion of the Dahomey kingdom from 1720 to 1780 and in the first decades of the nineteenth century, the slave trade in the ports of the Gbe-speaking area was constant, generating a continuous flow of Jeje slaves into Bahia. It is possible that until about the middle of the eighteenth century, the various coastal groups, such as the Hueda, Hula, Aizo, and Gun, and those of the interior such as the Ouemenu, Agonli, and Mahi, maintained marked ethnic differentiation and were relatively independent peoples. But in the second half of the eighteenth century, as Dahomey solidified its centralized power, these groups tended to mix, both in terms of residence (as a result of exogamic marriages, forced migrations, internal slave trading, etc.) and in terms of their cultural practices. For example, in regard to religion, Dahomey adopted a policy of assimilating the cults of the peoples under their control, imposing at the same time a hegemonic and hierarchized model of religious institutions. The ancestral cult of the royal family of Abomey (Nesuhue) gained the status of a "national" cult, to which other "public" vodun cults were subordinate. Eventually the organization of the voduns cult imposed by the Fon influenced the cults of the peoples under their rule (see chapter 3). This process of growing cultural homogenization that occurred in Dahomey might well have contributed to a situation in which the groups from this area, once in Brazil, assimilated with relative ease the generic denomination *Jeje* as a form of collective identity.

Thus, the denomination *Jeje*, initially restricted to a particular Adja group, probably located in the region of Porto-Novo or its environs, acquired a more generic meaning with the expansion of Dahomey and in the context of the Lusophone slave trade. It came to designate those peoples controlled by, or under the influence of, that kingdom, but that sometimes could embark in ports outside of Dahomean territory. In this semantic expansion of the term, certain cultural elements, such as linguistic similarity, became defining aspects of the content of the denomination, to the detriment of other factors such as ports of embarkation. In 1848, at the end of the period of the illegal slave trade, Francis Castelau, French consul in Bahia, wrote, "The Géjés or Dahomeans who form a powerful nation are quite numerously represented in Bahia; they previously embarked at Ouidah, but today they come mostly through Porto-Novo."[108] The next chapter examines the presence of the Jeje in Bahia.

2 The Formation of a Jeje Ethnic Identity in Bahia in the Eighteenth and Nineteenth Centuries

Some Notes on the Demographic Fluctuations of the Jeje in the Recôncavo and in Salvador

Having reviewed the Portuguese and Bahian slave trade on the Mina Coast, we can now examine the possible processes that led to the formation of a Jeje ethnic identity among the African population in Bahia in the eighteenth and first half of the nineteenth centuries. What was the demographic importance of this forced Jeje migration to Bahia?

Unfortunately, the data on the evolution and demographic structure of the Bahian population of the eighteenth century is either very imprecise or does not exist. According to Kátia Mattoso, the census information of this period is not to be trusted and does not allow us to quantify, with even a minimum degree of assurance, the total count or the proportion of freed or enslaved blacks and mestizos. The nineteenth century presents a different situation, however. Basing her figures on an 1808 census found in the Regional Archive of Cachoeira by the U.S. historian Catherine Lugar, and on the official census of 1872, Mattoso concludes that blacks and mestizos constituted 78.3 percent (43 percent free and 35.3 percent enslaved) of Bahia's population in 1808, decreasing to 72.4 percent (60.2 percent free and 12.2 percent enslaved) in 1872. The enslaved proportion of the population drops significantly as the century advances.[1] The insufficient data and very general figures make it more difficult to characterize the contingent of Africans within that population and more specifically the Jeje, one among the many African groups.

The most recent estimates suggest that between 1701 and 1810, Portuguese vessels destined for Bahia left the Slave Coast with approximately 656,000 Africans, of whom some 598,200 arrived.[2] Between 1801 and 1851, an estimated 328,500 African slaves arrived in the port of Salvador.[3] The estimates of the annual average importation for this period vary according to several authors, between 5,600 and 7,700 Africans, and show a marked increase commencing in the 1840s, when the trade was ostensibly prohibited by the English. For example, from 1846 to 1850, on the eve of the abolition of the Atlantic slave trade,

TABLE 1 Ethnoracial Composition of the Slave Population in the Tobacco-Producing Area of Cachoeria (1698–1820)

	1698–1729		1730–49		1750–79		1780–1800		1801–20	
	N.	%	N.	%	N.	%	N.	%	N.	%
Gentio da Guiné	32	9.3	—	—	—	—	—	—	—	—
Angola	59	17.1	51	16.6	85	21.9	87	29.8	155	19.3
Benguela	36	10.4	10	3.2	10	2.6	9	3.1	14	1.7
Other Central African	46	13.3	13	4.2	23	5.9	6	2.1	10	1.2
Mina	122	35.4	128	41.6	105	27.0	72	24.7	102	12.7
Jeje	**39**	**11.3**	**106**	**27.1**	**115**	**29.6**	**60**	**20.5**	**237**	**29.5**
Nagô	—	—	5	1.6	35	9.0	51	17.5	159	19.8
Hausa	—	—	—	—	—	—	2	0.7	81	10.1
Other West African	11	3.2	20	6.5	15	4.2	5	1.7	46	5.7
TOTAL AFRICANS	345	100.0	308	100.0	388	100.0	292	100.0	804	100.0
Central Africa Subtotal	141	25.2	74	12.4	118	9.4	102	11.7	179	8.0
West Africa Subtotal	172	30.7	234	39.3	270	21.4	189	21.7	625	27.9
Creole	192	34.3	225	37.8	645	51.2	365	42.0	1,005	44.9
Mestizo	55	9.8	62	10.4	227	18.0	214	24.6	429	19.2
TOTAL	560	100.0	595	100.0	1260	100.0	870	100.0	2,238	100.0

Source: For the period of 1698–1800 ARC inventories, 264 inventories were consulted: 173 from Cachoeira, 32 from São Gonzalo dos Campos, 26 from São Pedro de Muritiba, 12 from Belém, 7 from Santo Antônio de Tibiri, 5 from Nossa Senhora do Desterro do Outeiro Redondo, 3 from Santo Estevão de Jacuípe, 2 from Conceição da Feira, 2 from Capoeiruçu, 1 from São Félix, and 1 from Maragogipe. For the period of 1801–20 inventories, APEBa, Project Reis–Nigerian Hinterland. N.B.: "Mestizo" includes mulattoes, *pardos, cabras,* and mestiços.

the estimated annual average was 8,700 Africans.[4] A portion of this population was in transit to other destinations, housed at times for months in the city's warehouses built by the merchants for that purpose.

Few authors have presented information regarding the ethnoracial categories of the eighteenth-century slave population, and the available data is generally insufficient.[5] In order to fill this lacuna partially, I consulted the inventories from 1698 to 1820 that correspond to the tobacco-growing region of the Recôncavo (the municipality of Cachoeira and its districts), kept in the Arquivo Regional de Cachoeira (Regional Archive of Cachoeira, ARC), as well as those from 1750 to 1800 that relate to the sugar-producing area (the municipalities of São Francisco do Conde and Santo Amaro da Purificação) of the Arquivo Público do Estado da Bahia (Public Archive of the State of Bahia, APEBa).[6] The data from these inventories was complemented by similar research performed by João José Reis for the period 1801–20, from which

TABLE 2 Ethnoracial Composition of the Slave Population in the Sugar-Producing Areas of São Francisco do Conde and Santo Amaro da Purificação, 1750–1820

| | 1750–79 | | 1780–1800 | | 1801–20 | |
	N.	%	N.	%	N.	%
Angola	100	36.5	126	27.5	168	30.4
Benguela	4	1.5	34	7.4	25	4.5
Other Central African	10	3.6	4	0.9	12	2.2
Mina	26	9.5	15	3.3	28	5.1
Jeje	111	**40.5**	166	**36.2**	122	**22.0**
Nagô	10	3.6	97	21.1	102	18.5
Hausa	—	—	4	0.9	60	10.9
Other West African	13	4.7	13	2.9	35	6.3
TOTAL AFRICANS	274	100.0	459	100.0	552	100.0
Central African subtotal	114	21.3	164	15.8	205	18.8
West African subtotal	152	28.4	291	28.1	347	31.9
Creole	201	37.5	411	39.7	365	33.5
Mestizo	69	12.9	169	16.3	172	15.8
TOTAL	536	100.0	1035	100.0	1089	100.0

Source: APEBa inventories. For the period of 1750–1800, 48 inventories were consulted from Santo Amaro and 118 from São Francisco do Conde. For the period of 1801–20, data extracted from the Reis–Nigerian Hinterland Project.

resulted tables 1 and 2.[7] Although the sample is relatively dense, it is important to remember that the results represent mere approximations.

One may observe that during the second half of the eighteenth century, more than half of the enslaved population of the Bahian Recôncavo was "Brazilian," or Creole (blacks born in Brazil of African descent) and mestizo, which includes mulattoes, *pardos,** and *cabras* (dark-skinned people and those of mixed origin). Citing the estimates of Patrick Manning on the exportations from the Mina Coast to Bahia, Stuart Schwartz notes that the decrease in the importation of Africans coincides with the decline of the sugar economy between 1730 and 1780.[8] Thus, the demographic "creolization" of the slave population was influenced, and in fact stimulated, by the sugar crisis. It was only after 1790, with the recovery of sugar exportations, that the sugar-mill owners spent capital on renewing their slave workforce with fresh African levies. This situation led to a certain demographic "Africanization" in the sugar-producing area in the first decades of the 1800s, above all in Salvador (see table 3), though in the tobacco region the predominance of the Creole element continued, as did a growing process of racial mixing.[9]

Fernando Ortiz has said, in relation to agricultural exportation in Cuba, that "sugar cane and tobacco are all contrast." According to Schwartz, the eighteenth-century slave population of the Bahian sugar area was characterized by a high percentage of Africans, a scarcity of women, and few children. This distribution was greater in the larger mills (*engenhos**) than on the sugar plantations (*fazendas de cana*) and indicates the direct dependence of the sugar economy on the transatlantic slave trade.[10] The tobacco plantations, which generally had less economic power and access to credit, employed fewer slaves and probably absorbed those that were cheaper (women, children, and the elderly), because the cultivation of tobacco requires relatively less physical strength than does that of sugar. This circumstance favored a more balanced proportion between men and women and presumably the establishment of a greater number of family nuclei. Together with a richer diet (resulting from the raising of livestock and the production of cassava, beans, and corn on the tobacco farm), this resulted in greater fecundity, which yielded a growing number of Creole and mixed-race children. Thus, the tobacco economy seemed to depend less on the transatlantic slave trade than the sugar economy without, however, being entirely independent of it.[11] In any case, a great proportion of Creoles and mestizos (around 44 percent for the second half of the eighteenth century) were children of less than twelve years of age, and were not, in theory, part of the labor force.

The available data on African groups is made difficult to interpret by the wide range of meanings given to the ethnic categories and the variability in the use of this system of classification. Besides generic expressions such as "gentio da Guiné" or "gentio da Costa," the vast majority of enslaved population was referred to with a small repertory of names of "nations," including Angola, Benguela, Mina, Jeje, Nagô, and Hausa. A considerable number of additional terms—some referring to ports or regions of embarkation and others that can be properly identified as ethnicities in use in Africa[12]—were applied to a relatively small number of slaves (see "other" category in tables 1 and 2).

Ethnonyms such as *Arda* or *Lada* (*Allada*), *Coda* or *Codavi, Fon, Sabaru* (*Savalu*), and *Maki* (*Mahi*) refer to groups of the Gbe-speaking area, but they rarely appear in the inventories. The category "Arda" for example, was quite frequent in the first decade of the 1700s, but it became supplanted by the *Jeje* denomination, a process which, as I show above, corresponded to the decline of the Allada kingdom and the growing hegemony of Ouidah in the Mina Coast trade. The occasional use of terms such as *Sabaru* and *Maquim* reflected the regular incursions of the Dahomean army into the Mahi country in its search for prisoners of war.

The expression "gentio da Guiné," practically the only term during the seventeenth century, also declined drastically in use in the second decade of the eighteenth century, while other, more specific, denominations came into use to differentiate the growing diversity of the slave trade. However, certain generic categories seem to have been used more in specific regions. For example, the expression "gentio da Costa" was much used in the city of Salvador (see table 3) but was practically unknown in the Recôncavo. On the one hand, this suggests that Mina and many Jeje were classified in Salvador merely as "gentio da Costa"; on the other, it indicates that the *Jeje* denomination was particularly significant in the Recôncavo. Conversely, in the sugar area, especially in Santo Amaro, one notes the small percentage of Mina in comparison to the high percentages of Jeje and Nagô. More than indicating differentiated slave-trade networks for the sugar and tobacco areas, this difference suggests diversified regional usage of the ethnoracial classification system. Perhaps the sugar-mill owners, in their desire to identify their merchandise when buying large groups of captives, favored the more specific *Jeje* and *Nagô* denominations, rather than the more generic *Mina*.

This diachronic and geographic variability of the ethnic classification system makes its analysis difficult. A future, more detailed study will be required to unravel its complexity. However, the available data confirms the predominance in Bahia of slaves from West Africa, as opposed to those from Central Africa. In the sugar-producing areas, however, the proportion of Angola, Benguela, and other Bantu language groups was larger than that recorded for the same groups in the tobacco-producing areas. After 1750 in Cachoeira, the percentage of Central Africans in relation to West Africans varied between 22 percent and 35 percent, while in Santo Amaro and São Francisco it fluctuated between 35 percent and 41 percent. This difference shows that the relative proportion between Jeje and Angola, the two predominant African groups until 1820, varied not only by period, but also according to region.

One of the better-known changes of the first half of the eighteenth century is the significant increase in the number of Jeje, which climbs from 11.3 percent in the first three decades of the 1700s to 27.1 percent in 1730–50 (table 1). This increase reflects Agaja's conquest of the Gbe coastal area and the many prisoners of war consequently embarked in Ouidah. From 1750 until 1780, this group reaches its highest proportion, constituting the most numerous African nation, with almost 30 percent of the slave population in the tobacco regions and 40 percent in the sugar regions. The large exportation of Jeje corresponds, therefore, to the reigns of Agaja (1708–40) and Tegbesu (1740–75) in Dahomey.

With kings Kpengla and Agongolo in the last two decades of the century, the proportion of Jeje in the mills and sugar plantations of Bahia decreases to 36 percent, giving way to an increase in the number of Nagô, who begin to carry more demographic weight. This tendency can be explained by the decline of the slave trade in Ouidah, caused in part by its growth in the eastern ports in the Gulf of Benin (Porto-Novo, Badagri, and Onin), which, primarily after 1780, competed with, and limited the trade in, the largest Dahomean port. This fact would also explain the progressive growth in the number of Nagô after 1760, and also that of other West African groups, including the first Hausa, Tapa, and Bariba (Borgu) to arrive in Bahia. Despite all this, the Jeje continued to constitute the most numerous African group.

In the tobacco area of the Recôncavo at this time there was a decline in the number of Jeje, who constituted only 20 percent of Africans compared to 30 percent for Angola. The growth in the number of Angola, and to a lesser extent of Benguela, in the final decades of the 1700s, is confirmed by the numbers given by Carlos Ott, who for the period 1778–97 documents, for the interior of the state, a clear preponderance of "Bantu," with a count of 2,163, while the "Sudanese" (Mina, Nagô, Jeje) number only 681.[13] Although the proportion of "Bantu" derived from Ott's data seems inflated, there is no doubt that at the turn of the nineteenth century the Angola regained a significant presence. The revitalization of the subequatorial slave trade coincided, as I have said, with the recovery of the sugar economy and the demand for African slave labor.

In the first two decades of the 1800s, the slave trade continued to prosper on the Mina Coast. The Anglo-Portuguese treaty of 1810, which forbade the slave trade in the ports of Aného, Porto-Novo, Badagri, and Lagos (momentarily giving the advantage to Ouidah), had little effect, as did the subsequent prohibition in 1815 of the slave trade north of the equator. The traders continued the clandestine embarkation of Jeje and other neighboring peoples such as Tapa, Bornu, Carabari, Benin, Nagô, and Hausa. The latter began to arrive in Bahia in significant numbers in 1804, the year the Fulani waged an Islamic jihad against them.[14] The Jeje and Angola continued to be the most important African groups, however, though there appeared to be a new inversion in their relative proportion. While in the tobacco regions the Jeje regained demographic superiority, eventually constituting almost 30 percent of the African population, in the sugar regions there was an opposite movement, with a rise in the number of Angola and a decline in the number of Jeje. In Salvador, during the same period of 1800 to 1820, the Jeje and Angola maintain similar proportions (see table 3).

As a whole, these oscillations were a result of the dynamics of the Brazilian sugar economy and its interconnections with the fluctuations of the Atlantic slave trade, itself dependent on the international conjuncture and the varying politics of Dahomey. The reasons for the regional Bahian variability are more difficult to identify and might include such things as the dynamics of the internal slave trade, subject as they were to the law of supply and demand; changes in the slave owners' ethnic preferences, conditioned perhaps by slavers' marketing in favor of one or another African group; or even simple statistical distortions.

Whatever the case may be, it is interesting to note that between 1730 and 1780 the Jeje ranked second only to the Mina (who certainly included slaves from the Gbe-speaking area) as the demographically most important African group among the slave population of the Recôncavo and probably of Bahia as a whole. Between 1780 and 1820, despite the significant presence of the Angola, the Jeje continued to have prominence, maintaining or, at certain times and in certain places, regaining numeric supremacy. After 1820, however, the arrival of great numbers of Nagô led this group to surpass both Jeje and Angola.

But before commenting on this new period, it is appropriate to analyze certain characteristics of the Jeje population. For the period 1750–1800, 452 enslaved persons from this nation were counted out of a sample of 3,737 individuals, thus constituting 12.1 percent of the total slave population and 32 percent of the African slave population. In two cases it was not possible to identify the sex, and the remainder included 232 men and 218 women, giving a rate of ninety-five males for every 100 women in the tobacco region and 114 males per 100 women in the sugar region. These are low numbers in relation to those of the total slave population, which in the tobacco region would be approximately 123 males for every 100 women for the same period; in the sugar region during the eighteenth century as a whole, the number of males would be about 185.[15]

Seventy-seven individuals were identified as married, forty-seven women and thirty men, meaning that only 17 percent of the Jeje slave population was married formally in the church. The women's higher rate of marriage probably results from the relative lack of women among the slave population as a whole. This fact would also justify the high number of interethnic unions. Among the seventy-one married individuals for whom I identified the spouse's ethnicity, twenty-eight were members of the fourteen Jeje or intraethnic couples (including two Jeje-Savalu couples); the remaining forty-three Jeje were married to individuals of other ethnoracial categories. Some, more often women, married Creoles (fourteen cases) or even *cabras* and *pardos* (two cases), but most frequent were marriages with other Africans. In the sample I obtained, eight of the Jeje spouses were Angola, three Benguela, three Congo, one Masangano, four

Mina, five Nagô, and three São Tomé. The low proportion of ethnic endogamy (fourteen intraethnic couples as opposed to forty-three interethnic couples) and the high proportion of couples that include spouses from Central Africa do not seem to confirm the ethnic bias that Schwartz attributes to the choice of spouse in the slave marriages of the sugar region.[16] However, factors such as a master's imposition of marital partner or the lack of potential partners among smaller slave-holdings could easily compromise the endogamic ethnic preference.[17]

Among the forty-seven married Jeje women, little more than half (twenty-seven) had any children, giving a total of seventy-two Creoles (*crioulinhos*), an average of 1.5 children per couple. Though we lack the data—such as miscarriage, abortion, or infant mortality rates (which were probably quite high)—needed to estimate the Jeje fertility rate with precision, it seems that the Jeje population was far from sustainable through natural reproduction. However, seven of the Jeje mothers, interestingly belonging to intraethnic couples, produced thirty-seven children, or more than half of the estimated total. Likewise, forty "single" mothers with a total of seventy-five children were identified, which yields a fertility rate of 1.9 children per mother, somewhat less than the rate of married mothers, which was 2.6.[18]

As we have seen, in the second half of the eighteenth century the Creole and mestizo populations constituted the majority, which suggests that tobacco growers, and even some sugar-mill owners, allowed and probably encouraged marriage as a strategy for replacing their slave-holdings. If we add to this growth the interethnic mixing of Jeje marriages, we find grounds to question the division of the slave population according to culture of origin. In fact, the data suggests that in the second half of the eighteenth century there was a strong symbiosis of African values, which was certainly inherited by the Creoles.

The Jeje were also an adult population, and in many cases they suffered from serious health problems. I found only one reference to a Jeje boy (*moleque*) and a Jeje girl (*menina*), and while in general no ages are recorded, 22.5 percent of the slaves were identified as "old" or as of "advanced age." There also appears high number of sick or crippled, around 27.5 percent, a result of the harsh working conditions and the lack of any kind of medical attention. The ailments are varied, but there are many cases of groin injury, or hernia (*quebrados da virilha*), caused by carrying excessive weight on the head, as well as cases of gout, chest and stomach pain, asthma, "running of fluid down the legs" (*corrimento de baba*), "liver heat [*calor de fígado*] on the hands and feet" (a peeling of the skin), and illness simply described as "fatigue."

The great majority (72 percent) of Jeje slaves were employed in farming

TABLE 3 Ethnoracial Composition of the Slave Population, Salvador, 1702–1850

	1702–99		1800–1820		1821–50	
	N.	%	N.	%	N.	%
African	—	—	10	0.4	10	0.3
Gentio da Guiné	15	2.3	—	—	—	—
Angola	211	22.8	402	18.0	292	10.5
Benguela	53	5.7	91	4.0	44	1.6
Other Central African	41	4.4	57	2.6	280	10.0
Gentio da Costa	457	49.3	465	20.9	80	2.9
Mina	102	11.0	166	7.5	137	4.9
Jeje	32	**3.5**	420	**18.9**	331	**11.8**
Nagô	5	0.5	286	12.8	1204	43.2
Hausa	—	—	221	9.9	168	6.0
Other West African	11	1.2	109	4.9	243	8.7
TOTAL AFRICANS	927	100.0	2227	100.0	2789	100.0
Central African Subtotal	—	—	550	15.5	616	15.1
West African Subtotal	—	—	1667	47.0	2163	53.2
Creole	—	—	905	25.5	831	20.4
Mestizo	—	—	422	11.9	449	11.0
TOTAL	—	—	3544	100.00	4059	100.0

Source: APEBA Inventories. For the period 1702–99, Ott, "O negro . . .," 143. For the period 1800–1820, Project Reis-Nigerian Hinterland. For the period 1821–50, Andrade, *A mão-de-obra . . .*, 189–90. N.B.: The 20 "Africans" on the table's first line were deducted from the subtotals of Central and West Africans, and the "gentio da Costa" were counted as West Africans.

(*serviço de enxada*), that is, activities related to the cultivation of sugar cane, tobacco, or subsistence crops. The next most common category of employment was domestic services (*serviço da casa*). In fewer numbers appear more specialized occupations such as tobacco dryer, cook, carter, rope maker, or sailor. These skills are usually reflected in the higher prices of these slaves.

To this point, I have discussed primarily the Recôncavo Jeje slave population, but little has been said regarding slaves in Salvador or the freed population. To my knowledge, Carlos Ott is the only author to present data on the ethnoracial categories of the slave population in eighteenth-century Salvador. Because of the limited sample, this data should be considered with caution, but since Ott's numbers are the only data available, I include them in table 3 merely as an indication. Information for nineteenth-century Salvador is more plentiful, allowing an expansion of the period under analysis up to 1850, which is not possible for the Recôncavo. For this period in table 3, I adapted the data extracted from the inventories by Maria José Souza Andrade and João José Reis.

TABLE 4 Ethnoracial Composition of Freed Persons, Salvador, 1799–1850

	1779–1800		1801–20		1821–50	
	N.	%	N.	%	N.	%
African	1	0.3	1	0.1	119	6.9
Gentio da Guiné	8	2.2	15	1.6	5	0.3
Angola	61	17.0	108	12.0	122	6.7
Benguela	23	6.4	34	3.7	13	0.7
Other Central African	1	0.3	7	0.8	77	4.2
Gentio da Costa	11	3.0	22	2.4	2	0.1
Mina	169	47.0	314	34.8	138	7.6
Jeje	63	**17.5**	236	**26.2**	318	**17.6**
Nagô	20	5.6	96	10.6	754	41.7
Hausa	—	—	43	4.8	110	6.0
Other West African	2	0.5	26	2.9	150	8.3
TOTAL AFRICANS	359	100.0	902	100.0	1808	100.0
Central African Subtotal	85	10.4	149	7.7	212	6.0
West African Subtotal	265	32.7	737	38.2	1472	42.0
Creole/Mestizo	461	56.8	1043	54.0	1818	51.9
TOTAL	811	100.0	1929	100.0	3502	100.0

Source: Letters of manumission, APEBA, data taken from Mattoso, "A propósito . . .," tables 2, 3 (38–39). N.B.: "Jeje" includes 6 Dahomeans and 11 Maquinas (Mahi); "Other West Africans" includes 72 Tapas, 31 Bornu, 27 Calabari, 21 Benin, 9 Barbá, 7 Fulani, 7 São Tomé, 3 Camaroon, and 1 from the island of Príncipe; "Other Central Africans" includes 41 Cabinda, 29 Congo, and 15 Mozambique. The "Africans" and "gentio da Guiné" in the table's first two lines were not counted in the subtotals of West and Central Africans, and the "gentio da Costa" were counted as West Africans.

In table 4 I adapted the data presented by Mattoso on the ethnic origins of emancipated slaves in Salvador between 1779 and 1850. A comparative analysis of tables 3 and 4 shows which groups were most favored by manumission in the city. This information is important because, as we saw at the beginning of this chapter, in the nineteenth century the black and mestizo free and freed population was greater than the slave population.

My intent here is not to enter into a detailed discussion of this data but simply to point out certain important generalities. First, one may observe that the percentage of Africans among the freed population was less than among the slave population; from this one may infer that the Creoles born in the country and, above all, the mestizos, had a greater chance to obtain liberty. This uneven distribution indicates a hierarchized system of social relations that privileged the Creole to the detriment of the African foreigner.

In addition, we see that, among the Africans, those from Central Africa seem to have been the most disadvantaged. Also important is the different use of the ethnoracial terminology according to document type. While the inventories identify a high percentage of slaves as "gentio da Costa," this category is almost nonexistent in the letters of manumission, where the term *Mina* seems to substitute for it.

In Salvador the Jeje were one of the groups who most often benefited from manumission—in the first two decades of the century, when still the most numerous group (18.9 percent) among African slaves, they constituted more than a fourth (26.2 percent) of the emancipated African population. And even from 1830 to 1850, when their presence among slaves fell to 11.8 percent, they still accounted for 17.6 percent of freed Africans. The Jeje's apparent capacity to negotiate and obtain more letters of manumission than the expected average may be a result of their longer presence in the country and the creation of a wide social network of solidarity, principally in the urban context. In the tobacco region of the Recôncavo in the second half of the eighteenth century, the situation was the reverse. In that context, they made up approximately 25 percent of the African slave population but only 19 percent of the freed population.[19] The Jeje's fight for freedom was, therefore, won principally in the city, where it had the advantage of a long tradition of collective effort.

The greater number of Jeje among the freed Africans of Salvador in the first two decades of the nineteenth century is extremely important, for as we will see in chapter 4, freed Africans played the most relevant role in the formative process of Candomblé, which took place during this period. This demographic factor, though not determinant, might have contributed to a predominance of the vodun cult in the institutionalization of Candomblé.

In order to conclude this discussion of the fluctuations of the diverse ethnic groups within the black Bahian population, it is necessary to make some brief comments regarding the ascension of the Nagô. Mentioned in the Recôncavo since 1734, they were demographically significant in the second half of the eighteenth century, but their importation in great numbers came about in the first half of the nineteenth century, coinciding with the gradual disintegration of the Oyo empire, initiated by Afonja's revolt (c. 1797) and the Fulani jihad begun in 1804. In Bahia, however, the number of Nagô surpassed the Jeje and Angola only in the 1820s (table 3).[20] After 1830, with the definitive fall of the Oyo kingdom and the great social instability generated by the many civil wars that ravaged Yorubaland, Nagô captives were increasingly numerous. In 1848, Francis Castelnau, the French consul in Bahia, reports that "the Nagô ... form probably nine-tenths of the slaves in Bahia[,] . . . almost nearly all of them embarked in Onim (Lagos) or at Porto-Novo."[21] This percentage is certainly exaggerated, but the demographic superiority of the Nagô, however late, is unquestionable. Between 1840 and 1860 they constituted more than half of the African slave population in Salvador, between 56 and 69 percent, according to several sources.[22]

Another relevant phenomenon that begins in the 1840s but only becomes generalized after 1850 with the end of the transatlantic slave trade is the progressive and systematic utilization of the term *African* to classify slaves as well as freed blacks (table 4). The data Andrade extracted from the inventories show, in the ten years from 1851 to 1860, a rapid increase of the term, which is ultimately used to designate 58 percent of the non-Brazilian slaves, including and masking a majority of Nagô slaves. One concrete example is that of the slave José, who in 1835, during the trials following the Malê Revolt, was identified as José Nagô. But, in 1857, although still referred to as José Nagô, he is more frequently identified as José Africano or José da Costa da África (from the West African Coast).[23] The same process was identified by Maria Inês Cortes de Oliveira in the wills of the freed Africans from Salvador, in which the ethnic identification becomes increasingly vague and imprecise as the century advances. Between 1851 and 1890, *African* and *Costa da África* make up 77 percent of the self-identifications examined.[24]

One might suppose that the use of ethnic labels was closely related to the Atlantic slave trade, and that once it ended in 1850 identification based on nation names eventually lost its significance in a progressively more Creole and racially mixed society. For the white elite, this does appear to be true, since the records pertaining to them show a clear tendency toward homogenization, with the Creole-African distinction becoming the main dividing line by which whites classified the black population. Similarly, the formation of Brazilian nationalism, reinforced by independence from Portugal in 1822 and consolidated in subsequent decades, can be seen as contributing to the progressive irrelevance of "foreign" ethnic identities. And yet, the Africans did maintain their ethnic identities, but they restricted the use of these identities to the black population's cultural and social universe and principally, as we will see, to the religious sphere.

The preceding analysis allows one to argue that the Jeje in Bahia were demographically important between 1730 and 1820, coming to constitute, at various times and in different places, the most numerous African group. A sense of community or collective identity known as the Jeje nation probably developed in the first decades of the eighteenth century, and it was probably in the first decades of the nineteenth century that the Jeje, especially those who had been freed, made essential contributions to the institutionalization of Candomblé, though this process finds its roots in the second half of the eighteenth century. However, before addressing this topic, we must understand the initial process of identity construction and see how the nation names contributed to the formation of community ties. Moreover, in addition to the categories of classification, ethnic identity is lived and expressed through a whole range of behaviors and interpersonal interactions and, above all, through the capacity to create social institutions capable of bringing together members of a given community.

The Formation of a Multidimensional Identity Based on Alternative Processes of Denomination

When captured by traders, the enslaved Africans lost not only freedom but also family and social ties, as well as the cultural referents of their homeland. This process of "de-socialization," which Orlando Patterson calls "social death," was accompanied by another process—that of depersonalization.[25] Once sold to Europeans, either before embarking or upon arrival in the colonies, the Africans were normally baptized into the Catholic religion and received a Portuguese name. Once in Brazil, they were required to learn a new language and became merchandise in the eyes of the master, identified by their owner's name and by the nation name registered by the traders, which in most cases referred to the place of embarkation or of purchase, and not to the individual's place of origin. The slaves were also identified by their market price, which varied according to age, sex, physical condition, and skills. In short, their personal identity, if not entirely suppressed or substituted, was severely relativized by another created and imposed from without. At an individual level, or when socializing with fellow captives, certain traces of the original personal identity could be maintained, but in day-to-day relations with society at large the new identity imposed by slavery would reveal itself to be the most operational mode of presenting oneself to others. Thus, little by little, the nation-based metaethnic denominations were assumed by the black African population.

Simultaneous with the external identification used for them by the dominant class, Africans and their descendants developed new forms of solidarity and of collective identity, inasmuch as circumstances permitted. Within the social interaction of the slave quarters and that of the urban labor groups there developed a consciousness of new broader collectivities, gained by recognizing similarities in language and behavior and by identifying common or neighboring places of origin. That recognition of likeness was reinforced by the recognition of differences from others. At this level, obviously the linguistic component—the possibility of understanding one another even when speaking different dialects—created an immediate connection among certain groups that separated them from others with whom communication was not feasible. As a result, from the eighteenth century (or perhaps earlier) onward, recently arrived slaves found structured social networks in which collective identities based on nation were already in place and operational, allowing for accelerated assimilation.

In the historic dynamic that led to the construction of the African nations in Brazil, the processes of denomination—a dialogue of intersecting voices—played an important role. Let us consider the hypothetical case of the slave Joaquim. His master registers Joaquim in his inventory as Jeje because he was designated and sold to him as such by the trader who had brought him from the port of Ouidah or Porto-Novo on the Mina Coast. When Joaquim is captured in an attempt to escape and brought before a judge, or in any other civil or religious context controlled by the seigniorial class, he will be identified, or even identify himself, as Joaquim Jeje, using the denomination that was given to him by his master. This is the first level of articulation of Jeje identity, which corresponds to the vertical power relations of a dominant white class over a black-mestizo slave class, and in which the values and social customs of the dominant class are imposed on the subaltern one.[26]

Meanwhile, Joaquim is also a member of a black Catholic lay brotherhood, in which at times there are rivalries between Africans and Creoles. In this new antagonism, now restricted to the black population, Joaquim is more *African* (in the language of the time *preto*, or black or "not a national") than Jeje. Comparing himself to the black born in Brazil, Joaquim is reminded that he is not a "son of the land," that he was captured and comes from another place. In comparing himself to the Creole he is a *foreigner*.

Joaquim is Jeje, above all when interacting with other African groups—the Angola, Nagô, Hausa, Tapa—who speak other languages, come from other lands, and have different customs. This is the second level, one that corresponds to internal relations of cooperation and conflict among the blacks and mestizos and principally among the Africans. In some ways, these are dialectics of an essentially ethnic character rather than of race or class, as in the first level. Here the linguistic and cultural differences, and not those of color or position within the system of production, become the space of differentiation and contrast.

Additionally, in conversations with other hired-out Jeje slaves, Joaquim declares himself a Mahi from Dassa and quarrels with a Dagomé or a Savalu, neighboring, and at times rival, peoples. This is the third level and corresponds to the processes of differentiation among peoples included within the same metaethnic denomination. Here emerge the ethnic categories prevalent in Africa, all but invisible to the dominant class or other African groups. Some of these denominations—such as *Mahi*, for example—could have been meta-ethnic denominations already in use in Africa.

The intersection of these three levels of nomination, these three areas of contrast, seems to me most critical to understanding the construction of African nations in Brazil and the formation of a *multidimensional ethnic identity*. The dialogic process among the Africans themselves produced a progressive adjustment of the preexisting African terms of self-identification, which were multiple and had varied rates of demographic incidence, with the new meta-ethnic nation names imposed by the dominant class discourse, names more generic and fewer in number. These designations, which in Africa were in some cases restricted to a particular group, with time came to embrace a plurality of initially differentiated groups.

Ethnic identity often expressed itself through kinship metaphors. New kinship ties, not necessarily biological, were created. Africans who had traveled in the same boat during the Middle Passage, *malungos*,* came to consider themselves brothers for having shared this experience. As João José Reis points out, "African slaves and even freedmen and women had difficulty establishing their own families. This could explain why in Bahia the word *parente* [relative] was extended to include all members of the same ethnic group, Nagôs were said to be related to other Nagôs, Jejes to other Jejes, and so forth. In this strange land, Africans invented the concept of ethnic relatives."[27]

Associations of a religious nature, in their congregations and rituals, provided institutional forms of reinforcing this feeling of communalism and identification with an ethnic collectivity. The Catholic brotherhoods (in which the members are *brothers*), with their festivals (*folias** and *reinados**) organized according to African nation, seem to have contributed heavily to the formation of this new "ethnic-kinship" (see below). In addition to the brotherhoods, the *batuques** (African gatherings of drumming and dance) and, in the nineteenth century, Candomblé, with the creation of the "saint's family" (*família-de-santo*), also contributed significantly—the ties and mutual bonds established in the religious context becoming an alternative to consanguine relationships.[28]

It may also be that the more inclusive meaning of "kinship" in Brazil was favored by the concept of "extended families" prevalent in the majority of African societies. In the case of the Gbe-speaking area, for example, the family organization involves various social formations that operate on differentiated

levels, the principal ones being *huédo*, *hennu*, and *ako*. Each one of these formations implies varied ties of solidarity among its members, which are expressed
by the idiom of kinship. Leaving aside the *hué* (house) or the conjugal family, the *huédo* is the basic family collectivity, composed of the descendants
of a recent ancestor (three or five generations) through the patrilinear line.
The *huédo* constitutes a residential collectivity, and its members live in the
same family compound, recognizing one chief only (the *daa*), who reaches
this status through seniority. A series of *huédos* that recognize kinship ties or a
common geographic origin of their respective ancestors constitute a *hennu* or
lineage. There is also the *hennu daho*, or extended *hennu*, which may aggregate
certain clusters of other affiliated *huédos*, though not necessarily through genealogical ties. The *hennu* submits to the authority of a chief (*hennugan*) and
the "old paternal aunts" (*tanyi*). Finally, at the highest level is the *ako*, or the
clan, composed of those *hennus* that recognize a common mythical ancestor
(*tohuíyo*). The members of the *ako* share certain taboos (of food, for example)
and ceremonial religious obligations, but they do not submit to a chief, nor
do they necessarily establish a residential collectivity. In fact, the *ako* does not
constitute a group in itself but operates more as a referential category.[29]

In addition to the *huédo*, an individual can use the language of kinship with
the members of the *hennu* and the *ako*, though these are social formations of
flexible boundaries not necessarily connected by genealogical ties. Thus, the
"national" or ethnic kinship developed in Brazil would be merely an extension
of the same logic operative within African societies, according to which all
those who share a common ancestry, real or imagined, are considered "brothers." This idea is critical to understanding the topic at hand.

As I have stated, the process of Jeje identity construction, seemingly restricted to Bahia, appears to have occurred over many decades, adapting the
name of a particular ethnic group to the more generic and inclusive realm of
the entire Gbe-speaking people. Until the middle of the eighteenth century,
various groups from the coast—such as the Hueda, Hula, Aizo, and Gun—
gathered with others from the inland areas—such as the Ouemenu, Agonli,
and Mahi. In this initial phase these groups presented a great ethnic diversity.
This heterogeneity, probably invisible to the eyes of the Brazilian white elite,
appears to have been preserved among Africans.

In 1750s Rio de Janeiro, there existed various groups of "Mina blacks" (*pretos
minas*), both enslaved and freedmen, who had been brought from Dahomey.
Certainly, some of them came though the internal slave trade originating in
Bahia. These blacks formed religious associations such as the Brotherhood

of São Estevão (Saint Stephen) and Santa Efigênia (Saint Ephigenia) in the church of São Domingos. As Mariza de Carvalho Soares has documented, in the brotherhood's *comprimisso*, or statutes, addressed to the ecclesiastical powers in Lisbon, the Africans identify themselves with the metaethnic denomination *Mina*. In the 1750s, these Mina "entered into conflicts, dividing themselves into two groups: one composed of Dahomeans (Dagomé), and the other composed of small almost unknown groups, self-identified as Makii, Agolin, Sabaru, and Ianno."[30] "Dagomé" probably refers to the Fon or to other groups under Dahomean rule. The "Makii" are the Mahi. "Savaru" corresponds to Savalou, a city neighboring the Mahi region. The same is true with the "Agolin," or Agonli, peoples located to the northeast of Abomey and also considered Mahi. "Ianno" is a term that remains unidentified.[31]

Thus a plurality of ethnonyms was covered by the denomination *Mina*. It should be emphasized that it is only in the lesser congregations of the brotherhood, organized around the *folia* and *reinado* festivities and whose written records were not addressed to the ecclesiastic authorities, that these African denominations appear. It is clear that the metaethnic denominations were assumed by Africans in order to negotiate with white society, while the others had an internal function. The Africans negotiated with a variable repertoire of identities, based on denominations both internal and external, depending on the interlocutor or the social context.

There is another example, this time from Bahia, in the form of a civil judicial—and not religious—inquiry during the repression of the *calundu do Pasto* in Cachoeira in 1785. In the preliminary document of accusation, the clerk names the accused: "Sebastião, and Antonio, and Francisco, and Thereza and Anna, all Jeje," and a sixth woman, Marcella, Jeje, who was ultimately not tried. By the end of the inquiry a month later, the clerk had gained more information concerning the men: "Sebastião de Guerra, Francisco Rodrigues Leite, and Antonio Amorim, all freedmen, the first from the Dagomé nation, the second Marri, the third Tapa, and the negresses Thereza and Anna." The African owner of the house where the *calundu* was held, José Pereira, was responsible for providing the information concerning the origin of the prisoners, including the women: Thereza was a freedwoman of Mahi origin; Anna, was a Jeje slave; and Marcella, a freedwoman, was also Jeje. Thus, the six individuals, initially declared "all Jeje," were in fact one Dagomé, two Mahi, two Jeje, and one Tapa.[32] In addition to the term *Jeje*'s being able to include peoples outside the vodun area, such as the Tapa, what becomes clear is that among Africans *Jeje* was still a denomination restricted to a specific ethnic group within the vodun area that was distinguished from the Dagomé and the Mahi.[33] As we have seen, these Jeje may have been the coastal peoples of the vodun area, especially those located in the Porto-Novo region.

The *Jeje* denomination seems to have assumed its generic character quite early among the slave owners and slave traders, although sporadic mention in the inventories to Codavi, Makii, Sabaru, Fon, Dagomé, and in the nineteenth century, to Mondobi and Popo slaves was also possible. In some cases the documentation hints at the ambivalence of the repertoire of ethnic denominations. For example, in 1778, in the property inventory of Manoel Fernandes Pereira, resident of Maragogipe, appears the slave "Lourenço Sabaru," who, in two attached declarations referring to his manumission, identifies himself indiscriminately as "Gege" and "Mina."[34] Additionally, in an inventory from São Francisco do Conde, I found a reference to "a negress by the name of Josepha *Gege* or *Codavy*."[35]

The term *Jeje* was adopted by Gbe-speaking Africans in their dialogue with the broader society and in their contrastive relationships with other African groups, especially the Angola in the eighteenth century and the Nagô in the nineteenth. In this inter-African dialogue, linguistic and religious differences came to be more important. In the Gbe-speaking inner circles, however, at least in the religious sphere, more restrictive ethnic denominations associated with the term *Jeje*, such as *Jeje-Marrin* (*Mahi*), *Jeje-Dagomé*, *Jeje-Savalu*, and *Jeje-Mundubi* (*Mondobi*) persist even today. Once again, this hints at a *multidimensional identity* based on external (from the outside in and from the inside out) and internal dialogs (from the inside in).

Until now I have addressed primarily ethnic nomination processes and their importance in the formation of communal social relationships that are, in the words of Max Weber, "based on a subjective feeling of the parties, whether affectual or traditional, that they *belong together*." However, as I have mentioned, what is essential for the development of a collective consciousness and an ethnic identity is the community's capacity to generate social action of an associative nature, based on a "rationally motivated adjustment of interests or a similarly motivated agreement." Besides the discourses elaborated in the context of interpersonal interactions, it is in the social institutions that the simultaneous processes of inclusion (belonging) or exclusion are carried out, and it is in these associative relationships that ethnic identity can be better expressed. The participation in Catholic brotherhoods, work groups, and congregations of vodun worship are examples of these "group actions of an associative nature" that fomented the conscience of a collective Jeje identity.[36]

The Jeje in Relation to Whites, Creoles, and the Angola within the Catholic Brotherhoods

The Catholic brotherhoods were one of the social institutions that most contributed to the dialogic process that eventually created and defined the shape of the diverse African nations in Brazil. Several authors have pointed out that the black brotherhoods were divided according to the various African ethnicities, there being brotherhoods of Angola, Jeje, and Nagô.[37] This ethnic exclusivity, however, was very rare, and the brotherhoods almost always included a plurality of ethnoracial groups, though some may have enjoyed greater visibility or power. This heterogeneity *within* the brotherhoods was a source of repeated conflicts and tensions among the diverse groups, and it was precisely at these moments of conflict, or at times alliance, that the relations of contrast and the differential factor were made evident and that individuals became aware of their collective identity.

The most important criterion of exclusion operating among the brotherhoods reproduced the "racial" or "color" hierarchy prevalent in broader society, that is, it emphasized above all the separation between whites, blacks, and, later, the increasingly numerous mulattoes (*pardos*). In many fraternities, the "racial" distinctions were determining factors in the acceptance of brothers, though in the case of mulattoes a degree of ambiguity and mobility existed, depending on the individual's social status. Among the congregations of black men, in contrast, besides the "ethnic" distinction among the diverse African groups, the most striking internal division was that between Africans and Creoles.

The Creoles, like the mulattoes, having been born in Brazil and lacking any other cultural referent, more often had an assimilationist attitude. They had spoken Portuguese since birth, facilitating communication and the learning of "national" customs and habits. The Africans, for their part, came from another cultural world, and their original referents, despite the difficulties, were maintained or remembered, producing a greater degree of resistance. This resistance was more accentuated among the *boçais*, or newly arrived Africans who did not speak Portuguese, than among the *ladinos*, those more integrated into the slave system.

Though Creoles are often spoken of generically, it is important to point out that, like the Africans, they did not constitute a homogenous group. The first-generation Creoles, in many cases raised by African mothers, were able to maintain more marked emotional and sociability ties with their African progenitors than with other Creoles. But this proximity became lost with time. The second- and third-generation Creoles, raised by other native-born blacks, evinced a greater degree of adaptation to the dominant culture and came to constitute a more culturally homogenous social segment, with values and interests that differed from those of "foreign" Africans. Moreover, as I have stated, there was a high number of interethnic marriages, at least among the Jeje in the second half of the eighteenth century, principally with the Angola, Mina, and Nagô. It is probable that these couples communicated in Portuguese and that their Creole descendants were exposed to mixed cultural referents, Brazilian as well as African. This must have created quite varied processes of exclusion or inclusion by Africans for these Creoles.

The conflicts between Africans and Creoles go back at least as far as the eighteenth century and are evident in the probate records of the Catholic brotherhoods. One of the better-known examples in Bahian history is that of the Irmandade Senhor Bom Jesus dos Martírios (Brotherhood of the Good Lord Jesus of Martyrdoms), "established by Black men of the Gege nation," in the Carmo convent in the village of Nossa Senhora do Rosário of Cachoeira in 1765.[38] This Martírios is one of the very few black brotherhoods that explicitly referred in its name to an ethnic nation. We will return to this subject further on.

The brotherhood, despite being founded by Jeje Africans, was open to anyone of "good morals" who had the resources to pay, but it limited the admission of Creoles. The Africans left no doubt as to the animosity existing between them and "the black national men of this land whom are commonly called Creoles . . . because of the disputes that such men habitually have with those of the Gege nation who establish this brotherhood." The Creoles were admitted only if they could pay a fee of ten mil-réis (versus a two-*pataca* fee [a *pataca* being worth about 360 réis] for Africans); additionally, they could not, under any circumstance, hold any of the board offices. However, "this prohibition does not extend to Creole Sisters, who may serve in any office and enjoy all the privileges of the Brotherhood without reservation."[39] The acceptance of Creole women can be seen as an attempt to promote the "love market" in a society in which, among the African population, women were relatively scarce.[40]

This discriminatory policy of the Jeje against Creoles resulted from the aforementioned "disputes," among which the competition in the "love market" should not be excluded. This antagonism was not merely local, however, but played into a wider conflict. The Jejes' attitude likely also responded to similar policies practiced by the Creoles against the Africans in other brotherhoods. For example, in 1764, one year before the statutes of the Martírios brotherhood in Cachoeira were drafted, Felix Simões de Azevedo, contract administrator of the chancellery and of the slaves coming from the Mina Coast, donated the altar of Nossa Senhora da Caridade (Our Lady of Charity) in the Barroquinha church to a brotherhood of the same name also operating in the city, so that its members might place the sacred image of their patron on it. This brotherhood of the Martírios of Salvador had its original headquarters in the church of Nossa Senhora do Rosário dos Homens Pretos às Portas do Carmo (Our Lady of the Rosary of Black Men at the Carmo Gates). The brotherhood accepted Azevedo's offer in the same year of 1764, but it is not known exactly when they effected the transfer to the Barroquinha church. It is known, however, that in 1779, when the statutes were drafted, the brotherhood was already there. The statutes won royal approval on February 12, 1788.[41]

As João da Silva Campos notes, the official and older name used in the statutes is Irmandade do Senhor do Bom Jesus dos Martírios dos Creoulos Naturais da Cidade da Bahia (Brotherhood of the Good Lord Jesus of the Martyrdoms of the Creoles Born in the City of Bahia), and, contrary to A. J. R. Russell-Wood's belief, this congregation was not known for its flexibility in accepting new members.[42] In much the same way that the Jeje of Cachoeira discriminated against Creoles, the Creoles formed brotherhoods that discriminated against Africans.

Proof of this can be found in the statutes drafted in 1775 by the Irmandade do Senhor Bom Jesus das Necessidades e Redenção (Brotherhood of Good Lord Jesus of the Necessities and Redemption) established in the Corpo Santo church in Salvador. These statutes, printed in Lisbon in 1778, document an interesting exchange of letters between the prosecutor Antônio de Brito and the brotherhood's officers regarding chapter 12. This text explains that "experience has shown that, in order to avoid scandal, doubts, and discord, care should be taken only to admit brothers or sisters from among national blacks from outside the city, such as those from the Mina Coast or Loanda [Luanda] and that for no reason should any quality of Creole blacks be admitted." If the Jeje of the brotherhood of Cachoeira restricted the participation of Creoles, the Mina and Angola of the Corpo Santo brotherhood, some years later, excluded them definitively.

Brito, charged with recommending the statutes to Lisbon, questioned the propriety of this chapter, since one should not prohibit anyone from the worship of "God and his saints." The brothers, somewhat ironically, argued that they did not impede anyone from worship, "because any man, if his devotion so compel him, may give his alms without any impediment," but they insisted that the purpose of the exclusion was "to avoid partialities, hatreds, and dissentions, that frequently existed among them [the Creoles], and those from overseas." In fact, among the more weighty justifications, they alleged that in other brotherhoods of the city, such as "in that of Senhor dos Martírios, belonging to those excluded [Creoles] they observe the same prohibition with those from overseas."[43] Therefore, the policies of exclusion between Africans and Creoles in the brotherhoods were dialectically interrelated, some justified by the existence of others, and probably spread out through a region that included Salvador and the Recôncavo.[44]

More difficult to determine are the nature and the motives of the "controversies" and "hatreds" between these two groups, a subject deserving of a more detailed future study. What is important to emphasize here is that these conflicts and contrasts were precisely the occasions in which individuals were placed in, or took the side of, one or another group, reinforcing the processes of collective identification. In this case, the antagonism with Creoles seems to have favored inter-African solidarity.

The directorship of the Martírios brotherhood in Cachoeira was composed of "a President who shall always be a black man who is not a national of the Country: a Board Clerk, who, in the absence of a black who can read and write, shall be a white man, or mulatto of good reputation: a Treasurer and a Proctor who are blacks, but not nationals."[45] Hence, the most important offices, except that of clerk, were reserved for Africans, who, judging by the statute's title, we may assume were of the "Gege Nation."[46] In this context, the term *black (preto)* seems able to refer to both Africans and Creoles and needs to be qualified with the expression "not national" or "not a national of the Country" in order to refer specifically to Africans. Yet, in the statutes of the Redemption brotherhood of the Corpo Santo church, the Mina and Luanda Africans are referred to as "black nationals from outside the city," probably to indicate that, although foreigners, they had their own nations. This semantic ambiguity of the term *black (preto)* in the eighteenth century contrasts with its use in the nineteenth, when *black* was invariably synonymous with African.

Given that, the restrictions imposed on Creoles aside, any person could be admitted into the association, one can assume that with time the brotherhood in Cachoeira came to include, even among the directorship, Africans from various nations, thus contributing to a relative ethnoracial heterogeneity. For example, for the women's offices, such as the *juíza** or sister *mordoma*, white, mixed-race, and black women were considered "without any preference whatsoever." Nonetheless, the Jeje Africans, as founders of the brotherhood, must have maintained relative control, at least during the second half of the eighteenth century. It is important to remember that in this period in Cachoeira, the Jeje were the most numerous African group, and although there is not necessarily a direct relation between demography and cultural influence, their numeric superiority among the enslaved and probably freed blacks may have increased their social visibility.

One hypothesis regarding the term *Jeje* in the statute's title is that, in the eighteenth century, prior to the arrival of great numbers of Nagô, this denomination was used on certain occasions as a synonym for *Mina* and generically designated Africans from the Gulf of Benin, in contrast to the Angola from Central Africa. In the statutes of the Irmandade do Glorioso Senhor São Benedito (Brotherhood of the Glorious Lord Saint Benedict) in Itapagipe, written in 1800, for example, three *juízes** are named: one mulatto, one Creole, and a third Jeje or Angola.[47] This division among the offices reflects the ethnoracial classification system of the time, and the third judge would be the representative of the Africans, who, for their part, significantly, were divided between Angola and Jeje. It should not be forgotten, therefore, that in certain contexts *Jeje* was used as an umbrella term, comprising a larger group even than the Gbe-speakers. This could also explain its use in the inquiry into the *calundu* do Pasto in 1785, where it included the Tapa.

At the core of the Catholic brotherhoods, the Jeje and the Angola maintained a relationship that varied between conflict and cooperation. We have seen the case of the Redemption brotherhood of the Corpo Santo church, in which the blacks from the Mina Coast and Luanda—the former probably including a large number of Jeje (see below)—shared the offices of the directorship. There is another episode of apparent cooperation in the Irmandade de Nossa Senhora do Rosário dos Pretos da Rua de João Pereira (Brotherhood of Our Lady of the Rosary of the Blacks of João Pereira Street).[48] On November 9, 1784, Father José Joaquim Alvares, the brotherhood's clerk, drafts a petition "relative to the disturbances allegedly caused by the directorship in its government of said brotherhood." This document indicates that the directorship, composed of two *juízes*, was divided between "an equal number of Gege and Benguela or Angola." Besides the "Benguela and Gege blacks," the brotherhood welcomed members "of every condition," among them white clergy and mulattoes. In that year, however, the Africans united in order to displace the whites from the offices of treasurer and clerk.[49]

This incident suggests a case of solidarity or an alliance between the Jeje and Angola nations, intending to undermine the power of the whites within the institution. In the black brotherhoods, in Bahia as well as in Pernambuco, it was quite common to give the offices of treasurer and clerk to whites. As blacks became increasingly literate, however, the attempts to substitute the whites in these offices with blacks multiplied. In Bahia one finds this type of conflict in the Irmandade do Senhor Bom Jesus das Necessidades e Redenção (see below), and also in the Irmandade de Nossa Senhora do Rosário dos Homens Pretos (Brotherhood of Our Lady of the Rosary of Black Men) in Cachoeira in 1794.[50] The example of the Irmandade do Rosário de João Pereira is a clear example of how the antagonism of "class" and "race" between Africans and whites seems to take precedence over ethnic differences, and of how the experience of "class" (or of subaltern social position) could reinforce interethnic solidarity.

Another case is that of an apparent conflict between the Jeje and the Angola in the Irmandade de Nossa Senhora do Rosário dos Pretos às Portas do Carmo (in the Baixa dos Sapateiros neighborhood). The confraternity had existed since 1685 in the Sé parish. In 1700 the Portas do Carmo chapel was built, and to there the brotherhood moved and even now remains. Historians affirm that in the beginning this brotherhood was composed exclusively of Angola blacks, but that after the second half of the eighteenth century, they were obliged to admit Jeje and Creole brothers, as well as mulattoes and even whites.[51]

In the brotherhood's registry book between the years of 1719 and 1837, Sara Oliveira Faria finds a total of 3,175 entries, of which only a small minority is ethnically identified: 115 Creoles (3.6 percent), 103 Jeje (3.2 percent), forty-eight Angola (1.5 percent), thirty-seven Mina (1.1 percent), seventeen Benguela (0.5 percent), four Nagô (0.1 percent), and three Mozambique (0.09 percent). Among the remaining 2,848 (89.7 percent) entries there is no further declaration of origin.[52] The high percentage of entries lacking this information makes any estimate regarding the ethnic composition of the brotherhood questionable, besides suggesting that this criterion was not essential for the admission of brothers. Nevertheless, this data clearly shows the congregation's ethnic heterogeneity, while also indicating a relative Jeje majority among the Africans.

Perhaps because of this numerical threat, the Jeje were barred statutorily from the brotherhood's directorship, ethnic discrimination being an expression of subjacent tensions within the spheres of power. In the statutes of 1820, the offices of the directorship were restricted to Angola and Creole members, and it was specified that "in any year in which the clerk is an Angola, the treasurer must be a Creole."[53] As João Reis points out, the sociability between the Angola and Creoles in the Rosário brotherhood "perhaps indicates, on a micropolitical and institutional level, wider social allegiances between these two groups."[54]

With a significant presence since the seventeenth century, the Angola were the oldest nation in the Bahian slave population, which allowed the entrenchment of a close association with their Creole descendants. For their part, these

Creoles took in the new shipments of Angola slaves brought over in the eighteenth century, maintaining and reinforcing the ties of solidarity between the two groups. As I have mentioned, in the second half of the eighteenth century this relationship did not impede a certain degree of cooperation between the Mina and the Angola, encouraged by their common antagonism toward both whites and Creoles. But in the initial decades of the nineteenth century, in part because of the increased number of Africans arriving from the Mina Coast, the Angola sought to strengthen their ancient alliances with Creoles, perhaps in order to confront the new ethnic configuration of Bahian society.

Another interesting case in ethnic dynamics occurs in the aforementioned Senhor Bom Jesus das Necessidades e Redenção brotherhood, founded in the chapel of São Frei Pedro Gonsalves, commonly called Corpo Santo, a branch of the mother church Conceição da Praia, in the Cidade Baixa. This chapel was likely built in the early eighteenth century and was frequented principally by sailors. São Pedro Gonsalves, also called Sant'Elmo, was the patron saint of sailors.[55] A. F. Frézier, who was in Bahia in April 1714, described the churches of Cidade Baixa and indicated that the Corpo Santo was "for poor people."[56]

The statutes of this brotherhood, drafted in 1913, tell how on May 3, 1752, certain Jeje Africans instituted devotion to the Senhor Bom Jesus das Necessidades e Redenção in the Corpo Santo church, at that time the provisional headquarters of the Conceição da Praia parish. On October 4, 1775, the first statutes of the brotherhood were approved by the *doutor provedor de resíduos e capelas* (the administrator of chapels and goods bequeathed to the church) being confirmed by dispatch from the Tribunal da Mesa da Consciência e Ordem (Tribunal of Conscience and Order) on August 22, 1778.[57]

Based on this data, most scholars refer to the brotherhood of Senhor Bom Jesus das Necessidades e Redenção as being "Jeje," "exclusively Jeje," or composed of "Dahomean Jeje blacks."[58] However, the idea that the brotherhood was founded in 1752 and that its founders were Jeje appears only in the statute of 1913. There is no other contemporary documentary evidence of such events. In fact, as we have seen, chapter 12 of the 1775 statutes, wherein the admittance of Creoles is prohibited, makes explicit that black brothers and sisters from the "Mina Coast or Loanda" were admitted. If the congregation was founded by Jeje, they were already accepting Mina and Angola only a few years later. Additionally, among the members of the directorship of 1775, there appears as proctor a José da Silva, probably Portuguese, which would indicate the presence of whites as well.[59]

Campos claims to have consulted the "association's ancient book of resolutions"—a document I was unhappily unable to find—and presents information that makes clear the ethnoracial heterogeneity of this brotherhood's members and the Jeje's rivalry and conflicts with the whites, mestizos, and Creoles. According to Campos, only blacks from the Jeje nation could initially participate in the brotherhood. "Later they began to enlist white, mestizo, and Creole devotees, and blacks from other castes, though the Jeje constituted the majority." As was common, the white men little by little began to take charge of the principal administrative offices, "from which resulted some serious displeasure for the blacks, who eventually dismissed them from the association, which measure was later extended to the mestizos. From this, the sweet harmony hoped for by the Africans did not reign in the heart of the Brotherhood, as the Creoles who had remained came to sow disorder, until they too were eliminated. . . . From that time on, only Jeje blacks could be enlisted in the confraternity. And thus it went, rigorously enforced, until the society was reduced to a single individual, who died at an age of more than 100 in 1929. But prior to this, in 1927, many devotees of Senhor da Redenção, whites and mulattoes, took on the task of restoring the Brotherhood, which today is fully thriving."[60]

Although the chronology and sequential order of events are somewhat doubtful—since, for example, in 1775 the brotherhood seems to have included whites and non-Creoles—the case seems to demonstrate how Jeje identity was maintained and strengthened through relationships of contrast established with whites, mestizos, Creoles, and other African groups within the core of social institutions such as the brotherhoods.

Again, according to Campos, the procession of this brotherhood, which was Lenten and celebrated in the month of May, "was very solemn in former days, drawing together the whole of the city's African population, with many shows of devotion. The rich blacks even wore dress coats, top hats, and kid gloves. Meanwhile, the negresses made a show of luxury with gold and silk, which today would cause amazement."[61]

Numbering among these "rich blacks" was surely Joaquim d'Almeida, of the Jeje-Mahi nation, who once freed, dedicated himself to the slave trade. It was a reproduction of the image of the Senhor da Redenção kept in the Corpo Santo that he took when he returned to establish himself in Africa, in the city of Agoué, on the Mina Coast, after 1835. In this place he erected a Catholic chapel with the same name as the brotherhood.[62]

Just as the Redemption brotherhood of Corpo Santo has been identified a bit hastily as being exclusively Jeje, numerous other authors have identified the Irmandade do Senhor Bom Jesus dos Martírios of the Barroquinha church as blacks (pretos, i.e., Africans) or Nagô men.[63] This is again an unfounded assumption, since, as we have seen, this congregation was made up mostly of Creoles, at least in the eighteenth century. Oral tradition further suggests that Ketu African women of this confraternity, or devotees of its affiliated sisterhood of Nossa Senhora da Boa Morte (Our Lady of the Good Death), founded the first Bahian candomblé somewhere near the Barroquinha church at the beginning of the nineteenth century. However, there are reasons to doubt this narrative, at least as it relates to the supposed connections between the founders of the candomblé and the Martírios brotherhood, since the Martírios's discrimination against Africans seems to have lasted through the whole first half of the nineteenth century. Between 1800 and 1850, among a total of 145 wills of freed Africans who declared themselves members of some Catholic confraternity, only two Mina women belonged to that of the Martírios of the Barroquinha church.[64] This documentary evidence indicates that any significant presence of Africans (Nagô or any other) in this confraternity could only have been in the second half of the nineteenth century. Campos describes the devotees of the Boa Morte and sisters of the Martírios as "negresses of the *partido-alto* [upper-class], moneyed, and ostentatious, the youngest of whom were full of affectation and vanity," and mentions that the brothers of the Martírios would lead the procession, "followed in double rank by the aforementioned *Creole* women and, in former times, by *African* women." From what is said, one must infer that the participation of Africans could only have occurred after 1850. Yet oral tradition also supports that it was around 1850 when the Barroquinha candomblé was moved elsewhere in the city. Resolving these contradictions will require future studies.[65]

The Catholic brotherhoods, especially in the second half of the eighteenth century, were social institutions that offered the black and mixed-race population critical spaces for sociability and the establishment of collective processes of ethnoracial identification. Contrary to the supposed ethnic division between the black brotherhoods defended by historians, I have underscored their ethnic heterogeneity. Within them were varying dynamics of cooperation and conflict among the different ethnoracial groups: conflicts between whites and blacks, dominated by "class" and "racial" distinctions; conflicts between Africans and Creoles; and conflicts among the diverse African groups, in which "ethnic" or cultural distinctions prevailed. Additionally, as we saw earlier in the case of Rio de Janeiro, there could even exist dynamics of differentiation among various groups belonging to the same nation, which were expressed in the various *folias* and other festivities of the brotherhoods. This complex and dynamic dialogic system of internal and external contrasts seems to be at the base of the formation of the Jeje nation.

The Jeje and the Nagô:
Simultaneous Dynamics of Conflict and Cooperation

While in the eighteenth century Jeje interethnic relations of conflict and co-operation occurred primarily with the Angola and other groups from Central Africa, in the first half of the nineteenth century, with the massive influx of Nagô, the dialectic of contrast between this group and the Jeje became more noteworthy. As we saw in chapter 1, the Jeje-Nagô dialectic derives not only from the encounter of these groups once in Brazil but also from cultural contact that was long-standing and intense even in Africa.

The documentation of the Malê Revolt of 1835 is quite rich in information regarding this point and reveals some of the characteristics of this interethnic relationship. In this African insurrection, a total of only eleven Jeje Africans were detained or tried (3.8 percent of the total)—of whom four were slaves (2.3 percent), six were freedmen (5.4 percent), and one was of unknown legal status. This, as opposed to 212 Nagô Africans (72.6 percent of the total)—149 slaves (83 percent), sixty freedmen (53.6 percent), and three of unknown legal status. The minimal Jeje participation in the revolt has been interpreted as indicating animosity between Jeje and Nagô, inherited from the historic conflicts among the peoples of the kingdoms of Dahomey and Oyo.[66]

This animosity is explicit in some of the inquiry testimonies following the revolt. João Duarte da Silva, "freedman, Gege Nation," ship's cook, was arrested in his home, "in which also lives Dom Jozé, Gege Nation, ambassador of Agoumés," and declared that he did not participate in the Nagô revolt "because he does not understand their language . . . and because they are also enemies of the Gege and that if he had gone into the street on that occasion [the night of the revolt] he would certainly have been killed."[67] The freedman José da Costa also argued in his defense that he was "of a nation entirely the enemy of that of the blacks who caused unrest in the city." To prove his enmity with the Nagô, he declared that he had no friendships among them "not even those caused by human frailty [sexual relations] with the women of that nation."[68]

Other Jeje, without going to such lengths, declared simply that they did not understand the language of the Nagô. This was the case of Manoel Gomes Ferrão, "freedman of the Gege Nation, who makes his living carrying a palanquin at the corner of São Domingos, resident of Ferrão alley in the company of Narciza Barboza, and Thereza de Jesus, negresses of the same Nation."[69] And also from Ellena, a Jeje freedwoman, "who had belonged to the black Ignacio, and is now free, resident of the house of her patron Ignacio Jozé de Santa Anna, on Laranjeira St., and makes her living selling fish," who declared that the *alufá* (Muslim priest and teacher) Licutan, one of the leaders of the rebellion, and the slave Joaquim rented a room in a house neighboring her dwelling, where blacks would meet "who came there to eat and make merry, and that she understood no more as she is not Nagô."[70]

Simultaneous with this tradition of animosity or differentiation between the Jeje and Nagô are examples of cooperation, revealing that some Jeje could maintain long-term social relations with the Nagô, learning to communicate with them in their language. The slave Joaquim, "a native of the Gege African coast," for example, was accused of having "a room in the house of the insurgents," all of them being Nagô: Belchior Nagô from Cobi, Manoel Calafate Nagô, and Aprígio Ojô.[71] The black Angélica Gege also lived in the same house with Jozé Nation Nagô, "both forced to work in the streets in order to buy their Liberty." In the accusations it is specified that Angélica, "while speaking the Nagô language, is of the Gege nation."[72]

The youth Alexandre, of the Jeje nation, though a Nagô-speaker, dreamed of killing the whites and freeing himself from slavery in order to live with his lover, the Nagô Inês, who was also his *malunga*, a companion during the Middle Passage. He offers another interesting counterpoint to the traditional rivalry between the Jeje and Nagô.[73] Members of the new Jeje generation, Nagô-acculturated in Salvador, seemed to overcome the interethnic conflicts of their elders.

The familiarity of certain Jeje with the Nagô language could be the result of living with them in Salvador, but it is also worth noting that Nagô was a language commonly spoken in Dahomey, especially in the area of Porto-Novo. The Jeje could have learned the Nagô language, as well as assimilated other Nagô cultural elements, before arriving in Brazil. José, a forty-year-old partially freed Jeje—in 1835 he was still paying off his letter of manumission—worked as a butcher, but was reputed according to one witness to be a *curador de feitiço,** or a witchcraft healer. Despite being Jeje, José declared that he was "raised in the land of the Nagô," where he had probably learned to work with the world of orixás and their sacred healing leaves.[74]

There are further cases in which the Jeje seem to assume a Nagô identity, as we see with the freedman Luís. While in his 1828 letter of manumission his former master identifies him as a black (*preto*) of the Jeje nation, in the interrogations he claims to be Nagô, and the justice classifies him in the summary as "Luis of the Hausa Nation freed African in fact, Nagô."[75] Also, in the accusation of the aforementioned slave Joaquim, he is said to be a "native from the Gege African coast," whereas in the transcript of the prison sentence Joaquim "answered his name was Joaquim Nagô."[76]

These could be mere instances of confusion or clerical error, the result of the administration's limited knowledge of the African population's ethnic identity. Nevertheless, if the inquiries show a number of cases in which the same individual is identified as, or self-identifies as, belonging to different ethnicities, the last two cases appear to suggest a tendency of certain Jeje to identify themselves as Nagô. It is not improbable that Luis and Joaquim were in fact Nagô but were embarked "on the Gege African coast," that is, in Dahomean ports, and therefore identified as Jeje by their masters. But it is also possible that they were Jeje and that they had chosen to declare themselves Nagô as the result of processes of socialization and ethnic identification with the dominant and most numerous African group of the time.

In truth, the increasing semantic breadth of metaethnic denominations was conducive to this kind of inclusive dynamic. Renato da Silveira, who contends that the Malê Revolt was an essentially religious jihad inspired by African Muslims, suggests that the identification of these two Jeje as Nagô was the same as saying that they were Malê or people of Allah.[77] This interpretation highlights how ethnic identifications can be superimposed on, or confused with, religious identity—a topic to which we will return in later chapters.

To conclude the analysis of the relations of conflict and cooperation that shaped the Jeje nation, it is important to consider one other, more general aspect of the dynamics of assimilation and resistance that played out among Africans in their contact with Brazilian slave society. In recent decades, historical studies of the black population have privileged the binary opposition of assimilation and resistance, or negotiation and conflict, as the conceptual model through which to understand the social and cultural dynamics resulting from contact between Africans and their descendants with the European culture of the white colonizers. This tendency, assumed above all by the "new historiography" beginning in the 1980s, but with antecedents in the 1960s (such as in the work of Roger Bastide), tries to understand the black as a "historical subject" inserted into a complex web of social, political, and cultural ties, and no longer as part of a homogenous social class, defined only in terms of his or her position within the mode of production of the slave economy.[78]

However, this conceptual polarity—assimilation and resistance—despite pointing out the complexity of multiple relationships, is normally conceived of as mutually exclusive, that is, blacks, or the associations constituted by them, assume a position of *either* assimilation *or* resistance. However, many processes of assimilation, such as the Catholic black lay brotherhoods, for example, can also be seen as forms of camouflaged resistance. Bastide himself pointed out that all accommodation or syncretism is always more or less "counteracculturative."[79] In fact, on the level of the individual, in the field of social psychology, one could imagine that the same individual could, as one today can, at various times in his or her life, successively or even simultaneously adopt postures of both assimilation and resistance. Verger points out this "tendency of simultaneous acceptance of Brazilian and African cultures" in Bahia in the nineteenth century.[80]

Assimilation and resistance are complementary tendencies, and not necessarily opposed. They can occur simultaneously and, to a greater or lesser degree, are reproduced in any groups or individuals removed from their habitus or culture of origin. Depending on the circumstance and whenever the system of social relationships offers sufficient space, the individual negotiates and chooses the most suitable strategy from his or her repertoire of cultural references. The Jeje of the eighteenth and nineteenth centuries were no exception. Within this group existed the tendency of "Brazilianization," that is, individuals who adjusted and attempted to adopt the new customs dominated by the values of a white elite, and the contrary tendency of "Africanization" followed by individuals who sought to maintain and reproduce, as much as possible, the practices and customs of their land of origin. Both positions could function as strategies against the social exclusion created by the slave system.

The tendency toward "Brazilianization" is explicit in people who adopt Catholicism as their religion, or as one of their religions. A good example of a convert is the previously mentioned Joaquim d'Almeida, a freedman of Mahi origin and a member of the Corpo Santo brotherhood, who was a slave trader and constructed a Catholic chapel in Agoué, on the Mina Coast, around 1845.[81] Another example of the assimilationist attitude in the context of the Malê Revolt would be the case of the Jeje freedman José da Costa, who, in addition to declaring himself an enemy of the Nagô, attempts to demonstrate his innocence further by noting that he did not don the *abadá* (the white clothing of the Malê) at the time of the uprising, or any other African dress; quite the contrary, he was "dressed in a cotton overcoat and other items customary of the Brazilian Nation." An official craftsman of the Navy Arsenal, he was described as "assiduous in his work as a caulker. . . . a known friend of the land that congratulated him as obedient to all those superior officers and authorities and respectful of laws." Additionally, he was a "practitioner of the Roman Catholic Religion . . . and fiercely adherent to the customs and to the Nationals of this Empire, with whom he has always maintained social relations." The only thing he had "against him [was] the misfortune to be born in the Country of Africa," but his true affection was for Brazil, the "Homeland in which he was raised" and one whose side he would have fought if he had been called on to do so in 1835.[82] Perhaps this patriotism was exaggerated, acting as a strategy of self-defense against the accusations. But this dynamic and this malleability of the identification processes, which vary according to those involved and the circumstances, is essential to my argument.

Examples of resistance, in contrast, can be found in each situation in which the Jeje participated in religious practices of African origin, such as the previously mentioned partially freedman José, of the Jeje nation, who in the Malê Revolt was accused of being a healer, or the Jeje who were detained in the *calundu do Pasto* in Cachoeira in 1785. The list would be extensive, and in the next chapters we will discuss some of these cases in detail. Verger adds that other forms of "refusal to integrate" are expressed in the *quilombos*,* or maroon communities, in the revolts organized by Africans, in their conversion to Islam, and through their return to Africa after obtaining manumission.[83]

Assimilation, understood as the acceptance and reproduction of elements of a foreign culture, resides in the desire to identify with the dominant values that allow better adaptation and progress, whether on the group or the individual level. In other words, the processes of cultural adaptation are justified inasmuch as they offer mechanisms for upward social mobility. The labor market seems to be the privileged social space for processes of assimilation.

In contrast, the processes of cultural resistance of ethnic minorities or subaltern classes, based on maintaining cultural values and practices distinct from those of the dominant culture, offer mechanisms of struggle to those discriminated against by the spheres of power. Cultural resistance is primarily related to the mimetic behavior inherent to every learning process that accompanies the cultural transfer from one generation to another. The individual naturally tends to repeat or reproduce those values with which he or she is brought up. Cultural resistance is based on, or emphasizes, the conservative and gregarious nature of humans. But in the context of class struggle or interethnic conflict, in which the marginalized groups are kept from identifying with the values of the hegemonic group, cultural resistance appears as a dynamic of differentiation, as a mechanism of self-affirmation and defense against the threat of indifferentiation or that of invisibility, that is, alienation. The preservation, or the periodic reactualization of differentiating elements on which the construction of ethnic identity is based, somehow constitutes the political weapon of the excluded. In the context of the Africans and their descendants in Brazil, the field of religion, of beliefs and ritual practices associated with the invisible world, seems to have been the dominion par excellence of cultural resistance.

3 From *Calundu* to Candomblé

The Formative Process of Afro-Brazilian Religion

From "Ethnic" Nation to Candomblé Nation

The dialogic dynamic of ethnic differentiation among the diverse nations ana-lyzed here found a privileged context for expression early on in the blacks' festive gatherings and in their religious practices of African origin. As early as the eighteenth century, in a frequently cited letter from Martinho de Mello e Castro, Count of Povolide, dated June 10, 1780, there is talk of the festivities held in the Church of the Rosário, in Recife, where "the blacks divided by Na-tion dance with the instruments unique to each one."[1] As occurs even today in Candomblé, the nations divided and differentiated themselves according to ritual elements such as language, songs, dances, and instruments, especially drums. During Christmas 1808, in the town of Santo Amaro in the Bahian Recôncavo, this distinction among the *batuques* divided by nation persisted.[2] "During those Holy days of Christmas, many slaves of every nation descended from the sugar mills and plantations of this town's district, and gathering them-selves into three bodies together with many of this town, formed three drum-ming bands according to their nation, and performed their customary play, or dances; namely, the Geges, on the Sergimirim farm, the Angola behind the Rosário chapel, and the Nagô and Hausa in the street behind, next to the dis-tillery that Thome Corrêa de Mattos rents, the last band being the grandest."[3]

Thus ethnic identities have always found means of expression and differen-tiation within ritual. In a similar fashion, religious practices known as *calandus*, and later as candomblés, were one of the most important spaces for contrasting the various African nations and drawing the boundaries between them. So much so that the concept of nation eventually became limited to the sphere of these religious practices and the congregations organized around them.

In the second half of the nineteenth century, with the end of the slave trade and the progressive decline in the number of Africans in Brazil, ethnic denomi-nations of African groups ceased to function as categories for the ruling class, and yet they persisted among Africans and their Creole descendants within their networks of familial solidarity and above all in their religious practices. Ethnic identity was gradually accommodated to that territory of sociability that was controlled exclusively by the black-mestizo population, in which it was still possible to establish internal relations of contrast.

Vivaldo da Costa Lima, in his classic article "O conceito de nação nos Candomblés da Bahia" (The Concept of Nation in the Candomblés of Bahia), was the first author to call attention to how the term *nation* gradually "lost its political connotation to become a concept almost exclusively theological. Thus nation became the ideological and ritual model of the Bahian candomblé terreiros." In other words, *nation* came to designate a "ritual model," or an "organizational form defined according to a religious basis."[4]

Increasingly, the denominations of nation ceased to refer to individuals sharing the same land of origin or African ascendency. Whether a person belonged to a nation came to depend on his or her involvement, normally marked by initiation, with a terreiro where, within the cult, ritual and mythical elements originating from a given African region predominated. As Lima noted so well, biological kinship was replaced by spiritual kinship resulting from the initiation process. Consequently, the concept of "religious" nation became closely tied to the various lineages or genealogies of the *família-de-santo* (those initiated in the same group and sharing a *mãe-* or *pai-de-santo*,* or priestess or priest), through which "the ritual norms and the doctrine" are, one way or another, transmitted.[5]

Because of the fluidity and movement of religious experts and ritual practices from one cult house to another and the possibility of one individual being partially or successively initiated in terreiros of different ascendancies, it is difficult to accept the idea of the Candomblé nations as independent, homogenous, and mutually exclusive unities. Edison Carneiro, in 1937, had already noted the growing interpenetration of religious practices: "today many candomblés are no longer dedicated to a single *nation*, as in the past, whether because the current leader is from a different nation than his predecessor and naturally dedicates himself to both," or whether because religious experts visit other houses and their hosts are obliged "to pay homage to such people by drumming and dancing according to their respective *nations*. It is no longer rare to play after the manner of any *nation* in any candomblé."[6]

This flexibility led to a great eclecticism, one terreiro being frequently identified with various hypothetically exclusive nations (i.e., Ketu-Angola-Caboclo). Today it is also common for a terreiro to identify itself with the nation of the "traditional" houses that are more socially visible and prestigious (i.e., Ketu), regardless of any ritual connection with initiation. Increasingly, the category of nation is used ideologically as a strategy responding to interests of social legitimization and through which the group is able to establish alliances with prestigious congregations, or dynamics of contrast with competing ones.

Therefore, the category of Candomblé nation, though associated with a "ritual model," functions as an important factor in collective identification, both in the "traditional" houses as well as in those founded more recently. It *still* has, therefore, a political connotation (in the broadest sense of the term), while it reproduces mechanisms of competition and solidarity parallel to those that operate within the dynamics of ethnic identification.

The argument that I will attempt to make in the coming chapters, through the case of the Jeje, is that the identity of the "religious" nations of Candomblé, based on the articulation of a series of diacritical signs, shares the same logic and dynamic of contrast also inherent to the processes of ethnic differentiation. However, in order to establish this, we must first understand better the formative process of Candomblé, which is the primary subject of the next few sections.

Some Considerations on the Religious Institutions of the Vodun Area

Max Weber claimed that one of the principal functions of religion is to provide meaning to the existence of suffering and some means of overcoming or transcending it. Also, Bronislaw Malinowski calls religion an aid in bearing "situations of emotional stress." In continuing this line of interpretation, scholars of Central Africa in the 1960s and 1970s proposed the theoretical model known as the "fortune-misfortune complex," according to which religious activity has as its objective not only "to prevent misfortune" but also "to maximize good fortune." In conflict and in "times of difficult experience" (sickness, infertility, failure, destruction, death, etc.) one craves "health, fecundity, psychic security, harmony, power, status and wealth."

The conceptual range of the "fortune-misfortune" model, which is also applicable to the study of West African religion, "popular Catholicism," and Afro-Brazilian religions, calls into question its heuristic utility and its analytic interest if it is unable to distinguish between these different religious modalities. Nevertheless, this model helps to underscore and characterize a type of religiosity that is concerned with *sustaining* life in *this world*, as opposed to the emphasis of revelatory religions (Christianity, Islam, Judaism) on the afterlife and the eternal salvation of the soul.[7]

This is not the place to review theories of anthropology of religion. For explanatory purposes, it is enough to say that here we will view religion as that set of practices that establish an interaction between "this world" (that of humans) and the invisible "other world" inhabited (generally) by a series of "spiritual entities" responsible for the sustainability of life. Ritual, for its part, is defined as the structured and behavioral means that makes this interaction viable.[8] This concept of religion has the advantage of including a whole series of practices, such as the production of amulets, healing rituals, or witchcraft (*feitiçaria**) activities, which, from the point of view of anthropological tradition and also from that of revelatory religion, would be difficult to fit under the label of religion. However, in African societies they form an integral, sometimes central (rather than peripheral or marginal) part of the religious system.

We can now approach the question of the institutionalization of religious practices, understanding institution, as Sidney Mintz and Richard Price do, as "any regular or orderly social interaction that acquires a normative character and can hence be employed to meet recurrent needs."[9] In African societies diverse forms of religious activity were gradually institutionalized, that is, the values and practices aimed at communication with the "invisible world" were accommodated to some relatively stable forms of social organization that perpetuated themselves for recurring ends. For analytical purposes, we can establish a polarity distinguishing, on the one hand, those religious institutions that contribute to the reinforcement of the power structures and the development of mechanisms of social control and integration (in the Durkheimian sense) and, on the other, those more dynamic and transformative (in the Turnerian sense) that normally surface along the society's margins and convey a counterhegemonic discourse. Borrowing the terminology that Ioan M. Lewis uses in the field of possession cults, the first can be called central institutions, and the second, peripheral institutions.[10]

Let us consider as an example of a "central" religious institution, the vodun cult in the kingdom of Ouidah (Fida, Juda, Whydah), with its capital in Savi, in the final decades of the seventeenth century, of which there exist a number of accounts, such as those of William Bosman and Jean Barbot. In this kingdom, as in the neighboring kingdom of Allada (Ardra), the vodun cult was inseparably integrated into the sociopolitical organization and sanctioned the legal and moral authority of the king and the family chiefs. Although the ancestral cult, especially that of the kings, seems to have been central, Bosman identifies three principal "public deities": the snake, the trees, and the sea. "And each of these . . . hath its particular province . . . with this difference only, that the sea and trees are not permitted to intermeddle with what is entrusted to the snake; which on the contrary hath an influencing power over both the other." This means not only that the deities had specialized spheres of action but also that the priesthood was organized and divided according to what was probably a highly competitive hierarchal structure.

Dangbe the python, royal and supreme deity in Ouidah, was responsible, for example, for the rain invoked to obtain a "plentiful harvest." The trees were worshipped and received offerings "in time of sickness, more especially fevers, in order to establish the patients to health," although Dangbe could also fulfill this function. The sea was invoked "when it rages and hinders our bringing our goods on shore, when no ships have been there for a long time, and they impatiently wait for them." On these occasions, great sacrifices were made, throwing into the sea every kind of offering, including human beings. Robert Norris, in 1789, also mentions the intervention of the priests in the oracles and decisions concerning war. Therefore, members of the priesthood, given their power, real or imagined, over the agricultural cycles, health, trade, and war, were invested with the highest social status. This allowed them to establish a social pact with the political or civil power (the king and the chiefs of various family clans) obligating political leaders to provide them with the resources necessary for subsistence.[11]

For this purpose, the king of Ouidah organized annual processions to the temple of Dangbe, in the vicinity of Savi, spending a great fortune on offerings. The priests acted in alliance with the members of the nobility, who also received presents from the king. The civil power, represented by the chiefs of the various family collectivities, had a clear interest in supporting the religious cult, which allowed them to recoup a part of the heavy taxes imposed by the king. The religious institution functioned as a compensatory economic mechanism in the face of the king's absolute power. The offerings to the deities (i.e., the priests) normally consisted of "money, some pieces of silk or stuff, all sorts of cattle, good eatables and drinks."[12]

At the same time, the social pact between the civil and religious powers guaranteed the priesthood no small number of devotees consecrated to the deities, among them slaves. In the case of the Dangbe temple, in Savi, Bosman estimates more than 1,000 *vodunsi*,* or wives of the vodun. The religious institution, therefore, was structured largely on the periodic recruitment of these *vodunsis*, a recruitment justified by religious principles and having as its purpose the ritual consecration of these women into the service of the gods through a complex initiation process. But in addition to the religious dimension, this recruitment had a material motivation, as these women, or their relatives, contributed "with all manner of necessaries" to the activities of the temple, and "that so plentifully, that the priests can also handsomely subsist on it."[13] One can suppose that in the case of the *vodunsi* slaves, their contribution developed as agricultural work, domestic service, or other kinds of labor.

Therefore, the institution of the vodun cult, based on offerings to the deities and on the initiation process of the devotees, veils a dynamic of exchange of economic resources that justifies its existence and perpetuation; and this differs little from contemporary vodun cults in Benin as well as in Brazil. The initiation process is often one of the most important means of sustenance for a religious congregation. In the case of Ouidah, Bosman supposes that the king received a part of the revenue obtained from the *vodunsi*'s families. This suggests a circularity of resources, from the priests to the king and from the king to the priests.

Between ironic and sarcastic, Bosman's enlightened perception of the functioning of the religious institution in Ouidah could be called proto-Marxist because of its emphasis on unmasking the pecuniary motivations underlying the cult ("their religion seems only founded on the same principle, *interest*").[14] It should not, however, lead one to forget other complementary dimensions. Although the religious institution functioned as a mechanism of control and exploitation—Marx's "opium of the people"—it also guaranteed processes of social integration and offered moral assistance, solutions, and conceptual references consistent with the local worldview to meet the "times of difficult experience" (drought, war, sickness, death, etc.).

What should be emphasized here is that certain societies of West Africa, especially those located near the coast, developed progressively complex religious institutions fundamental to their sociopolitical and economic organization and, therefore, "central" to the system of social relationships. The vodun cults of seventeenth-century Ouidah are an example of this type of complex religious institution, a system based on (1) permanent sacred places dedicated to deities (temples and altars); (2) a hierarchized priesthood of mostly men in command; (3) a collectivity of devotees or *vodunsis*, composed of mostly women; (4) a series of periodic ritual activities, such as annual processions, public ceremonies of drumming and dance involving spirit possession; (5) initiation processes; and (6) offerings to the deities. These last two characteristics were a veiled strategy for the exchange of resources between the civil and the religious powers.

Alongside these "central" religious institutions, other cults that Lewis calls "peripheral" can also develop, establishing dialectic or contrasting relationships with the central ones. According to Lewis, the central possession cults, whose participants are normally men competing for power and authority, function as instruments of social control, while the peripheral cults, whose participants are normally subaltern groups—such as women or homosexuals—function as a ritualized form of protest or rebellion.[15] While this model is not easily applied to all contexts, it serves at least to point out the possible simultaneity, and even complementarity, of various competing religious institutions within the same society, and the consequent negotiations and conflicts between their social agents.

In order to illustrate this dynamic we can take the case of the Sakpata vodun cult in the kingdom of Dahomey. After the conquest of the kingdoms of Allada and Ouidah in the 1720s, Agaja and his successor Tegbesu adopted a policy of appropriating the subjected peoples' cults, often carrying their altars and priests to Abomey, the kingdom's capital. This policy of importing foreign cults, rooted in a strategy for the accumulation of religious power, also sought to placate the potential wrath and vengeance of the conquered peoples' gods. At the same time, it helped maintain control over this plurality of religious congregations, some of which were perceived as threats and potential focal points for contesting Abomey's central power. King Tegbesu was responsible for establishing the *ajahó*, the minister of the vodun cults and chief of the king's secret police. As Bernard Maupoil states, they elaborated a "plan of submission of the altars to the throne," or in the words of Maurice Glélé, the vodun cults were subjected to "the control of administrative police."[16] This process was accompanied by a hierarchical organization of the many existing deities that followed a genealogical model, placing the royal ancestral cult (Nesuhé) at the highest level, alongside the cult of the couple Mawu-Lisa, to which all other cults were subordinate (see chapter 7).

In this way, authorities hoped to neutralize the power of certain religious institutions or "peripheral cults" that could threaten the central power. The most notable example is that of the vodun Sakpata. With the appearance of smallpox, probably brought into the Gbe-speaking area by Europeans in the seventeenth century, this vodun, originally tied to the ancestral and earth cults, became increasingly associated with epidemics of this disease that regularly ravaged Dahomey. The priests of Sakpata were the only people capable of intervening in such cases, being responsible for individual cures, for the rituals to placate the deity's wrath, and for the festivities of thanksgiving for those who escaped death and usually became adepts of the vodun. For this reason, the Sakpata congregations experienced great expansion and popularity. If to this we add the belief that the priests of Sakpara possessed esoteric knowledge that allowed them to punish others with smallpox, one can understand why this much feared cult was viewed as a threat to the Dahomean monarchy. As

Claude Lepine points out, Sakpata eventually came to be seen as the only and true "king of the land," the only one to contest the power of the usurping Dahomeans who did not respect the kings or "masters of the land" of the conquered peoples. Dahomean tradition reports that in the time of Agaja there were "numerous conspiracies led by the Sakpata priests, many of them being banished from the country; many magical works were done in the Sakpata temples in order to bring an end to Agaja." In the eighteenth century alone, of the five Agasuvi kings who reigned in Dahomey, four were stricken with smallpox, and three of them died from it. Sakpata "quickly became a kind of symbol to all those who had been discontent with the Abomey monarchy."

The kings of Dahomey would not accept marriage with a woman consecrated to this vodun, and would never grant any office to one of its adepts. Some of them ordered the altars of Sakpata be taken from Abomey and placed outside the city walls. They oscillated between the desire to exterminate the cult and the fear of being unable to deal with the epidemics without the help of its priests. As Lepine observes: "during the reign of Agongolo (1789–97) the smallpox epidemics were very violent and the Sakpata priests gained considerable importance, so much so that the next king, Adandozan (1797–1818), commanded that they be expelled and carried in chains to Adamé, declaring that in Dahomey there could not be two kings. But Ghezo (1818–58), faced with the gravity of the epidemics that followed, and after having consulted Fa, commanded that Sakpata be brought back. Under the reign of Glélé (1858–89), the cult of Sakpata was prohibited."[17]

This example demonstrates how, when faced with a centralized hierarchical religious institution, peripheral, counterhegemonic, competing, and complementary institutions surface, institutions that historically can move from a marginal position to one of greater centrality, or vice versa. Beyond the relative stability of a religious system legitimized by the political power, religious institutions are always subject to internal dynamics of change. By now it should be apparent, however, that religious practices organize and perpetuate themselves based on the existence of social institutions that guarantee their expression.

Religious Practices of African Origin in Eighteenth-Century Brazil

The compulsory diaspora of the African population in Brazil is unique in that many groups were displaced from their societies and religious institutions and yet were able to transfer a plurality of cultures (values and practices in my terms, civilizations and superstructures in Roger Bastide's, collective representations in Émile Durkheim's) to a new social setting. That is, through memory and individualized experience, the enslaved brought with them "fragments of culture," but without the social institutions that gave them expression. As Mintz and Price point out—closely adhering to Bastide's general idea—the formation of an Afro-Brazilian society only occurred when new institutions were organized or, in Bastide's words, with the creation of complex social structures (infrastructures) capable of accommodating the various African cultures (superstructures) brought by individual, or groups of, slaves.[18] Likewise, one can say that the formation of an "Afro-Brazilian" religious community (what today is referred to as the *povo-de-santo*) was the result of the reconstruction process of new religious institutions through these many cultural fragments.

But which "institutions" were these? Bastide speaks of an initial stage of *adaption* occurring with the *batuques* (drumming performances), work crews, and Catholic brotherhoods, and a second stage of *creation* corresponding to the formation of complex social structures such as the *calundus* and candomblés, a process in which the freedmen played a decisive role. Actually, as we will see, the two stages seem to overlap, since the *calundus* of African origin were organized alongside or simultaneously with the recreational *batuques* and the Catholic brotherhood festivities. Bastide also notes that this process occurred principally in the urban context or on the sugar plantations, where greater concentrations of slaves were to be found, in contrast to the mining zones or to the semiarid backlands (where a cattle-based economy predominated), and, later, on the coffee plantations in the south of Brazil.[19]

To resume the initial argument of the "fortune-misfortune complex," one could say that this reconstruction, reinvention, or reinstitutionalization of African religions in Brazil occurred not only as a collective form of cultural resistance (asystematic in the majority of cases and conscious only in certain individuals or relatively restricted circles), but primarily as a necessity in the face of misfortune or those "times of difficult experience" of which slavery is undoubtedly one of the most extreme cases. The partial remodeling of religious practices of African origin, with its long and varied therapeutic traditions—encompassing what one might call today "social assistance"—became inevitable. It was not by chance that *curandeirismo*, or healing practices, and funeral rites were some of the African religious aspects most persistently reproduced in the Americas. It was also not by chance that the black population resorted to the Catholic brotherhoods that, in addition to other advantages, were primarily concerned with guaranteeing assistance to the sick and a decent burial.

Besides the therapeutic and funerary aspects addressed by religious activity, the congregations—whether Catholic brotherhoods or *calundus*—contrib-

uted to social cohesion and integration, a factor that became increasingly determinant in the perpetuation of these collective organizations. This is the other
side of the "fortune-misfortune complex," which seeks "to maximize good
fortune." Both the officially accepted festivities of the Catholic brotherhoods
and the semiclandestine (though relatively tolerated) *batuques* and *calundus*
constituted collective activities directed at the public. They were spectacular
events that promoted the social visibility of certain individuals or groups and
offered an institutionalized space for the competition for status and power. In
African cosmology, the accumulation of power and wealth was interpreted and
valued as a sign of the gods' favor and proof of the possessor's "strength." The
complex web of clientelism that existed in the brotherhoods, where a white
patron would establish a system of favor exchanges with his protected slaves
and freedmen, offered a space for social ascension and the quest for power.[20]
Also, within the restricted sphere of the black-mestizo community, in the organization of the *batuques* and *calundus*, there existed a space for micropolitical
dynamics, with the creation of hierarchies and forms of black clientelism parallel to those established by whites in the brotherhoods. The quest for social
visibility and power, one of the greatest human drives, accounting for a large
portion of our social life, undoubtedly strengthened the functioning of the
institutions that allowed its expression.

The black brotherhoods were a space of sociability, an institutionalized form
of black organization, accepted and even encouraged by the dominant classes.
Certainly, as Mary Karasch shows regarding the slaves of Rio de Janeiro, some
Africans, whether through their upbringing in Africa or upon arrival in Brazil,
could accept Catholicism and behave with "sincere" devotion motivated by
these cultural referents. In fact, the Catholic worship of saints, based on the
"vow contractual obligation" and on interpersonal relationships with spiritual
intermediaries capable of resolving daily problems, presents a notable similarity to the relationships between African devotees and their deities. This
homology certainly facilitated the more or less profound religious conversion
of certain individuals, and there is no reason to doubt the existence of devout
black Catholics.[21]

However, other Africans involved in the brotherhoods—perhaps the majority—did not undergo such a radical conversion. They could add, often su-
perficially, certain Catholic beliefs and habits to those with which they were
raised in Africa, establishing parallelisms or conceptual relationships, at times
even identifications, between the two referential systems. The accumulation of
differentiated spiritual resources, in fact a characteristic of many African religions and also of popular Catholicism, was lived not necessarily as a contradic-

tion but rather as an efficient strategy for dealing with adversity and obtaining good fortune. For these people, or at least for part of them, participation in the brotherhoods was not merely a façade or a means of hiding their "true" beliefs, for devotion to the saints was also an integral part of their religiosity. This does not mean that there did not exist another group of Africans who effectively used the brotherhoods to hide from the dominant class their "true" beliefs and practices. In both cases, within the intimacy of the brotherhoods and beneath the surface of baroque Catholicism, these people found an alternative space for the perpetuation of values, emotional dispositions, existential orientations, notions of self, forms of expression, gestures, and so on, of their own African cultures, and these aspects were an inextricable part of their religiosity.

In this way, the brotherhoods often hid practices—those of the *calundus*—that did not fit well into the canons and rules of Catholic theology. The social networks established by blacks in the Catholic brotherhoods were probably those that could guarantee the organization of the *batuques* and other religious practices that, in the eyes of the Africans, had as much efficacy—and for some even more—as devotion to Catholic saints. The double participation of many Africans and Creoles in the parades and processions of both the brotherhoods and the *calundus* or "superstitious" dances were experienced as a beneficial juxtaposition of conceptual resources to deal with daily adversity. The Afro-Catholic syncretism of contemporary Candomblé finds its roots in this duplicity of practices that appeared in the seventeenth century and were developed primarily in the eighteenth century.

In 1765, when the brotherhood Senhor Bom Jesus dos Martírios de Homens de Nação Gege in Cachoeira sent its petition requesting the ratification of their statute to the Mesa de Consciência e Ordens in Lisbon, the local ecclesiastical authorities were against the establishment of such an association. The petition was accompanied by a note recommending that the Portuguese authorities deny confirmation, alleging that the Jeje were "taken from the paganism of Africa and always retain a propensity for superstition," and that it was therefore best to keep them subject to the discipline of the bishop.[22] This "paganism" and "superstition" were perhaps an allusion to the recreational *batuques* that accompanied the Catholic processions and the brotherhood celebrations (*folias*), each nation with its own dances, songs, and instruments. However, it is more probable that the author of the note was hinting at clandestine practices involving forms of "idolatry" that the Catholic Church had been demonizing since the previous century and that were normally referred to as *feitiçaria** (sorcery or witchcraft).[23]

The Church never established a clear distinction between practices with preventive, propitiatory, and therapeutic ends, such as the production of amulets, or healing techniques, and those practices that, although similar to these in their manipulation of complex materials (*feitiços*), had harmful or antisocial *intent*, and that could be classified as *feitiçaria* in the strict sense of the term. It is noteworthy that the threat, real or imagined, of *feitiçaria* (in the aggressive or antisocial sense) played an important role in the relationship between masters and slaves, and also frequently in the micropolitical spheres of Africans, for example, in the brotherhood power struggles.[24]

The possibility that one might become the target of *feitiçaria* practice, or the desire to avenge oneself of a perceived mystical aggression, promoted an ambiguous mixture of defensive and offensive attitudes. Fear was the psychological substratum that supported *feitiçaria* and could be wisely manipulated by religious experts, who were also specialists of the human mind. As they had pharmaceutical knowledge and a long tradition of poison production, this fear was not always unfounded. Thus, Jeje *feitiçaria* was always one of the most reputed and feared. As we will see in following chapters, the dynamic imposed by the threat of *feitiçaria* persisted throughout the centuries among the Jeje religious congregations, surfacing especially at times of disputes over the succession of the leadership of these communities.

At the beginning of the seventeenth century there is mention of "slave sorcerers" (*escravos feiticeiros*) and their efficacy in the use of herbs. In 1728, Nuno Marques Pereira, the author of *Peregrino das Américas* (Pilgrim of the Americas) wrote of the "superstitious and heathen rites" of Africans, and in 1761 an Ilhéus magistrate ordered the arrest of black sorcerers, specialists in the "diabolical arts" of divination and performing cures.[25] Another term, of Angola origin, frequently used to designate these practices in seventeenth- and eighteenth-century Inquisition records was *calundu*. Laura de Mello e Souza studied this documentation in detail, recording nine cases of *calundu* accusations in Minas Gerais between 1725 and 1750.[26] In Bahia in the seventeenth century, the famed Brazilian poet Gregório de Mattos wrote "Que de quilombos que tenho / Com mestres superlativos / Nos quais se ensina de noite / Os cálundus e feitiços" (That from quilombos I have / with superlative masters / where at night are taught / the *cálundus* and witchcraft).

In 1685, the mixed-race Clara Garcez, a widow, was denounced for worshiping in her home a "creature or a clay stick" from which she made her living "curing all those who came to her house sick, with *calundus* and animated puppets." Among the healing practices were preventative activities—such as making amulets or *mandinga* pouches—and others that were primarily therapeutic—involving the preparation of remedies (both internal and external)—

and, most important, the practice of exorcism, frequently referred to as "taking the devil from the body." Techniques such as blowing, suction, scrubbing, or other forms of expulsion (vomiting, defecating) were used to expel from the body malignant spirits considered the cause of the illness. Although exorcism was common to the Amerindian, Catholic, and African traditions, only those cases that involved "African demons" or African practitioners were designated as *calundus*. In the 1740s, in Salvador, the Carmelite Frei Luís de Nazaré, himself an exorcist, recommended that slaves brought to him receive treatment in *calundus*, as "African demons" were not his specialty.[27]

In Rio de Janeiro in 1772, in the official proceedings against a *calundu* practitioner named Ana Maria da Conceição, *calundu* is defined as the act of "performing various dances." In 1753, for example, the slave Maria Canga earned some gold ritually telling fortunes; "she would invent a *batuque* dance, in the middle of which something would come in and out of her head, which she called wind, and she would begin to foretell what she wanted." The divination practices were, and continue to be, critical religious activities. The oracular methods allow the prediction, diagnosis, and prescription of the best strategy to be adopted when faced with a given conflict, and thus are an indispensable component of the healing practice. In the eighteenth century, divination, or "fortune telling" (*dar ventura*) occurred mainly through mediumship, or "spirit possession," experiences, as well as by other means such as water scrying. Only in the nineteenth century is there documentation mentioning the *Ifá** or cowry shell divination system. In 1739, in the village of Sabará, in Minas Gerais, the Angola freedwoman Luzia Pinta is accused of being a "*calunduzeira*, healer, and fortune teller." She made "diabolic apparitions with some dances . . . with her standing on a small altar with its dossal having a cutlass in her hand with a wide riband tied about her head with ends thrown back, and dressed in the manner of an angel," to the sound of small drums (*timbals*, or cymbals according to Souza) that three blacks, her slaves, played about her. She became "as one who has lost her senses, speaking things that no one understood, having those who had come to be cured prostrated on the ground, she passed over them a number of times, and it was on these occasions she would say she had winds of divination."[28]

Although Laura de Mello e Souza points out the similarities between this ritual and contemporary Candomblé—which seems pertinent only in relation to attire such as the riband tied to the head and the cutlass—it is important to point out that these dances and such mediumship experiences were generally restricted to the ritual officiant, and their chief aim was divination and healing. Also, Luzia Pinta would travel to wherever her services were required, having no exclusive fixed place for conducting her rituals. As I argue in greater detail below, these characteristics differentiated colonial *calundus* from the later candomblés inspired by the traditions of the Mina Coast, where the dances and "possession" experiences were collective, officiated by individuals ritually initiated for this purpose, involving what was essentially a dimension of celebration and worship, without such evident presence of other more pragmatic aims such as healing or divination. In this way, the eighteenth-century divination and healing tradition of *calundus* seems to evince a strong Central African influence.[29]

However, this tendency does not mean that there was not an equally important West African tradition of "healer-diviners" or *feiticeiros*. The Inquisition sources for the most part do not identify the ethnicity of those denounced. However, Luiz Mott did encounter the case of Tereza, a "black, Mina Gegê, freedwoman who had been the slave of Captain Manoel Barbosa," denounced and imprisoned in Bahia (Recôncavo), on February 4, 1778, while "her lover Luis, a Creole," fled. The *Mina Gegê* denomination proves the existence of Jeje religious experts who, just as the Kongo-Angola, were dedicated to relatively individualized religious activities. In the case of Tereza, who was "generally . . . believed, reputed, and feared as a *feiticeira*," the situation was one of antisocial practices, since "many had died through her spells, from diseases unknown to the art of Medicine, some families being entirely wiped out by her slaughter."[30] Similarly, at the beginning of nineteenth century, in 1807, a "Gege freedman" and "eminent healer [who] told fortunes" named Francisco Dossû was imprisoned in the town of São Francisco do Conde. In his deposition he declared "that many people came to him, whites, mestizos, blacks of both sexes to hear their fortune and be cured," and he confessed "that he often dances *tabaques*,* to effect cures, going about in many parts of the Recôncavo."[31]

Thus we see that in the eighteenth century *calundu* was a generic term used in reference to a variety of religious activities of African origin, as opposed to Catholic or Amerindian practices. Although the dancing and the drums were a part of ritual activity, their functionality was essentially healing or oracular, as *calunduzeiro*,* or *calundu* practitioner, could be used as a synonym for healer or diviner.[32] These practices were officiated by a religious expert, at times with a reduced number of assistants that, seconded or "embodied" by spiritual entities, often the "souls of their relatives," interacted in a interpersonal relationship with the "client" or patient, "telling fortunes," prescribing remedies or curing as well as performing "spells." It is also important to note that the *calunduzeiro* would travel to wherever his or her services were needed, normally having no fixed location in which to carry out his or her practice. This mobile and relatively independent method of operation facilitated the religious expert's access to the clientele, which was not restricted to the black population and could include mestizos and whites.

Altars and Offerings:
Beyond the *Curandeiros** and Diviners

Nevertheless, *calundu* could, in some cases, refer to organized groups with collective ritual practices that involved more participants than merely the healer-diviner and his or her clients. In 1738, the Benedictine prior of Bahia remarked that the slaves "gather together in *societies* to perform their *calundus*."[33] This allusion to "societies" is significant. In relation to the black festivities that emerged around the Recife brotherhoods, the Count of Povolide, in the above-cited 1780 letter, differentiated between "dances that although ... not the most saintly, I don't consider worthy of total censure," as "they are similar to the fandangos of Castile, the fofas of Portugal, and the lundus of the whites and *pardos* of that Country," and those other "superstitious dances" or "dances that I wholly condemn." The latter "are those that the blacks from the Mina Coast do in secret, or in homes or in the field, having a Master Negress with an altar of idols worshipping live goats and others made of clay, anointing their bodies with various oils, rooster blood, eating corn cakes after many superstitious blessings, making the rustics believe that those bread anointings give good fortune, and make women fall in love with men and men with women."[34]

These "dances," done "in secret" in homes or fields with "altars of idols," animal sacrifices, and food offerings, seem to go beyond simple healing or divination practices and are the antecedents of the future nineteenth-century candomblés. The animal sacrifices and ritual food offerings on altars dedicated to the gods constitute the base of African religiosity, especially that of the West African traditions.[35] It is important to note that in Povolide's letter these practices are explicitly associated with the "blacks from the Mina Coast," with no mention of Central African groups. This ritual complexity involving "idols" and offerings was replicated in the Tundá or *acotundá* dance, which occurred in Paracatu in around 1747 and is documented by Luiz Mott. Practiced by the *Courá* (*Courano, Curá, Curano*), a group from the Mina Coast, this ritual involved, together with possession experiences, the presence of a "puppet[,] ... a Saint from their land," to which they "offered" various pots of raw and cooked greens and around which they danced.[36]

Healing and *feitiçaria* practices were conducive to the production of amulets (*patuás**), charms (gris-gris), or *mandinga* pouches, which were portable personalized objects, considered mediating instruments for the achievement of a particular goal and whose African antecedents can be traced to, among other items, the Dahomean *gbo*.* Yet the emergence of the altar-offering system (which might also be called the *assento**-*ebô** complex) was a critical development. The shrines, or altars, are relatively fixed or stationary (often buried) consecrated material ensembles that are family or community property. They are considered the home or residence of named and well-defined deities that normally require the initiation of devotees.[37]

My hypothesis is that in the eighteenth century the Mina Coast traditions provided the means for the organization of some *calundus* that went beyond the mere healing and divination functionality. It is important to remember that during this century, among the Mina groups, the Jeje were demographically predominant. The worship of "idols" or "figures" in shrines implied the need for relatively stable spaces in order to conduct religious practice. It was probably from this West African tradition, rather than from the Kongo-Angola practice, more often based on the individual activities of the healer-diviner, that the first domestic cults were organized in "homes and fields." Their relatively more complex social and ritual structure could be described as an "ecclesiastic" type of organization.

In chapter 2, we considered the 1785 repression of the *calundu* do Pasto in Cachoeira, in which three women and three men were arrested, two Jeje, two Mahi, one Dagomé, and one Tapa, all apparently constituting three couples. This *calundu* seems to have been a domestic cult, set up in three rooms of a house rented by the freed African João do Espírito Santo from the Mina African José Pereira, also a freedman. The leader of the *calundu*, Sebastião de Guerra, sublet one of the rooms from João do Espírito Santo. As João José Reis points out, this type of living arrangement was common among the black population of Salvador and implies the existence of strategic networks of solidarity and cooperation among Africans. Having been previously condemned for practicing *feitiçaria* in Jacuípe, Sebastião was known as a powerful healer of spells or *feitiços*, but in addition to this, he succeeded in establishing in Cachoeira an incipient congregation around a cult that functioned with a certain regularity, since it was "public and notorious" that there "they danced *calundus*." Reis defines this *calundu* as "a religious community in formation."[38] This case exemplifies how the healer-diviners, who in some cases acted with relative independence, also managed to secure a minimal collective infrastructure through which to conduct their religious activities.

Though at the time of the police raid the six Africans were sleeping, with the exception of one who was bathing, one of the witnesses declared that there "would gather many negroes and negresses ... that they all carried out a dance within the said house and sang in the Jeje language, and played an iron instrument, and instead of the *tabaque* drum they played on the mouth of a pot and it was public knowledge that the said dance was a *calundu*." As Reis justly highlights, the absence of the *tabaque* could be related to the need for discretion, essential in that climate of repression, though the description most likely refers to a funerary ritual. There is an instrument in Jeje tradition that is used for this purpose called the *zen-li*, from which the sound is obtained by beating a fan of leather or straw on the mouth of a jar.[39]

In Sebastião's room, there was also found "a small arrow standing on end with a needle on top, and from the said arrow descended two tips, and on each one was a tuft of feathers, and it was stirring about with nothing on which to rest." When the white merchant Manoel de Almeida Cardoso, a participant in the *calundu* raid, tried to grab the arrow, it fell to the floor, and he was unable to set it up again. This strange object, which supported itself apparently by magic, was what most captured the attention of the witnesses. Around this mysterious arrow they found on the floor coins, cowry shells, gourds, leaves, ointments, small pieces of iron, other tufts of feathers, a bottle of liquor, gourd ladles with seeds, and other ritual ingredients, and "when they dug into the earth there appeared various objects, such as some small pieces of iron, some local wax balls with beans, rice, and [illegible] set into them."[40]

The buried objects indicate the presence of a shrine and the objects on the ground were the offerings arrayed before the "arrow," itself probably a material representation of the power of the deity enshrined there. In addition to healing and divination practices, we find here an element of apparent worship of spiritual entities. In Brazil, the Jeje tradition cultivated the practice of establishing *pejis** (shrines) or material ensembles consecrated to the deities, of which the dynamic of ceremonial offerings is complementary and typical. Some of the objects found in the *calundu*, such as leaves, cowry shells, and liquor, continue in contemporary candomblés as central elements of the offering system.

Written record gives no evidence of the existence of initiation processes of devotees or *vodunsis*, but the fact that this was a minimally organized congregation, controlling its own space, leads one to believe that within this context such rituals could have developed. This information suggests that in the last quarter of the eighteenth century the Jeje, in addition to being organized into Catholic brotherhoods and functioning individually as healer-diviners, already had the capacity to establish rudimentary religious congregations of the domestic sort, the majority of which were presumably established around a single deity.

We can now deal with the central problem of institutionalization, or re-institutionalization, of forms of black religious organizations in Brazil and the formation of an "Afro-Brazilian religion." My basic thesis for understanding this problem maintains that this process occurred through an increasing level of social and ritual complexity. From an initial stage in which "fragments of religious culture" were recovered and put into practice by charismatic individuals who acted alone and independently for the most part (in personal interactions, principally for healing and divining purposes), it passed to a further stage to form the first domestic or familial congregations generally devoted to the worship of a single deity. These finally evolved into extrafamilial congregations, more socially complex still in their hierarchical structures and ritual practices, which over time came to function with a certain stability in their own dedicated spaces, with a recurrent liturgical calendar and dedicated to the worship of a plurality of deities, enshrined in individualized sacred spaces.

It is important to note that this process, which for the purpose of analysis I characterize as linear, going from simplicity to complexity, from the individual to the collective dimension, should not be understood as a progression in which one stage supplants the other. In other words, simultaneous to the institutionalization of the more complex cults, individual practices and the minor congregations continued to exist, and quite expressively. As we will see in the next chapter, during the nineteenth century extradomestic congregations were still relatively rare and functioned, as still happens today, alongside individual practices and cults limited to the domestic sphere. In fact, according to circumstances or necessity, the same religious expert could alternate between working individually and as part of a larger congregation. The schematic and "evolutionist" character that I attribute to the process should not, therefore, minimize the complexity of the problem.

Another aspect worth highlighting is that, as we have seen in the case of the Tundá dance, as early as the eighteenth century there were extradomestic religious congregations operating with a "ecclesiastic" structure, and it is not unthinkable that they were more numerous than existing records implies. One could even speculate that some of them appeared quite early on, almost simultaneously with the proliferation of individualized healing and divination practices, contradicting therefore, the "evolutionist" or linear aspect of the process. However, the documentary silence leads one to believe that the possible functioning of these extradomestic congregations in the eighteenth century was likely sporadic and unstable.

Here it is worth remembering Bastide's warning against explicative models of Candomblé's formation that postulate the existence of primordial cults that survived unchanged through the centuries. He argues for "a chaotic proliferation of cults or cult fragments arising only to die out and give way to others with every new wave of arrivals."[41] Similarly, I believe that it was only at a later stage, probably at the start of the nineteenth century, that a *social network* of extradomestic congregations was developed. Only when these congregations, in sufficient number, began to establish among themselves cooperative, complementary, and conflicting interactions, could one speak of an "Afro-Brazilian religious *community*" and the emergence of Candomblé.

There is one other problem related to the African antecedents that might have intervened in this process. As I have suggested, I believe that the healing and divination practices, or at least some of their more significant elements, could have originated in either Central or West Africa, though Central African traditions seem dominant in this respect. In eighteenth-century Bahia, however, the *foundation* of the "ecclesiastic" organizational model that permitted the formation of the above-described extradomestic congregations found its antecedents in the traditions of groups who had come from West Africa, most particularly the Jeje. This is because the Jeje at this time were the most numerous group, and above all, because they had, as I have described in relation to the kingdoms of Ouidah and Dahomey, clear institutional precedents in this domain, something not so evident among the groups from Central Africa.

I am not suggesting here that the formative process of Candomblé should be explained exclusively by a direct and linear transference of West African elements to Brazil. It seems beyond doubt that in the reinstitutionalization of the religious values and practices of Africans in Brazil there was a reconfiguration and resignification of African elements from multiple origins (those from Central Africa included), of non-African elements, as well as the "creation" of other elements, resulting from the new social context and from the formative process itself. However, "bricolage" creativity is almost always the result of the combination and recycling of preexisting elements. Although other writers have argued for the influence of models such as the Catholic brotherhoods or even Masonic societies on the "ecclesiastic" type of organization that gave birth to the nineteenth-century candomblés,[42] it appears to me that the slaves coming from West Africa, with their vivid memory of the religious institutions in operation there, had the greatest probability of contributing directly, and creatively, to the process.

One could further argue that the similarity between certain practices, values, and forms of religious organization from West Africa and those from Brazil was the result, not only of lineal influences, but also of parallel, although independent, responses to similar conditions and social dynamics.[43] For example, the common structure of a slave system that favors the confluence of ethnically heterogeneous groups in cities such as Salvador and Ouidah could have generated similar, but independent, processes in the reconfiguration and aggregation of cults. In chapter 7, I explore this hypothesis in relation to the emergence of cults of multiple deities in West Africa and in Candomblé. The similarity of social contexts can create similar collective or institutional dynamics, but when the resulting systems found in different geographic areas present identical configurations of particular elements—as happens, for example, in the vodun pantheons of Benin and Brazil—it is more difficult to justify "convergences" merely in terms of a parallelism between the initial *conditions*. In these cases, the importance of lineal influences must not be ignored and one must identify which African groups, taking into account their social antecedents, would have more likely acted as agents of the cultural transfer, while keeping in mind that any element, once implanted in the new context, is subject to adaptations, transformations, resignifications, and appropriations by other groups.

4 The Jeje Contribution to the Institutionalization of Candomblé in the Nineteenth Century

The Emergence of a Network of Extradomestic Religious Congregations

Although they could be restricted to the domestic sphere, the religious practices based on the "altar-offering complex"—and their extension into public ceremonies of drumming, dance, and the manifestation of multiple deities in the bodies of their adepts—tended to be organized in private spaces reserved for such purposes. The increased ritual complexity and the maintenance of these sacred spaces required a greater outlay of resources and, consequently, the participation of a greater number of people. In this chapter, we will explore how a network of religious congregations with such characteristics emerged in nineteenth-century Bahia and examine their social interactions.

Until recently, the history of African religious practices in nineteenth-century Bahia was a topic little explored outside the work of Nina Rodrigues, Pierre Verger, and João José Reis.[1] Fortunately, the past decade has seen increasing interest in preabolition Candomblé, and at last a more systematic effort to examine the topic is developing.[2] Police records, including correspondence, housed in the Arquivo Público do Estado da Bahia (Bahian State Public Archive) and the newspapers of the time constitute the principal documentary sources; sources for the first half of the nineteenth century are still scarce, however, while those for the second half are more numerous and consistent.

Among the newspapers, *O Alabama*, "a humorous and critical periodical" founded in Salvador in 1863, stands out. Though the editors of this paper were Afro-descendants and abolitionists, they saw Candomblé as an expression of barbarism, superstition, and sexual promiscuity and launched a systematic campaign to denounce it. Despite this ideological bias, the articles of this paper offer valuable, almost ethnographic, descriptions of African religious practices, in some cases witnessed directly by the journalists, and document African terminology, names of leaders and participants, as well as the location of various candomblés. This material undoubtedly represents the richest documentary source on Bahian Candomblé in the 1860s and will be considered in greater detail further on.[3]

For the present, we will focus on the earlier 1800–1850 period. As we saw in chapter 3, on Christmas 1808 in Santo Amaro, there were simultaneous "gatherings" of Angola, Jeje, and Nagô-Hausa slaves held on separate streets. These *batuques*, dances, and banquets were celebrated in the open air or in abandoned houses appropriated for the occasion, and did not last longer than one day.[4] They were, therefore, gatherings that yet lacked an established organization and specific spaces dedicated to such activities.

However, it is known that one year earlier, in 1807, on lands of the Boa Vista farm, a part of Herminigildo Netto's plantation in the Madre de Deus district (near Santo Amaro), there was an apparently more established ritual congregation led by Antônio, a young Angola slave. Antônio was arrested and identified in the documents as "president of the candomblés' terreiro." This is the first known record of the word *candomblé*, probably a term of Bantu origin. In this use *candomblé* (or *candombleis* in the Portuguese) seems to be used as a synonym for *batuque*, and might refer to healing and/or divination, but the title of "president" suggests an incipient hierarchical organization of a religious collectivity. As Rachel Harding comments, the word *candomblé* emerges just as the term *calundu* falls from use.[5] This coincidence strengthens the analytic polarity, suggested in chapter 3, between the old colonial *calundus* and the new, more organizationally complex candomblés, and perhaps allows one to date, in very general terms, the emergence and greater visibility of the latter at the start of the century.

Harding's central thesis is that Candomblé came about in response to slavery and as a form of resistance against the dehumanization of the enslaved African. She emphasizes the concepts of "communion/community, refuge/resistance, and healing/reparation" as means of creating a sense of alternative black identity under slavery.[6] The shared condition of slavery and the communality of cognitive orientations would have led blacks to form a "pan-Africanist" interethnic solidarity. Although these two ideas synthesize important dynamics of Candomblé, I believe that the formative process of this institution cannot be reduced so simply to these factors.

In the first place, the "pan-Africanism" defended by Harding is questionable, as is clear in the example of the Santo Amaro gatherings of 1808. Existing ethnic divisions by nation were stimulated by the political powers, primarily in the first decades of the century. Following the end of the transatlantic slave trade in 1850, distinctions between nations are not so explicitly documented, though they do persist in some candomblés throughout the century, despite the growing ethnic and racial heterogeneity of Candomblé participants. It was only after abolition, with the decrease of Africans in Bahia, that an "African" identity was assumed by certain communities, and still this "Africanness" was closely tied to the Yoruba culture, making difficult its categorization as "pan-African."

Certainly the contrast between the interests and values of the black subaltern "class" and those of the white elite was a determining factor in configuring important aspects of this religious institution, through the resignification of old religious practices with new intentionalities (such as the production of *mandinga* pouches to offer protection from the abuses of masters) or the reinterpretation of new religious forms with old meanings (such as the syncretism of Catholic saints with African deities). In this confrontation with Iberian culture and Catholic hegemony, Candomblé emerged as a "peripheral" and socially marginal religious institution, with a parallel and sometimes counterhegemonic cultural discourse.

However, the genesis of Candomblé cannot be reduced to "class" opposition or to mere resistance to slavery; it should be viewed *also* as the consequence or effect of the intra-African encounter, relatively autonomous in relation to society at large, and resulting from its own *internal dynamic*. The reactualization of African religious practices could respond to strategies against adversity, which went beyond slavery, or be a way to satisfy the need for group solidarity or dialectic complementarity inherent to African micropolitics.

Another point to take into account is that, despite the candomblés' containing a significant number of slaves among their participants and despite their often serving as a refuge for fugitive slaves, the institution was not developed exclusively for this social segment. In fact, the formation of religious congregations was a phenomenon led essentially by freedmen and freedwomen. Of the total of eighty-one documented references to religious leaders collected by Reis for the period 1800–1888, only two concerned slaves.[7] This data demonstrates the critical role of the freed persons, with their greater mobility and resources, in the development and maintenance of Candomblé.

In fact, the freed African Candomblé leaders, like the eighteenth-century *calunduzeiros*, rendered religious services to clients from social backgrounds that extended well beyond the black community to include *pardos* (or mulattoes) and whites, poor and rich, free, freed, and slaves, which indicates that Candomblé, from the beginning and increasingly, based its activities on a strategy of social inclusion, at least as far as "clients" and participants (initiated members) went; it therefore cannot be considered simply as a space of "refuge" for blacks. I believe that this openness and the capacity to establish connections outside the black community also contributed to the consolidation and expansion of Candomblé.

This is not to deny the importance of religion in the processes of slave resistance, above all in the first half of the century. For example, the Hausa slave revolt in 1807 was inspired by religion. Information regarding the *quilombos* of this time indicates the presence of drums and religious activity in connection with revolts. Amulets and *mandingas*, often of Malê origin, were often found amid the weapons of the African conspirators. Revolts included the Itapuã rebellion begun on February 28, 1814, and led by Francisco, a slave called "king" and "president of the dances of his nation, and its protector and agent," and his companion, the "queen" Francisca. On February 12, 1816, slaves from Santo Amaro and São Francisco do Conde began a revolt "after a religious festival." In 1826, Africans, mostly of Nagô origin, who had been involved in the revolt of the Urubu *quilombo* in the suburbs of Salvador sought refuge in a "house called candomblé." The "queen" Zefereina is mentioned as one of the insurrection's leaders and the mulatto Antônio as the owner of the candomblé. Ritual objects found there included "shells" (cowry shells), drums, "a cardboard crown decorated with cowry shells" (which was strung to the head of the wounded black), statuettes of "cows painted red," and "a red hat with three feathers."[8]

In all of these cases, the rebellions seemed to be intimately connected to religious activity and indicate the existence of a number of African religious congregations. However, the documentation does not reveal the complexity and the degree of institutionalization of these "religious festivals" and "candomblés." The armed rebellions may have also benefited from other forms of politico-religious organization such as the black brotherhoods, but the candomblés, with their need for secrecy, could be advantageous to the organization of insurgent movements. It is not surprising, therefore that the authorities saw African religious manifestations as a threat and a potential focal point for insurrection that needed to be controlled.

The white elite's varying policies of tolerance and repression of these assemblies in the first decades of the nineteenth century had antecedents in the previous century. Already in 1728 one finds the polarity between a moderate and tolerant tendency and another more authoritarian and intransigent in the case of the traveler Nuno Marques Pereira and a farm owner who lodged him. The latter seemed to accept the entertainments of the slaves as a form of social control, while the traveler seemed repulsed, seeing the *calundus* as an offense against God. As Laura de Mello e Souza points out, "the tolerant and comprehensive paternalism of the master and the dogmatic and orthodox intransigence of the traveler constitute, therefore, two possible faces of the ideology of the slave-owning class."[9]

The history of religious persecution in colonial Brazil suggests that the last quarter of the eighteenth century saw greater indulgence in relation to popular religious practices, a tendency probably increased by the expulsion of the Jesuits in 1759.[10]

In the nineteenth century, this polarity between tolerance and repression is reflected in the policies of two Bahian governors, the sixth Count da Ponte, who governed between 1805 and 1810, and the eighth Count dos Arcos, who succeeded him, governing until 1818. The case is well studied by João José Reis and Renato da Silveira, among other authors. The Count da Ponte maintained a policy of systematic repression and considered the "African festivity subversive by nature because it created in the slave a taste for independence, stimulated his self-confidence, promoted libertinage and disdain for Western moral and aesthetic values." For his part, the Count dos Arcos considered it good politics to allow the African *batuques*, despite recommendations to the contrary from the central government in Rio de Janeiro. For him, these gatherings that regrouped the slaves by nation contributed to their internal division, separating the diverse ethnic groups. Along with recognizing the slaves' right to leisure, the count feared that repression would unify them against the slaveholders. That is, according to the Count da Ponte, the festivities amplified tensions with slave owners, while for the Count dos Arcos, they acted as an escape valve, and even contributed to disunion among slaves as well as the well-known strategy of divide and conquer.[11]

These questions continued to divide the representatives of postcolonial power. In 1829, António Gomes de Abreu Guimarães, justice of the peace in the parish of Brotas, and a believer in the repressive policy of the Count da Ponte, for whom he expressed admiration, ordered the raid of a candomblé located in his parish, in the place known as Accú, probably present-day Acupe.[12] This interesting episode is documented in a letter from Guimarães found by Reis and discussed in his article "Nas malhas do poder escravista: A invasão do candomblé do Accú na Bahia, 1829" (In the Web of Slavery's Power: The Invasion of the Accú Candomblé, Bahia, 1829). For our purposes here, this candomblé is worthy of attention because there is a reference to the worship of a "Vodun God," which could indicate that this congregation was of Jeje origin.[13] In addition to being the earliest written reference to the word *vodun* in Bahia, this letter provides evidence of a religious congregation with a complex organizational capacity, involving the participation of more than thirty-six people (three men were arrested and twenty-two women, while eleven women remained at the site and others fled) and festivities that lasted several days (in the words of the magistrate, "this festivity had been booming along already for three days").[14]

The ceremony that was interrupted by the raiding troops is described by the justice in the following manner: "Upon a fully prepared table, a puppet thoroughly trimmed in ribbons, and cowry shells, and a large gourd from the Coast full of cowries mixed with some copper coins as alms, playing drums (*tambaque*) and gourds adorned with cowry shells, some [women] dancing, and others sleeping in a room, or acting as if asleep."[15] Again in this description is found the "altar-offering complex": the worshipping of a "puppet," the representation of the "Vodun God," with offerings of money and cowry shells. Additionally, the reference to women "sleeping" or "acting as if asleep," suggests perhaps secluded *vodunsis* being initiated. All of this points to a ritual complexity similar to that of contemporary candomblés, and one that should be distinguished from the above-mentioned slave "gatherings" tolerated by the Count dos Arcos, which were no more than sporadic meetings lacking the infrastructure of an organized cult.

Within the chronological sequence of existing documentation on Jeje religious practices—which begins with the Mina-Jeje *feiticeira* of 1765, continues with the domestic congregation of Cachoeira in 1785, and carries on to this candomblé of 1829—one can clearly see the evolution from individualized activities of Jeje religious experts to organized cults with relatively stable congregations. The 1820s therefore mark the culmination of a process begun in the eighteenth century that leads to the consolidation of new religious institutions with an ever widening social base, including participants of every color and legal status, but dominated and controlled for the most part by the black population and, at this point in the century, principally by freed Africans. The Jeje case is emblematic of a process that likely also occurred among other African nations such as the Nagô or Angola, and that would allow one to speak of the emergence of an Afro-Brazilian *religious community* as early as the 1820s.

I will return to the Accú candomblé shortly. For now, I will continue to examine the divergent policies of the dominant "class" in regard to the proliferating African cults. The justice of the peace Guimarães, in the same letter (written to the Viscount de Camamu, then president of the province) that describes the raid at Accú, criticizes the justice of the neighboring district of Engenho Velho for tolerating a large festival with "banderoles, different factions, and cries of long live King Dom João, and Prince Dom Pedro, that was held at great cost, and there were so many people, that in only one day a Bullock was killed, besides others, and there were people of many colors."[16]

In 1832, on a farm called Batefolha, in the parish of Santo Antônio Além do

Carmo, which borders on the Pirajá parish, the "continual beating of drums," was heard and there was found a "great gathering of black, white, and *pardo* men and women, who took part in those *batuques*." The justice of the peace of Pirajá attempted to suppress the festival, but the participants presented a license issued by the justice of Santo Antônio.[17] This confirms the conflicting attitudes of the justices of the peace of the different parishes concerning the festive gatherings of blacks, however, it is not known for certain if these two festivals were of a religious or secular nature. Nevertheless, it is not improbable that they were accompanied by some kind of religious ritual activity.

In keeping with his policy of repression, in 1831, the same Antônio Guimarães, with thirty soldiers under the command of a Captain Matos, raided more than thirty African homes in the Engenho Velho district (despite being outside the borders of his parish). In them were found "drums, Saints, and instruments of their Diabolical celebrations, which the soldiers broke." On the same night, the soldiers raided a neighboring house located on a hill "where there were continually negroes and negresses with dances, drumming and fortune telling." There "many negroes and negresses" were taken prisoner.[18]

All of these episodes suggest that as early as the 1830s there were a number of well-organized religious congregations, with a certain degree of stability, with numerous participants, and with the capacity to react against repression. In both the Accú and the Engenho Velho candomblés, there is evidence that certain members had relationships with people of influence among the dominant class. In the case of Accú, the freed African Joaquim Baptista, resident, and perhaps caretaker, of the candomblé, complained to the president of the province, the Viscount de Camamu, of the theft of various objects and money that occurred during the raid on the terreiro. Another participant in this candomblé, probably an *alabé* or drummer, was a slave and at the same time, the slave overseer for the Viscount de Pirajá. When, together with other blacks, he went to protest the theft to Justice Antônio Guimarães, he alleged that he had come on behalf of his master—this in order to intimidate the justice. Regardless of whether this was true, the use of these strategies demonstrates that the congregations had a network of social contacts that they deployed when necessary to ensure the functioning of their activities.[19]

In the raid on the Engenho Velho candomblé, the soldiers found among those attending a white attorney by the name of Joaquim José de Oliveira. He was not just an occasional visitor to the terreiro, since he persistently sought the liberty of the blacks, and with some success.[20] This evidence suggests the existence of people connected with the candomblés, in some cases whites, who could intercede on their behalf with civil society. It was perhaps at this time that the position of *ogã** began to be institutionalized, with the function, which continues today, of representing the congregation to civil society.

It is difficult to determine the stability and continuity of these candomblés: whether they were centers in which festivals were periodically held and religious rituals performed with an established liturgical calendar, or whether festivals were celebrated only occasionally when circumstances were favorable. In the case of Batefolha, Reis points to a certain stability of the supposed candomblé, given that six years later in 1838, on a map of the government forces that fought the Sabinada rebels, a candomblé appears very close to the place where the 1832 festival was held.[21] In any case, these celebrations could last a number of days—one may recall that in the case of the Accú candomblé, "this festivity had been booming along already for three days." This would imply a complex organizational capacity and probably the existence of a liturgical structure that divided the celebration into various parts.

The Candomblés' Social Composition and Its Increasing Racial Mixing

The ethnic and racial heterogeneity of the participants at these gatherings and at religious festivals is an important element. In the Accú candomblé, to the surprise of the justice of the peace, they found Africans as well as Creoles, "three negroes, because the others fled, an immense number of negresses, and to our great displeasure, many Creoles native to this country." Documents pertaining to the raid on the Engenho Velho candomblé speak of *pretos* and *pretas*, or blacks, terms that in the language of the time referred to Africans, but we have already seen the presence of a white attorney among them. In criticizing the other Engenho Velho festival in his 1829 letter, Guimarães mentions the presence of "people of many colors." In the festival of Batefolha, "black, white, and *pardo* men and women" were found.

This ethnoracial heterogeneity becomes a growing tendency in the second half of the century. Harding and Reis analyze the social composition of the candomblés between 1800 and 1888. Searching through police records, Harding found a total of ninety-five documents, sixty-five of which have been positively identified as referring to candomblés and an additional thirty of which likely refer to African religious practices. Reis's analysis is based on references to candomblé leaders, of which he finds eighty-one individuals. In my analysis of *O Alabama* for the comparatively restricted time period of 1863 to 1871, I identified a total of sixty-five records referring to leaders or candomblés.[22] I also sought to differentiate between cases in which the existence of a complex religious congregation (candomblé) is made clear and those that imply a religious expert who apparently worked individually, primarily through healing and divination practices with no indication of a collective infrastructure or organized religious congregation ("individual practitioner"). Although this distinction is not always easy to establish, a provisionary classification identified thirty-seven "candomblés" and twenty-eight "individual practitioners."

The results of these three investigations do not always coincide, but they do converge invariably on certain facts. They confirm that the candomblés united people of varying legal status (slaves, freedmen, and free), ethnoracial identities (African, Creole, mestizo, and whites), and social conditions. However, in distinguishing between leaders, participants (i.e., initiated devotees), and clients (i.e., individuals looking for religious services), there appear more specific outlines. I have already mentioned the lack of slaves as candomblé leaders. The long periods of reclusion necessary for initiation were difficult to obtain for them and limited their involvement in large numbers and continued participation.[23] However, slaves did constitute an important part of the clientele, many times in search of charms that might pacify their masters, or in search of refuge (the elite always suspected the candomblés of harboring fugitive slaves).

Given these circumstances, it was the freed and free blacks, with their greater economic resources and mobility, who constituted the majority of leaders and participants. One of the characteristics of the Bahian slave system was the high percentage of people of color who were free or freed, an estimated 30 to 40 percent of the total population in the first decades of the nineteenth century.[24] This fact was a determinant, and perhaps necessary, condition for the formation of Candomblé. This seems to be confirmed when one looks to the United States, where the population of people of color did not surpass 6 percent of the total free population before 1850, or to Jamaica, where this population was only 3 percent in 1800, and indeed there are no religious institutions comparable to Candomblé in these countries. This hypothesis complements, rather than annuls, that of Bastide, who explains the difficulty of the institutionalization of African religious practices in Anglo-Saxon slave systems as being due to the influence and rigidity of Protestantism as compared with the greater flexibility of Catholicism in countries such as Brazil, Cuba, or Haiti.[25]

In relation to color, whites appear in the documentation in only two instances as leaders, occasionally as participants, and in the majority of cases only as clients. In 1868, in a terreiro in Campinas, the presence of two white women is mentioned and the journalist comments, "These villainous candomblés are so deeply rooted, that it is no surprise to see blacks involved, when even whites are the fiercest adepts of the thing."[26] The same pattern is also applicable to mestizos, with two examples as leaders, but their presence as participants or devotees was certainly greater than that of whites.[27]

The majority of candomblé leaders and participants were, therefore, black (Creoles and Africans). From the sixty-five documents positively identified as relating to candomblés, Harding concluded that for 1800 to 1850, 69 percent of those were candomblés composed exclusively of Africans, and 31 percent were mixed (African-Creole, African-Creole-*pardo*, African-Creole-*pardo*-white). From 1851 to 1888, the proportion is inverted, and only 37 percent are African candomblés, and 63 percent are mixed.[28] The growing tendency toward eth-noracial heterogeneity throughout the century seems to be clear.

This would seem to cast serious doubts on the persistence of national divisions among candomblés and would tend to support Harding's thesis regarding a certain "pan-Africanism," although the term does not seem to me particularly appropriate, emphasizing the "African" component when it is known that it was the Creoles, and to a lesser degree the *pardos* and whites, who contributed to the increase in racial mixing. If participants and clients were heterogeneous, however, this does not mean there were not emblematic ritual differences among the diverse African traditions that were, and are to this day, zealously maintained by congregational leaders.

Regarding candomblé leadership, the data confirms that Africans made up the majority in the first half of the 1800s, and that their numbers, although remaining significant, progressively declined in the second half of the century. Harding's data shows that for the period of 1800 to 1851, 88 percent of the leaders were African, while 83 percent were during the 1851 to 1888 period. As she points out, the Creole leadership may have been minimized by the ideological bias of those responsible for the written records, who, at least up to 1850, saw Candomblé as an essentially African phenomenon. Of the eighty-one leaders identified by Reis, thirty-three were African, six Creole, five mulatto, and two white. Of the remaining thirty-five cases, thirty-one are identified as black.[29] Of the fifty-five leaders identified through my analysis of *O Alabama*, twenty-seven were African or *preto*, one black, one Creole, and two *pardo*, while in twenty-four cases no ethnic-racial identity is provided. In any event, it is very probable that this African majority among the leadership contributed to the establishment and maintenance of distinct ritual practices according to their various "nations" or original religious traditions.

Another topic open to debate is the gender of both participants and leadership. Harding points out that between 1800 and 1888, women made up between 60 and 65 percent of participants (initiated devotees). Although the numbers can vary, this feminine majority among participants, maintained even today, seems beyond doubt. In examining the leadership, however, one sees that men, mostly Africans, retained a majority during the entire preabolition period. Harding identifies forty-one leaders for 1800–1888. Of these, 68.5 percent were men and 31.5 percent women. Among the eighty-one leaders identified by Reis for the same period, 61.7 percent were men and 38 percent were women. Dividing her data between 1800 to 1850 and 1851 to 1888, Harding shows how female leadership increased in the second half of the century, going from 12 percent in the first period to 41 percent in the second. My analysis of fifty-five leaders from 1863 to 1871, while generally coinciding with this tendency, indicates different percentages: thirty-eight men (69 percent) and seventeen women (31 percent).[30]

It is important to note one other aspect, mentioned by Harding only in passing, regarding the phenomenon of coleadership. Of the fifty-five examples of leadership for 1863 to 1871, nine of them consist of two or three people and all correspond to cases identified as "candomblés," that is complex congregations. Five cases refer to a man seconded by a woman. This phenomenon indicates that the leadership of the candomblés, though normally hierarchized, was often a shared responsibility. It is tempting to see in this fact some influence of the Gbe-speaking area's vodun tradition, in which it is known that temple leadership is normally shared by a man-woman *vodunon* (priests) couple.

This would indicate that the famous and much discussed "matriarchy" of contemporary Candomblé, legitimized in the 1940s principally by Ruth Landes,[31] is a relatively recent phenomenon, given that female superiority in the congregations' leadership was only attained in the postabolition period. The explanation for the phenomenon varies according to author. Reis believes that in nineteenth-century Bahia, gender bias was not a determining factor in the formation of religious leadership. According to him, the initial African male majority reflected a demographic in which men outnumbered women among the slave population. The subsequent increase of women in leadership was, therefore, determined by ritual and sociological reasons.

At the ritual level, "possession" is normally considered a symbolically feminine and passive role, in which the devotee is "mounted" by the deity. In *O Alabama*, the majority of references to initiation groups speak exclusively of women. Therefore, in addition to making up the majority of the candomblés' clientele, women were also initiated in greater numbers. It makes sense, then, that with the progressive decline in the numbers of African leaders, the new generation of Creole women formed the most numerous social pool from which to draw new leaders.[32] Furthermore, in the slave system, especially in the urban context, black women had greater economic independence and social mobility than men. They obtained manumission more easily and became low- or medium-level entrepreneurs, primarily in the food industry. Thus, the hegemony among the religious leadership would reflect the greater social status of women. Harding presents an alternative sociological explanation, relating the growing female hegemony in Candomblé as compensating for their exclusion within the political sphere of the Catholic brotherhoods.[33]

The only objection to such arguments is that the greater number of women among initiates and their higher status within society at large were conditions that were likely already in place in the mid-nineteenth century, while their increase in religious leadership only came to pass at the turn of the century. My own impression is that indeed in Bahia in the nineteenth century there must have certainly been some gender bias that favored men in the selection of religious leadership, something inherited both from West and Central Africa. The greater religious status of men in the African religious institutions was perpetuated in Bahia and was maintained as long as there were Africans. The efficacy attributed to the religious practices of African religious experts gave them a prestige that inspired respect and fear.[34] They took advantage of this notoriety and general perception of the "African sorcerer's power" to perpetuate their hegemony. It was only when the presence of Africans decreased, at the dawn of the twentieth century, that Creole women, for the reasons explained by Reis, came to assume leadership roles in numbers that gave them a majority.

It is therefore worthwhile to examine in greater detail the dialectic between Africans and Creoles in the context of the religious community. In the case of the previously mentioned Accú candomblé, the traditional animosity between Africans and Creoles manifest in, for example, the slave revolts in the first decades of the nineteenth century and, in the specific case of the Jeje, the Catholic brotherhoods of the eighteenth century (see chapter 2), was not always so rigorous and widespread. The expectation of the justice of the peace, probably coinciding with that of the dominant "class," was that the Creoles, having been born and raised as Brazilians, had attained a greater degree of "civilization" and therefore would have naturally distanced themselves from Africans subject to "superstitions and heathenisms." Africans always suffered more discrimination than Creoles, as indicated for example by the greater number of letters of manumission granted to Creoles. In the case of Accú, the Creole women, with their cries, were treated paternally and set free, while the African women remained in custody.[35] Despite the surprise it gave the justice of the peace, the event indicates that in fact, in the 1820s, Africans were already recruiting Creoles into their religious activities, not only as clients looking for services but also as devotees—participants whose presence was necessary to maintain the internal dynamic of the congregation.

As we saw in chapter 2, the Creoles cannot be considered a homogeneous group. There were those of the first generation, that is, raised in African families, who could easily be integrated into the religious activities of their progenitors. Reis remarks that this "ritual incorporation of a numerous group of non-Africans" was a "crucial strategy of survival" for Candomblé. Indeed, I believe it was precisely when Africans were able to establish kinship networks, based on their Creole descendants, that the formation of religious congregations was possible, first as domestic or family-based congregations and later as extradomestic congregations. As I will demonstrate below, some Jeje candomblés of the second half of the nineteenth century were founded by Africans in collaboration with Creoles, since biological kinship ties were essential in the recruitment of new adepts. In this sense, I would agree with Reis and say that, more than a "pan-African" tendency, what dominated Candomblé history in the second half of the nineteenth century was a growing process of creolization and racial mixing.[36]

However, it should be noted that this blending of Africans, Creoles, and mulattoes, despite being crescent and accentuated, principally in the last decades of the century, was probably not homogeneous; that is, more exclusive religious congregations coexisted with others that were more permeable. For example, there is news in 1859 of a candomblé in Quinta de Beatas, with a predominance of Africans (thirty Africans, eight Creoles, and four dark mulattoes). In 1862, there was the Pojavá candomblé in the second district of Santo Antônio with a predominance of Creoles (fifty-two Creoles and three Africans). Additionally, in 1866, in the Conceição da Praia parish, one finds "a Creole candomblé" directed by Anninha Sapoca. African terreiros persisted until the end of the century, as an old African woman attested to Nina Rodrigues. She said that she did not dance in Gantois because "her terreiro was one of people from the Coast [Africans]," while the Gantois terreiro was composed of "homeland people [Creoles and mulattoes]."[37]

Thus, just as attitudes of repression and tolerance toward Candomblé coexisted among the ruling class, the congregations themselves, perhaps in response to these policies, combined strategies of resistance and isolation (more frequent in the beginning of the century) with strategies of openness and social inclusion (increasingly common later). It is not yet known to what extent this alternation between attitudes of resistance and social integration could result in some congregations' being more closed while others were more permeable in regard to their memberships' ethnoracial composition. At the same time, one might ask if this polarity between the more closed "African candomblés" and the "national candomblés" more open to ethnoracial mixing was in direct relation to the maintenance of differentiated ritual modes (nations) and more "syncretic" ritual practices respectively.

The Occupation of Urban Space and Police Participation in Candomblé

With the decreased importance of the Catholic brotherhoods in the second half of the nineteenth century (which had previously marked the black presence in the city), the candomblés came to constitute one of the most important means of social aggregation, identity, and cultural resistance for the black-mestizo population. In this panorama, the occupation of urban physical spaces is a significant phenomenon, especially the proliferation of the candomblés in the city center.

According to Muniz Sodré, "territorialization is not defined as a mere imitation of animal territoriality but as a force for the exclusive appropriation of space (the result of a symbolic ordering) capable of engendering regimes of relationships, relations of proximity and distance. . . . the territory appears therefore as a given necessary for the formulation of group/individual identity, for the recognition of oneself by others." In the words of Wilson Roberto de Mattos, the conception of territoriality/territorialization "does not restrict itself merely to the identificatory analysis of the occupation of certain specific physical spaces but refers above all to the occupation of social spaces of greater reach singling them out through symbolic and cultural injunctions."[38] Without entering into this wider cultural dimension inherent to urban space occupation, here I simply wish to present an approximate topography of candomblés in the 1860s.

Discarding eight cases that cannot be precisely located from the available sixty-five records from 1863 to 1871, there remain fifty-seven recorded candomblés or individual practitioners. Of this total, thirty-one cases (54 percent) were located in semirural parishes bordering Salvador's urban nucleus. In this area, the parishes of Nossa Senhora de Brotas (eleven cases), Santo Antônio Além do Carmo (nine), and Penha (seven), stand out.[39] The remaining twenty-six cases (46 percent) were situated in the city center, primarily in the Sé parish (eleven cases) and in that of Sant'Anna do Sacramento (eight cases). Following those were the parish of São Pedro Velho (three cases), Passo (two cases), and Conceição da Praia (two cases). The great quantity of candomblé denunciations in the urban center, especially in the Sé area, were the result of *O Alabama*'s being located in this zone and having direct access to the happenings of its environs. Certainly, other terreiros existed in the periphery that carried on with greater discretion and that were never documented by this newspaper. Although this topography is only an approximate outline of what the reality must have been, it highlights the great number of terreiros or religious experts functioning in the urban center.

This was not a new phenomenon. Oral tradition recalls the functioning of the famous Ilê Iyá Nassô candomblé in the first decades of the nineteenth century, with its first headquarters in the Barroquinha church in the very center of the city.[40] However, as the articles from *O Alabama* and *O Óculo Mágico* make clear, the generalized proliferation of candomblés in the urban center was a phenomenon begun around 1850–60: "Previously these superstitious and frightful practices were carried out in the country, well outside the city limits; today they are performed with the boldest ostentation under the very nose of the police."[41] And: "If the police do not want candomblés, how is it that they allow them in front of their very noses? They send soldiers to *hunt them* in the backland and permit them within the city."[42] And finally: "The meetings here within the capital [São Miguel] are troubling, and unless we are not mistaken they are prohibited by a town council or a police regulation."[43]

And in fact, according to ordinance number 59, from February 27, 1857, "The *batuques*, dances and meetings of slaves, are prohibited in any place and at any time, under penalty of eight days in prison for each one found in violation."[44] This statute speaks only of slaves. Freemen and freedmen, by purchasing a license from the police, had some liberty to organize celebrations. The simultaneous and alternate tendencies of repression and tolerance characteristic of the first half of the century continued through the 1860s. To the indignation of those who supported repression, such as the journalists of *O Alabama*, these candomblés often enjoyed the collaboration and even active participation of the police and members of the army.

For example, in 1867 a funerary ritual was attended by an assistant to the local chief of police and two soldiers, who "ate, danced, and played in the *segun* [*sirrum*, a Jeje funerary ritual].*"[45] The *O Alabama* reporter complains: "I have never seen a police force more sympathetic to candomblé than this one! . . . They ask for license to play and to sing and the police grants it."[46] From a terreiro in Engenho Velho comes a report of the participation of a subchief of police, who, while attending a festival with his family, "became possessed . . . and there he was dancing about among the Creole women with a long staff and his panache in hand."[47] When the police went to free a woman who was being initiated in the Campinas terreiro, the *vodunsis* addressed the police as "nossa gente," or our people.[48] There are a number of reports of the tight relationship between candomblé leaders and the police. In a "farm of the Devotas" (probably in Quinta das Beatas, present-day Cosme de Farias), for example, the African Joaquim would receive a subchief of police, a "blind apologist of the *vodun* saint, showing up with his family whenever there was some festivity."[49] In the same area, Quinta das Beatas, the landlord of another candomblé was a member of the police force.[50]

In the 1860s, the authorities' selective tolerance of certain candomblés might also have been politically motivated: the elite saw in the congregations a significant number of potential votes. *O Alabama* reports on two festivals, in Barreiras and in Engenho Velho, celebrated in terreiros or by candomblé members following the victory of the conservatives in the local elections. The first, in 1864, was "a *feijoada* banquet given by the conservatives in thanks to their voters"; the second, in 1868, was "a great festive affair to celebrate the victory of the red party [conservatives] in the elections." The reporter is astonished to discover "that politics involved even the candomblés." The candomblés' support of conservatives elicits a sarcastic comment from the liberal journalist, who calls the conservatives "conservers of candomblé!"[51] Also, the "conservative Creole women organize[d] a pilgrimage to the Senhor do Bonfim church on the occasion of the triumph of the party in the recent elections."[52] This political alliance continued throughout the twentieth century, but it is important to note that the candomblés' conservative leaning was already in place in the second half of the nineteenth century.[53]

Returning to the analysis of the geographic distribution of the candomblés, it is noteworthy that the majority of the "candomblés" of the urban center were domestic congregations located in small spaces—homes, stores, warehouses, or hidden places—without forested or green areas. The more habitual practices were healing or exorcism, in order to "take the devil," or the *feitiço*, out of peoples' bodies, as well as fortune telling. These practices could alternate with occasional *batuques*, generally on Saturdays or Sundays. In the urban center the "individual" practices predominated, while outside the city "candomblés" were more numerous. Of the twenty-six records of the urban area, fourteen were classified as "candomblés" and twelve as "individual practitioners," while of the thirty-one records of the outlying area twenty-three were "candomblés" and eight were "individual practitioners." This indicates that although religious experts were more present in the urban center, congregations were able to develop greater organizational complexity in the semirural parishes.

Perhaps this explains the motive behind the greater police repression in the more rural areas. As *O Alabama* complained: "This police force has a weakness for candomblés! It allows them in the city by its own authority and orders to raid them outside of town!"[54] The paper also denounced the fact that candomblés in the outlying areas served "as a haven for runaway slaves, where they are protected for many days."[55] From the beginning of the century, the semirural parishes were favorite refuges for fugitive blacks, not only in the candomblé terreiros but also in *quilombos*. In 1814, for example, certain merchants and other Bahian citizens observed the weak policing of the Casa da Pólvora, or the armory, situated in Matatu, an area surrounded by "villages of fugitive slaves," as Verger described it.[56] In Brotas, the freed slaves were often accused of inducing slaves to flee their masters, then sheltering them and giving them work on their farms. The justice of the peace of this parish returned more than 400 slaves to their masters.[57]

In 1866, *O Alabama* requested that the police take measures to repress candomblés "in certain parts of the city and in its environs such as Cruz do Cosme, Engenho Velho, Campinas, Quinta das Beatas, Engenho da Conceição, Matatu, and others."[58] And indeed, Cruz do Cosme (with two cases)—today the neighborhood of Liberdade—in the Santo Antônio parish; Engenho Velho (with three cases) and Quinta das Beatas (with five cases), both in the Brotas parish; and Campinas (with three cases), in the Penha parish seem to be have been the peripheral areas with the highest concentration of candomblés.

The great landowners who constituted the white capitalist elite of Bahian society normally lived in mansions and townhouses in the urban parishes. Their properties in the semirural countryside, at times extensive *engenhos*, fruit plantations, and wooded areas, were exploited by the black population, mostly made up of free and freed blacks who worked as subsistence farmers cultivating manioc and vegetables. And so "great farms operated alongside small ones, while arrangements by which farmers would pay half of the harvest to the landowners were common." In many instances, these arrangements involved concessions of titled land that permitted certain freedmen and their families to act with relative autonomy as tenant farmers. There were also cases in which freedmen purchased small plots of land.[59]

In each of these situations, blacks could control certain physical spaces, at times in places difficult to access, in the bush, away from the eyes of the landowners and public forces, where they were able to organize religious activities and eventually form candomblés. This territorialization around an urban nucleus was not only a strategy to conceal activities, but it also responded to an internal imperative of African ritual, in which elements of nature (i.e., leaves and water) are indispensable to the worship of the deities.

In 1870, *O Alabama* printed an interesting case that illustrates the potentially conflicting relationship between landowners and tenants. Senhor Cotia Brandão, a landowner in Campina, in the Pirajá parish, wanted to double the rent he was charging the African *Pai* Thomaz, head of a candomblé located on the premises. In this case, the landowner had no problem with the religious activities, allowing them to play candomblé "until it stinks, as long as they pay their rent" of 20 réis per *tarefa* (4,356 square meters). If he did not pay the increased rent, *Pai* Thomaz, who had occupied that "huge plot of land" since 1847, ran the risk of losing three houses that he had built as part of the terreiro. Feeling that not only was his candomblé but also his own property at risk, *Pai* Thomaz threatened Cotia Brandão with death. Moreover, "the negro, having belonged to a certain house, [had] the free protection of a lawyer, who [was] a zealous apologist of candomblé."[60] This reveals how the possession or control over land by candomblé congregations was even at that time a source of conflict. I see access to the land as a crucial aspect of Candomblé's consolidation, since the terreiros required fixed and stable locations to "plant" their shrines. These could be kept in hidden rooms of the urban center, but only in the open spaces of the semiurban periphery could they be emplaced in natural sites with trees, rivers, and springs.

The Predominance of Jeje Tradition in 1860s Candomblé

If by the 1830s there were already clear indications of extradomestic congregations with significant social and ritual complexity, the documentation offered by *O Alabama* leaves no doubt that in the 1860s Candomblé had attained a level of institutionalization comparable to that seen today. In addition to the frequent activities of healing and divination conducted by individual religious experts, there was an extensive network of religious congregations, with relatively well-established sacred spaces—on the farms of the periphery as well as in the urban center—that maintained varying complementary and cooperative relationships. These congregations were hierarchically organized according to the principle of seniority, based on members' lengthy initiation process.

As I have emphasized, the ritual activity was developed along the lines of the "altar-offering complex," with periodic animal sacrifices and food offerings on the shrines. One important ritual characteristic of these extradomestic congregations that I have until now mentioned only in passing is that each of them was dedicated not to the worship of a single deity (as seems to have been the rule in the eighteenth century) but to a plurality of spiritual entities. In fact, this is a distinctive mark of nineteenth-century candomblés that ultimately confirms the growing ritual complexity that the institution of Candomblé experienced.

Although according to oral tradition the cult of multiple deities goes back to the first decades of the nineteenth century with the foundation of the Ilê–Iyá Nassô candomblé in Barroquinha, the first written records suggesting this date from 1858.[61] Contrary to the idea prevailing in Afro-Brazilian studies, however, my hypothesis is that the cult of multiple deities was *not* simply a Brazilian innovation resulting from the new conditions of a slave society and the encounters between different African ethnicities. I contend that this ritual practice has clear African antecedents in the Gbe-speaking area and that, logically, the Jeje vodun traditions played a determining role in the constitutive process of this model of Candomblé. This is a complex and controversial subject, and because of its importance, I give it special attention in chapter 7.

In any case, the Bahian multideity cults included public ceremonies, lasting many days with drumming, dance, and divine manifestations in the bodies of devotees. Note that these congregations shared a relatively homogeneous festival calendar. For example, after Carnival, in the period of Lent, they suspended ritual activities celebrating the *festa do balaio*, or basket festival. And in November, some terreiros celebrated the *festa do inhame novo*, or new yam festival, consisting of "the consecration of the first fruits of each year's harvest to the African deities," and in September, they would commemorate the festival of the twins Saint Cosmas and Saint Damian, syncretized with the Nagô *ibejis*, the Jeje *hohos*, or the Angola *mabaças*. The funeral rituals and the presents to the *mães d'água*, or water deities, were also regular activities in which members of different congregations could participate.

This recurrence of the same festivals across many congregations demonstrates the consolidation of Candomblé's institutional character in the 1860s, though of course this process of institutionalization had begun in previous decades. If festivals such as the *inhame novo* could be the result of an almost linear transference of specific African practices, others, such as the *festa do balaio*, which coincided with the Catholic calendar, indicate a distinctly Brazilian genesis. The two dynamics—persistence and resistance, on the one hand, and transformation and creative adaption, on the other—acted in conjunction with one another.

In Afro-Brazilian studies it has been emphasized that in the formative process of Candomblé, there was a strong interpenetration between the tradition of the Yoruba orixá cults and that of the Gbe vodun cults—an interpenetration that had already in fact been going on for centuries in Africa. Rodrigues was the first author to use the expression "Jeje-Nagô candomblé" to indicate this process of "intimate fusion" between the two religious traditions.[62] Without denying this evidence, or minimizing the importance of the processes of reinvention and resignification of African religious practices within the Brazilian context, what I wish to discuss here is the possible predominance of one or the other of these African religious sources in the constitutive process of Candomblé.

Before beginning this discussion, it is worth noting that the greater attention given to the Jeje and Nagô traditions, to the detriment of the Congo-Angola—whose history and ethnography have yet to be studied—results from the greater documentary evidence available for the first group. However, throughout the present analysis, as well as in the following chapters, when relevant, I will point out the influences of the Congo-Angola traditions, particularly in relation to their important interpenetration with the Jeje tradition.

The thesis I set forth in this section is that the religious tradition of the vodun cults originating in the Gbe-speaking area, that is, the Jeje tradition, constituted a determinant matrix in Candomblé's institutionalization process, and that until the 1870s this tradition was, if not hegemonic, at least as important as the Nagô tradition of the orixá cults. This idea runs counter to the theories of authors such as Dale Graden, Lorand Matory, and João José Reis, who maintain the hegemony of the orixá cult tradition. In order to support this argument, I use the method anticipated by Reis, which consists of a linguistic analysis of the terminology used by the journalists of O Alabama. As a development of, and complement to, this analysis, I then discuss the concept of "nation" in Candomblé, with the intention of assessing the presence of the Jeje "nation" terreiros in Salvador in the second half of the nineteenth century, suggesting, in support of my initial thesis, a predominance of these terreiros over those of the Nagô "nation."

In commenting on the stories from O Alabama, Graden assumes, with little grounding in the text, a hegemony of the Nagô orixá cult tradition and even a greater number Nagô terreiros in the Candomblé of that period. Graden speaks of the "predominant Yoruba Afro-Bahian traditions in Salvador" and of the "sense of Nagô superiority transmitted by the pages of O Alabama," that, according to him, anticipated by three decades the interpretations of Rodrigues—also a defender of the "superiority" of Nagô mythology over that of other Candomblé traditions. Matory also speaks of a "Nagô-dominated complex" and of the "Nagô-dominant Afro-Bahian religious parlance of the mid-nineteenth century." Reis, in a more thoughtful manner that recognizes the importance of the Jeje tradition, also suggests a Nagô-tradition hegemony, a supposition strengthened by his count of the African terminology of O Ala-

bama, according to which Nagô terms outnumber those of the Jeje.[63] My own analysis of *O Alabama* terminology, however, suggests a relative dominance of terms originating from the Gbe-speaking area.

Concerning contemporary Candomblé, Julio Braga, based on information from Yeda Pessoa de Castro and Vivaldo da Costa Lima, calls attention to "the presence of Fon ritual segments in the structure of the candomblés that are said to be of the Nagô-Queto nation, or pure Queto, which make them very close to the conventual and initiation organizations of that population in Benin." Braga adds that "the classification system based on the formation of the initiation group (*barco* das iaôs*), whose members are identified by the order of their entry into the conventual reclusive space by the terms '*dofono, dofontinha, fomo, fomotinha, gamo, gamotinha, domo, domotinha, vito, vitotinha,*' is an obvious example that demonstrates that the Nagô candomblé is created *at its most basic structural level* with the presence of other *non–Nagô-Yoruba* elements" (emphasis added).

These "non–Nagô-Yoruba" elements are essentially Jeje. As Lima suggests, citing Adolphe Akindélé and Cyrille Aguessy, the initiatory names used in Brazil roughly correspond to those used in the vodun cults of Porto-Novo: *houndjènoukon, dométien, nogamou, nogamoutien, yomou, yomoutien, gamou, gamoutien,* and *notien.*[64]

But Jeje linguistic influence goes far beyond this initiatory group classification system. The names of the *peji* (altar room or sanctuary) and of its *pejigã** (caretaker); of the *runcó* or *runco* (initiation room); of the place where the *assém* (votive object) is implanted, the *assento* (shrine); of the *amasi* (mixture of leaves and water); of the *rum, rumpi,* and *runle* or *lé* (drums); of the *aguidavi* (drum stick); of the *gã* (sacred idiophone); of the *adjunto* (guardian spirit); and probably of the *decá** (ritual that confers the status of seniority on an initiate), are all words of Gbe origin.[65] These terms, used today in the Ketu and Angola terreiros in reference to aspects of the rituals' "most basic structure," such as initiation processes, group hierarchy, sacred space, instruments, and others, indicate the irrefutable importance that the vodun cult tradition had in the formative process of Candomblé.

The linguistic analysis of African terms that appear in *O Alabama* confirms and reinforces this hypothesis pointed out by Lima and Braga. In the first place, and perhaps most important, the term *vodun* (as in "saint vodun" or "to dance vodun") appears seven times in reference to African deities, while there is no mention of the term *orixá,* except in the compound *baba-loixa* (from the Yoruba word *babalorixá**) to designate the high priest. It is very likely that at this time, and perhaps even from the first decades of the century (recall the "vodun god" of the Accú candomblé in 1829), *vodun* was used in the majority of the terreiros as a generic term in allusion to African deities. This extrapolation of the term *vodun* outside of the restricted sphere of the Jeje nation's terreiros is highly suggestive of the influence of the vodun cult tradition in the institution of Candomblé. Similarly, in relation to oracular practices, the term *Fa*, the denomination for the deity of divination in the vodun area, appears twice, and the word *Ifá* used by the Nagô does not appear at all.

As for the names of the deities, there are three explicit references to voduns (the number in parenthesis indicating frequency): Lebal (one), who is Legba; Soubô (one), the thunder deity, Sogbo; and Loco (five), the tree god, associated with the gameleira tree. The last appears also as *Loucose*, which is the name given to the devotees of this deity—in Fon, the suffix *-si* means "wife of" (*lokosi* = wife of Loko). Likewise, there appear indirect allusions to two other voduns: *Aguesa* (one), devotee of the hunter vodun Agué; and *Nanasi* (one), probably devotee of the vodun Nanã. If to this list we add the previously mentioned divination deity, Fa, we have a total of six Jeje voduns.

In contrast, only five Nagô deities appear: Xangô (three), the thunder orixá who corresponds to Sogbo, and in one case this orixá is mentioned in the context of a Jeje terreiro; Oiá (one), significantly named as "the wife of the greatest saint—Soubô," and not of the orixá Xangô; Oxalá (two), the "oldest *saint* (Eternal Father)"; Ogun (one); and Xapanan (one). There appear a number of references to Saint Cosmas and Saint Damian, in one instance referred to with the Angola term *mabaça*, as well as various references to the *mães d'agua*, which could also indiscriminately cover Jeje, Nagô, or Congo-Angola female water deities. One of the newspaper's articles speaks of "cults dedicated to the bedecked *mãe-d'agua*, to a snake, to a bird, etc." This mention of a cult of the snake might allude to the vodun Dan or to the orixá Oxumaré. The bird might be an allusion to the hunter vodun Agué, at times represented as a bird, or maybe to the worship of *iamis* (female ancestors associated with *feitiçaria*).

The slightly greater prevalence of vodun names over names of orixás is complemented by the greater Jeje occurrence in relation to hierarchical terms and titles. To refer to the female head of the terreiro, Portuguese terms such as *mamãe, mãe do terreiro, rainha, grã-mestra*, and *sacerdotisa* (momma, mother of the terreiro, queen, grand master, and priestess, respectively) are frequently used. For male leaders the terms are *papai, pai-do-terreiro, presidente, grande-mestre*, and *grã-sacerdote* (papa, father of the terreiro, president, grand master, and high priest). As to African terms, there are references to four individuals identified with the Nagô title *baba-loixa* (and the variants *baba* and *baba-louxa*), from which derived the Portuguese *pai-de-santo* (father-in-the-saint).[66]

However, the mention of hierarchical titles of Gbe origin are more numerous, such as *gumbônde* (and the variant *gombono*) (three), or its feminine form *gumbonda*, a phonetic evolution of the Fon term *hunbono*, designating the high priest; *guncô* (one), which designates the wife of the *gumbônde*; and *donunce* (one), described as "a kind of grand master of the order," a term probably derived either from *donusi*, meaning "initiated into the secret of amulets and pharmacopeia," or from *denoche*, composed of the term *noche*, meaning "my mother." In consonance with the generalized use of the term *vodun*, the term *vudunças* (and its variant *avudunças*) (five) a corruption of the term *vodunsi*, is frequently used to refer to the initiated adepts of the deities, and on no occasion do the Yoruba terms *iaô* or *ebome*, more frequently used nowadays, appear. There is even reference to the two women called Margarita *Gamotinha* and Maria *Doufona*, confirming the use at this time of the initiatory terms discussed above. In the context of a Jeje terreiro there appears the term *equede** (mistress of the novices), of uncertain etymological origin. The title *ogã* (six)—used sometimes as a synonym for the head of a terreiro and other times as the name for the male dignitaries who second the religious leader in various functions—is shared by Jeje and Nagô and is therefore irrelevant to this count. In summary, for one occurrence of Nagô hierarchical terms (*baba-loixa*), there are six of Jeje origin.

In relation to other African terms, such as names of rituals or foods, the proportion is inverted. There appear fourteen Nagô terms, nine Jeje, four Bantu (*milonga, missangas, zungu,* and *candomblé*) and seven that remain unidentified.[67] It is important to note that among the Nagô terms the majority are names of foods or animals probably used also outside of the sphere of religion: *atás* (*ata* or pepper) (one); *obi* (*obì* or kola nut) (five); *orobô* (*orógbó* or kola nut) (two); *eipou* or *êpu* (*epo* or oil) (two); *afurá* or *furá* (*fúrá* in Hausa, *afúrá* in Yoruba, drink) (two); *efó* (*èfó* or edible leaves) (one); *amalá** (*àmàlà* or votive food) (one); *acucó* (*àkùko* or rooster) (one); *etuns* (*etù* or guinea hen [one]); *abou* (*àgbò* or ram [one]); *foricanabou* (*f'orí kà àgbò* or "head placed on sheep," a ritual gesture made with the sacrificial animal) (one); *obacouçu* (*Oba Koso*, a name for Xangô that in *O Alabama* designates a "bird that Africans venerate and whose song warns them when someone approaches," perhaps the sparrowhawk, associated with Xangô) (one); *ebó* (offering) (one); and *ojá* (*òjá* or strip of cloth [one]).

In contrast, among the Jeje terms the majority refer to important spaces, activities, or ritual objects: *pegi* (*kpè jí* or altar) (three); *segum* (*sinhun* or funeral ritual) (two); *sapocan* (initiation ritual [two]); *von-siça* (*vòsísá* or sacrifice [one]); *mocan* (*mwen kan* or straw necklace [one]); *gés* (*jé* or beads [one]);

kessé (*kesé* or West African parrot [one]); *bobo* (*abobo* or bean dough [one]); and *agontè* (shoot of the ronier palm; appears as *aguntesa*, the ritual name for a priestess [one]).[68]

To summarize, my linguistic analysis of *O Alabama* shows a slightly greater number of Jeje terms than Yoruba terms.[69] Of course, this linguistic evidence is not conclusive proof of Jeje dominance in Candomblé, but it certainly indicates parity between the Jeje and Nagô traditions. Yet, with the Nagô making up the great majority of Africans in Bahia in the 1860s and the Jeje being but a minority, the linguistic equilibrium demonstrates the importance of the vodun cults in the formative process of Candomblé and its continuing critical role even in that decade. In other words, one might suppose that, in the field of Candomblé, the Nagô demographic superiority had not yet translated into cultural hegemony.

To support this idea further, let us evaluate the extent of Candomblé's division in terms of "African nations" during the second half of the nineteenth century, and within this context, the strength of the Jeje terreiro presence. As we have seen, at the beginning of the century the African population was grouped together in terms of collective identities that, while created in Brazil, resulted from cultural and linguistic identities of mostly African origin. Recall, for example, the groupings of Angola, Jeje, Nagô, and Hausa in Santo Amaro in 1808, or the policy of the Count dos Arcos that favored these ethnic divisions.

However, these distinctions appear to become somewhat diluted as the century advances. In *O Alabama*, for example, there is not a single explicit reference to African nations in relation to the candomblés of the time. As I have mentioned, in the second half of the century, the social composition of the candomblés presented a growing ethnoracial heterogeneity. This mixing process grew with the end of the Atlantic slave trade and the discontinuation of the arrival of new Africans. *O Alabama*'s silence about the ethnic distinctions among the various religious congregations may be misleading. In part, it can be explained by the fact that, after 1850, the ethnic classifications were no longer used by the dominant class and were replaced by the generic term *African* (see chapter 2). But this does not imply that Africans and their Creole descendants ceased to use these denominations in religious and familial contexts.

The growing ethnoracial heterogeneity of the candomblés' social base suggests a priori the existence of a parallel process of ritual heterogeneity, with a growing interpenetration of religious practices and values of Jeje, Nagô, and Angola origin. In the 1860s, the above-mentioned "Jeje-Nagô Candomblé" symbiosis was certainly in process, and it is likely that some terreiros or religious leaders no longer identified their practices in terms of "nation" or ethnic categories. An example is a report from *O Alabama* on the candomblé of the African Zé Rolavo in Quinta das Devotas. The leader is identified with the Jeje term *gombono* and has a *filha-de-santo*,* or initiated member, called *vudunça* (another Jeje term), but she is a devotee of *O'xalá*, the name of a Nagô orixá. This *vudunça*, possessed by her orixá, told the fortune of a military officer, her husband or lover, "that he was to be dismissed shortly and that, in order to avoid this, he should give [the *vudunça* (or her orixá)] an *abou* (ram), a liter of *êpu* (oil), two *acucó* (roosters), one *kessé* (West African parrot), *obis, colla, atás*, and *orobôs*, twelve of each, to make an *ebó* (fulfillment of precepts in order to obtain a favor) with which not only would the imminent evil be withdrawn, but he would be promoted to captain."

In the list of ingredients for the *ebó* (a Nagô term) there appears a mixture of Jeje and Nagô names (see above). After sacrificing the ram, a Nagô tradition (the Jeje do not sacrifice rams), and drinking some drops of its blood, "there followed the burlesque ceremony of *forican-abou*, which consists of giving light butts on the head of the dead animal, while the black mumbles certain words. After the *vonsiça* (sacrifice), there followed a kind of dance called *bonaduê*, and our very vain officer, decorated with *gés* (beads) took charge of the *nacucu cuim* (drum) and began to beat very strongly, while the *daughters of the house* [initiates] danced using nimble and extravagant postures."[70]

In this derisive description of the ritual, a mixture of Jeje and Nagô expressions again occurs, but the level of detail and the effort employed by the journalist to use and translate the African terms indicates that he was somewhat of an insider, or that he had an informant well-versed in the subject. This does not mean that his report is without errors, however; for example, the *forican-abou* is performed with a live animal, before the sacrifice. In any case, the narrative of this report indicates the possible interpenetration and mobility of terms and practices outside the borders of nation. In fact, this interethnic fluidity and ritual interpenetration would have been a constant, and even indispensable, factor in the genesis and continuity of Candomblé.

Having said this, it is probable that, alongside these religious experts who were more open to the assimilation of practices and values from a variety of sources, other experts existed who were equally aware of the diverse origins and uses of each of these practices, and were capable of recognizing differences and establishing selective criteria between them. It is important to remember that the majority of terreiros of this period were founded and led by Africans, religious experts predominantly initiated in Africa. In one way or another, they continued their religious careers in Brazil, adapting their knowledge and inserting their practices into the modus operandi that they encountered upon arriving in the colonial context. It is more probable, however, that some of them, as leaders, especially those aided by intraethnic social networks, were interested in maintaining certain rituals, deities, and specific terminology from their lands of origin in order to preserve identity and differentiation.

In other words, the distinctions between the different candomblé nations, despite the lack of documentary evidence, surely persisted within certain religious congregations, as happens today. With the eventual death of African leaders in the second half of the century, their Creole descendants, after inheriting the leadership of these congregations, continued to maintain their nation's identity based on these ritual practices. Therefore, though the ethnoracial heterogeneity of Candomblé participants had increased throughout the century, the identity of African nations remained anchored in certain liturgical characteristics that were emblematic of differentiated religious traditions.

Based on this premise, I attempt to evaluate the presence of liturgical elements from the various African traditions of the candomblés documented by *O Alabama* in order to infer the predominance of any given "nation." This exercise is quite complicated for a number of reasons. In the first place, the identification of a candomblé as belonging to a particular nation can be a rather ambiguous and even arbitrary determination, and for some terreiros it might be a consideration of little importance. The second reason is the potential unreliability of the *O Alabama* reports, written by outsiders to Candomblé. Despite at times being eyewitnesses to the events, they could make mistakes or distortions. The third reason is the absence, in the majority of the reports, of sufficient information to infer any identification. Finally, the possible identification of nations presented here is based on a combination of analytic strategies, such as the ethnic origin of the leaders, the use of hierarchical terminology, or the cult of certain deities, all of which are only indicative and not conclusive. More reliable are those identifications corresponding to the few terreiros mentioned in *O Alabama* that are still active today and whose nation can be verified by contemporary accounts. Despite these difficulties, I believe that the exercise, although tentative, reveals certain significant tendencies.

Of the sixty-five records identified in *O Alabama* that correspond to "candomblés" (collective religious congregations) or "individual practitioners" (religious experts who probably acted independently, lacking the infrastructure of an established group), only 20 present sufficient data to suggest an identification of "nation." Of these twenty, only eight can be identified with any degree of certainty, and are those that I call "positive," the remainder being merely "likely." Of the eight "positives," five are Jeje, two Nagô, and one Angola. Of the twelve "likely" cases, five would be Jeje, six Nagô, and one Angola. Adding the "positive" and "likely" cases together would yield ten Jeje, eight Nagô, and two Angola.[71] Thus we see that the quantitative analysis of the terreiros by "nation" presents proportions corresponding to those found in the linguistic analysis, where the Jeje represent the majority, followed closely by the Nagô and then by the Angola in smaller numbers. This fact supports the initial hypothesis of a relative predominance of the Jeje traditions in preabolition Candomblé.

Having presented the results of the analysis, we must detail how they were obtained. An initial criterion in evaluating the "nation" of a terreiro, which if not totally reliable is at least approximate, is to consider the ethnic origins of its leadership. Of the eighty-one leaders (including thirty-three Africans) identified by Reis for 1800–1888, only six could be identified with African nations: two Angola, one Mina, one Jeje, one Hausa, and one Nagô.[72] Of this number, only the two Angola and the Nagô appear within the 1863–71 period.

Let us examine the Angola cases. In 1864, a candomblé is denounced "in the place called Dendezeiro," in the Penha parish, "whose leaders are Anna Maria, African, of the Angola nation and a black known as *Pai* Francisco." Anna Maria, also called "*queen*, or *mãe* [mother] of the terreiro," was the leader of a congregation composed of at least thirteen members: six women and seven men (six of whom were drummers); three Africans, two Creoles, three *pardos*, and five unidentified; among them two freed persons and one slave. The second Angola case is that of "the Angola *preto velho*, *Papai* Mané, who casts out devils, puts in devils, sells devils, lends devils, and is the very devil." Given that in this report the information points only to healing and exorcism activities, I consider it only probable that "*Papai* Mané" was the leader of an Angola terreiro.[73]

Among the Nagô cases, the two I consider to be "positive" are the candomblé of Domingos Pereira Sodré and the candomblé called Moinho led by the African *Tia* Julia. Both Reis and Harding comment on the case of the freedman Domingos, and the former discovered a story in the *Diário da Bahia* from July 28, 1862, specifying that Domingos came from Onim (Lagos). Apparently seconded by two freedwomen, he told fortunes to a sophisticated clientele, while working to free slaves from their masters by way of *feitiçaria*. This is very probably the same "*Papai* Domingos" who appears in 1870, in the Acú alley in Brotas, leading, together with *Mamãe* Mariquinhas Velludinho, a "grand session, on a farmstead to evoke the soul of Chico Papai, high priest of fetishism."[74]

The second case is that of Moinho, which can be identified as Nagô by present-day evidence, since this was actually the same group as that of the Gantois terreiro (Ilê Iyá Omin Axé Iyamassé), recognized as one of the city's oldest Nagô-Ketu candomblés. On January 4, 1868, there appears the first report that mentions a *pagode* or *bando* (a festive group) on Rio Vermelho Road (today Avenida Vasco da Gama), composed of "people from the terreiro of *Tia* Julia in Moinho," and also refers to "Pulcheria, the second *mamãe* of the terreiro." These are doubtless the African Julia Soares de Sá and her daughter Pulcheria, the leaders of the Gantois terreiro, documented by Nina Rodrigues in the 1890s as "the mother of the terreiro, Julia, old African[, and] . . . her daughter Pulcheria who helps her in everything." Moinho was located near Rio Vermelho Road, probably in the environs of Dique do Tororó in present-day Garcia, and it was only after 1870 that it moved to its present location on the Gantois farm. Further reports on Moinho add interesting information, such as the celebration of the festivals of the new yam in November, and of Our Lady of the Conception at the end of December, followed by another involving the sacrifice of "an ox to the *Mãe d'Água*" (probably the water goddess Oxum).[75]

The criterion used to identify the other six cases of "likely" Nagô terreiros or "individuals" is the use of the *baba-loixa* title or the mention of Nagô deities in relation to their members. The six cases include (1) an unidentified *baba-loixa* with a terreiro in Cruz do Cosme; (2) *Senhor* Granada, *filho-de-santo* of the *baba-loixa* of Cruz do Cosme, consecrated to Xangô and Oxalá, "*feitiço* healer and exorciser of devils"; (3) the *baba-loixa* Turibio, with a candomblé in Quinta das Beatas, who passed away in 1864; (4) the "*baba-louxas* Azomé and Acromece retired teachers in the defunct school of Chico-Papai, who provide fortune telling and consultations, and cast out devils from the body, at easy prices," with a house on the Alvo Hill, in the Sant'Anna parish; (5) the "African healer Augusto," also called *baba-loixa*, with a terreiro in Campo Grande, dedicated to the practice of exorcism; and (6) the candomblé of Chico-Papai, located in Poeira Street, which could also be Nagô, since its leader had two *filhos-de-santo* (initiates) called *baba-loixas*, was a "colleague" of the Cruz do Cosme *baba-loixa*, and the session celebrated in 1870, five years after his death, was led by *Papai* Domingos, who was very probably the same Domingos Pereira Sodré, Nagô of Onim. It is important to note that at least three of these examples (2, 4, and 5) appear as "individuals" dedicated to healing and divination, without clear information as to whether they were leaders of a complex religious congregation.[76]

As to the ten Jeje candomblés, I identified five as "positive." The first is Bogum, a terreiro that is still active and the best-known representative of the Jeje nation in contemporary Salvador Candomblé. I discuss in the next chapter a number of reports that refer to this terreiro between 1867 and 1870. A second terreiro, in Quinta das Beatas, can be identified as Jeje. The names of the leaders are not given, there is merely the mention of a *papai* and a *mamãe*, but a report on the wife "of a businessman" describes her as being secretly taken there "hidden in a sedan chair" to "dance *vodun*" and "to worship *Loco*." Although the report says she held "the hatchet emblem of Xangô," this could be an allusion to the vodun Sogbo, since in this terreiro there is explicit mention of "*Gege negresses*, Creoles, and *mulatas*." This reference to the ethnicity of Africans is singular in the documentation of *O Alabama* and is strong evidence for the identity of this terreiro's nation.[77]

The identification of the other three "positive" cases derives from oral tradition maintained even today. The late Valentina Maria dos Anjos, better known as *Doné* Runhó, the leader, or *mãe-do-santo*, of the Bogum terreiro from 1960 to 1975, in remembering the old Jeje terreiros of Salvador, cited those of Kerebetan, the Campina de Boskejan, and Agomea.[78] The late *Ialorixá** Olga Francisca Régis, leader of the Alaketo candomblé, confirmed some of these names: "There was Agomé, there was Kanjira, there was [another] next to the Tapa terreiro, the Zerebetan, where they had *gaiaku*, but it was down by the beach area. . . . There is even the song '*Zerebetano zaro, zerebetano zaro.*'"[79] Oral memory in this case is faithful to the past, and in fact I found references to these Jeje terreiros in *O Alabama.*

Regarding the Zerebetan (or Kerebetan) terreiro, I found a report from May 15, 1867, denouncing the disappearance of a *parda* slave woman, Casimira, who "went with others to a terreiro in the Barreiras area, called in the African tongue *Querebetan*—fountain where all go to drink." If the journalist's translation is correct, the original term would be perhaps *Querebetò*—*tò* being the Fon term referring to a lake or watercourse (river, stream, etc.). There exists, even today, outside of Salvador, a neighborhood called Calabetão whose name may be a corruption of that of the old candomblé "in the Barreiras area." The Casa das Minas, in São Luís of Maranhão, one of the oldest and most important Jeje terreiros in Brazil, is also called Querebentã de Zomadonu. According to Sérgio Ferretti, in São Luís *querebentã* refers to the house of the people of Davice, big house, or terreiro of Davice. Davice (a kingdom that probably precedes that of Allada) in the Casa das Minas designates the vodun family of the royal ancestors of Dahomey, led by the vodun Zomadonu.[80]

The "Agomé terreiro" (or Agomea) was in the neighborhood of Campinas, near Pirajá, in the Penha parish, and is named in a report from November 11, 1871. The description of the *vodunsis* in the *camarinha*, or initiation room, is quite prejudiced and distorted. There is the mention of the "*mamãe* of the terreiro, (*gumbonda*)" and of the Creole Paixão, *equede*, or the one in charge of the initiates.[81] The name of the terreiro is probably derived either from Dagomé (a phonetic variation of Dahomey) or from the name of the former kingdom's capital, Agbomé, present-day Abomey. It is therefore reasonable to think that this candomblé was of the Jeje-Dagomé nation.

It is likely that the name of the neighborhood of Gomeia, located near São Caetano to the south of Campinas, was taken from this Agomé terreiro. Artur Ramos suggests that this toponym is "a corruption of the Portuguese form of Dahomey (Agomé, Dagomé in the old documents), the country of the Geges" and, in support of this interpretation, Carneiro adds that "two of the three Gege candomblés of Bahia—those of Manuel Menezes and Falefá—are located in the neighborhood of Goméa."[82] The terreiro of Joãozinho da Gomeia also operated there, and despite being of the Angola nation, presented, as Ramos notes, important "Jeje borrowings." Eyewitnesses of the festivities of that house recall that it "had many Jeje people, it was Angola, but played Jeje Candomblé, and had many initiates of Omolu, Oxumaré, Nanã."[83] It is unlikely, however, that this presence of Jeje terreiros, or Jeje influence, in the twentieth century, had any connection with the old Agomé terreiro.

The Campina de Boskejan (or Campina de Boskeji) terreiro would also, of course, have been located in Campinas. In *O Alabama* appear a number of reports on terreiros in this area, but it is difficult to identify them and to know whether these reports refer specifically to this Jeje candomblé. However, one report from 1867 speaks of "the Campina terreiro" (note the use of the singular, rather than the plural neighborhood name of Campinas), where they were carrying out the *segum* (*sirrum*) for the death of *Mãe Aguntessa* ("wife of" or devotee of Agunté, *agontè* being in Fon an edible sprout from a species of palm tree, perhaps deified as a vodun). There is also mention of the presence of gameleira trees, a *Pai* Dothé (*doté* is a Fon hierarchical title) divining with the *Fa* (note the use of the Fon term), Izabel Loucouce (Lokosi, devotee of the vodun Loco) performing the shaving of the deceased, and an Agueça (Aguesi, devotee of the vodun Agué). These elements indicate that this was a Jeje terreiro, very probably the same Campina de Boskejan preserved in oral memory. *Humbono* Vicente, for example, remembered that the Campina de Boskejan terreiro had a *Loco* tree (gameleira).[84]

We can identify the remaining five "likely" cases of Jeje candomblés, as in the case of the Nagô terreiros, from the use of Jeje hierarchical terminology, the mention of Jeje deities or devotees of Jeje deities, and from ties with other Jeje congregations. In 1868 in Engenho Velho, in the candomblé of the *preto* (i.e., African) *Papai* António, a great ceremony lasting more than a week was held, coinciding with the victory of the conservatives in the municipal elections. An ox was slaughtered and "more than 2,000 people of every class" congregated. There were Creole women "elegantly dressed in serge, some wearing little towels on top of their heads, with rattles and horsetails in their hands, and in their midst there were African negresses who, as senior *vudunças*, took part in the celebration." The description of the sacrifice speaks again of the presence of "many women, acting as a kind of bacchante, whom they called *vudunças feitas*," or initiated *vudunças*. It was at this event that an assistant chief of police "became possessed[,] . . . ate *boiling oil*, and beside the *Lôcco* tree, fell to the ground beating himself."[85]

In the Jeje and Nagô terreiros of Maranhão and Bahia, they speak of an ancient practice performed to demonstrate the vodun's power and to confirm the authenticity of the possession. The practice consisted of ingesting cotton balls soaked with boiling palm oil (*acará*). In the vodun cults of the Gbe-speaking area and in the Jeje terreiros another ritual, with the same purpose, was also common—in Bahia called the "Zo ordeal," "ordeal of fire," or "hand-cast"—which consisted of placing the hand in a clay pot with boiling palm oil, from where the vodun took a piece of meat from a previously sacrificed animal. Following this, the vodun showed the piece to all present but did not ingest it. *O Alabama* explicitly mentions this ritual "in which they place their hand in oil" in another candomblé in Quinta das Beatas.[86] Jehová de Carvalho, according to information from a former *equede* from Bogum, reports the same ritual in that terreiro and adds that it could be followed with that of "coal stepping," in which barefoot *vodunsis* put their feet on live coals, blown by the straw fans in the hands of the *ogãs*: "Sogbo saw and kept watch over all."[87]

The "Zo ordeal" in Brazil is associated with the voduns of the Hevioso family, of whom Loko is one. The fact that in the Engenho Velho festival the act of "eating boiling oil" was performed "beside the *Lôcco* tree" suggests that the ordeal of fire in which the subchief of police participated was the *acará* ritual, or perhaps the "Zo ordeal" more specific to the vodun tradition. The mention of this ritual, of the vodun Loko, and the allusions to senior African *vudunças* strongly suggest that it was a Jeje candomblé. Indeed, in Engenho Velho, an area neighboring Bogum, oral tradition recalls the Jeje terreiro Pó Zerrem, which we will discuss further on. Might the candomblé of *Papai* António be the same as that of Pó Zerrem? There is yet some doubt.

The African Joaquim, with a terreiro in Quinta das Beatas (perhaps the same mentioned above where the "Zo ordeal" was performed), is referred to as *gumbônde* (high priest) and his wife is called *guncô*, both Jeje titles, suggesting that this candomblé was of that nation. *Pai* Joaquim is denounced by his wife for supposedly sexually abusing "the girls" who were being initiated.[88] In São Miguel, in the parish of Sant'Anna, there is record of an African who "has in a room, prepared in the form of a temple, various types of idolatrous images . . .

and even the figure of the devil (Lebal) dressed in a large cape, which is one of the most miraculous." This Lebal is Legba, a Jeje deity corresponding to the Nagô Exu.[89] Lastly, police persecution led a group of Bogum initiates to be taken first to São Miguel, then to the house of Clara (an African), and later to a terreiro in Areias da Armação, probably led by Maria Velhudinha. It can be assumed that the *vudunças* of Bogum were taken to terreiros of the same nation in order to continue their initiation. And in fact it is known that the terreiro of Maria Velhudinha in Areias received visits from other Jeje priestesses and priests from Cachoeira, providing support for this hypothesis.[90] I will discuss this subject further in the next chapter.

One could say that from the second half of the nineteenth century, a network of Jeje congregations with complex hierarchical and liturgical organizations gradually formed in Salvador. Within this network various complementary, cooperative, and probably conflicting relationships were established. At the same time, the Jeje religious community functioned as an integral part of a larger black-mestizo religious community with whose congregations it also established relations of, on the one hand, competition and contrast based on their rituals and, on the other, solidarity and cooperation in organized resistance against repression and discrimination by the dominant classes.

Because of the inevitable limitation and partiality of the sources, the linguistic analysis and the quantitative assessment of Jeje terreiros presented here should be viewed with caution; future studies are needed to refine these results. However, the documentary evidence of *O Alabama*, in addition to confirming the idea, established by Afro-Brazilian studies, that the Jeje origins were among the most important in the genesis of Candomblé, suggests that the traditions of the vodun cults remained dominant until at least the early 1870s. This is not to diminish the contribution of other nations, such as the Congo-Angola *inquice** cults, and most important, the Nagô orixá cults, which, as we have seen, were nearly as influential and renowned as those of the Jeje.

Actually, what I am proposing is simply an inversion of the emphasis that exists in the Jeje-Nagô dyad, questioning the traditional interpretation current in Afro-Bahian studies that has privileged the Nagô. The Nagô-centric interpretation comes from the contemporary perception of a greater number of terreiros that self-identify as Nagô-Ketu, and especially from the historical memory preserved by oral tradition, which considers the Ilê Iyá Nassô the oldest terreiro in Bahia. Because of the current prestige of that house, and those that have sprung from it, such as Gantois and Axé Opô Afonjá, this myth of the Nagô-Ketu origin of Candomblé has been accepted without much examination, and over time has become hegemonic in the discourse of Candomblé practitioners and among intellectuals. New documentary sources such as *O Alabama*, however, present a much more complicated reality and offer sufficient indications to propose alternative interpretations.

The Process of "Nagô-ization" at the Turn of the Century

My thesis of the dominance of a Jeje tradition in mid-nineteenth century Candomblé poses an interesting problem: How does one explain the apparent disappearance, in approximately twenty years (1871–91), from the time of *O Alabama* to the beginning of Nina Rodrigues's work, of this standing of the Jeje, giving way to an obvious dominance of the orixá cult tradition? In his posthumous work, *Os africanos no Brasil*, Rodrigues recognizes that at the beginning of his studies he was unable to distinguish between Jeje and Nagô mythology, given the "intimate fusion" between them. And although he affirms that "it is a Jeje-Nagô mythology that prevails in Brazil rather than one that is purely Nagô," he concludes that "today the number of Jeje in Bahia is greatly reduced. If at any time their beliefs and their cult existed here free from mixture, I cannot now affirm it. In present-day Jeje candomblés and terreiros the Creole and mestizo element predominates and the practices are, as in the Nagô candomblés and terreiros, a mix of the two mythologies. What is beyond doubt is that today the Ewe [Jeje] mythology is dominated by the Yoruban."

Following Ellis, he explains the absorption of the Jeje by the Nagô culture as being due to the predominance of the Nagô language and the "more complex and elevated" nature of Nagô religious beliefs.[91] Although these presumptions are certainly debatable, this perception has persisted.

In 1937, Carneiro wrote: "If in the time of Nina Rodrigues, Jeje mythology had already fused with and even gave way to Nagô mythology, what is seen today is an almost complete absorption of Jeje practices, which are almost totally forgotten as independent practices, by Nagô mythology."[92] A decade later, Ramos reiterated that "the old assertion of Nina Rodrigues that the cults and practices of the Jeje were absorbed by the Nagô continues to be valid. Jeje religious survivals, when they exist, do not ever constitute, in Bahia, the Northeast, or in Rio, a cultural block that clearly evidences a wholly Dahomean heritage. In other words, there is not, in Bahia, a vodun cult established as such."[93]

It should be noted that this perception was partially the result of these authors' focus on the Nagô-Ketu terreiros, and that this bias caused the visibility of these terreiros to obscure the presence of the Jeje. If in fact the Jeje candomblés became a minority, as we will discuss in the coming chapters, some of them were able to maintain their differentiated ritual practices and worship of Jeje deities.

Nina Rodrigues concentrated his study of Candomblé on the Nagô Gantois terreiro, and just as he did in analyzing the labor groups of black porters, where he privileged the African ones to the detriment of the Creoles, it is probable that in his research on religion he was subject to a similar bias, somewhat distorting what was actually happening around the end of the nineteenth century. Nevertheless, his work contains clear indications that the Jeje indeed no longer enjoyed the high profile that they had in the 1860s. If the term *vodun*, for example, were utilized as in the time of *O Alabama*, Rodrigues would not have failed to note this fact. Yet, it was the term *orixá* that began to be used in a generic manner to designate the African deities.

Considering this, it is interesting to note a comment by Rodrigues himself. Speaking of the vodun Loko, associated with the gameleira tree, he says: "it so happened that in our studies published before becoming familiar with the work of Ellis, *black Nagôs* made us correct the name of Lôco[,] . . . alleging that it was simply a *Creole corruption* of its true name Irôco."[94] This example suggests that at that time, an ethnocentric movement of Nagô "purification" was being developed in opposition to the "Creole corruption," and shows how the agency of practicing Nagôs may have been instrumental in their own socioreligious promotion and consequently in the increasing invisibility of the Jeje. But what might have afforded this self-consciousness of Nagô identity and the subsequent effort to legitimize it?

The process that created Nagô supremacy in Bahian Candomblé cannot be explained as the effect of a single cause but should be understood as the result of the complex interaction of a plurality of factors that I can only tentatively outline here.[95] In the first place, the change seems to coincide with the great proliferation of terreiros that occurred in the postabolition period. As the newspaper reports collected by Rodrigues show, the terreiros spread throughout Salvador and also in the Recôncavo between 1896 and 1905 and were led principally by Creole women.[96] Despite the ideals of progress and civilization promoted by the new Republic, the great majority of the Bahian black-mestizo population continued to be excluded from exercising real citizenship. The social marginalization of the colored population reinforced the formation of a distinct racial and cultural identity and the search for spaces of alternative sociability such as Candomblé. In the construction of this black identity, assumed primarily by the Creole population, Africa, as a diacritic sign of origin and as a projection of the cultural imaginary, came to play a central role for at least some groups. It is in the 1890s, for example, that carnivalesque groups such as the Pândegos da África and the Embaixada Africana emerge.[97]

In the context of Candomblé, I believe that it was precisely in the postabolition period, coinciding with the gradual disappearance of the old Africans and the simultaneous idealization of Africa, that terreiros such as Gantois—which could assert a historic African foundation—began to lay claim to this ancestry, although at this time they were already essentially Creole congregations. Africanness constituted a differential factor, a symbolic asset with which to face competition from more recently founded terreiros. This reaffirmation of identity would also be reinforced by the belief that "African" religious practices were more effective and "stronger" than the disparaged "Creole" practices of the recently arrived religious experts.

But, in this claim of Africanness, why did the Nagô tradition become the most privileged? Perhaps because a particular idea of Africa was being forged at that time, intimately connected to the growing visibility of Yoruba identity. Motory observes that in the last decades of the nineteenth century "at the British-dominated crossroads of African/African American interaction, the Yoruba acquired a highly publicized reputation for superiority to other Africans."[98] Begun by the Protestant missionaries of Sierra Leone, and stimulated by the British colonial powers in their dispute with the French, the Yoruba ethnogenesis gained renewed vigor with the so-called Lagosian Renaissance of the 1880s and 1890s. The black bourgeoisie of this vibrant city, faced with social and racial exclusion imposed by colonialism, began to promote a "cultural nationalism"—the expression is Ade Ajayi's—as a form of resistance. Affirming the specificity of a Yoruba "race-nation," this movement "cultivated the Yoruba language, adopted African dress; . . . collected the ancestral wisdom of their communities in the form of proverbs, stories, and poetry; compiled historical narratives from the oral traditions; and even started to find merit in some aspects of traditional religion."[99]

Though already long established, the transatlantic communication between Bahia and the Mina Coast had been growing since 1835, with hundreds of African returnees settling on the African coast each year, many of them in Lagos, contributing, together with the Lucumi returned from Cuba and the Aku from Sierra Leone, to the "Yoruba Renaissance." Other Afro-Bahians traveled and carried out business regularly between the two coasts, and in the last decades of the century Lagos was the principal destination of vessels headed for West Africa. This means that the reports on "Yoruba cultural nationalism" could have reverted indirectly to Bahia, creating a favorable climate for the revalorization of the corresponding Nagô identity. Candomblé, with its ancient and latent ethnoritual division, offered fertile ground for "nationalist" revivalisms. It is also important to note that the city of Kétou, after being destroyed by the Dahomeans in 1883 and in 1886, was reconstructed in 1896, and that news of this event might have arrived in Bahia. Might the identification of certain terreiros in Salvador with the Nagô-Ketu nation date from this time?

Among the agents of this intercommunication between Bahia and Yoruba-land toward the end of the century, the case of the *babalaô*, or diviner, Martiniano Eliseu de Bomfim is the best-known. He was one Nina Rodrigues's informants and in his youth spent a number of years in Nigeria, becoming initiated into the Ifá tradition and later becoming one of the precursors of the "Africanization," or rather the "Nagôization," of Candomblé. In 1910, he probably helped his close friend Eugênia Ana dos Santos, *Mãe* Aninha, found Axé do Opô Afonjá and later establish the institution of the *obás de Xangô*, inspired by the honorific titles used in the Oyo kingdom.[100] Joaquim Francisco Devodê Branco (1856–1924), a Mahi freedman, resident of Lagos, and tradesman in Porto-Novo, was also a friend of *Mãe* Aninha and the godfather of her successor, *Mãe* Senhora.[101]

With his journeying, Branco could have brought information on religious events from the Mina Coast, but his influence could only have been tangential. However, as Lima recalls: "By the end of the nineteenth century, the trip to Africa by freed Africans and their children was an important legitimizing element of prestige and generator of knowledge and economic power. Even as they traded in a wide variety of merchandise brought from the Coast to Brazil and vice versa, they also, in today's language, 'recycled' the knowledge of the religious tradition learned from 'the elders' in the terreiros of Bahia."[102]

In its function of legitimizing prestige, the voyages (real or imagined) to Africa appear in a number of narratives referring to the foundation of some of Bahia's most famous terreiros.[103] Thus, the end of the nineteenth century seems to establish the conceptual basis for a notion of Africa as the original locus of a "tradition" that required recovery, reinventing continuities in order to overcome a "traumatic past." This idealization of Africa was also an alternative and a reaction to the assimilationist bias of Creole culture. In keeping with the growing visibility of Yoruba cultural supremacy in the Afro-Atlantic world, the process of "re-Africanization" consolidated itself as a process of "Nagôization." And at the same time, some sectors of the religious community saw this process as a strategy to obtain political power in an increasingly racialized society.

Intellectuals have also been seen as playing a role in "Nagôization." Beatriz Góis Dantas has defended the idea that it was the intellectuals, from Rodrigues through Carneiro and Ramos to Verger and Elbein dos Santos, to cite only the best-known, who systematically privileged the "pure Nagô" terreiros, exalting them "as true religion, in contrast with Bantu magic/sorcery."[104] While this may be true, Dantas's argument has the serious defect of undervaluing the agency of Candomblé practitioners in legitimizing their religious practices when faced with competing groups. The reputation of Gantois, for example, was well established long before Rodrigues began his research. In fact, this may have helped lead him to that terreiro in the first place. When, in the 1930s, intellectuals began to valorize more ostensibly the African "purity" of the Nagô-Ketu terreiros, they were merely recognizing, and strengthening, an internal hierarchy already established by Candomblé practitioners.

The combination of these many causes, merely outlined here, allowed certain Nagô-Ketu candomblés to be considered "models" or hegemonic references, while many others of lesser import increasingly assumed the "Nagô" identity in an attempt to legitimize their practices. This resulted in the decreasing visibility of the vodun tradition, which in the nineteenth century had constituted one of the most determinant formative forces in the institutionalization of Candomblé.

The next two chapters will examine the history and evolution of the Bogum terreiro and those of other Cachoeiran Jeje candomblés during the second half of the nineteenth century and in the postabolition period. Hopefully, the macrohistory presented in this chapter will serve to locate the microhistory that follows within its larger sociocultural context.

5 Bogum and Roça de Cima

The Parallel History of Two Jeje Terreiros in the Second Half of the Nineteenth Century

The Intersection of Oral Tradition and Written Sources

This chapter examines historical information from the second half of the nineteenth century regarding two Jeje terreiros: Bogum in Salvador and the terreiro known as Roça de Cima (which could be translated roughly as "the upper farm") in Cachoeira. Seja Hundé (also known as Roça do Ventura) arose from Roça de Cima at the end of the century. The two terreiros maintained close ties until around the 1950s. The data in this chapter comes in part from the scanty bibliography available,[1] but it derives principally from the historical documents I was able to find in notary records and archives, from certain reports in *O Alabama*, and from surveys of the Jeje oral tradition that I have collected over the past seven years.[2]

The methodology I used, based on cross-referencing oral tradition and written sources, was complicated by several factors. The first was the scarcity of documents on the religious activity of the black-mestizo population in general, and on the members of these Jeje congregations specifically. The second was the occasional reluctance of Jeje devotees and priests to speak of the history of their terreiros, great patience and persistence sometimes being necessary to gain their trust. The final difficulty was that the use of oral tradition for historical reconstruction presents innumerable problems, as Africanists have shown clearly.[3]

A common example is the possibility of "skipping generations" or of "selective simplification" when recalling undocumented historical genealogies.[4] The more relevant people are remembered while the less important intermediates are forgotten, resulting in incomplete chronological or genealogical sequences. It is often a case not of lying but simply omitting part of the truth. In other cases, there is the use of topoi, or narrative stereotypes, which cause the transposition of events; the same stories are used to refer to different geographical or chronological events, or variations of the same story are attributed to diverse groups. This "narrative economy" of orality can introduce distortions of both omission and invention. Oral discourse is always conditioned by the social interactions between the narrator and the listener, and often the discourse expresses the narrator's views and ideological biases, conscious or unconscious, and serves as a strategy for legitimizing present situations based on the past or resisting competing versions.

It is the subjective and operational "reality" of these "historical myths," independent of their historical veracity, that interests anthropology. But for historical reconstruction, it is important to go beyond the anthropological value of the "realities of the imaginary" and attempt to filter the information through a critical sieve, which reveals and corrects the ideological biases or distortions implicit in the discourse. To evaluate the historical reliability of oral evidence it is very important to ask the same person about the same topic on repeated occasions and to contrast this data systematically with the testimony of others. One must also identify whether the speakers were eyewitnesses to the facts or if they received the information from others. Finally, the correspondence between the oral evidence and written sources (when available) can decisively confirm an event.

The present experiment revealed recurring discrepancies between oral memory and documented memory. In these cases, the written information was privileged, after evaluating its historical reliability, according to conventional methods of historiography. This does not mean that documentary evidence is not subject to possible distortions and errors, as is oral evidence. But, being documents contemporary with the facts or events, they inspire more confidence in their veracity, or at least in the probability of their veracity. In any case, the following narrative's hypothetical "historical realism" should be read with a certain degree of caution. I merely attempt here to reconstruct or chronologically order the known facts, in order to offer a basis for more lengthy future research. The narrative begins with Bogum in Salvador.

The Origins of Bogum and Its Activities in the 1860s

The Bogum candomblé, or Zoogodô Bogum Malê Rundô, has been called the "oldest Jeje terreiro," "centenarian," "bicentennial," "more than three centuries old," and other appellations that highlight its great age.[5] In a 1961 interview, the late Valentina Maria dos Anjos, *Doné* Runhó, then *mãe-de-santo* of Bogum, said it with greater prudence: "The terreiro was founded by Africans and is more than 100 years old," which would put its foundation at around the first half of the nineteenth century.[6]

Another oral tradition of the terreiro dates its establishment to the end of the eighteenth century. According to this version, there was a plantation, or *engenho*, with a great concentration of slaves where today the Catholic University stands. It is believed that some of these slaves escaped from the sugar mill and established a *quilombo* in the bush, "planting," at some 800 to 1,000 meters from the aforementioned *engenho*, the first Bogum shrines. It is said that these slaves were of the Mahi nation, but there probably were Africans of other nations as well.[7] I imagine that at this beginning moment, given the conditions of a clandestine *quilombo*, the stability of the supposed terreiro must have been precarious and the religious activities sporadic. Perhaps it is this oral tradition that leads the inhabitants of present-day Engenho Velho da Federação, where Bogum is located, to believe that the neighborhood sprang up from a *quilombo*.[8] In 1724, in the lands of the São Bento convent, in Rio Vermelho, and adjacent to present-day Avenida Cardeal da Silva (formerly Caminho da Federação), there existed an *engenho* known as Pedra da Marca.[9] Perhaps this was the same *engenho* recalled by oral tradition.

Although the area of the terreiro has been seriously reduced in the last few decades, older Bogum members remember that, in the past, it covered a great area of bush that went from the top of Federação—presently Praça Valmir Barreto—and extended, descending the hill, between what is presently Ladeira Manoel Bomfim (also known as Ladeira do Bogum) and Rua Xisto Bahia, until coming to the former Caminho Dois de Julho—today Avenida Vasco da Gama—where the Lucaia River and the trolley line pass. In the nineteenth century, the Caminho Dois de Julho, which went from Dique do Tororó (Tororó Dam) to Rio Vermelho, was also known as the Caminho do Rio Vermelho and constituted a border between the Brotas and Vitória parishes. The area of Bogum was part of the Vitória parish, in what is presently the Engenho Velho da Federação neighborhood.

According to Rita Amélia, a researcher from the Projeto Fundiário do Engenho Velho da Federação (Engenho Velho da Federação Agrarian Project), in the past the so-called Engenho Velho was a huge property that extended from the Brotas parish, occupying part of the Vitória parish. At some point the Vitória parish portion was separated and, together with the lands of Fazenda Madre de Deus, came to constitute what is now the Engenho Velho da Federação neighborhood.[10] If this hypothesis is correct, the separation of the Engenho Velho da Federação section must have occurred before 1853, since the inventory of Captain Antônio Teixeira de Carvalho, who died in that year, indicates among his properties the "farm called Engenho Velho, situated in the parish of Brotas, which is divided by the São Pedro [aka Lucaia] River."[11] It is also quite probable that in popular use "Engenho Velho" referred to an area that covered land that went beyond the official borders of Engenho Velho de

Brotas. In the 1860s, *O Alabama* reports three candomblés located in "Engenho Velho," and at least one, Bogum, was in the present-day Engenho Velho da Federação, outside of the Brotas parish.[12]

According to João José Reis, in the first half of the nineteenth century, the parish of Brotas had only one justice of the peace. As we have seen, at the end of the 1820s, this would have been Antônio Guimarães. In the 1829 letter written to the Viscount of Camamu, which we discussed in chapter 4, the magistrate speaks of a festival in Engenho Velho "outside of my district" and in an 1831 letter mentions the raid on a candomblé in Engenho Velho, also outside of his jurisdiction.[13] Logically then, the Engenho Velho of the 1829 festival, and in particular that of the 1831 candomblé, would have been located within the parish of Vitória. If this is the case, these are references from as early as the 1830s to a candomblé in the area of present-day Engenho Velho da Federação.

The soldiers carried out the 1831 raid on the candomblé because at dawn, after they had spent a night invading the homes of Africans, "a man approached us and told us to ascend the hill, and that on top we would find a house where the presence of negros and negresses with dances, drumming, and fortune telling was continuous."[14] This description of an African candomblé at the top of a hill, in Engenho Velho da Federação, is perfectly compatible with the location of Bogum, located strategically at the top of Ladeira Manoel Bomfim. Of course this is not conclusive evidence, because there are a number of hills in the Federação area, and there may have been other candomblés. But for now, it is the strongest indication that Bogum could have been functioning in the 1830s.

Whatever the case, this indication, though imprecise, seems more convincing than other arguments that defend the same hypothesis that Bogum was operating in the 1830s. Antonio Monteiro and Jehová de Carvalho suggest that the candomblé existed in the time of the Malê Revolts of the first decades of the nineteenth century, based on the name of the terreiro, Zoogodô Bogum Malê Rundô. According to these authors, in what has already become a widely spread oral tradition among Salvador's *povo-de-santo*, Bogum was the name of a small house or annex located in front of the Quinze Mistérios church in the Santo Antonio Além do Carmo neighborhood, where the Malês hid "gold bars, arms, and gunpowder kegs" destined to fuel their revolts. According to Carvalho, the word *Bogum* referred to the chest (or *baú* in Portuguese) where the donations of gold and money were kept. According to Monteiro's account, a black Malê by the name of Aprígio, "captain responsible for the command of the [Malê] forces in the center of the city," was accused of denouncing the insurrection to "those of the government." Fleeing reprisals from his own religious brothers, he sought refuge in the forests of Engenho Velho, near the Jeje terreiro. Discovered by the Mahi Africans, Monteiro writes, Aprígio was accepted by the religious community, in which he came to be known as the "black of the bogum [chest]," an expression later used to designate the terreiro.

Carvalho's account, supposedly based on historical evidence, identifies the black Malê as Joaquim Jeje, who was involved in the rebellion of 1835 and had accepted "the Islamism of the Malês without renouncing the fetishism of the Jeje people." According to Carvalho, Joaquim Jeje, fleeing political repression following the failure of the insurrection, had found refuge in the Engenho Velho terreiro, there hiding the prized chest or *baú* (*bogum*) that contained the gold of the Malês. This would explain the inclusion of the terms *bogum* and *malé* in the name of the terreiro. These interpretations, despite their nearly novelistic appeal, are questionable. Besides the discrepancy between the two versions, there is a certain inaccuracy as to the dates. Although the event is normally associated with the 1835 revolt, Carvalho also associates it with the Malê insurrection of 1826 "that was extended in stages to the year 1835."[15]

The judicial inquest into the Malê Revolt of 1835 documents the slave "Joaquim from the coast of Africa, Gege" (even though elsewhere he declares himself to be Nagô, as we saw in chapter 2), but he was imprisoned and there is no reference to a chest in relation to him.[16] There is the case of the slave Belchior, of the Nagô nation, who, on the night of the revolt, being in the house where the Malê leaders were meeting and in disagreement with the insurgents' intentions, "took his box and went to Santo Antônio da Moraria to the house of his master." The majority of slaves had their "box," or chest, and in 1835 dozens of them were examined. In Belchior's case, nothing was found "to indicate that the named slave was an accomplice in the insurrection."[17] Might Belchior have been able to hide the original contents of the box before it was inspected? Is the reference to a different chest? The possibility remains for anyone wishing to speculate, but the documentary evidence places serious doubts on the possible relationship between an unknown chest of Joaquim Jeje and the name of the Bogum terreiro. We will examine other aspects of the etymology of the Bogum name below.

Although the idea that Bogum was operating in the 1830s should not be discarded, I found no conclusive evidence that this religious congregation existed previous to the 1860s. On May 2, 1867, the first reference to a funerary ritual performed "for the soul of one Machado, dignity of the Bogum who passed away," appears in *O Alabama*. The deceased was probably an important *ogã* from the terreiro, but it is important to note that the *zelim** or *sirrum*, as the funerary rituals in the Jeje nation are called, was performed on Rua das

Laranjeiras, in the city center, and not in Engenho Velho. A number of terreiros operated on Rua das Laranjeiras, and the fact that the *zelim* was performed there is the first indication of the connection that existed between Bogum and other religious congregations. The ceremony lasted nine nights and "they played some real candomblé. The orgy began at 9:00 and ended at 4:00 in the morning."[18] Although the celebration of funerary rites for congregation members in private homes or outside the home terreiro was not infrequent, in this case it is probable that it occurred because of an initiation was being performed at Bogum, and the rituals involving *eguns*,* or the spirits of the dead, are incompatible with those involving the voduns.

Not many days later, on May 10, there appears a second report, addressed to: "The Most Excellent Chief of Police, asking him to send to Engenho Velho, to the candomblé known as *Bogum*—whose leaders are the barber José Moraes, resident of the Cabeça; Isidoro Melandras; and the negress Rachel—to seek out a woman whose superstition and fanaticism, associated with the most crass ignorance, led her to deliver herself up to those wicked souls, who make use of her for hideous and repugnant practices."

This woman, a Creole named Andrelina, "whom they call Acadêmica, driven to the said farmstead, has lived there for ten weeks, locked in a room, completely naked, until she receives the *sapocã*."[19] The *sapocã* is certainly what is today called the *sarapocã*, an initial semipublic coming-out of an initiate in the Jeje tradition (see chapter 8).

Despite the report's ideological and pejorative bias, it contains important information regarding the Bogum leadership: it was shared by two men and an African woman. As I have already noted, coleadership was characteristic of the ecclesiastical organization of the Gbe-speaking area's vodun cults. It also confirms the period's general pattern of a predominantly male religious leadership. Regarding the barber José Moraes, a resident of Cabeça, I was unable to find further information, and it is unknown whether he was African or Creole. In the nineteenth century, African barbers often functioned as surgeons, administering various medical treatments, such as bleedings or cupping, these being "a favorite African remedy."[20] It is probable that José Moraes, being both a barber and the leader of a candomblé, would have had the skills of a healer.

Two years later, on April 14, 1869, *O Alabama* includes a new "letter to the Most Excellent Chief of Police, to bring to your attention the following: There is in Engenho Velho, among others, a candomblé terreiro known as *Bogum*, whose chief is José Barbeiro, with a stand in Cabeça." This is the same barber José Moraes. In this report, the mysterious death of a *vodunsi* during an initiation is denounced. According to the opinion of the "public voice," the journalist reports, "one of these unfortunates, whom ignorance and fanaticism led to believe in such witchcraft, had fallen into the *santo* [a trance] and found herself in the initiation room, in the company of others like her. In performing the *sapocã*, a ceremony that consists in cutting the hair and in being able to step beyond the threshold of this room, after six months, the neophyte was unable to perform correctly certain customary dances, and to teach her she was daily chastised by the *donunce*, a kind of grand master of the order," a chastisement from which she apparently died.[21]

Although punishment can be a part of the rigors of the initiation, once again, caution should be used in accepting such information (suspicions the journalist only heard secondhand) as truth. What is important to emphasize here is the reference to the *donunce*, as a "grand master of the order." This woman, the highest religious authority of initiations, was probably the "negress" Rachel, mentioned in the preceding report, which indicates the importance of the female figure in the shared Bogum leadership.

The same report indicates that other neophytes from the same group, or *barco*, were "immediately taken to a house in São Miguel, where they now find themselves, this precaution being taken for fear that, if the police had known of what happened, they would go there and find them." Two days later, "at two o'clock in the morning" on April 16, once again escaping police persecution, "the so-called *Vadunças* and all of the accessories of the candomblé arrived at Areias da Armação, taken from the house of the African Clara, in São Miguel, to that place." This certainly refers to the Bogum initiates who, after the report published on April 14 of their being in a house in São Miguel, transferred during the night to Areias da Armação, taking with them the initiation implements or other objects of candomblé belonging to the African Clara that could have compromised her. Very probably the candomblé in Areias was that of Maria Velhudinha, where we know that Clara from São Miguel and Jejes such as *mamãe* Ludovina from Cachoeira had participated that February in the *festa do balaio* (see chapter 8). Besides the above-mentioned connection between the Bogum terreiro and the candomblé on Rua das Laranjeiras; it can be seen that Bogum maintained a complex network of cooperative relationships with various religious congregations, also probably Jeje, both in the city center and the outlying areas. The last report from *O Alabama* regarding Bogum, dated June 23, 1870, says that "in Engenho Velho, at Bogum, there is a big candomblé on Saturday, the sacrifice will be [of] a bullock."[22]

From this evidence one can conclude that in the 1860s, Jeje candomblés such as Bogum had already achieved a liturgical complexity similar to that of contemporary candomblés. They practiced funerary rituals that lasted nine

In the Rio Vermelho region (c. 1890). Photo: G. Gaensly and R. Lindemann, in Gilberto Ferrez, *Bahia: Velhas fotografias, 1858–1900* (Salvador: Kosmos, 1988)

days (they now last seven) and structured their ritual activities in large festivals with the sacrifice of bullocks and complex collective initiation processes, which lasted a minimum of six months and involved possession or mediumship experiences. The cult's organization included a rigid hierarchy determining the ritual responsibilities of each member, and both African leaders and Creole devotees participated. In addition to this, the consecutive reports from 1867 and 1870 indicate significant stability in the congregation, where the ritual activity was prolonged throughout most of the year. If some of these elements seem to have been implicit in the candomblés of previous decades, such as the one of Accú in 1829, it is clear that from the 1860s they were completely consolidated.

It is worth adding two important terreiros that were neighbors of the Jeje-Mahi Bogum: Pó Zerrem, of the Jeje-Mundubi nation, now defunct, and the Nagô-Ketu nation's Ilê Iyá Nassô, better known as Engenho Velho or Casa Branca, which is still active.[23] These demonstrate how the area around Bogum became one of the most important points of candomblé concentration in the city. This stretch of Caminho do Rio Vermelho, known as Joaquim dos Couros, was in fact a strategic location.

In the nineteenth century, this zone was essentially wilderness, offering every type of leaf necessary for religious practices. Also, the proximity of the Lucaia River provided access to water, essential for the rituals of voduns and orixás. As the late Runhó affirmed, "One can only 'make the saint' if there is water and wilderness."[24] Additionally, the space of closed forest made access difficult for outsiders. The three terreiros were located on elevated hillsides, with Bogum at the top of the hill, which allowed for increased control over the arrival of undesired people.

At the same time, this location was the halfway point between the urban nucleus of Salvador and Rio Vermelho, at the time an important community of black fishermen, mostly freedmen, which surely favored the participation in these candomblés of both people from the city as well as those from this coastal village. The disadvantage of being isolated and relatively hidden was the risk of assaults on the "negresses passing by carrying burdens," which seems to have been frequent in the 1860s.[25]

The Pó Zerrem (Pau Zerrem or Pauzerré) was located on a slope parallel to that of Bogum, dividing the area from that terreiro. Nothing is known of its origins or founders, but some believe that this terreiro is older even than Bogum.[26] I have already suggested that the Engenho Velho candomblé, which was led by the African António and where the 1868 festival documented in *O Alabama* was held, may have been Pó Zerrem, as it presents various elements identifiable as Jeje.[27] Oral memory recalls only its most famous leader, Manoel Aprígio da Conceição, more commonly called Aprígio or Tata Aprígio of Sogbo, who was active perhaps during the last decade of the nineteenth century, and certainly in the first decades of the twentieth.[28] The terreiro ceased activities around 1945, probably because of internal disputes that emerged after Aprígio's death. The lands were sold, and in the 1960s the area was urbanized.[29]

Waldeloir Rego sees Pó Zerrem as a corruption of the Fongbe expression "kpo zeli," *kpo* being a panther, ancestral totem (*tohuiyo*) of the Agasuvi clan, from which the royal dynasties of Allada, Dahomey, and Porto-Novo emerged, and *zeli* (*zènli*), the name the Fons give to the percussive instrument, the funeral rhythm, and to the funerary rituals themselves. Other scholars identify the term *zerrem* as a deformation of *sirrum*, another name for the Jeje funerary rites.[30] This association between the name of the terreiro and funeral rites suggests the importance that the *egun* or ancestral cult may have in this candomblé.

In fact, Pó Zerrem is normally identified as Jeje-Mundubi, a "nation" in which the cult of the *eguns* would be included among its liturgical characteristics.[31] It is known, however, that in the religious context of the Jeje congregations, Mundubi is associated with the Kaviono (Hevioso) family. *Humbono* Vicente told me that Pó Zerrem was Kaviono, and the fact that its leader, Aprígio, belonged to the vodun Sogbo and that the terreiro preserved the cult of the vodun Averekete, who also belongs to this family (although Everaldo

Duarte identifies this Averekete as a form of *Legba*), confirms the importance of the Kaviono family and further supports identifying the terreiro as Jeje-Mundubi.[32]

This difference of "nation," with Pó Zerrem being Jeje-Mundubi and Bogum being Jeje-Mahi, could explain relationships both of conflict and of complementarity that appear to have existed between the two candomblés. Though the little information that exists on Pó Zerrem relates to the period of Aprígio, it suggests this fluctuation between ritual rivalry and cooperation. In 1988, *Mãe* Nicinha, the leader of Bogum, declared that the cult of Averekete was performed during the festivals of Sogbo and Badé but that Averekete's shrine was installed in the "Pozzerram" and that his cult in Bogum had ceased since the disappearance of that terreiro.[33] Again according to *Humbono* Vicente, in the lands of Pó Zerrem there was a grove of bamboo (an ancestral shrine in the Jeje tradition) in which the Bogum members carried out private rituals to open the liturgical activities of the terreiro, as well as used it as a dropping-off point for *despachos* (ritual offerings or belongings of a dead person).*[34]

Because Pó Zerrem was more involved with the egun cults, however, members from Bogum did not often attend, as the vodun cult tends to avoid contact with cults that deal with *eguns*. Everaldo Duarte remarked that there were more Pó Zerrem members who went up to Bogum.[35] Another possible cause for the mutual exclusion was that in Pó Zerrem, men as well as women were initiated as *vodunsi*, contrary to Bogum, where only women were initiated, at least since the postabolition period. In the words of *Humbono* Vicente, "Pó Zerrem was male, Bogum was female."[36]

The geographic proximity of Bogum and Pó Zerrem (and perhaps also Ilê Iya Nassô) seems, therefore, to have generated cooperation but also competition and potential conflict. The cooperation could have possibly favored the interpenetration of some practices and values between the religious traditions of the different "nations," a process that was undoubtedly at the heart of Candomblé's nineteenth-century formation. But the possible competition may have led to the opposite result, that is, processes of contrast that accentuated liturgical disparities as signs of differentiated identities.

Unfortunately, I was unable to find documentary information on Bogum after 1870. Its history in the postabolition period will be taken up again in the next chapter. Now it is necessary to move the narrative to Cachoeira, where in the in second half of the nineteenth century another important Jeje terreiro, Roça de Cima, operated and, as I have stated, maintained frequent contact with Bogum, demonstrating how the social network of Jeje Candomblé was not limited to Salvador but expanded to the Recôncavo as well.

The Legendary Obá Tedô Quilombo
and Candomblé in Cachoeira

As we saw in chapter 1, the third-quality tobacco cultivated in Cachoeira, São Félix, Muritiba, Maragogipe, and São Gonzalo dos Campos in the eighteenth century, especially in the second half, became the principal Bahian commercial export to the West African Mina Coast, creating a continuous flow of Jeje slaves from this area. The relationship between the cultivation of tobacco and the slave trade was so important that it induced some plantation owners to become directly involved in the lucrative trade in human flesh.[37] The production of sugar on the plantations of Iguape, Santo Amaro da Purificação, São Sebastião do Passé, and São Francisco do Conde was, however, the activity that sustained the economy of colonial Bahia. It was on these plantations that the greatest concentration of slaves existed. It is important to remember, however, that subsistence agriculture was also significant. It was therefore in the Recôncavo area that the great Brazilian families and landowners settled and prospered. These same families would come to constitute the landowning elite who would later organize the war of independence against the Portuguese urban merchants operating in the commercial center of Salvador.

The town, or *vila*, of Nossa Senhora do Rosário do Porto da Cachoeira, on the banks of the Paraguaçu River, besides being the greatest industrial center for tobacco, was the Recôncavo's economic hub, its river port and market being the point for exchange between Salvador and the country's interior. From Cachoeira issued the paths to Minas Gerais, Maranhão, and the semiarid hinterlands (*sertão*). The transhumance of cattle, the transport of gold, and the internal traffic in slaves passed through Cachoeira. As a result of this strategic location, Cachoeira became the place of residence for a great number of plantation owners, favoring the village's prosperity, as well as the concentration of the black population.[38]

The great contingent of Jeje Africans in Cachoeira and the surrounding area is evident, for example, in the establishment of the brotherhood of Senhor Bom Jesus dos Martírios de Homens Pretos de Nação Gege in 1765. Also, as we have seen, as early as the last decades of the eighteenth century, the Jejes began to organize domestic religious cults, such as the *calundu* of the Rua do Pasto (see chapter 3). Therefore, it is possible to suppose that the practices of the vodun cult in Cachoeira go back to this time and that they attained a greater organizational complexity during the first decades of the nineteenth century, as happened in Salvador. However, other than this reasonable conjecture, there is no evidence of a Jeje candomblé until the 1860s.

There are references in oral tradition to religious congregations previous to this period. In Recuada, the urban nucleus where the African population of Cachoeira lived and where their descendants still live today, there is an area known as Galinheiro, probably a reference to the Galinhas or Africans of Grunci origin who embarked from the Galinha River, and another known as Corta Jaca, in the locale of the present-day market. According to Ambrósio Bispo Conceição, *Ogã* Boboso, in the Galinheiro (or in the Corta Jaca) there existed a candomblé house of the "Mussurumi" nation (*Musulmi* or *Muçulmam* in the Hausa language). Its cult, associated with the *eguns*, in which they danced with a coffin on the head, was considered dangerous and only adults participated in it. From this house, the Africans, dressed in uniform and armed with cudgels or sharp tools, would prohibit strangers from entering. Based on this information, Luiz Cláudio Dias do Nascimento hypothesizes the existence of a *quilombo* called Obá Tedô, or Bi Tedô according to *Ogã* Boboso, on a steep hill between the Capapina road and the old road to Belém, above Recuada. Dias do Nascimento believes that a candomblé of the same name operated there around 1830 or 1840.[39]

Ogã Boboso claimed the Bi Tedô candomblé was led by an African named Quixareme or Tijaremi (a corruption of *tio*, or uncle, Xarene or Chareme) and it was there that the Jeje installed their first shrines in Cachoeira. *Ogã* Boboso said that *Tio* Xarene was Mahi and that he was the founder and pillar of the Jeje Candomblé, not only in Cachoeira, but in all of Bahia. *Ogã* Boboso also affirmed that the saint of *Tio* Xarene was Azonsu and that festivities were held for this vodun at Bi Tedô in October.[40] Dias do Nascimento adds that the Casa Estrela (House of the Star) located in the urban center of Cachoeira, on what is now Rua Ana Neri, number 41, functioned as headquarters for the African community, and especially as the headquarters for the Boa Morte sisterhood. He also argues that the Casa Estrela was associated with the Obá Tedô candomblé and says "it is believed that it was there that the initiation rites of new devotees were performed," while in Obá Tedô "only the drumming-dancing ceremonies were performed."[41]

Unfortunately, beyond these contemporary oral accounts, there is no documentary evidence on this supposed *quilombo* or candomblé. All that is known is that in 1876 the Batedor viaduct was constructed near Recuada, on the Central da Bahia train line.[42] Dias do Nascimento argues that the name of the viaduct is a visible corruption of the term *Obá Tedô*. João da Silva Campos, speaking of Salvador, comments that around 1875 the African population was concentrated on Rua do Alvo and Rua dos Nagôs, "*Nagô tedô*, as they named it." *Tédo* is a Yoruba word meaning "the place in which people settle for the first time." *Oba* is king, therefore, *oba tedô* would be "the place where the king settled" or, in Dias do Nascimento's looser version, "here lives the king."[43] The element *Ba-* in the word *Batedor* could also be a reference to the *Egbas*, one of the more numerous Nagô ethnic groups of Bahia, sometimes denominated by this term. Although the name Obá Tedô or Batédo is of Nagô origin, it is not impossible that in Cachoeira it referred to a gathering of Africans of various nations—Nagô, *Gruncis*, and Huassas—as the presence of the "Musulmi" candomblé in the Galinheiro seems to suggest.

The presence of other *quilombos* in the rural zone of Cachoeira is also spoken of. For example, in Terra Vermelha, to the south of the Caquende River, adjacent to the Engenho Tororó, there seems to have existed a *quilombo* called Malaquia or Malaquias. There is also talk that in these *quilombos* were organized some of the slave revolts that occurred in Cachoeira in 1826, 1827, and 1828. However, there is no historical documentation of this.[44]

The formation of *quilombos* in the area of Cachoeira seems certain, and it seems very probable that African religious cults were practiced in these secret backwoods spaces. It is common knowledge that the Batedor viaduct is in an area where *ebôs* and *despachos* were taken by the Cachoeiran *povo-do-santo*, and it is said that "there is much buried there." Despite this indirect evidence, nothing can be affirmed with certainty. In any case, it is important to note that, as in the case of Bogum, oral tradition agrees that the first Jeje candomblé in Cachoeira arose in the context of a *quilombo*.

Roça de Cima or the Farmstead of *Tio* Xarene

It is only in the second half of the nineteenth century that one finds more reliable information indicating the presence of a Jeje candomblé within a few kilometers of Cachoeira's urban center. This candomblé would have been located to the right of anyone ascending the "old road to Belém" (now Ladeira da Cadeia), before Lagoa Encantada, on the route to Engenho do Rosário. According to oral tradition, there existed there a candomblé of Africans known as Roça de Cima, led by Ludovina Pessoa, *Tio* Xarene, and probably at a later period also by José Maria Belchior, who went by Zé de Brechó.

Currently, the *povo-de-santo* identifies this place by the presence of a very leafy and ancient *jaqueira* or jackfruit tree. When people pass before it, they commonly greet the tree in an African language, and, at times, tap their foreheads against it. This jackfruit is the sacred tree where the spiritual master of Roça de Cima is enshrined, the vodun Dandagojí—or according to other accounts Dangorojí or Darangogojí—a kind of Sakpata that perhaps corresponds to the African vodun Dada Zodji or Daazodji.[45]

Roça de Cima bordered the old Ventura farm where today is located the Seja Hundé candomblé that, as we will see, derived from Roça de Cima. A land record dated March 18, 1860, mentions the Ventura farm, thus called because its proprietor was Luiz Ventura Esteves, a resident of the São Sebastião parish. The description of the property boundaries mentions, among other things, the section that went from "the foot of a large cashew tree," along the road from Engenho do Rosário, to "the foot of a jackfruit of the Vicente Ferreira farm," descending from there to the Caquende River.[46] This "foot of a jackfruit" is very probably the Roça de Cima jackfruit, which even today marks the boundary of the Ventura farm.

I found another land record, dated June 8, 1896, that verifies an earlier deed from August 5, 1882, showing that José Maria Belchior purchased for 200 milréis a farm called *Sítio* do Charema (or *Sítio* Charene), or Charema farmstead, from José Gonsalo Martins de Oliveira and his wife, Amália de Oliveira. The site of *Sítio* Charene, which neighbors the "entrance of Ventura," indicates that the location in question is without doubt Roça de Cima.[47] In fact, Charema or Charene is certainly a reference to *Tio* Xarene. It is probable that *Tio* Xarene had rented the spot from José Gonsalo and Amália de Oliveira, owners of the Boa Vista farm. If the *Sítio* Charene with its jackfruit was the same farm as Vicente Ferreira's, which appears in the 1860 document, one could speculate that the Portuguese name of *Tio* Xarene was Vicente Ferreira, although no documentation indicates that they were the same person.

In any case, it seems certain that before 1882, *Tio* Xarene controlled the land where Roça de Cima operated and that, from this date (perhaps coinciding with the death of *Tio* Xarene), José Maria Belchior assured the continuity of the terreiro, becoming the proprietor of the farm and perhaps also assuming the leadership of the congregation. This explains why today Roça de Cima is remembered as the candomblé of Zé de Brechó, even though it is known that Brechó was not a *pai-de-santo*. Roça de Cima is also known as the candomblé of Altamira, but this name only came to be used after the death of Zé de Brechó, when the land was sold and became part of a larger property known as Fazenda Altamira (see below).

The fact that *Tio* Xarene is recognized by Cachoeiran oral tradition as one of the "pillars of the Jeje community" and that his vodun was Azonsu (probably in the guise of Dada Zodji), indicates that he was the first *humbono*, or *papai de terreiro*, as they were called at the time, of Roça de Cima—it being common in Candomblé for the chief vodun of the terreiro to correspond to the "master of the head," or the orixá, of the terreiro's founder. In this context, *Ogã* Boboso affirmed that, in addition to Dandagojí (Azonsu), Ogun was also the "master of the terreiro," perhaps because Ogun was the "master of the head" of Ludovina Pessoa. Although there is no conclusive evidence, this information suggests a religious leadership shared between *Tio* Xarene and Ludovina Pessoa. In fact, oral tradition claims that *Tio* Xarene was Ludovina Pessoa's husband, though this could be a distortion of oral memory in order to express religious collaboration.[48] Independent of this possible marital relationship, as we have seen, in Benin and in many Bahian terreiros of the nineteenth century it was common for a man and a woman to share leadership of a vodun temple.

Ludovina Pessoa is the second, and perhaps the most important, figure in Roça de Cima's history. A number of reports from *O Alabama*, dated from 1866 to 1869, confirm that, in this period, *mamãe* Ludovina lived and carried out religious activities in Cachoeira, while at the same time attending and even organizing important ceremonies in various terreiros of Salvador. The first report from 1866 explains that during the period of the festival of Saint John, a number of women from Salvador went to Cachoeira and from there they "continued to a *roça* [small farm]" with a certain Lucrecia dos Pastéis being "taken captive and forced into a room of the house of an African named Ludovina." A second report, written in verse nine months later, indicates that during this time Lucrecia remained in the *casinha* (or *huncó*, the initiation room) and from there she left "dumb," no longer knowing how to speak the "language of the whites" (that is, during her initiation she spoke only the African ritual language), being placed by Ludovina herself in a house in Salvador in order to conclude her initiation and that, "after the passing of a year, and the cutting of her hair, ... her speech will reappear." It is possible that the "room in the house of an African named Ludovina," where Lucrecia was kept during the first part of her initiation, refers to the Casa Estrela of Cachoeira. As I have noted, Dias do Nascimento suggests that this was where the *vodunsis* were prepared during the long periods of initiation. Oral accounts attest that Ludovina Pessoa lived in the Casa Estrela, at whose entrance a shrine was "planted" for Legba, still visible today under a granite rock in the form of a five-pointed star. However, a farmstead near Cachoeira, where festivals were held, was undoubtedly the Chareme farm, which permits the conjecture that Roça de Cima was operating since at least the 1860s.[49]

Roça de Cima seems to have been the most important religious center of the Jeje community in Cachoeira, and the great high priestesses of Jeje Candomblé from the postabolition period were initiated there. It was probably in this con-

Warehouses in the city of Cachoeira (c. 1860–65). Photo: Camillo Vedani, in Gilberto Ferrez, *Bahia: Velhas fotografias, 1858–1900* (Salvador: Kosmos, 1988)

gregation that the liturgical model perpetuated at both Bogum in Salvador and at Seja Hundé was consolidated. Oral tradition confirms that it was at Roça de Cima that the first two *mães-de-santo* of the future Seja Hundé were initiated: Maria Luiza do Sacramento (Maria Agorensi) and Maria Epifania dos Santos (*Sinhá* Abalhe).[50] There is also some vague talk that it was there that the first two *mães-de-santo* of postabolition Bogum, Valentina and Maria Emiliana da Piedade, were initiated or underwent some preparatory ritual. And Maria Romana Moreira, who succeeded Emiliana, was certainly trained in Cachoeira.

The ultimate authority in these initiations, which would have involved various people, is not always clear. Oral tradition supports the idea that without Ludovina's consent "one could not *make saint* [perform initiations] in a Jeje terreiro." To Ludovina are normally attributed the initiations of Maria Agorensi, Valentina, and Maria Emiliana, although it is likely that some of them had been conducted at Bogum in Salvador, while *Tio* Xarene and/or Zé de Brechó are normally considered the *pais-de-santo* of Abalhe and Maria Romana, who were initiated together.[51]

According to *Humbono* Vicente, *filho-de-santo* of Maria Romana, at that time initiation lasted eighteen months, thus Abalhe began at fourteen and completed initiation at fifteen, and Maria Romana would have begun at eight and had her coming-out at nine and a half.[52] It is known that Abalhe, Maria Epifania dos Santos, died in December 1950, at the age of ninety.[53] If the age that appears in the obituary is correct, this would place her birth in 1860, and her initiation around 1874–75. However, it is said that the initiations of Maria Agorensi and Emiliana occurred before that of Abalhe, probably in the 1860s. It is clear that Ludovina initiated a number of other *filhas-de-santo*, such as the previously cited Lucrecia dos Pastéis, but what is important to emphasize is that the women who would decades later lead the most important candomblés of the Jeje-Mahi nation underwent training at Roça de Cima.

Ludovina Pessoa:
"The First Jeje Marrino *Mãe-de-Santo*"?

As I noted in chapter 4, the rise of a candomblé religious community is structured on relationships of cooperation, complementarity, and conflict among various congregations. In fact, the founding of a religious congregation or terreiro is always the result of the collective effort of religious leaders and a network of social relations that contribute to provide the necessary material resources, such as the land and the capital to bear the expense of the festivals. If Ludovina Pessoa and *Tio* Xarene were the religious leaders of Roça de Cima, they enjoyed the collaboration of influential figures among the emerging black elite, including Zé de Brechó, whom I discuss below.

However, Ludovina Pessoa seems to have attained a degree of leadership unparalleled among Jeje Candomblé of the third quarter of the nineteenth century. Although it is not improbable that a Jeje congregation existed previous to Ludovina, she appears as the uniting factor of this forming community, to the point that today oral tradition affirms that the African Ludovina Pessoa was "the first Jeje Marrino [Mahi] *mae-de-santo*." This version of history is summarized in a document dated January 12, 1943, on the occasion of *Humbono* Vicente's being awarded the *decá*. It describes the religious ascendency of his *mãe-de-santo*, Maria Romana Moreira: "Maria Romana Moreira of Possu Beta Pojaí, initiated by two legitimate Jeje Marrino Africans from the city of Cachoeira, from the terreiro of Tio Xarene, deceased, and Zé do Brechó, while the first Jeje Marrino *mãe-de-santo* was Ludovina Pessoa of Ogun Rainha, born in Africa. She had a terreiro in Cachoeira at Roça de Cima, with headquarters in Bougu. When she would come from Africa each year, she went to both terreiros. Without her permission, no one could make saint in a Jeje terreiro, so she would come to make vodun. And when she had finished, she would return to Africa."[54]

This 1940s version of the oral tradition presents many interesting pieces of information. It conveys the close relationship between Bogum in Salvador and Roça de Cima in Cachoeira. The fact that it speaks of Bogum as being the "headquarters" suggests, implicitly, that the Cachoeira terreiro was considered a branch and was founded later. This topic has spawned a long debate between the Jeje Mahi *povo-de-santo* of Salvador and that of Cachoeira. *Humbono* Vicente affirmed that actually it was "all the same terreiro, it was all united, but then the women argued with each other, and then it all became disunited. Some from Cachoeira say, here, this is freshwater Jeje and those from Bogum say that there it is salt water. It's a big mess. There used to be only one Jeje."[55] In 1961, the now deceased Runhó, *mãe-de-santo* of Bogum, declared that "the first *mãe-de-santo* [of Bogum] was Ludovina Pessoa, who was African."[56] However, those from Seja Hundé in Cachoeira and even some from Bogum maintain that the Cachoeira terreiro was founded first. The *Ogã* Celestino Augusto do Espírito Santo and the now deceased Nicinha of Bogum declared in 1987, "Ludovina Pessoa left Bogum (a city in Africa) and first opened a terreiro in Cachoeira de São Félix. . . . Ludovina Pessoa is one of the oldest *mães-de-santo*, but we know that she was not the first."[57]

The documentary evidence does not clarify which community came first. As we have seen, between 1866 and 1869 Ludovina lived in Cachoeira but received periodic visits from women from Salvador at Roça de Cima. At the same time, Ludovina traveled frequently to Salvador. A report in *O Alabama* from 1869 tells of the visit of "*mamãe* Ludovina, who lives in Cachoeira," accompanied by the "*Ogã* Ventura," to the terreiro of Maria Velhudinha in the "Barreiras" area on the outskirts of Salvador during the *fechar o balaio** festival, a ceremony that closes the annual cycle of ritual activities and coincides with the beginning of Lent. This *Ogã* Ventura, of whom I will say more below, was probably a tenant on the neighboring Ventura farm and must have participated in the religious activities of Roça de Cima. The prominence given to Ludovina, the first mentioned in a long list of attendees from Cachoeira, São Félix, Maragogipe, and Salvador, indicates her fame and prestige.[58] Another series of reports from May of the same year documents another festival, organized on a property in Cruz do Cosme (present-day Liberdade), which was led by Ludovina. This report was written in verse:

Know, with no exaggeration
That Ludovina's main function
Carried out at Cruz do Cosme
Was fulfilled with all compunction.

Apparently the festival involved a *zelim* "for the soul of a woman, *Totonia Fateira*," and the "candomblé" raged for many days. In the same week, Ludovina, "chief of the celebration," confirmed "in the house of *Bella*" an *ogã* by the name of Umbellino. It is not known if this house is the same candomblé as that of Cruz do Cosme, but at the end, the journalist describes there being "folk from Bahia, a multitude from Cachoeira, a herd from Sant'Amaro, and a throng from Feira." This indicates the amplitude of the religious community's social network and Ludovina's great capacity for drawing a crowd, confirming that she was one of the most respected Bahian Candomblé *mães-de-santo* of the time.[59]

These are the only contemporary records that I found concerning Ludovina Pessoa, and they certainly indicate close and periodic contact between Salvador and Cachoeira. However, there is no evidence of Ludovina's presence in Bogum, which, as we have seen, was led at that time by José Moraes, Isidoro Melandras, and the "negress" Rachel. This lack of documentary support does not invalidate the idea that Ludovina Pessoa, despite living in Cachoeira, had an important role at Bogum, as attested to by oral tradition.[60] In fact, the terreiro of Maria Velhudinha in Areias, visited by Ludovina, was the same one to which the group of initiates from Bogum was taken when they fled police persecution.

A legendary figure, Ludovina Pessoa has given rise to a great diversity of opinions regarding her life. *Equede* Santa from Bogum declared that Ludovina was the grandmother of Menininha (famous *mãe-de-santo* of the Gantois terreiro) and also that "Ludovina comes from the slave quarters."[61] Little is known of her past, however. In the archives I found four references to Africans named Lodovina or Luduvina who might correspond to Ludovina Pessoa.

The first reference records the baptism of a "Lodovina, Jeje adult, slave of Antonio José," in the parish church of Nossa Senhora do Rosário, in the city of Cachoeira, on January 12, 1810, with godparents Antônio Carvalho and Brazida Maria Trinidade, both Jeje.[62] If the "Gege" nation of this Lodovina favors her identification as Ludovina Pessoa, her age seems to complicate it. If she were an adult in 1810, by 1866–69, when hypothetically she appears in the *O Alabama* news stories, she would have already been very old.

The second document is the declaration of a "gege Luduvina," dated August 19, 1829, asking for clemency from the judge of Cachoeira after having been imprisoned as the result of an "enemy denouncement." Luduvina apparently wanted to ship twelve sacks of corn and beans belonging to her husband to Bahia without the necessary license, a problem that was finally resolved by the payment of a fine.[63] This Luduvina was married, perhaps residing on a farm, employed in agriculture and commercial activity, and thus very probably a freedwoman.

The third reference, incompatible with the previous, is a slave-payment record for a purchase that took place in São Félix on January 22, 1844: "Francisco Lopes de Faria paid [as an initial payment] half of ten percent of 350 mil-reis (17$500 reis), the price for which he purchased the African slave Luduvina from Antônio Manoel da Cunha."[64] The relatively low price suggests that the slave was rather old.

The fourth reference appears in a series of documents related to the letter of manumission obtained by a certain African Ludovina in Cachoeira in July 1858. Through her godmother, Carlota Maria da Conceição, Ludovina, a wage-earning slave above forty-five years of age, was able to buy her freedom for one *conto de réis* (1,000 mil-reis) from her mistress, the freedwoman Maria Jacintha Pereira, married to the African freedman Antônio Lopez Ferreira, who, in addition to Ludovina, possessed one other African slave. This letter of manumission was contested by Antônio Lopez, who wanted to sell Ludovina to a third party, but Maria Jacintha Pereira, having already received part of the money and alleging dementia on the part of her husband, won Ludovina's freedom.[65]

I am unsure whether one of these African Ludovinas is Ludovina Pessoa, but as Ludovina is a rather uncommon name, it is likely that one of them is. In the case of the last Ludovina, the date of manumission precedes by eight years the time when Ludovina Pessoa appears as the leader of Roça de Cima, at which time she would have been approximately sixty years old. The relatively high price, for the time, of the letter of manumission is noteworthy, and suggests a woman of demonstrated qualities. The intervention of the godmother Carlota Maria is in accordance with a common practice of the first half of the nineteenth century, by which the godparents of a slave assumed the responsibility of purchasing their godchild's freedom,[66] but it suggests also that Ludovina was part of a social network of solidary freed Africans, which included even her own mistress. The religious prestige of Ludovina Pessoa, certainly previously established in Africa, would have increased the solidarity that led to her freedom. The combination of these elements tends to strengthen the identification of this Ludovina, freed in 1858, as our protagonist.[67]

Another interesting piece of information from the 1943 document mentioned above is the claim that Ludovina would come "each year from Africa." This could be a legend, created to legitimize the authority of this priestess, but if it were confirmed, this fact could have important consequences in the religious sphere, for it suggests the introduction into Brazil of values and practices of the vodun cult after the period of the slave trade. However, examining the entry and departure records of declared African passengers in the inspection books of the Port Police of Salvador, between 1873 and 1889, I found only one Ludovina Maria da Encarnação, African, who departed Salvador on July 13, 1878, with Rio de Janeiro as the destination.[68] It is possible that Ludovina's trips occurred before 1873; in any case, the available evidence cannot confirm the oral tradition's version.

What appears certain is that Ludovina, moving regularly between Salvador and Cachoeira, must have been a freedwoman with certain economic resources, perhaps a *partido alto* or high-class woman, as they were called at the time. As to Ludovina Pessoa's saint or vodun, oral tradition is unanimous in affirming that it was Ogun, but some speak of Ogun Rainha, others of Ogun Tolo, and still others of Ogun Aíres.[69] Marcos Antônio Lopez de Carvalho, using information provided by Dias do Nascimento, affirms that "she was one of the African freedwomen who made up the Jeje [*sic*] sisterhood of the Senhor do Martírios, located in the Barroquinha Church [in Salvador]," and also "was a member of the Sisterhood of Nossa Senhora da Boa Morte [in Cachoeira]."[70] Dias do Nascimento adds that Ludovina was one of the founders of the devotion of Boa Morte. Though it is probable that she participated in one or more of these sisterhoods, there is as yet no documentary evidence of this.

One can be fairly confident that, in the 1860s, Ludovina Pessoa, together with other Jeje Africans and their descendants, founded, or at least consolidated, the leadership of Roça de Cima in Cachoeira, maintaining a strong collaboration with the Bogum candomblé, as well as regular contact with various other terreiros in the city. My hypothesis is that this was made possible by an elite of freed Africans and their descendants who, from the first decades of the nineteenth century, but particularly in midcentury, gained access to land and were able to establish a varied network of sociopolitical relationships with the white elite who could assure the functioning of these congregations. In the case of Roça de Cima, there is evidence of this in the third character of our microhistorical narrative: Zé de Brechó.

Zé de Brechó and the Emergence of a Black Elite in Cachoeira

José Maria Belchior, or Zé de Brechó, is legendary among the *povo-de-santo* of Cachoeira. He is famed as a feared sorcerer (*feiticeiro* or *ajé*) of "great power." He "knew how to make *feitiço*" and was "master of the *ebô*." He "could kill within twenty-four hours" any victim, or any client who owed him money.

The disputes between Zé de Brechó and his brother Salaco, or Antônio Maria Belchior, another renowned "macumbeiro," or sorcerer, are famous. According to Eugenio Rodrigues da Rocha, also known as Geninho: "When they would have a birthday, one would send a present to the other. And when they would receive the present, they would look and say: 'You tell him that there is still something missing.' It's just that no one knew what that thing was. One would test the other. At that time that's how things were. The sect had those wise men and the two most famous in Cachoeira were them."[71]

The story of the two brothers who did not get along lasted many years, and the now deceased Galdina Silva, better known as "*Mãe* Baratinha," of the Nagô-Ketu nation, told how "the two ended up dying from each performing so many works against the other." She would perform a ritual every May in the Rosarinho cemetery in honor of the two "babalawos Salachior and Belchior."[72] *Humbono* Vicente explained that Zé de Brechó "would turn into a heron and go to Africa." These "magic powers" of Jeje religious specialists are not unknown and it is believed that the *feiticeiros*, like the *Iyami Oxoronga*,* can transform themselves into birds. When the steamboat from Salvador would arrive at the Cachoeira dock and a heron would be spotted on the mast, people would whisper, "Here comes Zé de Brechó, returning from Africa."[73]

Certainly Zé de Brechó had profound knowledge of the religious practices and became an important Candomblé dignitary of Cachoeira, even buying the lands of Roça de Cima and leading the congregation. However, although it is said that he was responsible for the initiations of Abalhe and Maria Romana, it is not clear whether he actually became a *pai-de-santo*. *Ogã* Boboso recounted that he assumed the function of *olowô*, the priest who holds the secrets of Ifá; according to Dias do Nascimento, Zé de Brechó was consecrated to Dadá, a kind of Xangô, and had the title of *Dadá Runhó*.[74]

In addition to this image of the "sorcerer" preserved by oral memory, there is certain historical information concerning Zé de Brechó that reveals a more complex person. In reality, he was the descendant of an emerging black elite that appeared around the middle of the nineteenth century, and he eventually became a public figure of some repute, with free access to every social level in Cachoeira and Salvador.[75] Contrary to what oral tradition suggests, he was not African but Creole, the first-born son of an African couple—Belchior Rodrigues de Moura and Maria da Motta. He was probably born in Cachoeira in January 1836, when his father was still a slave.[76]

On August 14, 1855, the year of the "great epidemic" of cholera that devastated the Recôncavo, Belchior Rodrigues de Moura, "fearing death in consequence of the current epidemic," made his will in Salvador. In it he declares that he was "baptized in the dogmas of the religion of Jesus Christ" and that he was "born on the Coast of Africa, coming to this capital, while still a child, I was purchased as a slave at auction by Senhor José Rodrigues de Moura from whose power I freed myself with the amount of 600 mil-reis, on February 1, 1841." Belchior Rodrigues de Moura died, as he feared he would, on September 27, 1855, in Cachoeira, leaving Maria da Motta, an African with whom he was never actually married, and five children: José Maria Belchior, nineteen years and eight months old; Antônio Maria, sixteen years old; Maria Aniceta, thirteen years old; Magdalena, four years old; and Juliana, two years old.

At that time, Belchior Rodrigues de Moura possessed six African slaves, one "to work the land" and the rest "for wage-earning labor," two houses in Recuada, as well as "a piece of land in Capapina that occupies three farms, one belonging to the deceased, and the others to Joaquim So-and-So and José So-and-So." The total value of Belchior Rodrigues de Moura's properties amounted to the considerable sum of two *contos* and 548 mil-reis.[77] The lands were registered on August 17, 1858, by Maria da Motta in the name of her sons, specifying that they were bordered "to the south by the road to Belém, and to the north by the road to Capapina."[78] According to Dias do Nascimento, it was precisely on these lands that the legendary Oba Tedô *quilombo* operated. The designation of tenants as "So-and-So" (*de Tal*) indicates that they were Africans or Creoles, but besides suggesting a concentration of black farmers, there is nothing that points to the existence of a candomblé, much less a *quilombo*.

How, in the fourteen years from 1841 to 1855, was Belchior Rodrigues de Moura able to buy his freedom and purchase lands, two houses, and six slaves? At the time of his death, Belchior had debts of one *conto* and 391 mil-reis, that is, approximately half of his patrimony. It seems therefore that, besides the income from the land and wage-slaves, he retained the money for loans, normally "received in cash." However, it is not known how he invested his money or what his "business" was.[79] Is it possible that Belchior Rodrigues de Moura acted as a "banker" for Africans? Was he the "head of a manumission society," a kind of African economic fund created to make loans for the purpose of buying slaves' liberty? Another business that provided quick riches was the illegal trafficking in slaves. Might Belchior have been involved in such activities? Did he perhaps travel to West Africa during this time? These are questions with no answers at this time. What is conclusive is that, though his property was modest and his debts substantial, Belchior Rodrigues de Moura was a freedman belonging to an emergent black elite in Cachoeira, with land, the capacity to control economic resources, and a social network that extended from the Recôncavo to Salvador.

With the death of his father in 1855, José Maria Belchior, at almost twenty years old, inherited, in equal parts with his younger brother, Antônio Maria Belchior, the slave Felippe and the lands of Capapina. In the following years, his mother, Maria da Motta, who was, according to oral tradition, a *vodunsi* of Roça de Cima and a member of the Boa Morte sisterhood, faced serious difficulties in paying her husband's debts: two slaves died and others took advantage of the circumstances to free themselves. This situation fragmented and considerably reduced the family estate. At this time, her sons exchanged the old tenants at Capapina for new ones, perhaps in an effort to increase their income.[80] It is likely that the fact that they possessed one wage-slave and the lands of Capapina conferred on the Belchior brothers income and a certain social status in the local black community.

In the voter records of Cachoeira for the years 1871–75, José Maria Belchior and his brother Antônio Maria Belchior are listed in the Thirtieth Recuada district. The first declares his profession to be that of carpenter and the second, that of joiner. By 1880, the brothers claimed to know how to read and write and have an annual income of 400 mil-réis; they listed "business" as their profession, all of which indicates a certain social ascension.[81] In fact, in 1874, the brothers became members of the Sociedade Monte Pio dos Artistas Cachoeiranos (Cachoeiran Mount Pio Artists' Society), a society for aiding the arts and professions. The society was founded that year at the residence of the artist José Clarião Lopes but later held its meetings in the council room of the São Benedito Brotherhood, in an annex of the Nossa Senhor d'Ajuda chapel, where, in fact, the Boa Morte sisterhood also operated.[82] This connection between the Monte Pio society and the São Benedito brotherhood is significant.

The brotherhood or devotion of São Benedito was established in the Ajuda chapel by free and slave Creoles in 1818.[83] In it participated a number of amateur black musicians who made up the Banda Marcial de São Benedito (São Benedito Marching Band). But the Musical Corporation of Nossa Senhora d'Ajuda (later the Sociedade Lítero Musical Minerva Cachoeirana) operated in the same chapel and was created by "erudite" whites connected to the Cachoeiran oligarchy, who instituted the Nossa Senhora d'Ajuda brotherhood. Because of political conflict between the two groups, which culminated around 1871 in an inquest and lawsuit, the Banda Marcial de São Benedito had to abandon the chapel and move to the Conceição do Monte church, which was the religious center for the city's liberal faction. Because the brotherhood of Santa Cecília (patron saint of black musicians) had been founded in this church on May 13, 1872, the members of the former marching band became the Orféica Lira Ceciliana Philharmonic Society. The Monte Pio Society, the São Benedito brotherhood, and the Lira Ceciliana Philharmonic thus constituted a network of institutions in which the black elite of Cachoeira articulated their social visibility and their liberal and abolitionist interests, in opposition to the politically conservative faction, associated with the Minerva philharmonic, the Ajuda brotherhood, and the church of Nossa Senhora do Rosário, or Matriz.[84]

Although the Belchior brothers do not appear in the Record Book of Active Members of the Monte Pio Society, in May 1874, three months after the society's foundation, José Maria Belchior participated in the general assembly and spoke of "various points related to the statutes," and on October 18, after the ratification of the statutes, the two brothers paid their dues of twenty milreis. From early on, they occupied important positions. Antônio Maria was treasurer for 1877, 1879, 1880, and 1892, and a member of the Police Commission of the same society for the years 1884 and 1885. Antônio Maria participated more regularly than his brother in the activities of the society, but it was José Maria Belchior who attained greater notoriety. In addition to assuming the office of treasurer in 1878, on February 28, 1886, he was elected vice president; that November he appears as the interim president and, on February 20, 1887, he was elected president, a position he would maintain until March 10, 1889.[85] Again, he was owner of Roça de Cima and, in addition to his professional ascension, he must have enjoyed a certain social visibility as the director of an important religious congregation.

As the leader of the Monte Pio Society, José Maria Belchior faced a period of economic difficulties resulting from the loss of its endowment caused by failed financial transactions and by the society members' failure to pay their monthly dues. However, during the period of his administration, between 1886 and 1888, the society experienced a growth in members, going from ninety-one to 103 active members, from twenty-two to twenty-five honorary members, and from three to four benefactor members. In his reports he showed an apparent financial transparency with detailed calculations of accounts, attributing the deficits to the "accounting mistakes" of the previous administrations, and in his speeches he seems quite eloquent and well versed in the oratorical arts. On a number of occasions, he suggested that the Monte Pio Society had enemies who would like to see it fail, and he spoke of the "vicissitudes, obstacles, and animosity that had developed against the society in order to prevent it from becoming, as it has become, an institution."[86] This "animosity" very probably came from the conservative and traditional faction of the Cachoeiran oligarchy who saw in the society an organized threat from the black popular class, represented by its literate, liberal, and abolitionist elite.

On May 13, 1888, the day on which was "passed by vote and sanctioned the

Law that extinguishes and abolishes slavery within this Empire," José Maria Belchior, in his capacity as president of the Monte Pio Society, called a special meeting in which, after a number of speeches, a congratulatory telegram that he himself had signed was sent to Princess Isabel. Afterward, those present attended a popular demonstration "composed of more than 8,000 people" and accompanied by "two Orchestras." From the window of the society building, Pedro Vianna de Abreu, Cachoeira's public prosecutor, proffered "a luminous discourse . . . after which the Ceciliana Philharmonic, which was positioned in front of the building, performed a song worthy of the achievement, and then both orchestras played the national anthem."[87]

Even as ex-president, in September 1889, José Maria Belchior was named head of a Monte Pio Society commission to receive His Highness the Count d'Eu, husband of the Most Serene Imperial Princess, during a visit to Cachoeira. According to the society's proceedings, "His Highness was gratified and thanked Monte Pio for the proof of their consideration." This fact did not impede Belchior from joining the Republican Party and from, in October of the same year, becoming a candidate for municipal councilor representing that political party. He finished thirteenth in the voting, which conferred on him the post of secondary municipal councilor.[88] One month later, on November 20, José Maria Belchior signed, together with other Cachoreiran individuals, a declaration of allegiance to the Republic.[89]

Certainly because of his association with the Monte Pio Society, José Maria Belchior was named president and trustee of the Conselho Filial de Cachoeira do Centro Operário (Cachoeiran Subsidiary Council of the Workers Center) of the State of Bahia, an organization founded in 1896 and dedicated to the development of the arts, professions, and trades.[90] It is believed that Zé de Brechó was a Freemason and, although this cannot be confirmed, his association with the societies of arts and trades makes it quite probable.[91]

Among his many social relationships with the local elite, his friendship with Commander Albino José Milhazes—a Portuguese-born naturalized Brazilian, influential politician, wealthy businessman, exporter, tobacco industrialist, and large landowner—stands out. Milhazes was a trustee of the brotherhood of Nossa Senhora da Conceição do Monte, whose church, as I have noted, united the liberal political faction of Cachoeira, counting as allies other tobacco merchants such as Gerald Dannemann and Costa Penna, as well as the representative and abolitionist attorney Prisco Paraíso. It is also significant that on July 15, 1883, Milhazes was accepted as an honorary member of the Monte Pio Society, which tends to confirm that institution's liberal character.[92]

In addition to being the leading secondary municipal councilor, José Maria

Belchior, possibly toward the end of his life, was named a captain in the National Guard.[93] The Belchior brothers were also members of the Rosarinho Brotherhood, and Antônio Maria at least appears many times as a signee on the death records of Africans who were interred in the brotherhood's cemetery.[94] In fact, on April 16, 1902, Antônio Maria records the death of his brother, perhaps putting into doubt their legendary enmity. José Maria Belchior died a "victim of syphilis, on his farm in the site of Boa Vista," that is, at Roça de Cima, or Charema farm, which neighbors the Boa Vista farm. In this document, Zé de Brechó is named a "citizen," a term used only for distinguished individuals, and as "single, a landowner, first Secondary Municipal Councilor of this city, and a captain in the National Guard, his body being transported to the Mother Church where his funeral will take place, after which he shall be entombed in the Rosário cemetery of that brotherhood."[95]

Some days later, in a public notice in the *A Cachoeira* newspaper, the family of the deceased "shows their everlasting gratitude to those friends and acquaintances who, during his illness came to visit him and sooth the suffering of their much missed relative, never abandoning him, and who, after his death, took part in the numerous procession accompanying him to his final resting place." In this manner the family also gives thanks to "Vicar Heráclio Mendes da Costa; to the Municipal Council of this city, in which the deceased participated; to the various societies who left inscribed wreaths in homage—Montepio dos Artistas Cachoeiranos, Benefícia Cachoeirana, and Centro Operário. To the Minerva Filarmônica and União das Artes that played the funeral music and of which the deceased was a member. To the noble friends of the deceased, Drs. Emiliano and Joaquim Viegas, residents of Bahia, Joaquim Correia da Silveira e Souza, and Pedro Alexandrino Belmiro, who presented special wreaths" (APRC).[96]

This demonstrates how Zé de Brechó, son of a freed African, managed to consolidate and expand the social ascension begun by his father, eventually becoming a distinguished public figure with influential contacts among the elite of Cachoeira and Salvador. It is the resources and privileges of this black elite, in this case of a first-generation Creole, together with the religious experience of the last and old Africans, such as Ludovina and *Tio* Xarene, that explain the operation of terreiros such as Roça de Cima. The social prestige of Zé de Brechó and his position as a captain in the National Guard likely contributed greatly to the expansion of the terreiro and to assuring the tranquility of its activities without excessive repression. His enterprising and progressive character together with his demonstrated gifts as a leader led him to buy the lands of the Jeje candomblé in 1882, from which time he presumably directed the congregation.

The Founding of Seja Hundé on the Ventura Farm

If the Roça de Cima Jeje candomblé was operating by the 1860s, in the following decade, and especially after the 1880s, Cachoeira experienced an unprecedented phase in the growth of Nagô candomblés. In the second half of the nineteenth century, the sugar plantation economy of the Recôncavo entered into decline, leaving great numbers of the rural black population unemployed. But from 1870 to 1880, German investors installed mechanized cigarette and cigar factories in Cachoeira and São Félix that caused an important immigration of poor freed slaves seeking work in these new industrial centers.[97] This concentration of black urban population, the consolidation of a black elite of successful artisans and landowners, and the social ascension that religious activity offered to the unemployed black population in the postabolition period explain, in part, the progressive establishment of relatively stable religious congregations.

Based on interviews conducted in the 1980s, Fayette Wimberly identified two candomblés in the Cachoeira and São Félix area founded after 1850—Roça de Cima and the Capivari candomblé of Anacleto Natividade—and nine others, all Nagô, founded after 1870. Wimberly documented primarily the candomblé of Anacleto Urbano da Natividade, a Nagô slave and overseer of the sugar mill of Nossa Senhora da Natividade at the Fazenda Capivari, near São Félix, the property of Colonel Umbelino da Silva Tosta (1831–81). Through his skills as a "healer," demonstrated during the cholera epidemic in 1855, Tio Anacleto of Omolú was authorized by his master to maintain the terreiro, providing medical and spiritual assistance to both the slaves of the plantation and the free and freed clients in the area. The *barracão** of the candomblé, constructed around the trunk of an imposing cajá tree, consecrated to Saint Roch or Obaluayê, is still active today. According to oral testimony collected by Wimberly, this tree is dedicated to Iroko or to the vodun Loko. Wimberly also mentions that the stream that runs through the terreiro was protected by a great serpent that would appear and disappear according to the will of the gods. These indications led Rachel Harding to suggest a multideity cult strongly influenced by Jeje tradition.[98]

Although it is difficult to determine the date of the establishment of the other candomblés, it is likely that some of them existed only after abolition in

1888. In São Félix oral tradition recalls the terreiro of Neves Moreira of Ogun and that of Cajazeiras, founded by the Creole Luciano Barreto of Ogun Bomi, known as *Tio* Salu.[99] In the suburbs of Cachoeira, on the road to Terra Vermelha, José de Vapor, the grandchild of Nagô slaves, founded the Viva Deus terreiro. In the same area, *Tia* Judith, a descendant of Nagôs and a relative of Anacleto do Capivari, led the house of Aganjú de Deus, or perhaps Aganjú de Dê. In Cachoeira's urban center, on Beco do Sabão, the Nagô candomblé of Maria Agueda de Oliveira was already operating at the dawn of the twentieth century. *Sinhá* Agueda was of Iemanjá and was born at sea, when her mother, the African *Tia* Sofia of Olissá, was coming from Africa. Maria Felicidade da Conceição, of Nagô origin and known as *Tia* Malaqué de Xangô, opened an African house behind where the Chafariz, or main fountain, currently stands, and she was succeeded by her biological daughter, Maria Galdeça da Conceição, who died in 1910 (Maria Galdeça was the paternal grandmother of *Gaiaku* Luiza and *Seu* Geninho). At Lagoa Encantada, on the road to Belém, Porfira, better known as Aleijadinha, had another candomblé, which was famous for its presents to the *mãe d'água* (water spirit). According to legend, these presents offered at Lagoa Encantada later appeared in the Dique do Tororó (Tororó Dam) in Salvador. Other names remembered from this period are Canuto, who died at an advanced age in 1914; *Pai* João, a feared Jeje *feiticeiro*; *Tio* Luiz; and *Tio* Fado.[100]

In addition to the various Nagô "subnations" that are spoken of, such as Nagô-Agavi, Nagô-Tedô, Nagô-Congú, or Nagô-Jexa, it is worth noting that the Nagô ritual of the Recôncavo, which was characterized by its own songs and by the use of small drums played with the hands, was different from the Nagô-Ketu tradition known in Salvador. The Nagô ritual of Cachoeira, in addition to the singularity of its Yoruba origin, was influenced by the Jeje tradition, and the cult of the Jeje vodun Bessen was common in some of these establishments. However, it would be more accurate to speak of a mutual interpenetration of ritual elements, which at the end of the nineteenth century, gave way to the tradition called by the *povo-de-santo* "Nagô-Vodun" or "Nagô-*Vodunsi*." The predominant Nagô-Ketu ritual in Salvador only became popular in Cachoeira quite late, in the 1930s, with the establishment, in Portão near Muritiba, of the Ilé Ibece Alaketu candomblé of Manoel Cirqueira de Amorim, who was also known as Nezinho do Portão and was closely connected to *Mãe* Menininha of Gantois.[101]

In view of the great proliferation of Nagô terreiros at the end of the nineteenth century, the relative unity maintained by the Jeje in the Roça de Cima area is notable. It is only in the first decades of the twentieth century that there is talk of another Jeje candomblé in the region—the Jeje-Dagomé candomblé of Vitoria of Fazenda Caju, near Maragogipe—where one could arrive only by boat or horseback going along the road of the Bom Jesus beach.[102] However, in the last decade of the nineteenth century, there appears to have been a schism at Roça de Cima. As mentioned previously, along the border of Roça de Cima was the Ventura farm, which in 1860 was the property of Luiz Ventura Esteves. There worked an African or Creole remembered as *Vovô* Ventura, very probably the same "*Ogã* Ventura" who accompanied Ludovina Pessoa at Maria Velhudinha's candomblé in Salvador in 1869.

One version of oral tradition maintains that Ventura "married" Maria Luiza Sacramento, Maria Agorensi, Ludovina's *filha-de-santo*, while another claims that Ventura only took her as a mistress or that he was her "companion." It was probably because of this relationship that Maria Agorensi, with help from Ludovina, opened a new terreiro on the Ventura farm—Seja Hundé—known as the Roça do Ventura or the Ventura candomblé, which remains active to this day. Aguesi, also known as Eliza Gonzaga de Souza, niece of Maria Agorensi and an important *vodunsi* of Seja Hundé, related how, when she was born in 1903, *Vovô* Ventura had already passed away. She added that, when Maria Agorensi became the *gaiaku*, the couple separated, possibly for religious reasons that place sexual restrictions on the leader of a candomblé, and he went to live in a smaller house near the present-day *barracão*. "Ventura was said to have sold cassava, and everyone went to buy cassava from Ventura." Some affirm that Ventura had no religious position and that he was "only the landowner," while others claim that he was *alabê*, or drummer, of Seja Hundé and that his saint was Badé. The second hypothesis seems more probable when we recall his position of *Ogã*, which *O Alabama* referred to in 1869.[103]

The supposed ownership of the lands of the Ventura farm by Ventura, an idea maintained by scholars such as Dias do Nascimento and Carvalho, has not been proved. *Humbono* Vicente and *Ogã* Boboso claimed that Ventura was merely a tenant who took the name of the property's former owner, Captain Luiz Ventura Esteves, an *engenho* owner and resident of the São Sebastião de Passé parish.[104] However, in the friendly division of the goods of the captain (who died on February 26, 1885), there is no mention of the land in Cachoeira.[105] It is therefore likely that Luiz Ventura Esteves sold the Cachoeira lands to an unknown third party before his death.

Humbono Vicente, *Ogã* Boboso, and *Seu* Geninho all affirmed that the Ventura property was at some point part of the neighboring Engenho do Rosário. In the 1880s, this plantation belonged to the previously mentioned Commander Albino José Milhazes. After the death of Milhazes in 1891, the property was inherited by his wife, Silvia Milhazes, who in 1895 sold it to the Francisco Cardozo & Silva Company. In 1900, however, Captain Albino José Milhazes, the commander's son and owner of the neighboring Faleira farm, again purchased the land and buildings of the Engenho do Rosário.[106] It is likely that, thanks to the friendship between Zé de Brechó and the Milhazes family, Maria Agorensi was able to purchase the portion of the Engenho do Rosário that today makes up Seja Hundé. *Ogã* Boboso said that the document of purchase is dated 1901 or 1909. *Seu* Geninho confirmed that Maria Agorensi bought the Ventura land for 200 mil-reis, and that the document was drafted by a notary called Sapocaia. Following Agorensi's death, this document passed through the hands of *Pejigã* Miguel Rodrigues da Rocha, and should today be in the hands of *Ogã* Boboso, but it was never presented to me, nor did I find any record of it in the court registry. The ownership of the land is a very delicate subject, and the information regarding it is quite confusing. *Humbono* Vicente suggested that Maria Agorensi and her successors had only tenant rights to the land and not the property's deed.[107]

Although some believe that Ludovina Pessoa was the first *doné* or *gaiaku* of Seja Hundé, most affirm that the first *mãe-de-santo* was Maria Agorensi, it being Ludovina's duty merely to direct the rituals in order to "plant the *fundamento*."* Oral tradition affirms that Maria Agorensi was able to purchase the lands of the candomblé some years after it opened, which would imply that it occurred previous to 1901. The most conservative conjecture would date the establishment of the terreiro in the late 1890s. As we have seen, in 1896 Zé de Brechó officially registered the property of the Charema farm, which until then had only been recorded in private documents. It is likely that this indicates a certain fear on the part of Zé de Brechó of losing possession of the lands as a result of the succession disputes at the candomblé.

It is also unknown when Roça de Cima ceased to operate. Oral tradition is contradictory as to whether Roça de Cima and Seja Hundé operated simultaneously for some years. *Humbono* Vicente asserted that Roça de Cima existed first "where the Africans lived. . . . later the saint [the vodun Bessen] asked that the terreiro below be opened. . . . it started up, and then went down. . . . among the Jeje there is only one terreiro." In contrast, *Ogã* Boboso maintained that both terreiros operated simultaneously for some time and that there existed a liturgical connection between the two. "There is only one Bessen, but he has the power to look after both."[108] According to this opinion, the *vodunsis* of Seja Hundé, during their initiation and the festival cycle, would go up to Zé de Brechó's Roça in order to carry out certain rituals, among them perhaps the *boitá** (see chapter 8). According to *Ogã* Boboso, Maria Agorensi "left amiably and went to follow her own path." Aguesi said that "Agorensi founded it and the people of Ludovina joined."[109]

What seems clear is that when Ludovina Pessoa and Maria Agorensi opened Seja Hundé, they did so with the participation of a significant number of members from Roça de Cima. This may have complicated the simultaneous operation of both terreiros. I do not know if the split was spontaneous and harmonious. But the transference of a number of dancers from one house to another generally indicates internal dissent. There is also talk that at that time Zé de Brechó had taken the young Maria Epifania dos Santos, *Sinhá* Abalhe, as a mistress, and that she, apparently, did not follow Maria Agorensi. My own impression is that, after Maria Agorensi left, Roça de Cima continued to operate, perhaps rather precariously, for some years yet, with the help of those who remained faithful to Zé de Brechó. Certainly, with his death in 1902, Roça de Cima definitively ceased to exist.[110]

One other question remains as to the nation or ritual modality practiced in these two terreiros. While there is unanimity that Seja Hundé was a Jeje-Mahi terreiro (Marrin or Marrino), some assert that the Roça of Zé de Brechó was Jeje-Mundubi. How does a house with religious ancestry in a Mundubi terreiro change its nation and come to be Mahi? Aguesi insisted in distinguishing between the initiation of Maria Agorensi, carried out by Ludovina, and that of Abalhe, carried out by Zé de Brechó, as if they had been performed not only at different times, but perhaps also in accordance with different religious precepts.[111] Everything seems to indicate that Jeje Africans of diverse origins gathered at Roça de Cima, and that maybe these differences of religious tradition explain the breakup and departure of Ludovina Pessoa and Maria Agorensi.[112] In any case, Seja Hundé, since its inception, and certainly after Roça de Cima ceased to operate, inherited some of the Roça de Cima shrines and came to juxtapose the Mundubi and Mahi vodun cults (see chapter 7).

The history of Seja Hundé thus begins with Maria Agorensi, probably in the postabolition period. The era of terreiros such as Roça de Cima, led largely by African men, had ended, and the epoch of candomblés led largely by Creole women had begun. As *Seu* Geninho affirmed, in the past "Jeje was a Mason's lodge, there were only men, there were no women."[113] It is worth pointing out that probably at about the same time, in the 1890s, in Salvador, the Bogum terreiro recommenced activities under the leadership of the Creole Valentina, whose family name is not remembered and who was perhaps initiated in Cachoeira by Ludovina. These facts coincide with a general expansion of candomblés in the postabolition period that included, as we have seen, an increase in Nagô terreiros, as well as others exhibiting a Congo-Angola influence, that for their part aided the expansion of the so-called *Cabaclo* Candomblé. Before presenting the histories of Seja Hundé and Bogum in the postabolition period in the next chapter, I should present some side notes examining the etymologies of these terreiros' African names.

Etymologies of the African Names of Bogum and Seja Hundé

The African name of the Bogum candomblé is unanimously recognized as *Zoogodô Bogum Malê Rundô*, while that of the Seja Hundé candomblé is normally identified as *Zoogodô Bogum Malê Seja Hundé*. The similarity of the two names only confirms the close relationship between both terreiros and the idea maintained by oral tradition that at some point in the past they constituted a single religious community, divided into two congregations. This similarity also implies that the founders or members of one community participated in the establishment of the other. It is important to point out that *Zoogodô Bogum Malê Seja Hundé*, sometimes rendered as *Ceja Undé*, is the name of the candomblé of Ventura, and there is no evidence that Roça de Cima or the farmstead of Xarene ever had this name. For this reason, in the present study, I avoid the use of this name in relation to Roça de Cima. My hypothesis is that Seja Hundé received this name because of Ludovina Pessoa's participation in its founding. She is also recognized as a founder or active member of Bogum. In this sense—and this is also maintained by part of the oral tradition—Seja Hundé (but not Roça de Cima) can be seen as a "branch" of Bogum, which because of its historical precedence is the "original source."

Lébéné Philippe Bolouvi analyzes in detail the etymology of the *Zoogodô Bogum Malê Rundô* name for Bogum. I agree with him in that, from a linguistic point of view, the absence of identifiable grammatical monemes probably indicates a juxtaposition of isolated forms, perhaps from different linguistic origins. Bolouvi speaks of a "strategic" juxtaposition of terms that lie in more or less direct relation to the cult house's establishment, that is, in relation to the ethnic diversity of the terreiro's founders.

For Roger Bastide and Waldeloir Rego, the term *bogum* is a corruption or alteration of the term *vodun*, but, as Bolouvi points out, this is a questionable interpretation if one considers that *vodun* is one of the phonetic forms of African origin introduced into the Americas that most resisted change, having preserved itself in its original form despite orthographic variants in Bahia, Maranhão, Haiti, Cuba, and other regions of the New World.[114]

I have already discussed the interpretation offered by Antônio Monteiro and Jehová de Carvalho in which they identify the term *bogum* as the name of a coffer or chest (*baú*) in which was kept the gold to finance the Malê Revolts in the early nineteenth century, and which the Malê slave Joaquim, of Jeje origin, hid at the candomblé. Bolouvi, discounting the idea of *bogum* as an alteration of *baú*, but accepting the idea of the presence of Malê fugitives at the terreiro, further suggests that this Malê Joaquim would have been of Borgu origin, a region located to the north of Benin whose population was partially Islamic, and suggests that *Bogum* is a deformation of this toponym.[115] Alternatively, for some members of the terreiro, Bogum is the name of one of the house voduns, and indeed one of the three terreiro's *atabaques** is said to be consecrated to Bogum. This would be a version of Dan, associated with a type of black serpent with a red crest and common in the terreiro's region until the 1950s.[116]

My own hypothesis is that, initially, Bogum referred to a small village of the Mahi country, probably located between present-day Agouagon and Soklogbo, to the east of Savalou (see map 4 in chapter 1). In 1926–28, J. A. M. A. R. Bergé, a French colonial administrator who wrote on the history of the Mahi peoples, described the exodus of the Guedevi who, forced from the Abomey plateau by the arrival of the Agasuvi, were scattered throughout the Mahi country. At some point, probably in the eighteenth century, a group of Guedevi led by Djerho and departing from Agouagon, found along their way, in the middle of the forest, "a small Adja village called Bogoun," where they stayed for some time. Allied with the Adja of Bogoun, Djerho later drove out the Nagô of Soclogo Mountain (now Soklogbo), where he settled permanently. The people of Ouoko, another group of the Abomey plateau, under the leadership of Dossa-Glé also passed a long period of time in Bogoun during their northern migration.[117] If one trusts the oral traditions collected by Bergé, it is possible to suppose that some of the Bogum founders, whom we know identified themselves as being of the Jeje-Mahi nation, had come from the Bogoun village in the Mahi country. At the same time, it is not uncommon in the Gbe-speaking area for toponyms to be derived from the names of voduns and vice versa.

As to the term *Zoogodô*, Antônio Monteiro believes that it is an onomatopoeic vocative in praise of Xangô.[118] This interpretation is quite credible, and seems even more convincing when one considers the term as a compound of two names: Zò and Ogodô. Zò, which in Fongbe means fire, is also the name of a *hunve* vodun in Benin, literally "red vodun," associated with the family of thunder deities, principally Sogbo. As for Ogodô, it is known that, along with Afonjá, they were two names given to Xangô in the land of the Tapa.[119] Therefore, there is a reiterative duplication alluding to thunder deities in both the Jeje and Tapa traditions, which might indicate a simultaneous Jeje/Tapa participation in the founding of the terreiro. There is, for instance, the presence of a Tapa among the various Jejes in the repression of the Pasto *Calundu* in Cachoeira in 1785, which was mentioned above. The allusion to these thunder deities in the name of the terreiro makes more sense when one considers that the family of Sogbo, the thunder vodun of the Jeje, is regarded as the Bogum "royal family" (see chapter 7).

Furthermore, the duplication of ethnic denominations of the same god seems also to reproduce itself in a variant of the Seja Hundé name, which, according to some, is *Zo Ogodo Dangara Seja Hundé*.[120] In this instance, the term *Dangara* is a contraction of Dan and Angoro, these being the Jeje and Angola names, respectively, for the vodun associated with the serpent, in the case of Seja Hundé, the deity that is the "master of the terreiro." As happens with Zo and Ogodô, one finds in the name of the Cachoeira terreiro the duplication of ethnic variants of the gods central to the cult, which, once again, suggests the participation of various African "nations" in its founding. In Seja Hundé, as we will see, this is not the only evidence of the possible interpenetration of elements of the Angola tradition.

The meaning of *Rundô* is not known. The root *run* is clearly an alteration of the word *hun*, which, in high tone, is a synonym for vodun and, in low tone, means drum. However, the word *hundo* has no clear meaning. It may be a variant of *hunto*, which can designate the *atabaque*, or drum, player or the one responsible for the sacrifices, or it may be an evolution of *hundé*, the term that appears in the name of the Cachoeiran terreiro. However, there is also no convincing interpretation of the expression "Seja Hundé," though some believe it to be a name for, or a quality of, Dan, the serpent-vodun. *Ogã* Romão of Bogum, in transcribing information related by *Humbono* Vicente in 1964, renders the term as "Sôyan-ôdei."[121] Yet again the first term seems to be an allusion to the thunder voduns, as *sô* means thunder in Fon and *ayyan* or *soyan* is the name of the bush consecrated to Sogbo.[122] Might *ôdei* be a reference to the hunter vodun Odé? Alternatively, Felix Iroko documents Hundé as one of the most important mythical ancestors of the city of Hevié, the birthplace of the Hevioso thunder cult.[123]

There is therefore no satisfactory interpretation and the subject remains open to future, more detailed, studies. I agree with Bolouvi's general thesis that the names of these terreiros seem to be a juxtaposition of independent terms, most of them references to major voduns of the cult, whose origin should be sought outside of Jeje or Gbe linguistics. And this very fact seems to reflect the ethnic hybridity that existed in the founding of the terreiros.

6 Leadership and Internal Dynamic of the Bogum and Seja Hundé Terreiros in the Twentieth Century

Continuing with the historical reconstruction of the Bogum and Seja Hundé terreiros, this chapter examines the leadership and internal dynamic of these congregations in the twentieth century. Additionally, the end of the chapter presents information on other Jeje terreiros that operated during the same period. I discuss Seja Hundé first, beginning with table 5, which presents the names, nicknames (or names by which they were commonly known), voduns, and the likely period of leadership of its successive *gaiakus* (one of the titles used among the Jeje to designate the *mãe-de-santo* or leader of the house).

The Period of Maria Agorensi

The first *gaiaku* of Seja Hundé, Maria Luiza do Sacramento, whose *ruim* or ritual African name was *Arrunsi* Missimi (probably a deformation of *Hunsi Mesime*), was known as Agorensi Mesime or Maria Agorensi. *Agorensi* is the title given to those *vodunsi* consecrated to the vodun Bessen, the head of the Jeje-Mahi nation.[1] It is believed that she was initiated by Ludovina Pessoa before 1875, and, according to the *vodunsi* Aguesi, her initiation lasted two years. Though she is considered African by some, she was born in Nagé, near Maragogipe, in approximately 1840. Those who knew her in her old age, in the early decades of the twentieth century, say she had grey hair, used a cane, and had the habit of sitting on a four-footed stool that had a small hole in the center. *Seu* Geninho recalled her as a "grumpy old black. . . . she was stern and always went about with a stick. . . . she was thin, very rigid, and serious, hard in her old age, everyone feared her."[2]

It is likely that she belonged to the Irmandade do Senhor Bom Jesus dos Matírios (Brotherhood of the Martyrdoms) and to Cachoeira's sisterhood of Boa Morte (Good Death), which we know included many women from the Jeje terreiro. In her obituary, dated May 3, 1922, Aristides Gomes Conceição, former *ogã* and resident of Roça do Ventura, declared that: "At two o'clock in the afternoon, on the Ladeira da Praça, passed away from long suffering, his

TABLE 5 Seja Hundé Leadership

Period	Name	Alias	Vodun
c. 1896–1922	Maria Luiza Sacramento	María Agorensi	Bessen
1934/37–50	Maria Epifania dos Santos	Abalhe	Bessen
1957/62–69/71	Adalgisa Combo Pereira	Pararasi	Parara
c. 1978–94	Eliza Gonzaga de Souza	Aguesi	Agué
1994–2007	Augusta Maria da Conceição Marques	Lokosi	Loko

kinswoman Maria Luiza do Sacramento, at over eighty years of age, parents unknown, single, a native of Nagé, resident of this city; she will be buried at the Misericórdia cemetery, in a tomb of the Irmandade dos Matírios."[3]

Little is known of the early years of Maria Agorensi's governance at Seja Hundé. The available information indicates that the highlight of her leadership occurred in the 1910s, when she turned out two *barcos*, or groups of initiates. In the decades previous to this, the candomblé must have functioned basically with members from Roça de Cima, but the long period necessary to organize the first initiations is significant, probably indicating a gradual consolidation process of the congregation's social network. According to *Gaiaku* Luiza, Maria Agorensi was assisted by three *derés*, *mães pequenas* or seconds in command. The best-known *deré* was Custódia of Oiá, but *Deré* Madalena and *Deré* Isidora are also remembered. These positions were assumed simultaneously, but each *deré* had separate responsibilities.[4]

According to Aguesi, Maria Agorensi's first group of initiates consisted of eight *vodunsis* and the second of twelve. At that time the initiation lasted six months, three months inside the *hunco* and three months outside, a substantially shorter period than those of the Roça de Cima's initiations, which, as I have mentioned, lasted two years or a year and a half. The first group was probably secluded in 1914 and consisted of (1) *Dofona* Bela of Azonsu, (2) *Dofonitinha* Milu of Oiá, (3) *Fomo* Eliza Gonzaga de Souza of Agué, (4) *Fomotinho* Antônio Pinto of Oxum Dei, (5) *Gamo* Edwirgem of Oxum Nike, (6) Dagmar of Akotoquem, (7) Joana Boca da Noite of Sogbo, and (8) Virginia Moreira of Olisá.[5]

For the second group of twelve, I do not have the date, but logically the initiation must have occurred between 1915 and 1921. I am also ignorant of the names of those who constituted it; *Gaiaku* Luiza, however, in a show of her admirable memory, provided me with a list of the *vodunsis* from Seja Hundé during the time of Maria Agorensi. In addition to the eight initiates already mentioned, she cited the following names: (9) Leonidia of Oxum, (10) Lizarda of Oxum, (11) Antonia of Oiá, (12) Maria Custódia de Assis of Oiá, (13) Virgilio of Bessen, (14) *Dofona* Esmeralda of Azonsu, (15) *Dofona* Gina of Nanã, (16) Miúda of Nanã, (17) Naninha of Nanã, (18) Cecília of Aziri, (19) Marciana of Aziri, (20) Miúda of Kposu, (21) Raimunda of Odé, (22) Santinha of Badé, (23) Fausta of Badé, (24) Arcanja of Badé (Badesi Arcanja), (25) Joana Delfina of Sogbo, and (26) one whose orixa was Akorombe.[6] This is a high number of *vodunsis*, which indicates the importance and the success of the candomblé during that time. Systemizing the number and names of the voduns, we have: one of Odé, one of Agué, two of Azonsu, four of Oxum, three of Oiá, two of Aziri, one of Kpo, two of Sogbo, three of Badé, one of Akorombe, three of Nanã, one of Olissá, one of Bessen, and one of Akotoquem.

Besides the *mediums*—those who dance possessed or entranced during rituals—a terreiro cannot survive without the aid of *ogãs* and *equedes*. In 1914, before the first group of initiates had been gathered, five *ogãs* were confirmed, some of whom became eminent figures among the congregation: (1) *Pejigã* Miguel Rodrigues da Rocha; (2) *Ogã Senevi* Tomas de Aquino Bispo, better known as *Ogã* Caboco Acaçá; (3) Fernando; (4) Ermírio; and (5) Agapito.[7] In addition to these, the following are also remembered: (6) Aristides Gomes Conceição, a "relative" of Maria Agorensi; (7) *Ogã* João, *hunto* (drummer), the son of *Deré* Custódia and younger brother of *Ogã* Caboco; (8) Sergeant Endinho; (9) *Ogã Minazon* Luís Gonzaga, the father of Aguesi; and (10) Renato Gómez Conceição, the son of Aristides, known as Congo de Oro, of Iemanjá and Sogbo. This last was a suspended, or unconfirmed, *ogã*, but he later left the terreiro. Among the *equedes*, *Gaiaku* Luiza remembered Doninha and Tatu, daughters of *Ogã* Aristides, Cecília, Antonia, Neném, Cotinha, Zelina, Ana, and Isabel. *Seu* Geninho also mentioned Dadi, the sister of his father, Miguel Rodrigues da Rocha, and Masu, his paternal half-sister.[8] From this approximate survey of the composition of the Seja Hundé congregation some important names should be highlighted. Eliza Gonzaga de Souza, Vivi of Agué Aboro, *Etemin* Aguesi, the daughter of Luís Gonzaga (the *ogã minazon* of the candomblé) and the biological niece of Maria Agorensi, was nine or ten when she was selected as a member of the first *barco*. She became *gaiaku* of Seja Hundé in the 1970s. Her sister, Maria Ana do Carmo, was an *equede* of Bessen; her brother, Fernando, was confirmed as an *ogã* of Bessen in 1914, and her sister, Valentina was initiated later, during the time of Abalhe, as a *fomotinha* of Nanã.

Among the *vodunsis*, who were for the most part women, the presence of two men is worth noting: Antônio Pinto, *fomotinho* of Oxum Déi, initiated with the first group, and Virgilio of Bessen, initiated in the second.[9] The *fomotinho* of Oxum attained greater renown. It seems that the decision to initiate a man caused quite a debate, and it did not happen until Oxum possessed Antônio, who spent an entire night in the spring of Oxum, so that the old women would accept him into the initiation room. However, it is said that "*fomotinho* did not complete his ritual and fled to Rio still wearing his *kele** necklace."[10] There, he made many *filhos-de-santo*, and though he modified many ritual aspects, he became the "carioca root" of Jeje-Mahi candomblé (see below).

One of the most influential figures at Seja Hundé during this time was *Seu* Miguel Rodrigues da Rocha, who was married to Nagô descendant Cecília Ovídia de Almeida. They were the parents of *Gaiaku* Luiza, *Seu* Geninho, and Joana (the latter initiated to Azonsu during the time of Pararasi). In 1914, *Seu* Miguel was confirmed as a *pejigã*, or *ogã* in charge of the *peji*, a position corresponding to second-in-charge after the *mãe-de-santo*. His participation in the religious activities of the candomblé, together with his post as protector, mediator, and maintainer of the terreiro, reminds one in many ways of the charisma of Zé de Brechó.

According to the account given by his daughter *Gaiaku* Luiza, *Seu* Miguel was of Badé with Oxalá and Iemanjá. He was a physically imposing man, tall and strong, and had a butcher's shop in Cachoeira. Around 1918, he worked as a sailor, and it is said that he sailed to Africa. He was involved in politics and was a bodyguard of Commander Ubaldino Nascimento de Assis. His daughter claimed that "he was a Getúlio Vargas," adding that "he lived with bullets in his belt." The elections of the time involved frequent disturbances and shots being fired between the rival factions.[11] After one of these elections, *Seu* Miguel was forced to flee to Rio, working there as a foreman and mason on the construction of the Palácio do Catete (the presidential palace), only returning to Cachoeira in 1922. He died in 1966 as a city inspector. He obtained a certain degree of political and economic power and helped to finance the festivities in the times of Maria Agorensi. Whenever *Pejigã* Miguel arrived at the terreiro, he was greeted with drumming.[12]

Ogã Caboco, known as Caboco Acaçá and whose real name was Tomás de Aquino Bispo, was the son of *Deré* Custódia and of *Ogã Seu* Agapito, but his nursemaid was Dona Cecília, the wife of *Seu* Miguel. At eleven years of age he was confirmed as an *ogã senevi*, along with his biological father, *Seu* Agapito, and *Seu* Miguel. He was also a very good *hunto* (*atabaque* drummer). With time, *Ogã* Caboco would come to be an *ogã impe*, in charge of the animal sacrifices. He also "gave his hand," that is, he would help in other Jeje houses such as Bogum, the house of *Gaiaku* Luiza, his adoptive sister, or that of *Humbono* Vicente. According to *Humbono* Vicente, it was *Ogã* Caboco who was most knowledgeable at Seja Hundé, "when his life ended, everything ended." *Ogã*

Pejigã Seu Miguel (seated), *Ogã Senevi* Caboco Acaça (with watch), and two other *ogãs* from Seja Hundé (c. 1960)

Caboco died in the 1970s, in Belo Horizonte.[13] His brother, João, was also *ogã hunto* and his sister, Gina, was a Nanã *vodunsi*.

From this information one can make out a complex web of kinship ties among the congregation's members, which would only grow throughout the terreiro's history. This seems to be characteristic of Jeje terreiros in general, in Bahia as well as in the Casa das Minas in São Luís, Maranhão. A significant number of *vodunsis*, *ogãs*, and *equedes* are recruited from among the members of certain families of African descent and these blood ties are perpetuated through the generations. *Seu* Geninho spoke of the *povo de veia*, or "people of the vein," to refer to these people as opposed to the visitors or participants who did not belong to such families. In the early days of Seja Hundé, the important participation of relatives of Maria Agorensi and of *Deré* Custodia, as well as the influence of *Pejigã Seu* Miguel, stands out. This associative dynamic based on kinship, perhaps the most basic form of intergroup solidarity, is generally wisely used by the religious leadership to strengthen and maintain power.

This phenomenon is neither recent nor exclusive to the Jejes. As I suggested in chapter 4, it was precisely these kinship ties (in the nineteenth century between Africans and their Creole descendants) that permitted the formation of domestic congregations and, later, the rise of the candomblés. Together with blood ties, the religious kinship established by way of the initiation processes contributed to the formation of internal alliances among various groups of the congregation that, during the periods of conflict, such as the succession disputes, can manifest in the form of competing factions.

The period from 1914 until the death of Maria Agorensi in 1922 thus seems to mark one of the highest points in the history of Seja Hundé. Perhaps two decades after its founding, the terreiro attained one of its "golden ages." *Seu* Geninho, born in 1906, witnessed these events in his childhood. In testimony collected by Marcos Antônio Lopez de Carvalho, he remembered vividly and with longing the splendor of the Ventura candomblé of that time.

> We lived in Ventura for a long time. . . . our house was in front of the higher *peji* [altar]. It was a two-room house with a straw roof built by my father. There was a row of houses, all of straw, where the old-timers like Senhor Aristides, Tia Custódia, and *Dofona* Gina lived. . . . The candomblé there on Ventura Farm began the day. There were those sellers who would come from Cachoeira to sell their little treats. All night long, with the kerosene lamps lit, they would sell boiled peanuts, pastries of coconut and sugar, and *pé-de-moleque*. . . . At the farm, during festival time, there was a dive joint that sold cigars, cookies. . . . Roça do Ventura, in Cachoeira, there was nothing like it. During the time of the Boitá festival, you don't even want to know! All Cachoeira came up, all those businessmen: Senhor Ricardo Pereira, Senhor Luís Reis, and all those families would come to enjoy the Boitá. It was the candomblé that shook up Cachoeira. Many authorities would come, such as *Sinhá* Porfiria from Terra Vermelha, Aleijadinha from Lagoa Encantada, Zé de Vapor from Terra Vermelha. . . . He had a *filho-de-santo* called Edgar of Oiá, who was very highly regarded at Roça do Ventura. . . . *Sinhá* Abalhe was always present, she never abandoned Maria Agorensi; the same was true of Possusi Romaninha. The latter only spoke in Jeje, no way would she speak in Portuguese! Everyone from Bogum would come, and when there was a festival there, everyone from here would go there. There was an *ogã* called Bomfim, and he spoke Jeje very well. He would come to Caquende, to bathe with *Ogã* Caboco, and they would speak only Jeje. As a boy, I remember them passing leaves over their bodies and speaking Jeje.[14]

This testimony evidences the extensive social network that existed between the candomblé and the civil society, it also especially highlights the indispensable communication and exchange of visitors among the various terreiros of the region, many of them Nagô, but some of them also Jeje from Salvador, such as Bogum, and Campina de Boskeji. Through these ties of complementarity the social visibility of a candomblé is measured and legitimized, and the more varied they are, the greater the prestige of the congregation. Regarding the visits from people from Campina, *Humbono* Vicente commented that, when they arrived, they would sing, requesting permission to enter, ritually saluting Seja Hundé, which, according to him, is the name of the vodun Azonsu, head of the household:

Ere ere bi oyo
Campina tere na do
Ere ere bi oyo
Seja Hundé mina do.[15]

When Maria Agorensi died in 1922, this closed one of the most notable chapters in the history of Seja Hundé. As is customary in the Jeje tradition, with the death of the *mãe-de-santo* the funerary rituals (*sirrun* or *zelin* in the Jeje tradition, *axexé* in the Nagô tradition) are initiated. The first ritual requires the presence of the deceased body and lasts one week, with others following after one month, three months, six months, one year, three years, and seven years. In these seven years the activities of the candomblé are normally on hold, that is, the public festivals are not celebrated, nor are new *vodunsis* initiated, although certain internal rituals, such as nonblood food offerings at the altar, may be maintained. In any case, these periods of transition in which the new *mãe-de-santo* must be selected are normally characterized by internal power conflicts.

The Period of Abalhe

After 1922 Seja Hundé ceased activities for more than a decade. Some say that it was eleven years, others that is was fifteen.[16] According to *Gaiaku* Luiza, "Agorensi died. The terreiro remained closed for eleven years. The people left and many did not return. Abalhe gathered up her own."[17] It was therefore around 1933 or 1937 that Maria Epifania dos Santos, *Sinhá* Abalhe, was finally able to take charge as the new *gaiaku* of the candomblé.

It is worth noting that the 1920s, when both Seja Hundé and Bogum were inactive, was the period of the greatest police repression of Candomblé, in Salvador as well as in the Recôncavo.[18] It is also significant that the 1930s, when both terreiros recommenced their activities, was a time of progressive tolerance of Afro-Brazilian cults. In 1937 intellectuals such as Edison Carneiro and Aydano do Couto Ferraz, with the participation of *pais-do-santo* such as Eliseu Martiniano do Bomfim, promoted the Second Afro-Brazilian Congress in Salvador, which contributed much to the social recognition and valorization of this religious tradition. One year later, in 1938, "the practice of candomblé, *batuques*, and other black religious manifestations, was liberated, thanks to the intervention of the chief of staff of the Vargas government, Oswaldo Aranha, who had connections with the Axé Opô Afonjá branch in Rio."[19]

I do not know to what extent this external factor contributed to the reopening of Seja Hundé and Bogum, but other internal dynamics, besides police repression, seem to have been more critical in explaining an interregnum that lasted more than the seven years of mourning. Everything indicates that this delay resulted from internal dissent regarding who could and should assume the post of *gaiaku*. Lopez de Carvalho sums up the account told him by *Gaiaku* Luiza, which agrees with the one I heard:

> The *vodunsis* of the house, or rather, the *filhas-de-santo* of Maria Ogo-rensi, would not accept that *Sinhá* Abalhe assume the leadership of Ventura, and that was the reason it remained closed for so long. No one is sure of the reason why the old *filhas* of Maria Ogorensi would not accept *Sinhá* Abalhe, but the population of Cachoeira says that it was because she was initiated not at Ventura but rather at Roça de Cima. That the heir of the terreiro should be a daughter of the house and not a sister of Maria Ogorensi (in this case the "aunt" of the *vodunsis*). They also say that *Sinhá* Abalhe suffered much in order to gather all of the house *vodunsi* back around her, and that in taking charge she was confronted with someone who threateningly drew a line in the ground with a knife, and she was even slapped with a slipper on her face by her "nieces." According to *Gaiaku* Luiza, [the person] who succeeded in getting the *filhas-de-santo* to support her was the Azonsú of one of the old *vodunsi* [Luiza Moreira of Avimaje][20] who, manifesting through her medium, said that Bessen's terreiro should not become a cow pasture, and that it was about time that the *filhas* returned and accepted the new *Gaiaku*. And thus it was that the *vodunsi* came back little by little.[21]

But not all of them returned. *Pejigā Seu* Miguel, with his family, for example, withdrew from Seja Hundé from that period on. It is known that after the death of Maria Agorensi, the *peji*'s key, perhaps the greatest emblem of power in a terreiro, was passed first to *Pejigā* Miguel, but later, highlighting the differences that had arisen between Abalhe and Miguel, it was passed to the *Ogā Impe* Caboco Acaçá.[22]

This is a good example of the "social drama" with its four phases as described by Victor Turner: breach, crisis, redressive action, and, in this case, a combination of reintegration and schism. Thus we can see, confirming Turner's theory, how the group resorts to ritual (divination, divine manifestation, and probably other activities) to settle the conflict and reestablish the internal order of the congregation.[23] As a last resort, the divinities, appealing to the *communitas* or union of the group members, sanction the solution of the problem. Ritual and the belief system operate in a dialectic manner, as both mechanisms of transformation and overcoming conflict and as maintainers of cohesion and social order. However, as we will see below, this reparation is but partial and, beneath the group's apparent reintegration remain latent divisions and tensions between rival factions, dissent that reappears with new breeches, generally occasioned by the death of the congregation's leader or the weakening of religious power.

The rivalry between Abalhe and the *filhas-de-santo* of Maria Agorensi perhaps derived from the old differences between Abalhe and Maria Agorensi herself. As I have noted, it is possible that early on, Abalhe remained faithful to Zé de Brechó in Roça de Cima. It is also probable that after his death, Abalhe functioned as an independent religious specialist. Aguesi recounted how a Jeje man by the name of Epifânio Santa Rita gave the *decá* to Abalhe and that this ceremony was performed in Corral Velho (present-day Praça Marechal Deodoro); it of course could not have been performed in Seja Hundé "because of the other woman [Maria Agorensi]." This festival lasted three days and was very well attended.[24] At some point, Abalhe came to participate in the Seja Hundé terreiro. According to *Seu* Geninho, from what he heard from older participants, Maria Agorensi performed a ritual with Abalhe to "take the hand from the head" of her original *pai-de-santo* (*Tio* Xarene or Zé de Brechó), who was Mundubi. From then on Abalhe was Agorensi's lieutenant, helping with and accompanying her in all the activities of the candomblé.[25]

In any case, after assuming the position of *gaiaku*, around 1934 or 1937, Abalhe was able to return Seja Hundé to what it had once been, with many *filhas-de-santo*, many tenants, and many domestics living there and working for the good of the terreiro, with well attended festivals that attracted important members of other congregations from the Salvador area. *Sinhá* Abalhe's rule, from 1935 to 1950, constituted the second and perhaps the last "golden age" of the Seja Hundé terreiro.

Like her forerunner, Maria Epifania dos Santos was of the vodun Bessen, and her African name was *Arrunsi* Lufame (*Hunsi* Lufame), better known as *Fomotinha* Agorensi Abalhe, or simply Abalhe, sometimes pronounced "Abalia," "Abalha," or "Abalié," which was an honorific title.[26] Her obituary says she was born in Cachoeira, where she lived in various houses. *Ogã* Boboso

Maria Epifania dos Santos, *Sinhá* Abalhe, member of the Nossa Senhora da Boa Morte Sisterhood (c. 1950). Photo: Pierre Verger

mentioned one in Recuada that had one room that was "closed because of the amount of sacred stones kept there." He adds that Zé de Brechó, who had taken her as a mistress in the 1890s, lived upstairs.[27] She was a sister in the Boa Morte devotion and a member of the Martírios and Rosarinho brotherhoods.[28]

According to *Seu* Geninho, "everyone feared the tongue of *Sinhá* Abalhe," but she did not make her living from religion; in the words of *Humbono* Vicente, "she did not perform divination or religious services for clients."[29] According to Miguel Santana, a respected businessman and *ogã* at Axé Opô Afonjá, "she was small, black, quite dark. . . . she had a stall next to the Rosário church where she sold peanuts, tapioca cakes, bits of dried meat, sugar-apples. She did not sell goods from West Africa, no one did in Cachoeira, everything was sold here in Salvador."[30] Miguel Santana was at that time seeing Maria Cidreira da Anunciação, whose ritual name was Badesque (probably Badesi, a devotee of the vodun Badé) and who, according to him, was "second in charge after the *mãe-de-santo* there at Engenho do Rosário." Because of this, he was a guest for eight days at Seja Hundé, where he had the opportunity to confirm Abalhe's reputation as a devotee of the vodun Bessen: "There was something going on there, and I didn't know what it was, I only heard this noise: *shee . . . sheee . . . shee . . .* and nothing more. Later I found out that it was the snake that Abali took care of. But what a strange thing, huh? Frankly it scared me, but she said: 'Don't be afraid, nothing to be scared of, here you may rest easy.' She also bred some snakes in the Caquende River, so in the morning she would carry cut meat in a basket and go to the river; near the foot of some mangabeira trees she would take some leaves; I don't know what kind of leaves they were;

Ambrósio Bispo Conceição, *Ogã* Boboso (c. 1999). Photo: Fernando Araújo

she would mash them, spread them over her body, get herself all ready, and then she would sniff and then blow into the water and call the snakes by name. Then they would come out of the water, sticking their heads up. Whenever one would come out that she hadn't called, she would say: 'No, this one first, you wait.' And didn't it just wait? It was there at the famous Caquende."[31]

I have been unable to gain precise information regarding how many groups of initiates *Sinhá* Abalhe turned out. *Humbono* Vicente said that the number was two or three; *Gaiaku* Luiza claimed it was three. The *vodunsis* initiated during that period who are remembered without doubt include (1) *Dofona* Adalgisa of Parara (Pararasi), who would succeed Abalhe in the 1960s; (2) *Fomotinha* Valentina of Nanã, biological sister of Aguesi; (3) *Gamo* Augusta Maria da Conceição Marques of Loko (Lokosi), the last *gaiaku* of Seja Hundé; (4) a man, *dofono* of Bessen; and (5) Edith Moreira, the daughter of *Ogã* Caboco. Those who were also probably initiated by Abalhe are (6) Maria José of Oiá, (7) *Tia* Dada of Azonsu, (8) Valentina of Bessen, and (9) her biological daughter, of Akotoquem, who was born in the initiation room.[32]

Between 1936 and the early 1940s, the following were confirmed simultaneously: (1) Ambrósio Bispo Conceição, *Seu* Boboso of Sogbo, as *ogã kutó*, and (2) *Seu* Bernardinho of Lissá, cousin to Aguesi, as *pejigã*.[33] These are the two oldest members still active and preserving the knowledge of the Seja Hundé rituals. Others also remembered as participants from this time are (3) *Ogã* José de Abalhe, Abalhe's nephew raised by her in Recuada; (4) Sátiro Humberto da

Bernardino Ferreira dos Santos, *pejigã* of Seja Hundé (c. 1999). Photo: Fernando Araújo

Silva, better known as Pássaro Preto, *ogã minazon* and *ogã* of the vodun Loko of Augusta da Conceição Marques; (5) José Magno Ferreira dos Santos, more commonly known as Zé Careca, *ogã* of the Oiá of the above-mentioned Maria José, brother of *Seu* Bernardinho and of Sergeant Edinho, *ogã* during the time of Maria Agorensi; and (6) *Ogã* Baba, who lived in Rio. Among the *equedes*, some of those remembered include *Tia* Dadi, sister to *Pejigã Seu* Miguel; Maria Ana do Carmo of Bessen, paternal half-sister of Aguesi and niece to Maria Agorensi; her daughter, Maria São Pedro dos Santos, known as Valdelice of Agué, confirmed as *equede* of Bessen; and Bela, wife of *Ogã* José de Abalhe, who is still active.[34] It is worth noting how, in Abalhe's time, kinship ties remained important in the recruitment of members and in the social structure of the candomblé.

As *Ogã* Boboso recalled, *Sinhá* Abalhé was a much loved *mãe-de-santo* who got along very well with people. The Nagô candomblé of Anacleto, in Capivari, in São Félix, had a strong connection with the Ventura candomblé. She was also a good friend of *Seu* Aprígio of Sogbo, of the Jeje-Mundubi Pó Zerrem terreiro. The strong ties with the leader of the Pó Zerrem terreiro are understandable, since *Sinhá* Abalhe was religiously descended from the same tradition. The visits of Tata Aprígio to Seja Hundé are fondly remembered, and it is said that on these occasions *Sinhá* Abalhe, wearing clogs made of hoof, would dance the *mundubi*, the name of a dance specific to that nation.[35]

The Mundubi tradition was characterized as one giving much importance to the ancestral cult, and, in fact, *Seu* Aprígio helped Abalhe to install (*assentar*) the *kututo*, the "house of souls" or of the spirits of the dead, in Seja Hundé. This innovation is seen by some religious specialists as an unwanted change, as it is a practice that is foreign to the Jeje-Mahi tradition, in which everything is done "in Aizan, all obligatory rituals to the dead are done through Aizan" (see chapter 8).[36] At Seja Hundé there existed Maria Agorensi's original altar, located in a room toward the back of the *barracão*, but Abalhe was also responsible for the installation of a second altar, in an annex constructed to the side of the *barracão*. It is likely there that she installed the shrines that she had had in the Recuada house, some perhaps coming from Roça de Cima, a fact that, again, suggests important alterations of the terreiro's liturgy.

Although Seja Hundé was still closed at the beginning of the 1930s, Abalhe and those close to her helped in the founding and initiation of the first group of initiates of Ilê Ibece Alaketu Axé Ogun Megege, the first terreiro of the Ketu nation to function in the Cachoeira region.[37] Its collaboration with those of the Jeje terreiro is a good example of the flexibility that existed within the dynamic of religious cooperation outside of the supposed "borders" of the Candomblé nations. Concurrent with these "transnational" collaboration processes, the people of Seja Hundé could maintain contentious relations with terreiros of their own nation. The disputes between Abalhe and the feared Badesi Arcanja, the old Ventura *vodunsi* initiated by Maria Agorensi who had a "Jeje-Dahomey" terreiro in Maragogipe, are well known. *Gaiaku* Luiza spoke of "war" and "bad politics" between the two terreiros. The death of Badesi Aranja in the 1940s is attributed by some to these quarrels, which included activities of "witchcraft."[38]

The highly hierarchized structure of the candomblé congregations is always centered on the *mãe-de-santo*. The dynamism and the social visibility that Seja Hundé acquired under Abalhe's management were especially notable for her skill in articulating and manipulating a network of political relations that involved, depending on the time, alliances or dissidence with both individuals and groups that extended outside the realm of Candomblé. Abalhe's participation in the sisterhood of Boa Morte of Cachoeira, for example, offered her a parallel space for the management of these micropolitics. In any case, with the death of a candomblé's leader, it is as if the community loses its center of reference, the magnetism that holds its members together.

At five o'clock in the morning on December 1, 1950, Silvia França de Jesus, an old *vodunsi* from Roça de Cima, a friend and neighbor of Abalhe in Recuada,[39] declared that at "number 15, Rua dos Remédios [formerly Rua Belchior], in the city of Cachoeira, died Maria Epifania dos Santos, female, black, age ninety— single, worked from home, resident of Cachoeira and born in Cachoeira, parents now dead—her death was natural, and its cause was confirmed: sudden death with no medical attendance, by Doctor Agualdo Sampaio, and the burial will occur in the Piedade Cemetery. She left no goods, and no heirs—either legitimate or otherwise."[40] Her initiation-mate, Romana Moreira, took charge of the ritual that precedes burial, this despite having arrived late from Salvador, at a point when the coffin was already at the cemetery.[41]

With the passing of *Sinhá* Abalhe came the end of an epoch in the history of the candomblé, and Seja Hundé would never again know such splendor. With the death of Abalhe came new succession and leadership disputes. On November 10, 1950, three weeks before Abalhe's death, Maria Emiliana da Piedade, *doné* of Bogum, had died. This caused important changes in the internal dynamic of Bogum, one result of which was a disruption of the strong relationship that had traditionally existed between the two Jeje-Mahi terreiros of Cachoeira and Salvador. The 1950s, therefore, seems to mark a transition point in the history of these terreiros and the beginning of what one might call their "modern period," as opposed to the "olden times." Taking advantage of this circumstance, I will now return the narrative to Salvador to take up again the history of the Bogum terreiro, from its reopening in the postabolition period until the 1950s.

Bogum in the Postabolition Period: From Valentina to Emiliana (c. 1890–1950)

As we saw in chapter 5, until 1870 Bogum was operating under the direction of José Moraes, Isidoro Melandras, and the "negress" Rachel, probably also relying on the help of Ludovina Pessoa. What occurred at Bogum during the last three decades of the nineteenth century is still a mystery. The oral tradition of Bogum claims that, after Ludovina, the candomblé closed until around 1890.[42] Although there is no confirming evidence for this date, it does coincide with the period during which Seja Hundé was supposedly founded. On January 17, 1961, in an interview given to researchers from the Centro de Estudos Afro-Orientais (CEAO), Valentina Maria dos Anjos (Runhó), at that time the head of Bogum, and her son, *Ogã* Amâncio de Melo, when asked about the house's religious ancestry, answered: "The *mãe-de-santo* is Valentina, her last name has been forgotten. Her saint is Adaen [Sogbo Adan], which corresponds to Xangô

TABLE 6 Bogum Leadership

Period	Name	Alias	Vodun
c. 1890–c.1920	Valentina	—	Sogbo Adaen
c. 1937–c.1950	Maria Emiliana da Piedade	Miliana	Agué
1953–56	Maria Romana Moreira	Romaninha	Kpo
1960–75	Valentina Maria dos Anjos	Runhó	Sogbo Adaen
1978–94	Evangelista dos Anjos Costa	Nicinha	Loko
2002–present	Zaildes Iracema de Mello	Índia	Azonsu

in Ketu. The *pai-de-santo* is Manuel da Silva, who was of Ogun, but the saint did not descend upon him."[43]

Valentina and Manuel da Silva were certainly active in the first decade of the twentieth century, but very little is known regarding the process and the moment of the reopening of Bogum in the postabolition period. Before proceeding with an examination of this period and in order to help organize the account, I present in table 6 a chronological list of the *donés*,[44] or *mães-de-santo*, who led Bogum in the twentieth century.

Nothing is known regarding Valentina's origins. Some say that she was a Creole and was initiated by Ludovina Pessoa. Some say that Valentina and Manuel da Silva lived together as lovers, although another tradition would have Manuel da Silva as married to Dominguinha.[45] Runhó and her son spoke of Manuel da Silva as a *pai-de-santo*, but according to Everaldo Duarte this was merely a courtesy title. *Equede* Santa of Nanã, Runhó's biological sister, claimed that "Manoel da Silva lived in front of Bogum, was a young boy, and had a house there. He made his living cutting palms to make oil, he took care of the terreiro. . . . it happened that he went to Bogum . . . and was suspended as *ogã*." The same sources note that when Bogum was reopened, Manuel da Silva was not yet a confirmed *ogã*. According to Duarte, Manuel da Silva "managed those lands. He made a promise to Oxalá that if he won a court case, he would reopen the terreiro." It would seem that he achieved the desired results with justice and kept his promise.[46] This collaboration in the opening of the terreiro and his alleged romantic relationship with Valentina could explain why Manuel da Silva, although officially a suspended *ogã*, enjoyed great power among the congregation, to the point of being remembered as a *pai-de-santo*.

As is the case with Seja Hundé, the early years of Valentina's leadership at Bogum are obscure, but it is reasonable to think that, in the first decade of the twentieth century, the terreiro was already functioning with a certain stability, for around 1910 Valentina gathered her first group of initiates, consisting of eight *vodunsis*, celebrating the completion of their initiation in June 1911.[47] Oral memory recalls only the names of three of the women from this group: Runhó of Sogbo, Dadu of Ogun, and Anita.[48] All remained active until the 1960s.

Runhó emphasized that "at the time that I made saint there were still Africans in the house.... Tianna Gege, the *mãe-pequena* here, she's before Emiliana, she had the mark of her tribe on her face. Tiana is from the time of my *pai-de-santo* [Manuel da Silva]." The interviewers commented that Runhó and her son "make quite a distinction when they speak of Africans and Brazilians. Valentina shows true veneration when she refers to Africans."[49] Therefore, in Bogum, the coexistence of Africans and Creoles lasted well into the twentieth century.

The historical reconstruction of the transitory period between Valentina's governance and that of her successor, Maria Emiliana da Piedade, is complicated by the lack of reliable documentary evidence. According to the house's oral tradition, Valentina and Manuel da Silva died in approximately 1920 and the terreiro remained inactive for some years until 1935, when Emiliana took over.[50] Runhó explained that "there was the first house that belonged to the Africans, then we, the *caboclos** [Brazilians], came along. This house was built in 1927."[51] There is nothing to imply that the new house was not constructed during the interregnum, in order to satisfy the congregation's housing needs. But, if what was built was a new *barracão* or dance hall, such an undertaking could indicate a recommencement of religious activities, when Emiliana assumed the post of the new *gaiaku*. It remains to be seen whether Runhó's memory, which dates this event to 1927, is completely reliable.

The Portuguese writer Edmundo Correia Lopes, the first author to write of Bogum in the postabolition period, visited the terreiro in September 1937 during the celebration of a *zelim*, or a funerary ritual. He commented that at that time "Bôgúm was awaking from a long sleep. I saw the house being worked on, though whether simply to enlarge it or to retrieve it from ruins, I cannot say. One year or more after the passing of she who reigned as *mãe-de-terreiro*—I heard tell she was an African woman who had come from Dahomey to work for an Englishman—the community was about to celebrate her funerary rites, to perform the final and solemn *despacho*."[52]

According to this account, Emiliana came to power in 1937, which seems to be a plausible hypothesis, for, besides being in rough agreement with the terreiros' oral tradition, which dates the event to 1935, it is contemporary evidence of the facts provided by an eyewitness. The fact that the house was, at that very time, under construction suggests that the building of the new *barracão* occurred in 1937, and not in 1927, though, as Correia Lopes points out, the construction could have been merely an addition to the building. More problematic seems to be the identification of the deceased as the *mãe-de-terreiro*, who "reigned" a "one year or more" ago. This would imply that Valentina lived until approximately the 1930s and that she was African, which contradicts the oral versions that have her as a Creole and dates her death to around 1920.

On this point the information of Correia Lopes, which he himself recognizes as somewhat uncertain as he only "heard tell," seems a bit unreliable. One could speculate that the "African woman who had come from Dahomey to work for an Englishman" was not Valentina but the African Tiana Gege, who, according to Runhó, was active in 1911 and was the *mãe-pequena* of Bogum, "previous to Emiliana." Despite the proverbial longevity of Africans, to find an African in Salvador in 1911 would have been something exceptional; to find one in the 1930s, even more so, and if she arrived in Brazil before the cessation of the slave trade (1850), she was very probably a centenarian.[53]

As to the date of the death of the woman I presume to be the *mãe-pequena* and not the *mãe-de-terreiro*, it could be 1936, though Correia Lopes leaves it somewhat doubtful with his "one year or more." Yet one should not exclude the possibility that the funerary ritual was one of the *zeleins*, performed three and seven years after the death, as happens in Candomblé with members of the upper hierarchy. Moreover, it would not be unthinkable that Tiana Gege, as *mãe-pequena*, had acted as regent after Valentina's death, and that certain religious activities were directed by her during the interregnum period, which might also explain the construction of a new *barracão* in 1927, as Runhó suggested.

In any case, in addition to the possible chronological concurrence with the interruption of religious activities in the beginning of the 1920s, the reopening of Bogum under the leadership of Maria Emiliana da Piedade in 1937 coincided approximately with the reopening of Seja Hundé under Abalhe, which may suggest a joint strategy in the operation of the two congregations. As we have seen, there are those who affirm that the two terreiros were united and, at that time, the people of Bogum made annual visits to Seja Hundé, and those from Cachoeira repaid the visits by going to Salvador.

Correia Lopes writes that "Bogum is the name by which the adepts of the Gêge ritual in the City of Salvador refer to the house of that cult. The branch in Cachoeira, in the same State of Bahia has the same name. This branch was founded by an adept from the Salvador terreiro."[54] Who this Bogum adept was is unknown; perhaps it was Manuel da Silva. But this comment suggests that members of Bogum participated in the founding of Seja Hundé, which, in turn, would imply that the Salvador terreiro was probably already operating under Valentina's leadership in 1896, the year I estimate as the date of the opening of Seja Hundé (see chapter 5).

Maria Emiliana da Piedade
(no date)

Maria Emiliana da Piedade's leadership is remembered as one of the most important times for Bogum. She was a black Creole, the daughter of Manoel Ramiro and Maria Claudina Magalhães; she was born between 1858 and 1867 and would have been approximately seventy years old when she assumed leadership of the house around 1935. She was illiterate and remained unmarried.[55] As Miliana of Agué, she was consecrated to the vodun Agué, the hunter and master of the forests.[56] In 1987 *Ogã* Celestino Augusto do Espírito Santo and *Doné* Nicinha declared that "Emilia was born and raised in the [Bogum] terreiro." *Humbono* Vicente corroborated this opinion and said, "Emiliana had both mother and father at Bogum," both of whom were of Agué. He added that she was to be initiated at Pó Zerrem, but she became possessed by her vodun at Bogum during a Zo ritual and she was "made" there by Ludovina. Everaldo Duarte also suggested that Ludovina had initiated Emiliana at Bogum during the preabolition period, though it is not impossible that she also performed some rituals in Cachoeira.[57] Duarte remembered her as "tall and strong" and also as "quarrelsome." In the last years of her life she had knee problems and walked with a cane. *Humbono* Vicente told how Emiliana divined with cowrie shells that she would drop into a wooden dish, and that she had a gourd through which she made Agué whistle.[58] It is likely that Romana, *filha-de-santo* from Roça de Cima, attended Bogum during the time of Valentina, but it is certain that she helped Emiliana reopen the house in the 1930s, becoming from then on the *mãe-pequena*, or second-in-command to Emiliana. According to *Humbono* Vicente, Romana's regular participation at Bogum, sometimes accompanied by *Ogã* Caboco Acaçá, did not sit well with Abalhe at Seja Hundé, and this was one of the factors that contributed to the later difficulties between the two terreiros.[59]

According to its bylaws, the Sociedade Afro-Brasileira Fiéis de São Bartolomeu (Afro-Brazilian Society of the Faithful of Saint Bartholomew), a civil organization of the terreiro, was founded on July 28, 1937.[60] Unfortunately, I did not find the society's original registry, but this information does strengthen the hypothesis that, in the same year (also that of Emiliana's takeover), there was a serious effort to consolidate the terreiro's internal organization. The establishment of the society followed the celebration of the Second Afro-Brazilian Conference in January 1937, and preceded the organization, under the direction of Edison Carneiro, of the União das Seitas Afro-Brasileiras (Union of the Afro-Brazilian Sects) that September. It is therefore, not improbable that the founding of the Sociedade Afro-Brasileira Fiéis de São Bartolomeu was incited by the organizers of the conference.

In any case, Bogum was one of nine Jeje candomblés (eight Jeje and one Dahoméa), among a total of sixty-seven, registered with the Union of Afro-Brazilian Sects of Bahia in September 1937. By 1948, the year of the publication of *Candomblés da Bahia*, Carneiro markedly reduces the number of Jeje terreiros: "The candomblés of this nation, in Bahia, number only three—that of old Emiliana, at Bôgúm, the most important of all, the Pôço Bètá (Manuel Falefá), in Formiga, JêJe-Marrin (Mahi), and that of Manuel Menez, in São Caetano. These houses have bravely guarded the purity of the Jêje cult."[61] I will discuss these and other Jeje terreiros toward the end of the chapter.

For now, what is important is that the 1940s was one of the most splendid and important periods for Bogum. And in fact, it is during this period that the first studies begin to take interest in the terreiro. I have already mentioned the case of Correia Lopes and Carneiro, but Bogum also received the U.S. anthropologists Frances and Melville Herskovits, who recorded numerous ritual songs in 1941–42.[62] It is also from the time of Emiliana onward that the oral tradition of Bogum begins to retain a more precise memory of the terreiro's history.[63]

Emiliana prepared at least three groups of initiates, or *barcos*—the first included seven *vodunsis* and second and third had three—which confirms the congregation's positive dynamic and its capacity for recruiting new members. The first group celebrated its coming-out on July 28, 1940,[64] and included: Nicinha of Loko (the biological daughter of Runhó); Martinha of Ajonsu (Azonsu); Tomázia of Oxum; Teresa of Ogun; Lourdes, and one other daughter of Bessen. The festival in celebration of the group's coming-out was well

Luiza Franquelina da Rocha, *Gaiaku* Luiza (February 2002). Photo: Photini Papahatzi

attended, which indicates that the terreiro had already secured a certain degree of social visibility and popularity under Emiliana's leadership.[65]

In the second group, which must have had its coming-out in 1944, the initiates were Roxinha of Oxum, known as *dofona* from Vitória; Maria of Azonsu, and Luiza Franquelina da Rocha of Oiá.[66] Luiza Franquelina, or *gaiaku* Luiza, to whom I have already referred a number of times, was raised at Seja Hundé and taken to Bogum by Maria Romana, becoming a member of this second *barco* after it had already been formed. This fact caused some talk and it seems that certain differences between Romana and Runhó arose as a result of it.[67]

The third group of three celebrated its coming-out on September 21, 1947, and included Dezinha of Oxum (*hunsó* or *mãe-pequena* during the time of Nicinha's leadership), Clarice of Ajonsu, and Luizinha of Ossaim.[68] In 1999, of these thirteen *vodunsis*, Roxinha, Tomazia, and Luizinha had passed away. It is worth noting that since Emiliana the number of *vodunsis* in the initiation groups was always odd, while during the time of Valentina, and of Maria Agorensi and Abalhe at Seja Hundé, it was always even, normally eight or twelve. Today the practice of initiating an odd number of *vodunsis* in Jeje-Mahi terreiros seems prevalent.

Velho Romão, from the time of Emiliana, is remembered as the most knowledgeable *ogã* at Bogum. Also remembered is Gregório Bigodeiro, and *Ogã* Salu, who even without being confirmed, was very respected.[69] As at Seja Hundé during the time of Emiliana's leadership, there existed a complex network of social relations with other terreiros in the city and in the Recôncavo. As we have seen, Romana and Caboco Acaçá were present at many of Bogum's rituals. When members from Cachoeira visited Bogum in groups, they would climb the hill of the terreiro singing and asking for permission to enter, being received with other songs of welcome. The group could spend more than a month as guests at Bogum and its members would participate in the festivals and rituals of the house, such as the *quitanda** and the "pilgrimages" to São Bartolmeu Park to honor the vodun Bessen.[70]

There were also relationships with the neighboring terreiro of Pó Zerrem, under the direction of *Seu* Aprígio, and with Antônio of Oxumaré and Cotinha, from the Oxumaré terreiro in Mata Escura da Vasco da Gama. The famous *pai-de-santo* Procópio, "of Jeje descent" but head of the Ogunjá terreiro, of the Ijexá nation (Ketu, according to Carneiro), also frequented Bogum. There, he participated in the initiation of a *vodunsi*, whose saint required specific preparation unique to Procópio's nation.[71] There were also contacts with the Cacunda de Yaya terreiro of the Jeje-Savalu nation and with the most famous Nagô-Ketu terreiros, such as the neighboring Casa Branca or Engenho Velho. Menininha from Gantois and Mariquinha Lembá of Angola also attended the festivities of Bogum.[72] It is therefore during the period of Emiliana that Bogum was established as one of the most important terreiros of Salvador. The prestige of the terreiro was based on the ritual proficiency of its leaders, but it was assured and legitimized by this social network of contacts and collaboration with the priests of other "candomblé nations" that contributed to the increased social, ritual, and spiritual recognition of Bogum among the *povo-de-santo*.

Conflicts of Succession and Schisms:
The Regency of Romana at Bogum

Emiliana died at age ninety-two, on November 10, 1950.[73] Three weeks later, Abalhe passed away in Cachoeira. Bogum closed its doors for three years, and this transitional period was marked by disputes over leadership. From what I know, the antagonism centered on two of the most influential people of the congregation at that time: Romana and Runhó. Given her seniority and the fact she was *mãe-pequena* or *hunsó*, Romana should have been the one to succeed Emiliana.[74] Before her death, Emiliana was to name Romana as her successor, but Runhó, with whom Romana always had trouble (I have already mentioned certain differences caused by Luiza's initiation), opposed the succession.[75] Runhó alleged that Romana had not been initiated at Bogum and was there as a guest participant—the same argument used against Abalhe at Seja Hundé. It seems that the quarrel also involved mutual accusations of *feitiçaria*, or witchcraft. It is said that following Emiliana's sixth-month *zelim*, Romana left Bogum taking her sacred saints' shrines to the house of *Humbono* Vicente, one of her *filhos-de-santo*, while the community at Seja Hundé, in Cachoeira, claimed the right to keep them. As is frequently the case in such situations, it seems that Romana abandoned Bogum accompanied by a group of congregation members.[76] Another version recounts that Runhó had not yet fulfilled all of the rituals necessary to becoming *doné* and that, finally, it was Romana who, after reconciling with Runhó, assumed the role of regent for the time necessary for Runhó to complete her obligations.[77]

In approximately 1953, Maria Romana Moreira effectively assumed the governance of Bogum, though she never became *doné* or initiated any *vodunsi* there.[78] Maria Romana Moreira of Kposu Batan Ajaí was better known as Romaninha Pó or Romaninha Pósu (Pó-Ossum).[79] *Humbono* Vicente said that she "was of Oxum, but it was Kpo who ruled her head and that she was the first Kpo to be initiated in Brazil. As I have noted, she was initiated around 1875, at Roça de Cima, with *Tio* Xarene and Zé de Brechó. *Humbono* Vicente related how one day Zé de Brechó found a package at a crossroads, but being as he was "master of the *ebó*," he was unafraid and opened it, finding inside a little girl. It was Romana and he "raised her and made her saint."[80]

Romana was a seller of *acaça* cakes, popcorn with coconut, and other such fare. She had a biological son who was a lieutenant in the army and a daughter through whom she had a number of grandchildren.[81] Romana was a charismatic woman with a vast store of esoteric knowledge, or *fundamento*, not only from the Jeje nation, but also from other "nations." She moved freely between Bogum, where she was a regular participant, and Seja Hundé, where they would do nothing without her presence. Additionally, Romana was also *mãe-pequena* of the Bate Folha terreiro, of the Angola nation (Muxicongo), a fact that once again points to the close relationship between the Angola and Jeje nations.[82] She diligently attended the Oxumaré terreiro. Some say that Romana conducted an initiation ritual for Antônio Oxumare, one of the first heads of that house.[83] Romana also had free access to Cacunda de Yaya and to the Pinho candomblé of the Nagô nation in Maragogipe.

This mobility of an experienced priestess among the candomblés of various nations in the first half of the twentieth century points to a factor that may help explain how values and ritual practices are assimilated or transferred from one nation to another. For it is precisely religious specialists such as Romana, familiar with the esoteric knowledge of various rituals (another example would be *Gaiaku* Luiza, her *filha-de-santo*), who are most aware of and sensitive to

Maria Romana Moreira, Romaninha de Pó (1941)

liturgical differences. However, the giving of services to different terreiros, which at times could be motivated by material interests, was not always well regarded, and some accused Romana of being a "bohemian of the religion." This attitude was apparently one of the motives for the disputes that arose with Runhó and also earlier with Abalhe and Emiliana.[84]

Romana participated in the initiation of many *barcos* in different terreiros but only had four *filhos-de-santo* of her own. The first was Vicente Paulo dos Santos, initiated in 1935, at the age of twelve. He underwent his first ritual at Bogum with Emiliana but was later initiated by Romana at his house in Matatu, where he lived until his death in 2001. Romana was helped by Velho Romão, a Bogum *ogã*, and by *Ogã* Caboco from Seja Hundé. Luiza Franquelina da Rocha was initiated in 1944. Her last two *filhos-de-santo* were Vitorino, who lived in Minas Gerais, and Mário, who lived in the Bahian backlands.[85]

In the final years of her life, Romana lived with *Humbono* Vicente in his house, but she died of diabetes in the home of her biological daughter on Ladeira do Canto da Cruz in October 1956.[86] Her *filhos-de-santo* Vicente and Luiza claimed that she was between 115 and 120 years old at that time, but it is probable that she was around ninety. Prior to her death, Romana left all of her religious paraphernalia to Vicente, including Kpo's shrine, a *xaxará** of Azoani,

Vicente Paulo dos Santos,
Humbono Vicente of Ogun
(2001)

and an *itacara** of Bessen. The handing over of these items was done before the people of Seja Hundé. Also previous to her death, a number of Bogum *ogãs* went to ask her for the key to the terreiro's shrine room, which was closed at that time, but she died without giving up this symbol of power.[87] These events suggest that Romana, supported by the people of Seja Hundé, maintained until the end of her days a tense relationship with the Bogum faction led by Runhó.

Romana also faced certain difficulties in Cachoeira following the death of Abalhe in 1950. Romana supported the candidacy of Pararasi, *filha-de-santo* of Abalhe, for the position of *gaiaku*, but she faced competition from *Gamo* Edvirgem of Oxum, *filha-de-santo* of Maria Agorensi. The rivalry between the faction of Maria Agorensi and that of Abalhe, begun in the 1920s, continued in the 1950s. Finally, it seems, *Gamo* Edvirgem gave up the fight and left the path open for Pararasi's succession, which must have taken place in the late 1950s, after Romana's death.[88] It is said that Pararasi assumed the post "on her own" and that she was not "very well accepted by the Cachoeiran community."[89] In Salvador, Runhó also refused to legitimize the succession of Pararasi, perhaps because of her connection with Romana. Thus, the "social drama" of the past reemerged with new actors but similar characteristics, and the partial reintegration of the congregation was accompanied by a new schism.

During the 1950s, and more precisely during the latter years of Romana's regency in Bogum, relations between Bogum and Seja Hundé grew cool and communication between the two terreiros ceased. The causes are vague, but it is said that there were mutual accusations of ritual incompetence.[90] What was once "only one terreiro" breaks into two because of micropolitical quarrels in the search for religious power. With the death of Romana, who still functioned as a link between the two congregations, Runhó withdrew and broke off relations with Seja Hundé. Some say that she wanted independence from Seja Hundé, which had been the domain of Romana.

When Runhó took over as the new *doné* of Bogum in 1960, no one from Cachoeira attended the ceremony.[91] Her biological daughter, Nicinha, was chosen as *mãe-pequena*; Runhó placed people on whom she could rely in the terreiro's highest posts.[92] From this point, other members of the dos Anjos family began to occupy positions of authority, and biological kinship became a way of guaranteeing the stability of religious power and the continuity of the terreiro.

"Modern" Times at Bogum: From Runhó to Nicinha

Maria Valentina dos Anjos, better known as Runhó, was born in 1877, daughter of Ana Maria dos Anjos. She probably went to live at the Bogum terreiro after her initiation in 1911, when she was about thirty years old. Runhó was either married to or lived with Gonçalo Alpiniano de Melo, *filho-de-santo* of Mariquinha Lembá of the Angola nation. At this time Runhó already had two of her four children—the firstborn Amâncio Ângelo de Melo, who would come to be one of the most important *ogãs* of the house, and Evangelista dos Anjos Costa (Nicinha), who would come to succeed her biological mother as the terreiro's chief.[93]

Valentina dos Anjos was consecrated to the vodun Sogbo Adan, and her African name was Mere Doji.[94] Her nickname, Runhó, not to be confused with *hunsó* (the title of Bogum's *mãe-pequena*), derives from the Gun or Aizo term *hunyó*, the name of a person consecrated to a deity, or a synonym for *hunsi* (i.e., *vodunsi*).[95] Those who knew her describe her character as firm, responsible, joyful, and marked by great faith.[96] She was a self-declared Catholic and had "sympathy for Saint Geronimo," which is not surprising if one remembers the syncretism of Saint Geronimo with Xangô and Sogbo.[97] Runhó did not like Candomblé as a girl but accepted her religious responsibilities with complete dedication following her initiation. *Equede* Santa, her biological sister, commented that "Runhó's Sogbo did not accept invitations from anyone," alluding to the sobriety of her behavior. The famous Brazilian novelist Jorge Amado praised her as an example of the "discretion and prudence traditional among the Jeje nation," and others point out the "austerity with which she guided her Candomblé."[98]

Valentina Maria dos Anjos,
Doné Runhó (1975)

It is possible that Runhó had initiated two *filhas-de-santo* around 1918, before assuming the post of *doné*, as she stated, "I myself made two *filhas* after seven years [of being initiated]."[99] I know nothing further regarding these two *filhas-de-santo*, but at that time initiations could be performed outside the terreiro, frequently in private homes or in isolated places outside the city. Capone also mentions the case of *Mãe* Lindinha (Arlinda Lopes dos Santos), the biological daughter of Cristóvão of Ogunjá, head of Ilê Ogun Anauegi Belé Ioman, an Efon nation terreiro located in the Ubaranas neighborhood of Salvador. Candomblé prohibits a *pai-de-santo* from initiating his immediate biological relatives. This would have led Cristóvão to ask Runhó, as a friend of the terreiro, to initiate his daughter. This ritual would have occurred before 1947.[100]

In 1961, Runhó mentioned that of those initiated with her, there were only three *vodunsis* still living and that "together with those of the house, initiated by the late Emiliana, there are about six still active."[101] This scarcity of *vodunsis* was somewhat resolved in the following year, 1962, when Pararasi, the Romana candidate, assumed the leadership of Seja Hundé. Her takeover was considered illegitimate by some of the *vodunsis*, and it is said that a group of approximately ten women left Seja Hundé to attend Bogum. With these events, the relations between Bogum and Seja Hundé worsened, and contact between the two definitively ceased. Meanwhile, remediating the lack of *vodunsis* seems to have been one of Runhó's priorities.

Between 1964 and 1972 Runhó initiated six *barcos*, with a total of sixteen *vodunsis*. I present here the list of initiates and the dates of their coming-out ceremonies as cited by Everaldo Duarte. On July 22, 1964, the first *barco* of two *vodunsis* graduated: Maria of Omolu and Teresa of Aziri Tobosi. In 1966, there was the coming-out of the second *barco* of three *vodunsis*: Maria Odília of Ajonsu, Eunice of Ogun, and Jacira of Badé. In 1967, the third *barco* of three came out: Marlene of Toquem, Margarida of Oiá, and Anita of Agué. On December 21, 1970, was the fourth *barco* of three: a daughter of Aziri, Adelina of Bessen, and Zildete of Ode. On August 1, 1971, came the fifth *barco* of two: Nizette of Logun and Arlinda of Lissá (Oxalá). On October 20, 1972, the coming-out of Runhó's sixth and last *barco* was celebrated; it constituted of three *vodunsis*: Ivone of Ogun, Beatriz of Oxum, and Nilce da Silveira of Ajonsu.[102]

Thus there was a great deal of activity at this time and also quite a diversity among the voduns, as each one is different, with the exceptions of two Aziri (Iemanjá), two Ajonsu (Azonsu), and two Ogun. This indicates, to a certain degree, an implicit desire to preserve the richness of the Jeje pantheon and at the same time Runhó's high level of ritual expertise. She tried to preserve this esoteric knowledge from outside curiosity: "Those who don't know, don't understand, but I won't change, and I won't teach."[103]

Mãe Runhó, who suffered from heart problems, passed away on Saturday, December 27, 1975, at nine o'clock in the morning. It was precisely on the night before the beginning of the cycle of festivities of the terreiro. According to the press of the time, Runhó was ninety-eight. Her interment occurred on Sunday morning, at Quinta dos Lázaros; "the coffin, the wreaths, the chants and the cries descended upon the hill and, on foot, they traversed the streets and avenues, with Iansã opening the way before them with her terrible cry."[104]

At nine o'clock in the evening the *sirrum* began at the terreiro. On the last night of the ritual, on Saturday, January 3, there came representatives of many terreiros and important figures from Bahian culture, such as Valdeloir Rego, Jorge Amado, and Caribé. The seventh-day mass, on the following morning, was celebrated in the Church of São João Batista in Vila América. At this point it was already known that her daughter *Gamo* Lokosi would be her successor. "In fact, the governance of the Bogum terreiro was already in her hands since the time of the illness of Maria Valentina dos Anjos, 'Runhó.' But while this was true, it was not evident, for 'of course a child cannot act before his or her elders'"[105] For the first time, Bogum experienced a transition without discord.

Runhó's *Sirrum*: *Mãe* Nicinha (standing) together with Runhó's son Edivaldo dos Anjos Costa. *Jornal da Bahia* archives (12/12/75)

The policy of allying religious power within the same family appears to have yielded some results.

On January 2, 1979, three years after the death of Runhó, the terreiro re-opened, and on January 21, "the successor Gamo Lokosse received her office." It was *Humbono* Vicente who presided and handed the office over to Nicinha. On February 20, "Mayor Edvaldo Brito was honored at the conclusion of the cycle of festivities that marked the reopening of the candomblé."[106]

Evangelista dos Anjos Costa, Nicinha of Loko, was born and grew up at Bogum. Her birth occurred under peculiar circumstances. She herself explains that her mother often said "that I was born in the street, under a gameleira tree." This is why Nicinha was later consecrated to the vodun Loko, an initiation conducted by Emiliana in 1940. Jehová de Carvalho adds that she received some additional later preparation with Runhó, probably in order to be able to assume the role of *doné*.[107]

During her management of the terreiro, Nicinha initiated four *barcos*. The first was gathered in June 1985 and had its coming-out in January 1986, the initiation lasting seven months. *Humbono* Vicente participated as *pai-pequeno*. This *barco* included *Dofona* Zaildes Iracema de Mello, a niece of Nicinha's, known as Índia of Ojonsu (Azonsu), age fourteen, and *Dofonitinha* Kelba Carvalho of Agontolu, the daughter of *Ogã* Jehová de Carvalho. The second *barco* was probably put together following the festivity cycle, in February 1986, and had

Evangelista dos Anjos Costa,
Doné Gamo Lokosi (Nicinha)

its coming-out in October of the same year. It included *Dofona* Sara Jesus of Oxum and *Dofonitinha* Gislene Jesus of Bessen. The third *barco* came out in September 1989, with *Dofona* Valdete Jesus of Gun, *Dofonitinha* Jubiacira Jesus of Nanã, *Fomo* Rita de Cassia of Kpo, and *Fomotinha* Conceição Gonçalves of Iansa. The fourth and last *barco* came out in February 1990, with *Dofona* Georgina of Sogbo and *Dofonitinha* Albertina of Agué. There were therefore ten *vodunsis* with ten different voduns.[108]

During Nicinha's time the terreiro lost some of its most important members, such as *Equede* Santa, who died a little after 1981, and *Ogã Huntó* Amâncio Ângelo de Melo, the son of Runhó, who died on December 26, 1983. Consequently, Nicinha had to face difficulties with great determination. Encouraged by Ordep Serra's Project Mapeamento de Monumentos Negros da Bahia (MAMNBA, Mapping of the Black Monuments of Bahia), she was responsible for the reorganization of the Sociedade Fiéis de São Bartolomeu, the terreiro's lay civic organization. She placed at its head the oldest *ogã*, Lídio Pereira de Santana, who was assisted by two of his sons, Edvaldo and Hamilton dos Anjos Costa, as well as Everaldo Duarte, Jaime Sodré, Celestino Espírito Santo, Ana Maria Costa, and Gilberto Leal.[109]

As I will show in greater detail below, this period was marked by a consistent community effort to promote greater social visibility of the terreiro. With

The visit of Hunon Dagbo to Bogum (July 1988). Seated, from left to right: Everaldo Duarte, *Mãe* Nicinha, Hunon Dagbo, and Pierre Verger. Photo: Arlete Soares

this purpose in mind, *Mãe* Nicinha hosted the "Primeira semana de palestras: O povo malê e suas influências" (First Seminar on the Malê People and Their Influences) at the terreiro from July 21 to 26, 1986. This forum began to devise measures to combat real estate speculation and organized a campaign to fund the terreiro's restoration.[110]

Nicinha also promoted meetings with high-ranking African religious dignitaries. On July 23, 1983, following the end of the Second World Conference on the Orixá Tradition, which took place in Salvador, Nicinha received at the terreiro the Obá (king) Oyesis Xagulan of Ejigbo, Nigeria.[111] In July 1988, she received the visit of Hunon Dagbo, the highest authority of the vodun cults in Benin, who had come to Salvador to participate in the inauguration of the House of Benin.[112] On both occasions, *Mãe* Nicinha sang songs to the voduns in the African language, which were immediately recognized by her African visitors.

Nicinha, who suffered from acute anemia and had already been hospitalized on two occasions, died at two o'clock in the morning on Wednesday, October 5, 1994, at the age of eighty-two. The funeral procession, which took place on foot as prescribed by Jeje tradition, went from the terreiro to the Quinta dos Lázaros Cemetery, where she was interred. The *zelim* lasted seven nights, counting from the day of the *mãe-de-santo*'s death, and a mass was celebrated on the seventh day at the church of Nossa Senhora do Rosário dos Pretos

(Our Lady of the Rosary of the Blacks) in the Pelourinho.[113] In the absence of the *doné*, the *mãe-pequena*, *Hunsó* Dezinha of Oxum, temporarily assumed leadership of the house.

The terreiro remained closed to the lay public for more than seven years. These were difficult times for the congregation, who suffered further loss in 1995 with the death of *Ogã Hundeva* Edvaldo dos Anjos Costa, Nicinha's biological son. There arose certain difficulties between the more traditional and conservative faction and another faction of younger members who wanted to reinitiate activities at a faster pace.

One of the most admirable characteristics of the congregation has been its capacity to withstand long periods of inactivity, sometimes lasting more than fifteen years and caused by succession disputes. As Runhó said in 1961: "People want to end it but there are so many *saints* around that we have to continue. . . . We had no particular interest in continuing but they said—the terreiro is Gege!"[114]

In 2001, taking advantage of the campaign launched by the Palmares Foundation for the preservation of the terreiros of Salvador, Bogum obtained some resources from the Ministry of Culture to restore the *barracão* and the altars, which at this time were in very bad shape. When the work was finished, *Humbono* Vicente Paulo dos Santos passed away on December 16, 2001. He should have been the one to toss the cowry shells to confirm the new *doné*. Faced with this adversity, the famous diviner or *olowo*, Agenor Miranda Rocha, ninety-four years of age, was invited from Rio de Janeiro. On May 30, 2002, the day of Corpus Christi, after examining the cowry shells of Ifá, he appointed *Dofona* Zaildes Iracema de Mello, thirty-eight, known as Índia of Ajonsu (Azonsu), niece of Nicinha and granddaughter of Runhó, as the new *doné*. Legitimized by the powers of the most prestigious and respected *olowo* of contemporary Candomblé, the religious leadership of Bogum continued to be bound to Runhó's family into the third generation. The public activities of the house were recommenced in December 2002, and on August 17, 2003, the successor assumed the post of *doné* with the title of Naa Doji, inaugurating a new phase in Bogum's history.

"Modern" Times at Seja Hundé: From Pararasi to Lokosi and the Carioca Immigration

For now we will return to Cachoeira to examine the period from 1960 to the present. The management of Seja Hundé by Pararasi, or Adalgisa Combo Pereira, marks a new period in its history. Pararasi was born in Castro Alves, near Muritiba in the Recôncavo. She was initiated by Abalhe and consecrated to the vodun Parara, a type of Sakpata or Azonsu; "she danced wearing *palha da Costa*," the straw costume associated with her vodun. According to *Humbono* Vicente, she was "modern."[115] As we have seen, her taking over as *gaiaku* was contested by some members of the congregation. As Lopez de Carvalho writes, "according to the Cachoeiran population, the reign of Pararasi as *gaiaku* was not one of the best. They say she had a very difficult, authoritarian personality. Many of the *vodunsis* of the house had died and Pararasi had some difficulty with the administration of the terreiro.[116]

The duration of her leadership is difficult to estimate. She must have taken over either in the late 1950s or very early 1960s. Certainly by 1962 she was functioning as leader with a certain regularity. It was in this year that *Gaiaku* Luiza bought land in the Caquende neighborhood of Cachoeira and began the first activities of the Rumpayme Agono Huntoloji terreiro.[117] This led to a series of disputes between the two candomblés, as Seja Hundé could not accept the installation of another terreiro of the same nation in Cachoeira. The disagreements and misunderstandings continue to the present day. The idea that a certain location can have only one Jeje-Mahi candomblé, and therefore only one *gaiaku* or *doné*, is replicated at Bogum. This custom seems to be associated with the notion that the shrines installed by the Africans in Seja Hundé and Bogum cannot be duplicated in other places, for the "stones" supposedly brought from Africa ought to be the only and the legitimate home of certain voduns. But also it seems that this "rule" would be used and emphasized as an argument to avoid the division of the Jeje-Mahi congregations in the successive internal disputes during the periods of succession. This would explain, in part, the success of the expansion of the Nagô houses, which are not so rigid in this respect.

According to *Ogã* Bernardino, Pararasi initiated four *barcos*, while according to *Ogã* Boboso there were only two or three. The first *barco* was organized in 1964. In it were (1) *Dofona* Maria da Conceição of Azonsu, the wife of *Ogã* Zé Careca; (2) *Fomotinha* Joana of Azonsu, the biological sister of *Gaiaku* Luiza and *Seu* Geninho; (3) a *vodunsi* of Averekete; (4) a *vodunsi* of Oxum; (5) a *vodunsi* of Logun Edé. It is known that there are another three *vodunsis* prepared by Pararasi: (6) *Dofono* Edivaldo of Bessen, (7) *Fomo* Alda of Oiá, and (8) *Dofonitinha* Alaíde of Oiá. The latter two live in Rio, but until recently traveled regularly to participate in the festivities of Seja Hundé. Still, the mention of a second *Dofono* (Edivaldo) would indicate the existence of at least two *barcos*.[118]

The first *barco* caused serious problems for Pararasi and, according to some "caused the ruin of the terreiro." One explanation given by Luís Magno, the biological son of *Dofona* Maria da Conceição, is that there was one *vodunsi* of Oxum and another of Logun Edé, voduns that in the Jeje tradition, according to Luís Magno, could only be consecrated upon the head of a *vodunsi* after the *mãe-de-santo* had initiated a number of *barcos*—"She began where others finish."[119] Alternatively, others explain that, within a group of initiates, the novitiate of Averekete should be done at the end: "Averekete is the last; Pararasi put it at the front, and that's what caused the ruin of the house."[120] Neither of these arguments is entirely convincing, but they point to the fact that Pararasi had problems with, and received criticism regarding, the way she organized this group of initiates.[121]

Coinciding with the migratory movement of the northeastern population to the cities of the South, Pararasi was the first *mãe-de-santo* from Seja Hundé to travel outside of Cachoeira and professionalize her religious activities. She lived for some time in Rio, in the house of a Seja Hundé *ogã* called José, and also in Belo Horizonte, where she lived by offering her religious services.[122] Her time in Rio was the beginning of the development of a social network that ended up significantly changing the social base of Seja Hundé in the following decades. The date of Pararasi's death, from all indications, is between 1969 and 1971, when she was eighty-four years old. Some say that she died in Cachoeira and others that she died in Belo Horizonte, but *Humbono* Vicente affirmed that it happened in Salvador: "She died from a stomach illness; they say it was the result of witchcraft." However, the seven-day *sirrum*, directed by Nezinho do Portão, took place in a rented house on Rua do Carmo in Cachoeira.[123]

After Pararasi's death, Eliza Gonzaga de Souza, Vivi Aguesi, Maria Agorensi's *filha-de-santo*, assumed the post of "regent" of Seja Hundé.[124] *Humbono* Vicente, in what was perhaps a political maneuver in the process of finding a successor for Pararasi, apparently performed a ritual to confirm Aguesi into that position, but he also claimed that "she was not invested with the leadership," for she could not take the position of *gaiaku*.[125] According to Jeje tradition, Agué Aboro, the young vodun to whom Aguesi was consecrated, does not allow his *vodunsi* to become *gaiaku*. It is also said that a person of this vodun, although authorized to direct or supervise initiation processes, cannot ritually shave or paint initiates, that is, "lay hands on the head" of anyone. However, in 1980, Aguesi initiated two *filhos-de-santo*, a *dofono* of Azonsu, and a *dofonitinha* of Oxum, which is considered by some to be the cause of her infirmities and subsequent dementia.[126]

During the 1980s, it seems that Seja Hundé maintained a certain stability and held ceremonies annually, although with a reduced number of *vodunsis*.

On May 9, 1992, Aguesi was invited to Rio de Janeiro by *pai-de-santo* Zezinho da Boa Viagem, one of the *filhos-de-santo* of *Fomotinho* Antônio Pinto, initiate-mate, or *barco*-brother, of Aguesi. She was received at the airport by more than 100 people and the local media, causing a good deal of hubbub among Rio's *povo-de-santo*.[127] Yet, she was later forgotten and remained unremembered when, in her old age, she needed it most.

As the niece of Maria Agorensi, Aguesi was the legitimate heir of the lands of Seja Hundé, and for this reason some considered her the true "owner of the terreiro." In the early 1990s, she began to suffer from health problems, a situation of which some congregation members took advantage to distance her from the candomblé's leadership. At that time she lived in the area on Ladeira da Cadeia (in the house that had belonged to her aunt, Maria Agorensi), and later she lived alone on Ladeira Manoel Vitorio, in Recuada, where she was eventually forgotten and abandoned.[128]

During this time Augusta Maria da Conceição Marques, *Gamo* Lokosi, Abalhe's *filha-de-santo*, took over as the new *gaiaku*. *Humbono* Vicente passed this office onto her in his house in Matatu, Salvador.[129] As Aguesi was still living at this time, there are those who suggest that "the throne of Ventura was occupied . . . by two *gaiakus* at the same time: Aguesse and *Gamo* Lokossi."[130] But this is merely rhetorical euphemism, for by this time Aguesi had ceased to participate in religious activities. She passed away on January 14, 1998, at the age of ninety-five.

Lokosi was initiated at Seja Hundé because the nature of her saint, Loko, required being made in a Jeje house. She had already been consecrated to Xangô, however, in an Ijexá-Nagô terreiro, where her biological mother danced. Besides being *gaiaku* of Seja Hundé, she also led an Ijexá-nation terreiro in Salvador. This simultaneity of religious adherence is significant and indicates the permeability among the various Candomblé rituals. The liturgical differences between nations can be maintained in each terreiro; for example, in the Salvador terreiro Lokosi could receive *caboclos*, but this did not occur in Seja Hundé, where *caboclos* are not accepted. However, at least one *filho-de-santo* initiated in the Ijexá tradition accompanied Lokosi regularly in her obligations at Seja Hundé.[131]

Since 1995, when I first witnessed the rituals at Seja Hundé, the activities of this candomblé have been carried on with regularity. In this same year, two *ogãs* were confirmed and one individual recruited for a *barco* of one person only—a grandson of *Ogã* Boboso—belonging to the vodun Bessen. The young Netinho, as he was known, was predestined to assume the future leadership of Seja Hundé, for his saint, head of the Jeje-Mahi nation, had chosen him.

Unfortunately, he died a year later, cutting short such prospects. For Lokosi this was not a good omen and seemed to confirm the terreiro's decline begun in the time of Pararasi. In June 2003, in an evident effort to correct this situation, two new *ogãs* were confirmed and a new *vodunsi* from Rio de Janeiro was chosen to be initiated for Bessen.

Like Pararasi, *Gamo* Lokosi also maintained periodic contact with Rio de Janeiro, which contributed to the ever increasing presence of people from that state and, to a lesser degree, from São Paulo—*ogãs* as well as *vodunsis*. The complex network of kinship that structured and, to a certain degree, assured the resources necessary for the operation of the candomblé in the first half of the century began to give way to an influx of participants from Rio and São Paulo, who for a while seemed to be taking over this function. Although some members of the families of *Ogã* Boboso and *Ogã* Bernardino continue to play a central role in the liturgical activities, the participants from Rio, many of them *filhos-de-santo* or *netos-de-santo* of *Fomotinho* Antônio Pinto of Oxum, began to change the social structure and the internal dynamic of the religious congregation.

If Seja Hundé was characterized in the past by a majority of black women initiated within the terreiro and residents of Cachoeira or its surrounding areas, recent years have seen a growing participation of male *vodunsis*, generally *adés* (homosexuals), relatively young, white, and initiated in Brazil's southern cities. In the festivity cycle of January 2000, for example, three men from Rio, one from São Paulo, and another two men visiting from the local area, danced, accompanied by only a single local woman from Seja Hundé. The change in the social provenance of the agents of religious ritual has affected certain liturgical aspects (quicker drum beats, which are viewed as an influence of the Rio candomblés), certain forms of sociability (the *ogãs* of today have their own house with two rooms, beds, and a bathroom and no longer sleep in the *barracão*), and, indirectly, the internal power relations.

Everaldo Duarte noted that devotees from Rio and São Paulo had begun to attend at Bogum before its cessation of activities in 1993. The connections between Seja Hundé and the Rio Jeje, however, are much older. It is said that in Rio de Janeiro the first Jeje terreiro was Kwe Simba of *Gaiaku* Rozenda, an African woman who arrived in Brazil around 1850.[132] However, the person who contributed most to the diffusion of Jeje ritual in Rio de Janeiro Candomblé was Tata, *fomotinho* of Oxumila (Oxum), initiated in 1913 by Maria Agorensi. He had not yet completed his initiation when he moved to Rio, settling in São João de Niterói, where he initiated a great number of *filhos-de-santo*. Among the best-known of these was Zezinho da Boa Viagem, who himself initiated some of the present-day participants in the festivities of Seja Hundé. *Fomotinho* also trained many *filhos-de-santo* in São Paulo, such as Jamil Rachid of Obaluaê, an influential leader of São Paulo Umbanda.[133] As his *netos* and *bisnetos-de-santo*, or religious descendants of those whom he initiated, tell it, "*Fomotinho* even messed with Ketu and Angola," and this would be one of the reasons that they would have been brought to Seja Hundé—as part of the search for "authentic" Jeje-Mahi roots.[134] In more recent times, *Gaiaku* Luiza's *filhos-de-santo* have also contributed to the spreading of Jeje-Mahi ritual in Rio de Janeiro. For example, Doté Nelson of Azunzu opened a popular terreiro in São José Belford Roxo Park and was the head of Radio Marrym FM, which was devoted to the "airing of spiritualist programs" from 1996 to 1998. There are also Amaori of Oxóssi and Marcos Antônio Lopez de Carvalho of Bessen, both trained by *Gaiaku* Luiza, who have Jeje-Mahi terreiros in Rio.[135]

Besides the ritual knowledge acquired in Cachoeira, it is above all the contact with the "origins" that confers on these religious specialists valued prestige and status in their respective communities. In truth, the influx of devotees from the South into the Jeje terreiros of Bahia is part of a much broader and more complex movement that has been affecting Afro-Brazilian religions since the 1970s. Candomblé has gone from a marginalized religion that has been discriminated against to a cultural practice perceived as worthy of social recognition. The religious institution's new visibility and prestige, rooted in the value given to the "tradition" and "African purity" of the oldest Bahian houses, has led to a process of "re-Africanization" expressed through the discourse against Catholic "syncretism," the increase in travel to Africa by religious specialists, and the implantation of Yoruba language courses, to cite only a few of the better-known aspects. In southern cities, these circumstances together contributed to a gradual transfer of practitioners from Umbanda to Candomblé, now viewed as a "stronger," more effective tradition, which in the religious market also meant the chance for a larger clientele. In this context, Africa, or the "traditional" Bahian Candomblé houses, which were closer and more accessible, became highly valued as the source of esoteric knowledge and "African purity" that could legitimize the practices and, ultimately, the power of the new religious experts.[136]

In Jeje nation circles, Seja Hundé and Bogum, as early houses with African roots, fit into and associated with this ideal of purity that generated the influx of devotees from the South. In the case of Seja Hundé, many of these visitors justify their choice, basing it on its religious genealogy, which through *Fomotinho* connects them by "lineage" to this house. Also, devotees from Seja Hundé, with their trips to Rio, São Paulo, Minas Gerais, and other parts of the country, strengthen a social network that encourages (through the material benefits it brings) these visits during festival periods. At the same time, the considerable presence of outsiders does provoke certain tensions and some resistance from older members. More than once I heard "visitors" complain that "the old-timers don't explain anything" and also of having been excluded from certain internal rituals. However, the "old-timers" are also aware of the need to yield somewhat and arrive at some compromise or consensus, for they know that the activities of the terreiro depend on these people for material resources and participants. In the midst of such transformations, *Gamo Lokosi* passed away on December 2, 2007, creating space for new inner power arrangements. The Jeje people have amply demonstrated their capacity for persistence and adaptation, overcoming difficult times such as the long succession conflicts. The challenges of the current times are quite different, however, and the consequences unforeseeable.

To Whom Does the Land Belong?
Bogum's Property Problems (1960–90)

Bogum's problems appear to be of another kind. The urban context has been the great enemy of this congregation. Coinciding with Runhó's leadership, the 1960s marked the beginning of what I called Bogum's "modern" epoch, a period characterized by important changes related to Salvador's urban growth and real estate speculation.

The 1890 property inventory of Maria Julia Figueiredo, high priestess of the Ilê Iyá Nassô terreiro, says that the "place called Engenho Velho, Caminho do Rio Vermelho [was] on leased land and the property of Doctor José Carneiro de Campos." Since Ilê Iyá Nassô neighbored the Bogum terreiro, one could infer that Carneiro de Campos had been the owner of the property on which both candomblés stood until at least the 1890s.[137] It is likely that at the beginning of the twentieth century[138] the lands of Engenho Velho da Federação were bought by Commander Bernardo Martins Catharino, whose property included the terreiros of Bogum, Pó Zerrem, and Casa Branca and extended as far as Gantois. Around 1930, this area of 226,526 square meters was inherited by Eduardo Martins Catharino, son of the commander; in 1953, after Eduardo's death, it came to be owned by the commander's daughter, Maria Laura Martins Catharino, and her husband, Hermógenes Príncipe de Oliveira. After the couple's separation in 1989, the lands became the property of Príncipe de Oliveira, the current owner.[139]

As we saw in chapter 5, the Bogum terreiro originally occupied a large area

MAP 5 The site of the Bogum Terreiro, approximate original area (dotted line) and current area (shaded). Source: Sicar/Conder; Project MAMNBA, Salvador City Hall, September 1981.

of bushland. This area went from the top of Federação—today Praça Valmir Barreto—and extended, descending the hill, to the former Caminho Dois de Julho—today Avenida Vasco da Gama—where the Lucaia River passed. Near the river were two springs used for rituals. The *barracão*, located at the top of the hill, was separated from the rest of the land by the Ladeira do Bogum, a former public road. At the end of the 1950s or the beginning of the 1960s, this road was paved by the city of Salvador, becoming the current street, Ladeira Manoel Bomfim. Since then, Bogum "has had its physical space diminished to one-fifth of what it was originally."[140]

The progressive loss of space occurred primarily because of the construction of houses and huts, which began in the late 1950s and increased throughout the 1960s. The lands that were on the other side of the Ladeira Manoel Bomfim were gradually occupied by outsiders to the community, as the result of the selling of land by the Catharino family (the nominal owners), concessions made by Runhó to people who would come to her asking for help, and the occasional sale that Elísio, Nicinha's brother, himself made. At the same time, a degree of negligence by the city allowed the situation to get out of control.[141]

In January 1961 Runhó was already complaining that some of the sacred trees, or *atinsas*, had been "separated" from the terreiro, and she protested against the real estate problems suffered by the terreiro. She commented that "it looks like Senhor Catarino wants to sell the plot where the *barracão* is situated," adding that the community could not buy it because "we can't pay what he's asking."[142] In the early 1970s it seems that Bogum possessed only the plot where the *barração* stood and, on the east side of the Ladeira Manoel Bomfim, only two small plots: one, separated from the *barração* by some fifty meters, was where the sacred tree of the vodun Azonodo stood, and another where the house of Agorensi, an old Bogum *vodunsi*, was located. A few days before her death, Runhó told Juarez Paraíso during the filming of *Tenda dos Milagres* (Tent of Miracles) by the filmmaker Nelson Pereira dos Santos: "Every day it gets harder for the Gege to perform rituals to our voduns (orixás). The problem is we lack forest and river close to our terreiro. Before we had a river here; but it was blocked up. We can't 'make saint' without leaves and water."[143]

In 1978, while the terreiro was still mourning Runhó's death, the tree of Azonodo, of great ritual importance, fell under the winter rains; some say it was injected with chemical agents that ended its life (see chapter 8). A short time later, this small piece of land of Azonodo was sold, and the proceeds were distributed among various members of the terreiro. *Ogã* Celestino stated: "We got rid of part of the land because when we would build a fence, they would tear it down, as well as throw trash on it."[144]

Mayor Edvaldo Brito's visit to the terreiro on February 20, 1979, typified Nicinha's effort to build political alliances at the highest level, although Jehová de Carvalho, in his address, affirmed that "this candomblé has never before honored any authority and receives the mayor, not because of the post he occupies, but because of his position as one who is involved with the candomblé."[145] Nonetheless, these actions indicate the community's desire to call the attention of the public powers to the terreiro's situation and to convey its requests.

In 1981 the city of Salvador, in an agreement with SPHAN/Pró-Memória of the Ministry of Culture and under the direction of Ordep Serra, launched Project MAMNBA, whose goal was to preserve, through the patronage of public agencies, the sacred areas of the terreiros of Salvador. This project succeeded in having the Casa Branca terreiro registered as a cultural heritage site in 1984, and in having work begun to preserve São Bartolomeu Park. Ordep

Serra and Project MAMNBA contributed greatly to the reorganization of the Sociedade Afro-Brasileira Fiéis de São Bartolomeu, which would be instrumental in coordinating the terreiro's fight for survival. The contributions of *ogãs* such as Everaldo Duarte, Jaime Sodré, and Gilberto Leal, among others, were greatly important in this process.

In 1985, through the initiative of Project MAMNBA, the then mayor of Salvador, Manoel Figueiredo Castro, submitted to the city council the proposed ordinance number 3,591/85 designating Bogum, Casa Branca, Gantois, and the Ipatirió Gallo candomblé as Cultural and Landscape Protection Areas. This ordinance declared the whole of the candomblé and its surroundings used for religious and residential purposes, as well as the isolated trees and the area immediately around them, as an Area of Strict Protection. It also established that no buildings larger than two stories could be built in the vicinity.[146]

A second piece of legislation from the same period determined that the terreiros would no longer pay city taxes. There are copies of receipts for taxes paid by Bogum in the 1960s, in Maria Emiliana da Piedade's name, which suggests that these taxes were paid from the times of her leadership in the 1940s. In addressing the newspaper *A Tarde*, Nicinha said proudly, "At least we won't be paying taxes. Nowadays, besides the taxes, we make lease payments; because so far the land has not been ours." Taking advantage of the circumstances, and following the advice of Project MAMNBA leaders, Bogum stopped making lease payments on the land. Since then, the Príncipe de Oliveira family, the land's official owners, have also ceased seeking payment. However, the residents of Bogum still do not have a deed to the lands.[147]

The ordinance declaring Bogum a Cultural and Landscape Protection Area was passed but not ratified. Because of the city's lack of control and lack of means to implement the law, buildings of more than two stories have proliferated in the area surrounding the terreiro, seriously jeopardizing the privacy of religious practices. In the context of the above-mentioned First Seminar on the Malê People and Their Influences, held in 1986, Jaime Sodré noted the shrinking area belonging to the terreiro, and Nicinha complained that "this usually ends up compromising the secret ceremonies, as they are exposed to the eyes of the curious." The law existed, but its effectiveness was null. Sodré also complained of the "precarious state of the physical facilities of the terreiro," in need of urgent repairs, and suggested having the terreiro registered as a heritage site in order to preserve it.[148]

Although an internal decision by Bogum members, who feared they would be unable to protect the privacy of the sacred areas, kept the heritage-site project from succeeding, the campaign launched through the press and other

Sideview of the Bogum terreiro before the restoration of the roof (7/22/1987)

political initiatives seemed to have an effect. In March 1987, the Gregório de Matos Foundation, under the presidency of Gilberto Gil and the direction of Antônio Risério, launched a campaign to restore the city's principal terreiros. At Bogum, this initiative contributed principally to renovating the roof of the *barracão* and to constructing walls around the property, because, as *Ogã* Celestino Santos pointed out, "the house's money is insufficient for the repairs." At that moment of enthusiasm there was still some hope of obtaining further support at the state and federal levels. Unfortunately, it was only during the administration of Mayor Lídice da Matta, in November 1993, that some improvements were made in the vicinity of the terreiro, in the Praça da Federação, which thereafter was called Praça de Mãe Runhó, and where a bust of *Doné* Runhó was erected.[149]

Therefore, in the 1980s Bogum mobilized itself through political contacts and the use of the media to fight off real estate speculation and obtain aid from public agencies. The use of the press by the terreiros (and vice versa), which began in the 1970s, deserves a small sidenote. In 1973, for example, the newspaper *A Tarde* began regularly to advertise a number of the city's most famous terreiros, Bogum among them, "in order to make it easier for those wishing to visit the Candomblé terreiros."[150] This is also the period during which the Bahian government began to portray Candomblé as a symbol of Bahian cultural identity, and the terreiros began to be promoted as a tourist attraction and a product of cultural marketing. Simultaneous with this external manipulation, the religious communities, mostly through their *ogãs*, took advantage of this opportunity, and used the press for their own purposes—as a weapon to gain public support and demand aid from public agencies. The 1980s seems to be most intense period of this activity. In the case of Bogum, the antiquity of the terreiro and its claim to be "the *only* candomblé of the Jeje nation in the state of Bahia," "the *last* of a number of *historic sites*," or "a kind of Jeje *museum*" (emphasis added), in addition to being ways of legitimizing religious authority among the *povo-de-santo*, were critical points used in the terreiro's strategy to give credibility to its demands, defend its rights, and win the support of public agencies.[151]

Similarly, another idea that contributed to creating the house's prestige through the press was to portray Bogum as a "matriarchy." Female leadership of Bogum dates from the postabolition period, while in the second half of the nineteenth century, despite the significant presence of Ludovina Pessoa and the "negress" Rachel, the leaders seem to have been predominantly male.[152] Even leaving aside these historic facts, the contemporary representation of Bogum as a "matriarchy" to the public powers is, in part, a response to the perception that a female religious power would appear more attractive and acceptable to the white elites, being less threatening than male power.

In this context, Lorand Matory's suggestion that since the 1930s intellectuals such as Gilberto Freyre have contributed to the creation in Brazilian society of the image of the "black mother" as maternal, kind, and protective, is pertinent. Authors such as Edison Carneiro or Ruth Landes associated this favorable image of the black woman with the "purity" of the African rituals, principally Nagô, in opposition to the image of the *feiticeiro*, or male sorcerer— homosexual and involved in syncretic practices—associated primarily with the Angola tradition.[153] Bogum, in its claims to matriarchy and to being the most ancient terreiro, and implicitly of "African purity," seems to align itself with the ideology of the more "traditional" Ketu-nation hegemonic houses.

Other Twentieth-Century Jeje Terreiros

At the end of the nineteenth century, Nina Rodrigues, despite recognizing the Jeje tradition in Candomblé and coining the term *Jeje-Nagô*, did not explicitly cite any terreiro of this "nation." In fact, he did not even speak of Candomblé nations and only mentioned the terreiro of Livaldina, "where the Jeje influence was most accentuated," because he had found in that house a figure of a serpent that he identified as belonging to the cult of Dan.[154] It is not until the 1930s that the first references to Jeje terreiros occur. Correia Lopes, in a work published in 1943, documented his visit to Bogum in 1937, and Carneiro, in a 1948 publication, mentioned Bogum, Poço Béta, and the candomblé of Manuel Menez as being registered, in 1937, with the Union of Afro-Brazilian Sects of Bahia.[155] Unfortunately, I was unable to find any further information regarding the Manuel Menez terreiro in São Caetano.

The Poço Béta terreiro, which continues to be active, was founded by Manuel Vitorino da Costa, better known as Manuel Falefá or Manuel da Formiga. He was born in Santo Amaro, on December 21, 1900, and died on May 18, 1980. There are contradictory accounts of his initiation. According to Falefá's own testimony, he was "made" at age eleven and consecrated to the vodun Nanã, probably in São Francisco do Conde. However, according to Itamoacy, his first-born son, his father was initiated at age seven by his grandmother, Clarice Constanza Barbosa, in Pojuca, on Pau Grande farm, near Santo Amaro.[156]

The available information, though confusing, seems to suggest the existence of an earlier terreiro, "founded by Xangô," perhaps in Mata de São João, called Poço Bêtá. Falefá's grandmother, Clare Borbosa, was in line to assume the leadership of the house but did not accept the position, appointing Falefá as "heir." Later, Falefá opened a candomblé in Salvador, called Poço Béta (with a difference in accentuation from the original name), with the "house patron saint" being the vodun Sogbo Adan, spelled by Falefá himself as "Cô bô Adân da Virdê." Though consecrated to Nanã, Falefá claimed: "I am heir of Sogbo." This suggests that he initially had some responsibility in the Recôncavo terreiro, founded by others.[157]

Various etymologies for Poço Béta have been offered. *Poço* is probably a phonetic evolution of Kposu, the panther vodun. *Bêtá*, or *béta*, is more difficult to identify, although in the Jeje terreiros of Bahia the vodun Kpo is also known as Poçu Batan Ajaí, who according to *Gaiaku* Luiza is the father of the vodun Sogbo. This seems to be the most plausible etymological hypothesis, but there are others.[158]

According to Itamoacy, Falefá opened his first Salvador house, called Ori Funji, in the neighborhood of Barra. A short while later, probably in the 1930s, the terreiro moved to Rua da Formiga, number 118, in São Caetano, where it stayed until 1970, when Nanã asked that the terreiro be closed for lack of space, and it was relocated to Rua São Martins, in the São Marcos neighborhood in Pau de Lima, where it remains today.

In his youth, Manoel Falefá was in the navy, traveling on various occasions to Africa. He learned to speak Yoruba and dealt in West African cloth, *orobô*, *obi* (two types of kola nuts), and other African products. Falefá was a popular figure among the *povo-de-santo*, although among the Jeje experts his liturgical

Manuel Falefá (in the hat) and his first wife (c. 1950). Photo: Pierre Verger

knowledge of that nation still elicits some reservations. In 1937 he wrote an essay titled "O mundo religioso do negro da Bahia" (The Religious World of the Black Bahian) for the Second Afro-Brazilian Conference, and his terreiro was registered with the Union of Afro-Brazilian Sects of Bahia.[159] In 1968, by that time a teacher of Yoruba, he received a grant to travel to the Popo region of Togo, and to Lagos, Nigeria. Following his return, he drew images of snakes, the emblem of Bessen, on the walls of the terreiro. These were later removed. Although Carneiro in 1948 identifies the candomblé as "Jêje-Marrim (Mahi)," it is likely that it was after this trip that Falefá began to identify his house as being of the "Mina-Popo" nation. It is also interesting to note that in the CEAO records he already identifies his grandmother as "Gêge Popo."

Manoel Falefá was married to two women and had at least seventeen children with them. In the 1960s, nine of these children were already participating in the terreiro's activities, which suggests the important dependence of the congregation on kinship. He founded, within the candomblé, the Ayaba Okere Civil Society which is still in operation.[160] With Falefá's death in 1980, his oldest filha-de-santo, Sibeboran, of Aziri Tobosi, assumed the terreiro's leadership, changing its name to Ilê Omó Kétá Posú Bétá (House of the Children of Posú

Bétá) and enshrining Iemanjá or Aziri Tobosi as the terreiro's new spiritual "regent." When Sibeboran died in 1992, her biological daughter, Edvaldina Alves de Souza (Dona Vadinha), became the new leader, a post that she maintains today. Currently the calendar of festivities goes through the months of May, July, August, October, and December.[161]

Another important terreiro in the early decades of the twentieth century was Cacunda de Yaya (Yava). Matory speaks of the origins of Cacunda as emerging from another terreiro in the village of Acupí, near Santo Amaro. Jaime Montenegro, initiated at Cacunda, heard that the Santo Amaro congregation was Casarangongo (which seems to be a Bantu term) and was said to be Jeje Agabi.[162] Cacunda de Yaya was initially founded in the Sussuarana neighborhood in Salvador on January 6, 1920. Later, when the government expropriated the land, the terreiro was transferred to São Caetano. It was led by Sinfrônio Eloi Pires, a devotee of Obaluaê who descended from Africans and whose ritual name, or *dijina*, was Zuntôno. Sinfrônio died on June 1, 1938, leaving as his successor his wife, Constança da Rocha Pires, better known as *Mãe* Tança, a devotee of Nanã whose *dijina* was Ajuasse. *Mãe* Tança died on October 2, 1978, and was succeeded by her biological daughter, Maria Pires, of Oxum, whose *dijina* was Ia-Omi-Ni-Que. She had as her *pejigã* (and *axogum*) Pedro de Alcantara Rocha (Pedrinho). He was a devotee of Ogun whose *dijina* was Ogun Leé, and was confirmed in April 1933. Being an illegitimate son of *Mãe* Tança, Pedrinho was called after her death *babalaxé*, or high priest. The most important festivities were the *Festa das Frutas* (Fruit Festival) and the *Amalá* of Xangô, both celebrated on January 6, and the Obaluaê Festival, on Holy Saturday, following Good Friday, with ox and goat sacrifices. Although the house continues to maintain the shrines, it has not celebrated festivities since 1991.[163]

In the time of *Mãe* Tança there was close communication with Seja Hundé while it was led by Abalhe and Pararasi. *Mãe* Tança also traveled to Rio, and it seems that two factions formed, which gave way to internal disputes. *Mãe* Tança's first group of initiates was organized in 1954 with seven *vodunsis*, and later there was even a second group with four *vodunsis*.[164] *Mãe* Hilda Dias dos Santos's Ilê Axé Jitolú terreiro, founded around 1960 in Curuzu—the spiritual center of the famous Ilê Ayé Carnival group—and the Inlegedá Jigemin terreiro of *Pai* Amilton Costa, founded in 1974 in Boca do Rio and moved in 1985 to Curuzu, are both descended from Cacunda de Yaya.

Cacunda de Yaya and those terreiros affiliated with it are normally identified as Jeje-Savalu. The liturgical differences between Jeje-Mahi and Jeje-Savalu are not very great, though there are blessings, sacrifice songs, songs for the coming-out of *iaôs*, and nation hymns that are different. In general, present-day Jeje-Savalu traditions reveal a strong liturgical Nagô-Ketu influence. In *Pai* Amilton's Jigemin terreiro, for example, devotees perform rituals such as the "procession for Odudua," similar to the waters of Oxalá of the Ketu nation, which are not typically celebrated among the Jeje-Mahi. In this terreiro, the *zandró* and the *biotá* rituals, important to the Mahi ceremonial tradition (see chapter 8), are rarely celebrated, and the *biotá*, for example, is private and includes no procession around the sacred trees, characteristic of Mahi terreiros. The Jeje-Savalu recognize Omolu (Azonsu) and Nanã as "the true masters" of their nation, and not Bessen, as the Mahi do. With the exception of these elements, the ritual language, drum beats, holy songs, and ritual practice are very similar.[165]

In the 1920s and 1930s a number of Jeje houses in Salvador emerged as extensions of terreiros located in the Recôncavo (Santo Amaro, São Francisco do Conde, Mata de São João). The Jeje-Dagomé terreiro of Fazenda Caju (which we discussed in chapter 5), was located on the banks of the Paraguaçu River near Maragogipe. It was led by Dona Vitória, who was about ninety years old in 1970, and must have been operating in the first decades of the century. According to Luiz Magno, Dona Vitória, "was of Aberigã with Nanã. Aberigã is the name they call the vodun Bessen there in Jeje-Dagomé." Despite the difficult access, during the time of the candomblés, there were many canoes and boats to take people to the terreiro.[166] In Maragogipe, in the 1930s and 1940s, the feared Badesa Arcanja, daughter of Maria Agorensi, opened a terreiro. We have already discussed the serious disputes she had with Abalhe during the last years of her life.

Gaiaku Luiza also remembered the existence of a "Jeje-Efon" terreiro on the island of Itaparica.[167] Uvaldo Ossório, despite claiming that "on the island the influence of the Geges was practically nothing," writes that "with slavery abolished, they remained in the old village of Ponta das Baleias, working as day laborers for the *cachaça* distilleries. They were mostly coopers and smiths," and he mentions the "terreiro of *Mestre* Evódio, an old worshiper of Avrikiti, a sea deity," and his companions *Tio* Cassiano, *Mestre* Jorge, *Tia* Henriqueta, and *Mestre* Antônio Laê. In this congregation they also worshipped Obessém (Bessen) and Iroko (Loko).[168] Ossório gives no more details, but the reference to their leader as one who worshipped the vodun Averekete permits the supposition that the terreiro was descended from the peoples of the coast of the Gbe-speaking area.

In Salvador in the 1930s there is news of *Tio* Vidal, with a candomblé in Engenho Velho de Brotas. Some say that he was Ketu and others that he was

Jeje. *Mestre* Didi remembers that on March 10, 1937, *Mãe* Aninha of Axé Opô Afonjá performed "a great ritual for *Babalorixá* Vidal, who was of Xangô in the Jeje nation, and made Oxalá (Oxaguiã)." A few years later, between 1941 and 1942, Frances and Melville Herskovits recorded a number of songs identified as "Gêge" interpreted by the "Vidal group." The change of saint and of nation (from Jeje to Ketu), together with *Tio* Vidal's command of ritual repertoires of multiple nations, points to the relative permeability and fluidity of individuals among the various nations of Candomblé.[169]

To this border territory belong a number of terreiros, such as Ilê Maroialaje or the candomblé of Alaketo, in Matatu, and the Oxumaré terreiro, in Mata Escura, which, without explicitly declaring themselves Jeje, exhibit a strong Jeje influence. In the case of Alaketo, one of the oldest terreiros of Salvador, this juxtaposition of rituals has its antecedents in the city of Kétou, from which its founders came, for there the orixá cults lived alongside the vodun cults of their neighbors from time immemorial. Although Afro-Brazilian studies generally identify Alaketo as a Nagô-Ketu candomblé, its late leader, Olga Francisca Régis, identified it as Nagô-Vodun and explained: "Nagô-Vodun is Jeje and Ketu, part Jeje and part Ketu, that is to say, the two things together. . . . We may make a candomblé that is only Jeje, or one that is only Ketu, or we can mix the two—perform a Jeje ritual, or perform a Ketu ritual. We perform a ritual to Oxumaré, more to the Jeje part; and to Azoónu, more to the Jeje part; and to Iroko more to the Jeje part. We also do Xangô, which is more to our Ketu part. . . . In the songs, in the rituals, [the Jeje] is different, the dances are different from those of Ketu. But now the people don't separate anything, so they sing a bit of the Jeje, and a bit of the Ketu, meaning there are those who do things differently. . . . we distinguish between them."[170]

This interesting commentary illustrates that, despite the increasing "Nagoization" of Candomblé, there still exist various degrees of "Jeje-Nagô syncretism," and in some houses the coexistence does not imply pure and simple identification or substitution of voduns for orixás.

The case of the Oxumaré terreiro, in Mata Escura (today Vasco da Gama), is something different. It was founded sometime before 1911 by the legendary African *Tio* Salacó of Xangô and by Antônio Oxumaré, his *filho-de-santo*.[171] Vivaldo da Costa Lima mentions that Antônio Oxumaré is "remembered even today by the 'eldest members' for his connections with the Bahian political leaders during the time of the Civilist Campaign." Dona Cotinha (Maria das Mercês), Antônio Oxumaré's *filha-de-santo* and *mãe* of the terreiro during the 1930s, was of Euá and married *Seu* Jacinto.[172] Lima asks why Carneiro omits Continha's name in his work "since Carneiro himself cites, in *Religiões negras,*

TABLE 7 Statistics of Jeje Terreiros in Salvador

Year	Jeje	%	Ijexá	Ketu	Angola	Caboclo	Umbanda	Other	Total
1937	9	13.4	6	13	22	15	—	2	67
1969	14	4.57	16	107	61	105	2	1	306
1981	4	0.27	14	660	350	271	50	—	1,349
1983	30	2.47	47	447	384	41	1	261	1,211
1992	19	2.02	22	415	200	245	37	—	938
1998	18	3.60	8	282	137	14	11	26	500

Sources: For 1937, Carneiro, *Candomblés . . .*, 44. For 1969, "Pesquisa sobre os candomblés de Salvador," directed by Vivaldo da Costa Lima, CEAO, 1960–69, in J. T. dos Santos, *O dono . . .*, 21. For 1981, Federação Baiana do Culto Afro-Brasileiro (Barbosa, 1984), in J. T. dos Santos, *O dono . . .*, 21. For 1983, adapted from data of survey conducted by SIC-IPAC in the Metropolitan region of Salvador, in J. T. dos Santos, *O dono . . .*, 19. For 1992, Registry books, Federação Baiana do Culto Afro-Brasileiro, Salvador, June 1992. For 1998, Mott and Cerqueira, *As religiões . . .*, 13.

the terreiro of Oxumaré, which he attended," including, in the book's appendix, a colorful description of the "Present to the Mother of Water" festival celebrated in 1934.[173]

This candomblé, today self-denominated as Ketu, initially evinced a strong Jeje influence. Pierre Verger comments that "the Gegê and Nagô cults were fused in terreiros such as that of Oxumaré." It is known that in the early decades of the twentieth century there was a strong relationship between the Bogum and the Oxumaré terreiros, and that men who could not be initiated at Bogum, since only women danced there, were "made" at Oxumaré. It is possible that Antônio Oxumaré performed a Jeje ritual with Romana, who frequently attended his terreiro. The terreiro's current leader, Silvanton da Mata, declared in 1995 that "in the beginning the terreiro was Jeje. But, because of changes, today the worship is Ketu. The terreiro went through great difficulties, and it was necessary to change nations." This must have occurred in the 1940s, perhaps following the death of Dona Cotinha, but the motives were never identified.[174]

In addition to the terreiros referred to here, there were, and still are, a number of others that identify themselves as Jeje. Adapting a series of statistics of terreiros in Salvador according to nation, I created table 7.

The data in the table should be viewed cautiously, since self-denomination by nation is sometimes more a result of a given leader's interest in legitimization than of any real connection to religious descent. For example, in the 1998 statistic, there are terreiros with names that include apparently Jeje terms, such as Ilê Savaluê de Azanssun (in Liberdade) or Ilê Axé Gêge, yet claim to be Ketu. There are also terreiros that claim to be Jeje, but that have *donos da casa,* or head orixás, that belong to another nation or whose affiliation with Jeje candomblés would be questionable.

Despite these nuances, the table shows a clear decline in the percentage of Jeje terreiros throughout the century. Since the 1930s, when the Jeje had a significant presence of 13 percent, until the 1980s and 1990s, when they represented only about 2 or 3.6 percent, the tendency has been a decrease in number. This is due, in part, to the great expansion of terreiros that has occurred since the 1970s, when many terreiros with no defined religious affiliation claimed to be Ketu, being as this was the most prestigious and socially visible "nation." This would explain the 0.2 percent of Jeje terreiros in 1981, when the Ketu houses demonstrated great growth, achieving almost 50 percent.

As the late Runhó declared, "the Gege terreiros came to an end," a nostalgic perception shared by *Humbono* Vicente, who affirmed that "in Bahia, the time of the Jeje is over. Nowadays no one knows how to answer the songs."[175] The memory of the Jeje rites is being lost, but, paradoxically, the Jeje "nation" still enjoys great prestige among the *povo-de-santo* and a presence in the media, principally the press, comparable to the Nagô-Ketu or Congo-Angola nations. This in part results from the social visibility of terreiros such as Bogum, but the prestige is also rooted in the very history of Candomblé, which recognizes the vodun worship tradition as one of its constitutive sources.

It is difficult to foretell the future evolution of the "Jeje nation." There is an ongoing process of revitalization of this nation in the Jeje-Mahi terreiros of Rio de Janeiro and other cities in the South. Additionally, in Salvador, Bogum is recommencing liturgical activities and, together with terreiros such as Huntoloji of the late *Gaiaku* Luiza in Cachoeira, or the Jigemin terreiro of *Pai* Amilton in Curuzu, which also enjoys a certain degree of social visibility, may contribute to a renaissance of this nation's identity. As I have noted, a number of researchers, such as Matory, Lopez de Carvalho, and Dias do Nascimento, have published works in the last few years dedicated to Jeje terreiros. My book is also a part of this trend. This new and growing interest in a nation previously largely ignored may contribute to the consolidation of a tendency, perceptible among certain sectors of the *povo-de-santo*, that protests against the Nagocentrism of contemporary Candomblé. At this time, the construction of identity based on a "differentiated specificity" that contrasts with the dominant referents can be seen as an alternative strategy to increase the attraction to, and legitimize the prestige of, certain terreiros. Thus, the tradition of the vodun cult, with its undisputed historical antecedents and its simultaneous "rarity," is an option with potential that may still be developed.

7 The Jeje Pantheon and Its Transformations

Multideity Cults, Pantheons, and Hierarchies

Having reconstructed the microhistory of the Jeje-Mahi terreiros of Salvador and Cachoeira, I will now examine their religious system, beginning, in this chapter, with the spiritual entities or voduns, and the internal dynamic of the "pantheons" into which they are organized. Continuing with a topic highlighted in chapter 4, in the first part of this chapter I analyze one of the aspects that contributed significantly to the process of increasing ritual complexity that occurred in the institutionalization of Candomblé. This aspect is the gathering of cults corresponding to various deities within a single congregation, the consequent juxtaposition of different shrines, or *assentos*, in the same physical space, and the organization of forms of serial performance to celebrate, simultaneously or consecutively, this spiritual plurality. It is therefore important to distinguish the *multideity* cults from the *monotheistic* cults dedicated to a single spiritual entity.[1]

Previous to the nineteenth century there is no documentary evidence, in Bahia, of congregations that worshipped more than one deity, although this is not sufficient to infer that no such congregation existed. As I have noted, oral tradition claims that it was during the foundation of Ilê Iyá Nassô—which occurred, according to the most liberal calculations, in the last decade of the eighteenth century, or, according to the most conservative calculations, in the first decades of the nineteenth—that the simultaneous aggregation of cults of various deities in the same terreiro occurred for the first time in Bahia. Yet the first documentary indication of a multideity cult only appears in 1858, when, in a candomblé in Quintas da Barra, in the Salvador district of Vitória, police found various vestments and ritual emblems suggestive of a collective cult.[2]

Authors such as Pierre Verger or Roger Bastide, in comparing this Bahian situation with ethnographic evidence of orixá cults from the Yoruba area, which at least in the precolonial past were generally monotheistic (a single deity per temple or congregation), conclude that the aggregation of cults of deities of diverse origin in the same physical space, as happened with Ilê Iyá Nassô, was the result of a genuinely "Creole" process or an essentially Brazilian innovation brought about by the new sociocultural conditions imposed by the slave society, the interethnic encounter of heterogeneous social groups, and the necessity of economizing and sharing resources in times of oppression. Other authors, such as João José Reis, have maintained that the devotion to manifold saints practiced in the Catholic churches also would have served as a model or referent for the establishment of cults of multiple deities in Candomblé.[3]

Without denying the possible influence of these factors, it is important to note that some of the African groups that arrived in Bahia had clear religious antecedents in this domain. In effect, one of the characteristics of the vodun religion is the conceptualization of the spirit world in *constellations* or *groups* of deities, and one of its structural elements is the organization of congregations dedicated to the collective cult of a varying number of voduns, with public rituals that use forms of serial performance. Similarly, the historic and ethnographic analysis of the vodun cult clearly shows the essentially dynamic nature of these *groups* of divinities. There is a recurring tendency to include, assimilate, or aggregate new deities to the existent "pantheons." What one could call the "aggregation principle" would be, therefore, a third property of the vodun religious system.

The process of interethnic joining of deities that characterized the formation of Ilê Iyá Nassô and that, very probably, occurred during the same period in other contemporary terreiros, could be interpreted, in part, as the intrinsic result of the confluence of socially heterogeneous groups that took place in the slave colonial society. Thus the aggregation processes occurring in Bahian Candomblé and in the vodun cults of the Gbe-speaking area could be interpreted as parallel, although independent, responses to similar social conditions. Centers such as Ouidah or Abomey, for example, shared with Salvador the same social heterogeneity, movement, and stratification, which would have in some way contributed to the synthesis or juxtaposition of cults.

Given the historical precedence of this phenomenon in the Gbe-speaking area, however, one could argue that the multideity cults in Candomblé were *also* the result of linear and direct influences of the "aggregation principle," characteristic of the vodun cults, although applied to a more extensive ethnic diversity. In other words, certain enslaved Jeje religious experts in Bahia had the ritual referents and esoteric knowledge to organize multideity cults and, more important, were accustomed to aggregating new divinities in these cults. In a social context that favored the gathering of heterogeneous human groups, this experience of African Jejes was undoubtedly of great use to religious specialists from other origins who, whether through association with Jeje priests or through imitating their practices, replicated similar collective cult forms. These considerations corroborate, from another angle, the thesis I presented in chapter 4, that the vodun tradition played a determining role in the formative process of Candomblé.

Let us examine these questions in greater detail. Alongside the deified ancestors of the various lineages (*hennu-voduns*) and the "personal gods and forces" (Fa, Legba), Melville Herskovits divides the Dahomean "public" or "great gods" into four main categories: the sky pantheon of Mawu-Lissá, the earth pantheon of Sakpata, the snake pantheon of Dan, and the thunder pantheon of Hevioso. Herskovits states that "the Dahomean does not conceive of a single deity as performing all the functions of each of the elements. He rather envisages *groups of deities*, with each group forming a pantheon ruled by a *pantheon head*" (emphasis added).[4] As Bernard Maupoil explains, "the thunder, the earth, all of the great voduns possess a set of *satellites* among whom they share out the duties for which they are responsible."[5] What is important to highlight is the idea that the voduns are conceived of as forming *groups*, at times connected by genealogical ties, and that their shrines or altars are aggregated in a given temple, following a logic of religious efficacy and of accumulation of spiritual power (*acè*).*

Olabiyi Yai warns that calling these groups of deities "pantheons" may be misleading because the word *pantheon* "surreptitiously introduces the new and potentially subversive twin concepts of verticality and hierarchy as definitional dimensions/features of divinity in the world view of the people of the region"—features that may not always have existed.[6] However, one must concede that ideas of verticality and hierarchy, in a variety of forms, were not alien to the vodun religion.

As we saw in chapter 3, William Bosman observed in seventeenth-century Ouidah the supremacy of the snake cult over the trees and the sea cults, suggesting an analogous hierarchy among its priesthood. However, it was the Fon kings who were reputed to have established, beginning in the eighteenth century, a highly centralized and hierarchical religious system in Dahomey. Maupoil writes of a "plan of submission from the altars to the throne," and Maurice Glélé, of the state's "control by administrative police" over the vodun congregations.[7] This political control over religious life resulted in the centralization and hierarchical organization of the vodun priesthood. King Tegbesu's mother, Na Hwanjile, is generally held to be responsible for the introduction, in around 1740, of the Mawu-Lissá cult in Abomey, transforming this vodun couple into the supreme creator gods, occupying the apex of an increasingly vertical and hierarchized pantheon. At the same time, the introduction of the male-dominated Fa divination system and the promotion of the Nesuhue cult of royal ancestors into a "national" cult, with precedence over other "public" cults, contributed to a growing pyramidal structuring of the religious system.[8]

The progressive establishment of an "official pantheon" in eighteenth- and nineteenth-century Abomey was accompanied by the elaboration of conceptual and ritual ties between its constitutive parts, the "public" or "state deities." The cults of Mawu-Lissá, Hevioso, and Dan, for example, until then independent, became associated through myths with the intent to establish coherent cosmologies. These efforts aimed at creating a cohesive system were primarily restricted to Abomey and its sphere of influence.[9] Though the impact of these forces outside of Abomey should not be underestimated, what seems to have prevailed in the region is a series of what John Peel, referring to the Yoruba area, calls "local cult complexes," each defined as "the ensemble of cults . . . , which is likely to include both a good many of the *orisa* [voduns] found widely . . . and others of more local currency, perhaps even unique to that place."[10] For analysis, it is therefore useful to distinguish between a "national cult complex," established by Abomey, promoting a highly hierarchical vertical pantheon, and various "local cult complexes," capable of assimilating elements of the official model, but also of deviating from it.

Generally speaking, the priests of each vodun temple or congregation had relative autonomy to install shrines or *assentos* of the gods that they found most suitable. Though the majority of the voduns worshipped in a temple tended to belong to the same generic category (*hunve* or red voduns, such as Hevioso; *atimevodun* or tree voduns; Dan; Sakpata; Nesuhue; etc.), new voduns, for various reasons, could be "acquired" or "purchased" and added to already existing ones as "satellites." This dynamic resulted in a continual movement and transformation of the "pantheon" of any given temple and, consequently, of any "local cult complex." A comparison of lists of voduns gathered in various regions of the Gbe-speaking area, both from within and outside Dahomey, shows recurring contradictions in the number, identity, gender, attributes, function, and the relative kinship position of the deities of any particular "pantheon." This evidence clearly indicates that, despite the centralized religious organization that prevailed in Abomey, the "pantheons" were never static or homogenous. I will further analyze below this dynamic in relation to the voduns worshipped in the Jeje candomblés of Bahia.

Regardless of this variability, in each vodun temple a god is normally identified as the head of the spiritual group. This minimal hierarchical element is generally, but not always, expressed in genealogical terms. The figure of the father or of an original genitor couple frequently expresses the preeminence of certain voduns over the rest of the group. In some cases, the hierarchies prevalent among the deities reflect corresponding hierarchies among their priests. Narratives that emphasize certain hierarchies are often elaborated or constructed in order to legitimize a god or a group of gods (normally those with whom the narrator is connected) over those of competing congregations. One can conclude that the concept of *groups* or "families" of interrelated gods, led by a principal figure and worshipped in the same temple, generally under the centralized supervision of a male-female couple of *vodunons* (priests, literally "owners" of the vodun), constitute fundamental features of the vodun religion.

These characteristics of the cult of voduns in the Gbe-speaking area seem, to a certain extent, to contrast with the orixá cults of the Yoruba area, where the interconnectivity among orixás is apparently less strong. According to Verger, each orixá cult constitutes an independent institution, which results in what he calls a series of "juxtaposed monotheisms." In other words, each congregation, or even each village or city, would be dedicated to the exclusive veneration of a single autonomous deity. Though in the Yoruba area one finds ensembles of various cults in any given town, and in some cases even the worship of more than one orixá within the same congregation, Verger's hypothesis of a certain independence among the various orixá cults seems to be confirmed in a study by P. R. Mckenzie. Based on an analysis of orixá *orikis** and of Ifá verse, Mckenzie concludes that, with the exception of Xangô, Obatalá, and the "Ifá triad" (Exu, Orunmilá, and Olodumaré), the orixá cults present almost no verbal allusion to other deities, suggesting a relative "separatism" among them and the absence of a fixed or established pantheon. Mckenzie, who criticizes previous unitary models of the Yoruba pantheon, is less radical than Verger and adopts a more conciliatory middle ground, speaking of "*constellations* of orixás around a few prominent ones"; he finds that there existed among them "partial uniformities, but without ever completing a cosmological whole."[11]

Verger's hypothesis leads to the conclusion that the juxtaposition of a plurality of individual cults within the same congregation, as found in Brazilian Candomblé, Haitian Vaudou, and Cuban Santeria (what he calls "polytheism" as opposed to "juxtaposed monotheisms"), was fundamentally a New World creation resulting from new sociocultural conditions imposed by slavery, where limited human and material resources would have encouraged the merging of otherwise separate cults. This phenomenon would thus constitute a critical difference between Candomblé and West African orixá traditions. Verger's Nagôcentric interpretation has been uncritically accepted and reproduced by most Afro-Brazilian scholarship, most notably by Bastide, to cite only one of the more significant authors.[12] However, this interpretation does not take into consideration the ample evidence collected in the Gbe-speaking area (some of it by Verger himself) showing a long and fecund tradition of multideity worship.[13]

Furthermore, as documented by Andrew Apter in the kingdom of Ayede, in the Ekiti Yoruba Highlands, and by Margaret Thompson Drewal in Igbogila, a village in the Egabado region, one finds multideity orixá cults and forms of serial performance, at least in present times, in the Yoruba area, too. Apter goes so far as to conclude that the multideity orixá cults may have been a common characteristic throughout Yorubaland, and this supposition also leads him to question Verger's hypothesis and suggest that Candomblé's multideity cults might find their antecedents in the religious practices and institutions of Yorubaland. While a more detailed historical analysis is needed, it is important to note that the multideity orixá cults of Yorubaland seem to be a relatively recent phenomenon, perhaps the result of migrations and social restructuring that occurred after the fall of the Oyo kingdom in around 1830. In the case of the Ayede kingdom, for example, multideity cults centered on certain major orixás only appeared after 1845, during this kingdom's formation. Given that the Brazilian transatlantic slave trade ended in 1850, is seems unlikely that the religious practices of Ayede had any influence on the formation of Candomblé. With the case of Igbogila, however, as Drewal suggests, multideity orixá worship may have been, in its origin, a vodun practice, appropriated by the Ahori (Hollidjè) from the Gun of Porto-Novo and subsequently replicated by their Egbado neighbors.[14]

A characteristic of these Yoruba multideity cults is that the ritual is conducted by a plurality of religious experts, each one responsible for one orixá, while in the vodun temples one finds a centralized leadership, often a male-female pair of *vodunon*, responsible for the entire group of deities. According to Nina Rodrigues, there were no specialized priests in Bahia at the end of the nineteenth century; each *ialorixá* or *babalorixá* directed the worship of all deities enshrined in the terreiro, except on special occasions, such as an important festival, when several priests would gather together in the same house.[15] This new structural similarity between the vodun tradition and Candomblé reinforces my basic hypothesis that there existed a significant continuity between the two religious systems.

The emphasis here on the importance of the vodun tradition, which results from the direction of my research, should not lead us to minimize the problem's complexity. To think in terms of a polarization between a vertical "polytheistic" Dahomean system of religious organization and a horizontal "multi-monotheistic" Yoruba one is certainly reductionist and analytically misleading. Hierarchization and centralization processes were not unique to the Fon, and the historiographic and ethnographic evidence proves that centralized forms of religious organization were also common among the Yoruba groups.[16] Similarly, multideity cults and forms of serial performance were not exclusive to the vodun cults. However, the available documentation suggests that these practices were common in the Gbe-speaking area since at least the eighteenth century, while in Yorubaland they appear relatively late and in a more restricted form.

It is also clear that the formative process of Candomblé was not simply a replica of a given African tradition; instead, a whole series of sociocultural conditioners required and stimulated a "creativity" that resulted in uniquely Brazilian institutional characteristics, beyond, or alongside of, possible processes of continuity. However, the "principle of aggregation," based on the inclusion of new deities in a preexisting ritual complex, a principle that is the rule in the vodun religious system (rather than the exception, as it seems to be in the precolonial orixá cults), persisted as a Jeje influence that offered an important organizational model in the establishment of Candomblé.

The Cult of Sea and Thunder Voduns in the Gbe-Speaking Area

In addition to the ritual practices that we will examine in chapter 8, the "pantheon," or the identity of spiritual entities, is perhaps the most important factor differentiating the "Candomblé nations." Nowadays, the various Jeje-Mahi terreiros in Bahia can worship a complex variety of deities—voduns as well as orixás—with certain details differing from one house to another. However, a certain consensus exists in highlighting three main groups of voduns as both dominant and characteristic of this "nation." These three groups, or "families," are led by the "kings of the Jeje nation": (1) the snake vodun Bessen (the family of Dan), (2) the thunder vodun Sogbo (the family of Hevioso or Kaviono), and (3) the smallpox vodun Azonsu (the family of Sakpata). As the late Netinho, a *vodunsi* from Seja Hundé, explained, the three families are like the index, middle, and ring fingers; the three belong to the same hand (the same nation), but the middle (Dan) is the largest. *Gaiaku* Luiza, for her part, altered the hierarchy by stating that Sogbo is the king, Bessen the prince, and Azonsu the count.[17]

Nanã is "the oldest of the mothers of the water"; Loko is associated with the gameleira tree; Aziri, Agué, Lissá, Aizan, and Elegba are other well-known voduns, and many others are preserved in memory, but the three families mentioned above, each one including a varying number of voduns, constitute the most important identity markers of the contemporary Jeje pantheon. Juxtaposed with these voduns, a series of Nagô orixás, especially the *yabas* or female orixás, are worshipped, resulting in a mixed pantheon frequently referred to as "Nagô-vodun." This interethnic juxtaposition, which characterized not only the Jeje houses but in a general sense the formative process of Candomblé as well, could be interpreted, as I suggested above, as a dynamic inspired by the "aggregation principle," operative within the vodun religious system of the Gbe-speaking area.

In order to understand better this principle, we should analyze a specific case from a historical perspective. The example of the voduns associated with thunder and the sea, which in Brazil correspond to the Hevioso family, illustrates how these deities were gradually inserted into increasingly inclusive multiethnic pantheons, initially in the Gbe-speaking area and later in the Jeje terreiros of Bahia. This example also suggests that such changes, transpiring at the level of the spiritual entities, in which new entities are added and others "forgotten," associating them within different hierarchies, may express distinct ethnic interactions of their social agents as well as changes in the corresponding priesthood organizations. In other words, the organization of the spiritual world may mirror certain aspects of the social dynamic.

A simplified scheme of this case study can be divided into four stages. First, the sea and thunder vodun cults were independent religious institutions ascribed to particular lineages or ethnic groups—namely, the Hula and the Aïzo-Seto, respectively. Second, the sea and thunder cults were progressively appropriated by other ethnic groups, spreading throughout the Gbe-speaking area and becoming "public" cults. In this process the two vodun groups became conceptually and ritually related in varying forms, depending on the region. In many cases, the sea and thunder voduns were integrated into a single "pantheon" and worshipped in the same temples. Third, in Brazilian Jeje terreiros, at least in Bahia and Maranhão, the thunder-sea group of voduns, which were already integrated and known as Kaviono or Hevioso, became an inclusive "pantheon" incorporating a series of deities, which in the Gbe-speaking area belonged to different groups. Fourth, in the Bahian Jeje-Mahi terreiros, the Kaviono family (also known as Mundubi), although identified as a distinct group of voduns, is ritually juxtaposed with other groups of Mahi voduns, such as the snake vodun Dan, the earth vodun Sakpata, as well as certain Nagô orixás, such as the *yabas* Oyá and Oxum, for example.

The first problem in confronting this gradual and variable aggregation of deities is how to locate this movement in time and space. The historical analysis of any vodun group, in particular that of the thunder and sea voduns, presents serious methodological difficulties because of the absence, until the second half of the nineteenth century, of precise and reliable data. These difficulties can only be circumvented by resorting to a linguistic analysis, oral tradition, and by projecting twentieth-century ethnographic data onto the past. The cautious combination of these forms of indirect evidence, together with what documentary evidence is available allows the creation of a reasonably plausible geographical and chronological outline.

Sea worship is documented in various parts of the Gulf of Benin since the second half of the seventeenth century.[18] In many cases offerings to the sea were performed to invoke the arrival of European vessels, or to calm the waters' fury and allow the embarkation of goods and slaves. In this way, the worship of the sea was apparently linked to commerce with Europeans and its economic advantages. However, there is also evidence that suggests that veneration of the sea was associated with earlier autochthonous beliefs, since in landlocked kingdoms such as Allada, Oyó, and Dahomey explicit religious precepts prohibited their kings from entering into, or seeing, the sea.[19]

In the Gbe-speaking area, sea worship seems to have initially been a Hula prerogative; significantly, the sea voduns are known as *hulahun,* and today the Hula claim to be their original "owners." The Hula, also known as Popo, Fulao, Pla, Flà, or Afla, were mainly lagoon fishermen and salt producers, with their political capital in Agbanankin, in the Mono delta. Given their navigational skills and the lagoon's commercial importance as a local trade route, they quickly expanded along the entire Gbe-speaking coastal area. The available data suggests that by at least 1630 they were already established in various coastal settlements from Aflawu to Jakin, and probably as far east as Apa (Badagri).[20] Therefore, despite the absence of written documentation, it is probable that the sea cult was also spread over this region by that period.

Thunder worship is less documented, and the earliest sources from the seventeenth century speak primarily of the Gold Coast. Jean Barbot documents the association between thunder and a sky deity known as Jean Goeman or Jankomé (*Onyankome*) in the Akan territory. Bosman, referring to the same region, mentions that "the Negroes [are] of the opinion that the force of thunder is contained in a certain stone," and suggests its association with "super-natural things."[21] Although these comments do not allow us to affirm the existence of an organized thunder cult, they do indicate an ancient deification of thunder in the region. In the Gbe-speaking area the first explicit reference to the thunder cult appears in a French manuscript dated between 1708 and 1724. It mentions, in the kingdom of Ouidah, the worship of thunder and the belief that it killed thieves with its "stones," implying an association as a deity of justice.[22]

It is only in the latter half of the nineteenth century, however, that the names of the thunder gods are first documented. F. E. Forbes is the first author, in 1851, to mention the name of So ("Soh") as a thunder god. Hevioso is mentioned for the first time by Francesco Borghero in 1863: "In the Gegi language, the thunder god is called Kevioso. He is the same as the god Schango of the Nagôs." Richard Burton, who visited Ouidah and Abomey the same year, also speaks of "So or Khevioso, the thunder fetish . . . worshipped at Whydah, in a So Agbajyí, or thunder closet."[23]

According to A. Le Hérissé, a number of Sô or thunder cults (sô = thunder) coexisted in the Gbe-speaking area. There was the Djisô (the thunder from the sky), worshipped by the Djetovi, presumably a proto-Yoruba group living in the Abomey plateau. And there was the Hevieso or Hevioso, the Sô from Hevie, whose worship, at least from the nineteenth century onward, seems to have been the most popular thunder cult in the region. In Hevie, a village in the Aïzo region between Allada and Ouidah, the Hevioso voduns are also called Setohun, or deities of the Seto. According to Serpos Tidjani, the Seto were an ethnic group from Athiemé, along the banks of the Mono River, who migrated to Hevie in the seventeenth century. According to Roberto Pazzi, the diffusion of the Sô cult from Hevie into the neighboring regions did not occur until the nineteenth century.[24]

Although information based on twentieth-century oral tradition should be used with care, what emerges from this brief outline is that the sea and thunder vodun cults were initially independent religious institutions, coupled with specific ethnic groups. In other words, they were *hennu* or *ako* voduns and their worship was the exclusive responsibility of certain lineages. In addition to linguistic evidence—the sea voduns are called *hulahun* and those of the thunder are *setohun*—contemporary ethnographic documentation corroborates this fact. Verger gathered lists of voduns worshipped in Hevie and in various eastern Hula villages. In Hevie, he found no mention of sea gods (except Ahuangan, identified either as a sea or a thunder vodun), while in Hula cities such as Ketonou, Godomey, and Avlekete, the vodun Hevioso is unknown or merely peripheral, apparently being a late appropriation associated with other "public" voduns such as Lissá or Sakpata. In Allada, in Aïzo territory, Herskovits also documented the presence of Hevioso voduns and only a single independent shrine dedicated to the sea vodun Agbé. This data supports the idea that the Hula sea cult and the Aïzo-Seto thunder cult were, in the past, distinct, separate religious institutions.[25]

Regional Variations and the Internal Dynamic
of the Sea-Thunder "Pantheons"

Over time, however, the sea and thunder cults were increasingly appropriated by other ethnic groups, such as the Hueda, Fon, Gen, Ewe, and Anlo, spreading throughout nearly all of the Gbe-speaking area and thus becoming "public" or interethnic cults. Through this process, the two vodun groups became, to differing degrees depending on the region, conceptually and ritually related. In many cases, the sea and thunder voduns became integrated into a single "pantheon," worshipped in the same temples, which could be considered an early stage or expression of the "aggregation principle."

In Ouidah, although Hevioso is worshipped among certain Hueda families, the most important temple is found at the compound of Hunon Dagbo, the high priest of the sea voduns. The Hunon kinship collectivity is Hula in origin, but its presence in Hueda territory precedes the arrival of the Dahomeans in the 1720s. It is said that Hunon Dagbo "personally owns" the Hevioso voduns, but their juxtaposition with the sea voduns of his lineage suggests that, from the beginning, the thunder voduns were subordinate to the sea gods. This hierarchical relationship was expressly sanctioned when Hunon Dagbo was promoted by the Dahomean king as the supreme religious authority in Ouidah, and all of the Hevioso cults came under his jurisdiction. The subordination of the thunder voduns to those of the sea is conceptually expressed when Hunon affirms that all of the Hevioso voduns are sea voduns, children of Agbé.[26]

The opposite seems to have taken place in Abomey, where the sea voduns appear under the religious jurisdiction of the thunder priests. Le Hérissé, in 1911, is the first author to note that the sea pantheon was integrated into, and implicitly subordinate to, the thunder pantheon. "In the court of Hevioso are included Hu, the sea and his family. Hu, or Agbé or Hualahun, is, as his last name indicates, of Huala origin [Grand-Popo]. . . . Hu is the husband of Na-èté, together they are the parents of Avrekete; this trinity is worshipped in the thunder temples and uses the same seven leaves consecrated to the thunder." Indeed, in the thunder temples, Agbé and Naeté are considered "children" of Sogbo (the great So).[27]

In Agbanankin and Heve, in Hula territory and home of Agbé and the sea voduns, the Hevioso cult is also found, but in separate temples. In Heve, among the Hevioso congregations, the thunder voduns are called *yehwe*, suggesting an interpenetration with the Togoland *Yehwe* cults. As Herskovits notes, "the Yehwe cult is in terms of Dahomean culture but *vodu* worship with particular regional emphasis on the gods of Thunder and the Sea, and less separatism in the worship of other affiliated deities" (such as Gbade, Loko, or Dan).[28]

Indeed, in Togoland, probably among the Anlo or Ewe, Jacob Spieth recalls the leadership of the *Yehwe* pantheon being shared by the male thunder vodun So, imported from Hevie, and his wife, the sea vodun Agbui (Agbé), imported from Avlekete (a Hula village). Thus, outside the Hula territory, Agbé can become a female deity, symbolically subordinate to her husband, the thunder vodun. Besides variations in gender and kinship links, the integrated thunder-sea vodun group, such as in Abomey, presents an apparent hierarchical superiority of the thunder side.[29]

Lastly, in Aného (Petit-Popo) and Glidji, in Gen territory, one finds a mixed pair of thunder and sea voduns, the male Hevioso and the female Takpadoun, who give birth to a mixed offspring of sea voduns (Avlekete, Agboe, or Anatê) and thunder voduns such as Gbede (Gbadé) and Aklobè (Akolombé), the latter considered to be the father of other thunder voduns such as Sogbo and Da Ahwanga.[30]

The evidence collected in Ouidah, Abomey, the Mono River delta, and Togoland clearly demonstrates the mobility of practices and values associated with voduns across both geographic and ethnic borders, and the myriad regional variations resulting from this movement. In Ketonou, capital of a royal Hula lineage, the sea cult is dominant and there is no evidence of a Hevioso cult, while in Gen territory one finds a mixed sea-thunder couple with an equally mixed progeny. Moving westward, from Ketonu to Togoland, there seems to be a greater interpenetration, as if the integration of both groups of deities became easier outside the home area of each cult.

While commenting on a similar dynamic among the orixá cults, Peel observes: "the mobility of *orisa*, whether as a consequence of the migration of their ordinary adherents or through the promotional zeal of their priests, also promotes shifts in the character of *orisa*. An incoming *orisa* may find its special niche ... already occupied, or it may seek to carve out a new niche for itself."[31] The gender, kinship, and hierarchical shifts noted in relation to the sea-thunder voduns may follow a similar principle. The male Agbé, for instance, may undergo a change in gender and kinship position when he becomes newly appropriated into communities that already had a dominant male thunder god.

In this way, the inversion of hierarchical status among sea and thunder voduns in Ouidah and Abomey might be explained in chronological terms; the latecomer deities are always subordinated to the previously established group. This is clear in Ouidah, where the Hevioso voduns were the "guests," while the sea voduns were those proper to the Hula lineage. This would also imply that the sea voduns were imported to Abomey at a time when the Hevioso cult was already established there.

Other than this generality, much about the moment when this sea-thunder aggregation and its movement across ethnic and geographic borders occurred is open to speculation, and little can be said with certainty. It was undoubtedly an asystematic process that took place in successive moments in different areas. The same vodun might even have been imported to different temples in the same village by different families in different periods, whether by violent means such as wars and the capture of slaves, or by more peaceful means such as through marriage, kinship alliances, or the migration of priests.

According to Christian Merlo, the inclusion of Hevioso voduns in the Hula sea temples of Ouidah predated the invasion of the coast by Agaja in 1727. Certainly this Hueda-Hula assimilation of Hevioso voduns is very old, given that the devotees of Hevioso are called *huedanu* (people of Hueda) at the end of their initiation, and their secret ritual language is Huedagbe. This ethnic terminology associated with the initiation can at times indicate the cult's place of origin, but in this case it indicates one of its points of diffusion.[32]

Oral tradition varies as to the date of the installment of the Hevioso cults in Abomey and Kana, placing it either during the reign of Agaja, Tegbesu, or Agonglo, which probably reflects the successive importation of different Heviosos. Oral tradition is also contradictory regarding the place from where the Hevioso cult was imported. Although Ouidah is one possibility, Hevie is the place most frequently cited. Other versions cite the Hula regions of Heve, Ahla Heve, Jakin, and Agbanankin, indicating, as in Ouidah, an early Hula appropriation of the Aïzo-Seto voduns. Over time, Hevioso became the most important "public deity" in Abomey and, as a warrior vodun and god of justice, was a symbol of Dahomean domination. The importance conferred on Hevioso in Abomey—also known as Agbohun, or "god of Abomey"—is comparable to the importance given to Xangô in Oyo.[33]

As for the sea voduns, Le Hérissé claims they were imported to Abomey during the reign of Tegbesu and later introduced into the thunder temples. However, in 1727, during the reign of Agaja, there are already indications that members of the Dahomean elite were participating in the sea cults of Jakin. In the mid-nineteenth century, the appropriation of the sea cult by the Fon royalty seems to have been institutionalized.[34]

The coastal Hulas and Huedas were probably the first ethnic groups to integrate the two "pantheons" and were responsible for their subsequent geographic diffusion. However, during the mid-eighteenth century—the period in which the Atlantic transfer of these cults might have begun—and certainly in the beginning of the nineteenth century, when they presumably contributed to the formative process of Candomblé, these sea and thunder cults were already spread along the entire coast from the Volta River to Badagri and practiced by a number of ethnic groups including Hula, Hueda, Fon, Aïzo, Tori, Dovi, Gen, Ewe, and Anlo.

Yet, as we saw in chapter 1, in Bahia the thunder-sea voduns came to be known as *Mundubi*, an ethnic denomination recorded in the first decades of the nineteenth century. Similar to what occurred with Mahi, Savalu, and Dagomé, Mundubi came to designate a specific ritual modality associated with the voduns of the Kaviono family. The term *Kaviono* is interpreted by various Jeje religious experts as a phonetic evolution of Hevioso or Kevioso, although there may also be an association with the expression "kaviecile" (or "kawo kabiyecile"), which is used to greet the thunder voduns and orixás. As *Humbono* Vicente explained, "mundubi is Kaviono, and they sing: *ooo, ooo, ooo, Dahomé, o Kavieceli vodun Dahomé.*"[35]

The Hevioso, Kaviono, or Mundubi family in Brazil always refers to the integrated pantheon of thunder-sea voduns, with hierarchical and numeric priority given to the former as the name suggests. The most important vodun of this group is Sogbo (Sobo), followed by the descendants (Badé, Akolombé, etc.), while the sea voduns, Averekete, Agbé (Abé), and Naeté (Naté) are less known and normally relegated to secondary positions. This hegemony held by the thunder voduns reproduces the pattern found in Abomey, along the lower Mono River and Togoland (and not the inverse, prevalent in Ouidah), which might suggest the identification of the term *Mundubi* with groups from these areas.

The "Aggregation Principle" in the Bahian Jeje-Mahi Pantheon

To continue with the analysis of the "aggregation principle" characteristic of the vodun cult tradition, we will move to Brazil to examine the final two stages of the process. In the Bahian Jeje terreiros, as well as those of Maranhão, the Hevioso or Kaviono "family" became an inclusive niche or conceptual category, aggregating a series of deities such as the panther-vodun Kpo, or the tree-vodun Loko (or Lissá and Nanã in Maranhão), who in the Gbe-speaking area did not necessarily belong to this group. It is important to point out that in Africa spiritual entities such as Legba, Kpo, Loko, and Dan, do not designate a single vodun but are generic terms that include a plurality of individualized entities that can be associated with a number of different voduns. For example, there might be one Kpo who is manifested as, or "comes along the path of" the Sakpata earth voduns and another who "comes along the path of," or is physically manifested by way of, the Hevioso thunder voduns. Both are Kpo or panthers but are manifested in different temples as distinct "qualities" with their own attributes. Similarly, certain voduns may have their Dan, Loko, or Legba "quality." This fact would explain the inclusion of Kpo and Loko in the Hevioso family in Brazil. But in addition to this first-level aggregation, the Kaviono or Mundubi "family," though identified as a distinct group of voduns, was ritually juxtaposed with other groups of Jeje-Mahi voduns and Nagô orixás.

The organization of the present-day Bogum pantheon can be used as a point of departure. In this terreiro three groups of spiritual entities stand out: (1) the Kaviono, considered the "royal family," who include voduns such as Sogbo, Badé, Loko, Kpo, and others;[36] (2) the *Voduns*, who include different "qualities" of the snake vodun Dan (Bessen, Toquem, Quenquém, etc.), of the smallpox vodun Sakpata (Azonsu or Ajonsu, Azoani, etc.), and others, such as Tobosi, Agué, and so on; and (3) the *Nagô-voduns*, who include female Nagô orixás, such as Nanã, Iansã, Oxum, Iemanjá, as well as other male orixás such as Omolu, Oxóssi, and so forth. Different "qualities" of the same spiritual entity can correspond to different groups and have separate shrines. For example, the vodun Ajonsu belongs to the "vodun" group, but Omolu, his corresponding Nagô orixá, belongs to the "Nagô-vodun" group and has his own shrine. The same occurs with the vodun Agué and the orixá Oxóssi. It is also said that the Nagô entities "are orixás but have Jeje precepts."[37]

Certain voduns such as Bessen or Ajonsu, because of their hierarchical importance, are sometimes confused with members of the "royal family," but it would perhaps be more accurate to speak of them as "subjects" or "guests" of Sogbo. Jehová de Carvalho documents a house myth that might explain the friendship between Sogbo and Dan. "Sobô was on his land when suddenly up comes a caravan. And this caravan had a leader called Dâ. And Dâ comes to the land of Sobô and asks for shelter for the night. But Sobô became worried about the weariness of those who followed Dâ and told him: 'You may stay here for more than one day.' From the time of this contact, stories were told between the two peoples so that they discovered that there were common interests between them. ... So Dâ said: 'If you will allow me, I will never leave this place.' And Sobô gave consent. From this point in time, the land of the Jeje-Mahins, the land of Sobo, came to be also the land of Dâ."[38]

This refuge given to the people of Dan in the land of Sogbo finds a parallel in the mythic tradition of the corresponding Nagô orixás Oxumaré and Xangô, in which, as we will see below, the former, responsible for the rains, is considered the "servant" of the latter. This mythic tradition that ties and subjects Dan to Sogbo (or Oxumaré to Xangô) perhaps emerged from the centralization and hierarchization of the vodun cults established in Abomey, in which the cults of Dan were introduced into the Sogbo temples. Alternatively, this narrative might be a Jeje adaption of the Yoruba myth that came about in Brazil, and perhaps reflects the meeting and collaboration of Mundubi and Mahi priests.

Gaiaku Luiza, leader of the Huntoloji terreiro, which closely follows the Seja Hundé tradition, explained that "in our house we have the Modubi or Kaviono, Dan, and the Nagô vodun. And we follow the right path, such as when we begin the *zandro* 'valu, valu, valu nu kulu . . .,' and it goes on, when it ends, then begins the Nagô-vodun 'ago, ago nilê,' asking permission from the Kaviono because the Jeje is intertwined with all three. There was no *merê* [woman] in the Jeje. There were only men. That was why the Nagô-vodun came in, such as: Oiá, Iemanjá, Oxum, Nanã, so that there might be *iabás* [female vodun in Nagô]. That's why when the *zandro* ends and the *dorozan* begins we sing, 'Ago nilê, nilê madá, ago ni bibi o e ki iu ile madá ago,' asking permission from Kavioso, the head of the nation."[39]

Indeed, the juxtaposition of Mundubi and Mahi voduns with Nagô orixás finds expression at the ritual level, in the sequence in which the *zandró* songs are sung, the *zandró* being the opening ritual of festivities in the Jeje-Mahi candomblés that we will examine in chapter 8. The *zandró* begins with a series of songs, associated with Bessen, after which follow others to Legba and Ogun Xoroque, deities who open the paths. These are then followed by songs to Aizan, Tobosi, and the Kaviono family. Lastly, with the song "Ago Nilê" begins the sequence that corresponds to "Nagô-vodun."

The "Nagô-vodun" part of the *zandró*—that in fact constitutes the sequence that structures the public festivities—actually contains songs praising voduns as well as orixás, and closely follows, though not exactly, the order of the *xirê* (the initial sequence of songs in the Nagô-Ketu candomblés): (1) Ogun, the orixá of war and metals; (2) Agué and Odé, the hunter voduns; (3) the earth and smallpox voduns, Sakpata-Azonsu; (4) the *yabas* or female orixás, Oxum-Iemanjá-Oiá; (5) the thunder voduns Sogbo-Badé-Loko-Kpo; (6) the oldest mother of the waters, Nanã; (7) Olissá-Oxalá; and (8) Dan-Bessen, the snake vodun. This last, considered as being the "master" or "king" of the Jeje-Mahi nation, ends the sequence as a sign of distinction, a characteristic unique among the Jeje terreiros of Cachoeira and not replicated in the Nagô-Ketu

Jeje (voduns)   +   Nagô (orixás)

Mundubi   +   Mahi

Hevioso +	Dan +	Sakpata +	Other +	Yabas +	Other
Sogbo	Bessen	Azonsu	Legba	Oiá (Iansã)	Ogun
Badé	Bafono	Azoani	Agué	Oxum	Oxóssi
Loko	Toquem	Avimanje	Aziri	Iemanjá	Omolu
Kpo	Akotoquem	...	Nanã	...	Xangô
Averekete	...		Olissá		Oxalá
...			...		...

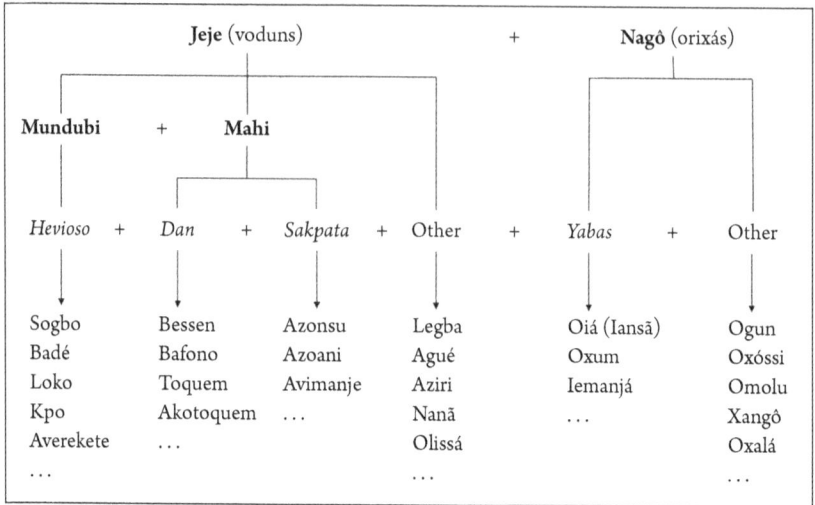

FIGURE 1 Jeje-Nagô and Mundubi-Mahi aggregation processes within the Jeje-Mahi terreiros

candomblés, which end the *xirê* by singing to Oxalá. This complex multiethnic aggregation process is represented in figure 1.

The "aggregation principle" operates on two main levels: (1) the juxtaposition of the Mundubi group with that of the Mahi, and (2) the juxtaposition of the Jeje voduns with the Nagô orixás. The former was probably the result of the grouping of religious specialists from diverse ethnic groups from the Gbe-speaking area, a consequence of the need to share the limited resources available during the slavery regime. An example of this dynamic can be seen in Roça de Cima, which is normally identified as Jeje-Mundubi, but which undoubtedly also included the presence of Mahi religious experts such as Ludovina Pessoa, who later helped to found Seja Hundé, a terreiro identified as Jeje-Mahi. In any case, it is certain that this interethnic grouping was fostered by the Gbe-speaking area's vodun cult tradition, where the "aggregation principle" was a habitual practice. This was merely an extension of the inclusive structure of the multideity cults and forms of serial performance that operated in a more restricted manner in Africa.

The juxtaposition of Jeje voduns with Nagô orixás can be interpreted in a similar way. This second level of aggregation presents more complex characteristics. During public ceremonies, songs in praise of Nagô orixás can be inserted into segments that correspond to their vodun counterparts (i.e., they might sing to Oxóssi during the Agué segment and to Omolu during the Sakpata segment, etc.). This practice tends to increase given the contemporary Nagô hegemony, and religious specialists attribute to it the loss of knowledge by the *povo-de-santo*, who no longer know how to respond to Jeje songs, thus requiring them to use the more popular Nagô-Ketu repertoire. More significant is the inclusion in the Jeje pantheon of the *yabas*, especially Oiá and Oxum, female entities who have no clear equivalent in the vodun tradition. This penetration of Nagô elements into the Jeje liturgy undoubtedly results from the importance of the orixá cult tradition in Candomblé's formation, and explicating it will require a new historical analysis.

It is difficult to know if the Mundubi-Mahi juxtaposition preceded or was contemporary with the Jeje-Nagô juxtaposition, but it is clear that the heterogeneous aggregation of gods that can be observed today was already latent in the mid-nineteenth century and was certainly consolidated by the end of the century, as Rodrigues attests in his remarks regarding the "intimate fusion" of the Jeje and Nagô mythologies, to the point "that today it is impossible to distinguish them."[40]

By the 1860s *O Alabama* was explicitly documenting the names of Sogbo, Legba, and Loko, and the names of Agué and Nanã indirectly. It also referred to the "serpent" and "smallpox" cults (see chapter 4), all of which suggests that the essence of the contemporary Jeje pantheon was already in place by that time. In fact, when a journalist arrived at the festival led by Ludovina Pessoa in Cruz do Cosme in 1869,

> All were eating *amalá*
> And intoned a hymn
> In thanks and praise to *Oiá*[41]

Ludovina's participation as head of this festival suggests a Jeje candomblé, or at least one with a strong vodun influence. The mention of Oiá indicates that, even by this time, the Nagô orixás were part of the Jeje "pantheon." In fact, in a footnote to the original text, this commentary glosses the name of Oiá: "The wife of the greatest saint—Soubô." Contrary to Nagô tradition, in which Oiá is considered to be Xangô's wife, in Jeje terreiros she is identified as the wife of the vodun Sogbo.

Despite the "intimate fusion" of the Jeje and Nagô mythologies, at the turn of the century Rodrigues recorded the names of a number of voduns worshipped in the Jeje terreiros of Salvador: "Besides Mawu, Khêbiosô, Legba, Anyi-ewo, Loko, Hoho, Saponan, and Wu (the sea), confused with the corresponding Nagô orixás Olorum, Xangô, Elegbá, Oxumarê, Irôco, Ibeji, Xaponã, and Olokum, a great number of lesser-known voduns or Jeje deities exist, such as Dsô, the fire, and Nati and Avrikiti, sea deities; Bá, god of warriors; and animals such as the crocodile, the leopard, etc."[42]

The mention of Hevioso, Anyi-ewo (Aido-Hwedo or Dan), and Saponan (a Yoruba name for Sakpata) confirms the veneration of what are currently the three hegemonic groups in the Jeje terreiros. The "confusion" Rodrigues alludes to concerning the Nagô orixás could indicate the growing predominance of Nagô cosmology in Bahian Candomblé at the end of the nineteenth century, but it could also be interpreted as an effort by Rodrigues's Jeje informants to speak in terms more easily understandable to someone familiar with the Nagô tradition. The other voduns Rodrigues mentions, such as Legba, Loko, Mawu, the leopard, and other sea deities (Wu, Nati, Avrikiti, and the crocodile), I will discuss below. For now, what is important is that as early as the second half of the nineteenth century the three principal families of the present-day pantheon were worshipped in Jeje terreiros, and that they were ritually juxtaposed with a group of Nagô orixás.

A given deity's degree of persistence or importance in the religion can be determined by the presence or absence of four criteria, in order of increasing importance: the deity (1) is remembered by name only; (2) is praised in ritual song; (3) has a shrine in the terreiro; and (4) has consecrated devotees and is manifested through "possession" in public festivities and internal, in-house rituals. The last criterion, which implies the existence of the previous three, expresses the highest level of presence of a deity in the religious community.

As we saw in the previous chapter, between 1913 and 1920 there were twenty-six dancers at Seja Hundé (twenty of whom were initiated during this period).[43] Seven of them, more than one quarter of the total, were consecrated to voduns belonging to the Kaviono family (two to Sogbo, three to Badé, one to Kpo, and one to Akolombé). At the same time, an equal number of initiates was consecrated to the female orixás Oxum and Oiá, a fact that indicates an increasing penetration of the *yaba* cult into the Jeje cult. This situation is reproduced in Bogum during the postabolition period, where, significantly, two of the four *mães-de-santo* were devotees of Sogbo and the presence of Oiá and Oxum devotees is also well-known.

Although *yabas* had already been included in the Jeje liturgy by the mid-nineteenth century, as the above citation from *O Alabama* suggests, it is probable that the number of devotees of these female orixás had grown because of women's numerical superiority among initiates, particularly when Creole women assumed leadership of the terreiros at the turn of the century (see chapter 4). As *Gaiaku* Luiza explained, among the Jeje, there were only male voduns, and the absence of female voduns was the reason for the appropriation of the *yaba* cult, thus instituting in the Jeje pantheon the "Nagô-vodun" group.[44] Although it is not entirely correct to say that there were no female voduns among the vodun cults of the Gbe-speaking area, it is true that most were male. My suggestion is that the growing importance of Oiá and Oxum devotees in the Jeje terreiros was directly related to the increasing female control of the congregations. In this case, the aggregation of Nagô *yabas* and the consequent transformation of the Jeje pantheon reflects or expresses, not the interethnic interactions of the religious experts, as in the case of the juxtaposition of the Mundubi and Mahi voduns, but alterations in the proportions of the gender of the participants and, more important, of the congregations' leadership.

The increasing importance of female orixás within the Jeje spiritual universe may also have been caused by complementary conceptual factors. In Nagô mythology, Oiá and Oxum are held to be wives of the orixá Xangô, and, by association, as we have seen, in the Jeje terreiros they are also conceived of as the wives of the corresponding vodun, Sogbo.[45] In addition to the central role of the snake-vodun Dan and the smallpox-vodun Sakpata, the hegemony of Xangô that prevails in the Nagô terreiros and in the wider religious community may have contributed to the privileging of the Mundubi vodun Sogbo in the Jeje-Mahi terreiros and, by extension, the assimilation of his wives.

While new deities are incorporated into the pantheon, others disappear; in other words, the aggregation principle inherent to the multideity cults is complemented by a parallel principle of selectivity or exclusion that might explain the progressive forgetting of certain gods. The decreasing importance of Jeje sea voduns in Bahia is an example of this dynamic. Rodrigues mentions at least four sea voduns: Hu, Naeté, Averekete, and Tokpodun (the crocodile, normally included in the Gbe-speaking area sea pantheon). But among the list of Seja Hundé dancers, it is noteworthy that there is not a single dancer of any one of these sea voduns. Hu (Agbé) and Tokpodun were completely forgotten; the name of Naeté is vaguely remembered but rarely invoked in ritual song. Averekete is the only vodun from the sea family praised in the songs and having a shrine at Seja Hundé, but not at Bogum, which celebrated Averekete's rituals at neighboring Pó Zerrem. However, the ritual knowledge necessary to initiate devotees of Averekete seems to have been lost little by little.[46] It is noteworthy that in Maranhão the persistence of the sea voduns is stronger, and Agbé (Abé), Naeté, and especially Averekete, are still important and popular voduns.

The male orixá Olokum, the Nagô sea god in the Ijebu Awori and Egbado area, like his Jeje counterparts, lost his standing in Bahia to the female Iemanjá, goddess of the Ogun River, originally worshipped by the Egba of Abeokuta. She gradually became the most important sea orixá in Brazil. In the Jeje-Mahi terreiros, the female Aziri Tobosi, originally a river spirit worshipped by the Mahi-Agonlis, was associated with Iemanjá and as such continued to be the most important water deity among the Jejes (see chapter 8).

These interrelated transformations, as in the case of Oxum and Oiá, suggest that there was a gradual "feminization" of the orixá-vodun pantheon, in which male sea gods such as Agbé and Olokum were slowly replaced by female freshwater deities. In much the same way that the juxtaposition of sea and thunder voduns in eighteenth-century Dahomey reflected the appropriation of outside cults, and that in nineteenth-century Bahia the ritual juxtaposition of Mundubi and Mahi voduns reflected the collaboration of religious experts from differing ethnic groups from the Gbe-speaking area; it is reasonable to think that the "feminization" of the orixá-vodun pantheon, which occurred primarily at the end of the nineteenth century, responded to women's growing importance in Candomblé leadership. This comports with Bastide's idea that the selection of and emphasis on certain deity attributes in the New World were conditioned by the sociocultural characteristics of the new context.[47]

Candomblé, therefore, despite being a genuinely Brazilian creation, conditioned and molded by slavery and colonial society, has been shown to have reproduced and adapted the basic principles of the multideity cults and forms of ritual serial performance characteristic of the vodun religious system. These principles persisted in Bahia as essential features that provided the structural means of aggregating a plurality of multiethnic cults into a relatively cohesive religious institution. It has also been my intent to demonstrate, through a historical analysis of the internal dynamic of a particular group of gods in the Gbe-speaking area and in the Jeje terreiros of Bahia, how the transformation of any "pantheon" is always based on simultaneous processes of accumulation/integration and selection/discrimination of deities. In fact, these processes, which occur on the conceptual level of the spiritual entities, reflect ethnic interactions and specific changes in the organization of the corresponding priesthood. It is furthermore possible that a historical analysis of the internal dynamic of the "pantheons" might reveal aspects of the sociopolitical organization of their devotees, and in particular, of their religious leaders. We can now examine other groups of voduns, such as the families of Dan and Sakpata, in order to complement the analysis of the Hevioso family.

Fluxes and Refluxes of Sakpata-Shapana, Omolu, and Nanã Buruku in Africa and Their Continuity in Nagô-Vodun Candomblé

A well-known myth in Nagô-Ketu Candomblé tells of Nanã Buruku, "the oldest mother of the waters," syncretized with Santa Anna as the mother of Omolu (Shapana) and Oxumaré, since these three deities are generally considered to be of Jeje or Jeje-Mahi origin. In the Axé Opô Afonjá terreiro, for example, these three entities have shared ritual ceremonies on Monday, and during the *xirê* they are sometimes praised consecutively.[48] To a certain degree, this ritual association, also explicit in terms of mythological kinship, contains yet another example of the aggregation principle.

Verger sees in this tradition of the Nagô-Ketu terreiros a direct continuity with what happens in the city of Kétou, where "Nanã Buruku is in the same temple as Osumare and is considered the mother of Omolu (Soponna)." This last orixá is also represented alongside the emblems of Oxumaré and Iroko in a separate temple. Shapana came from the Gbe-speaking area, where he is known as Sakpata; according to Verger, Kétou was the only city where this entity is identified with Omolu.[49] Faced with this parallelism, one cannot discard a possible continuity between the Kétou traditions and the practices of Bahian Candomblé. Yet, it is important to note—leaving aside the case of Oxumaré discussed in the next section—that Nanã Buruku, Shapana, and Omolu form a complex triad of deities in Africa, with innumerable cults interrelated in the most diverse ways and distributed throughout a vast area that extends from the Nupe country in the east, to beyond the Volta River, in the northeast region of the Ashanti country, in the west. To reduce the influence of this triad in Candomblé to the traditions of a single location would be unwise.

To this point, I have referred to Sakpata as the "earth vodun," but it would be more accurate to speak of him as the "master of the earth." According to Claude Lepine, the Sakpata-Shapana cults (and those of other variants such as Obaluaê, Ainon, Iye, and Buruku) were originally cults dedicated to the "king of the earth," associated with the ancestral founders (born from or living in the depths of the earth) and the agricultural cycles, and had origins in an ancient, pre-Odudua religious system. These cults would then have accompanied the migrations of the descendants of Odudua and the Adjas, around the year 1000, spreading throughout the whole Yoruba and Gbe-speaking area. This movement would imply an "origin" in the Tapa (Nupe) region, in the east, and it would have progressed westward, passing through Oyo-Ifé, Kétou, Savè, Dassa Zoumé, and Savalou before reaching Tado and Atakpame in the west.

Verger exhaustively describes the distribution of the cults of Sakpata-Shapana, Omolu, and Nanã Buruku in the Gbe-speaking area as well as in different Yoruba areas, demonstrating the intricate regional diversity, though there is a noticeable relative separation between the Sakpata-Shapana cults and those of Omolu and Buruku. As I have noted, only in Kétou is Shapana identified with Omolu, since in many cases the origin of Omolu, Molu, or Moru is placed in the west, in the Adja-Popo area.[50] Verger suggests two hypotheses: "Might this be a case of syncretism, perhaps lost today, between two deities of different origin and belonging to different ancient cultural groups, one coming from the east (Soponna) and the other from the west (Omolu or Molu), uniting and assuming a single character in Kétou? Or, to the contrary, might this be a single deity, of *Yoruban* origin and of more remote *Tapa* (Nupe) origin, brought westward by one of the many ancient migrations that tradition mentions, and upon this deity's subsequent return to his point of departure, he carries a new name [Omolu], which, originally, was nothing more than an epithet?"[51]

The second hypothesis of the "emergence" of Omolu in the western area of the Bight of Benin, based on the new characterization of an older eastern deity, would also apply to Nanã Buruku. This deity might have come from Ilê Ifé, as Verger suggests, and its cult would have become increasingly associated with earth gods such as Shapana. This connection with the earth element persists in contemporary Candomblé, for Nanã Buruku is associated with mud and is considered the "venerated *yaba* of death and depths" or "a monster who comes from the bottom of the earth."[52]

In the Yoruba area, Buruku (Buku) is normally identified as a male entity, being frequently associated, and even confused, with Shapana and at times with Omolu. Like them, Buruku can be associated with smallpox, and it is said that Buruku's cult was brought from the Egun country or Dahomey, while other versions point to Savé or Dassa Zoumé, in Mahi country, as Buruku's place of origin.[53] The variations that juxtapose or even identify Shapana with Buruku, as well as Buruku's male gender and association with smallpox as seen in the Yoruba area, contrast Buruku's characterization in the Gbe-speaking area.

In the latter region, Buruku is female, known by many names, such as Nanã Buluku, Anaburuku, or Minona, associated with notions of maternity and fecundity and quite distinct as a goddess from Sakpata. It is conceivable that this transformation and feminization of Buruku occurred, as with Omolu, in the western part of the Bight of Benin, in the Ashanti country. In fact, there are indications that suggest an "origin" there, or at least the passage of Buruku through the Ashanti country. For example, the Nanã Buruku priestesses in Pira and Djagbalo, north of Savalou, use an Ashanti throne, and *Nanã* is the respectful term used by Ashantis for elderly women. Through subsequent migrations, the cult of Nanã would have returned to the east, acquiring greater importance in the Atakpmé area in Togo. From there, the cult would have spread through the Mahi country and into Abomey and Kétou, perhaps supplanting older similar local cults.[54]

It is only after the "feminization" of Nanã Buruku in the Ashanti area, and her being brought back to the Gbe-speaking area, that she would have been transformed into the "mother" of Sakpata. As we have seen, the conceptualization and union of voduns into families is habitual in the Gbe-speaking area and less common in the orixá cults. In Abomey and Zangnanado, Nyohwe Ananu is mentioned as the foremother of the Sakpata family. In another version from Abomey and in Vedji, in the Mahi country, Nanã Buruku is considered the matriarch of the Sakpata family. Minona, whose name in Fon means "our mother Na," is a female deity known in the Gbe-speaking area who can be associated with the Nanã symbolic field. In Brazil it is said that Shapana is the child of Nanã Buruku or of Iyabayin (Yabanhi). These are probably two names for the same entity, as Iyabayin derives from the Yoruba expression "ìyá àgbà yin," the oldest mother of all.[55]

If in Kétou Nanã Buruku is associated with Shapana-Omolu and Oxumaré, in Abomey tradition—although viewed as the mother of Sakpata in some temples—she is also tied to the sky pantheon of Mawu and Lissá, and is sometimes considered the mother of this primordial couple, or even identified with Mawu, the female half responsible for the creation of the world.[56] In certain traditions of Abomey, therefore, Nanã Buruku has the role of primogenitor connected with notions of fecundity, as in Togo, having no direct correlation with smallpox as occurs in the Yoruba area. Within the Abomey religious system's area of influence, she is closer to Lissá (Olissá) than to Sakpata.

These regional variants of Nanã Buruku's transformation are perhaps still perceptible in certain ritual elements of contemporary Candomblé. If, as shown, the Nanã-Omolu-Oxumaré triad is important to Nagô-Ketu Candomblé; Nanã is also held as the wife of Oxalá (Lissá) on certain occasions.[57] Thus one could argue for the presence of not only Kétou traditions, but others from Dahomey as well. In the Jeje-Mahi nation, they sing to Nanã at the end of the ceremonies before singing to Lissá (Oxalá), which conveys the relationship prevalent in Abomey, but the filial relationship between Sakpata and Nanã is also recognized. This is a clear example of the interpenetration of vodun and orixá cults, developed during centuries in West Africa and transferred to Bahia, where it greatly contributed to the formation of a religious system that the participants themselves do not hesitate to call Nagô-Vodun.

But to return to Sakpata, although in various places of the Yoruba area such as Kétou Shapana is considered to have been brought from the Mahi country, the Sakpata cult in the Mahi country was very probably imported originally from the Nagô area. In Savalou it is said that the Sakpata Agbosu cult was appropriated or assimilated by Ahosu Soha (founder of the royal dynasty in Savalou), sometime during the second half of the seventeenth century, while passing through the Ouemé River region, home of the Kadjanu, who were Nagôs from the Egbado area near Badagri. The kingdom of Dassa was another important center for the Sakpata cult. Its royal dynasty goes back to at least 1700, and its inhabitants are also said to be from the Anagô region near Badagri. In fact, even today the Sakpata initiates are called "anagonu" (Anagô people), and their ritual language is an archaic form of Yoruba. It is said in Dahomey that the Sakpata cult was imported by King Agaja, while Savalou, Dassa Zoumé, and later Pingini Vedji (near Dassa Zoumé), are cited as possible points of origin for the cults introduced into Abomey. The Mahi country was, therefore, one of the cult's points of diffusion, and for that reason, Sakpata, despite his ancient Nagô origin, is normally considered a Mahi god.[58]

As we saw in chapter 3, it was only in the seventeenth century that the Sakpata-Shapana-Omolu complex of deities (and also Buruku in the Yoruba area) began to be associated with the smallpox epidemics brought by the Europeans, to the point that in contemporary Fongbe *sakpatá* means small-pox and *sakpatá kpevi* or "little sakpata," means chicken-pox. R. P. B. Segurola adds that because of the fear the smallpox epidemics inspired, no one dared to pronounce the name of Sakpata and instead used other words such as *me* (person), *ahosu* (king), *aihosu* (king of the earth), *dohosu*, *dokuno* (lord of death), or *àzon* (illness or infirmity). Devotees consecrated to Sakpata are called *sakpatasi*, *anagô*, or *azonsi*.[59] In chapter 3 we also saw the varied ways the Dahomean kings appropriated and controlled the Sakpata cults, as well as how Sakpata temples became centers of resistance for those peoples subjugated to Dahomey. Among other things, this circumstance may explain the high number of Sakpata priests sold as slaves to the Americas.

In 1870 Bahia, *O Alabama* records the first reference to "Xapanam," the Nagô name for Sakpata, and in 1871 there is a second reference to "smallpox worshipped as a god" in the Nagô candomblé of Moinho (Gantois).[60] In relation to the Jeje, we have already discussed the case of Roça de Cima in the

1860s and the jaqueira tree consecrated to Azonsu or Dandagoji, the vodun of *Tio* Xarene. In the Capivari candomblé, in São Félix, *Tio* Anacleto of Omolu acquired fame as a healer during the cholera epidemic that devastated the region in 1855. Thus one can assume that the cults of orixás and voduns associated with the earth and epidemics were already instituted in Bahia by at least the middle of the nineteenth century.

Rodrigues, at the end of that century, mentions the names of "Saponan, Wari-Warú, Afoman, and Omolu."[61] In the 1950s in Salvador, Verger collected a list of twenty-one names, from a number of informants, associated with these deities; it includes some Nagô terms, though a majority are Jeje terms, among them various toponyms from the Mahi country, such as *Savalu* (from Savalou) or *Dassa*.[62] As in Africa, speaking the name of Sakpata is avoided in Jeje terreiros for fear of possible punishment from this deity. Although the name does appear in some songs, the name Azonsu, or its phonetic variants (Azonze, Azunzu, Azunsum), is used more frequently to designate the head of this family. *Azon* (illness) is also the root of the name of other voduns of the same category, such as Azoani (of which Azoanu is a variant), and Ajonsu (Ajansur, Ojonsu, Ajunsó) or Azonodo (Azoanodo, Azaunoodor, Zanodô, Azanaodô, Ozana Ado). We will discuss the ritual of the latter deity in detail in chapter 8. In Seja Hundé, Azonsu (enshrined in a mulungu or omolongu tree) and Azoani are considered to be two separate voduns, but in other terreiros some of these "qualities" can be confused. In Bogum for example, Azonsu seems to be identified as Ajonsu. Other voduns from the same family that are remembered in contemporary Jeje terreiros are Sakpata Logua, Parara, Avimanje, Dada Lansu (associated with Kpo), Ajagonu, and Jagun.

In present-day Bahia, the characteristic clothing of Sakpata-Omolu consists of a hood and a skirt of *palha da Costa* (straw) that covers the entire body, supposedly to hide his sores and physical deformities. This dress may be a relatively recent creation, for there is no clear evidence of its use among the cults of these deities in West Africa, and in Brazil the practice is not documented until the 1930s.[63] In the Jeje terreiros *palha da Costa* is used for other voduns such as Kpo and Loko, in addition to Azonsu, and it is normally dyed a "wine color," a technique that has parallels in the Gbe-speaking area and constitutes a distinctive element of Jeje dress.

The ritual emblem of Sakpata-Omolu is a broom with straw or palm-stem bristles called *xaxará*, a symbol that in Africa seems associated principally with the Omolu cults.[64] Sakpata also sometimes carries small closed gourds (*adô*) that hang from his clothes and wears necklaces of white cowry shells crossing his chest.[65] At times he wears a black necklace called *laguidibá*. Sometimes his necklace contains alternating black and red beads. His colors therefore are, as in Africa, white, red, and black.

Following the ambivalent principle characteristic of most African deities, Sakpata, Shapana, Omolu, and Obaluaê, gods of pustules, skin disease, contagious diseases, and in present times, also associated with AIDS, have both the power to inflict these punishments, and, more important, to cure them. Sakapta-Omolu, also known as the "old man" or the "lord of flowers," in allusion to popcorn, one of his ritual foods and also a representation of skin pustules, was syncretized according to his various "qualities" with Saint Roch, Saint Lazarus, Saint Sebastian, and, formerly, with Saint Benedict. Flies, mosquitoes, beetles, and black butterflies are insects associated with him. He is denominated "doctor of the blacks,"[66] "doctor of the poor," or "wounded doctor" because of his healing gifts. The therapeutic dimension of Sakpata-Omolu, who acquired his curative powers through having been sick himself, has been dealt with in detail in Afro-Brazilian scholarship; I refer the reader to the most recent works of Claude Lepine, Pedro Ratis e Silva, and Andrea Caprara.[67]

The Family of Dan and Bessen, Master of the Jeje-Mahi Nation

The third major group of deities within the Jeje-Mahi terreiros is the family of Dan (or Odan), led by the snake-vodun Bessen (or Obessén), considered by many to be the "king," "prince," or "master of the Mahi nation." His greeting is "Arobobo Bessen"; he is also addressed with the expression "seu aholo Bessém Dokumi, Ogorensi Misimi, Ogorensi Nujami"—*aholo* being derived from the Gbe term *aholu*, meaning prince.[68] If, at Seja Hundé, Azonsu is considered the "master of the *barracão*" or dance hall, Bessen is held to be the "master of the terreiro." Similarly, at Bogum, while the Sogbo family is considered to be the "royal family," the vodun Bafono Deka (*Bafon no de ka*) "very well regarded because he has Bessen" is identified as the "patron" or "head of the house." One member of Bogum put it thus: "Bessen is the master of the nation, of the terreiro, but Sogbo is at the top."[69] Bessen's importance is expressed ritually by the position his songs occupy within the ceremonies. In Cachoeira, the first songs of the *zandró* are associated with this vodun, and in the "Nagô-vodun" part of this ritual and in the public festivities Bessen is the last god to be praised. This position of Dan at the end of the repertoire of songs is one of the elements that distinguish the Jeje sequence from the Nagô-Ketu *xirê*, which ends with songs to Oxalá. The *boitá*, a ritual that marks the high point of the Jeje-Mahi ceremonial cycle, and which we will examine in chapter 8, is also dedicated to Bessen.

Dan is a Fongbe generic term meaning snake or serpent. In the Gbe-speaking area, voduns from different categories can be associated with a given individualized "quality" of Dan, in the same way that each vodun has its own Legba. It implies a multiple and multiform deity, worshipped in different forms by diverse ethnic groups. In Brazil, *Dan* continues to be a generic term designating voduns that manifest in the form of a serpent. Although religious experts can distinguish between land and water snakes, any ophidian, whether a river anaconda, a land coral snake, or a boa constrictor, is identified as Dan.

Dan, or in his individualized "quality" the vodun Bessen, is paired with the Nagô orixá Oxumaré and the Angola *inquice* Angorô. Besides their ophidian aspect, these deities are also identified with the rainbow; in the Gbe-speaking area, when Dan assumes this "quality," he is called Ayido-Hwedo, Fongbe for "rainbow." The reciprocal identification between "Outchou-Marè" and "Aidokouédo" was noted in West Africa by Father Bouche in 1868.[70] The same reciprocal identification between "Anyi-ewo" and Oxumaré is replicated by Rodrigues in Salvador. Currently, Ayido-Hwedo is sometimes remembered as Aniêvo. While Bessen is identified as a male vodun, Oxumaré is believed to be part male and part female.

Bessen, Oxumaré, and Angorô are normally syncretized with Saint Bartholomew, who appears with a snake in Catholic iconography. For this reason, important processions were carried out in Saint Bartholomew Park in Pirajá to glorify these deities. In the 1930s, Edison Carneiro remarks on how these were celebrated "noisily, on August 24, in the village that, in the area of Pirajá, bears his name and is one of the largest convergence centers of negro-fetishist worship in Bahia." Also, Donald Pierson mentions the "sacred" fountain known as "Saint Bartholomew's Miracle."[71]

Within Candomblé, Bessen, Oxumaré, and Agnorô symbolize the continuity and life force that sets the world in motion. This "mobility principle" is expressed in a cosmological myth shared at Bogum, according to which in the beginning of time there was only one gourd composed of the symbiosis of the Mawu-Lissá couple, a hermaphrodite or a undifferentiated male-female god. Dan, the serpent, coiled about this primordial gourd and, like the string of a top, made it spin, generating the movement that gave origin to the world and nature. Then Mawu granted control of the various natural environments—earth, fire, lightening, the sea, the rivers, the trees—to different voduns such as Sakpata, Sogbo, and Loko. Associated with natural forces, the voduns preceded men and, therefore, their cult should not be confused with the ancestral cult.

When man was created, new problems arose, such as illness, as well as new activities, such as hunting and fishing. Mawu created new deities to deal with these issues, withdrawing afterward to a place far from the world. These late-comer gods are the orixás such as Oxóssi, associated with the hunt, or Ogun, associated with metal civilization.[72] A Jeje-centric attitude is noticeable in this legend in which the Nagô orixás are relegated to a secondary position in comparison to the voduns, who were primordial agents of the dynamic of nature.

Following the creation of the world, Dan became identified with the rainbow, residing simultaneously on earth and in the sky, uniting the domains of Sakpata and Sogbo and being responsible for the rain that fertilizes and assures natural life. Therefore, Dan, Oxumaré, and Angorô are deities that promote wealth, good fortune, and prosperity. According to Rodrigues, Oxumaré is "the servant of Xangô," transporting water from the earth to the clouds, the abode of his master.[73] This idea is repeated with Angorô. According to Valdina Pinto: "*Angorô* is responsible for the water cycle, the continuity of life, the life force contained in water. It is *Angorô* who transports the water to the heavens and makes it fall in the form of rain; and that is why in the Angola terreiros we make a circle of water in the middle of the *barracão* when we sing to *Angorô*, and in some terreiros of other nations, they place a pitcher of water in the center of the *barracão* when they sing to Oxumaré."[74]

This convergence of ideas around Dan, Oxumaré, and Angorô as gods of movement, wealth, the rainbow, and as responsible for the water cycle suggests a very old interpenetration of values among the different "nations," making probable an influence of the Jeje tradition on the Angola conception of Angorô. For example, in the Gbe-speaking area the transformation of the snake Dan into the rainbow (perhaps a myth of Mahi origin) is mentioned by Burton in 1863. Dan's association with wealth derives from a Gbe belief, documented by Alfred Ellis, that "his excrement is believed to have the power of transmuting grains of maize into cowries." Verger explains that "blue beads, called *Nana* or stones of *Aigry*, were called *Dan Mi* (excrement of Dan) and are left on the ground by him as he passes; they are said to be worth their weight in gold." As a symbol of continuity, Dan is represented in a number of bas-reliefs in the Abomey palace, where Ayido-Hwedo appears as a serpent swallowing its tail. This circular symbol that synthesizes the idea that every end is a beginning, and vice versa, finds an exact correspondence in the figure of the *Ouroboros* from the European alchemy tradition. Le Hérissé mentions two other figures of this vodun among the collection of the kings of Abomey: two wooden serpents, gently curved into an arch and painted red and white. These are the colors of Hevioso and signal the connection between Dan and the thunder vodun and the water cycle, a mythological relationship likely developed in Abomey and maintained in Brazil, where Dan-Oxumaré is considered "the servant of Xangô."[75]

However, other indications suggest a simultaneous influence of the Angola tradition on the Jeje snake cults. As we saw in chapter 6, the term *Agorensi* (and its variants Angorinse, Ungoroci, Ogorensi, Angorense, and Gorencia) is a title used since at least the second half of the nineteenth century by the devotees of Bessen in the Jeje-Mahi terreiros. The word appears to be a compound of Angorô plus the suffix *-si*, which in Fongbe means "wife of," and would indicate that Angorô was an *inquice* known even at that time and suggests a long-standing process of Jeje-Angola interpenetration. According to *Hunbono* Vicente, Agorin and Angorô are the same, "the Jeje united with the Angola."[76] In fact, Gisèle Binon-Cossard offers an Angola etymology for Angorô that derives from *ãngolo*: "This name comes from the term *ngolo*, an abbreviation of *kongolo* or *nkongolo*, which means rainbow. Bittremieux, who cites Mgr. A. Declerq, says: 'the rainbow is a large serpent *nkongolo* that lives in the clouds and the rain.'"[77] Hence, Angorô's association with the serpent, the rainbow, and rain would also be of Central African origin.

In addition to the attributes associated with the generic vodun Dan or Bessen, we must not forget that in the Jeje-Mahi terreiros this god is merely the most visible head of a numerous "family." Some of the members are (1) Bafono Deka (Bofun); (2) Dan Akaçu (Akassu); (3) Ajaçu; (4) Toquém (Toquen, Toquein); (5) Doquém; (6) Quemquem; (7) Cotoquem (Acotoquem); (8) Cóquem (perhaps a variant of Cotoquem); and (9) Jiku. *Gaiaku* Luiza said that Bessen is the father of Cotoquem, husband to the female Quenquém. And Aguesi said that Acotoquem was the father of Bessen.[78] It is important to note that these names do not appear in the ethnographies of the Gbe-speaking area, most of them corresponding to the coast or to Abomey. This would indicate that these were little-known voduns from the interior, the Mahi country being the most likely region of origin, given its tradition in relation to this cult.

In Seja Hundé and at Huntoloji, the vodun Dangibi, or Danjebê, a phonetic evolution of Dangbe, is also worshipped as an individualized deity, differentiated from Bessen and having his own shrine. This is significant, for Dangbe is the python vodun, mythic ancestor of the Hueda of Ouidah in the coastal area. The juxtaposition of serpent voduns of Mahi and Mundubi origin within the Dan group is another example of the "aggregation principle."

Euá, a female orixá of Nagô origin, is the goddess of a river of the same name (Yewa or Iyéwa) in the Egbado area, but in present-day Brazil, she is sometimes identified as a snake vodun of Jeje origin, and the wife of the orixá Oxumaré.

As *Gaiaku* Luiza pointed out, Euá "is called Jiku in Jeje."[79] The association between Oxumaré and Euá derives perhaps from the Oxumaré terreiro in Mata Escura. Antonio Oxumaré, one of the house founders, had as a *filha-de-santo* Dona Cotinha of Euá, who succeeded him and with whom, some say, he had a liaison.[80] Might the ritual, and perhaps romantic, connection between the two leaders explain the later mythological association of their respective saints? Even today, during the festival of Oxumaré (Bafono), in August, Euá's presence is prominent, and there is a choreography in which the two orixás dance on the ground like serpents, sucking water from a wooden bowl and then spraying it into the air. This ritual gesture is probably a relic of a myth known in the area of Porto-Novo according to which Ayido Hwedo-Oxumaré "only appears when he wants to drink, and seated on the ground on his bottom, thrusts his mouth into the water."[81] In the Oxumaré terreiro it is said that water sprayed into the air by Euá and Oxumaré represents the rainbow, and whoever is wetted by this water is possessed instantly.

In the Jeje terreiros, Bessen and other members of the Dan family dress in white and wear, as in the Gbe-speaking area, necklaces made of a number of strings of cowry shells crossing the chest. Bessen's emblem, which looks like a knife, is called *takara, itakara*, or even *hungo*. *Humbono* Vicente said that Bessen's beads are white and not striped with green and yellow, as are the ones that Oxumaré's devotees generally wear.[82] Bessen dances to the sound of various drum rhythms, such as the *bravum* or the *sato*, and at times dances lying on the ground or kneeling, imitating the sinuous movements of a serpent with arms extended above the head.

I conclude this section with the presentation of some brief historical comments on the ophidian cults in Bahia. At the turn of the century, Rodrigues affirmed that the Jeje serpent cult "appears not to have existed in Brazil, at least not in any properly organized way." In his research, he only found one "vestige" of the cult in Livaldina's terreiro, where he found as one of the idols a pole or blade of iron "having the undulations of a snake and terminating at each end in the tail and the head of a serpent." Although Livaldina identified the object with the orixá of iron, Ogun, these serpentine figures of metal normally form part of the shrine of Dan or Dangbe, as is the case at Seja Hundé even today, where this emblem is called *pé dagomé*.[83]

In any case, from the 1930s on a number of authors such as Artur Ramos, Donald Pierson, and Aydano do Couto Ferraz began to identify elements of the ophidian cult in various terreiros. Carneiro, for example, in speaking of Oxumaré and the festivals of Saint Bartholomew Park, wrote that "not even Nina Rodrigues could have imagined the importance that the cult of this orixá would come to have in the present day." In 1948, he affirmed, "In old Emiliana's candomblé [Bogum] there is a serpent painted on the wall of the *barracão*; Manuel Menez assured me that 'the snakes don't bite him'; and Manuel Falefá, telling me of the birth of the rainbow, named him Sôbôadã, which I suppose is merely a special Dã [Dan] of Sôbô (Sogbo), for, in Dahomey, all the voduns have one. In any case, Dã is present in all of the Jeje candomblés left in Bahia. A study on him is yet to be done."[84]

This documentary evidence, which according to Rodrigues suggests the absence of the Dan cult at the turn of the century, and its later appearance in the 1930s, has led Lorand Matory to affirm that "the communication at the start of this century [the twentieth] between Bahia and the Gulf of Guinea implies the revival of the Jeje nation and its worship of the snake-god as its emblem." According to Matory, the Mahis "practiced *rarely* the worship of the snake-god" in their country of origin, but, when they returned from Bahia to Africa, they settled in the coastal cities where the ophidian cults were very common, and they appropriated elements of them. This fact and the subsequent contact of those who had returned with the Bahian "relatives" would explain the "revival," not only of the Dan cult but also of the Jeje-Mahi identity in Candomblé.[85] While this idea may be useful for discussing the transnational dynamics in the construction of ethnic identities, it presents some problems.

First, the idea that the Mahis from the Gulf of Guinea "*rarely* practiced the worship of the serpent-god" is debatable. Certainly, since the seventeenth century the serpent cult is documented principally among coastal groups, such as the Hula and the Hueda.[86] This does not mean that the ophidian cult was not important among the Mahis of the inland mountainous region. Religious ethnography from the Gbe-speaking area is unanimous in attributing Mahi origin to Dan, or Ayido-Hwedo, although it is possible that he was imported from the Hueda in the second half of the seventeenth century and that from that point the Mahi country became one of the points from which the cult was disseminated. In fact, only a very early implantation of the cult in the Mahi country could explain why, in the whole of lower Dahomey, the adepts of the vodun Dan are, following initiation, called *mahinu* (inhabitants of Mahi).[87]

Second, the supposed absence of the cult of Dan in Bahia at the end of the nineteenth century is also questionable. *O Alabama* in 1870, for example, explicitly documents cults devoted "to a serpent."[88] There is other indirect evidence, unwritten but no less convincing. The "spiritual master" of Bogum, which was in operation from at least 1867, is the serpent-god Bafono or Bessen. The identification of the "spiritual master" of any candomblé is a process that is always determined during the founding of the terreiro, and normally coincides with the founder's vodun or orixá, their *dono da cabeça* or "master of the head." It is logical to suppose that the cult of Bessen would date from at least this time. The same argument is applicable to Seja Hundé, founded in the 1890s, whose "spiritual master" is also Bessen and whose first two *gaiakus* or *mães-de-santo* belonged to this vodun. Indeed, they were initiated at Roça de Cima in the 1860s and 1870s.

The available data thus suggests the presence of the serpent cult in the Mahi country since at least the eighteenth century, and in Brazil there is clear evidence of homologous cults in the Jeje-Mahi terreiros from the second half of the nineteenth century. Although Rodrigues may have been unaware of it, these continued to have an important presence into the first decades of the twentieth century. These facts allow us to presuppose the continuity of the cult from the time of the slave trade, and they are sufficient to question Matory's argument of the cult's alleged "death" and "revival" in Bahia in the first decades of the twentieth century. This does not invalidate his idea of the importance of transatlantic communication in the transnational construction of ethnic identities, but the effects of this communication on religious practices should not be overemphasized.

Some Final Considerations
concerning Other Jeje Voduns

In concluding this chapter, I will briefly consider certain other voduns known in the Jeje terreiros. For example, Querino mentions the name of Niçasse as a Jeje synonym for Olorum or Zambi, the supreme god.[89] This is, very probably, a corruption of Lissasi, an allusion to Lissá or Olissá, the Jeje version of Oxalá, the god of creation. Although the mythology of the Mawu-Lissá couple prevalent in the religious system of Abomey is not completely unknown in Bahia (see the Bogum cosmological myth above), its ritual expression does not seem to be significant. Lissá has devotees and is worshipped in close association with Oxalá, but the presence of Mawu seems to have lost importance. As I have noted, Nanã Buruku has perhaps assumed the female role formerly occupied by Mawu.

I should emphasize the importance within the Jeje cult of two entities previously mentioned and related to the Kaviono family, that is, Loko and Kpo. I have noted the significance of tree worship in vodun cults in relation to the kingdom of Ouidah in the seventeenth century. The sacralization of trees and other vegetable species is not exclusive to vodun cults, but it is undoubtedly a valorized and cultivated feature in Jeje terreiros, where many shrines or altars are ritually fixed at the foot of certain sacred trees, called *atinsa* by the Jeje. I will discuss their significance in the *boitá* ritual in chapter 8.

In Bahia, the panther-vodun Kpo, who dances with his fingers in the form of a claw, is normally associated with the Hevioso family, but he can also be manifested as a distinct "quality" of the Sakpata family. In the Gbe-speaking area, the figure of the panther represents the voduns Agasu in Abomey and Ajahuto in Allada, which are deifications of the mythic ancestors of the royal lineages of these kingdoms (see chapter 1). The image of the panther associated with royalty constituted a strong icon of power, which certainly contributed to Kpo's ability to "infiltrate" or be appropriated by other cults, such as those of Hevioso and Sakpata. Similarly, in the Jeje terreiros of Bahia, Kpo or Kposu sometimes appears as the father of Sogbo, associated with the thunder voduns, and may have his shrine outside the house, in the bush, receiving offerings similar to those of Sakpata.

Although Agasu is not known in Bahia, the vodun Ajauntó (variants include Junto, Jaunto, and Ujaunto) is one of the most singular deities of the Jeje pantheon. This entity has no consecrated adepts but presides over an important initiation ritual called "drinking *hunvé*" or "drinking *ajauntó*," which I will discuss briefly in chapter 8. In the Gbe-speaking area, its cult is documented at the end of the nineteenth century in Porto-Novo, but it was in Allada that it traditionally acquired greater relevance and probably inspired the royal cults of the panther-vodun Agasu in Abomey.[90]

Among the hunter voduns of the forests worshipped in the Jeje terreiros, Agué and Odé stand out. The former is normally associated with the Nagô orixá of the leaves, Ossaim, and the latter with the hunter orixá Oxóssi.[91] Agué, besides being the god of the forest, is a hunter and the animals are under his control. According to Herskovits, in the Gbe-speaking area "those who dance for Agué climb the trees as do hunters." He is sometimes represented as a bird, or as an animal that can transform itself, according to what was explained to me in Ouidah. Agué is worshipped in the temples of Mawu-Lissá and maintains a close relationship with Ogun, a characteristic that persists in the Jeje terreiros, where Agué is always praised after Ogun.[92]

In Yoruba *odé* means hunter, and it is interesting to see how a common Yoruba noun becomes a proper noun referring to a vodun. Odé is, therefore, a Jeje appropriation or adaptation of a Nagô hunter deity. However, in Jeje terreiros such as Bogum or Poço Béta, there is a vodun known as Agangá-Tôlú (Gongatolu and Ontolu being variants), who is considered a Jeje Oxóssi. In the Oxumaré terreiro in Salvador and at Kwe Simba in Rio de Janeiro, this vodun is known as Atolu. A hunter vodun, at Poço Béta he danced with colored cloths bound about his waist like a skirt, and with a ribbon adorned with feathers on his forehead.[93]

According to *Gaiaku* Luiza, "there is no Logun Edé among the Jeje."[94] However, *Humbono* Vicente remembered a particular vodun of the Jeje terreiros who had been long forgotten. That vodun is Bagô, a water saint who would wear a small bell about his neck and when he wanted water would stammer like a child. He was worshipped only at Seja Hundé and not at Bogum. Herskovits mentions Bagbó as a "deity related to Sagbata." In the Hula pantheon of sea divinities there is one Saho, but a phonetic evolution from this name to Bagô seems unlikely.[95]

I would be remiss if I ended this chapter on Jeje deities without mentioning the *caboclos*. Afro-Brazilian scholarship has until recently suffered a certain tendency to privilege the terreiros that supposedly have preserved the "purity" of African tradition, emphasizing their African gods, such as orixás and voduns, while neglecting the importance of local influences and adaptations in the more "mixed" candomblés. The proliferation in Candomblé of "Brazilian" entities called *caboclos*—whether they be Indian spirits or other entities called *encantados*, associated with popular types such as the cowherd, fisherman, sailor, and so on, but in any case, entities, "created" in Brazil—seems to have occurred primarily at the end of the nineteenth century, although their presence in some cults of African origin might be much older.

When in 1937 Camargo Guarnieri gathered 152 Candomblé songs in Salvador, forty-six were specified as being of the Ketu, Jeje, or Ijexá nations, fourteen as Angola-Congo, and ninety-two as *caboclo*.[96] The fact that the majority of the songs were *caboclo* could indicate the importance of these entities in the Candomblé of the time. However, certain Nagô-Ketu terreiros considered "traditional," until the 1950s and even more recently, attempted to hide or even deny that some of their *filhas-de-santo* on certain occasions could be possessed by *caboclos*. In the three principal terreiros examined in this study—Bogum, Seja Hundé, and Huntoloji—there is also a relative silencing of the possibility of some *vodunsi*'s being possessed by a *caboclo*, though more than one case has been confirmed.

In any case, in these terreiros, it is said that the *caboclos* never manifest themselves in the *barracāo*, at least during the *vodun* rituals, which according to my own observations is true. It is also said that the *caboclos* have no initiation, that is, the *vodunsis* do not go through any special preparation in order to be consecrated to their *caboclos*. It is accepted, however, that these entities may manifest themselves in specific situations in order to warn of some danger, give counsel, or admonish. At Bogum, for example, it is known that *Mãe* Nicinha was possessed by a *caboclo*.[97]

The Nagô-vodun pantheon of the contemporary Jeje-Mahi terreiros, despite the peripheral presence of the *caboclos* and the complex aggregation of Nagô orixás—a dynamic that had been occurring in the Gbe-speaking area for many centuries and that continued to develop in Brazil throughout the nineteenth century—thus continues to be characterized by the identity of certain deities classified as voduns, which are associated with differentiated names and ritual practices. Despite the many transformations and mimetic processes related to the Nagô orixás, voduns such as Sogbo, Azonsu, and Bessen continue to be the most important differential factor in demarcating the Jeje nation within Candomblé. The next chapter will examine other elements, this time related to ritual aspects, that help distinguish the Jejes from other nations.

8 The Ritual

Characteristics of the Jeje-Mahi Liturgy in Bahia

How to Define a Jeje Liturgy?

The objective of this final chapter is to examine certain liturgical characteristics of the Jeje-Mahi terreiros of Salvador and Cachoeira in order to evaluate those elements that differentiate the "Jeje nation" from other religious traditions within Candomblé. This highly ethnographic and descriptive task is not easy. As in many other social institutions, in Candomblé knowledge is power, and the logic of the secret is the strategy that sustains the initiation processes and the hierarchical organization of the group. In this sense, the Jeje religious experts have the deserved reputation of being the most "closed" and enigmatic in the preservation of their "secrets." As *Seu* Geninho said, "Jeje is like Freemasonry."[1] The effort put into hiding their practices from the eyes of the curious is proverbial, not only for the researcher, with whom they deal with a certain facility, but more especially with initiates who come from other terreiros and are suspected of being present in order to "spy." This reserved and suspicious attitude, intrinsic to any religion requiring initiation, was exacerbated by long years of repression and secrecy to which the religion was subjected. However, it seems the Jeje pride themselves in, and make an issue of, maintaining this reputation and tradition.

Faced with this situation and given my uninitiated status, the "methodology" I adopted in my fieldwork was to observe "actively" and participate "passively." In this way, I was following a piece of advice that was given to me many times during my research on Tambor de Mina* in São Luis: "With *Mina*, you go about with an open eye, an attentive ear, and your mouth shut." This attitude, based on "being there," creating minimal interference and avoiding any formal interview or too many questions, undoubtedly resulted in a slow learning process and required patience and persistence. However, over time, I gained access to certain private ritual practices and information held secret, or "deep knowledge." The dividing line between what can be told and what should be kept secret is ambiguous, and rarely discussed with practitioners, leaving me with the difficult work of establishing these limits. Although it is possible that for some the narrative that follows goes beyond what might be permissible, it is my hope that, for those with whom I spoke, what I have written here does not exceed the limits of what is tolerable.

Besides this delicate exercise in ethnographic self-censorship (an example of how the scholar becomes contaminated by the behavior of the subjects studied), my position in relation to the religion was essentially one of an "outsider," or perhaps that of one from the "border," with the consequent limitations in relation to a whole body of fundamental esoteric knowledge necessary to understanding the religion's deep meaning. To this is added the extreme complexity and the unending wealth of details that compose the ritual universe of Candomblé, which can only be learned through close proximity over many years. These difficulties and limitations are insurmountable, and the reader should take them into account in evaluating the content of this chapter. Having conveyed these reflexive reservations, to which should be added the more general epistemological problem of the subjective nature inherent to any representation of reality, the difficulties of analyzing the Jeje liturgy derive from a whole other series of more objective facts.

Candomblé is not a religion subject to an institutional hierarchy that imposes dogmas to be followed by all, and, as it is said, "every house has its own ways." Everything is done according to "tradition," but this allows, even requires, a constant adaptation to current circumstances. In reality, the Afro-Brazilian religion is characterized by great flexibility and eclecticism, and the Jeje terreiros are no exception to this dynamic of progressive change. Despite being a smaller group, the Jeje houses present a rich variety of ritual practices and deities that differentiate one congregation from another.

The problem worsens when one discovers that, in addition to this "internal" diversity, the Jeje terreiros practice rituals and worship deities of other nations and when, at the same time, one finds that terreiros not identified as Jeje perform Jeje rituals and worship Jeje deities. Therefore, it would be inaccurate to speak of a Jeje liturgy as a homogenous, static, and contained unity, practiced only by the terreiros that identify themselves as Jeje. This is a serious obstacle to any effort to define what is meant by a Jeje liturgy. Should that liturgy be those ritual practices found in the terreiros that identify themselves as Jeje, or those ritual practices associated with voduns found in the terreiros of various nations? In this book, I have opted to study those practices associated with the voduns in the terreiros that self-identify as Jeje and that, according to the participants, express and characterize the Jeje liturgy in comparison to other nations.

Thus, the study is not an exercise in identifying "Africanisms," deposits, or cultural survivals from the Gbe-speaking area, but an attempt to analyze those liturgical elements that shape the contemporary identity of the Jeje terreiros vis-à-vis other terreiros such as the Angola or Ketu. Since this identity is a dialogic and contextual construct always created in relation to "others," it is important to understand what Jeje practitioners consider to be from their own nation and to understand how they problematize their difference. Similarly, it becomes necessary to analyze other elements that, while not explicit in the discourse of Jeje practitioners, constitute, in fact, elements genuinely Jeje because they have their origin in the Gbe-speaking area.

As we saw in chapter 7, the identity of the Jeje terreiros is articulated primarily through their deities, the voduns. In turn, the cult of voduns involves various modes of expression, such as language and songs, drum rhythms, dances, dress, the behavior and social interactions of the voduns and the members of the religious community, offerings (animal sacrifices, food, seeds, leaves, etc.), as well as a whole series of ritual segments or *obligations*, in which it is possible to identify elements that distinguish Jeje practices from those of other terreiros. Of course, all of these modes of expression are interconnected and integrated into what could be called a "religious culture," but for explanatory purposes, it is useful to maintain these distinctions or analytical categories. Therefore I will analyze these different aspects of ritual activity for the purpose of highlighting elements particular to the Jeje tradition.

Jeje Language or Dialect: Blessings and Hierarchical Terminology

Since the time of Nina Rodrigues's study, an erroneous tendency has persisted in Afro-Brazilian studies to associate the Jeje language with Ewe. *Ewe* was a term popularized by Alfred Ellis beginning in 1890 to designate, principally in German works, the totality of peoples from the Gbe-speaking area, but in reality it is the name of only one of the groups originating in Notsé. As Rodrigues points out, at the turn of the twentieth century Jeje included five dialects: "1.- Mahi; 2.- Dahomê or Effon [Fon]; 3.- Aufueh [Agoué]; 4.- Awunã or Aulô [Agouna or Anlo]; 5.- Whydah or Wetá [Hueda]." In this list, only Aulô, perhaps a variant of the ethnonym *Anlo*, could be considered Ewe. In the 1940s, Edison Carneiro wrote that "Jeje (including the Mahi variation, which is pronounced Marrim)" was still spoken.[2]

As I demonstrated in chapter 3, the "nationalism" of the Brazilian African Diaspora, in the absence of the territorial factor (which could only be experienced as the remembrance of a lost origin), was structured primarily as a "linguistic nationalism." In the same manner, the African languages persisted in the religious sphere as one of the most important diacritic signs in the formation and imagination of the Candomblé nation. In chapter 4 I analyzed the influence of Jeje religious terminology in Candomblé as a whole. In addition to the Jeje words that have crossed the borders of nation, however, the Jeje terreiros maintain their own speech or "dialect" that contributed to establishing an identitary specificity of this religious tradition in comparison with other nations. In present times, the songs in praise of the deities, the songs of animal sacrifice, the songs of the "coming-out of the initiate," and so on, and the prayers (which differ from the songs) are one of the most important areas on which Jeje difference is structured.

Although it is difficult to speak of an actual "language," the Jeje "dialect" is seen in the hierarchical and liturgical terminology; in certain oral formulas such as blessings, greetings, and other expressions used to converse with the voduns, to call the *gaiaku*; and to ask permission to enter the terreiro, or the house ("ago nu kwe vi" or "ago no kwé vé"). Other formulas are used by the *gaiaku* to determine whether a *vodunsi* is ill, and so on. The linguistic repertoire is quite extensive, and a provisional, and certainly incomplete, vocabulary compiled during this research includes more than 100 words, among them terms to designate different parts of the body, animals, foods, leaves, ritual objects, sacred spaces, and so on. For the purpose of illustration, this study examines only the blessings or ritual greetings and the terms of priesthood hierarchy.

To ask for and receive a blessing (*benção*, from the Latin *benedictione*, the act of blessing) is a very common practice in Brazil's patriarchal society, given its heavy Catholic influence. In the context of Candomblé, this ritual gesture is combined with a no less extensive African tradition of ritual greetings and compliments. In general, the asking of a blessing expresses subordination and respect on the part of the person doing the asking toward the person granting it, and is therefore determined by the hierarchical principle of seniority, an essential rule of West African cultures.

At present, in Jeje Candomblé the request for a blessing can take various forms. Outside the ritual context, it can consist of a simple kiss of the hand; if the other person is of the same hierarchical level, the gesture is reciprocated. During ceremonies, in front of senior members, the person might simply slightly curve the body, lowering the gaze, while at the same time extending the arms with the palms up, without any physical contact involved in the interaction. In cases where the intent is to express a greater degree of subordination or respect, the individual might kneel before the superior, kissing or touching the ground with the forehead, while the superior might lightly touch with his or her hand the neck or the back of the person. It should be noted that among the Jeje of Cachoeira, the complex *dobale* used in the Ketu terreiros, in which an individual prostrates him- or herself in different ways before the superior, is not observed, at least in present times.[3] These corporal gestures are normally accompanied by an oral formula characteristic of, and differentiated according to, the nation or the category of vodun to which the superior is consecrated. The request for a blessing always requires an answer, which would the actual blessing.

In the Jeje-Mahi terreiros three principal formulas are distinguishable, corresponding to the three main vodun categories: Nagô-vodun, Mahi, and Kaviono. In the Nagô-vodun tradition they say "colofé," and the response might be simply "colofé" or "Olorum modokwé." It is likely that "colofé" is an expression of Yoruba origin, as this blessing request can also be heard in some Ketu houses. Gisèle Binon-Cossard, for example, refers to the expression "Olorum kolofe" as Nagô.[4]

"Benoi" is the Mahi blessing request and is used when addressing those consecrated to Dan or Bessen. The response is "Benoi é ganji." Then there is the expression of greeting to this vodun, "from the Nagô-vodun to Dan," which would be "arrobo benoi, eborrei é ganji," or the variant "o benoi, arrobo benoi." It should be pointed out that "aroboboi" is the Ketu greeting for Oxumaré. As for the Kaviono side, for those individuals who belong to the family of the vodun Sogbo, the expression "aóoo" is used, followed by the answer "aotí" or "aotín."[5]

It is important to note that the requests for blessings are normally preceded by the hierarchal title of the person to whom the request is made (i.e., "*ogã* colofé," "*equede* colofé"). When dealing with the *mãe-de-santo*, the title corresponding to this position, according to each tradition, is used. In Nagô-vodun it is "*gaiaku* colofé"; in Mahi, "*mejito* benoi"; and in Kaviono, "*doné* aóoo." As *Gaiaku* Luiza said, "I am *gaiaku* in Nagô-vodun; I am *mejito* in the land of Dan; in the land of Kevioso, I am *doné*."[6] This diversity of blessings and hierarchical titles demonstrates and corroborates the above-mentioned division within the Jeje pantheon into the three traditions of Mahi, Mundubi, and Nagô-vodun. For the titles *doné* and *gaiaku* (probably a Nagô term) I did not find a clear etymology, but the term *mejito*, used in the "land of Dan," comes from the Fongbe (or Mahigbe) *mejitó*, which means mother, "she who brings someone into the world."[7]

Surely as a result of his reading of Ellis, Rodrigues speaks of the term *vodunon* or *vodunō* as the "name given to the Jeje priestesses of the Dãnh-gbi cult." Although, in translating *-nō* to mother and *vodu* to saint or orixá, he sees in the term *vodunō* an antecedent of the Brazilian term *mãe-de-santo*, it is important to note that in Fongbe the suffix -nõ, besides meaning "mother of," expresses the idea of "possessor of, proprietor of, holder of." Therefore, if in the Gbe-speaking area the term vodunõ is not feminine, and it is used primarily to designate the male religious head, the translation of the term with the Portuguese words dono (owner), proprietário (proprietor), or zelador (overseer) of the vodun would be more correct. It is noteworthy that the use of this term is very rare in contemporary Jeje terreiros and seems restricted to people familiar with studies on Dahomey.[8]

Humbono is the term more commonly used to designate the male religious head. In chapter 4 I mentioned the use of its phonetic evolutions gumbônde or gombono, and its feminine form gumbonda, in nineteenth-century Candomblé. These variants derive from the Fon term hunbonõ, which translated literally means the owner or overseer (-nõ) of the "talisman" (bô) of the deity (hun). Other feminine hierarchical titles that appear in O Alabama, such as guncô or donunce, seem to have been forgotten.

At Seja Hundé, the term deré is used to designate the mãe-pequena or the second-in-command to the gaiaku.[9] At Bogum the term hunsó is more frequently used to refer to this position. In Benin, according to R. P. B. Segurola, the hunsó can be a woman or a man and means the assistant to the vodunon, responsible for important ritual functions such as dancing "carrying the animals to be sacrificed on his shoulder. At this time, they say, é só hun: he has grabbed the fetish."[10] This function, unique to the ritual called vodun só gbo (the vodun grabs the goat), is always reserved for the older and more experienced members.

Then there is the term hungan (literally, the chief of the deity) used in Benin to designate the second-in-command, or right hand, of the vodunon. It can be a man or a woman who, in addition to acting as a substitute for the vodunon when needed, serves as his spokesperson to the vodunsis. This term is known at Bogum but apparently refers to those in the lower levels of the hierarchy.

In addition to the male or female head of a congregation, there are ogãs, or male dignitaries, who, without dancing or "receiving" the vodun on their heads (becoming possessed), were initiated to assist the leader in various functions. In the Jeje terreiros, the titles of higher status are pejigã, ogã huntó, and, in Cachoeira, ogã impé. Strictly speaking, the pejigã is the overseer or person in charge of the peji (shrine room), the huntó is in charge of the atabaque drummers, and the ogã impé is responsible for the animal sacrifices and other internal rituals and corresponds to the axogum of the Nagô-Ketu terreiros.[11] Depending on the circumstances, the same person can assume various functions. For example, Amâncio Melo was ogã huntó of Bogum, "the chief of the drums and responsible for the slaughtering of sacrificial animals to the voduns."[12]

At other times these titles can acquire variable meanings. For example, *huntó*, the "owner of the drum," might, at times, be employed as a synonym for *pai-pequeno*, or it can designate a mere drummer.

The term *doté* is also used in various ways, at times as a synonym for *ogã*—from which comes the term *doté impé*, used for *ogã impé* or as a synonym for *humbono*, overseer of the saint, or *pai-de-santo*. In Porto-Novo, Adolphe Akindélé and Cyrille Aguessy note the term *douté* as a synonym for *vodunon* or head of the temple.[13] In Petit-Popo, John Duncan wrote of "a caboceer, or *dootay*, who is acknowledged as hereditary chief magistrate or ruler."[14]

Another title known in the Jeje terreiros of Cachoeira is that of *obajigan* or *bajigan*, the second to the *pejigã*.[15] It is perhaps a corruption of *agbajigan*, a title used at Bogum, which in Fongbe indicates the person in charge of the interior courtyard (*agbaji* = interior patio, veranda). Other terms of Gbe origin have also been documented, such as *ganto*, the person in charge of the *gã*, or sacred idiophone; *ogã kutó*, the person in charge of the house for the *eguns* or ancestors of the terreiro (*kú* = death); and *ogã minazon*, the one in charge "of the candomblé's artillery, the sets of *tabaque* drums."[16] Other titles about which I was unable to gather more information are *oganvi, ogã senevi, alavi, agosun,* and *ogã tenequites.*[17] In Cachoeira, I also heard the term *hundeva* applied to an *atabaque* player. In Benin this term refers to a person who does not "receive" the vodun on the head (is not possessed), but who, being initiated, helps in various ritual activities.

Regarding the *equedes* or female assistants, although they can serve different functions relative to the preparation of ritual foods, serving the voduns, and so on, I was unable to document specific titles for them. I know only that, at Bogum, the person in charge of ritual food preparation is the *dogan*.[18] It is noteworthy that both *ogãs* and *equedes*, in addition to having their own *dono da cabeça*, or principal deity, are generally also consecrated to the voduns who choose them for these posts. For example, an individual of Ogun can be chosen to be an *ogã* by the Oxum of a given *vodunsi*, and thereby becomes an *ogã* of Oxum, being required to help her *vodunsi* in whatever is necessary.

The use of this complex hierarchical terminology thus helps differentiate the Jeje nation from other rites of Candomblé. As a number of other scholars have already noted, the hierarchical organization of the congregation and the division of labor by gender are of fundamental importance to the functioning of the cult. As *Mãe* Stella of Oxóssi, of the Axé Opò Afonjá terreiro, stated, "Hierarchy is everything: beginning, middle, and end. Without it there is chaos" or

"Hierarchy means discipline."[19] However, one notices that often the "official hierarchy," based on the various titles and the principle of seniority, does not necessarily correspond to the hierarchy of real power, and that individuals with relatively insignificant titles, such as *equedes* or *ogãs*, can, at times, exercise great influence on decisions made or sanctioned by the governing body. In other words, alongside the "official hierarchy" there is always an "informal hierarchy" that actually wields the power.

Instruments and Drum Rhythms in the Jeje Terreiros

The percussive instruments and the musical language (rhythms, beats, drumming styles) are considered as other areas that reveal liturgical differences between the Candomblé nations, especially between the Angola and Jeje-Nagô rites, given that there is greater interpenetration and similarity between the styles of the Jeje and Ketu terreiros. The contemporary Candomblé orchestra of Bahia is composed of the *ferro* (a handheld idiophone composed of one or two bells) ritually referred to as the *gã* or *agogô*, and of three drums of different sizes called, from largest to smallest, "*rum, rumpi,* and *lé,* corruptions of the Fon words *hum* and *humpevi* for the first two, and of the Nagô word *omele* for the third."[20] In the Jeje terreiros of Cachoeira, the *gã* is a small iron bell, played with a piece of iron or wood. In the Ketu terreiros, and in those of other nations, the *agogô* is generally a small double bell.

Until around the beginning of the twentieth century, the Candomblé orchestra also included the *cabaça* (gourd; *gò* in Fon or *xequere* in Nagô) covered by a net of strings, from the knots of which beads or cowry shells are hung, and to which Rodrigues attributed a "notable role." This instrument's use, which in Maranhão is still important, in Bahia gradually disappeared, becoming restricted, in the Jeje terreiros, to the *zandró* ritual (see below). Additionally, Carneiro mentions the *chocalho*—a cylinder or type of rattle made of tin with pebbles inside—also all but forgotten today. Only in the Sogbo and Xangô cults is the *xeré,* a ritual *chocalho* made of copper or from a gourd, used for the invocation of greeting of the deity. The *adjá*—a metal bell used to reverence or to invoke the deities—which in the 1960s Carneiro mentioned as "less used," is today a very common instrument emblematic of the power of the *pai* or *mãe-de-santo.*[21]

The drums and the *ferro* (iron bell) are conceived as "beings endowed with a soul and personality."[22] They are baptized and consecrated to certain spiritual entities, the *ferro* normally to Legba or Exu. The *atabaques* at Bogum, for example, are consecrated to Sogbo, Oxum, and Iemanjá.[23] They receive food offerings periodically during the *zandró* ritual. At Bogum the drums were "made of a single piece of jack tree" and, since the time of Runhó, were varnished. At Seja Hundé wood from the palm, coral, or coconut tree is used. The fabrication of drums is the responsibility of certain *ogãs*. The person to cut and carve the tree trunk must do so at a certain time and also practice sexual abstinence. The instruments' skins are made of hide from ritually sacrificed goats.[24]

According to Pierre Verger, "the forms and systems of *atabaque* skin tensioning vary according to the nation of the terreiro. The system employing wedges is frequent in the candomblés of Bantu (Congo and Angola) origin. The system using rods inserted into the body of the drum is in Brazil characteristic of the Nagô and Djèdje nations."[25] The latter system is used at Bogum and in the Huntoloji terreiro, where the skin is stretched with strings tied to pegs inserted into the body of the drum. This technique was also used long ago at Seja Hundé, but today they use metallic tensioners, as in the majority of Nagô terreiros.

Another difference between the various nations relates to the manner in which the drum is played. Among the Jeje nation, the *huntó* (drummer) playing the largest drum strikes it with his left hand, while in the right he holds an *aguidavi* (a Fon term meaning a stick of guava, tamarind, or cipó wood, of between twenty-five and thirty centimeters in length) that is used to strike not only the drum skin but also the body of the drum. The *rumpi* and *lé* players use two *aguidavis*. Among the Nagô-Ketu nation it is the same, although the strokes of the *aguidavi* on the body of the *hun* are distinctively Jeje. Among the Congo-Angola and Ijexá nations drummers normally play with their hands, as done formerly in the old Nagô terreiros of the Recôncavo.

The different rhythms or beats are appeals or "rhythmized locutions," "words of summoning," invocations.[26] The sound of the drums is considered a language that establishes communication with the invisible world of deities. As *Gaiaku* Luiza explained, it is through the wind that circulates in the drums when they are played that the gods manifest themselves. The rhythmic element of the music is created by the drums and the *agogô*, and the singing expresses the melodic element. According to *Ogã* Joãozinho, it is the song that sets the speed of the rhythm, in his words: "I play according to the tone of the song." And he observes: "It's not always quick, it's a question of education: Nanã dances slowly; Oiá, accentuated; Ogun, quick." According to him, the *hun* improvises variations on the *rumpi* and the *lé*, which are meant to combine their different rhythms as if they were entwined fingers.[27] The job of the *ferro* is to set the meter and the tempo of the rhythmic cycle, which I will call the time-line.[28]

The ethnomusicologist Xavier Vatin identifies twenty "rhythmic formulas" in contemporary Candomblé; eight come from the Nagô-Ketu nation (*agabi, aguerê, alujá, batá, daró, igbí, opanijé, tonibobe*), seven from the Jeje nation (*adarrum, avaninha, ramunha, bravum, satô, jicá, vassa*), four from the Angola nation (*arrebate, barravento, cabula, congo*), and one from the Nagô-Ijexá nation (*Ijexá*). As with other liturgical aspects, here there is also a strong interpenetration among the various nations, as well as variations in terminology, and also controversy regarding the origin of some of the rhythms.[29]

Here I will merely identify the time-line and comment on some of the characteristics of the most important rhythms that are considered Jeje. The timeline of the *avamunha* (*avamunia, hamunyia, ramunha*), also known as *avaninha* (*avanía*), consists of twelve pulses and five strokes, "/x.x.x. .x.x. ./." This timeline is subtly different from the Cuban *clave*, which has sixteen pulses and five strokes "/x. .x. .x . . . x.x . . ./." Vatin identifies the first as *avaninha* and the second as *ramunha*. The *avamunha* "is a marching beat, but it is a fast march," used to call the voduns to the *barracão* (dance hall) or for their departure. In these cases, it is not accompanied by song, but there is an *avamunha* with song for many voduns. In some terreiros, this rhythm can also be used (without song) to invoke the manifestation of the gods.

The *adarrum* is perhaps the best known and most frequently cited Jeje rhythm in Afro-Brazilian scholarship. It is a highly accelerated summoning beat, without song, used to induce "possession" in the dancers on occasions when the deities are slow to manifest themselves. As Artur Ramos was told, "There is no *saint* who can resist the *adarrum*," or as I heard, "Play the *adarrum* and everyone gets possessed." *Adarrum* is a corruption of the Fon word *adahun*, which can be translated as "rhythm of wrath." It is only played on special occasions, but it has crossed the borders of Candomblé nations and can be heard in the Nagô-Ketu terreiros and more rarely in the Congo-Angola. Its time-line is eight pulses and four strokes, "/x.x.x.x./," increasing to seven strokes "/x.xxxxxx/," which, when added to a very fast beating of the sticks on the drums, creates a sensation of acceleration.[30]

The *satô* (or *huntô*) and the *bravum* (or *brarrum*) are two other rhythms unanimously recognized as Jeje. The *satô* is the "official" rhythm of Bessen, but it is also played in songs for Azonsu, Nanã, and Iemanjá.[31] The *bravum*, without song, can be used as an "entrance beat," "departure beat," and as a "greeting beat" to salute those priests of high standing when they arrive at the terreiro, but it can also accompany the songs of a number of deities. Both rhythms share a metric cycle of six pulses. According to Vatin, both have four strokes "/x.xxx./," with the difference that in the *bravum* the six pulses are grouped in a binary form (three times two) and in the *sató* they are grouped in a ternary fashion (twice three). These divisions of the pulses into pairs or triads affect the dance steps and not necessarily the beat. In the houses included in this research, the *bravum* normally has only two strokes, "/x.x . . . /," a pattern not recorded by Vatin in his classification.[32]

In the Jeje-Mahi terreiros of Cachoeira members speak of the *quebrado* and of the *mundubi* (or *kevioso* or *voduvi*) beats as most characteristic of their nation. In truth, they are rhythms whose principal time-lines correspond, respectively, to the *sató* and to the *bravum* (the latter of two strokes), but that alternate with rhythmic variations and have their own choreographies. These beats and dances invariably accompany the song repertoire of the first part of the *zandró*, when they greet the Jeje voduns, and therefore constitute one of the distinctive ritual elements of this liturgy. The *quebrado* accompanies the songs of Bessen, Azonsu, and others. The *mundubi*, as the name suggests, sustains many songs of the Hevioso family of voduns, but it is also used in songs of other voduns such as Bessen.

The beats and dances of the *quebrado* and *mundubi* are divided into two parts or alternating movements. During the first movement, the time-line of the *quebrado* is "/x.xxx./" (*sató*) and that of the *mundubi* is "/x.x . . . /" (*bravum*). The dance coincides with the movement of the *vodunsi* from the starting position in front of the drums to the *barracão*'s doorway, from there to the opposite side of the room (where the *gaiaku* is seated), and from there again to the drums, forming a triangular path that moves counterclockwise. At the moment when the dancer is before the drums, the door, or the *gaiaku*, a variation in the time-line occurs.[33] During this second movement, the dance also changes; the hands move as if beating a drum on the lower abdomen, or sometimes the torso bends forward while the arms and legs open and close along the sides, as if weighed down.

The transitions from the second to the first movement are normally marked by what is called the *jiká*, a gesture that consists of a light genuflection and a shaking of the shoulder blades—a movement that only the most experienced *vodunsis* are able to execute gracefully. Although *jiká* is a Yoruba word meaning shoulder, in Candomblé it is a distinctive sign of the voduns, sometimes considered their greeting. The *jiká* gives its name to another Jeje rhythm sometimes called *ijika* or *jinká*, whose time-line is "/x.xx. ./," which corresponds to the *ilú* rhythm played to Iemanjá. I have also heard some speak of *azakun* (also *azançu* or *azanhuna*)—likely a corruption of *azanhun*—which is a beat used "mostly as a summons" but that can also be used for the departure.[34]

The last rhythm identified as Jeje by Vatin, the *vassa*, is one of the most popular among all of the Afro-Brazilian religions. Its time-line consists of twelve pulses with seven strokes, "/x.x.xx.x.x.x/." In the Jeje terreiros it is also called *nagô* or *alujá* and generally accompanies songs to the *Nagô-vodun* deities (Ogun, Oxum, etc.). In the terreiros of other nations this time-line is also known as the *vassi* or *ketu* beat, and among those of the Tambor de Mina of Maranhão it is called *dobrado*. These names, added to the fact that it is used for a great many orixá songs, call into question the supposed Jeje origin of this rhythm, which in fact is extensively documented all over West Africa.

Last but not least, there is a group of *Nagô-Ketu* rhythms that can be heard in the Jeje terreiros. For example, the *alujá* associated with Xangô, which always has a time-line of twelve pulses and four strokes, "/x. .x. .x. .x. ./," although it may present variations that coincide with the *vassa* (thus the term *alujá* used to designate the *vassa* in Jeje terreiros). Other beats are the dramatic *opanije* of Omolu "/xxx.xxx.xx.x.xx./"; the lively *aguerê*, associated with Oxóssi, Oiá, or Ogun, "/xx.xxx./," and the *igbí*, played to Oxalá, "/x.xx.x.xx.xx/."

One can conclude that, although members of the *povo-de-santo* speak frequently of drum beats as one of the distinguishing characteristics of the liturgy of a given nation, these currently circulate from one terreiro to another with great fluidity. While there are beats and specific choreographies of the Jeje-Mahi terreiros, such as the *quebrado* and the *mundubi* of Cachoeira, the "rhythmic" frontiers between the Jeje and Ketu nations are tenuous, while the differences in relation to the Angola nation are more noticeable, because of that nation's practice of playing the instruments with the hands rather than with sticks. It is therefore among the songs and their language that clearer demarcations between different religious traditions can be traced.

Some Considerations on the Initiation of the *Vodunsis*

The initiation of adepts for their consecration to the gods constitutes one of the central characteristics of Candomblé and carries with it a change in the individual's role and status in relation to the social group. Following Victor Turner, who elaborated on the concepts developed by A. Van Gennep to analyze rites of passage, one can divide the initiation process into three phases: separation, transition (opposition, marginality, or liminality), and subsequent social reintegration. In the vodun cults of the Gbe-speaking area, the initiation of a *vodunsi* presupposes a radical rupture with her past; the previous person "dies" to be "reborn" under the auspices of the deity, with a new personality. This process of "existential" transformation is expressed in various ritual stages and in the terminology associated with them.[35]

First the neophyte or candidate experiences a "ritual death," of which it is said that *vodun hu asi* (the vodun kills the woman), and she remains for some days prostrate on the ground. At this point the *vodunsi* is called *hun ciò* (the corpse of the vodun). This state is followed by a "ritual resurrection," known as *hun fínfòn* (waking the vodun), which inaugurates the new spiritual life of the *vodunsi*. This phase is followed by a training period, in which, by enduring a number of ritual and learning processes, the *vodunsi* acquires a new personality or "spiritual identity." During this period, the *vodunsi* can alternate between states of "possession" by the vodun and a psychological and behavioral state, difficult to define, but that is conceptually associated with the amorphous and infantile stage of the new personality, which Verger calls the "state of mental dullness."[36]

In Benin there is yet another, later stage in which the *vodunsi* is prepared to act as a beggar (*nubyoduto*). This state includes childish behavioral character-istics and is called *ahwansi, tobosi, agamasi, yomu,* or *kuvi,* depending on the cult, but it is necessary to distinguish this state of *nubyoduto* from the "state of mental dullness" referred to above, despite the fact that both are associated with an infantile state. In contemporary Candomblé these two states tend to be confused with the state of *erê,* the child or assistant of the deity. The *erê* state allows the neophyte to withstand long periods of reclusion in the *huncó* and formerly was also connected to the activity of ritual begging. The initiation culminates in the *vodunsi's* public presentation to the community, a ritual in which the vodun "proclaims his or her name." This ritual name is called the *huin* in Jeje or *orunko* in Ketu. Nowadays, the *vodunsi's* return to secular life is almost consecutive to the "giving the name" ceremony, but previously social reintegration was a slower process.

The duration of the initiation process has been progressively reduced. In the Jeje terreiros it is said that formerly it lasted two years, a year and a half, or one year. In the 1860s *O Alabama* mentions most commonly six months. Today the seclusion time might still last six months or more, but a shorter period of between three weeks and three months is not uncommon. The initiation is divided into an initial period, in which the *vodunsi* remains secluded in the *huncó* (initiation room), and a secondary period, during which she may leave the *huncó* but must still remain in the terreiro. For example, during a six-month initiation, she spends three months "inside" and three "outside."

Let us examine in greater detail certain initiation aspects of the Jeje-Mahi terreiros. As *Gaiaku* Luiza explained, "the Jeje do not put together a *barco* (group of initiates) every year, but every few years. The Jeje do not go looking for novices, we wait for them to come to us, but if you don't sow, you don't reap."[37] There are certain annual rituals, such as the *boitá* or the bonfire of Sogbo, that are considered favorable times for the "fall" or the "ritual death." In the *boitá*, as the procession rotates around the sacred trees (*atinsa*), the new candidates can become possessed for the first time. The *atinsa* before which the candidate becomes possessed is generally taken as a sign indicating to which vodun she belongs. In the *barracão* the candidate throws herself on the ground, expressing her "ritual death." She is covered with a white cloth (*ala*) and then is "suspended" by the *ogãs* in front of the door and the drums, before being gathered into the initiation chamber. With this gesture, the candidate is merely "asking to be made," without necessarily implying that she will actually be initiated. The final decision is left to the religious experts.

The state produced by the "ritual death" can go on for a number of days, and it is said that in the past it lasted seven nights and seven days, but today it normally lasts from one to three days. During this period, the candidate remains in a state of total atony, "without eating, drinking, or doing her necessities. The vodun is incarnated through her[,] ... really stuck to her." If the candidate endures this test she is submitted to certain initial rites, "to fix the saint," but if she "awakens" the initiation might be suspended. Normally, after a week of this ritual death, the *sapocã* or *sarapocã* is celebrated. This is a semipublic ritual in which the novice who has overcome all of these trials is presented in the *barracão*. The *sarapocã* marks the formal "entrance" of the *vodunsi* into the initiation process, and also indicates that the family of the novice has accepted this commitment. According to *Ogã* Boboso and *Gaiaku* Luiza, the *sapocã* is "a farewell from the family," though the *vodunsi*'s head has not yet been consecrated, that is, it has not yet been shaved or painted.[38]

The period of seclusion and instruction in which the novice is "acculturated into the Jeje religion" begins from the time of the *sarapocã*. There is a behavioral apprenticeship for learning to eat, sit, speak, pray, and so on. "The saint learns to grind on the rock to make *acaçá* (a white corn dough), to thread beads, the dances, the dialect." As *Gaiaku* Luiza said, "the Jeje have schooling," and it involves a lengthy apprenticeship, "without books," based on the imitation and repetition of what the elders do. However, the initiation varies from individual to individual. Each person receives his or her different markings (scarification), and the leaves and other elements used in the initiation rituals also vary according to the vodun to which the person is consecrated.

After this seclusion period, which can last a number of months, there is a second ritual presentation of the *vodunsi* in the *barracão*. This is a private, internal ceremony that marks the coming-out from the initiation chamber, or *huncó*, and begins the second period of initiation, the "outside" period.

The *vodunsi* are allowed to circulate through certain areas of the terreiro but without going beyond its limits, except on special occasions. In the past, for example, the novices went out to sell acarajé (fried bean cakes) or some other item, according to the wishes of their vodun, and with the proceeds they would pay the costs of their initiation.

Gaiaku Luiza fondly remembered the old times in the Jeje terreiros. During initiation, "the vodun would come on Sunday morning and would only let go on Thursday night. . . . On Fridays no saint descends among the Jeje." It is a holy day and no drums are played; as tradition states, "On Friday one neither pays nor is paid." The saint, alternating with its *erê*, "incorporated the novice during five days in order for her to be instructed. Nowadays, things have changed and today their bodies are not healthy or strong enough." According to *Gaiaku* Luiza, the novices' training is easier when they are "awake" (in their normal state) than when they are in their *erê* state or with the vodun. According to *Humbono* Vicente, the *erê*, referred to by him at times as *esin* (from the Yoruban *esin orisa* = the god's horse), comes "always after the saint, and they are there until the day of the name [i.e., during the whole initiation]. . . . the *erê* song is different from the vodun song. . . . the Jeje *erê* is different from the Nagô *erê*, they are different songs. . . . there is an [*erê*] shrine for each person."[39]

As *Gaiaku* Luiza described it, the daily routine of the novices was intense. At about five o'clock in the morning, the *vodunsis*, already embodied by the saint, would take a bath in the river (*to*) and begin the first prayers. During a ritual called *kpole*, they would move in around the sacred trees in single-file procession. "The *donfona* performs the prayers . . . there are more than thirty songs, three per vodun. . . . the *donfona* sings the song and the voduns keep responding." Following the *kpole* there were other prayers until nine o'clock in the morning. At around eleven o'clock, the voduns would *tomar o rum*, that is, they would dance to the sound of the drums; "the morning *rum* is simple: there are three songs." This was followed by a rest period until three o'clock in the afternoon, when the *vodunsis* would take another purifying bath. At four o'clock, once again the drums would beat and the voduns would dance until around six o'clock, at which time they would begin praying again. In Candomblé six in the evening and six in the morning are praying times. At this time the *vodunsis* cannot sit beneath the sacred trees, for it is believed that at that time the voduns are present there. Then the novices would rest, "they would relax a bit to recuperate their energy," but the *erê* remained embodied. On another occasion, *Gaiaku* Luiza remarked that over time and as a result of Ketu influence, the four o'clock dance "rehearsal" was moved to nighttime, from nine in the evening until one o'clock in the morning.[40]

Through this intense regime of activities, especially the daily "rehearsals," the *vodunsi* learns the songs and dances of the voduns, as well as the "dialect" or "talk," for "nothing is said in Portuguese." Formerly, during the entire time that the novice lived in the terreiro she would wear the typical *baiana** clothes, white long skirts, and embroidered blouses. It was forbidden to wear makeup, jewelry, watches, high-heeled shoes, or any other similar profane item. Only after seven years would this prohibition be lifted, and only after this time would the candidate acquire the rank of *vodunsi*. This is in stark contrast to today's practices.

Of course, during the initiation period a whole series of internal and external rituals take place that involve the body of the *vodunsi* and her shrine at the *peji*, which progressively "fix" the deity's *axé,** on the altar and on the head of the devotee. Some Ketu practitioners claim that the Jeje initiation is characterized by the absence of the *oxu* or *adoxu*, the wax cone, herbs, and so on that cover the ritual cut on the top of the novice's head. These are aspects about which I can say little and which the Jeje take pride in maintaining secret. One ritual distinctive to Jeje initiation is the "taking *hunvé*" or "taking *ajauntó*" associated with the vodun Ajauntó (Junto, Jaunto, Ujaunto), the mythical ancestor of the Agasuvi (see chapter 7). According to *Humbono* Vicente, "without it one cannot make saint, it is a sacrament," "to be able to enter the *peji*, only those who have taken it; otherwise, you can't enter." This ritual that includes the drinking of a liquid is probably a continuation of the *enon kpe vodun nuye* (drinking the vodun) ritual, practiced in the Benin vodun temples. The ingestion of the sacred drink is like an alliance with the deity, with fatal consequences if the pact is broken.[41]

One of the external rituals (performed outdoors) characteristic of Jeje initiation is the *gra, grau* or *taking grau*. It normally takes place during the last stage of the initiation, after the *quintanda das iaôs* (see below), and consists of an "ordeal" or a "trial of the vodun" in which the *vodunsi*, embodied by the *gra*, endures three to seven days in the wild, part of the time alone, but watched from afar by the *mãe-de-santo*, the *ogãs*, or *equedes*. The *gra*, also called "the beast," is believed by some to be an elemental spirit of nature, by others to be like an aggressive manifestation of the *erê*, or even like a version of Exu. For this reason, there is a certain mystification of the danger and difficulty associated with this "wilderness ordeal." When the *vodunsi* returns occasionally to the vicinity of the terreiro, the congregation members mock her to provoke her aggressiveness in a confrontation that mixes playfulness with fear. The *vodunsi* attempts to spit on them and hit them with a stick, while they either hide inside the house or defend themselves, striking the ground hard with sticks.[42]

The *vodunsi*'s choleric attitude and the community's joking and avoidance relationships constitute a clear persistence, though in a somewhat altered form, of an African ritual segment. In Benin, the end of the initiation and the beginning of the *vodunsis'* gradual social reintegration are expressed through the metaphor of slave capture. It is said that the *vodunon*, in a symbolic war marked by the firing of a canon, captured the novices from the "vodun's country," bringing them as slaves (*kanumo*) to the secular world. In the ritual segment called "the war will capture them" (*ahwan wa uli ye*), the novices ritually exteriorize their frustration and anger—for having been taken from the "vodun's country," where they enjoyed all kinds of privileges—by attempting to beat all passersby with stones and sticks, while these in turn mock them, saying that they will never again return to the "vodun's country." In Bahia the same dynamic and ritual behavior persisted, but the logic of its meaning was transformed. The metaphor of the slave war was forgotten, perhaps because this practice was not part of the colonial social reality, and the anger of the *vodunsi* came to be explained as a manifestation of the aggressiveness of a given spiritual entity.

The idea of the *gra* is also known in Angola ritual under the name of *inkita* or *enquite*. For Binon-Cossard, "the originality of the Angola initiation resides principally in the *inkita*, a wilderness ordeal that has not been practiced since the 1950s."[43] It is impossible to determine if there was an Angola assimilation of Jeje practices in Brazil or if this was merely a case of convergence. In any case, this is another example of early interpenetration of Jeje and Angola religious practices. In the Jeje houses of Cachoeira that have an area of forest, the *gra* is still practiced.

The initiation process culminates with a third appearance of the *vodunsi* in the *barracão*: the "giving of the name" (*huin*). The celebration is public and one of the best attended and most important of any terreiro. In some ways it demonstrates everything that a *vodunsi* has learned during the initiation process and, at the same time, assesses the expertise of the leadership that oversaw the process. The ritual is similar throughout the various nations of Candomblé, though with difference in the details. Normally, it is divided into three comings-out or presentations of the possessed *vodunsi* in the *barracão*. Shaved and embodied by her deity, she emerges painted on various parts of her body, differently on each occasion, with *efun* (white paint), *wuaje* (blue paint), and *ossum* (red paint). Finally, the vodun appears in its full ritual clothing and carrying its emblems and, after being asked a number of times, suddenly jumps into the air and proclaims its name in a loud voice, producing great enthusiasm among the audience and the manifestation of other gods among the *filhos-de-*

santo present. A common drumming ceremony follows with songs and dances for all of the deities.[44]

There is some controversy regarding the capacity of voduns and orixás to speak. Generally, during initiation, while possessed by their deity, the *vodunsi* does not speak, and it is only at the end of initiation, before the giving of the name, that the rite to "unlock the speech" of the vodun is performed. Some religious experts point out that, "among the Jeje, the saint sings its song after the name," that is, the voduns can speak and, in the rituals, they themselves draw out their songs, a behavior also seen among the vodun cults of Maranhão and in the Gbe-speaking area. However, in Bahia, this rule has some exceptions, as some voduns do not speak and others only sing. In Nagô-Ketu Candomblé, *in general*, the orixá does not sing, and his or her songs are incited by others. Some religious experts say that the rite of "unlocking the speech" is unique to the Ketu and that it is performed prior to the giving of the name; others say that speech among the Ketu is only unlocked for the *ebomes* (*vodunsi* with more than seven years as an initiate).[45]

After the "giving of the name," the *vodunsi*'s gradual reintegration into secular life and into her biological family begins. In Benin, this process can last months and is marked by a complex sequence of rituals. After her third and final public presentation, called *hun su dide* ("the lifting of prohibitions"), follows a week of public festivals, at the end of which the *vodunsi* receives her ritual name. Then is performed the *ahwan wa uli ye* (the war is going to capture them), the ritual referred to above in describing the *gra* ritual. In their capacity as slaves, the *vodunsis* remain three days in the temple. As people who were born again into a new spiritual life, they forget everything regarding common life and must relearn everyday activities, especially relating to commerce and conjugal duties. For this purpose, a number of rituals are performed, such as the so-called *vodunsi lè na sa gi* (the *vodunsis* will sell *acaça*), in which they go to the market to sell *acaça*; and the *e na da asu* (the novices get married), also called *zan kpíkpé* (the mat encounter), in which the *vodunsis* perform a pantomime of the sexual act with a child of the opposite sex on a mat.

After this process, the family must pay a symbolic amount to the *vodunon* to buy the slaves' freedom in a ritual called *kanumò xì xò* (the purchase of the slaves), and, thus the *vodunsi* returns home, though normally she shows some resistance. After three months, they perform a ceremony called *du lè gbe* and, six months later, another called *jô gbe* (loosing the tongue), which allow the *vodunsi* to speak once again the common language instead of the ritual language of the vodun. Other ceremonies with votive sacrifices sometimes occur in the following years. The social reintegration of the *vodunsi* is thus a gradual process.

In Bahia, one finds a good deal of resonance of and correspondence with these African practices, though in a fragmented form. This confirms the importance of the vodun cults as an organizational model of Candomblé. In the case of the *gra*, as previously noted, the angry behavior of the *ahwan wa uli ye* ritual persists, although the explanatory metaphor of war has been forgotten.

Still, if the reference to the *capture* of slaves has been lost, the metaphor of slavery has not. *O Alabama* recorded how the *vodunsis*, "at the end of this time [of initiation], leave and will still serve as slaves to the person who buys them in the saint."[46] In fact, the African ritual *kanumò xì xò* (the purchase of the slaves), in which the *vodunsi* was ransomed by the family, continued in Bahia until recently, but under the name of *a compra das iaôs* (the purchase of the iaôs). This ritual consisted of a pantomime of an auction in which the *mãe-* or *pai-de-santo* would sell the novice to a member of the congregation, whom the *iaô* would then serve. In the absence of a buyer, the novice would remain in the service of the *mãe-* or *pai-de-santo*.[47] *Gaiaku* Luiza remembered that the *vodunsi* was considered a "slave" and that only after seven years "she would become freed, emancipated."[48] In many cases, it was during this period of "slavery" that the *vodunsi*, like the hired-out or *ganho* slaves of old, would sell *acarajé* and other foods in order to pay the costs of initiation, or rather, their manumission.[49]

Even today among the Jeje houses the role of the street peddler is replicated in the *barracão*, through the ritual called the *quitanda das iaôs* (market stall of the iaôs). Though not exactly the same, this ritual evokes the African ritual of the *selling of acaça* mentioned above. Even Carneiro spoke of the *quitanda*, "this ceremony in which they sell (or steal) foods or fruit prepared or acquired by the iaôs, some weeks before the completion of their initiation." At Bogum and Seja Hundé the *quitanda* was celebrated after the *vodunsi*'s giving of the name. As *Humbono* Vicente explained: "You would throw a mat and a cloth on the ground" and the *erês* would call to the people to come buy the fruit, saying "*emi lé ó; e alejo hun bo.*" They would name the fruits and sweets in the African language and, in a very casual and jovial mood, "people would pretend to buy while sticking out their hand as if to steal, and at that point the *erê ogo jo*, strikes with a stick[,] . . . hits them with a stick." This caused great confusion until "the *aniban*, the soldier, the person dressed as soldier" entered and, pretending to fire shots into the air, attempts to impose order in the room. It is at this time of panic that the *erê* flees into the wild, starting the *gra* (or the *inkita* for the Angola) ritual.[50]

It is important to note that the *quitanda* is also a distinctive ritual segment of the Angola nation, which indicates the long-standing Jeje-Angola symbiosis that I have noted in relation to other elements. Binon-Cossard supplies a description of the ritual in that nation and confirms that the *quitanda* "does not exist in the Ketu candomblés."[51] In this discourse on similarities and contrasts, some religious experts also insist that among the Jeje nation "there is no *panã* as with the Ketu." The *panã* is a ritual that, in the houses of that nation, precedes the auction or the *compra das iaôs* (purchase of the *iaôs*) and consists of simulating a series of daily actions, such as carrying water on the head, ironing, sewing, cooking, and so on. The *erê* tries to demonstrate her abilities, although usually with a good deal of joking around and with little success. This ritual also includes imitating the selling of foods in the market and a mock mass, with the subsequent acting out of conjugal duties. In fact, although nowadays it is considered a Ketu ritual, the *panã* includes elements of rituals that are clearly from the Gbe-speaking area, such as the *e na da asu* (the novices get married). This exemplifies how diacritical signs of one nation can be borrowings of another that has already forgotten them as their own.

Whatever the case may be, the *vodunsi*'s learning process lasts an entire lifetime, throughout the daily social intercourse within the religious congregation. The spiritual identity of the person will be configured and constructed based on the successive ritual addition of secondary spiritual entities that accompany the "master of the head." Normally, these spiritual aggregations occur during the ceremonies that the *vodunsi* must perform one, three, seven, and twenty-one years after initiation. After seven years, the *vodunsi* obtains seniority. It is from this moment that, among the Ketu, the *ebome* receives the *decá*, a title that conveys the right to open a new terreiro. Although this term is of Gbe origin, alluding to the gourd (*ka*) containing the tools given to the new *mãe-de-santo* to initiate her *filhos-de-santo*, it is said that with the Jeje, there is no *decá*.

Orthodox sources claim that "with the Jeje there is no election of new leaders, it is by hierarchy," that is, when the *doné* or the head of a terreiro dies, she is replaced by the most senior *vodunsi*, and in theory it is not possible to open new offshoot houses. A *vodunsi* with seven years seniority is only permitted to "shave and paint" new *filhos* but cannot open her own house. As we have seen, this rule—common in Salvador, Cachoeira, and São Luis—could have been elaborated and legitimized by the leaders of the oldest Jeje houses in order to avoid internal dissent during the succession process. This would also explain the difficulty Jeje houses have experienced in seeking to expand. However, the exceptions to this rule are numerous, and the founding of new terreiros that proclaim themselves to be Jeje continues even today.

Initiation in the Jeje-Mahi nation is thus characterized by performing a series of rituals, such as the *sarapocã*, the *kpole*, and the "taking the *hunvé*," that are specifically Jeje, and by sharing others with the Angola, such as the *gra* and the *quitanda*, that are not practiced among the Ketu. Also differentiating the Jeje ritual from the Ketu is the discourse of its practitioners, insisting on the absence of the *panã* and the *decá* rituals that seem to have antecedents in the vodun cults of the Gbe-speaking area. The *panã* and *decá* examples demonstrate how a nation can assimilate and adapt foreign ritual segments, which eventually come to be considered its own. In this case, the diacritical signs are the result not necessarily of historical continuities but of a process of dialogic contrast that occurred between competing congregations in Brazil. These are some of the aspects identified in the study, but of course there are others that only an insider, intimately familiar with the inner rituals of the various Candomblé nations, could reveal.

The Festival Cycle Structure: Calendars and Ritual Segments

Complementary to the initiation rituals, each year the terreiros celebrate a cycle of ceremonies that include a number of both private and public rituals. The private rituals revolve around the "altar-offering" complex and principally consist of shrine cleansing rituals (*ossé*) and animal and food offerings to the voduns, at the altars or at the sacred trees. These propitiatory offerings are intended to regenerate the *axé* of the gods, and thereby the *axé* of the congregation. This is the principle of reciprocity, of giving in order to receive. It is not by chance that these private ceremonies are considered the most important. The public drumming-dancing rituals with the manifestation of the voduns on their *vodunsis*, performed in the *barracão*, constitute the social part of the ritual activity and aim to demonstrate and share the deities' "strength" with the general community. The public festivals contribute in this way to the congregation's social visibility within the larger society and include, in addition to their religious aspect, a dimension of spectacle absent from the private rituals.

As in the initiation processes, within the annual festival cycle, the Jeje-Mahi terreiros are distinguished by the celebration of a series of ritual segments that are unique to them, such as those for Aizan, Legba, and Ogun Xoroque, the *zandró*, the *boitá*, the Aziri Tobosi ceremony and, at Bogum, the Azonodo feast. The Jeje practitioners also identify their liturgy by the absence of certain rituals that are typical of the Ketu nation, such as the *padé*,* the *Cabeça de Boi* (Ox Head) of Oxóssi, the *olubajé* of Omolu, and the *Waters* of Oxalá.

The annual festival cycle in the Jeje-Mahi terreiros happens between December and February, complemented in June by Sogbo's bonfire, during the period of the Saint John celebrations. During the rest of the year, occasional ceremonies can be performed for the benefit of congregation members or even "clients" requiring a particular service. Nevertheless, in the majority of terreiros, during Lent, after Carnival, activities are suspended for a number of weeks. The concentration of Jeje-Mahi ritual activity from December to February also coincides with the period in which, in Benin, the majority of vodun temples carry out their festivals, December marking the end of the rainy season. Jeje ritual activity therefore seems to adapt itself to the Catholic calendar imposed by the colonial context, while at the same time preserving traces of the earlier African calendar.

Table 8 shows a basic outline of the annual ritual cycle in the Seja Hundé and Huntoloji terreiros of Cachoeira. The order, schedule, and length of ritual activities are subject to the rhythm of each house, and there is a certain flexibility for variation according to circumstances and the needs of the moment. In the last few years, for example, the calendar was reduced in both terreiros, concentrating the activities within two or three weeks, a modification that can be attributed to the advanced age of some of its religious leaders. In the past, when ceremonies would extend over a month, the animal sacrifices in the first weeks generally included only fowl, while during the week that preceded the *boitá*, four-legged animals would be immolated. However, the ritual concentration and relative brevity of the calendar are also important characteristics of Jeje liturgy.

While in most Candomblé terreiros the calendars are organized in a series of successive festivities, each dedicated to a particular deity, among the Jeje-Mahi nation of Cachoeira all of the deities are celebrated together. In other words, during a single sacrificial session, offerings are made to all the voduns, and during the public festivals all gods are praised. This ritual structure of collective sacrifice and celebration supports the hypothesis that the multideity cult was rooted in Jeje Candomblé since its beginning.

The festival calendar of Bogum, however, departs from the Cachoeira model to follow a structure similar to that of the Nagô-Ketu terreiros, with rituals specific to each deity, performed during consecutive weeks. The liturgical year begins with the *ossé* (shrine cleansing) and the festival of Olissá, an apparent imitation of the Waters of Oxalá celebrated in the "traditional" Ketu terreiros. The ritual sequence is also divided, as in Ketu houses, into one part dedicated to the "white" deities (Olissá, Dan) and another part dedicated the "red" or palm oil gods (Sogbo, Ojonsu).[52] This important difference in calendar and ritual structure between the Cachoeira and Bogum terreiros may result from the terreiros' rural and urban contexts and from Bogum's greater contact with

TABLE 8 Basic Structure of the Ritual Cycle in the Jeje-Mahi Terreiros of Cachoeira

Week	Day	Schedule	Ritual
1	Saturday	after 6:00 P.M.	Aizan[1]
		night	*Zandró*
	Sunday	morning	Legba and Ogun Xoroque
		—	votive sacrifices and offerings
		night	public festivity
	Monday to Thursday	—	prayers and other private rituals
	Friday	—	rest
2	Saturday	night	*Zandró*
	Sunday	afternoon	*Boitá*
		night	public festivity
	Tuesday	—	conclusion of the *Boitá*
	Wednesday	morning	Aziri Tobosi ritual
	Friday	—	rest
3	Carnival Sunday	—	housecleaning and conclusion

1. The ritual activities at Huntoloji begin on Saturday morning with rituals to Legba and Ogun Xoroque, followed by the Aizan ritual, which normally occurs before 6:00 P.M. The sacrifice occurs in the early morning at around 6:00 A.M. on Sunday, after the *zandró*. According to some sources, the sacrifice at Seja Hundé also was performed early in the morning in former times.

the Nagô-Ketu houses of Salvador. This case is also a good example of the possibility of diverging processes of change within the Jeje nation itself, which makes it difficult to speak of a single liturgy.

Legba, Ogun Xoroque, and Aizan: Opening Rituals

In the Jeje-Mahi terreiros of Cachoeira, despite possible inversions of order, the annual festival cycle begins with the offerings to Aizan, Ogun Xoroque, and Legba, deities characteristic of, and exclusive to, the Jeje nation. None of these deities "shaves anyone" and, therefore, having no initiates, do not manifest themselves in a human body.[53] Aizan is associated with ancestors of the community, and Ogun Xoroque and Legba are messengers who open the pathway to the other voduns, and are therefore honored at the beginning. These three voduns also act as guardians of the terreiro.

Legba corresponds to Exu or Elegbará in the Nagô nation. He is a multi-faceted entity, with a number of attributes and functionalities that make definition difficult. Legba, like Exu, is considered the dynamic principle of the universe, the agency that activates all processes. He is the messenger between men and the gods, who carries the message and returns with the answer; he is the intermediary, the linguist, the translator, and it was he who revealed the secrets of divination to humans. Legba is also the master of all paths; he opens them and closes them; he always precedes the other voduns and orixás when they manifest themselves on Earth. He is the trickster par excellence, jovial, cunning, vain, susceptible, irascible, capricious, churlish, and indecent; he can help to solve any problem, or confuse and cause disorder, fights, and accidents; he can unite enemies or separate friends, work for good or for evil. Neglecting him can have the worst of consequences. Legba also symbolizes the masculine principle and can be represented, as in Benin, by a figure with a phallus of great proportions.

In 1741, in *Obra nova da língua geral de Mina*, António da Costa Peixoto identifies "Leba" as "Demon."[54] In Salvador, in 1871, *O Alabama* denounces an African resident of São Miguel, who had "a room prepared in the form of a temple with idolatrous images of various kinds" and among them, "the figure of a devil (Lebal) dressed in a long cape, which is one of the most miraculous."[55] This identification of Legba with the devil, though incorrect and prejudiced, persists to the present day. It is only with the work of Nina Rodrigues that one finds the first reference to Exu (Exu Bará or Elegbará) in Bahia.

Currently in the Jeje terreiros, in addition to Legba, a number of "qualities" referred to as Exus are known and worshipped, thus indicating a gradual penetration of the Nagô referents in relation to this figure. These Exus include Lalu; Tiriri; Birigui; Agbo, "master of leaves"; Obará, "master of money"; Mirim, "of the Ibeji"; and Vereketu (perhaps a phonetic evolution of Averekete), who accompanies Legba and Ogun Xoroque.[56]

Ogun Xoroque is another very well-known deity among the Jeje terreiros. His shrine is always placed at the entrance of the terreiro, within a group of sticks planted into the ground to form a circle, which protrude some thirty centimeters from the ground and are interlaced with vines. Ogun Xoroque fulfills a function similar to that of Legba or Exu and, to a certain degree, that of Ogun in the Nagô-Ketu terreiros. He is the "attendant of the saint, owner of the terreiro, and master of the paths, he opens and closes paths" and is associated with Bessen, Ogun, and other voduns. Ogun Xoroque does not appear to be documented in the Gbe-speaking area's ethnography. This suggests that he could be an entity assimilated from another nation and later transformed; perhaps a juxtaposition of the name of the orixá Ogun with that of *iami* Oxoronga (ancestral mother), or with that of the orixá Oloroquê of the Efon nation.[57]

The role of Aizan, Legba, and Ogun Xoroque as "entities who come at the forefront" is expressed on at least three levels: (1) the position of precedence that their rituals occupy in the festival order; (2) in the *zandró* ceremony, in which their songs precede those of other voduns; and (3) the placement of their shrines in physical space, occupying the frontal area of the terreiro. In the case of Legba and Ogun Xoroque, this position at the entrance and doors is in keeping with their role as guardians.

The rituals dedicated to this triad of "messengers" have as their principal aim to facilitate the opening of paths and, through their mediation, to call and channel the offerings to the other deities. As occurs with the Nagô Exu, it is usually said that Legba is "dispatched" (sent out) to avoid his contentious intervention in the progress of later ceremonies. But in fact, according to the religious experts, Legba remains present the entire time and he is "attended to" (another meaning of *despachar* in Portuguese) so that he can protect and drive away any other troublesome spiritual entity. In all, the opening function of these three entities' rituals is reminiscent of certain aspects of the *padé*, or "Exu's dispatch," performed in the Nagô-Ketu terreiros, but it is not the same thing.

Juana Elbein dos Santos describes in detail the *padé* (from the Yoruba *ìpàdé*, for gathering) in the Axé Opô Afonjá terreiro. The ceremony is officiated by the *iamorô* and her assistants, the *dagã* and the *sidagã*. Exu, in his "qualities" of Iná (fire), Ojisé (the messenger or executor), and Agbo (the guardian), is invoked to carry the offerings to the male ancestors (*baba eguns*), the founders of the terreiro (*esa*) and the female ancestors (*iami*). Each one of these groups, through Exu, receives different offerings. Because the *padé* deals with the *eguns* and, above all, with *iami* Oxoronga—the representative of the ancestral mothers and associated with the *ajés* (witches) and the most aggressive feminine forces—this ceremony is considered to be fraught with danger. In the more recently founded Ketu terreiros, the *padé* can take less complex forms, but the invocation of Exu and the request to convey the propitiatory offering to the ancestors always includes the act of spilling water on the ground, in an appropriate place outdoors.[58]

The act of spilling water on the ground is also replicated in the Jeje ritual during the *zandró*, when devotees sing to Legba and Ogun Xororque, and the homage paid to the founding ancestors of the terreiro corresponds, among the Jeje, to the Aizan ritual. Therefore, while there are resonances of the *padé* in Jeje liturgy, or vice versa, both the identity of the mediating deities and the ritual practices associated with them are different, so that the absence of the *padé*, as Jeje practitioners point out, constitutes one of the distinctive marks of Jeje liturgy.

The Aizan ceremony is of fundamental importance in the Jeje-Mahi liturgy of Cachoeira, although Verger mentions that "in Brazil, this vodun is hardly spoken of anymore." Aizan, or Ayizan, as he is called in Benin, is a very old vodun, probably of Allada origin. Verger documents two traditions regarding his origin. According to Verger, some "say he was taken there [to Allada] by Adjahuto, when he arrived from Tado. Others affirm that Ayizan was already in the region before his arrival." A. Le Hérissé seems to support the second version when he says that the original inhabitants of Allada were the *Aïzonou* (*Aïzo* inhabitants), and that the ethnonym derives "from the name of the fetish of the land," that is, "Aïzan." As early as 1668, Olfert Dapper describes the offerings performed in the kingdom of Ardra to a *Fetisi* "covered by a pot with holes," through which the priest carries out oracular consultations. As Verger points out, "this seems to correspond to Ayizan," and in fact, even today the shrine of this vodun "consists of a mound of earth [and sand from different origins], on top of which is placed a jar with small orifices, surrounded with palm leaves (*azan*)."

Ayizan is closely connected to the earth element. In fact, *ayi*, or *aí*, the root of his name, in Fongbe means earth or ground. Verger says that he is "owner of the earth" and that he represents "the mat of the earth, the earthly crust." In a manner similar to Legba, Ayizan is considered the protector of the country, the cities, as well as, and most important, the "guardian, or more correctly, lord of the market." He is found in the markets of big cities, such as Abomey and Ouidah. Besides this public dimension, "certain families have their own Ayizan, who supports them, guides them, and chastises the bad behavior of the children." Taking into account these familial or domestic cults, Verger concludes that Ayizan "is a type of ancestor" identified with "the earth."[59]

In this way, one might think that Ayizan was yet another regional variant of the ancient earth and ancestral cults, as were those of Sakpata and Shapana initially, before becoming identified with the smallpox epidemics (see chapter 7). To consider the earth a "kind of ancestor" stems from a combination of two associated and recurrent ideas common in various parts of West Africa. The first is the belief that the mythical founding ancestors of the family collectivity (*hennu*)—the so-called *tohwíyo* in Benin—emerged from or were born from the earth. Herskovits comments that, in some cases the *tohwíyo* are believed to have Aizan as a supernatural ancestor.[60] The second is the belief that the earth is the abode of dead ancestors, given that it is in the earth that they are buried and in it they receive their offerings.

This long-standing connection between Aizan and the earth and ancestors is what endures in Bahia, for at the beginning of his ritual the names of the terreiro's founding ancestors are invoked as well as those of the most illustrious members of the congregation who have passed on. It is perhaps because of this connection between Aizan and the *kuvito* (spirits of the dead or *eguns*) that it is also said that "Aizan is death," but, more accurately, in addition to being the guardian of the house, this vodun acts as a mediator between the living and the terreiro's ancestors, and here, as I have previously suggested, one finds a parallelism between the Aizan ceremony and the Nagô-Ketu *padé*.[61]

Let us examine some of the more important aspects of the Aizan offerings.[62] Although this ritual can be performed before sunset (as happens at Huntoloji), Aizan is the only vodun who can also "eat" (receive offerings) at night, and the ceremony is performed around a cactus (*Cereus jamacaru*), where the vodun is enshrined. Following the cleansing, or *ossé*, of the altar and the lighting of a candle, which is the light that illuminates the god's path, the oracular consultation takes place. While the two parts of the *orobô* (a type of kola nut) are rubbed together, the *ogã impé*, or master of ceremonies, invokes all of the terreiro's ancestors (i.e., *ago* Ludovina Pessoa, *ago* Maria Agorinsi, *ago* Abalha, etc.). Lastly, the *orobô* is tossed, thus requesting permission to perform the ritual.

This being done, the assistants are "cleansed," in hierarchal order, with a varying number of fowl, which the *ogã impé* passes numerous times over the head and body of each person. This is a common form of purification in the vodun cults of Benin as well and works by transferring the body's pollution into the fowl. Then begins the animal sacrifices. Aizan always "eats" chicken, and the cut must be made in a specific manner. Following this comes a series of three songs. The first begins with the phrase "Ê Aizan, vodun Aizan bereo . . .," asking the vodun to accept the sacrifice.[63] Following the sacrifice, the *ogã impé* proceeds to the food offerings (beans, corn, *caruru*, and others). After some forty-five minutes, the participants collect the utensils and return to the *barracão*. Later, the cooked chickens are "laid down" or presented at Aizan's feet.

The rituals for Ogun Xoroque and Legba are consecutive and also consist of food offerings and sacrifices performed at their shrines, but they are always carried out in the morning, as it is said that food is not given to Legba in the afternoon. At Seja Hundé, the ritual is carried out on Sunday after the first *zandró*, while at Huntoloji it is performed on Saturday, preceding the Aizan ritual and the *zandró*. At Seja Hundé, the ritual begins in the *barracão* with the "cleansing" of all the congregation members, using the sacrificial animals, normally young black and red chickens. The first ritual is that of Ogun Xoroque, and near his shrine at the crossroads near the terreiro entrance, a second offering to Exu Tiriri can also be performed. In both cases, "the meat is left there."

The ritual for Legba, performed at the foot of an imposing gameleira tree or *pé de Loko* located at the front of the *barracão*, is similar to that for Ogun Xoroque. It begins with the cleansing of the shrine, using water and leaves. A candle is lit and the first food offerings (*acaçá*, cachaça, and palm oil) are laid out. Once the necessary requests are made, whispering the words into the ears of the animals, the sacrifice of the chickens (sometimes roosters) is carried out. At this time the Jeje songs to Legba, Varaketu, and Ogun Xoroque begin, as well as some in the Nagô language to Exu. Following certain actions with parts of the animals' bodies, their remains are deposited at the shrine. Following this, the other food offerings (*farofa*, roasted corn, palm oil, honey, *cachaça*, white corn, water, and others) are set out. The ritual ends before noon, when there is a break before beginning the main sacrificial session for the voduns.

Between the Legba and Ogun Xoroque ritual and that of Aizan, a certain parallelism is observable: both include animal and food offerings at a given shrine, and they share certain ritual gestures, such as the cleansing of both the shrine and the participants. However, these rituals do present significant differences in the songs, food offerings, and their preparations, as well as in the type of cut performed on the sacrificial animals and their color.

The *Zandró*: The Invocation Announcing the Animal Offerings

The *zandró* is the Jeje ritual that opens the drumming cycle in the *barracão*. Currently, the *zandró* is always performed on Saturday night, beginning at around ten or eleven o'clock. Formerly, it would last until dawn on Sunday morning, but it now normally ends at around two or three o'clock in the morning. *Zandró* is a Fon name that includes the term *zan* (night), which refers to the watch or night vigil previous to a religious ceremony. The *zandró* ritual is the invitation, the call to, or invocation of, the voduns. It is carried out with prayers, songs, and drumbeats whose purpose is to proclaim to the voduns the animal offerings that will be set out on the following day. This same functionality is found in Benin, where the *zandró* also inaugurates the annual festival cycle and is coupled with the announcement of animal sacrifices. This diacritical sign of the Jeje liturgy is, therefore, based on the continuity of a ritual segment from the Gbe-speaking area.

Among the Jeje-Mahi of Bahia this ritual can be repeated on various occasions, preceding the terreiro's most important ceremonies, especially the *boitá*. In this case, there is no clear connection between the *zandró* and the "slaughter," given that the *boitá* ritual does not include animal sacrifices, despite bearing a relation to them (see below). In any case, the various *zandró* rituals do not present significant differences. The ceremony is divided into various parts that are given specific names by the participants: the toss of the *obi*, the feeding of the drums ("the drums are baptized"), and the *zandró* songs, which are divided into a first part with Jeje songs exclusively to voduns and a second part, sometimes called *dorozan*, with songs to voduns and orixás (the so-called Nagô-vodun side).

At the sound of the *avania* rhythm, the *vodunsis* enter the room in a line, bringing various objects with them.[64] The first woman carries in one hand a plate of kola nuts (*obi* or *orobô*), malagueta pepper (*atakun*), some coins (*akwe*), and a candle, and in the other a pitcher of lustral water (*esin* or *abô*); the others carry four small bottles of palm oil (*omi* or *epô*), honey (*oi*), wine and cachaça (*ahém*), a bowl (*aban*) of white flour mixed with water,[65] and six plates of black beans, black-eyed peas, or kidney beans (*aikun*), *farofa*, roasted corn or popcorn (*dobu* or *doburu*), white flour (made from yam or corn) (*ifun*), and boiled white corn (*ebô*). After leaving all of the food on the ground, the *vodunsis* remain kneeling in a line before the drums.

Normally, some member of the house announces in Portuguese the reason behind the *zandró* (i.e., "this *zandró* is for the *boitá*); the *ogã impé*, or whoever is officiating the ritual, then lights a candle before beginning the *obi* session. The consulting of the oracle begins by naming the terreiro's voduns and their ritual greetings ("this *zandró* is for Bessen, Ogun, Odé, Oké, Agué . . ."), evoking those present and excusing those who are absent. When the two halves of the *orobô* fall facing up, indicating a positive response, the ceremony continues.

The devotees then proceed to the ritual of feeding the musical instruments, the *gã* (*ferro*), and the drums, a ritual at times referred to as "feeding the leather." As mentioned above, the instruments are consecrated to certain deities and require periodic offerings of food to renew their "strength." The *ogã* places a small quantity of each liquid and solid in the *ferro* and leaves equal quantities at the edge of the top of the drums. Each one of the foods is related to certain spiritual entities. The order in which they are offered roughly follows the sequence in which the voduns are praised during the rituals. For example, the white corn of Oxalá is usually the last food to be set out, and Oxalá is always venerated in the final part of the song sequence. However, this order can vary from one ritual to another. The whole procedure is carried out in great silence and concentration, only interrupted by the occasional requests for blessings, made by the *vodunsis* to the *gaiaku*, to the *ogãs*, or to the *equedes*.

After the "baptism of the drums," the *ogã* cuts the *obi* into small pieces, and in a kind of communion, he distributes them according to a strict hierarchical order among the congregation members. Some also drink a bit of lustral water from the pitcher and might eat some of the grains of the malagueta pepper. At this point the requests for blessings are repeated. It is noteworthy that the baptism of the drums is not exclusive to the Jeje terreiros but is also practiced in Ketu Candomblé, although with some variations.

When this part is finished, and after a brief pause, the *vodunsis* reenter the room and seat themselves on mats on the ground. Each one takes a gourd covered in beads (*go*), and accompanying the rhythm of the drums and the *ferro*, begins to sing. The sequence of the *zandró* songs always follows a solo-chorus structure and begins with five songs, the first three of which are transcribed here.[66]

1   Olu Baba   Valu vava
    Valu nu kwé ée lo   Valu no quelo
    Valu nu kwé ée lo   Valu no quelo
    Valu nu kwé le dí   . . .
    Olu Baba   Valu vava
    Valu un kwé ée lo   Valu no quelo

2   Olu Baba   Valu vava huntó
    Huntó mona valê mixó   maian valê . . . é,
    Huntó mona valê mixó   mixó é maian, maian, é mixó
    Mona valê huntó é   maian maian huntó
    Olu Baba   Valu vava huntó
    Huntó mona valê mixó

3   Xen xen xen   Que qué o que qué
    Mona valê du kia   maian valê do kia
    Avalê du kia   do kia . . .
    Mona valê du kia   maian vale

According to *Gaiaku* Luiza, these songs are for Bessen, but other religious experts do not associate them directly with him and say that they are to all the voduns. Following them come songs to Legba, Ogun Xoroque, and Varaketu (Averekete). At this point, one *equede* or *vodunsi*, using a gourd, throws a small amount of water three times on the ground outside the *barracão*. This is done as an offering similar to that of the Ketu *padé*. During this sequence, no one may leave the room. Following these songs, the *vodunsis* kneel in a line before the drums and sing to Aizan. The dances done while kneeling constitute an important characteristic of this deity. After this comes a collective circular dance before the *vodunsis* are again seated on the mats to then begin a series of individual dances in which each *vodunsi* dances during a song. These *zandró* songs are begun with a series dedicated to Tobosi and other voduns, in particular those of the Hevioso family, such as Sogbo, Badé, Akolombé, Kpo, and Averekete. This part of the *zandró* is concluded with a circular dance and the song "Ago, ago, ago nilé o," requesting permission from the head of the Hevioso nation to enter into the Nagô-vodun portion of the ritual. Therefore, this song signals the transition to a new ritual segment.[67]

This part begins with songs of greeting and praise of orixás and voduns, similar to the Nagô-Ketu *xiré* sequence. In the Jeje terreiros some call this ritual segment Nagô-vodun, and others *dorozan* (*dorosan* or *dorozu*). Some Jeje experts use the term *dorozan* to refer to the *zandró* songs in general, without applying it specifically to the Nagô-vodun segment, which seems more correct. In fact, *dorozan* is a phonetic evolution of *drozan*, itself an inversion of the syllables of the word *zandró*. In Fongbe *zandró* is the noun that means nocturnal vigil, while *drozan* is the verb that designates the action of vigilance, of remaining awake during a nocturnal religious ceremony.[68] For the sake of analytical clarity, and to distinguish this ritual segment from the *zandró* songs that come before the change in drumbeat, I will use the term *dorozan* to designate this Nagô-vodun sequence.

At this point, each vodun or orixá is praised with three songs and the most important with six or multiples of three. Among the Jeje-Mahi of Cachoeira the sequence begins with Ogun and ends with Bessen, and not with Oxalá as is typical of the Nagô-Ketu *xiré*. The order is normally the following: Ogun, Agué (Ossaim), Odé (Oxóssi), Azonsu (Azoani, Sakpata, Omolu), Oxum, Iemanjá, Iansã, Sogbo (Badé, Loko, Kposu), Nanã, Oxalá, and Bessen.[69] It is important to note that it is precisely this sequence of the *dorozan* that constitutes the basic structure of the public festivities that follow the *zandró* over the subsequent days. The *zandró* can end after the *dorozan*, or it can continue with a sequence of songs called *mundubi*, dedicated, of course, to the Kaviono family. Finally, there are some songs to conclude the ceremony, and for the withdrawal of the *vodunis*. At Huntoloji the last song is normally the *koro koro*, in allusion to the cock's crowing at the arrival of dawn.

In the Jeje terreiros of Cachoeira, as well as at Bogum, they no longer sing exclusively in Jeje, and many of the *dorozan* songs (i.e., those for public festivities) are performed in Nagô. It is only when Jeje entities, such as Azonsu, Sogbo, or Dan, are addressed that one hears songs in the Jeje language. Jeje participants claim that the knowledge has been lost and that the public no longer knows how to respond to the Jeje songs, and that for this reason they are obliged to sing in Nagô. Other explanations argue that this is merely a precaution to avoid Jeje songs' being replicated in non-Jeje houses, or in profane contexts such as Carnival.

From a choreographic point of view, it is interesting to note that, while some collective circular dances are performed, such as in the Ketu *xiré*, the majority of the songs are danced individually or in small groups of *vodunsis* belonging to the same class of vodun. If there is no *vodunsi* of the vodun being sung to, another *vodunsi* dances or, more rarely, the song is played with no dancing. Contrary to Ketu tradition, among the Jeje, all entities should be played to, regardless of whether any of their *vodunsis* are present. When beginning a series of songs to a new entity, all of the *vodunsis* perform greetings to the drums, to the door of the *barracão*, and to the high dignitaries. In doing so, they kneel, touching the ground with their heads, and requesting a blessing. Others might put their hand to the ground, afterward touching their forehead and right ear with their fingers. The Jeje in Cachoeira do not observe the *dobale* typical among the Ketu, in which the dancers prostrate themselves on the ground.

The choreography with its different steps and gestures varies according to the instrumental rhythms and the content of the songs, which often refer to certain fragments of the deities' mythology. However, many of these dances present a choreography that could be considered characteristic of the Jeje tradition and that contrasts with the collective circle dances of the Nagô-Ketu nation. This choreography, which I described above in discussing the *quebrado* and *mundubi* drumbeats, in addition to its characteristic rhythm and gestures, has a "triangular," rather than circular, pattern: the *vodunsis* move from the drums to the doorway of the *barracão*, from the doorway to the other end of the room, and from there, again to the drums.

The *zandró* can be held without any *vodunsi* becoming possessed by their saint. However, when this happens, the voduns are not attired in the ritual dress typical of public ceremonies; instead, there is a simple change of clothing, such as the wearing of a piece of cloth (*ojá*) around the chest. Possession can occur when singing to the vodun of a certain person, however, at Huntoloji I observed on more than one occasion that it occurred following the last songs to Bessen, during the *mundubi* part of the ritual.

Some of the *zandró* characteristics, such as the "baptism of the drums" and the use of gourds by the *vodunsis* while seated on the mats, are clearly descended from practices from the Gbe-speaking area. In the vodun cults of Benin, previous to the *zandró*, devotees perform a ritual called *hun do dji*, which is done to suspend or open the drum. While it does not include the food offerings performed in the Jeje terreiros, the *hun do dji* seems to have a similar function in that it ritualizes the initial drumbeats.[70] After the *hun do dji* and, in order to begin the *zandró*, the *daa* or head of the family, gives to the *vodunons* a number of ritual objects, among them some *kplakpla* mats. The mats are spread out and all the priests sit upon them. At this point they say, "E do zan nu dohué," which means, "He set out the mat for the *dohué*." The *dohué*, which is the name of a rhythm, designates by extension the *zandró* ceremony. The dances and the songs, which go on until four o'clock in the morning, are invariably accompanied by the sound of the *asogwes*, the gourds covered in strings of beads or cowry shells. Interestingly, the *zandró* in Benin does not involve the manifestation of voduns. In the past, this nocturnal ceremony was complemented by a segment called *dohué na cò kanlin* (the *dohué* will keep watch over the animal). The *vodunons* would spend the rest of the night watching over the animals that were to be sacrificed the following morning, indicating the connections between the *zandró* and the sacrificial ceremonies.[71]

The animal sacrifice, as symbolic transference and regeneration of the *axé* of the deities (and by extension of the religious congregation) is the most important act of the "altar-offering complex," and probably of the religion as a whole. The sacrificial ritual that follows the *zandró* is private and restricted to initiated members, and, therefore, I will comment on it merely in general terms. It has already been stated that in the Jeje ritual in Cachoeira, contrary to what happens in the Ketu version, all deities receive offerings or are "fed" in the same ceremony. The central deities of the pantheon: Azonsu, Sogbo, and Bessen, receive four-legged animals, normally goats of either sex, rams being prohibited in Jeje terreiros. This is another difference from the Nagô-Ketu ritual, where the ram is the most emblematic votive offering (especially in relation to Xangô). On rare occasions, an ox is sacrificed in the Jeje ritual.

The moment of the "cut" is the most favorable time for the voduns to manifest on the heads of their devotees. The animal blood pouring over the shrines opens a channel between the tangible world of humans and the invisible one of the gods, and, as proof of the consummation of this communication and the acceptance of the offerings, the gods reveal themselves in their human receptacles. Once possessed during this sacrificial ceremony (performed in the predawn hours at Huntoloji and at around noon at Seja Hundé), the *vodunsis* remain in this state until night, when, at the moment of the public drumming segment, they present themselves to the community. Once again, this is a feature of the Jeje ritual that differs from the Nagô-Ketu tradition.

While the moment of sacrifice is also one of the principal occasions for possession in the Ketu nation, once the ritual is completed, the *iaôs* generally return to their normal dispossessed state. The public drumming, performed at night, begins with the *xiré*, in which the orixás are invoked, and it is during this circle dance that the orixás will manifest themselves. The *iaôs* that get possessed are carried out, only to reappear in the second part of the feast, adorned in their ritual attire. However, among the Jeje-Mahi the *vodunsis* are possessed during the sacrifices and remain in this state until the beginning of the public ceremony, when they appear fully dressed for the ritual. In the Jeje liturgy, the calling upon or invocation of the deities, which in Nagô-Ketu tradition occurs during the *xiré*, is done during the *zandró*, performed the previous day.

The animals' immolations are subject to complex rules; the type of animal, its color, and its sex depend on the deity to which it will be offered. The knife or instrument used for the killing, as well as the cut and the accompanying songs, also vary according to the god. Some voduns such as Ogun Xoroque, receive raw meat, but the majority of deities require specific processes for the preparation of the various parts. This activity is also subject to numerous rules. There are, for example, specific places and people to skin the four-legged animals, or specific requirements and forms for taking the meat from the altar room (*peji*) to the kitchen. Each animal is quartered and cooked in a different manner, according to the deity to whom it is offered. The so-called *exés* (parts) of the animal, such as the head, heart, lungs, gizzard, feet, tail, wings, or testicles, are charged with *axé* and are associated with certain properties and receive special treatment. After the offerings in the *peji*, part of the blood and the entrails are offered to the deities in the sacred trees outdoors, while other four-legged animal *exés*, such as the head and the feet, are reserved for another *fundamento* ritual, which culminates in the *boitá*.

The Boitá Ritual:
The Main Public Festival of Jeje-Mahi Liturgy

The *boitá* is the principal public ceremony of the Jeje-Mahi liturgy and is performed on the Sunday following the sacrifice of the four-legged animals. Because it involves the preparation of certain *exés*, or animal parts, the *boitá* can only be performed after the immolations. The *boitá* is performed in homage to Bessen, the chief vodun of the Jeje-Mahi nation, but it can also be dedicated to other voduns. This ceremony is always well attended by both members and outside visitors. The public portion of the ritual consists of a procession in which the *fundamento*, a series of consecrated objects, is carried on the head of an Ogun *vodunsi* (Ogun being an attendant of Bessen)[72] around various tree shrines and ritually presented at the shrines of Bessen and Azonsu. The *boitá* objects are carried on a large tray, basket, or wooden bowl covered by a white cloth (*ala*), decorated with angelica flowers and *mariwo* palm leaves. The preparation of these sacred empowered objects is itself a secret rite and, once concluded, divination with *obi* is performed to confirm the voduns' approval. The term *boitá* might be a corruption of *gbota*, which is part of an expression used in the Benin vodun cults ("gbota gbigba") to designate a ritual involving offerings to ancestors.

I attended the *boitá* on numerous occasions in different terreiros and present here a synthetic description in the "ethnographic present," though this stylistic convenience does not imply a uniform and unchanging practice.[73] In the *barracão* the voduns manifest themselves through their *vodunsis* to the sound of the *adarrum* at around 2:00 P.M., "the time at which the voduns come to earth." Shortly afterward, they go down to the river to bathe before being dressed in their ritual attire. At approximately 5:00 P.M., after all necessary preparations, the procession enters the *barracão*. The drums and the *gã* play, and the *huntó* sings:

> Aê a ito,
> aê ba ito,
> aê a aito,
> aê aba ito.

This song, chorused by the participants, is hypnotically and monotonously repeated during the greater portion of the ritual. In single file appear the *ogãs*, the *gaiaku*, the embodied voduns, and the *equedes*. All are dressed in white—the *ogãs* with a towel wrapped about the waist, dropping down in the front to their bare feet. Four *ogãs* come at the front, the first carrying a wooden vessel full of *amasi* (a maceration of water and leaves), the second a vessel of *farofa*, the third one with manioc flour, and the final *ogã* with toasted corn or popcorn. As the procession advances, the first *ogã* sprinkles the *amasi* with a cluster of leaves, and the others go along tossing small bits of food on the ground. Behind the *ogãs* comes the *gaiaku* with the *adja*, followed by Ogun, who carries the *boitá*. The *ogã impé*, who directs the group, keeps close to the *boitá* objects. Then come the remaining voduns, all barefoot and dressed in white—in the *avô funfun*, as they say in Ketu. Some *equedes* assist the voduns and conclude the procession.

After dancing in a circular pattern three times around the *barracão* (and presenting the *fundamento* objects before the drums), the procession goes outside and begins to make its way around the terreiro, circling once, twice, or three times around various sacred trees (*atinsa*). As it arrives before the shrine of Bessen (or Dangbe), which is not an *atinsa* but rather a mound of earth covered in pieces of ceramic, the *boitá* is taken from the head of Ogun and presented to the vodun. At this point a new song is sung:

Eta jero ita kaia
beta besi
Eta jero ita kaian
beta besi[74]

After some minutes, the procession resumes its course until it arrives at the shrine of Azonsu, where the same pause and song are repeated. The march then continues to the sound of the first song and, returning to the *barracão* after a half hour, concludes the outdoor portion of the ritual, which must always end before sunset. The *boitá fundamento* is then presented at the altar or placed in the center of the *barracão*, where the voduns dance in a circle during a number of songs. At this point the Nagô-vodun song sequence may be initiated, before the departure of the voduns. As I have noted, the *boitá* is one of the most important times for the recruiting of new initiates and the sudden possession of candidates by their voduns, provoking their violent fall to the ground, is not infrequent.

At approximately 8:00 P.M., the ceremony recommences with a regular public drumming-dancing festival in which the voduns, this time dressed in their colored ritual attire, dance until about 11:00 P.M. Throughout this segment the order of songs typical of the *dorozan*, or of the Nagô-vodun portion, is followed, beginning with Ogun and ending with the Bessen dances. Two or three days after the *boitá* ceremony there is a rite "to unbind the *boitá*." This is the closing ritual in which the *boitá* is taken apart. It is believed that during this interval no member of the religious community may leave the terreiro—to leave is to risk death—but this precaution is no longer observed.[75]

The *boitá* is also celebrated in the Bogum and Oxumaré terreiros of Salvador, with some differences. In the case of the latter, for example, it is a private ritual; the *vodunsi* who carries the *fundamento* is consecrated to Oxum, and apparently the voduns do not participate in the procession but only manifest themselves in the *barracão* at the end of the procession.[76] According to Jeje practitioners, the *boitá* ritual is also different from, and more complex than, the ceremony called *ita*, or *Cabeça de Boi* (Ox Head), a ritual that honors the orixá Oxóssi, performed in the oldest Ketu terreiros, such as Engenho Velho, Gantois, Axé Opô Afonjá, and in others of more recent foundation such as Portão d'Aguas Claras, in the Recôncavo. This Ketu ritual, performed on the day of Corpus Christi, involves the sacrifice of an ox to Oxóssi, as well as the ritual consecration of its head, which is later presented in the *barracão*. However, as far as I know, this ritual does not include the procession around the sacred trees as happens in the Jeje houses. *Gaiaku* Luiza stated, "*Ita* is part of Queto. We have the *boitá*."[77] The carrying of various ensembles of empowered sacred objects in public processions is something common in vodun cults of Benin and the orixá cults of the Yoruba area. However, there is, as far as I know, no ritual that can be clearly identified as an antecedent of the Jeje *boitá*.

The Azonodo Ritual: The Festival of Fruits at Bogum

If the *boitá* is the central ceremony of the Jeje-Mahi terreiros of Cachoeira, the ritual for Azonodo (Azoanodo, Azonado, Azaunoodor, Zanodô, Azanodô, Ozanado) is one of the principal festivals of Bogum. In fact, this ceremony is exclusive to the terreiro, demonstrating that the search for uniqueness is not restricted to the level of nation but occurs more precisely at that of the individual congregation. The vodun Azonodo was enshrined in an immense tree—two or three people together would not be able to wrap their arms around the trunk. Descending the Ladeira Manoel Bomfim, this tree was located to the right. In September all of the leaves would fall and it would seem to be dying, but, little by little, from the thorns that covered the trunk and branches, white flowers would bloom. In January, during the time of the ritual, everything would still be white. "People would come to have their picture taken," *Ogã* Ailton explained. "There was no other tree like it in Salvador." During the Primeiro Encontro de Nações de Candomblé (First Meeting of the Candomblé Nations), held in June 1981, Jehová de Carvalho spoke of the importance of the vodun Azonodo in the Jeje terreiro and criticized the real estate speculation that led to the death of the sacred tree in 1978: "We have Zonodô, or Azanodô who, according to what I am told, does not manifest in humans. . . . This tree was around 200 years old. That is what is assumed. . . . And because of a very serious problem, which is the sacrifice of the sacred soil of Bahian Candomblé, because of this problem of speculation in that area, in order to construct large buildings. . . . this tree was poisoned [they injected the trunk with harmful chemical agents]. That tree, about two years ago, just before the great Azanodô festival, fell. Before this happened we publically warned that the tree might fall, that it was part of Bahia's cultural heritage. That it was a part of the sacred heritage of Bahian Candomblé."[78]

Ogã Ailton said that "the tree fell very slowly, groaning like a sick person, and came to fall in the middle of the street, without damaging a single house." As to the age of the tree, the estimate of 200 years seems exaggerated. According to *Equede* Santa, the original tree was brought from Africa, planted in a cask by the grandfather of Escolástica da Conceição Nazareth, the famous Menininha of Gantois. Menininha's grandfather, named Salaco, must have been a freedman who, like other Africans of that period, probably traveled between the two Atlantic coasts. If one figures that he was born approximately fifty years prior to his granddaughter (c. 1844), and that the trip to Africa had occurred in his youth, one can speculate that the tree arrived in the second half of the nineteenth century, perhaps in the 1860s.[79] At this time, as we have seen, both Bogum and Moinho (Gantois) were operating, and this fact further confirms the close ties of complementarity between the Ketu houses and Bogum.

The Azonodo festival is celebrated on January 6, the Day of Epiphany, or Three Kings Day. The vodun Azonodo is associated with the black king Melchior (or King Balthazar) and, as Carvalho points out, this is a "very unique manifestation of Bahian religious syncretism."[80] The relationship between Azonodo and the epiphany of the Three Kings, and the idea that this vodun does not manifest itself in the human body or receive blood sacrifice, is all very well known.[81] However, the bond between Azonodo and the main vodun families incites differing opinions. Many, perhaps the majority, believe that Azonodo is a type of Dan, a snake from the Bessen family. *Humbono* Vicente mentioned a song that expresses this connection: "Bessen Azonado; [pause] Bessen no gueré déuá; Bessen Azonado; Bessen no gueré déuá."[82] Other sources seem to have confused Azonodo with Azoani, the vodun from the Azonsu family.[83] Although the Jeje make a clear distinction between these two voduns, the common phonetic root of *azon*, which in Fongbe means illness and is at the base of many Sakpata vodun names, suggests an early connection between Azonodo and the earth pantheon. Segurola records the name Azowano as another name for Sakpata. For Rego, "Azon non do" means the plant that causes illness.[84] In Ouidah, a priest of Sakpata, after hearing a description of the tree of Azonodo, which is perennial with thorns and white flowers, identified it as the *clontin* tree, associated with the Sakpata vodun Sodji. Its leaves, *cloma*, are used for the preparation of *amasi* and are associated with a purification ritual to keep away illness (*eno nyi azòn*).[85] Everaldo Duarte, on a journey to Benin in 2002, identified the Azonodo tree as being of the same species as the famous "tree of forgetfulness" (*l'arbre de l'oubli*), that grows on the way from Ouidah to the shore. According to legend, before embarking for the New World, the slaves were made to walk around the tree a number of times in order to forget any memory of their past.[86]

But let us examine how the Azonodo festival was held at Bogum. The ritual would begin at dawn on January 6, with the washing of the trunk and the placement of a white piece of cloth around the point where the first branches began.

Throughout the entire day, *pais* and *mães-de-santo* from various Candomblé nations would bring their fruit trays to the foot of the Azonodo tree. At around 5:00 P.M., before the sunset, these fruits were distributed among the Bogum members and visitors.[87] Raul Lody, an *ogã* of Bogum, describes the ceremony: "At this festival all of the initiates dress in white and wear light-colored beads. The women in the procession carry wooden bowls and trays filled with many different kinds of fruit. Later these fruits are placed on the branches and roots of the 'Azanodô,' the sacred tree. On this day there is no sacrifice of animals, and the only sacrifice offered to Azanodô are the fruits themselves. At the close of the ceremony, a table of fruit is offered to the participants and guests. N.B.: The Azanodô festival is practically forgotten, even among the most traditional Afro-Brazilian cults."[88]

According to *Equede* Santa, in the past at the entrance to the Azonodo tree enclosure was—an area "of closed-off brush, with *peregun* shrubs and a lot of secrets"—which was restricted to the most senior *vodunsis*. Only they participated in the fruit consecration ritual at the *atinsa*, and only when this was finished would one of them come out to distribute the fruit among those who waited outside. *Equede* Santa adds that during the ritual, Runhó's Sogbo would wander around "carrying a snake outside the enclosure. Today [is different] and everybody comes in [within the enclosure]."[89] As is clear from Carvalho and Lody's descriptions, in more recent times the ritual was no longer private, and the sharing out of the fruit was done within the enclosure of the sacred tree.

Everaldo Duarte mentions that Azonodo is "a fruit-giving tree; he is wind and protector of harvests." His ritual was performed to commemorate the first fruit harvest of December. "No one could eat fruit prior to this ritual," but this rule was in force only until the 1960s and is no longer observed.[90] This prohibition is reminiscent of others pertaining to rituals associated with agricultural cycles, such as the yam festival, celebrated in September in Benin and in November in Bahia. Recall that *O Alabama* speaks of the "festivity of the new yam" in the Moinho terreiro (Gantois) in 1871: "It consists of the consecration of the first fruits of the harvest of each year to the African deities. Before celebrating this ceremony, the members of the African sects are forbidden to eat of it."[91] According to Duarte, the yam festival was not practiced at Bogum, or among the Jeje nation in general.

With the death of the Azonodo tree in 1978, its remains were buried beneath a yellow flamboyant tree planted at the front of Bogum's *barracão* by Nicinha with the help of Duarte and *Equede* Santa, and it is there that the rituals are performed to this day.

The Aziri Tobosi Ritual: The Agonli Water Vodun

The narrative now returns to Cachoeira. The Aziri Tobosi ritual, in the past as well as today, marks the end of the annual festival cycle of the Cachoeiran Jeje-Mahi calendar, but not necessarily those of other Jeje terreiros in Salvador, such as Bogum or Poço Béta.[92]

Aziri Tobosi has a clear antecedent in Benin in Azili, or Azili Tobo, a *tòvodun*, a water vodun or a vodun who inhabits the waters. This deity is directly associated with the lake of the same name, Azili, on the east bank of the Ouemé River, some eight kilometers northeast of Zagnanado, in the Agonli region. Some *vodunons* say that the vodun Azili comes from the Wo or Wogbo River (the great Wo), an autochthonous name for the Ouemé River. As the Agonli region is located to the north of the Zou River, the border of the Mahi country, Azili is also considered a Mahi vodun.[93] The second element of the name, Tobo, could be a compound of the words *bô* (empowered object or medicine) and *tò* (water, or any body of water, such as a river, spring, or lake). *Tobo* is, therefore, the preparation or spell whose power is infused by the water spirits, normally contained in a gourd.[94] Other sources believe that *tobo* is a contraction of *tògbo*, the great (*gbo*) body of water (*tò*), which would be an allusion to the Wo (Ouemé) River or to Azili Lake. Both interpretations entail an association with water.

Mahi ritual practices associated with river deities such as Azili were assimilated or appropriated by the Fon as early as the eighteenth century, contributing in great measure to the institutionalization of the royal Nesuhué cult in Abomey. For example, the *tohosu* (princes of the water) and the initiation ritual called *Yivodo*, two important elements of the Nesuhué cult, are closely associated with Azili Lake. It is precisely at the end of the *Yivodo* ritual that, in the presence of a religious expert from the Azili country, the Neshué *vodunsis* are prepared to act as *tobosi*. This is an ambiguous transitional state between vodun possession and the person's normal state (not to be confused with the manifestation of a second deity), which can last a number of days and is characterized by feminine and childlike behavior (similar, but not identical, to the *erê* state in Candomblé). Following the public festivals, the *tobosi* go to the market and other places to beg. They constitute a unique characteristic of the Nesuhué cult and the cult of Dan.

Aziri Tobosi is a Jeje spiritual entity unknown in the Nagô-Ketu and Angola candomblés of Bahia. The Jeje experts speak of Aziri Tobosi (or Tobosi Aziri) and Aziri Kaia (or Tobosi Akaia) as two female spiritual entities associated with the waters, the former being more widely known. As Aguesi of Seja

Hundé declared, "every source of water has its master," and Aziri Tobosi "is an entity of the depths"; she lives in the deepest of water. Aziri Tobosi is normally associated with freshwater and for this reason is sometimes compared to, but not identified with, the Nagô River orixá Oxum. Aziri Kaia, in contrast, is most frequently associated with Iemanjá and saltwater. According to *Gaiaku* Luiza, Aziri Tobosi is associated with both fresh- and saltwater and dresses in white and wears crystal and silver beads like Iemanjá. Like the Azili vodun of Benin, in every case the association with water is explicit.[95]

The gender of a vodun is always difficult to determine, and despite Aguesi's assertion that Aziri Tobosi is for six months female and for six months male, she is most frequently considered a female vodun in Bahia. This is also the case in Haiti, where Azili, known as Ezili or Erzulie, is held to be a woman. In Abomey there is documentation of the name Azili Nyòho Awui, *nyòho* being translatable as "old woman," suggesting that the female nature of Azili in Haiti and Bahia has precedent in Benin. However, at Casa das Minas in Maranhão Azili is considered a male vodun, clearly differentiated from the *tobosi*, which are considered female spirits.[96]

Nowhere in Bahia does the word *tobosi* refer to the childlike state of transition following possession, which is characteristic of Benin, nor a spiritual class of girl princesses as at Casa das Minas. In 1916, Manuel Querino wrote: "Saint Anne in Nagô is Anamburucú, and in Dahomean, Tobossi."[97] One might be led to think that, in Bahia, *tobosi* became a generic term among the Jeje to designate female and/or water voduns, such as Aziri or Nanã. My own hypothesis is that, as in Haiti, the initial use of the term to designate water entities was eventually substituted by a reference to the female "quality" of the gods, an attribute that gained dominance. The ritual of Aziri Tobosi, as practiced in the Jeje-Mahi terreiros of Cachoeira, is the *last* ceremony and marks the end of the annual calendar of ritual activities, and this final position in the ceremonial structure corresponds to the same final manifestation of the *tobosi*, or mendicants, in the African rituals. This concurrence may not be mere coincidence and might be a vestige of the Agonli cult of the vodun Azili Tobo.

The Aziri Tobosi ceremony in Cachoeira, which basically consists of "giving food" to this god, is an outdoor ritual, performed normally in the morning. The *assento* of Aziri is always enshrined in a sacred tree near a stream, pool, or spring. The proximity of water is significant, and at Seja Hundé the *assento* is enshrined within the water on the bank of the Caquende River, under a *dendezeiro*, or palm tree. The rituals at Seja Hundé and at Huntoloji present some variations, whether in the schedule, in the order of the ritual segments, the food offerings, or in other elements. However, they do share some similarities in the general structure, which is divided into two parts.[98]

As in other rituals, one or a few candles are lit, and an oracular consultation is done with the *obi* to confirm that the vodun accepts the ceremony. Subsequently, the initial food offerings are made. As the chickens are sacrificed to the sound of the first songs, the voduns manifest themselves in their *vodunsis*. In a wooden bowl, or at the trunk of the sacred tree, are placed foodstuffs such as *farofa*, *acaçá*, honey, palm oil, and water. During this initial stage, there are songs to Aziri Tobosi such as:

Aé, aé, Tobo;
Tobosi lé, Tobo.

Makobo, makobo
Tobosi lé makobo

At Seja Hundé, they continue with the song sequence of the *zandró*, with songs to different voduns, while at Huntoloji they sing the *dorozan* (or the Nagô-vodun part) sequence. The voduns, all together, dance at the front of the sacred tree for approximately one hour. Thus concludes the initial stage of the ceremony, when the voduns return to the house while the *equedes* cook the sacrificial animals.

Following this recess all of the participants return to the *atinsa*, or sacred tree, and perform a second offering, with the meat now cooked and with the other foods such as beans, *abara*, *caruru*, fried banana, popcorn, white corn, and so on. The same foods that are offered to the god are then distributed among the participants in banana leaves. During this second stage at Seja Hundé the voduns dance to the sound of the *dorozan* and only partake of the ritual food at the end of the ceremony, once they have regained their "normal" state. In contrast, at Huntoloji, the *vodunsis* appear possessed by their *erês* during this part and, seated on mats, share in the ritual food along with the other participants.

Initially this fact, in that particular ritual context, led me to believe that there might be a relationship between the *erê* and the *tobosi* states, but in comparing it with the Seja Hundé ritual, in which there is no presence of *erês*, I was led to conclude that this manifestation at Huntoloji is most likely a mere functional strategy to allow the *vodunsis* to eat the ritual food, since the *erê*, unlike the vodun, has the ability to eat. Actually, this food communion, accompanied by personal requests to the god, creates a moment of *communitas* and constitutes the true essence of the ritual.

Thus it is apparent that the Cachoeira ritual, Aziri Tobosi, has nothing that can be said to correspond to the *tobosi*, as known in the Nesuhue cult and at Casa das Minas. The only continuity between the *tobosi* of the Nesuhue cult with Aziri Tobosi and her ritual is her aquatic and female nature, and perhaps her ritual's being last in the liturgy. This fact, together with the evident similarity between the names, suggests a common cultural origin of the Aziri Tobosi cult of Cachoeira and the Nesuhue cult, which, as I have noted, corresponds to the Agonli Azili Tobo cult. This example suggests that the regional differences found in relation to Aziri and to the *tobosi* in São Luis and in Cachoeira derive, in part, from differences in their African antecedents. In other words, the different ethnic origin and religious affiliation of the social agents responsible for the transatlantic transfer are at the root of certain Brazilian regional variations. This case highlights the fact that within the Jeje tradition itself there was a heterogeneity of religious practices that have yet to be critically examined.

The Old Ceremony of "Closing the Basket" and the Bonfire of Sogbo

Finally, we will examine the annual cycle's closing ceremony, the so-called *encerramento*. This ritual, formerly known as "closing the basket" (*fechar o balaio*) is not exclusive to the Jeje and therefore does not contribute to the discussion of what differentiates this nation. However, its analysis contributes to highlighting, alongside the maintenance of the differences, the persistence of a series of shared rituals and hence of a consensus among all Candomblé congregations that cuts across specificities of nation.

As an *O Alabama* article of February 16, 1869, described it, "during these three days of Carnival, the drum is beating; they are closing the basket for Lent is just around the corner." Another news item states that "the closing of the sect's festivals during the weeks of Lent lasts eleven days, beginning on the Saturday before Carnival.[99] The interruption of liturgical activities during Lent (also observed, for example, by the Tambor de Mina of Maranhão), following the Catholic calendar, suggests a ritual segment "invented" or institutionalized in Brazil without any direct connection to African practices. This ceremony indicates Candomblé's ability to adapt to the local conditions of a slave society.

In the 1860s, the *fechar o balaio* ceremony was already a festival of great importance, involving many days of drumming, the sacrifices of oxen and sheep, and other rituals. It was practiced in many terreiros and was an occasion for the gathering of religious experts from many different places. The importance of this festival, "created" in Brazil, celebrated recurrently in many terreiros, and involving a dynamic of cooperation and complementarity among the various nations, indicates the high level of institutional consolidation attained by Candomblé at the beginning of the second half of the nineteenth century.

Nowadays, it is frequently said that during Lent the voduns and orixás return to Africa, but this does not seem to have been the original meaning given to the interruption of religious activities. The *fechar o balaio* ceremony was associated with the idea that the deities would go to war during this period. Thus in 1867 it was said in relation to a woman who was being initiated at Bogum that "the *saint left* her during Carnival, the time during which *he leaves for the war*, and only returns around Easter." On the Rua do Sodré, the reporter from *O Alabama* relates the presence of a "true *quilombo*" of Africans, where "the drums are constantly seething" to celebrate the fact that the "saint has gone to war, or that he has returned from war."[100]

The term *fechar o balaio* has been forgotten by the contemporary *povo-de-santo*, but it seems to have been an allusion to female sexual abstinence, and some of the older members, in an interesting semantic turn, still remember it as meaning "not to seek out women during Lent."[101] Currently, the ritual that signals the conclusion of activities during Lent is better known by the Nagô term *loroogun* (or *olorogun*), translated by Francisco Viana as "he who performs the war ritual." Maintaining the old tradition documented in *O Alabama*, the *loroogun* still symbolizes the deities' departure for war. In this ritual "the cohorts of Oxalá (Senhor do Bonfim) and Xangô (Saint Jerome) fight in the candomblé terreiros to the sound of the drums and religious songs. The group that first allows an orixá to manifest itself in the terreiro is the one to lose."[102]

In the Jeje-Mahi terreiros the old *fechar o balaio* is today generally referred to as the *encerramento* or "the closing." It is considered a minor ritual, restricted to a few congregation members and performed on Carnival Sunday (or on the first Sunday following Carnival). The voduns manifest themselves in the morning, and until not many years ago, this was followed by drumming in the afternoon. Then there comes a general house cleaning using *peregun* palm fronds. The *barração* floor is wetted with water and the space is purified with incense. The *mariwo* palm leaves are removed from the doors and windows and other decorations from the walls. The voduns carry bags with white corn (associated with the sky deity Oxalá or Olissá), which is spread on the roof, and roasted corn or popcorn (associated with the earth god Azonsu), which is spread on the floor. During the procession the *avania* rhythm is played, accompanied by a farewell song that announces the departure of the voduns.

According to *Gaiaku* Luiza, "they know they won't return. . . . it is as if there were going to war." The bags are later hung on the sacred tree of each deity, and only after Lent, with the recommencement of activities, are they taken down. As far as I know, this use of bags is characteristic of the Jeje terreiros and is not practiced in the Nagô houses. Seven-day candles are lit for each of the voduns in the indoor shrines and at their sacred trees ("they are lit outside and inside"). Others are also lit for the initiated members of the house. The *peji* shrines are covered with white cloths (*ala*), and the sacred trees are wrapped in colored cloth. Two days after this ritual, the scraps and leavings of the cleansing are cleared out (the white corn, roasted corn, *peregun*, *mariwo*, etc.). The whole of this is carried out in the afternoon to a distant place in the woods and abandoned in the shadows. During Lent the saints will not respond (i.e., manifest themselves in their *vodunsis*). Olissá is the only one who remains (and perhaps some other entity such as Nanã) to provide aid in case of some emergency.[103]

Thus the decline of the old *fechar o balaio* festival can be seen. Currently, at least in the Jeje terreiros, it seems reduced to a private house-cleaning ritual, lacking animal sacrifice and, increasingly, drumming and vodun manifestation. In houses engaged in re-Africanization, it is said that the *loroogum* was a tradition imposed by Catholic hegemony, and the interruption of this festival is not infrequent as they now practice various activities during Lent.

After Lent, the only important ritual in the Jeje terreiros is the so-called bonfire of Sogbo, occurring in June, during the Saint John and Saint Peter feast days. Although this ceremony presents unique aspects that differentiate it from homologous rituals practiced in candomblés of other nations, it is not (like the *encerramento*) a ritual segment that practitioners identify as exclusive to the Jeje nation. However, given the importance of this festival in the Jeje calendar, it should be briefly discussed.

The bonfire of Saint John, a tradition of Iberian origin, is also associated with the harvest in the Recôncavo of green corn, a crop of Amerindian origin. As elsewhere in the country, in Cachoeira the festival is hugely popular and all families prepare bonfires on the eve of Saint John's Day. This tradition, which can probably be traced to the earliest times of the colonial period, together with other elements unique to the June festivities (such as the preparation of the Brazilian sweet dish *canjica* and the consumption of genipap and passion fruit liquors) was appropriated by the Candomblé community regardless of nation. However, among the Jeje houses the bonfire became one of the most important regular ceremonies of the ritual calendar, being associated with the voduns Sogbo and Badé, who in Jeje hagiology are deities associated with fire.

June 24, Saint John's Day, is normally associated with Badé and Bessen, while June 29, Saint Peter's Day, is associated with Sogbo.

There might exist an interesting connection between Badé and the Saint John festival, a link that derives from the festival's association not so much with fire as with corn. In fact, as Segurola points out, Gbadé, in addition to being a vodun of the Hevioso family, in Fongbe means corn, "in Ouidah they say *gbadé*; in Abomey the form *agbadé* is used." In 1741, Peixoto mentions the term *abádè* as corn. According to Edmundo Correia Lopes, "Keibiossô, the Gêge Xangô, became Badé, Badé is corn, and nothing would be more natural than to unite the Keibiossô cult with the cultivation of corn, in one of those agricultural celebrations of slaves such as the charming peanut festival of which we find early notice in Gabriel Soares."[104] If the June festivities correspond to the green corn harvest, it is not improbable that this would contribute to the celebration of Badé during the Saint John festival.

Here is a synthetic description of the ceremony given by *Gaiaku* Luiza: On the eve of Saint John's Day, before lighting the bonfire, the *canjica* for Bessen is prepared, made with ground green corn—from which the "straw" is removed—water, sugar, clove, butter, cinnamon sticks, and coconut milk as desired. The preparation of Bessen's *canjica* on Saint John's Day causes some to identify the bonfire of this day with the snake-vodun. The preparation of the bonfire, made with wood from the sacred trees, is, as a rule, the responsibility of the *ogãs*. Once the fire is lit, which can take time because of the rain, the members of the house go around the fire three times with the *canjica* and the fruits, especially oranges, which will later be presented at the "feet of the saint." While the fire burns there is drumming and the voduns, especially Sogbo, whether at this point or during the previous sacrifices, take possession of the *vodunsis*. Once manifested, they dance around the bonfire. In the past this ritual, together with the *boitá*, was a prime occasion to gather new *vodunsis* into the initiation room. At the end of the ritual, the *canjica* and the fruit is divided among those in attendance. *Humbono* Vicente added that in the old times there would be dancing with the *canjica* around the fire and they would throw corn and oranges into it.[105] At Seja Hundé the Saint John bonfire is kept lit until Saint Peter's Day, when Sogbo is paid homage.

If, on the one hand, Azili Tobosi is an example that demonstrates how cult differences from the Gbe-speaking area can persist as regional variations within Jeje ritual in Brazil, and if the Azonado ritual shows how ritual differentiation can be found within the restricted area of a single terreiro, then the *fechar o balaio* ceremony and the Saint John bonfire, as rituals created in Brazil and therefore the result of consensus, tend, on the other hand, to be ritual spaces where the particularities of nations are not evident. The broadest conclusion that can be derived from this evidence is that the diacritical signs chosen to articulate differentiation between nations, though they can sometimes be elements "created" in Brazil, are more frequently anchored (though perhaps readapted and given new meanings) in differentiated African elements.

Conclusion

Despite the detail given to certain aspects of Jeje liturgy, this book is far from exhaustive. There are yet other important rituals, such as the *zelim* funeral rites, which present singularities that differentiate them from homologous rituals performed in the candomblés of other nations. However, they do not constitute ritual segments that practitioners identify as exclusive to the Jeje nation, so I have left them as material for future studies.

One of my more general conclusions is that the processes of religious identity, which are articulated within contemporary Candomblé from liturgical differences, reveal a clear parallel with the processes of ethnic identity operating among Africans and their descendants in the eighteenth and nineteenth centuries. Both are cases of relational identity processes, that is, differentiation processes based on contrast with the "other" and on the dichotomization of diacritical signs. Difference is expressed in a double movement by the valorization of singularities not shared by others, as well as through the absence of certain values and practices that are typical of others. In fact, the processes of religious identification observable in Candomblé today were, in the past, an integral part of ethnic identification, and there exists a certain relation of continuity between them.

Moreover, processes of religious identification are multidimensional in a manner similar to the process I pointed out in relation to ethnic identity. In other words, a member of a Jeje terreiro has recourse to various categories in order to express his or her religious belonging. At the most basic level such a person can describe his or her religion as "African," aligning him- or herself with an increasingly valorized ethnoracial black identity. This type of identification occurs primarily in interactions with people belonging to religions that lack African referents, or that, if they have them, do not value them in the same way, such as practitioners of Caboclo Candomblé, Umbanda, spiritism, or evangelical churches. On a second, intermediate level, our terreiro member can use "metaethnic" categories to describe his or her terreiro as being of the Jeje nation. This type of identification-description is normally produced in interactions with members of other Nagô or Angola terreiros, and in a context of awareness of differences in liturgy and spiritual genealogies. On a third level, within each nation there is a series of categories with more specific references to African lands or cities. Among the Jeje, as we have seen, there is Mahi, Savalu, Dagomé, Mundubi, and so on. Unlike the "metaethnic" labels, these categories no longer express much difference at the ritual level, but they persist as diacritical signs of particular congregations. In the case of the Jeje nation, the Mahi variant seems to have persisted with greater visibility than other "subnations" that were eventually forgotten. With the Nagô nation, Ketu is the dominant "subnation."

Thus, the multidimensionality of ethnic identification among blacks in the eighteenth and nineteenth centuries finds parallels in the religious sphere, although the importance and social visibility of the various identifying levels is dynamic and historically variable. While there were Africans in Bahia involved in candomblés, the third level—that of "subnations"—must have had a significant relevance; as those Africans died and were substituted by Creoles, "metaethnic" denominations by nation became more important. In more recent decades, the more generic level of Africanity seems to have become the most used because of the importance that negritude ideology has gained as an ethnoracial identity.

All of these identifying dimensions associated with Candomblé, based on conceptual and ritual differences that are more or less recognized, are operative as long as there is a basic consensus, that is, while they occur within, or in relation to, the same religious institution. As I have repeatedly highlighted, difference is only possible where there is a minimal level of similarity, and this similarity—the result of long processes of symbiosis—is also reflected in the classificatory system. Thus the term *Nagô-vodun* (or its intellectualized version, *Jeje-Nagô*)—expressing the interpenetration of these two great ethnoreligious traditions—is frequently used by Jeje practitioners to refer to their practices.

The classificatory system outlined above should not be understood, however, as rigid or stratified into autonomous levels. There are innumerable possibilities of combinations of this nation terminology to designate the rites of contemporary Candomblé houses, creating compounds such as *Ketu-Angola-Caboclo* or *Ijexá-Ketu-Angola*, and so on. The plasticity and eclecticism in using these religious identifications suggest a constant movement of practices and values across groups and indicate that such identifications are frequently the result of efforts to legitimize one group over others, rather than to express a direct continuity with specific African traditions.

Since Bogum and Seja Hundé are congregations with histories going back to the nineteenth century, however, it is possible in their cases to examine these questions from a broader historical perspective. By analyzing ritual activity and the configuration of their pantheons, it is possible to evaluate the degree of continuity or discontinuity of the diacritical signs that mark the borders of the Jeje-Mahi nation. This is not an easy task given the lack of precise historical information, and it is very difficult to make projections on the past based on contemporary ethnographies. Additionally, persistence and change occurred in separate domains and discreet aspects of ritual practices. Nevertheless, based on the available evidence it was possible to present some hypotheses regarding general tendencies.

The most visible diacritical signs of the Jeje liturgy are the identity of the deities, the voduns, as well as the language used in the songs and prayers associated with them. These elements, despite the possibility of transformations undergone over time, seem to present a clear relation of continuity with antecedents from the Gbe-speaking area, which in most cases go back to the time of slavery. Regarding the deities, we saw the aggregation dynamic that seems to organize them into increasingly broader groups, while a similar dynamic of selectivity forgets lesser gods.

Despite sharing the "altar-offering" structure common to Candomblé and bearing some functional similarity with the Nagô *padé*, the Legba and Ogun Xoroque sacrificial offerings constitute a singularity of the Jeje liturgy. These deities are nominally differentiated from their Nagô counterparts Exu and Elegbara. There can be a homogenization of their ritual practices—Legba receives palm oil, *farofa*, and *acaçá* like Exu—but this homogenization derives in part from Africa, where these deities already shared certain attributes. In fact, the nominal division between these two classes of entities (or perhaps one should speak of a single category) can be tenuous and, through the dominance of Nagô referents, some people, even in Jeje houses, refer to Legba as Exu. However, despite this, in the discourse of the *povo-de-santo*, Legba and Ogun Xoroque are considered Jeje. Hence, the dichotomization between Legba and Exu, which contributes to the demarcation of the border between the Jeje and Nagô liturgies, derives from an opposition already existing in Africa, and thus, in this case one sees a more or less adapted retention.

Also in the case of Aziri, we saw how local variants of vodun cults from the Gbe-speaking area persist as regional variants within the Jeje liturgy in Brazil, which indicates a continuity not only of the conceptual and ritual complex associated with specific voduns, but also a continuity of their relative differences. In other words, in Brazil there was not only the preservation of the divisions between the vodun and orixá cults, but in some cases differences between distinct vodun cults also persisted. This indicates the importance of particular social agents in the transference, reactualization, and transmission of African religious practices in Brazil.

Furthermore, we saw the continuity of complex forms of ritual activity in relation to certain ritual segments such as the *zandró* that, despite changes, additions, and forgotten elements, find obvious antecedents in the vodun practices of the Gbe-speaking area. It can therefore be said that an important part of the diacritical signs that establish the borders of the Jeje nation is anchored in vodun cult practices imported during the period of the slave trade.

However, with regard to other ritual elements that today represent singularities of the Jeje nation, it is not easy to find such antecedents. The *boitá* homage to the sacred trees, for example, has no clear correspondence that I know of in African vodun practices. Also, despite the fact that the Azonado tree at Bogum was probably imported from the Gbe-speaking area and that it is associated with some Sakpata cult as its name suggests, no version of the fruit festival such as the one in Salvador is performed in Africa. It is obvious that the religious ethnographies of the Gbe-speaking area leave significant gaps, and that what I have considered to be an absence of antecedents may be merely a lack of awareness of undocumented cults. Furthermore, it is possible that practices that have persisted in Brazil later disappeared from the Gbe-speaking area. There is also, however, the possibility that these are ritual segments that were gradually "created" in Brazil—in the case of the *gra*, for example—by symbiosis with Angola practices or, in the case of the *boitá*, as a result of the formation of multideity cults, since its processional structure seems designed to pay homage to the plurality of shrines.

The same lack of ethnographic data impedes the assessment of the potential degree of continuity of other ritual elements, such as the *mundubi* and *quebrado* choreography and rhythms of the Jeje-Mahi in Cachoeira (though intuitively one could speculate as to some kind of continuity). Regarding those articles of clothing distinctive to the Jeje, such as the red-dyed *palha da Costa*, or straw, one does find antecedents in the Gbe-speaking area. However, the use of these articles in relation to the vodun Sakpata seems to have been an essentially Brazilian creation. These examples suggest that certain diacritical signs of Jeje liturgy are the result of elements stemming from the Gbe-speaking area that underwent complex processes of change and adaptation to meet new ritual conditions.

At the same time, it has been demonstrated that ritual segments elaborated in Brazil—such as the *fechar o balaio* ceremony, or the Saint John bonfires, which resulted from the interpenetration of African practices with Catholic, or Iberian, traditions and, therefore the product of the consensus of heterogeneous Africans, rather than Africans of a particular nation—constituted ritual spaces less conducive to sustaining differentiating diacritical signs, although, obviously any individual house might have developed its own particular details.

Finally, I pointed out the *decá* and the *panã* ritual segments, which might have been original vodun cult practices gradually forgotten by the Jeje until contemporary times, when their absence was claimed as a distinctive characteristic of the Jeje liturgy. Simultaneously, the same elements were appropriated, reelaborated, and valorized by the Nagô in the orixá cults, becoming their diacritical signs. This movement of practices from one group to another and their later reelaboration to the point of becoming the identity signs of another group is a perfect example of the plasticity and historical dynamic to which ethnoreligious identity processes are subject.

The analysis of the distinctive signs of Jeje liturgy thus suggests that they are the result of many different processes, including simple survivals but to a greater degree retentions that were partially readapted and resignified, or even idiosyncratic "creations" emerging from the cultural assemblage produced under the new Brazilian conditions. In any case, the Jeje example indicates the rich interface between continuities and discontinuities, as well as the hybrid and heterogeneous nature of the practices and values of any Candomblé nation.

The historic analysis of the formation of Candomblé also reveals, however, the critical importance of the vodun cult traditions—in relation to, for example, the centrality of the "altar-offering" complex, the initiation structure, the group conventual organization, and the multideity cult—although this contribution remains below the surface, silenced in the memory of today's Candomblé practitioners, who privilege more than anything the traditions of the orixá cults of the Nagô-Ketu nation. As I noted in the introduction, in this study, I have tended to highlight the Jeje, not in an attempt to "purify" or reify this tradition but in order to recognize and properly demonstrate its contribution to the formation of Candomblé. The diachronic or historic perspective adopted here is important inasmuch as it reveals the play between continuities and changes. Again, it has not been my intention to use History ideologically in order to justify or legitimize any given hierarchy.

My purpose in exploring the differential factor of the Jeje also stems from the awareness that this is a dynamic that operates among the practitioners themselves. In the relational contrast with competing groups, the Jeje congregations, like the Angola, must inevitably measure themselves against the Nagô-Ketu, who are socially more visible. This comparison can result in differing attitudes or reactions depending on the individual and the religious party to which they belong. Obviously, members of the "traditional" Nagô-Ketu houses (or those who identify themselves as such) do not like to speak of Nagô hegemony or of Nagocentrism. Aware of their general influence in Candomblé, they tend toward a certain intra-African ecumenism, underscoring the similarity between orixás, voduns, and *inquices*. In contrast, members of terreiros of other nations, while aware of and accepting of the predominance of Nagô-Ketu referents, can insist on their difference and, when this is ignored or marginalized, they might have recourse to the idea of Nagô hegemony. These antagonistic attitudes are rarely made public, and in general a dynamic of cooperation and complementarity reigns among the terreiros of different nations. However, privately, there also persists a dynamic of competition that cannot be ignored.

It is not my intention to problematize this Nagô "hegemony," but it is also true that in the face of so many studies of Nagô-Ketu Candomblé, this work on the Jeje nation presents an alternative view. I am fully aware that this contribution is limited, merely a partial and provisionary attempt that will require further study in order to correct and refine the hypotheses presented here. Nevertheless, if I succeeded in pointing out the plurality of influences that took part in the formation of Candomblé and, within this context, if I was able to give an indication as to the Jeje contribution, then I count myself as satisfied. *Humbono* Vicente said that "the time of the Jeje is over," yet I suspect that the tradition of vodun worship, through its constant transformation, continues to act as a driving force within Candomblé.

GLOSSARY

Acè (Yoruba), *ace* (Gbe), *axé* (Portuguese): life energy, life force or power
Amalá: ritual and votive food of Xangô, Iansã, Obá, and Ibêji
Assento: sacred space or shrine ritually prepared for the worship of a deity
Atabaque: Afro-Brazilian wooden drum

Babalorixá (Yoruba): male high priest in the orixá cults
Baiana: regional stereotype of the black or mixed-race Bahian woman,
   often associated with street-food venders
Barco: group of devotees initiated by the same priest(ess) during the same
   period
Barracão: dance hall or part of the terreiro where public ceremonies are held
Batuque: drumming and dance performance
Boitá: one of the most important ceremonies in the Jeje Candomblé liturgy

Caboclo: spiritual entity of non-African origin, usually associated with
   Amerindian spirits, but also with spirits of the Brazilian popular classes
   (sailors, ranch hands, etc.)
Calundu: generic term used in colonial Brazil to designate a variety of
   religious activities, often involving divination and healing, and associated
   with Africans
Calunduzeiro: calundu practitioner
Crioulo: Creole—a term used in Brazil to refer to blacks or descendants of
   Africans born in Brazil
Curador de feitiço: witchcraft healer
Curandeiro: healer

Decá: ritual that confers senior status to initiated members of Candomblé
   allowing them to open their own terreiro
Despacho: ritual offering placed at the crossroads or, in funerary rituals, when
   the belongings of the dead person are "dispatched," or done away with

Ebô (Yoruba): animal sacrifice or offering
Egun (Yoruba): spirits of the dead

Engenho: sugar mill plantation

Equede: initiated woman who aids in the rituals, but does not become possessed

Fechar o balaio: name formerly given to the ceremony closing the annual ritual cycle

Feitiçaria: witchcraft or sorcery

Feitiço: charm or spell

Filho- or *filha-de-santo*: an initiated person

Folia: festivity celebrated in the Catholic black lay brotherhoods

Fundamento: esoteric or "deep knowledge" regarding the meanings and procedures of the secret rituals of Candomblé

Gbo or *bô* (Gbe): personalized and personified empowering object

Ialorixá (Yoruba): orixá high priestess

Ifá: divination system among the Yoruba

Inquice (Bantu): deity

Itacara: sacred emblem of the vodun Bessen

Iyami Oxoronga: orixá representing the power of the witch

Juiz, juíza: title of a member of the directorship of a Catholic brotherhood

Kele: necklace worn by initiates worn until their coming out

Mãe-de-santo: mother in the saint, high priestess, same as *ialorixá*

Malungo: name given to those who experienced the Middle Passage on the same boat

Ogã: initiated man who aids in rituals but does not become possessed

Oriki: Yoruba praise poem

Orixá (Yoruba): deity

Padé: Opening ritual in the Nagô Candomblé liturgy

Pai-de-santo: father in the saint, high priest, same as *babalorixá*

Pardo: Mestizo or mixed-race individual

Patuá (Tupinamba): charm or amulet

Peji: room where Candomblé shrines are kept

Pejigã: man responsible for the *peji*

Povo-do-santo: the Candomblé religious community

Quilombo: clandestine community of maroons or fugitive slaves
Quitanda: ceremonial market festival that takes place after the initiate's coming-out

Recôncavo: area surrounding the Bay of All Saints in Bahia where the main sugar and tobacco plantations were located
Reinado: festivity celebrated in the Catholic black lay brotherhoods

Sirrum: Candomblé funerary ritual

Tabaque: see *atabaque*
Tambor de Mina: name by which Afro-Brazilian religions are known in Maranhão
Terreiro: Candomblé house or temple, usually comprising a piece of land with several buildings

Vodun (Gbe): deity
Vodunsi: devotee who has been initiated and consecrated to a vodun and who gets possessed by it

Xaxará: a sheaf of palm branches decorated with divination shells, emblem of the orixá Omolu, who is also known as Obaluaye

Zelim: Candomblé funerary ritual

NOTES

PREFACE

1. Throughout this book, I use *Candomblé* to refer to the religious institution and *candomblé* to refer to specific congregations or terreiros.

2. Capo, *Comparative. . . .*

3. Fredrik Barth defines a *polyethnic society* as one "integrated in the marketplace, under the control of a state system dominated by one of the groups, but leaving large areas of cultural diversity in the religious and domestic sectors of activity." Barth, "Grupos . . . ," 197.

4. Ibid., 196, 200.

5. For Weber, "ethnic communion" ultimately comes down to the subjective belief in a common origin, real or imagined (*Economy . . . ,* 270). For Geertz, "the congruities" of ethnic connection "are seen to have an ineffable, and at times overpowering, coerciveness in and of themselves" and result from "some unaccountable absolute import attributed to the very tie itself" (*Old Societies . . . ,* 109). For the distinction between primordial and relational theories, see Rex, *Raça . . . ,* 49).

6. Barth, "Grupos . . . ," 194. For constructivist studies of ethnicity as social interaction, with special attention given to historical depth, see, among others, Roosens, *Creating Ethnicity . . .* ; Eriksen, *Ethnicity and Nationalism*; and Carneiro da Cunha, "Etnicidade. . . ." In Afro-Brazilian studies, see Dantas, *Vovó . . .* ; Oliveira, "Retrouver . . ."; and Slenes, "Malungu. . . ."

7. Carneiro da Cunha, "Etnicidade . . . ," 35–39 (emphasis added).

8. Cohen, *Urban. . . .* For theories of ethnicity as an expression of interests, see also Glazer and Moynihan, *Beyond. . . .*

9. For instrumentalist theories of ethnicity, see, for example, Banton, *Racial. . . .* There are two types of "others" in relation to the individual: those of his or her own group and those of other groups.

10. Herskovits, "African . . . ," 635–43; Herskovits, *The Myth . . . ,* xxxvii; Bastide, *Sociología . . .* ; Verger, *Orixás . . .* ; J. E. dos Santos, *Os Nagô. . . .*

11. See, e.g., Dantas, *Vovó . . .* ; and Capone, *La quête. . . .*

12. Mintz and Price, *An Anthropological . . . ,* 5–7; Barnes, *Africa's . . . ,* 9–10.

13. Herskovits, *Man . . . ,* 553.

14. Sahlins, *Ilhas . . . ,* 7, 17.

15. See, e.g., Verger, *Notas . . . ,* 15; Verger, "Raisons . . . ," 144–45; and Bastide, *Sociología . . . ,* 113, 316.

16. V. W. Turner, *Schism. . . .* See also Maggie, *Guerra. . . .*

CHAPTER 1

1. Peel, "A Comparative . . . ," 263.

2. Akinjogbin, *Dahomey . . . ,* 213.

3. Rodrigues, *Os africanos . . .*, 35; Freyre, *Casa-grande*, 301. According to Rodrigues, the letter is dated 1648.

4. Antonil, *Cultura . . .*, 123; qtd. in Freyre, *Casa-grande*, 389.

5. Oliveira, "Viver . . . ," 175.

6. Mercier, "Notice . . . ," 30; Smith, *Kingdoms . . .*, 55, 70–71; Lima, "A família-de-santo . . . ," 16; Law, "Ethnicity. . . ."

7. Pérez, "Contribución . . . ," 3–4. The term is also used in Sogbossi, "Mina-jeje . . . ," 19.

8. Soares, *Devotos . . .*, 114ff., 189.

9. Ibid., 45, 47, 49; cf. D. P. Pereira, *Esmeraldo . . .*, 69–70; Pazzi, *Introduction . . .*, 74–75; Law, *The Kingdom . . .*, 10.

10. Pazzi, "Aperçu . . . ," 13.

11. Verger, *Os libertos . . .*, 17; Rodrigues, *Os africanos . . .*, 35, 108. See also Oliveira, "Quem eram . . . ," 58–60.

12. Soares, *Devotos . . .*, 66, 116–17; Debret, *Voyage . . .*, 2:76; Oliveira, "Quem eram . . . ," 59; Karasch, *A vida . . .*, 63–66.

13. Peixoto, *Obra nova . . .*, 20, 29, 69.

14. N. Pereira, *A Casa . . .*, 24; Eduardo, *The Negro . . .*, 10.

15. Soares, *Devotos . . .*, 118. Sogbossi, "Mina-jeje . . . ," 41. Matory suggests that the language could be Fon (*Black Atlantic . . .*, 308n6). Correia Lopes identifies it with the *Gunu* or Ewe ("Os trabalhos . . . ," 45ff.). Yeda Pessoa de Castro considers the vocabulary to be predominantly Fon (*A língua . . .*, 68).

16. Lepine, "As metamorfoses . . . ," 122.

17. Johnson, *The History . . .*, 8; Merlo and Vidaud, "Dangbé . . . ," 272; Iroko, *Mosaïques . . .*, 59.

18. Pazzi, "Aperçu . . . ," 18; Lepine, "As metamorfoses . . . ," 122–23.

19. Lepine, "As metamorfoses . . . ," 123; Costa e Silva, *A manilha . . .*, 535–38.

20. Verger, *Notas . . .*, 540.

21. Akinjogbin, *Dahomey . . .*, 22.

22. Le Hérissé, *L'ancien . . .*, 106, 274, 279; Akindélé and Aguessy, "Contribution . . . ," 20–28.

23. Law, *The Kingdom . . .*, 29–32, 37–40. For example, in relation to the Aligbonon-Agasu episode, Law claims that Agasu is an autochthonous Fon deity and that Aligbonon is essentially associated with the area of Wassa, near Abomey, having no connection with Tado; cf. Burton, *A Mission . . .*, 297; Le Hérissé, *L'ancien . . .*, 277; Blier, "The Path . . . ," 401–2.

24. Pazzi, "Aperçu . . ." 15–16.

25. Capo, *Comparative . . .*, xxv. For an analysis of the terms *Adja-Ewe-Fon*, see Medeiros, "Le couple . . . ," 35–46; and Asiwaju, "The Aja-Speaking . . . ," 87–102.

26. Tidjani, "Notes . . . ," 36–38. Smith, *Kingdoms . . .*, 55–72. Elisée A. Soumonni states: "The Yoruba of Dahomey are made up of the following subgroups: Sabe, Ketu, Awori, Ifonyin, Ohori, Idaisa, Ife, Isa, Manigri, and Ajase (Porto-Novo)" (*Daomé . . .*, 19).

27. Dapper, *Naukeurie . . .*, 307.

28. Van Dantzig, *Dutch Documents . . .*, 1.

29. Bosman, *A New . . .*, 397; Dalzel, *The History . . .*, 13; Verger, *Fluxo . . .*, 128; Dunglas, "Contribution . . . ," 143–44.

30. Asiwaju, "The Aja-Speaking . . . ," 87–102.

31. Aguessy, "Convergences . . . ," 235.

32. Pazzi, *Introduction . . .* , 51, 158.

33. With the intent of attracting European commerce to the Jakin port, and in order to decrease commerce at Ouidah, the king of Ardra, Tohonu, sent two ambassadors to the court of Philip IV in Madrid in 1658: Bans, who spoke Portuguese, and his servant. The Spanish Capuchins, hoping to convert the African king to Catholicism, took advantage of the linguistic ability of the two ambassadors to translate the *Doctrina christiana* from Spanish into Arda. In this text, there are sixty references to terms such as *vodu* (God), *vodugue* (the Holy Mother Church, from *vodunhue* = vodun house), *voduno* (priest), *vodunu, voduti, voduto*, and so on (Labouret and Rivet, *Le royaume . . .*).

34. For analysis of the term *vodun* and its etymologies, see Maupoil, *La géomancie . . .* , 52–54; and Blier, *African . . .* , 37–47.

35. For the *yehwe*, see Herskovits, *Dahomey . . .* , 2:190, 192. See also Burton, *A Mission . . .* , 292.

36. Verger, *Notas . . .* , 439. Another example is the orixá Iroko, known as the vodun Loko among Gbe-speakers.

37. Aguessy, "Convergences . . . ," 236.

38. The Fa divining practices were taken from the Yoruba area to the Gbe-speaking area, first to the coastal cities in the seventeenth century, then to Abomey at the start of the eighteenth century (Maupoil, *La géomancie . . .* , 4, 45–56).

39. Hazoumé, "L'âme . . . ," 65–86; Tidjani, "Notes . . . ," 33.

40. Akinjogbin uses the expression "slave raiding ground" (*Dahomey . . .* , 93).

41. Akinjogbin has in French "les démangés de la rage" or "les damages de la rage"; Bergé, "Étude . . . ," 711; Cornevin, *Histoire . . .* , 47, qtd. in Lima, "A família-de-santo . . . ," 42.

42. Verger, *Fluxo . . .* , 154; cf. AHU–Lisbon, São Tomé, cx. 4.

43. Norris, *Memoirs . . .* , 138.

44. See, e.g., Verger, *Fluxo . . .* , 251n26. See also Burton, *A Mission . . .* , 147, 262.

45. Bergé, "Étude . . . ," 712, 723.

46. Smith, *Kingdoms . . .* , 59.

47. Merlo and Vidaud, "Dangbé . . . ," 287–90. Bergé presents a variation of the same tradition in "Étude . . . ," 733–55. Regarding the Ifè, see Iroko, *Mosaïques . . .* , 98.

48. Duncan, *Travels . . .* , 2:222, 229–30. *Caboceer* is a title derived from the Portuguese term *cabeceira*, used in West Africa to refer to people of high rank.

49. Karl, *Traditions . . .* ; Merlo and Vidaud, "Dangbé," 287–90; Bergé, "Étude," 710–11.

50. Parés, "O triângulo . . . ," 193–96.

51. Ott, "O negro . . . ," 144–45; Andrade, "A mão-de-obra . . . ," Tabela 4 (2); Verger, *Fluxo . . .* , 670; Querino, *Costumes . . .* , 72.

52. In Angola there are phonetic forms similar to Mundubi, such as Mundómbe (Ndombe), an ethnic Bantu group located in the interior of Benguela: Curto, "The Story of Nbena . . . ," 44–64; Figueira, *Africa Bantu . . .* , 241–64. In Brasil, Ramos, in *As culturas . . .* , 224, refers to the Mundombe as "Bantu *Cafres* in Angola."

53. Verger, *Notícias . . .* , 228.

54. In both Bahia and Maranhão, *mindubim* (or the variant *midubi*) is a popular term meaning peanut (*Arachis hypogaea*, Lin., or *amendoim* in Portuguese). Interestingly, the

peanut is one of the ritual foods of the Hevioso voduns. According to the *ialorixá* (high priestess) Olga de Alaketu, the scarification of the Mundubi consisted of seven dots on each side of the face and one on the chin, and because of the similarity between the facial dots and the size and shape of peanuts, popular parlance created this ethnonym (Olga de Alaketu, Salvador, interview, March 1, 1996). In the Casa das Minas terreiro in São Luis in Maranhão, the term *mindubim* also refers to the Hevioso vodun family. The primary meaning of the word is peanut (*amendoim*); the secondary meaning is mute, or *mudo* in Portuguese. With the exception of Averekete and Abé, the Hevioso voduns, known there as the Nagô family, are considered mute (*mindubim*), and it is believed that they did not speak in order to hide Nagô secrets from the Jeje: Ferretti, *Querebentan . . .*, 300, 120–26. Alternatively, for Yeda Pessoa de Castro (*A língua . . .*, 146), *mundubi* comes from *xogbonuvi*, children of Xogbonu (i.e., Porto Novo).

55. During fieldwork, I heard at times the term *Jeje-Agabi* (in relation to a Santo Amaro terreiro), and at other times the term *Nagô-Agabi* (in relation to an old terreiro of the Recôncavo): Jaime Montenegro, August 10, 1999; *Gaiaku* Luiza, February 26, 2001). In Afro-Brazilian scholarship, the term *Jeje-Efon* (Efan) is also used, but identifying the Efon with the Jeje is erroneous despite the phonetic similarity between the Fon and Efon ethnonyms. Querino speaks of the "Efon or burned face," and Rodrigues considered the "Efan" to be blacks from Dahomey, though he correctly notes that they "show themselves to be different from the Dahomeans," as it is known that the Efon were a Yoruba-Ijexá group located near Ekiti in Nigeria: Querino, *Costumes . . .*, 31; Rodrigues, *Os africanos . . .*, 105; Akinjogbin, *Dahomey . . .*, 10. On Efon Candomblé ritual or nation as a variant of the Nagô, see V. G. da Silva, *Orixás . . .*, 84–88; and Capone, *La quête . . .*, 126–29.

56. Viana Filho, *O negro . . .*; Verger, *Fluxo . . .*, 9.

57. Law, *The Kingdom . . .*, 5, 87; cf. Brásio, *Monumenta . . .* 2, no. 97, Jácome Leite, São Tomé, August 8, 1553. The Popo were peoples predominantly from the Hula ethnic group and were fishermen and producers of salt, carrying on their commerce along the coastal lagoons.

58. Law, *The Kingdom . . .*, 87; cf. Bowser, *The African . . .*, 40–43; de Marees, *Description . . .*, 224–25. Brásio, *Monumenta . . .* 5, no. 197, Relação da Costa da Guiné, 1607, vol. 6; Garcia Mendes Castelo Branco, "Relation de la Costa de África," 1620; vol. 7, no. 39, Decree of Council of State, Lisbon, June 27, 1623.

59. Law, *The Kingdom . . .*, 87. Estimates taken from data given by van den Boogaart and Emmer, "The Dutch . . .," 353–75.

60. Rodrigues, *Os africanos . . .*, 35–36; Freyre, *Casa-grande . . .*, 301, 389; cf. Barlei, *Res gestae . . .*, 128; Antonil, *Cultura . . .*, 123. Rodrigues gives a translation of Barlei's text that differs from Freyre's: "with the exception of a limited number that, due to their excessive patience in labor, contributes to an increase in their value."

61. Labat, *Voyage . . .*, 2:125. The same idea is emphasized on page 124: "One should not imagine that all captives purchased in Juda and Ardres originate from these kingdoms. These two kings do not sell their subjects. . . . they are brought from neighboring kingdoms," often by Muslim (Malê) merchants.

62. Law, *The Kingdom . . .*, 6–9, 53–54, 87–88.

63. Verger, *Fluxo . . .*, 30–38, 49, 77; Pazzi, *Introduction . . .*, 208.

64. Barbot, *A Description* . . . , 321–22. The same reference to the low-quality Portuguese slave trade in Petit-Popo is documented in 1698 by Bosman, *A New* . . . , 334.

65. Van Dantzig, *Dutch Documents* . . . , 106.

66. Verger, *Fluxo* . . . , 19–30; Pazzi, *Introduction* . . . , 208; Wimberly, "The African . . . ," chap. 4.

67. Amaral, "As tribos . . . ," 57; Verger, *Fluxo* . . . , 63.

68. Lara, "Linguagem . . . ," 6; cf. "Carta do governador do Rio de Janeiro ao rei de 5 de julho de 1726," in *Documentos interessantes para a história e costumes de São Paulo*, no. 50 (1929): 60–61; "Parecer do Conselho Ultramarino de 18 de setembro de 1728," in *Documentos históricos*, no. 94 (1951): 28–30. On the same incident, see Verger, *Fluxo* . . . , 68.

69. Inventory of Antonio Sardinha, Muritiba, 1711–13, fl. 3v; Seção Colonial Judiciária, 01/56/56/442, ARC. In the division of property (fl. 10), it appears as "Luzîa gege."

70. Inventory of Ana da Silva Andrade, São Gonzalo dos Campos, 1714–49, Seção Colonial Judiciária, 01/65/65/495, ARC.

71. Last will and testament of Manoel Barbosa de Abreu, resident "of the other side of Paranaíba, São Bento das Balzas Parish, state of Maranhão," September 5, 1758, qtd. in Mota, Silva, and Mantovani, *Cripto maranhenses* . . . , 102–6.

72. Karasch, *A vida* . . . , 94. Another reference to a black of the "Gege nation" comes in April 7, 1835, in the *Diário do Rio de Janeiro*, 4, qtd. in Soares and Gomes, "Gênero . . . ," 22. In 1879, there is a reference to a "Mina Gègi," "*gunhôde*," or priestess by the name of Leopoldina Jacomo da Costa: "Desacato à Realeza—Tiramos da 'Gazeta' de 28," *Província de São Paulo*, September 30, 1879, pasta 16.017, *O Estado de S. Paulo* archives qtd. in Matory, "Man . . . ," 166–67.

73. Borghero, "Relation . . . ," 419–44; Desribes, *L'Évangile* . . . ; Bouche, *La Côte* . . . ; d'Albeca, "Essai . . . ," 2:5, 83, 129–37. Hansen, *Dahomey*. . . .

74. Cornevin, *Histoire* . . . , 79; Segurola, *Dictionnaire* . . . , 264.

75. Matory, *Black Atlantic* . . . , 79–81, 299–300; Matory, "Jeje . . . ," 62–63.

76. Van Dantzig, *Dutch Documents* . . . , 66–67.

77. Verger, *Fluxo* . . . , 59–61.

78. Schwartz, *Segredos* . . . , 282; cf. Verger, *Fluxo* . . . , 651.

79. Verger, *Fluxo* . . . , 129–30.

80. "Acquérat" refers to slaves connected to the French fort that could not be sold given that they were part of the property of the fort: Verger, *Fluxo* . . . , 207.

81. Labat, *Voyage* . . . , 2:125–27.

82. Rodrigues, *Os africanos* . . . , 103.

83. Rodrigues's thesis seems to be corroborated by members of the "Mina-Popo" terreiro, Poço Béta, of Salvador. The first-born son of Manoel Falefá, the house's founder, explains that Jeje is a corruption of *guégué*, which is the language of the Popo (Gen): Itamoacy Falefá, personal communication, Salvador, December 13, 1998.

84. Akindélé and Aguessy, "Contribution . . ."; Lima, "A família-de-santo . . . ," 14–15; N. Pereira, *A Casa* . . . , 68; cf. Abraham, *Dictionary* . . . , 38. Additionally, Bolouvi suggests that Jeje derives from the Yoruba adjective *jéjé*, which means "softly, silently, noiselessly." According to him, the name was given by the Yoruba to the Fon because of the surprise attack tactic employed by the Dahomeans against the cities of Abeokuta, Ketu, and so

on (Bolouvi, *Nouveau* . . . , 102). Sogbossi refutes this idea ("Mina-jeje . . . ," 44). For a detailed analysis of the subject, see also Oliveira, "Quem eram . . . ," 67–72.

85. Law, *The Kingdom* . . . , 16, 112; cf. Law, *Further* . . . : Arthur Wendover, Apa, July 17, 1682; Pazzi, "Aperçu . . . ," 14; Pazzi, *Introduction* . . . , 202–3.

86. Van Dantzig, *Dutch Documents* . . . , 89.

87. Akinjogbin, *Dahomey* . . . , 64; Law, *The Kingdom* . . . , 16, 112; cf. Law, *Further* . . . : Du Colombier, Ouidah, April 17, 1715.

88. Verger, *Notas* . . . , 23. Sogbossi proposes that the term *jeje* comes from the word *ajaji* ("Mina-jeje . . . ," 47). Raymond Oké claims that *ajaji* comes from an aphorism: "Ajahuto ton wè honja ta-do ton; aja-huto wè axolu aja ton, wè jan nyi ajaji [The royal throne of Tado belongs to Ajahuto; Ajahuto is king over all Aja; he sat over the Aja [Ajadji]." From this was taken the name Ajaji-Honja, which designates a region approximately twelve kilometers from Davié-Sèmè (Allada), where Ajahuto defeated the Adja of Tado (Oké, "Les siècles . . . ," 57). Yeda Pessoa de Castro puts forth yet another hypothesis, a bit "forced" in my opinion, according to which *jeje* originates from *gédéji* (descending from or born of Guede, ancestor of the Guedevi) (*A língua* . . . , 62).

89. "Étude sur la région. . . ," 26; Sogbossi, "Mina-jeje . . . ," 48; Pazzi, *Introduction* . . . , 41, 74. Le Hérissé (qtd. in Verger, *Notas* . . . , 524) and Herskovits (qtd. in Maupoil, *La géomancie* . . . , 65) speak of the Djetovi.

90. "Étude sur la région. . . ," 17–19. Merlo and Vidaud, "Dangbé . . . ," 269–70; Tidjani, "Notes . . . ," 17; Laffitte, *Le pays* . . . , 90. For the tradition of Idjé independence and later resistance to French domination, see Soumonni, "A Iorubalândia . . . ," 13–14.

91. Parés, "The Jeje . . . ," 95.

92. The Adja continued to call their new capital Allada (Ardra, or Ardres for the Europeans), and their coastal port Little Ardra or New Ardres (Porto Novo for the Portuguese).

93. Akinjogbin, *Dahomey* . . . , 214; Pazzi, "Aperçu . . . ," 15; Akindélé and Aguessy, "Contribution . . . ," 17, 18, 71; Dissou, "Essai . . . ," 83, 87; Oke, "Notice . . . ," 89. Bancolé and Soglo, "Porto Novo . . . ," 76; Verger, *Os libertos* . . . , 10–11.

94. Verger, *Fluxo* . . . , 59–70.

95. Akinjogbin questions the claim, supported by Snelgrave, Norris, and contemporary historiography, that this search for outlet to the sea was exclusively in response to the interests of the slave trade (*Dahomey* . . . , 73–81).

96. Snelgrave, *A New* . . . , 14–15, 20–23, 149–52; Verger, *Notas* . . . , 540; Verger, *Fluxo* . . . , 150–55; van Dantzig, *Dutch Documents* . . . , 176–78; Akinjogbin, *Dahomey* . . . , 91–92, 97–100.

97. Verger, *Fluxo* . . . , 144, 154.

98. Schwartz, *Segredos* . . . , 283–84.

99. Verger, *Fluxo* . . . , 211–23, 257–63 (for the embassy of Tegbesu); Verger, *Os libertos* . . . , 10–11, 101–4 (for João de Oliveira). See also Manning, *Slavery* . . . , 36, 43.

100. Rodrigues, *Os africanos* . . . , 31; cf. "Dois embaixadores africanos mandados à Bahia pelo rei do Dagomé. Carta de D. Fernando José de Portugal ao Exmo. Sr. Luís Pinto de Souza em 21 de outubro de 1795 [Two African embassadors sent to Bahia by the king of Dagomé. Letter from D. Fernando José de Portugal to His Excellency Sr. Luís Pinto de Souza on 21 October 1795]," *Revista do Instituto Histórico e Geográfico do Rio de Janeiro*

69, part. 1 (1895): 413. There is a "Carta do embaixador do rei do Dahome. Pedido para casar-se. Palácio de Queluz 3 abril 1796, Núcleo Governo da Capitania da Bahia [Letter from the ambassador of the king of Dahomey. Request to marry. Queluz Palace 3 April 1796, Central Government of the Captaincy of Bahia], série Ordens Regias 1763–1822, vol. 81, doc. 07, APEBa (qtd. in Verger, *Fluxo . . .*, 265–71).

101. Verger, *Fluxo . . .*, 271–75; Verger, *Os libertos . . .*, 14, 106–10.

102. Johnson, *The History . . .*, 193–205; Akinjogbin, *Dahomey . . .*, 188; Videgla, "Le Royaume . . .," 137–38. For the slave revolts in Bahia for 1807–35, see J. J. Reis, *Rebelião. . . .*

103. Akinjogbin, *Dahomey . . .*, 197–98; Law, "Francisco Felix . . .," 5–11.

104. Akinjogbin, *Dahomey . . .*, 193.

105. Aného (Petit-Popo), Agoué, and Porto Seguro were also important ports of the Gen or Mina-Popo area from the 1830s (see Jones, "Little Popo . . .").

106. For the *retornados*, see, among others, Verger, *Fluxo . . .*; and J. M. Turner, "Les Brésiliens . . ."; Carneiro da Cunha, *Negros . . .*; and Guran, *Agudas. . . .* For the transition to the palm-oil economy, see Manning, *Slavery . . .*, 50–55.

107. Oliveira, "Retrouver . . .," 120–21; cf. Presidencia Provincia, Escravos assuntos, maço 2.880/1, caderno 1.861, and maço 2.891, cadernos 1.863–79, APEBa. Verger, *Fluxo . . .*, 434–38.

108. Verger, *Fluxo . . .*, 15.

CHAPTER 2

1. Mattoso, *Bahia: a cidade . . .*, 82, 97, 119 (tables 9 and 17).

2. Eltis, Behendt, and Richardson, "A participação . . .," 39. The same authors calculate that a total of 1,454,200 slaves were shipped by the Portuguese from the ports of Luanda and Benguela between 1701 and 1810, of which only some (no estimate given) would have arrived in Bahia (ibid.).

3. Eltis, "The Volume . . .," table 3.

4. Mattoso, *Bahia: a cidade* , 117–19; Verger, *Fluxo . . .*, 662–63. Eltis et al., *The Transatlantic Slave Trade. . . .*

5. The most important historical sources in achieving this objective are the postmortem inventories, letters of manumission, wills, documents related to the purchase and sale of slaves, and censuses. Ott examined various sources related to the slave population of Salvador and the state's interior for the periods of 1702–99 and 1778–97, respectively ("O negro . . .," 141–53). Verger tallied the data from the "Livro de tutelas e inventários da Vila de São Francisco do Conde" (1739–1841), published in the *Anais do Arquivo Público da Bahia*, no. 37 (*Fluxo . . .*, 669–75). Schwartz presents data on the ethnic categories of the slave population of nine Bahian sugar mills, in 1739, and of Sergipe de El-Rey in 1785 (*Segredos . . .*, 287, 291). He also presents the ethnic origins of emancipated slaves in Salvador between 1684 and 1745 ("A manumissão . . .," 87). The same was done by Mattoso for the period 1779–1850 ("A propósito . . .," 39).

6. This research was part of the project O Processo de Crioulização: Antecedentes Históricos da Identidade Negra na Bahia (The Creolization Process: Historical Antecedentes of Black Identity in Bahia) carried out between 2003 and 2004, with a grant from the CNPq.

7. The research project directed by João José Reis had the support of the Nigerian

Hinterland Project of York University (Canada) and involved an analysis of the inventories held in the APEBa. I am grateful to Reis for giving me a copy of this data (hereafter referred to as Project Reis–Nigerian Hinterland).

8. Schwartz, *Segredos* . . . , 283–85; Manning, *Slavery* . . . , 28.

9. For a detailed analysis of the process of demographic creolization of the Recôncavo, see Parés, "O processo de crioulização. . . ."

10. Schwartz, *Segredos* . . . , 289; Ortiz, *Contrapunteo.* . . . , qtd. in Barickman, *A Bahian* . . . , 4. However, Schwartz seems to have underestimated the presence of Creoles on the sugar mills and farms.

11. Barickman, *A Bahian* . . . , 157–60. Barickman examines the period 1780–1860, but his thoughts on the contrast between the slave population of the tobacco and sugar zones are applicable to the eighteenth century. See Wimmer, "Ethnicity . . . ," 17.

12. In the Recôncavo inventories (some of which are not accounted for in tables 1 and 2), I found ethnonyms from Central Africa such as (the year of the first mention being in parenthesis) Loango (1698), Congo (1699), Luanda (1699), Rebollo (1699), Pombo (1701), Monjollo (1704), Quisamba (1704), Ganguella (1709), Massangano (1709), Dongo or Comondongo (1713), Moçambique (1715), Cangico (Angico) (1718), Casange (1720), Boticongo (1724), Muxicongo (1760), Pemba (1785), Tembu (1785), and Cabinda (1797). Among those of West Africa: Arda or Ladá (1699), Cabo Verde (1699), São Tomé (1713), Cacheu (1717), Bamba (1720), Calabar (1727), Courana (1733), Codavi or Coda (1746), Fon (1746), Lagoa (1760), Malet (1763), Xamba (1778), Sabaru (Savalu) (1778), Benim (1786), Maquin (Mahi) (1785), Ossá or Ussá (Haussa) (1785), Oyo (1797), Tapa (1797), and Barba (Bariba) (1797). I also found other categories, such as Ganga (1766), Grumã (1788), and Danum (1785), that I was unable to identify.

13. Ott, "O negro . . . ," 143.

14. Though they were Muslim, the Haussa were seen by the Fulani as pagans or infidels because of their religious practices, which sometimes assimilated rites and beliefs that did not sit well with Islamic orthodoxy. Also known in Bahia as *muçulmis*, the Haussa, together with the Nagô, led various slave revolts between 1807 and 1835. See J. J. Reis, *Rebelião* . . . , 68–121.

15. Wimmer, "Ethnicity . . . ," 7, 21; Schwartz, *Segredos* . . . , 289.

16. Schwartz, *Segredos* . . . , 319.

17. For an analysis of ethnoracial exogamy and endogamy in the black-mestizo family of the Recôncavo, see Parés, "O processo de crioulização. . . ."

18. It is possible that "single" mothers—woman about whom there is no reference to a mate—had stable relationships, though not sanctioned formally by marriage.

19. Páres, "O processo de crioulização . . . ," 38.

20. According to the inventory data presented by Andrade, *A mão-de-obra* . . . , 189–90, it was from 1825 that the Nagô became the most numerous African group among the slave population. In 1824–25, for example, on two sugar mills in Iguape, the Nagô were the majority among African slaves. On the list of slaves at the Santa Catarina sugar mill, there were twenty African slaves, mostly Nagô, who were purchased in 1824. That is, it was at that time that the richest mills were importing Nagô: "Alistamento das pessoas que habitam desde o Engenho da Cruz até o Engenho Novo," caderno 7, documentos avulsos, ARC. J. J. Reis confirms this transition in the years 1820–35: *Rebelião* . . . , 308–9.

21. Verger, *Fluxo* . . ., 14–15, 432. For the Fulani jihad and the fall of the Oyo empire, see J. J. Reis, *Rebelião* . . ., 158–74.

22. Ott, "O negro . . .," 141–53; Oliveira, "Retrouver. . . ." Taking into consideration the total slave population for 1830–50, the Nagô made up 36 percent (Andrade, *A mão-de-obra* . . ., 189–90).

23. "Devassa do levante de escravos ocorrido em Salvador em 1835," *AAPBa*, no. 53 (1996): 33, 35, 37.

24. Oliveira, *O liberto* . . ., 53–54.

25. Patterson, *Slavery.* . . .

26. In colonial times the divisions between class and race practically coincided. However, there was the possibility of a certain degree of social upward mobility, primarily for those of mixed race.

27. J. J. Reis, *A morte* . . ., 55.

28. For an analysis of the homology between kinship and religious ties within Candomblé, see Lima, "A família-de-santo. . . ."

29. Houseman et al., "Notes . . .," 530–41.

30. Soares, *Devotos* . . ., 92.

31. Soares recognizes that the transcription of this term is merely tentative—the printing of the original text is confusing. My own hypothesis is that the term transcribed as "Ianno" is actually *Lanno*, a variant of *Lanu* and contraction of the ethnonym *Hulanu* (resident-*nu*, Hula). *Lanu* appears as an ethnonym in Minas Gerais in 1747 (Mott, "Acotundá . . .," 93). Yeda Pessoa de Castro presents another idea—that *Lanu* comes from *Alladanu* (resident of Allada) (*A língua* . . ., 131).

32. J. J. Reis, "Magia . . .," 57–81. Source: Seção Judiciária, Cachoeira, *Devassas*, 1785, maço 1624, APEBa. The document was discovered and is discussed by Aufederheide, "Order . . .," 164. Reis's full transcription of the document is found in the section "Documentação—Documents," *Revista Brasileira de História* 8, no. 16 (1988): 233–49.

33. This distinction between the Jeje and the Dagomé seems to be maintained into the beginning of the nineteenth century. The Count dos Arcos writes "those of the Agomé came to be brothers to the Nagô, and the Jeje with the Haussa"; Verger, *Notas* . . ., 21.

34. "Inventário de Manoel Fernandes Pereira, 1778–1798," 01/24/24/242, ARC, fls. 102, 109, 110.

35. "Inventário de Caetana de Freitas, 1750," 03/1264/1733/19, APEBa (emphasis added).

36. All quotations from Weber, *Economia* . . ., 25 (emphasis added).

37. Russell-Wood, "Aspectos . . .," 151; Mattoso, *Ser escravo* . . ., 148; Verger, *Fluxo* . . ., 525; J. J. Reis, *A morte* . . ., 55.

38. "Compromisso* da Irmandade do Senhor Bom Jesus com o soberano título de Senhor dos Martírios, erecta pelos Homens pretos de nação Gege, neste Convento de Nossa Senhora do Monte do Carmo da Vila de Nossa Senhora do Rosário da Cachoeira, este ano de 1765," Lisbon, AHU, códice 1.666. The document is transcribed in Mulvey, "The Black . . .," appendix C, 264–72. The responsibilities of the brotherhood included: celebrating the festival in praise of the *Senhor Bom Jesus* on January 15 (chap. 9), the procession, performing the stages of the martyrdom on Palm Sunday (chap. 10), performing vows for the dead on Lent (chap. 11) and a weekly mass on Fridays (chap. 15), helping

slaves to buy their freedom (chap. 11), attending to the poor and sickly (chap. 13) and being responsible for burials, having four sepulchers in the convent's church (chaps. 14, 15). The brotherhood remained in the Carmo Convent during the whole of the nineteenth century, but interestingly, in 1877, the festival and procession were celebrated on September 23 (*O Progresso*, September 23, 1877, ARC).

39. "Compromisso da Irmandade do Senhor Bom Jesus dos Mártírios. Chap. 2: Da entrada dos Irmãos," qtd. in Mulvey, "The Black . . . ," 265. Also qtd. in J. J. Reis, *A morte . . . ,* 56; and by Oliveira, "Quem eram . . . ," 70.

40. J. J. Reis, "Identidade . . . ," 16.

41. Campos, "Procissões . . . ," 328–32.

42. Ibid., 16; Russell-Wood, "Aspectos . . . ," 152.

43. "Bom Jesus das Necessidades e Redenção, Lisboa, na Ofic. de Antonio Rodrigues Galhardo, Impressor da Real Mesa Censória, Ano 1778," doc. 38, cx. arq. 162-As1, est. 1, cx. 32, ACMS. I am grateful to Lucilene Reginaldo for having given me a copy of the manuscript version of the Statutes, dated August 28, 1778 (book 5, fls. 51–60, comuns 432, Chancelaria da Ordem de Cristo, Portuguese National Archive [Torre do Tombo], Lisbon).

44. For example, in 1804, a brotherhood of the Senhor Bom Jesus das Necessidades e Redenção (The Good Lord Jesus of Necessities and Redemption) was established on the island of Itaparica. Its statutes are copied almost verbatim from those of the brotherhood of the same name in Corpo Santo, accepting brothers from the Mina Coast and Loanda and excluding Creoles. I am grateful to Renato da Silveira for having given me a copy of these statutes.

45. "Compromisso da Irmandade do Senhor Bom Jesus dos Mártírios," qtd. in Mulvey, "The Black . . . ," 265.

46. In the body of the text, the Jeje nation is referred to only once.

47. "Compromisso da Irmandade do Glorioso Senhor São Benedito colocado na Capela de Nossa Senhora do Rosário, Filial a Matriz de Nossa Senhora da Penha de França de Itapagipe de Baixo. Feito no ano de 1800. Cap. 2: Dos juízes e suas obrigações," códice 1.929, AHU. I am grateful to Lucilene Reginaldo for the reference to these statutes.

48. This devotion was established in the mother church of São Pedro in 1689, but in May 1746, the brothers of the congregation are authorized to build their own chapel "at the place of João Pereira St.," next to the current-day Piedade Square: "Ereção da Capela de Nossa Senhora do Rosário da Rua do João Pereira, Freguesia de São Pedro desta capital, ano 1746," document no. 175, cx. arq. 362, est. 1, cx. 91, ACMS; Pondé, "A Capelinha . . . ," 316, 322.

49. "Parecer do desembargador ouvidor geral do crime a d. Rodrigo José Nunes, 9–11–1784," *Cartas ao Governo, 1780–84,* maço 176, APEBa.

50. Campos, "Procissões . . . ," 418–21; cf. *Revista do Instituto Arqueológico e Geográfico Pernambucano,* no. 55 (c. 1901): 285; "Carta da Rainha de Portugal D. Maria I ao governador da capitania da Bahia, sobre o pedido da construção de uma capela na Vila de Cachoeira pela Irmandade de N. S. do Rosário dos Homens Pretos. Lisboa, 13 de fevereiro de 1794," Núcleo Governo da Capitania da Bahia, série Ordens Regias 1763–1822, vol. 80, doc. 99A, 99B, 99C (years 1794, 1796), APEBa.

51. Campos, "Procissões . . .," 493–94; Russell-Wood, "Aspectos . . .," 152; J. J. Reis, *Rebelião* . . . , 332; Faria, "Irmãos . . .," 19.

52. Faria, "Irmãos . . .," 33. See also J. J. Reis, "Identidade . . .," 14.

53. "Compromisso de Nossa Senhora do Rosário das Portas do Carmo, 1820," chap. 5, cx. 1, doc. 1/R14, qtd. in Faria, "Irmãos . . .," 29–30.

54. J. J. Reis, *Rebelião* . . . , 332.

55. Campos, "Procissões . . .," 495–503; Campos, "Tradições . . .," 488.

56. Frézier, *Relation* . . . , 2:521, qtd. in Verger, *Fluxo* . . . , 84.

57. "Compromisso da Irmandade do Senhor Bom Jesus das Necessidades e Redenção [1913]," cx. arq. 446, est. 2, cx. 112, ACMS; Campos, "Procissões . . .," 418–21. The same information is found in "A Igreja do Corpo Santo," *A Tarde*, January 6, 1934, qtd. In Barbosa, *Retalhos* . . . , 92–95; Barbosa, *Efemérides* . . . , 43, 57, 58.

58. Verger, *Fluxo* . . . , 525; Mattoso, *Bahia* . . . , 401; Oliveira, *O liberto* . . . , 81; Russell-Wood, "Aspectos . . .," 151; J. J. Reis, *Rebelião* . . . , 333; J. J. Reis, *A morte* . . . , 55; Mulvey, "The Black . . .," 292. Ott attributes the creation of the brotherhood to the Nagô ("A Irmandade . . .," 20). Pierson gives 1829 as the date of its founding and specifies that the brotherhood required "pure African ascendency" (*Brancos e pretos* . . . , 81).

59. "Bom Jesus das Necessidades e Redenção, Lisboa, na ofic. de Antonio Rodrigues Galhardo, impressor da Real Mesa Censória, Ano 1778," doc. 38, cx. arq. 162-As1, est.1, cx. 32, ACMS. "Inventário de José da Silva, 1817," 03/1219/1688/05, Judiciário, APEBa.

60. Campos, "Procissões . . .," 418–21.

61. Ibid.

62. Verger, *Os libertos* . . . , 47, 48; Verger, *Fluxo* . . . , photo no. 27.

63. Verger, "Orixás da Bahia . . .," 238; Mulvey, "The Black . . .," 293. According to Renato da Silveira, the brotherhood included, in addition to Creoles, Africans from the Mina Coast, such as Jeje, Nagô, and Ketu ("Iyá . . .," 25; personal communication, September 13, 1999).

64. "Testamentos de africanos, 1800–1888," Judiciário, APEBa. Data generously shared by Maria Inês Cortes de Oliveira. In fact, both Mina women, with wills dated 1805 and 1811, belonged to seven and five brotherhoods respectively.

65. Campos, "Procissões . . .," 328–32. For the founding of the Barroquinha candomblé, see Silveira, "Iyá. . . ." It is important to remember that Mãe Aninha, head of the famous Axé Opô Afonjá, of the Nagô-Ketu nation, occupied the offices of *provedora* and *juíza* in the Martírios brotherhood at Barroquinha during the first decades of the twentieth century. Might the Martírios association with Nagô Africans be a relatively recent development resulting from Mãe Aninha's participation in the brotherhood?

66. J. J. Reis, *Rebelião* . . . , 326–28; Law, *The Oyo* . . .

67. *AAPBa*, no. 38 (1968): 140; J. J. Reis, *Rebelião* . . . , 328. According to Verger (*Fluxo* . . . , 519), Agoume would be Abomey.

68. J. J. Reis, *Rebelião* . . . , 447.

69. *AAPBa*, no. 38 (1968): 140.

70. *AAPBa*, no. 38 (1968): 7–8; J. J. Reis, *Rebelião* . . . , 233; Verger, *Fluxo* . . . , 520.

71. *AAPBa*, no. 40 (1971): 19, 24–25. Belchior, a Nagô from Cobai, also appears as "African," "Nago" and "Aossá nation" (*AAPBa*, no. 40 [1971]: 83, 86 and ff.).

72. *AAPBa*, no. 38 (1968): 20, 77.

73. *AAPBa*, no. 54 (1996): 105–21.

74. J. J. Reis, *Rebelião . . .*, 379–80.

75. *AAPBa*, no. 53 (1996): 59.

76. *AAPBa*, no. 53 (1996): 57.

77. Renato da Silveira, personal communication, October 5, 2000.

78. See Thompson, *A formação . . .*; and Bastide, *Sociología. . . .*

79. Bastide, *Sociologia . . .*, 173.

80. Verger, *Fluxo . . .*, 530.

81. Ibid., 525, 527, 600, 601, 635. This fact is also documented by Bouche, who was in Agoué in 1874, by Lafitte, and by Borghero.

82. J. J. Reis, *Rebelião . . .*, 447–48.

83. Verger, *Fluxo . . .*, 529.

CHAPTER 3

1. Biblioteca do Estado de Pernambuco, "Correspondência da Corte, 1780–1781," fl. 23–23v, qtd. in Soares, *Devotos*, 158–59. For a similar 1786 case in Bahia, see Verger, *Fluxo . . .*, 531; and J. J. Reis, "Identidade . . .," 26.

2. The term *batuque* was used frequently in the eighteenth century to refer to meetings of blacks involving dances and drumbeats. It loosely indicated both religious rituals and secular diversion. Other terms from the nineteenth century were *brinquedo, tambaque,* and *batucajé.*

3. "Correspondência do capitão José Roiz de Gomes para o capitão-mor Francisco Pires de Cavalho e Alburquerque, 20 de janeiro de 1809," Capitães Mores, Santo Amaro, 1807–22, maços 417–21, APEBa. This document is analyzed in detail in J. J. Reis, "Identidade . . .," 7–9; and in J. J. Reis, "Tambores . . .," 104–9. See also Harding, "Candomblé . . .," 286–87.

4. Lima, "A família-de-santo . . .," 21. This work was first presented at the conference organized by the government of Senegal together with UNESCO, "Négritude en Amérique Latine," held in Dakar in January 1974. It was published for the first time in *Afro-Asia*, no. 12 (June 1976), and later revised and published as part of an introductory chapter of Lima's master's thesis, "A família-de-santo nos Candomblés Jeje-Nagôs da Bahia: Um estudo de relações intragrupais," in 1977. In 2003, Corrupio published this text. In this book, the page references to Lima's work correspond to the 1977 thesis.

5. Lima, "A família-de-santo . . .," 20.

6. Carneiro, *Candomblés*, 44, 46. Carneiro was the first author to speak of candomblé nations in terms of differences in ritual practice. Rodrigues uses the term *nation* to refer to the group of origin, whereas in the religious context he refers only to "brotherhoods [*confraria*]" or "schools [*colégios*]" distinguished by "special precepts related to food, clothing, and religious duties unique to the cult of this or that saint or orixá" (*Os africanos . . .*, 101, 234).

7. Weber, "The Social . . .," 271–75; Malinowski, *Magic . . .*, 67. For the "fortune-misfortune complex," see V. W. Turner, *The Drums . . .*; Janzen, *The Quest . . .*; Janzen, *Ngoma*; and Craemer, Vansina, and Fox, "Religious . . .," 460–61, 463, 475. Karasch

(*A vida* ..., chap. 9, 354–56) and Slenes (*Na senzala* ..., 143) take the point of view of Craemer, Vansina, and Fox for the study of Brazilian religiosity.

8. These concepts of religion and ritual were inspired by the course "Religions of Africa" offered by the historian of African religion Louis Brenner at the School of Oriental and African Studies (University of London), in which I participated as an assistant in 1997–98. For a broader discussion of the topic, see, among others, Durkheim, *Les formes* ..., 31–66; Geertz, *A interpretação* ..., 101–42; and Spiro, "Religion ...," 187–222.

9. Mintz and Price, *The Birth* ..., 23.

10. Durkheim, *Les formes* ..., 60; V. W. Turner, *The Ritual* ..., chap. 3; Lewis, *Êxtase* ..., 32–36. For an analysis of periphery cults as counterhegemonic discourse, see Boddy, *Wombs* ..., 156–58; and Stoller, *Embodying* ..., 23–26.

11. Bosman, *A New* ..., 368a, 369, 382–83; Norris, *Memoirs* ..., 45, 54.

12. Bosman, *A New* ..., 371, 369.

13. Ibid., 371–72.

14. Ibid., 367a.

15. Lewis, *Êxtase* ..., 32–36. For a critique of "theories of marginality, see Giles, "Possession ...," 234–57.

16. Maupoil, *La géomancie* ..., 64; Glélé, *Le Danxomé* ..., 76.

17. Lepine, "As metamorfoses ...," 134–36; cf. Le Hérissé, *L'ancien* ..., 128; Herskovits, *Dahomey* ..., 1:20; Verger, *Notas* ..., 244–45.

18. Mintz and Price, *The Birth* ..., 18–19; Bastide, *Sociología* ..., 92–93, 107.

19. Bastide, *Sociología* ..., 314–16.

20. For an interesting analysis of clientelism within the Catholic brotherhoods, see Silveira, "Iyá ...," 45–51.

21. Karasch, *A vida* ..., 342–50; J. J. Reis, "The Politics ...," 15.

22. Mulvey, "The Black ...," 149.

23. For a discussion of the construction of the concept of fetishism, derived from the Portuguese term *feitiço*, see Pietz, "The Problem of the Fetish," vols. I, II, and IIIa.

24. See, e.g., Soares, *Devotos* ..., chap. 6, esp. 206 and 217.

25. J. J. Reis, "Nas malhas ...," 41. This article was expanded and published under the title "Nas malhas do poder escravista: A invasão do Candomblé do Accú," in Reis and Silva, *Negociação e conflito* ..., 32–61.

26. L. de Mello e Souza, *O diabo* ..., 263–69, 385.

27. Ibid., 263; J. J. Reis, "Magia ...," 62.

28. L. de Mello e Souza, *O diabo* ..., 264–67; Mott, "O Calundu-Angola ...," 73–82.

29. Mott shows the striking similarity between Luiza Pinta's *calundu* in Sabará and the healing-divination *xinguila* cults of Angola described by the Italian Capuchin João Antonio Cavazzi de Montecucculo in the second half of the seventeenth century. He also notes its structural differences compared with West African religious traditions. In one of the inquest hearings, Luzia Pinta declared, regarding her experiences as a medium, that "the said illness is called *calundus* in her land and that it can be transmitted from one person to another ... and that it can only be cured and remedied by playing certain instruments and doing [other things]," among which would be scrubbing and the external and internal use of powder for the purpose of exorcising the sickness (Mott,

"O Calundu-Angola . . .," 75, 80–81). Experiences of mediumship as a symptom of illness, which needs to be cured through rituals that involve the playing of drums and practices of exorcism and in which the patient comes to function as a healer following the cure, are known characteristics of many of the Bantu area cults, which Janzen generically calls *ngoma* (Janzen, *Ngoma* . . . ; V. W. Turner, *The Drums of Affliction* . . .).

30. "Caderno do Promotor, no. 129." Lisbon, ANTT, fl. 490. I want to thank Luiz Mott for generously giving me a copy of this document, and Tânia Pinto for calling my attention to Tereza's case.

31. Harding, *A Refuge* . . . , 81–85, 177–86.

32. L. de Mello e Souza, *O diabo* . . . , 263.

33. J. J. Reis, "Magia . . . ," 62.

34. Biblioteca do Estado de Pernambuco, "Correspondência da Corte, 1780–1781," fls. 23–23v, qtd. in Soares, *Devotos* . . . , 158–59.

35. The practice of animal sacrifice is documented in Brazil from the beginning of the seventeenth century. In 1618 during the visit of the Inquisition to Bahia, Sebastien Barreto denounced "the custom that the blacks had of killing animals in their funerals to wash in their blood, saying that the soul then left the body to rise up to heaven" (Bastide, *Sociologia* . . . , 249; Verger . . . , *Fluxo*, 530).

36. Mott, "Acotundá . . . ," 124–47. Also cited in L. de Mello e Souza, *O diabo* . . . , 268–69. *Courá* could be an evolution of "Kouramo," a term that appears in seventeenth- and eighteenth-century records as a river, lake, sea island, or village near present-day Lagos (Nigeria): Mott, "Acotundá . . . ," 136. See also Verger, *Fluxo* . . . , 204, 207, 209.

37. On *mandinga* pouches, see L. de Mello e Souza, *O diabo* . . . , 204–26; Mott, "A vida . . . ," 85–104; Harding, *A Refuge* . . . , 27–33. On the *gbo* and *bocíò*, see Bosman, *A New* . . . , 367a, 368; Herskovits, *Dahomey* . . . , 2:256–88; and Blier, *African* . . . . *Ebô* is now a polysemic term that in Yoruba basically means animal sacrifice or offering.

38. J. J. Reis, "Magia . . . ," 75.

39. Ibid., 70–71.

40. Ibid., 73.

41. Bastide, *Sociología* . . . , 78.

42. Ferretti, *Querebentan* . . . , 227.

43. I would like to thank Robin Law for calling my attention to this possibility; personal communication, August 26, 2001.

CHAPTER 4

1. Rodrigues, *Os africanos* . . . ; Verger, *Fluxo* . . . ; J. J. Reis, "Nas malhas . . ."; J. J. Reis, "Magia. . . ." The initiatic nature of African cults that imposes strict secrecy and the fact that these constitute, at least until recently, a religious culture based on orality, contribute to the almost complete lack of documentation written by Candomblé practitioners themselves. Most available sources were written by outsiders to Candomblé who were generally involved in its denouncement or persecution and therefore frequently contain prejudice, distortions, and errors. Among the documents written for freed Africans are the wills and petitions studied by Mattoso ("Testamentos") and Oliveira (*O liberto* . . .). Others that stand out because they were written by Africans themselves include the exceptional "Tratado dos escravos do Engenho Santana em Ilhéus," first published by

Schwartz ("Resistance," 69–81), and the documents written in Arabic by the Malê (J. J. Reis, "Magia . . . ," 58). The so-called *cadernos de fundamento*, or personal notebooks, kept by certain Candomblé practitioners would be another possible source, but this material is difficult to access, and there are no indications that such *cadernos* were kept prior to the first decades of the twentieth century.

2. J. J. Reis, "Candomblé . . ."; J. J. Reis, "Tambores . . ."; Harding, *A Refuge* . . . ; Silveira, "Iyá. . . ."

3. *O Alabama* circulated between 1863 and 1900, but unfortunately all that remains is the complete collection from 1863–1871 and a few issues subsequent to this period. The editor in chief was Aristides Ricardo de Santana, but between 1887 and 1890 new editors took over. In a piece from December 17, 1870 (page 7), the editors are referred to as "blacks" and "mulattoes." I would like to thank João José Reis for indicating to me this important source and for giving me a copy of the articles referring to the Bogum candomblé. In 1998, the U.S. historian Dale Graden published an article, "So Much Superstition. . . . ," based on the material in *O Alabama*.

4. "Correspondência do capitão José Roiz de Gomes para o capitão-mor Francisco Pires de Cavalho e Alburquerque, 20 de janeiro de 1809," Capitães mores, Santo Amaro, 1807–1822, maços 417–21, APEBa.

5. Capitães-mores, June 19, 1807, maço 417–1, APEBa, qtd. in J. J. Reis, "Recôncavo . . . ," 103; Harding, "Candomblé . . . ," 80. For possible etymologies of the term *candomblé*, see Y. P. de Castro, *A presença* . . . , 4; and Castro and Castro, "Culturas . . . ," qtd. in Karasch, *A vida* . . . , 573n98.

6. Harding, *A Refuge* . . . , 1.

7. J. J. Reis, "Candomblé . . . ," 121–22. One was the previously mentioned Antônio, of the Angola nation; the other was the slave Manuel, with a candomblé along the Caminho do Inferno, in Salvador, denounced by *O Alabama* (June 1, 1871, 1).

8. J. J. Reis, *Rebelião* . . . , 73–75, 85–86, 102–4; Reis and Silva, *Negociação e conflito* . . . , 41; Verger, *Notícias* . . . , 227. On the coronations of African kings and queens in Brazil, see, among others, Rodrigues, *Os africanos* . . . , 31–34; M. de Mello e Souza, *Reis* . . . ; and Schwarcz, *As barbas* . . . , 247–94.

9. L. de Mello e Souza, *O diabo* . . . , 266.

10. J. J. Reis, "Magia . . . ," 62–63; cf. Mott, "Acotundá . . . "; Higgs, "The Inquisition . . . "; L. de Mello e Souza, *O diabo* . . . , 323–24.

11. Verger, *Fluxo* . . . , 334–35; J. J. Reis, *Rebelião* . . . , 82; J. J. Reis, "Tambores . . . ," 109–12; Silveira, "Iyá . . . ," 8–21. The letter from the Count dos Arcos, from April 10, 1814, allowing the gathering of slaves in Graça and Barbalho, is transcribed by Rodrigues, *Os africanos* . . . , 156; Verger, *Notas* . . . , 21; Silveira, "Iyá . . . ," 17.

12. *Accú* perhaps derives from the African term *aku*, a ritual performed seven years following the death of an *ialorixá* in order to pass the mantle of leadership to the successor (D. M. dos Santos, *História* . . . , 18). In Fongbe, *kú* means death, the beyond, the place of the dead and also, as in Yoruba, the verb *to die*. In West Africa, *aku* became an ethnic denomination designating Muslims descended from liberated Yoruba slaves who arrived in Sierra Leone in the nineteenth century. This was probably due to the fact that many Yoruba greetings begin with forms of *E ku* or *A ku*. The Fon also use *kú* in many greetings such as *O kú* (Segurola, *Dictionnaire* . . . , 309).

13. As I will show, the term *vodun* or *vudun* was used during the second half of the nineteenth century as a generic designation for African spiritual entities. Therefore, while it is not certain that this was a Jeje candomblé, we should not exclude the possibility.

14. Reis and Silva, *Negociação e conflito . . .*, 36, 42, 128–29. The first reference to the term *vodun* in Brazil appears in the work of Peixoto, in 1741, in Minas Gerais.

15. Ibid., 36, 128.

16. Ibid., 44, 129.

17. Ibid., 61.

18. Ibid., 55–57; cf. Antônio Guimarães ao President Barros Paim, June 24, 1831, Juizes de Paz, maço 2.681, APEBa.

19. Reis and Silva, *Negociação e conflito . . .*, 48–50, 129.

20. Ibid., 57–58.

21. Ibid., 61.

22. Of the sixty-five records, fifty-five contain some information concerning the leadership, forty-five of which reveal the leader's name. This number does not include the many records referencing "*batuques, batucajés, sambas,* and *algazarras*" in which no religious connotation could be identified. Also excluded were any records that might have been religious, yet did not evidence an established congregation, and that were presumably sporadic celebrations such as festive or funerary gatherings. Any record that might have duplicated a preexisting case was also disregarded.

23. J. J. Reis, "Candomblé . . .," 129.

24. Schwartz estimates the percentage of freed blacks at "40 percent or more" of the total population of Bahia in 1816–17 (*Segredos . . .*, 373). In the Reconcôvo in 1808 blacks and mulattoes made up 43 percent of the population: Mattoso, *Bahia: a cidade . . .*, 119. According to J. J. Reis, the free and freed Africans and Creoles constituted 30 percent of Salvador's 65,000 inhabitants in 1835 ("Candomblé . . .," 122).

25. For data on the United States and Jamaica, see Schwartz, *Segredos . . .*, 373. Bastide, *Les Amériques. . . .*

26. *O Alabama*, September 29, 1868, 4.

27. J. J. Reis details the two cases of white leadership (in 1859 the Portuguese Domingos Miguel and his mistress of mixed race Maria Umbelina and, in 1873, the white Maria Couto) and one of a mixed-race leadership (in 1865, Belmira) ("Candomblé . . .," 120–21). There is additionally another example of "a woman of mixed race by the name of Umbellina, known as *Mamã* Balunce, resident of Coqueiros," in the Pilar parish, "fortune-teller and remover of spells," denounced in 1871 (*O Alabama*, February 18, 1871,1). It may be the same Maria Umbelina from 1859.

28. Harding, *A Refuge . . .*, 71.

29. Ibid., 72; Reis, "Candomblé," 120.

30. Harding, *A Refuge . . .*, 72–74; J. J. Reis, "Candomblé . . .," 120. When, for 1800–1888, Harding adds her sixty-five documents of positive identification and the remaining thirty probable ones along with the two cases of probable coleadership documented by Verger, she arrives at gender percentages similar in terms of leadership to those of J. J. Reis: 61 percent for men and 39 percent for women.

31. Landes, "A Cult . . .," 386–97.

32. This idea is also supported by Harding, *A Refuge . . .*, 97.

33. J. J. Reis, "Candomblé ...," 120, 131; Harding, *A Refuge ...*, 127.

34. See, e.g., Marques, *O feiticeiro....*

35. Reis and Silva, *Negociação e conflito ...*, 46–47, 128.

36. J. J. Reis, "Candomblé ...," 131.

37. *Jornal da Bahia*, Salvador, February 12, 1859, qtd. in Verger ..., *Fluxo*, 532. Also "Polícia," April 21, 1862, maço 6.234, APEBa, qtd. in Harding, "Candomblé ...," 320; *O Alabama*, September 13, 1866, 3; Rodrigues, *O animismo ...*, 171.

38. M. Sodré, *O terreiro ...*, 14–15; Mattos, "Negros ...," 19, 70.

39. In the parishes of Nossa Senhor da Vitória two recorded cases, and in the Pilar parish one recorded case, correspond to the area of Barreiras. The references to the Quinta das Devotas (there are two) were identified with the Quinta das Beatas, now Cosme de Farias, in Brotas. The great size of these parishes is important to note. In the case of Santo Antônio, there was the First District, neighboring Passo, which could be considered part of the urban center, and the Second District, which extended to the north in the semiurban area.

40. Silveira, "Iyá ...," 51–52.

41. *O Alabama*, May 2, 1867, 2–3.

42. *O Alabama*, August 25, 1869, 2.

43. *O Óculo Mágico*, October 11, 1866, qtd. in Costa, "Ekabó ...," 134.

44. Verger, *Fluxo ...*, 532; *O Alabama*, April 19, 1864, 1.

45. *O Alabama*, May 2, 1867, 2–3.

46. *O Alabama*, May 2, 1867, 2–3.

47. *O Alabama*, September 29, 1868, 3.

48. *O Alabama*, October 11, 1871, 4.

49. *O Alabama*, September 23, 1869.

50. *O Alabama*, March 19, 1869, 6.

51. *O Alabama*, September 23, 1864, 1–2; September 26, 1868, 4.

52. *O Alabama*, September 19, 1868, 1.

53. Significantly, the two great periods of Candomblé resurgence, in the 1930s and 1970s, corresponded to the Estado Novo and the Antônio Carlos Magalhães government during the dictatorship, that is, to politically conservative periods. The alliance of the conservative elites with Candomblé, or their paternalist and clientelistic relationship, results from a populist policy that attempts to placate the subaltern classes with symbolic gestures. But this policy is also motivated by the elite's dependence on (or fear of) black spiritual power.

54. *O Alabama*, October 2, 1869, 3.

55. *O Alabama*, August 9, 1866, 4. There is also a case of two runaway women slaves who took refuge in a candomblé on Bangala Street in the Sé parish: *O Alabama*, April 19, 1866, 1–2; November 26, 1867, 1.

56. Verger, *Fluxo ...*, 335.

57. Costa, "Ekabó ...," 153; cf. Nascimento, *Dez freguesias ...*, 89.

58. *O Alabama*, August 9, 1866, 4.

59. J. J. Reis, *A morte ...*, 31; Costa, "Ekabó ...," 151; Mattoso, *Bahia ...*, 124–25.

60. *O Alabama*, February 12, 1870, 7.

61. During that year the police found, in a candomblé in Quintas da Barra in the

Vitória district of Salvador, clothing and ritual emblems that suggest that this was a multideity cult: "Correspondência do Secretário de Polícia ao Presidente da Província," April 13, 1858, maço 2.994–1, Polícia, Delegados 1842–1866, APEBa (document discovered by Alexandra Brown and João José Reis), qtd. in Harding, *A Refuge . . .*, 59. There is a transcription of the original document in Harding, "Candomblé . . . ," 316.

62. Rodrigues, *Os africanos . . .*, 230.

63. Graden, "So Much Superstition . . . ," 69; Matory, *Black Atlantic . . .*, 86; J. J. Reis, "Candomblé . . . ," 124–25. Graden's analysis contains various errors, among which is the identification of a number of candomblés as Nagô where there is no indication to justify such. For example, a candomblé in Engenho Velho, which appears in an article in 1869, is identified by Graden as being the present-day Nagô-Ketu Casa Branca or Engenho Velho candomblé. However, *O Alabama* makes it clear that the Engenho Velho neighborhood contained so many terreiros that such an identification would be impossible. In fact, the same article relates certain linguistic and ritual clues that indicate this might have been a Jeje terreiro.

64. Lima, "A família-de-santo . . . ," 72–73; Y. P. de Castro, "Língua e nação . . . ," 75; Braga, *Na gamela . . .*, 38–39, 56 (emphasis added).

65. Y. P. de Castro, "Língua e nação . . . ," 75; Braga, *Na gamela . . .*, 56. The etymology of the word *decá* remains vague. In the *decá* ritual, the calabash contains the initiation utensils (knife, scissors, seeds, leaves, etc.) delivered up to the priest who has achieved seniority and independence. As in Fongbe *ka* means calabash, or gourd, the term *decá* (*deka*) is usually considered to be of Jeje or Gbe origin. However, in contemporary Fongbe, the word *deka* does not exist. Vivaldo da Costa Lima, citing Akindélé and Aguessy, points to the expression "dô non dé ka mè" as a possible etymology of the term. This expression is used in Porto Novo to refer to a ceremony in which the families of the newly initiated thank the *vodunon*, offering him all kinds of food (Lima, "A família-de-santo . . . ," 133–34, 177). Nina Rodrigues (*Os africanos*, 138) translates the term *ogã* as "lord [*senhor*], chief," which according to him is Jeje; but it is important to note that the term *ôgán*, with the same meaning, is Yoruba, while the Fongbe use the word *gan*.

66. The term *pai-de-santo* appears once, though used outside of a religious context (*O Alabama*, July 28, 1868, 1–2). I thank João José Reis for having called my attention to what is the earliest documented occurrence of this word. *Mãe-de-santo*, which derives from the Yoruba term *ialorixá*, does not appear in the 1860s. Other Portuguese hierarchical terms that appear in *O Alabama* are *segunda mamãe do terreiro* (second mother of the terreiro), *secretário* (secretary), *cabo de esquadra* (squadron corporal), and *tocador de tabaque* (drummer).

67. The seven terms of unknown linguistic origin are (with number of occurrences in parenthesis) *congu* (2), a term synonymous with candomblé or *batucajé*, as is probably also *cundúm* (to play *cundúm*) (2); *colla* (a large species of African tree of the *esterculiáceas* family whose capsular fruits contain nut-shaped seeds with a high level of caffeine and other alkaloids) (2); *nacucu cuim* (tabaque drum) (1); *luge* (1); *bonadué* (a dance, probably a Jeje term) (1); and *caruru* (food, perhaps a term of Tupi origin) (3).

68. *Segun* is a phonetic evolution of the term *sirrum*, the name given to the funeral rituals in Brazilian Jeje terreiros, for its part a corruption of the Fon term *sinhun* (*sin* = *asin* = water; *hun* = drum; *sinhun* = water drum). *Sinhun* is the name of one of the percussion

instruments used in the funerary rituals (an inverted half-gourd placed over a clay basin containing water, played with sticks called *aguidavis*). The other percussion instrument is the *zènli*, a jar or a pitcher played with a fan over the mouth (from Fongbe, *zèn* = ceramic jar; *li* = *ali* = the opening, the way; *zènli* = the jar's opening, mouth of the jar). *Zènli* refers to the instrument, the funerary rhythm or music, as well as to the funerary ritual. Yeda Pessoa de Castro documents the term *sal-apocā* (variants include *cāo-da-costa* [West African dog] or *sal-da-costa* [West African salt]) (*Falares . . .*, 333). However, Jeje religious experts do not recognize this word, nor do they identify it with the *sapocā* (or *sarapocā*) initiation ritual. *Mocan* appears in the *O Alabama* article as a ritual object of a Fa fortune-teller. In the Fon language, *mwenkanto* (the owner of the *mwenkan*) means diviner, or seer. In contemporary Candomblé, *mocan* refers to a "necklace of West African straw [*palha da Costa*] braided and decorated with cowry shells, having two ends tied with a kind of broom-end made of the same straw."

69. The discrepancy in J. J. Reis's count ("Candomblé . . . ," 124), which concludes that "Nagô beats Jeje," is due to the fact that Reis, though basing his numbers primarily on *O Alabama*, includes some Nagô terms found in other documentary sources in his sample.

70. *O Alabama*, February 23, 1870, 3–4.

71. Nine Jeje cases correspond to records classified as "candomblés" and one as "individual"; of the eight Nagô records, among the "likely" cases are three classified as "individual"; the "likely" case of the Angola is an "individual."

72. There is also the African *Pai* Jebù, who might be Ijebu (*O Alabama*, November 15, 1864), cf. J. J. Reis, "Candomblé . . . ," 120.

73. *O Alabama*, November 8, 1864, 3–4; November 18, 1864, 3–4; February 21, 1865, 3–4. In 1868 there is the report of the case of the teenaged Paulina, who was bewitched, being as "the *milonga* [charm] was made in the *Bate-Folha* terreiro" (*O Alabama*, October 15, 1868, 2). The present-day Bate-Folha, Mansu Bandu Kenkê, of the Angola (Muxicongo or Congo-Angola) nation, in Mata Escura in Salvador, was founded in 1916 by Manoel Bernardino da Paixão (Ampumandezu). Therefore, references to Batefolha previous to this date should not be associated with an Angola candomblé.

74. J. J. Reis, "Candomblé . . . ," 128; Harding, *A Refuge . . .*, 93–94, 200, 203; *O Alabama*, September 14, 1864, 1; June 3, 1870.

75. *O Alabama*, January 4, 1868; December 24, 1870, 8; December 29, 1870, 3; December 31, 1870, 6; November 24, 1871, 4; Rodrigues, *O animismo . . .*, 157. Afro-Brazilian studies in the 1930s identify Tia Julia as Maria Julia Conceição Nazaré, but recent research reveals her real name to be Julia Soares de Sá; Lisa Earl Castillo, personal communication, April 22, 2012. It is probable that Ilê Iyá Nassô of Barroquinha—a Nagô-Ketu terreiro from which Gantois branched off—was already operating at this time in Engenho Velho, but *O Alabama* does not verify this. It is the same situation with Ilé Maroialaje, the candomblé of Alaketo, of the "Nagô-vodun" nation, an identification that implies the coexistence of Nagô and Jeje ritual traditions (see chaps. 6 and 7), which must have been operating since the first half of the nineteenth century in Matatu (Brotas). *O Alabama* alludes to the existence of candomblés in Matatu, without giving further details. Given this lack of conclusive evidence, I have preferred to limit my analysis to the information present in *O Alabama*, and thus have not counted these two terreiros.

76. *O Alabama*, December 24, 1863, 2; March 12, 1864, 4; August 2, 1866, 3–4; June 23, 1870; November 18, 1871, 1; November 21, 1871, 2, 3; December 19, 1871, 4.

77. *O Alabama*, February 27, 1866, 4.

78. Valentina Maria dos Anjos (Runho), file no. 1, CEAO, 1961: "Pesquisa sobre os candomblés de Salvador," directed by Vivaldo da Costa Lima between 1960 and 1969, Centro de Estudos Afro-Orientais (CEAO)–UFBa. I am very grateful to Vivaldo da Costa Lima for having generously facilitated my access to the records (*fichas*) of the 113 terreiros researched for this project. Henceforth, references to this material will appear as "file no. . . . , CEAO, [year]."

79. Olga of Alaketo, Salvador, interview, March 1, 1996.

80. *O Alabama*, May 15, 1867; Ferretti, *Querebentan . . .*, 304.

81. *O Alabama*, November 11, 1871, 4.

82. Edison Carneiro, "Lembrança do negro da Bahia," *A Tarde*, March 29, 1949, 15. The two terreiros mentioned by Carneiro were in the São Caetano neighborhood.

83. Carneiro, *Religiões . . .*, 62; Ramos, introduction, 12–13; Nancy de Souza e Silva, May 14, 1999.

84. *O Alabama*, March 2, 1867, 3. *Humbono* Vicente, February 17, 2001.

85. *O Alabama*, September 22, 1868, 2; September 26, 1868, 4; September 29, 1868, 3 (Author's italics).

86. *O Alabama*, May 23, 1871, 2. This report mentions that "the owner of the land appeared in order to accommodate the noise and was carried by the saints on the heads of the voduns [*vodunsis*]." The mention of the "Zo ordeal" and the allusion to vodun suggest that this was another Jeje candomblé.

87. J. de Carvalho, *Reinvenção . . .*, 37. In the temple of Avimanje, in Ouidah (Benin), I witnessed a similar ritual called *ahwan dida*, in which, after cooking a goat in a clay pot with palm oil, the voduns pull out the pieces of meat with their hands (Ouidah, September 1995). The films made by Frédéric Gadmer in Benin in 1929 and 1930 document a similar ritual in the temple of Agasu in which the voduns, held by other people, place their feet over a steaming pot (Gadmer, *Dahomey . . .*). For a description of various ordeals by fire in the temples of Mawu and Hevioso in Abomey, see Herskovits, *Dahomey . . .*, 2:124, 165–66. Also, in the cult of the orixá Xangô a ritual called *ajeré* is performed in which the orixá carries a vessel of burning coals on his head.

88. *O Alabama*, December 24, 1870, 5. There is also the case, discussed above, of the African Zé Rovalo, also called *gumbonde*. However, since the *ebó* ritual performed there contains strong Nagô elements, I did not include it here.

89. *O Alabama*, November 21, 1871, 1.

90. *O Alabama*, April 14, 1869; April 16, 1869, 2.

91. Rodrigues, *Os africanos . . .*, 230–31.

92. Carneiro, *Religiões . . .*, 33

93. Ramos, introduction, 13.

94. Rodrigues, *Os africanos . . .*, 231 (emphasis added).

95. For a detailed analysis of the discussion in this section, see Parés, "The Nagôization . . ."; and Parés, "The Birth. . . ."

96. Rodrigues, *Os africanos . . .*, 240–45.

97. See Albuquerque, "Esperanças. . . ."

98. Matory, "Afro-Atlantic Culture. . . . ," 102.

99. Peel, *Religious . . .*, 279. See also Ajayi, "Nineteenth-Century Origins . . ."; Matory, "The English Professors . . ."; Matory, *Black Atlantic . . .*, 57–61, "Jeje . . . ," 60, 64; and Law, "The Atlantic Slave Trade. . . ."

100. Braga, *Na gamela . . .*, 37–58; Lima, "O candomblé . . . ," 45; Lima, "Os obás . . . ," 5–36.

101. Matory, *Black Atlantic . . .*, 88, 95–96.

102. Lima, "O candomblé . . . ," 52.

103. On the narratives related to the founding of Ilê Iyá Nassô and the role of the travels to Africa, see Carneiro, *Candomblés . . .*, 48; Verger, *Orixás . . .*, 28–29; and Bastide, *Sociologia . . .*, 323. For the same topic related to the Egun cult of the island of Itaparica, see Capone, *La quête . . .*, 250.

104. Dantas, "Pureza . . . ," 125.

CHAPTER 5

1. Since the 1940s, a few comments regarding Bogum have been published in newspaper articles and specialized publications. I will cite these as the opportunity arises. On Roça de Cima and Seja Hundé, see Wimberly, "The Expansion . . . ," 74–89; Dias do Nascimento, *Candomblé . . .*; and Dias do Nascimento, "Presença . . ." Marcos Antônio Lopez de Carvalho wrote an untitled and unpublished text on the Jeje Candomblé of Cachoeira, henceforth cited as Lopez de Carvalho, Documento. . . . Some of this data was subsequently published in Lopez de Carvalho, *Gaiaku Luiza.* . . . The research by Dias do Nascimento and Lopez de Carvalho was done at the same time as mine, and periodically we had the opportunity to share and discuss information.

2. I discussed the history of the terreiros with many people, but the elders were the most helpful to my research, especially the late Vicente Paulo dos Santos, better known as *Humbono* Vicente do Matatu, one of the most famed religious experts of the Jeje tradition; Ambrósio Bispo Conceição, or *Ogã* Boboso, one of the most highly regarded experts of Seja Hundé; the late Luiza Franquelina da Rocha, or *Gaiaku* Luiza, leader of the Rumpayme Huntoloji candomblé in Cachoeira; her biological brother, the late Eugenio Rodrigues da Rocha, also known as *Seu* Geninho; and Everaldo Conceição Duarte, the *pejigã* of Bogum.

3. See, for example, Vansina, *Oral . . .*

4. Lima, "O candomblé . . . ," 55.

5. "Bogum quer tombamento para preservar o seu bissecular terreiro," *A Tarde,* August 24, 1986; "Sepultada mãe-de-santo do mais antigo terreiro jeje," *A Tarde,* October 6, 1994; "Terreiro do Bogum inicia cerimônias de preparação," *A Tarde,* October 7, 1994. Some Bogum members even estimate the founding of the terreiro to have been in 1620 (Butler, *Freedoms . . .*, 191).

6. File no. 1, CEAO, January 17, 1961.

7. Everaldo Duarte, December 13, 1998; February 7, 1999; November 11, 1999. It is also said that some of these slaves of the quilombo might have gone toward the Recôncavo.

8. "Moradores lutam pelo Engenho Velho," *A Tarde,* May 5, 1997.

9. Rego, "Terras beneditinas," iv–18.

10. Rita Maia, personal communication, Salvador, April 6, 2001; Maia, *Projeto Fundiário* . . . ; "Moradores lutam pelo Engenho Velho," *A Tarde*, May 5, 1997.

11. The transcription of the inventory appears in the inventory of his wife and heir, Ana Francisca Texeira de Carvalho, who died in 1898. "Inventário de Ana Francisca Texeira de Carvalho," 1/7/7/1, Série Judiciária, APEBa.

12. The extensive use of the place name Engenho Velho and the confusion regarding the borders of the Brotas and Vitoria parishes persist until the end of the nineteenth century. In 1890, in a document listing the property of Maria Julia Figueiredo, *ialorixá* of Ilê Iyá Nassô, a terreiro also known as Engenho Velho or Casa Branca, located next to Bogum in the Vitoria parish, it is reported that she had three houses "in the place called Engenho Velho, Caminho do Rio Vermelho, Brotas parish": "Arrecadação da propriedade de Maria Julia Figueiredo," 03/1011/1480/20, Série Judiciária APEBa.

13. Reis and Silva, *Negociação* . . . , 44, 55–56, 129; cf. "Antônio Guimarães ao presidente Barros Paim," July 24, 1831, Juízes de Paz, maço 2.681, APEBa.

14. Reis and Silva, *Negociação* . . . , 56–57; cf. "Antônio Guimarães ao presidente Barros Paim," July 24, 1831, Juízes de Paz, maço 2.681, APEBa.

15. Monteiro, *Notas* . . . , 61. J. de Carvalho, "Nação jeje . . . ," 55–56; J. de Carvalho, "Mundo jeje comemora cinqüentenário de sua mãe-de-santo," *A Tarde*, July 26, 1988.

16. *AAPBa*, no. 40 (1971): 24–25, 57, 70.

17. *AAPBa*, no. 40 (1971): 86–92.

18. *O Alabama*, May 2, 1867.

19. *O Alabama*, May 10, 1867.

20. Karasch, *A vida* . . . , 353.

21. *O Alabama*, April 14, 1869, 1.

22. *O Alabama*, February 16, 1869, 2–3; April 14, 1869, 1; May 16, 1869, 2; June 23, 1870, 2.

23. After moving from Barroquinha, Ilê Iyá Nassô seems to have been temporarily established in a number of other places in the city before becoming permanently lodged in Engenho Velho. Carneiro says that "later, almost simultaneous with the founding of Gantois, Engenho Velho moved to the area called Joaquim dos Couros, along the Caminho do Rio Vermelho" (*Candomblés* . . . , 49). Since Gantois (Moinho) was already in operation in 1868 (see chap. 4), it would appear that Ilê Iyá Nassô moved to Engenho Velho in the 1860s. Verger and Silveira suggest that the terreiro had moved there in around 1855. To support this hypothesis, they argue that among those "who were in the place called Engenho Velho, in a gathering called a candomblé," mentioned in a *Jornal da Bahia* news article from May 31, 1855, appear the names of Leopoldina da Conceição and Escolástica Maria da Conceição, free Creoles, who were, according to them, relatives of Maria Julia da Conceição Nazaré (whose real name was in fact Julia Soares de Sá), a member of Ilê Iyá Nassô before her founding of Gantois (Verger, *Orixás* . . . , 29; Silveira, "Iyá . . . , 113). It should be remembered that Escolástica Maria da Conceição was also the name of *Mãe* Menininha, leader of Gantois since 1922, but Conceição is also one of the most common family names in Brazil. Verger and Silveira's argument, while possible, does not seem conclusive.

24. "Ruinhó quer mato e rio para 'voduns' do Bogum," *A Tarde*, December 5, 1975.

25. *O Alabama*, July 27, 1870, 1; March 11, 1871, 2.

26. *Humbono* Vicente, February 23, 1999; Everaldo Duarte, November 11, 1999.

27. *O Alabama*, September 22, 1868, 2; September 26, 1868, 4; September 29, 1868, 3.

28. Campos, "Tradições," 416; *Gaiaku* Luiza, August 25, 1996; Aguesi, August 9, 1996.

29. Everaldo Duarte, February 7, 1999.

30. Rego, "Mitos . . .," 186. For the etymological hypothesis of *sirrum*, my source is Dias do Nascimento, December 24, 1998 (see chap. 4, n. 68, for an etymology of *zènli* and *sirrum*).

31. *Gaiaku* Luiza, August 21, 1996. However, *Ogã* Boboso said that the *Pó Zerrem* "was not Mahi, but Dahomea. . . . These two Jejes are very similar, but their dances [those of the Dahomea] are rougher and more violent" (*Ogã* Boboso, interview, February 4, 1999). The interviews with *Ogã* Boboso, Luiz Magno, and Francesa Arlinda da Silva on February 4, 1999, were recorded in Cachoeira by Dias do Nascimento and Lopez de Carvalho. I am grateful to Dias do Nascimento for giving me access to this material, which hereafter will be referred to as "interview, February 4, 1999."

32. *Humbono* Vicente, February 23, 1999.

33. "Pierre Verger comenta reportagem sobre Jêje," *A Tarde*, July 31, 1988.

34. *Humbono* Vicente, July 3, 2000; *Gaiaku* Luiza, November 7, 1999.

35. Everaldo Duarte, November 27, 1999. At Bogum there is the *kutito*, or house of the dead for the terreiro's ancestral cult, but these practices are separated from the vodun rituals.

36. *Humbono* Vicente, November 13, 1999. Nelson José do Nascimento, known as *pai-pequeno* of Oxum Abotô, one of those initiated by *Seu* Aprígio, remembers that he was initiated in 1933, together with another man consecrated to Iansã (Oya Kebê): pai-pequeno, file no. 48, CEAO, 1966.

37. One of the better-known examples is that of Commander Pedro Rodrigues Bandeira, a wealthy merchant and *engenho* owner of the region, who traded in tobacco and liquor between Cachoeira and Salvador at the start of the nineteenth century, and at the same time had a number of vessels involved in the slave trade; Wemberly, "The African Liberto." In 1827, there was a slave insurrection on his property, Engenho da Vitória.

38. For a historic study of Cachoeira, see P. C. da Silva, "Datas . . ."; and Dias do Nascimento, "Presença. . . ."

39. *Ogã* Boboso, March 24, 2001; interview, February 4, 1999. Dias do Nascimento, *Candomblé . . .*, 16–17.

40. Based on a February 4, 1999, interview with *Ogã* Boboso, Dias do Nascimento and Lopez de Carvalho suggest that the Oba Tedô candomblé worshipped "the vodun Asansur Azoano, whose name was Nagopé (Dias do Nascimento, *Candomblé . . .*, 17; Lopez de Carvalho, Documento . . . , 1, 7). My own interpretation of this interview is that the term *nagopé*, also pronounced "nagobe" or "modobe," is a corruption of *mundubi* and refers to the nation of Roça da Cima (a subsequent Jeje candomblé).

41. Dias do Nascimento, *Candomblé . . .*, 16–17.

42. Milton, *Ephemerides . . .*, 387.

43. Campos, "Ligeiras notas . . . ," 291; Akin Adé, personal communication, September 5, 1999; Dias do Nascimento, December 17, 1998. Gavoy ("Note . . . ," 115) speaks of a "compound" founded by Chacha Félix de Souza in the Zomai neighborhood of Ouidah, called Batédo, where there lived 600 Nagô and Hausa slaves.

44. J. J. Reis, *Rebelião*, 100, 105–12. In 1814, there was another important slave revolt in the sugar mills and plantation of Iguape; ibid., 86–87.

45. *Gaiaku* Luiza, November 7, 1999; *Ogã* Boboso, interview, February 4, 1999: Garangogoji (my transcription), Dangoroji (Lopez de Carvalho's transcription); Dandagoji (*Humbono* Vicente's, June 30, 1999); Dahosi or Dadahosi (*Ogã* Boboso, March 5, 2000). Dada Zodji or Daazodji is a very old quality of Sakpata, though not documented in Abomey and Ouidah until the 1930s. He is considered the son of the androgynous entity Mawu-Lissa and twin brother to the female vodun Nyohwe Ananu, with whom he fathered the other Sakpata. As father, he is chief among the voduns of the earth pantheon. It is also he who kills with smallpox. Herskovits, *Dahomey*..., 2:129, 139, 142; Merlo, "Hiérarchie...," 20, 24. Alternatively, the name Dandagoji derives perhaps from *agogoji*, a deformation of Agbogboji, "the very name of Sakpata," according to an informant of Maupoil's, qtd. in Herskovits, *Dahomey*..., 2:139, 140.

46. "Cachoeira 1858–1860," record no. 97, Presidência da Província, Série Viação, no. 4.677, APEBa. Document found by Dias do Nascimento.

47. Book 4, no. 585, 180; book 7 ("Indicador Real"), no. 913; "Registros de Imóveis," FTFC. The description of the land's boundaries mentions the Belém road, the Virginio rock landmark, the entrance to Ventura, the Caquende River, the bamboo grove, the Boa Vista farm, the three sisters ("which are three very tall trees"), the lake, and the lands of the widow Melquíades.

48. *Ogã* Boboso, interview, February 4, 1999, August 20, 1996.

49. *O Alabama*, July 12, 1866, 1; March 23, 1867, 4. As Dias do Nascimento points out ("Presença...," 86), the name of Casa Estrela might derive from the name of Arlindo Estrela, who in the 1930s owned a neighboring property known as Solar dos Estrelas. *Gaiaku* Luiza (February 26, 2001) states that the Casa Estrela name is recent and that it was formerly known as "basement of the late Julia's daughter," Julia Guimarães Viana being the former owner of the property.

50. The Portuguese names of these women cause great confusion in the oral tradition. According to *Gaiaku* Luiza, the name of Maria Agorensi was Maria Luiza Gonzaga de Souza and the name of Abalhe was Maria Dionísia da Conceição. For his part, Lopez de Carvalho (Documento..., 2) gives Maria Diunísia do Sacramento as Abalhe's name; *Equede* Bela used Maria Epifania do Sacramento, and *Ogã* Boboso (November 7, 1999) spoke of Maria Epifania Dionísio dos Santos. In this work, I employ the names found in the respective death records: Maria Luiza do Sacramento and Maria Epifania dos Santos. For comments on the terms *Agorensi* and *Abalhe*, see chap. 6.

51. *Gaiaku* Luiza, December 17, 1998; Aguesi August 9, 1996. *Humbono* Vicente suggested that Emiliana was initiated by Ludovina in Salvador (August 3, 2000).

52. *Humbono* Vicente, 1996; January 29, 1999; December 7, 1999. On May 4, 1999, he stated that Abalhe entered at the age of fifteen and came out at sixteen.

53. Registros de Óbito (Death Records), vol. C37, no 4771, FTFC.

54. This document was typed by the Cachoeiran *pai-de-santo* José dos Santos Silva of Ogun Megege Dajarrum and preserved by *Humbono* Vicente in his house in Matatu.

55. *Humbono* Vicente, December 14, 1999, December 12, 1999.

56. File no. 1, CEAO, January 17, 1961.

57. Valéria Auada, "A rica história dos terreiros de candomblé da Bahia que o tempo

ameaça destruir," *Tribuna da Bahia*, March 28, 1987. *Ogã* Boboso affirms that Ludovina Pessoa "founded Bogum, Roça de Cima and Roça de Baixo" (interview, February 4, 1999).

58. *O Alabama*, February 16, 1869, 2.

59. *O Alabama*, May 13, 1869, 2; May 19, 1869, 3. According to *Ogã* Boboso (February 24, 2001), Totonia Fateira was the spiritual daughter of Ludovina Pessoa and was initiated in the same group, or *barco*, as Emiliana.

60. *Humbono* Vicente mentioned that he heard it said "to the elders," including his own *mãe-de-santo*, Maria Romana Moreira, that the Portuguese name of Ludovina Pessoa was Rachel: Vicente, May 4, 1999 (Aké); August 13, 1999 (Raqué); March 24, 2000 (Raquel). Given that Ludovina Pessoa is a Portuguese name, this allusion to Raquel in relation to Ludovina might refer to the "negress Raquel," a likely collaborator of Ludovina's.

61. Everaldo Duarte, November 10, 2001.

62. "Livro de Batizados da Paroquia de Cachoeira, 1805–1817," f. 144, est. 3, cx. 33, ACMS. In the same book, fl. 22, dated November 8, 1805, I found record of "Lodovica [written as "Lodovia" in the margin], Gege adult, slave of Ignacio de Figuereido Mascarenhas, her godparents were Agostinho [illegible] and his sister Mariana da Costa." The difference in the pronunciation of the name makes identifying this person with Ludovina Pessoa more difficult. For the entire period 1805–35, I found record of only five other Ludovinas (Lodovina, Lugduvina), but all were Creole children, the daughters of slaves.

63. "Cachoeira, 19 agosto 1829," Miscellanea, ARC. Document found by Dias do Nascimento.

64. Book "Contas-Pagamentos de escravos e alugues de casas. S. Félix 1842–1869," record no. 182, ARC.

65. "Ludovina Africana," Cachoeira, 1858, Autos civis, Judiciário, 78/2801/09, APEBa.

66. Karasch, *A vida . . .*, 344–45.

67. I found yet a fifth reference to a Maria Luduvina, African, age ninety, interred in the Santa Casa da Misericórdia cemetery on May 2, 1884: "Livro de óbitos, Cachoeira 1776–1885," cx. 35, est.3 ACMS. Interestingly, it was the only record of a Ludovina for the period 1870–85.

68. Port police inspection books, passenger departures and arrivals, vols. 1, 2, 3, 50, 51, 52, 53, 54, 55; APEBa.

69. Ogum Rainha: *Gaiaku* Luiza, 1996; Lopez de Carvalho, Documento . . . , 3. Ogum Tolo: Aguesi August 21, 1996. Ogum Aíres: *Ogã* Boboso, qtd. in Lopez de Carvalho, Documento . . . , 3; Dias do Nascimento, *Candomblé . . .*, 17.

70. Lopez de Carvalho, Documento . . . , 2, 4.

71. Ibid., 9. It is also said that Zé de Brechó prepared an *ebó* with the head of a pig, which was buried in the city square so that Cachoeira would be flooded. Salaco took apart the *ebó*, but the Paraguaçu River's occasional overrunning of its banks are still explained by this *ebó* (Mister, Cachoeira, February 25, 2001).

72. "Ruínas guardam história da cidade de Cachoeira," *Correio da Bahia*, September 4, 1999, 19.

73. *Humbono* Vicente, August 22, 1999.

74. Dias do Nascimento, *Candomblé . . .*, 17. According to Jehová de Carvalho, Dadá is a female deity of plants (*Reinvenção . . .*). Rodrigues describes her shrine made of cowry

shells and a mirror, but she is not associated with any other orixá (*O animismo . . .*, 51). In Fongbe, *dadá* refers to the king of Abomey, but on the coast the word frequently means the oldest sister (Segurola, *Dictionnaire . . .*, 111).

75. Dias do Nascimento provides some interesting data from other individuals of the "black intellectual and social elite" of Cachoeira, such as the Africans Antônio Domingues Martins and his wife Júlia Guimarães Vianna, the abolitionist Luís Osanah, the abolitionist lawyer Prisco Paraíso, and the councilman Colonel José Ruy Dias d'Afonsecca ("Presença . . . ," 35–36).

76. When his father died on September 27, 1855, Zé de Brechó was nineteen years and eight months old: "Inventário de Belchior Rodrigues de Moura, 1855–1869," Série Judiciária, 2/602/1056/10, APEBa. This reference is held as the most reliable, though other documents reveal notable discrepancies, dating his birth between 1829 and 1843.

77. "Inventário de Belchior Rodrigues de Moura, 1855–1869," Série Judiciária, 2/602/1056/10, APEBa.

78. "Cachoeira, 1858–1860," record 66, maço 4.677, Presidência da Província, Série Viação, APEBa.

79. "Inventário de Belchior Rodrigues de Moura, 1855–1869," Série Judiciária, 2/602/1056/10, APEBa.

80. "Cachoeira, 1858–1860," Presidência da Província, Série Viação, maço 4.677, records 77, 81, APEBa. Maria da Motta lived in the family home on Rua dos Remédios, no. 38, in Recuada until it was sold in 1901: book 3, no. 920, Registro de Imóveis, FTFC. She died in 1904 (Death Records, FTFC).

81. "Atas do conselho da qualificação dos votantes, 1871–73"; "Qualificação dos votantes da Freguesia de Nossa Senhora do Rosário da Cachoeira, 1871–1875" (fl. 26); "Lista de Cidadãos aptos para votarem, 1880," Miscellanea, ARC.

82. "Livro de Atas da Assembléia Geral da Sociedade Monte Pio dos Artistas Cachoeiranos. 21 fev. 1874 a 12 março 1893," ASMPAC.

83. P. C. da Silva, "Datas . . . ," 334.

84. Ibid.; Dias do Nascimento, *A Capela . . .*, 20–32; Dias do Nascimento, "Presença . . . ," 40. See also Milton, *Ephemerides . . .*, 360.

85. "Livro de Atas da Assembléia Geral da Sociedade Monte Pio dos Artistas Cachoeiranos. 21 fev. 1874 a 12 março 1893," ASMPAC.

86. "Relatório do Conselho do Monte Pio dos Artistas. Cachoeira, 1885–1887, 1887–1888," "Relatório do Conselho do Monte Pio dos Artistas. Cachoeira, 1885–1887, 1887–1888," document no. 57, ASMPAC.

87. "Livro de Atas da Assembléia Geral da Sociedade Monte Pio dos Artistas Cachoeiranos. 21 fev. 1874 a 12 março 1893," ASMPAC.

88. *A Cachoeira*, October 29, 1899. Document found by Dias do Nascimento.

89. "Livro-Relatório, 1889–1890," document no. 58, ASMPAC. Milton, *Ephemerides . . .*, 375.

90. "Conselho Filial do Centro Operário n'este Estado da Cidade de Cachoeira," 1900, loose documents, box "Atuação," ARC.

91. Aristides Milton mentions the installation of the Masonic lodge Caridade e Segredo (Charity and Secret) in Cachoeira on November 9, 1879 (*Ephemerides . . .*, 363).

92. "Documentos da Câmara Municipal de Cachoeira," Miscellanea, ARC; "Livro Lista de Associados 1874–1897," document no. 52, ASMPAC. Milton, *Ephemerides* . . . , 312; Dias do Nascimento, *A Capela* . . . , 30; Dias do Nascimento, "Presença . . . ," 40.

93. Death Records, Book C9, no. 396, FTFC. He appears already as "capitão José Maria Belchior" in a mortgage from May 21, 1901 ("Inscrição especial," Book 2B, no. 1.075, 39v, FTFC).

94. Death Records, Books C1-C9, FTFC.

95. Death Records, Book C9, no. 396, FTFC.

96. "A pedido," *A Cachoeira*, May 1, 1902, 2. Document found by Dias do Nascimento.

97. Barickman, "Até a véspera . . . ," 186–93; Wimberly, "The Expansion . . . ," 77–78.

98. Wimberly, "The Expansion . . . ," 82–84. Harding, *A Refuge* . . . , 58. Following the death of *Tio* Anacleto, the Capivari candomblé was led by his daughter Maria Felizarda and then by *Dona* Gina of Obaluayê (1933–95), *Tio* Anacleto's great granddaughter, initiated in 1945 in the Ketu candomblé of Nezinho do Portão (Velho, São Félix, February 3, 1999). According to *Ogã* Boboso and *Gaiaku* Luiza (February 16, 1999), the terreiro was "pure Nagô." According to Velho (February 3, 1999), the grandson of *Dona* Gina and present-day caretaker, the terreiro "was Nagô-*vodunsi* and became Ketu, and has also been Jeje and Angola," though he identified its current nation as "pure Ketu."

99. When *Tio* Salu passed away in 1949, he was more than ninety years old. He was succeeded as leader by his wife, Maria Ambrosia da Conceição (1907–92), a member of the Boa Morte sisterhood. The terreiro is identified as Jeje-Nagô or Nagô-*Vodunsi* (Rita Maria Barreto Soares da Conceição, Muritiba, February 17, 1999). According to *Ogã* Boboso and *Gaiaku* Luiza (February 16, 1999), the terreiro was Nagô.

100. Aguesi, August 8, 1996; *Gaiaku* Luiza, September 26, 2000, March 24, 2001; *Ogã* Boboso, May 5, 2002. Geninho said that the first terreiro in Terra Vermelha was that of Jerónimo, which "played Nagô and Angola beats" (Geninho, January 1, 2000, March 5, 2000, May 5, 2002). Dias do Nascimento mentions the Macambira candomblé in Caquende (*A Capela* . . . , 39).

101. *Gaiaku* Luiza, February 26, 2001.

102. Luiz Magno, interview, February 4, 1999.

103. Aguesi, August 9, 1996; *Gaiaku* Luiza, 1996, November 7, 1999; *Ogã* Boboso, November 7, 1999, January 1, 2000.

104. *Ogã* Boboso, November 7, 1999; *Humbono* Vicente, November 10, 1999.

105. "Partilha amigável de Luiz Ventura Esteves," Série Judiciária, 06/2596/3096/21, APEBa.

106. Book 4, no. 539; Book 3, no. 1.133; Registro de Imóveis, FTFC. In 1858, the Engenho do Rosário was the property of Major Antônio Olavo de Meneses Doria ("Registro de terras de Cachoeira, 1858–60," Série Viação, no. 4.677, APEBa). From 1878 to at least 1880, it belonged to Bernardo Mendes da Costa, a merchant ("Inventário de Manoel Nunes de Freitas Costa," fl. 139–40, 02/120/120/1162, ARC). On January 31, 1890, an ad appeared in a local paper reporting the theft of two horses "in the hands of the herdsman of Commander Albino José Milhazes at Engenho Rozario" (*O Tempo*, Cachoeira).

107. *Humbono* Vicente, August 22, 1999, January 19, 2000; *Ogã* Boboso, January 31, 2000, March 5, 2000, May 5, 2002; Geninho February 1, 2000. Helvecio Vicente Sapocaia

was a notary and in 1886 was named an honorary member of the Sociedade Monte Pio dos Artistas Cachoeiranos. This was at the time that Zé de Brechó assumed leadership ("Relatório do Conselho do Monte Pio dos Artistas. Cachoeira, 1885–1887, 1887–1888," document no. 57, ASMPAC).

108. *Humbono* Vicente, n.d. ; *Ogã* Boboso, December 18, 1998.

109. *Ogã* Boboso, interview, February 4, 1999; Aguesi, August 20, 1996.

110. In approximately 1904, Zé de Brechó's sisters, Maria Ancieta and Maria Juliana Belchior, sold Roça de Cima to the sisters Zilda and Elza da Nova Milhazes, both minors and nieces of the Portuguese Albino Milhazes. And in 1912, Zilda and Elza sold the "Altamira Farm," composed of the Chareme farm and a second "piece" of neighboring lands, to Pedro, José, and Clovis da Costa Pimentel, also minors. They in turn, in 1921, sold it to Judge José Nascimento Costa Falcão (Tabelionato de Notas, March 1910–October 1912, 73; August 1920–June 1922, 24v. Livro de Escrituras, FTFC). I would like to thank Dias do Nascimento for providing this information. It is commonly held among the populace of Cachoeira that this farm is haunted, given that there are many things buried there by the Africans.

111. *Gaiaku* Luiza, 1996, December 17, 1998; Geninho, January 22, 2000; Aguesi, August 9, 1996.

112. According to this hypothesis, Ludovina's supposed trips to Africa would have been critical. She could have brought back to Brazil, together with specific religious precepts, the renewed Mahi identity that was being assumed by Brazilian returnees in Agoué and other cities along the Mina Coast (Matory, "Jeje . . .," 66–67; Strickrodt, "Afro-Brazilians . . .").

113. *Seu* Geninho, March 5, 2000.

114. Bolouvi, *Nouveau* . . . , 59–61; Bastide, *Sociologia* . . . , 375; Rego, "Mitos. . . ."

115. Bolouvi, *Nouveau* . . . , 60.

116. Everaldo Duarte, January 4, 1996. Regarding the *atabaques*, "one is of Oxum, another of Bogum, and the other [missing word]" (file no. 1, CEAO, January 17, 1961. Ailton, October 4, 2001).

117. Bergé, "Étude . . .," 713, 717.

118. Bolouvi, *Nouveau* . . . , 60. Also interesting is Dunglas's comment that in Fongbe, *Zou goudo* means "derrière le Zou," or behind or to the north of the Zo River, thus designating the Mahi country.

119. At Bogum, Zò is not recognized as a vodun, though there is a ritual of the same name associated with Sogbo (see chap. 4). As to Ogodô, Lima states: "When asked about this second initiation [of *Mãe* Aninha], Senhora answered that 'this was necessary because Xangô was given two names in the land of Tapa, *Ogodô* and Afonjá.' These were the two qualities of Aninha's Xangô" ("O candomblé . . .," 55).

120. Jaime Montenegro, August 10, 1999; Dias do Nascimento, January 23, 1999.

121. "Obrigação de Vicente," manuscript, February 19, 1964. Copy provided by *Humbono* Vicente.

122. Burton, *A Mission* . . . , 78, says that in Ouidah, "the thunder fetish shrub" is called *Ayyan* or *Soyan*. Baudin, in *Fetichism* . . . (p. 23), relates that *Ayan* is the name of the tree from which, according to Yoruba legend, Xangô hanged himself.

123. Iroko, *Mosaïques* . . . , 15–18.

CHAPTER 6

1. *Hunsi* is synonymous with *vodunsi*. The term *agorensi*, which I use throughout this book, is pronounced and spelled in a number of different ways, including "ogurinsi," "agorinsi," "ogorinse," "ogorensi," "ungoroci," "gorência," and "angorense." It is probably a corruption of *angorôsi*, the woman (*si*) of Angorô, given that this is the name of the snake deity in the Angola terreiros, which corresponds to the Jeje Dan or Bessen and to the Nagô Oxumaré. For a discussion of the term and the possible interpenetration of the Jeje and Angola traditions, see chap. 7.

2. Aguesi, August 21, 1996; *Gaiaku* Luiza, December 17, 1998, February 16, 1999; Geninho, March 5, 2000.

3. Death Records, Book C23, no. 460, FTFC.

4. *Gaiaku* Luiza, November 7, 1999. *Deré* Isidora was a biologoical cousin of Luiza's mother: *Gaiaku* Luiza, May 5, 2003.

5. Aguesi, August 9, 1996; *Gaiaku* Luiza, December 17, 1998, August 8, 2001. The titles *dofona*, *dofonitinha*, *fomo*, and so on indicate the order in which the initiates entered the initiation group (*barco*) and correspond to the order of their ritual preparation. They indicate different hierarchical levels: the first to enter is considered the oldest and the last, the youngest (see chap. 4).

6. *Gaiaku* Luiza, November 7, 1999. Badesi Arcanja and Miuda of Kposu at least were initiated in the second *barco*. For a different version of this *barco*'s composition, see Lopez de Carvalho, *Gaiaku Luiza . . .*, 82. *Gaiaku* Luiza also mentioned the names of Luzia Moreira of Azonsu or Avimaje (January 3, 2000) and of Norberta of Iemanjá (May 5, 2002). As we have seen, there are a number of other *vodunsis* besides the twenty that supposedly make up the two *barcos*. This is because the list given by *Gaiaku* Luiza might include older members from Roça de Cima, such as *Deré* Custódia of Oiá, or members initiated in other terreiros (perhaps Bogum) who, for whatever reason, ended up at Seja Hundé. The fact that two *dofonas* appear on the list can be explained in the same way and does not necessarily imply a third *barco*.

7. *Gaiaku* Luiza, December 17, 1998, November 7, 1999. Geninho mentioned *Alabe* Leardino in this group of five, perhaps the same Ermírio: Geninho, June 23, 2000, May 5, 2002.

8. *Gaiaku* Luiza, November 7, 1999; Geninho, March 5, 2000.

9. According to *Humbono* Vicente (November 13, 1999), it was Virgilio of Oxóssi and he had a food stall in the Gravata neighborhood.

10. *Humbono* Vicente, August 22, 1999. The *kelé* is a ritual necklace worn by the neophytes during initiation; it signifies subjection and obedience to the deity and the *mãe-de-santo*.

11. See, e.g., "Ubaldino de Assis e pleito presidencial," *A Ordem*, March 15, 1922, ARC.

12. *Gaiaku* Luiza, December 17, 1998, July 29, 1999.

13. *Gaiaku* Luiza, December 17, 1998; *Humbono* Vicente, February 19, 1999, January 16, 1999. According to *Seu* Geninho, *Ogã* Caboco passed away in Belo Horizonte in 1977 at the age of seventy-seven (May 5, 2002).

14. Geninho, qtd. in Lopez de Carvalho, Documento . . . , 8–9.

15. *Humbono* Vicente, April 29, 1999, July 7, 2000.

16. Aguesi said activities ceased for fifteen years; *Gaiaku* Luiza claimed it was only

eleven; and Geninho said only seven: Aguesi, August 9, 1996; *Gaiaku* Luiza, December 17, 1998, August 16, 1999.

17. *Gaiaku* Luiza, November 7, 1999.

18. Braga, *Na gamela . . .*, 22. See also Lühning, "Acabe. . . ."

19. Dias do Nascimento, *A Capela . . .*, 16. Matory comments on this initiative of Aninha's, also attributed by some *pais-de-santo* to Joãozinho da Gomeia or Procópio; *Black Atlantic . . .*, 186.

20. *Gaiaku* Luiza, January 3, 2000.

21. Lopez de Carvalho, *Documento . . .*, 6; confirmed by *Gaiaku* Luiza, August 16, 1999, November 7, 1999.

22. Dias do Nascimento, February 16, 1999. The succession was confirmed by *Humbono* Vicente, February 19, 1999.

23. V. W. Turner, *Schism . . .*

24. Aguesi, August 20, 1996. According to *Ogã* Boboso, Epifânio Santa Rita was Abalhe's *pejigã*.

25. Geninho, January 22, 2000. On another occasion he suggested that it was actually Ludovina who "performed the work" on Abalhe, May 5, 2003.

26. *Ogã* Boboso, interview, February 4, 1999. On December 26, 1999, a song was sung during the Bessen segment at Seja Hundé that mentioned the name of *abalha*. Hunbono Vicente also spoke of *abalha*, which should not be confused with Abalé or Balé, which is a quality of Oiá (*Humbono* Vicente, December 7, 1999). *Ogã* Joãozinho, from *Humbono* Vicente's house, said that the correct pronunciation is "abalié" (Joãozinho, April 16, 1999). In Benin, *agbalia* can refer to the "recade" or scepter of King Tegbesu (Glélé, *Le Danxomé . . .*, 56); however, the term more likely corresponds to *agbálè*, the name given to the daughter born following the initiation of her mother or father in a Sakpata convent (Segurola, *Dictionnaire . . .*, 17).

27. Death Records, Book C37, no. 4.771, FTFC. *Mãe* Baratinha claimed that she was the illegitimate daughter of the poet Castro Alves (Dias do Nascimento, June 25, 1999). *Ogã* Boboso also said that Brechó and Abalhe lived on the second floor of a building known as Sete Portas, near the present-day market (interview, February 4, 1999). The stone eagle on the upper part of the façade is, according to some, a vulture or a heron into which Zé de Brechó would transform himself (Anália, March 2, 1999). This idea is doubtful given that Sete Portas was built in 1902, the year of Zé de Brechó's death. According to *Gaiaku* Luiza, it was Salaco, Zé de Brechó's brother, who lived there (*Gaiaku* Luiza, November 7, 1999).

28. *Ogã* Boboso, November 7, 1999; Dias do Nascimento, *Candomblé . . .*, 18.

29. *Seu* Geninho, March 5, 2000; *Humbono* Vicente, December 7, 1999.

30. J. G. da C. Castro, *Miguel Santana . . .*, 27.

31. Ibid.

32. Interview with Francesa Arlinda da Silva, Cachoeira, February 4, 1999.

33. *Humbono* Vicente, February 19, 1999, July 11, 2000. In 1996, *Ogã* Boboso said that he had been confirmed sixty years ago, that is, in 1936, while *Seu* Bernardinho said it was about fifty years, or in the early 1940s. *Ogã* Boboso would have been born on December 8, 1912 (*Ogã* Boboso, February 16, 1999).

34. In addition to these, *Gaiaku* Luiza mentioned *Ogãs* Nozinho, Gregório, and

Matias, as well as *Equedes* Nininha and Marcelina (*Gaiaku* Luiza, November 7, 1999, January 3, 2000). *Ogã* Jeninho from Casa Branca said that his father, Benzinho, was *ogã* of Seja Hundé (June 14, 2001).

35. Aguesi, August 20, 1996; *Ogã* Boboso, interview, February 4, 1999; Geninho, February 1, 2000.

36. *Gaiaku* Luiza, January 3, 2000, September 26, 2000.

37. The leader of this terreiro, Manoel Cirqueira de Amorim, nicknamed Nezinho do Portão, was raised by *Tio* Anacleto in the Nagô terreiro of Capivari, but his spiritual affiliation was closely linked to *Mãe* Menininha's Gantois in Salvador. He also actively participated in the festivals and funeral rituals of Ilê Axé Opô Afonjá (Kadia Tall, April 26, 1999; *Gaiaku* Luiza, June 25, 1999; Dias do Nascimento, June 22, 2000; D. M. dos Santos, *História* ..., 29, 32).

38. *Humbono* Vicente, October 8, 1998; *Gaiaku* Luiza, December 17, 1998; *Ogã* Boboso, December 18, 1998.

39. *Ogã* Boboso, November 7, 1999.

40. Death Records, Book C37, no. 4.771, FTFC.

41. *Humbono* Vicente, August 8, 1999; November 13, 1999.

42. Everaldo Duarte, August 23, 1996.

43. File no. 1, CEAO, January 17, 1961.

44. This is another title the Jeje use to denote the *mãe-de-santo* or head of the terreiro (see chap. 8).

45. Everaldo Duarte, November 10, 2001. Information obtained from *Equede* Santa.

46. *Equede* Santa, Salvador, interview, 1981; Everaldo Duarte, December 13, 1998, April 21, 1999. Unfortunately, the search for any reference to Manoel da Silva among the legal documents of the APEBa was unfruitful. At one time *Ogã* Batuta of Casa Branca stated that Manoel da Silva was also *ogã* at Casa Branca, which would indicate an interestingly fluid relationship between Bogum and the Nagô-Ketu terreiro. However, on another occasion, he would not confirm this: *Ogã* Batuta, June 3, 1999; October 8, 1999.

47. File no. 1, CEAO, January 17, 1961.

48. Everaldo Duarte, December 13, 1998. Everaldo Duarte remembered having heard that in the time of Valentina a priest with two virgins went to bless the terreiro (November 10, 2001).

49. File no. 1, CEAO, January 17, 1961.

50. Everaldo Duarte, August 23, 1996.

51. File no. 1, CEAO, January 17, 1961. The old *barracão* was called "bosteiro," or dung heap, due to its packed-earth floor being mixed with cow manure, pitaga tree leaves, and palm seeds (J. de Carvalho, *Reinvenção* ..., 37; Everaldo Duarte, December 13, 1998).

52. Correia Lopes, "Exéquias ...," 559. In the same year of 1937, when Correia Lopes went to visit the Casa das Minas in São Luis, he recounts that he introduced himself to *Mãe* Andresa saying, "I know some Gege songs from Bahia," commenting in parenthesis "(I knew little; Bogum of Engenho Velho had not yet rebuilt at that time)." This comment confirms that in September 1937 Bogum was under construction and suggests a reopening of the terreiro, or at least that religious activities were irregular and infrequent, before this date (Correia Lopes, "A propósito ...," 79).

53. According to *Humbono* Vicente, Tiana Gege was consecrated to Oxum and lived

in Barroquinha. Her Exu and Oxum are still enshrined at Bogum (*Humbono* Vicente, September 13, 2000).

54. Correia Lopes, "Exéquias . . . ," 559. In 1945 Correia Lopes asserted that Bogum "had a branch in Cachoeira" ("Os trabalhos . . . ," 53)

55. "Rascunhos de filhos dos terreiros de seita africanas e cabocla existentes na Bahia," a manuscript produced by Deoscóredes Maximiliano dos Santos for the CEAO in 1966. Record no. 532, dated September 25, 1946, says that Emiliana was seventy-five years old—which would date her birth in 1871—but in the margin "January 6, 1867" is written as the probable date of her birth. The year she died, 1950, is more certain. According to Runhó, she was then ninety-two. This would place her birth in 1858 (see chap. 6, n. 73).

56. *Humbono* Vicente, November 12, 2001; *Gaiaku* Luiza stated that Emiliana was a devotee consecrated to the vodun "Aman Beunim Ló," (CEAO, *2º Encontro . . .* , 70). According to Everaldo Duarte (November 10, 2001), Emiliana was consecrated to Bafono and had the title of *Donaci*. Deoscóredes dos Santos, in record no. 532 of the previously cited "Rascunhos de filhos dos terreiros de seita africanas e cabocla existentes na Bahia," reports "Miliana of Ôgum."

57. Valéria Auada, "A rica história dos terreiros de candomblé da Bahia que o tempo ameaça destruir," *Tribuna da Bahia*, March 28, 1987. *Humbono* Vicente, July 3, 2000, September 22, 2001, November 12, 2001; Everaldo Duarte, November 27, 1999, August 23, 1996, December 13, 1998. *Ogã* Boboso said that Emiliana was initiated before Abalhe, together with Tatiana Fateira, who passed away in 1869. Other less reliable information claims that Emiliana was a "sister-in-the-saint" (*irmã-de-santo*) of Abalhe and Romana and therefore initiated by *Tio* Xarene and/or Brechó.

58. *Humbono* Vicente, January 18, 1999, November 12, 2001.

59. *Humbono* Vicente, September 8, 2001.

60. Statutes of the Sociedade Afro-Brasileira Fiéis de São Bartolomeu, published in *Diário Oficial* nos. 10.777 and 10.778, on October 16, 1977.

61. Carneiro, *Candomblés . . .* , 44–45, 64.

62. Herskovits and Herskovits, "Afro-Bahian Religious Songs. . . ."

63. Valéria Auada, "A rica história dos terreiros de candomblé da Bahia que o tempo ameaça destruir," *Tribuna da Bahia*, March 28, 1987.

64. Everaldo Duarte, December 13, 1998; "Cirrum começou no Bogum e Gamo é a nova yalorixá," *A Tarde*, December 30, 1975. Other sources give 1941 or 1938 as the coming-out date: "Sepultada mãe-de-santo do mais antigo terreiro jeje," *A Tarde* October 6, 1994; J. de Carvalho, "Mundo jeje comemora cinqüentenário de sua mãe-de-santo," *A Tarde*, July 26, 1988. I consider 1940 as the most likely date for the coming-out of this group.

65. Everaldo Duarte, December 13, 1998. Tomázia of Oxum was nephew to Regina of Oxum, who came from the Pó Zerrem terreiro (*Equede* Santa, interview, 1981). Tomázia's Oxum confirmed Everaldo Duarte as *ogã* (Everaldo Duarte, November 27,1999).

66. *Gaiaku* Luiza, February 16, 1999, January 3, 2000. This *barco* does not appear in Everaldo Duarte's chart.

67. Ibid. Luiza Franquelina da Rocha was initiated in the Ketu ritual in 1937, in Nezinho do Portão's Ilê Ibece Alaketu terreiro, and by 1944 she had already initiated a *filha-de-santo* in the Angola and Ijexá ritual. Luiza's initiation in the Jeje ritual was performed by Romana outside of Bogum, and one year later, in 1945, she received the *decá* at the

hands of Romana in the presence of some who had been initiated by Maria Agorensi (not by Abalhe). Luiza said that her saint (Oiá) did not accept staying "in either the east or the west," referring to Seja Hundé and Bogum, and commanded her to open her own terreiro. She operated out of her own home in the Liberdade neighborhood until 1952, when she was able to open a candomblé in Cabrito and became known as *Gaiaku* Luiza.

68. Everaldo Duarte, December 13, 1998, November 27, 1999. The quality of Luizinha's Ossaim was not Agué but was probably a Nagô quality.

69. *Equede* Santa, interview, 1981; *Humbono* Vicente, February 23, 1999. Nicinha also mentioned having heard of other old *ogãs* of the house who were born to African parents, citing the names of Romão, Basilio, Mariano, and Bonifacio ("Terreiro Bogum, testemunho vivo da resistencia jêje," *Jornal AfroBrasil*, year 2, no. 37, November 6–12, 1985, 12).

70. Everaldo Duarte, December 13, 1998; Duarte, "O terreiro . . . ," 19–22.

71. Pierson, *Brancos e pretos . . .*, 324; Carneiro, *Candomblés . . .*, 45; Everaldo Duarte, November 27, 1999.

72. *Equede* Santa, interview, 1981. In the 1930s it seems that Emiliana also helped Manuel Ciriáco de Jesus initiate his first *barco* in the precepts of the Jeje nation in Santo Amaro, although Ciriáco later became the leader of the Congo-Angola Tumbajuçara terreiro (Cleo Martins, August 17, 2003).

73. On March 3, 2000, *Gaiaku* Luiza showed me the *in memoriam* card for Maria Emiliana da Piedade, who passed away on November 10, 1950. In January 1961, Runhó declared that "Emiliana died ten years ago and at the age of ninety-two" (file no. 1, CEAO, January 17, 1961).

74. *Humbono* Vicente, February 19, 1999.

75. *Gaiaku* Luiza, February 16, 1999, January 3, 2000. Everaldo Duarte remembered that a group led by *Equede* Raimunda and *Ogã* João Bernardo also questioned Runhó's aspirations.

76. *Gaiaku* Luiza, February 16, 1999; *Humbono* Vicente, December 7, 1999.

77. According to *Humbono* Vicente (February 23, 1999), the rituals were performed in Cachoeira. Everaldo Duarte (February 16, 2003) claimed they happened at Bogum in Romana's presence.

78. *Humbono* Vicente, February 23, 1999.

79. *Humbono* Vicente, May 4, 1999; *Gaiaku* Luiza, in CEAO, *2º Encontro . . .*, 70.

80. *Humbono* Vicente, December 6, 1998, May 4, 1999.

81. *Humbono* Vicente, February 23, 1999.

82. *Gaiaku* Luiza, January 28, 1998. It is said that there is a shrine in the area of Batefolha that predates the founding of Manoel Bernardino da Paixão's terreiro. Perhaps Romana was called to take charge of the rituals associated with this early Jeje shrine. Bernardino passed away in 1946 (*Gaiaku* Luiza, March 2, 2000).

83. Everaldo Duarte, December 13, 1998.

84. Ibid.

85. *Gaiaku* Luiza, November 28, 1998.

86. *Humbono* Vicente, February 23, 1999. According to *Gaiaku* Luiza, the obituary date was October 16, 1956; Lopez de Carvalho gives it as October 23, 1956.

87. *Humbono* Vicente, February 23, 1999. The key seems to have first passed through the hands of *Ogã* João Bernardo, who, together with *Equede* Raimunda, opposed the

succession of Runhó, but it was later recovered by Antonio Monteiro, who delivered it into the hands of the new *doné* (Everaldo Duarte, October 10, 2002).

88. *Gaiaku* Luiza, December 17, 1998; Dias do Nascimento, January 23, 1999; *Humbono* Vicente, February 19, 1999.

89. Everaldo Duarte, December 13, 1998.

90. Ibid.; *Humbono* Vicente, January 18, 1999.

91. Everaldo Duarte, December 13, 1998; Jaime Montenegro, August 10, 1999.

92. "Cirrum começou no Bogum e Gamo é a nova yalorixá," *A Tarde*, December 30, 1975.

93. Runhó was ninety-eight when she died in 1975. At that time, in one of the first reports in *A Tarde*, it was said that Nicinha was about to celebrate her sixty-sixth birthday, but another report in the same paper on the following day wrote that it is her sixty-fourth birthday: "Ruinhó quer mato e rio para 'voduns' do Bogum," *A Tarde*, December 5, 1975; "Calam-se atabaques do Bogum: começa o 'Cirrum' por Ruinhó," *A Tarde*, December 29, 1975; "Cirrum começou no Bogum e Gamo é a nova yalorixá," *A Tarde*, December 30, 1975; file no. 1, CEAO, January 17, 1961; Everaldo Duarte, January 4, 1999.

94. *Gaiaku* Luiza, December 17, 1998. "From the place of sacrifice the order arrived soon, repeated by a female voice: 'Mêrê dô ji' (Hanji, singing). And the chorus began" (Correia Lopes, "Exéquias . . . ," 560).

95. Segurola, *Dictionnaire . . . ,* 250.

96. Neném de Mello, November 3, 1999.

97. File no. 1, CEAO, January 17, 1961.

98. *Equede* Santa, interview, 1981; "Acabado Cirrum, o Bogum fica fechado por um ano," *A Tarde*, January 5, 1976; Jorge Amado, "A solidão do povo jeje," *Manchete*, February 7, 1976, 38.

99. File no. 1, CEAO, January 17, 1961.

100. Capone, *La quête . . . ,* 126–27. According to Everaldo Duarte, this initiation occurred more recently (October 21, 2001).

101. File no. 1, CEAO, January 17, 1961.

102. Everaldo Duarte, November 27, 1999. In Duarte's chart, the date of the last group of initiates is October 20, 1974, but Ivone of Ogun (Ogunsi) on October 20, 1998, celebrated twenty-six years as an initiate, *Humbono* Vicente being the *pai-pequeno* (Ogunsi, *Humbono* Vicente, October 8, 1998).

103. "Mãe Ruinhó vai bem, graças aos orixás," *Jornal da Bahia*, September 23, 1975.

104. Jorge Amado, "A solidão do povo jeje," *Manchete*, February 7, 1976, 38; "Ruinhó quer mato e rio para 'voduns' do Bogum," *A Tarde*, December 5, 1975; "Calam-se atabaques do Bogum: começa o 'Cirrum' por Ruinhó," *A Tarde*, December 29, 1975; J. de Carvalho, "Nação jeje . . . ," 58.

105. "Acabado Cirrum, o Bogum fica fechado por um ano," *A Tarde*, January 5, 1976; "Sucessão" and "Cirrum começou no Bogum e Gamo é a nova yalorixá," *A Tarde*, December 30, 1975.

106. "Candomblé do Bogum faz festa em homenagem ao prefeito da cidade," *A Tarde*, February 20, 1979, *Humbono* Vicente, December 7, 1999.

107. "Cirrum começou no Bogum e Gamo é a nova yalorixá," *A Tarde*, December 30,

1975; J. de Carvalho, "Mundo jeje comemora cinqüentenário de sua mãe-de-santo," *A Tarde,* July 26, 1988.

108. Everaldo Duarte, February 16, 2003.

109. J. de Carvalho, *Reinvenção . . . ,* 37. *MAMNBA Project (report and other documents).* Prefeitura Municipal de Salvador, Casa Civil, Grupo de Coordenação de Assuntos Culturais, 1981–85. In the statutes of the Sociedade Afro-Brasileira Fiéis de São Bartolomeu (established in July of 1937), published in the *Diário Oficial* nos. 10.777 and 10.778 on October 16, 1977, Edvaldo dos Anjos Costa signed as president; Everaldo Conceição Duarte as vice-president; Ailton Conceição Nascimento as first secretary; Renato Gonzaga dos Santos as second secretary; Hamilton Domingos dos Anjos Melo as first treasurer; Celso Santana as second treasurer; and Lydio Pereira de Santanna, Roverval José Marinho, Celestino Augusto do Espirito Santo, Jorge Antonio Fontes Santos, and Jorge Gusmão dos Santos as members of the Deliberative Council.

110. July 22, 23, and 25, 1986, *A Tarde*; J. de Carvalho, *Reinvenção . . . ,* 37.

111. J. de Carvalho, *Reinvenção,* 38.

112. "Pierre Verger comenta reportagem sobre Jêje," *A Tarde,* July 31, 1988.

113. According to the press, Nicinha died at the age of eighty-three: "Sepultada mãe-de-santo do mais antigo terreiro jeje," *A Tarde,* October 6, 1994; "Terreiro do Bogum inicia cerimônias de preparação," *A Tarde,* October 7, 1994.

114. File no. 1, CEAO, January 17, 1961.

115. *Humbono* Vicente, February 19, 1999.

116. Lopez de Carvalho, *Documento . . . ,* 11.

117. After closing the Cabrito candomblé in Salvador, *Gaiaku* Luiza returned to Cachoeira in October 1961. At Oiá's order, and with the financial help of her father, *Seu* Miguel, she bought the new lands for 176 *cruzeiros* in 1962 and celebrated a number of masses there. In 1964, using cowrie-shell divination performed by *Humbono* Vicente, she determined to which vodun each sacred tree corresponded and performed the first rituals. In 1966 her father passed away, and in 1967 she traveled to São Paulo and Rio de Janeiro where she stayed until 1970, when she performed her first confirmation of an *equede* at Huntoloji and began celebrating festivities there. In 1980 the first group of initiates was gathered and *Humbono* Vicente planted the *abassa*'s *axé* (*Gaiaku* Luiza, August 16, 1999, November 7, 1999, January 3, 2000.)

118. Bernardino, February 16, 1999; *Ogã* Boboso, February 16, 1999, November 7, 1999; Luis Magno, interview, February 4, 1999; *Gaiaku* Luiza, November 28, 1998. According to *Humbono* Vicente, Pararasi prepared only one group of initiates (January 16, 1999, July 11, 2000). According the *Seu* Geninho, Alda and Alaíde were part of the first group, made up then of seven *vodunsis* (Geninho February 1, 2000, March 5, 2000); according to Aguesi, Alaíde was *fomotinha* and "sister-in-the-saint" of a "fominho" (*sic*) of Azonzu (Aguesi, August 20, 1996).

119. Luiz Magno, interview, February 4, 1999; Dias do Nascimento, January 23, 1999.

120. *Gaiaku* Luiza, May 6, 2003.

121. For example, Luiz Magno attributed the death of his mother, one year later, to mistakes made in this initiation (Luiz Magno, interview, February 4, 1999).

122. *Humbono* Vicente, January 16, 1999; *Ogã* Iasana of Seja Hundé, June 23, 1999.

123. Antonio Moraes, November 14, 2004; *Humbono* Vicente, July 11, 2000, January 1, 2001. Without citing any source, Lopez de Carvalho claims that the death occurred on March 3, 1969, in Salvador; Lopez de Carvalho, *Gaiaku Luiza . . .*, 50. Bernardinho also states that Pararasi died in Salvador (June 23, 1999).

124. According to *Humbono* Vicente, the terreiro closed for fifteen years, which seems an excessively long period.

125. *Humbono* Vicente, January 16, 1999, February 19, 1999, November 13, 1999.

126. *Gaiaku* Luiza, February 16, 1999.

127. Olu Ayé, "Nação Jeje Marrym perde gaiaku Aguêsse, 1900–1998," *Orixás & Africanos*, no. 45, year 11 (1998): 3.

128. *Humbono* Vicente, February 19, 1999, June 30, 1999.

129. *Ogā* Joãozinho, April 16, 1999; *Gaiaku* Luiza, November 7, 1999.

130. Olu Ayé, "Nação Jeje Marrym perde gaiaku Aguêse, 1900–1998," *Orixás & Africanos*, no. 45, year 11 (1998): 3.

131. *Humbono* Vicente, February 23, 1999, October 6, 2001.

132. Nilton Feitosa's presentations on Candomblé in Rio, qtd. in Capone, *La quête . . .*, 125. The Kwe Simba house, still active, is of the Jeje-Kaviono nation, or *axé podaba*. Rozenda was succeeded by Natalina of Aziri Tobosi and later by the current leader, Helena of Oxumaré (Nancy de Souza e Silva, August 27, 1999). Some of the characteristics of the *podaba* nation are the cult of deities such as the vodun Jo, a kind of Iansã, or the vodun Gotolu, a kind of Oxóssi; the absence of Badé or Averekete (which would raise doubts about this house being of the Jeje-Kaviono nation); the initiation of novices to Ogun Xoreque (which does not occur in the Jeje-Mahi ritual); and the songs to Ogun and Nanã in "Jeje" (not in Nagô as in the Jeje-Mahi ritual) (Eduardo of Olissá, Cachoeira, December 26, 1999).

133. V. G. da Silva, *Orixás . . .*, 91. There was also *Pai* Dancy's Dâmbalá Kuere-Rhó-Becem Akóy Vodu terreiro operating in São Paulo. Although he was initiated into the Haitian Vaudou tradition, *Pai* Dancy has been another active participant at Seja Hundé in recent years.

134. Dadu de Olissá, December 26, 1999; *Pai* Francisco, December 26, 1999.

135. *Gaiaku* Luiza, June 22, 1999; *Orixás & Africanos* (the official institution for the distribution of Afro-Brazilian cults and culture), no. 45, year 11 (1998): 15.

136. See Prandi, *Os candomblés . . .*, for the passage of Umbanda to Candomblé in São Paulo. For an analysis of the competitive dynamic that occurs in the "re-Africanization" process among those who seek the roots of tradition in Africa and those who seek them in Bahia, see V. G. da Silva, *Orixás . . .*; Capone, *La quête . . .*; and Parés, "The Nagôization. . . ."

137. "Arrecadação da propriedade de Maria Julia Figueiredo, 1890," 03/1011/1480/20, APEBa.

138. There is mention of the land of Commander Bernardo Martins Catharino in Vitória since at least 1930: "Inventário de Joaquim José da Silva Fialho, 1930," 6/2366/2866/2, APEBa. However, there is no mention of this property in his wife's will ("Testamento de Ursula Martins Catarino, 1922," 7/2950/0/8, APEBa).

139. Cartório do 1º Ofício de Registro de Imóveis de Salvador, qtd. in Maia, "Projeto Fundiário . . . ," Miscellanea.

140. "Bogum quer tombamento para preservar o seu bissecular terreiro," *A Tarde*, July 24, 1986.

141. Everaldo Duarte, November 11, 1999.

142. File no. 1, CEAO, January 17, 1961.

143. "Ruinhó quer mato e rio para 'voduns' do Bogum," *A Tarde*, December 5, 1975.

144. "Mataram árvore africana adorada no terreiro gêge" (from an unidentified newspaper), 1978; "Locose toma assento na cadeira de Ruinhó," *A Tarde*, January 6, 1979; J. de Carvalho, *Reinvenção* . . . , 69; Valéria Auada, "A rica história dos terreiros de candomblé da Bahia que o tempo ameaça destruir," *Tribuna da Bahia*, March 28, 1987. In this article, *Ogã* Celestino says the land was sold in 1977, but, according to Duarte, the problems with the wall and the refuse happened where the Azonodo tree stood, and therefore the sale must have occurred after 1978 (Everaldo Duarte, September 22, 2001).

145. "Candomblé do Bogum faz festa em homenagem ao prefeito da cidade," *A Tarde*, February 20, 1979.

146. "Projeto de Lei no. 3.591/85"; cf. *Projeto MAMNBA* (report and other documents), Prefeitura Municipal de Salvador, Casa Civil, Grupo de Coordenação de Assuntos Culturais, 1981–1985. "Terreiros querem proteção para manter culto a orixás," *A Tarde*, December 10, 1985.

147. "Terreiros querem proteção para manter culto a orixás," *A Tarde*, December 10, 1985. Everaldo Duarte, August 1, 1999.

148. "Bogum quer tombamento para preservar o seu bissecular terreiro," *A Tarde*, July 24, 1986.

149. "Gil vai lançar campanha para recuperar terreiros," *Tribuna da Bahia*, March 13, 1987; "Campanha para recuperar terreiros de candomblé," *A Tarde*, March 13, 1987; "O chamado do Bogum," *Jornal da Bahia*, March 18, 1987; Valéria Auada, "A rica história dos terreiros de candomblé da Bahia que o tempo ameaça destruir," *Tribuna da Bahia*, March 28, 1987; "Trono de Ruinhó," *Cidade da Bahia*, August 28, 1993; "Decreto de Lídice autoriza monumento à Revolta dos Malês," *Diário Oficial do Município*, year VIII, no. 1.145, November 22, 1993. In 2001, thanks to the work of Everaldo Duarte, Gilberto Leal, and Raul Lody, Bogum gained the resources necessary for the restoration of the terreiro from the Fundação Palmares, making possible its reopening in 2002.

150. "Seção Serviço Total," *A Tarde*, January 19, 1973.

151. "Bogum quer tombamento para preservar o seu bissecular terreiro," *A Tarde*, July 24, 1986; "O chamado do Bogum," *Jornal da Bahia*, March 18, 1987.

152. Statistics collected in 1983 show, that for the twentieth century, the percentage of male leaders who claimed to be Jeje made up a very significant 40 percent, versus 60 percent for female leaders (J. T. dos Santos, *O dono* . . . , 19). Also cited by Matory, *Black Atlantic* . . . , 230.

153. Freyre, *Casa-grande* . . . , 283; Matory, *Black Atlantic* . . . , 191–207, 229–30; Carneiro, *Candomblés* . . . , 96–98; Landes, "A Cult . . . ," 386–97. See also Dantas, *Vovó* . . . , chap. 4; and Parés, "The Nagôization. . . ."

154. Rodrigues, *Os africanos* . . . , 230–34.

155. Correia Lopes, "Exéquias . . . "; Carneiro, *Candomblés* . . . , 45, 64.

156. File n. no., CEAO, n.d. [1961–1968]. Interview with Falefá conducted by Vivaldo da Costa Lima. In the section "Religious Antecedents" appear the names of Maria Julia

(Duke) of Oxum and of "*pai-de-santo* Manoel [or] José Domingos, of Ogun (dead twenty-four years) (Ife) (Jakáibê)." In the same record is mentioned Maria Nenem, the famous Angola *mãe-de-santo* who intended to initiate Falefá, but "the saint fled, not accepting the duties of the nation" (Itamoacy da Costa, December 13, 1998).

157. File n. no., CEAO, n.d. [1961–1968].

158. In eighteenth-century Ouidah, for example, Labat documents *beta* as the name given to the *vodunsis* of the snake vodun Dangbe (*Voyage* . . . , 2:188). Father Steinmetz reports, in relation to the etymology of the term *Nesuhue* in Benin, the use of the expression "Lensu-hue Kpo-vêta," which would mean the house (*hué*) of the great (*su*) Len, son of the panther (*kpo*) of the red (*vê*) head (*ta*) (Falcon, "Religion . . . ," 143). In the Sogbo family pantheon there is also the vodun known as Abetá Yoyo (*Gaiaku* Luiza, in CEAO, *2º Encontro* . . . , 70, 75).

159. M. V. dos Santos, "O mundo. . . ."

160. Itamoacy, December 13, 1998; Gambovi, Manoel Falefá's nephew, December 6, 1998.

161. *Gaiaku* Luiza, in CEAO, *2º Encontro* . . . , 73–74; Mott and Cerqueira, *Candomblés* . . . , 157. There are doubts as to the religious ancestry of Sibeboran. According to Yeda Machado, she was initiated in Ketu Candomblé; she was a friend of Falefá's family, though not initiated by him. According to one of the *ogãs* of the house, she actually was initiated by Falefá in São Caetano. He adds that Sibeboran's Portuguese name was Josefina (December 13, 1998).

162. Jaime Montenegro, August 10, 1999. Yet, in my fieldwork, I heard talk of Nagô-Agabi (in relation to the old terreiros of the Recôncavo) (*Gaiaku* Luiza, February 26, 2001).

163. Matory, "Man . . . ," 211–13; cf. Pedro de Alcântara Rocha, interview, September 10, 1992; *Pai* Amilton, December 26, 1995.

164. Jaime Montenegro, August 10, 1999.

165. *Pai* Amilton, interview, December 26, 1996.

166. Luiz Magno, interview, February 4, 1999. According to another transcription of the interview, Averigã is a name for Oxaguian.

167. *Gaiaku* Luiza, 1996. In chapter 1, I comment on the frequent association that candomblé practitioners make between the ethnic denomination *Efan* or *Efon* (people from the Ekiti country in the Yoruba area) and the *Fon* ethnonym, and the tendency to confuse their terreiros for Jeje terreiros.

168. Ossório, *A ilha* . . . , 130. I am grateful to Renato da Silveira, who called the existence of this text to my attention (June 16, 2001).

169. D. M. dos Santos, *História* . . . , 14; Lima, "A família-de-santo . . . ," 140; Herskovits and Herskovits, "Afro-Bahian Religious Songs. . . ."

170. Olga of Alaketo, Salvador, interview, January 3, 1996.

171. The first known reference to "Antonio, alias *Euxumaré*" appears in the *Diário de Notícias*, September 18, 1911, 1 (qtd. in M. L. A. dos Reis, "A cor . . . ," 133). I found a second report that refers to the "well-known healer *Osumaré*" in *A Tarde*, October 3, 1922, 2. In 1934, João da Silva Campos mentions among the "older *feiticeiros* from Bahia from 1875 to the present," the "most feared . . . Salocó, mulatto and Antônio Oxumaré (The Spellbound Snake) Creole" ("Ligeiras notas . . . ," 305). File n. no., CEAO, 1960.

172. The information on the relationship between *Seu* Jacinto and Cotinha come from Milton Moura, September 1, 2001.

173. Lima, "O candomblé . . .," 41; cf. Carneiro, *Religiões* . . . , 106–9. In "Uma revisão na ethnographia religiosa afro-brasileira," a paper presented at the 1937 Afro-Brazilian Conference (page 66), and in *Negros bantos*, Carneiro cites the candomblé of Oxumaré in Mata Escura, "of *Pai-de-santo* Jacinto" (*Religiões* . . . , 166–67). But as I have noted, Jacinto was merely Cotinha's husband.

174. Verger, "Orixás da Bahia . . .," 208; Silvanilton da Mata, in CEAO, *2º Encontro* . . . , 26. Cotinha passed away on July 2, 1944. Francelina assumed leadership, or regency, until around 1950, when she was succeeded by Simplicia, who died on September 18, 1967 (Milton Moura, September 1, 2001).

175. File no. 1, CEAO, January 17, 1961; *Humbono* Vicente, November 17, 1994.

CHAPTER 7

1. I use the term *multideity cults* to emphasize the plurality of deities in each congregation and avoid the term *polytheist* normally associated with the religion as a whole. An extended version of the first part of this chapter has been published elsewhere (Parés, "Transformations . . .").

2. Silveira, "Iyá . . ."; Harding, *A Refuge* . . . , 59; Harding, "Candomblé . . .," 76, 99, 316. Harding also cites *Pai* Anacleto's terreiro in São Félix (Recôncavo), as evidence of a multideity cult in the mid-nineteenth century (*A Refuge* . . . , 58); cf. Wimberly, "The Expansion . . .," 82–83.

3. Verger, *Notas* . . . , 15; Verger, "Raisons . . .," 144–45; Bastide, *Sociología* . . . , 113, 316; J. J. Reis, "The Politics . . .," 15.

4. Herskovits and Herskovits, "An Outline . . .," 9–10, qtd. in Maupoil, *La géomancie* . . . , 56.

5. Maupoil, *La géomancie* . . . , 56.

6. Yai, "From Vodun . . .," 246.

7. Bosman, *A New* . . . , 368a; Maupoil, *La géomancie* . . . , 64; Glélé, *Le Danxomé* . . . , 75.

8. Le Hérissé, *L'ancien* . . . , 126–27; Herskovits, *Dahomey* . . . , 2:103–5; Yai, "From Vodun . . .," 254, 256; Bay, *Wives* . . . , 92–96.

9. Herskovits, *Dahomey* . . . , 2:150–51, 163.

10. Peel, "A Comparative . . .," 275–76.

11. Verger, *Notas* . . . , 15, 39; Verger, "The Yoruba . . .," 24; Mckenzie, "O culto . . .," 134–35, 137, 139.

12. Bastide, *Sociologia* . . . , 113, 316; Verger, *Notícias* . . . , 228–29.

13. See, e.g., Merlo, "Hiérarchie . . ."; and Herskovits, *Dahomey* . . . , 2:304.

14. Apter, "Notes . . .," 373, 392–93, 396–97; Drewal, "Dancing . . .," 211, 230–31. The circular choreography used in Igbogila and the order in which the deities are celebrated (Elegba, Ogum, Eyinle, Iroko, Ondo, Omolu) are surprisingly similar to the *xirê* (the initial sequence of songs and dances) practiced in the Ketu candomblés of Bahia. Possibly the practices seen in Igbogila were introduced by returnees from Brazil, or alternatively, it is possible that the Egbado were also important social agents in the formation of Nagô-Ketu candomblé.

15. Rodrigues, *Os africanos* . . . , 236. This is also confirmed by *O Alabama*, from 1863 to 1871.

16. For example, in relation to the orixá Xangô, in Oyó, see Apter, *Black Critics* . . . , 24–25.

17. *Gaiaku* Luiza, February 26, 2001.

18. For the kingdom of Benin, see Dapper, *Naukeurie* . . . , qtd. in Verger, *Notas* . . . , 50. For the Popo region, see Barbot, *Barbot on Guinea* . . . , 620–21. For Ouidah, see Bosman, *A New* . . . , 383. For the Gold Coast, also see Bosman, *A New* . . . , 153; and Isert, *Voyage* . . . , 45.

19. In relation to Allada, see Bosman, *A New* . . . , 383. For Oyo, see Snelgrave, *A New* . . . , 59. In relation to the Fon, see Borghero, *Journal* . . . , 123. See also Isert, *Voyage* . . . , 123.

20. Pazzi, "Aperçu . . . ," 13–14; Pazzi, *Introduction* . . . , 172–74, 199–200; Mouléro, "Histoire . . . ," 43; Law, *The Kingdom* . . . , 6–9; Gayibor, *Les peuples* . . . , 29–30.

21. Barbot, *Barbot on Guinea* . . . , 581, 589; Bosman, *A New* . . . , 113. Burton (*A Mission* . . . , 78) says that in Ouidah, "the thunder fetish shrub" is called *Ayyan* or *Soyan*. Recall that according to Baudin (*Fetichism* . . . , 23), *Ayan* is the name of the tree on which, according to Yoruba legend, Xangô hanged himself. Adam Jones (qtd. in Barbot, *Barbot on Guinea* . . . , 582–83) notes that *Jean Goeman* or *Jankomé* corresponds to the Akan term *Onyankome*. If the root of this term, *onyan*, is an Akan phonetic evolution of *ayyan* or *soyan*, then it is indirect evidence of the expansion of the thunder cult from the Yoruba area to the Gold Coast as early as the seventeenth century, taking for granted that the cult expanded from East to West.

22. An anonymous source (52), cited by Law, *The Slave Coast* . . . , 111. For another reference to the cult of "stones falling from thunderbolts" in Ouidah, see Archives Nationales, Section d'Outre-Mer, Dépôt des Fortifications des Colonies, Côtes d'Afrique, ms. 111, "Réflexions sur Juda par les Sieurs de Chênevert et Abbé Bullet," June 1, 1776, 74. I would like to thank Robin Law for pointing out the existence of these documents to me.

23. Forbes, *Dahomey* . . . , 1:171. Forbes also relates an incident with the thunder priests in Agoue in February 1850 (102–3). In April 1863, the lodgings of the Catholic French missionaries in the Portuguese fort at Ouidah were struck by lightning. Borghero, faithful to his antifetishist principles, refused to pay the fine demanded by the Hevioso priests and was temporarily jailed (Borghero, *Journal* . . . , 129–34). Burton also points out that Hevioso is an "adaption" of the Yoruba Xangô of thunder (*A Mission* . . . , 295). The first explicit reference to Xangô in the Yoruba area comes in Bowen, *A Grammar* . . . (1858), 16.

24. Le Hérissé, *L'ancien* . . . , 115–16; Tidjani, "Notes . . . ," 35; Pazzi, *Introduction* . . . , 123.

25. Le Hérissé, *L'ancien* . . . , 108; Herskovits, *Dahomey* . . . , 2:157. For the vodun lists, see Verger, *Notas* . . . , 521, 528–29, 542–45; and Herskovits, *Dahomey* . . . , 2:304.

26. Merlo, "Hiérarchie . . . ," 6–8; Hunon Daagbo, Ouidah, interview, July 16, 1995.

27. Le Hérissé, *L'ancien* . . . , 109; Herskovits, *Dahomey* . . . , 2:151, 302.

28. For Agbanakin, see Karl, *Traditions* . . . , 236. For Heve, see Verger, *Notas* . . . , 529, 541; and Herskovits, *Dahomey* . . . , 2:193.

29. Spieth, *Die Religion* . . . , 173, qtd. in Herskovits, *Dahomey* . . . , 2:193.

30. Fio Agbonon II, *Histoire* . . . , 164, 168; Verger, *Notas* . . . , 529.

31. Peel, "A Comparative . . . ," 275.

32. Merlo, "Hiérarchie . . . ," 6–8; Verger, Notas . . . , 105; Herskovits, Dahomey . . . , 2:188; Segurola, Dictionnaire . . . , 482.

33. Le Hérissé, L'ancien . . . , 108; Segurola, Dictionnaire . . . , 484; Verger, Notas . . . , 525–30.

34. Le Hérissé, L'ancien . . . , 108; Snelgrave, A New . . . , 101, 104. In 1851, Forbes describes a ceremony in which soldiers posted on the road between Abomey and Ouidah would fire their rifles in succession as "a salute to the Fetish of the Great Waters, or God of Foreign Trade" (Forbes, Dahomey . . . , 1:18). In 1860 human sacrifices to the sea were encouraged by King Glele from Abomey as part of the funeral ceremonies in praise of his father, Ghezo (Peter Bernasko, Ouidah, November 29, 1860, Archives of the Wesleyan Methodist Mission Society—SOAS). I am thankful to Robin Law for calling these references to my attention. See also Burton, A Mission . . . , 295.

35. *Humbono* Vicente, October 8, 1998.

36. Among the Jeje-Mahi of Bahia, the Kaviono family includes other voduns such as Zo (the fire vodun); Sogbo Baba Guidi (or So Baguidi, perhaps a phonetic evolution of Gbaguidi, the ruling family of Savalou. In Oyo, Verger [Notas . . . , 129] gives Baba Sigidi as a form of Exu associated with the *ilari* royal messengers); Jogorobossu (Jogoroboçú at Casa das Minas is the son of Zomadonu and thus belongs to the Davice family); Bossu (perhaps a phonetic evolution of Besu, a vodun of the thunder pantheon in Benin, or of *bossum*, a generic name for deities in the Akan territory. Maupoil [La géomancie . . . , 73] mentions Bosu Zoho as a Sakpata vodun, and in the Avimanje [Sakpata] temple in Ouidah, the vodun Bosú, guardian of the temple gate, is worshipped); Jokolatin (*joko atin*, the joko tree); and Betá Yoyo (or Beta Oyo). As far as I know, these secondary deities do not have devotees consecrated to them and do not manifest themselves in public festivals.

37. Everaldo Duarte, January 4, 1996, August 21, 1996, November 27, 1997.

38. J. de Carvalho, "Nação jeje," 51.

39. *Gaiaku* Luiza, in CEAO, 2º Encontro . . . , 81–82.

40. Rodrigues, Os africanos . . . , 230.

41. *O Alabama*, May 19, 1869, 3.

42. Rodrigues, Os africanos, 234.

43. *Gaiaku* Luiza, November 7, 1999.

44. *Gaiaku* Luiza, in CEAO, 2º Encontro . . . , 82.

45. In West Africa, the myth of the three wives of Xangô—Oiá, Oxum, and Oba—appears documented for the first time in 1858 in Bowen, A Grammar . . . , 16.

46. In the Gbe-speaking area, Averekete is considered the youngest son of Agbé and Naeté and as the youngest is reputed to be spoiled, cunning, capricious, and a trickster. Averekete is believed to be the messenger between humans and the gods and in the rituals is always at the front, opening the way for the other voduns; he likes to play, spread rumors, and comically mimic the other voduns (Herkovits, Dahomey . . . , 2:155, 158). Sharing with Legba the same ritual functionality and changing character, in the Jeje-Mahi terreiros of Bahia, Averekete is rarely praised in the sequence of songs dedicated to Sogbo, but he is never forgotten when Legba is sung to. This is perhaps a contributing factor to his persistence.

47. Bastide, Sociología . . . , 120–21. Bastide discusses, for example, how forced labor on the plantations favored the disappearance of agricultural deities who brought no

benefits to the slaves, and also how social inequality and oppression by masters favored the hegemony of deities of justice, such as Xangô; of war, such as Ogun; and of communication, such as Exu.

48. Verger, *Notas . . .*, 276; D. M. dos Santos, *História . . .*, 67–69.

49. According to some versions, Sakpata was imported from Dassa Zoumé, Adja Popo, or Aise, in the Hollidjé region. Verger, *Notas . . .*, 249–50, 272.

50. For example, a myth from the kingdom of Fitta, in the Mahi area, tells that the voduns Morou (Omolu), Dan, and Loko arrived from Adja-Popo and settled there in the time of the first King Oba Tchérékou ("Le royaume des Fittas," 78, 83). The same myth is cited in Bergé, "Étude . . . ," 724. However, it is important to note that Omolu is a Yoruba expression ("òmò òlù").

51. Verger, *Notas . . .*, 252.

52. *Gaiaku* Luiza, November 28, 1998; M. S. de A. Santos, *Meu tempo . . .*, 54.

53. For evidence of the regional diversity of the cult of Buruku, see Burton, *A Mission. . . .*, 297; Burton, *Abeokuta . . .*, 107; Ellis, *The Yoruba-Speaking . . .*, 73; Frobenius, *Mythologie . . .*, 191, 218; Verger, *Notas . . .*, 257–59. The fact that no iron knife is used for the sacrifices to Omolu and Nanã Buruku would indicate the existence of these cults previous to the Iron Age. This is a characteristic that is continued in the Nanã cults of Brazil and has been previously noted by Querino (*Costumes . . .*, 94). The topic is discussed in detail by Verger, *Notas . . .*, 272, 278.

54. Verger, *Notas . . .*, 274.

55. Ibid., 239–40; Y. P. de Castro, *Falares . . .*, 246; Rodrigues, *O animismo . . .*, 50.

56. Herskovits, *Dahomey . . .*, 2:101–2.

57. D. M. dos Santos, *História . . .*, 67.

58. Lepine, "As metamorfoses . . . ," 126–28; Verger, *Notas . . .*, 240; Le Hérissé, *L'ancien . . .*, 128; Herskovits, *Dahomey . . .*, 2:38.

59. Segurola, *Dictionnaire . . .*, 456.

60. *O Alabama*, October 29, 1870, 2; November 24, 1871, 4.

61. Rodrigues, *O animismo . . .*, 50. Saponan and Omolu are Nagô names. There is some doubt in the case of Wari-Warú and Afoma. Cacciatore attributes a Yoruba etymology to the latter: *afomó*, contagious or infectious: *Diccionario . . .*, 40. However, Verger documents a Sakpata song in Abomey that talks of Afomado Zogi (*Notas . . .*, 247).

62. These names are (1) Jagun Agbagba, (2) Omolu, (3) Obaluaye (literally, the "king of the earth"), (4) Soponna, (5) Afoman, (6) Savalu, (7) Dassa, (8) Arinwarun (the same Wari-Warú cited by Rodrigues), (9) Azonsu ou Ajansur, (10) Azoani, (11) Posun or Posuru (Kposu or Kpo, the panther vodun in his Sakpata quality), (12) Agoro (probably a confusion since Angorô is the snake god of the Angola), (13) Telu or Etutu (probably from the Nagô *ile titu*, the same as "cold ground"), (14) Topodun (probably a confusion given that Tokpodun is the crocodile vodun of the thunder or sea pantheon), (15) Paru, (16) Arawe (a place in Mahi country), (17) Ajoji (at Bogum there is memory of an Ojoji *vodunsi*, "a Jeje Omolu," perhaps of corruption of Daa Zodji), (18) Avimaje, (19) Ahoye, (20) Aruaje, and (21) Ahosuji (a corruption of the Fon term *ahosusi*, "wife of the king") (Verger, *Notas . . .*, 252). Other names for Sakpata are Jeholu (lord of pearls) or Ainon (lord of the earth).

63. In the early decades of the twentieth century, neither Rodrigues nor Querino

mention straw from West Africa (*palha da Costa*) when describing Omolu or Shapana (Rodrigues, *O animismo*..., 74; Querino, *Costumes*..., 38). In *Religiões negras*, published in 1936, Carneiro also does not broach the topic. It is only in *Candomblés da Bahia*, when Carneiro mentions that Omolu "always wears a hood of *palha da Costa* (*filá*), that falls to his shoulders and hides his face" (*Candomblés*..., 59). Pierson was the first author to comment on "the Omanlu [*sic*] initiates were dressed primarily in red tones. Fiber threads, belts of reddish brown, went from their heads to below the knees, completely covering the face" (*Brancos e pretos*..., 327).

64. Rodrigues, *O animismo*..., 50; Querino, *Costumes*..., 38–39; Carneiro, *Religiões*..., 40; Ortiz, *Los bailes*..., 216; Verger, *Notas*..., 258–50.

65. In the Gbe-speaking area, the Sakpata necklaces (*hunkan*) alternate pairs of white cowry shells with the black seeds of the *atinkuin* or *atekun* fruit. This is something that seems to have disappeared from the Jeje terreiros.

66. Carneiro, *Religiões*..., 59.

67. Ratis e Silva, "Exu-Obaluaiê..."; Lépine, "As metamorfoses..."; Caprara, "Médico...."

68. *Gaiaku* Luiza, in CEAO, *2º Encontro*..., 78.

69. File no. 1, CEAO, January 17, 1961; Neném de Mello, November 3, 1999.

70. "Letter from Father Bouche in Ouidah to the Father Superior in Porto Novo," *Archives de la Société des Missions Apostoliques*; ref. 20.393, rubric 12/80200, July 31, 1868, 3–4, qtd. in Matory, "Man...," 161–62.

71. Carneiro, *Religiões* (*Negros bantos*), 166–67. Pierson, *Brancos e pretos*..., 307. For a recollection from the 1940s on the pilgrimages of the members of Bogum to Saint Bartholomew Park, see Duarte, "O terreiro...," 19–22.

72. Everaldo Duarte, December 18, 1994.

73. Rodrigues, *Os africanos*..., 223.

74. Valdina Pinto, in CEAO, *2º Encontro*..., 56–57.

75. Ellis, *The Ewe-Speaking*..., 47–49; Verger, *Notas*..., 231, 235; Le Hérissé, *L'ancien*..., 118; Burton, *A Mission*..., 298; Hazoumé, *Le pacte*..., 143; Maupoil, *La géomancie*..., 73.

76. *Humbono* Vicente, December 6, 1998. The presence of Angorô in the Angola cult is documented since at least 1937 (Carneiro, *Religiões* [*Negros bantos*]..., 166–67). Braga mentions *angorossi* as a "form of praise in the Angola candomblés" (*Na gamela*..., 185).

77. Binon-Cossard, "Contribution," 24; cf. Bittremieux, "La société secrète des Bakhimba au Mayombé...," 245. For another etymology, see also Valdina Pinto, in CEAO, *2º Encontro*..., 56.

78. *Gaiaku* Luiza, in CEAO, *2º Encontro*..., 75, 82; J. de Carvalho, "Nação jeje...," 52. Waldeloir Rego (November 19, 1994) mentioned Abalu as a "form of Dan." There is also word of Toqüéni, perhaps a variant of Toquem. According to Waldeloir Rego, Toqüéni is a poisonous snake of the surucucu, or South American bushmaster, type. At Casa da Minas in São Luís, the term *toqüém* is used to denote the youngest voduns, children or adolescents, principally from the royal family of Davice, who come at the front, opening the way for those who are older, and they carry messages (Ferretti, *Querebentan*..., 307). According to Olga of Alaketo, "Tokuenu is not an entity. Tokuenu is a ritual that is done at the root of a tree and then come the senior qualified people, they come to lay on hands and such" (interview, January 3, 1996).

79. *Gaiaku* Luiza, in CEAO, *2º Encontro . . .*, 82.

80. File n.d., CEAO, 1960; Nancy de Souza e Silva, October 28, 98. Milton Moura, September 9, 2001.

81. Baudin, *Fetichism . . .*, 44, 47; Ellis, *The Ewe-Speaking . . .*, 47–48. Personal observation: Bafono and Euá rituals, Oxumaré Terreiro, August 18, 1996.

82. *Humbono* Vicente, October 20, 2000, November 12, 2001; *Gaiaku* Luiza, in CEAO, *2º Encontro . . .*, 72, 74. *Gaiaku* Luiza calls the cowry shells *ajés* and the necklaces of strung cowries, *balajás* (or *barajás*). The *balajás* are also attributes of Nanã, Azonsu, and Euá: *Gaiaku* Luiza, October 8, 2001. In Fon, *ajé* means "shells," derived from *jé*, pearl or bead (Segurola, *Dictionnaire . . .*, 34, 260).

83. Rodrigues, *Os africanos . . .*, 231–33.

84. Carneiro, *Religiões . . .*, 166–67; *Candomblé . . .*, 64–55; Ramos, "Introdução . . .," 12–13 (cf. Ramos, *O negro . . .*, 43; and Couto Ferraz, "Vestígios . . .," 271ff.).

85. Matory, "Jeje . . .," 66–67; Matory, *Black Atlantic . . .*, 87–89, 93, 96–98, 101–2. Matory takes up the idea endorsed by Dantas, adding that intellectuals such as Carneiro, familiar with the work of Herskovits on the religion of the Gbe-speaking area, could have passed information to the Jeje priests, contributing to the process of "revivalism." The supposed agency of intellectuals is not applicable in the context of the Jeje terreiros in the early decades of the twentieth century, since these houses received only occasional visits from intellectuals, and only after 1937.

86. See, among others, de Sandoval, *Naturaleza . . .*, qtd. in Gayibor, *Les peuples . . .* ; Bosman, *A New . . .*, 368a–82 ; Barbot, *A Description . . .*, 340–45; Labat, *Voyage . . .*, 2:163–99, Pommegorge, *Description . . .*, 195; Snelgrave, *A New . . .*, 11–12; Atkins, *A voyage . . .*, 113–18; Norris, *Memoirs . . .*, 69, 105; Duncan, *Travels . . .*, 1:126–28, 195–97; Burton, *A Mission . . .*, 73–76; Le Hérissé, *L'ancien . . .*, 110; Herskovits, *Dahomey . . .*, 2:240–55; Falcon, *Religion . . .*, 66–70; and Verger, *Notas . . .*, 503–16. On the induction of Dangbe as a Hueda deity, see Labat, *Voyage . . .*, 2:163; and Law, *The Kingdom*, 24–25.

87. Le Hérissé, *L'ancien . . .*, 118; Verger, *Notas. . .*, 105, 231, 235; Jacques Bertho, qtd. in Merlo, "Hiérarchie . . .," 12. Merlo and Vidaud, "Dangbé . . .," 287–90; Falcon, *Religion . . .*, 38; Bergé, "Étude . . .," 720–21, 724, 740. Ritual practices of the Nesuhue cult, involving the voduns Dan and Dambada Hwedo, were appropriated from the Agonli in the Mahi country. Given that the Nesuhue royal cult was established in Abomey in the eighteenth century, it is likely that the snake cult in the Mahi country dated from at least this time (Parés, "O triângulo . . .," 193ff. ; Verger, *Notas . . .*, 232). For Dambada Hwedo, see Herskovits, *Dahomey . . .*, 2:203, 207–8.

88. *O Alabama*, May 28, 1870, 3. There is also in the same newspaper a reference to a certain Luis Gomes da Saúde, "snake breeder" (December 10, 1870, 5). See also *Jornal da Bahia*, March 13, 1854, qtd. in Verger, *Fluxo . . .*, 532.

89. Querino, *Costumes . . .*, 37.

90. Baudin, *Fetichism . . .*, 37; Ellis, *The Ewe-Speaking . . .*, 83, 89.

91. Some authors identify Agué with Oxóssi (Verger, *Notas . . .*, 215).

92. Herskovits, *Dahomey . . .*, 2:107, 121; Verger, *Notas . . .*, 215–18. Frobenius, commenting on the orixá Enjille (Erinle, Inle, associated with Oxóssi), says that he is "represented by small figures of forged iron, in the form of a candelabrum on the point of which is a forged bird" (*Mythologie . . .*, 222).

93. Nancy de Souza e Silva, September 27, 2000.

94. *Gaiaku* Luiza, April 28, 2001.

95. *Humbono* Vicente, October 8, 1998, March 30, 1999, December 7, 1999. Herskovits, *Dahomey . . .*, 2:271.

96. Lühning, "O compositor . . .," 66.

97. Everaldo Duarte, August 10, 1996.

CHAPTER 8

1. *Seu* Geninho, March 5, 2000; *Ogã* Boboso, September 5, 2002.

2. Rodrigues, *Os africanos . . .*, 137, 139. Regarding the confusion between Jeje and Ewe, see, for example, the comments of Raul Lody in Querino, *Costumes . . .*, 81. Carneiro, *Candomblés . . .*, 44.

3. At Bogum, however, the *vodunsis* can perform the *dobale* before the *doné*. For commentary on the *dobale* and the *ikákó*, the *foíbalè* (gestures of praise and respect) of male and female orixás, respectively, see M. S. de A. Santos, *Meu tempo . . .*, 54–57.

4. Binon-Cossard, "Contribution," 12. Some people might even respond "colofé mi" or, if from the Angola nation, "colofé muzambi," expressions that certain Jeje religious experts find incorrect. The response "Olorum modokwé" seems to be an adaptation of "Olorun mo dupe" (thanks be to God), a classic response to every kind of salutation in Yoruba (Felix Ayoh Omidire, September 13, 2003). However, the use of the Fon word *kwé* (house) makes the expression translate to "may God receive you in his house."

5. *Benoi* perhaps comes from *gbenò*, which in Fon means master of life, creator of the world. From the Jeje-Savalu nation I found two possible blessings: (1) "se mina ho" (*Gaiaku* Luiza, December 17, 1998); and (2) "imbaloim," answered with "son fosu nafó" or, more likely, "so kposu apo" (*Humbono* Vicente, December 14, 1999, May 16, 2001). In Ketu, the expression "motubá" ("matubá") is currently used, with the answer being "motubaxe" ("matubaxé"); also used is "túmbá mi," answered with "túmbá ase, o."

6. *Gaiaku* Luiza, in CEAO, *2º Encontro . . .*, 77; and December 17, 1998.

7. Segurola, *Dictionnaire . . .*, 384.

8. Rodrigues, *Os africanos . . .*, 236; Segurola, *Dictionnaire . . .*, 408. Carneiro more correctly indicates the Nagô terms *ialorixá* and *babalorixá* as antecedents of *mãe-* and *pai-de-santo* (*Religiões . . .*, 56).

9. *Gaiaku* Luiza, in CEAO, *2º Encontro . . .*, 79.

10. Segurola, *Dictionnaire . . .*, 249.

11. *Humbono* Vicente, February 19, 1999.

12. J. de Carvalho, "Mundo jeje comemora cinqüentenário de sua mãe-de-santo," *A Tarde*, July 26, 1988.

13. Akindélé and Aguessy, "Contribution . . .," 114, qtd. in Lima, "A família-de-santo . . .," 134.

14. Duncan, *Travels . . .*, 1:101. In Bahia, *O Alabama* mentions a "papai Dothé," *olowo* or Fa fortune-teller (*O Alabama*, March 2, 1867, 3). In the Nesuhue cult in Abomey, the term *vodunsi hundoté* (literally, "deity's *vodunsi* standing up") is used to refer to those *vodunsis* consecrated to the vodun but relatively inexperienced (Adoukonou, *Jalons . . .*, 2:68, 191–95).

15. *Gaiaku* Luiza, in CEAO, *2º Encontro . . .*, 77; *pai-pequeno*, file no. 48, CEAO, 1966.

16. The last two terms are known in Cachoeira (*Ogã* Boboso, August 7, 2001). Bernardinho confirms *ogã minazon* as an *atabaque* drummer (August 18, 2001). The term *minazon* probably derives from *binàzón*, which in Fongbe means "he who commands all = minister of the finances and goods of the king" (Segurola, *Dictionnaire*...).

17. *Pai-pequeno*, a *filho-de-santo* of Pó Zerrem, additionally mentioned the titles *citoí* and *sinoí* as synonymous with *babalaxé* and *ialaxé* (*sic*), respectively, within the Jeje nation (*pai-pequeno*, file no. 48, CEAO, 1966). Another title known in Cachoeira is *ogã perê*, or the overseer of the *barracão*. This might be of Nagô origin.

18. Everaldo Duarte, September 30, 2002. In the Ketu terreiros, *dagan* means assistant to the *iamorô* (in charge of the *padé* ritual).

19. M. S. de A. Santos, *Meu tempo*..., 26, 28. For an analysis of Candomblé's hierarchical organization and the principle of seniority, see Lima, "A família-de-santo...," 49–118.

20. Verger, *Notas*..., 28. The Fon term *hun* is polysemic and, besides *atabaque* drum, means heart (for it too beats) and any kind of vehicle (boat or otherwise). The term *hunpevi*, used for the smallest drum, means the small (*kpe*) son (*vi*) of the drum (*hun*) (or the small son drum). In the Angola terreiros, the drums can be called *rum, contra-rum*, and *rumpi* (Binon-Cossard, *La musique*..., 160–79).

21. Rodrigues, *Os africanos*..., 160; Rodrigues, *O animismo*..., 80–81. Carneiro, *Religiões*..., 75. Regarding the use of *chocalhos* and *agogôs*, see Rodrigues, *Os africanos*..., 240, 248.

22. Verger, *Notas*..., 25.

23. During the time of Runhó, one drum was consecrated to Oxum, and another to Bogum (file no. 1, CEAO, 1961).

24. File no. 1, CEAO, 1961; Everaldo Duarte, August 31, 2002; Bernardinho, August 14, 1999, January 9, 2000; *Humbono* Vicente, November 29, 2000.

25. Verger, *Notas*..., 28.

26. Ortiz, *La africania*..., 374, 376, qtd. in Verger, *Notas*..., 25, 28, 29.

27. Joãozinho, January 7, 1996.

28. "The so-called time-line patterns [...] constitute a specific category of struck motional patterns, characterized by an asymmetric inner structure, such as 5 + 7 or 7 + 9. They are single-note patterns struck on a musical instrument of penetrating sound quality, such as a bell" (Kubik, *Theory*..., 44). In transcribing the time-lines I follow the conventional annotation system used by Kubik in which "/" marks the beginning of the rhythm cycle, and in which "x" (the beat), and "." (the silence) have the same duration.

29. Vatin, "Étude...." I am grateful to Xavier Vatin for the enlightening interview he granted me on June 27, 2001.

30. Ramos, *O negro*..., 163; Segurola, *Dictionnaire*..., 4. The *adahun* was a rhythm used to encourage the warriors before or during the wars and is still played in the vodun cults of Benin. See also Binon-Cossard, *La musique*..., 160–79; and Vatin, "Étude...."

31. In Fongbe a *satô* is a large drum that is part of certain funeral or recreational orchestras, whereas a *satò* is a courtyard area in front of the vodun convents or the royal palace (Segurola, *Dictionnaire*..., 457).

32. Vatin, "Étude..."; J. Sodré, *Música sacra do Candomblé*....

33. At Seja Hundé, the variation of the *quebrado* presents a change in the beat structure that I was unable to identify. At Huntoloji the time-line changes to the *avamunha* (or a

faster version), going from a six- to a twelve-pulse cycle. Whereas the *mundubi* time-line at Seja Hundé becomes a "/x.x.x./" beat, at Huntoloji the sequence is more complex and again I was unable to identify it precisely.

34. Olga of Alaketo, interview, January 3, 1996; Waldeloir Rego, December 31, 1995.

35. Van Gennep, *Rites . . .* ; V. W. Turner, *The Ritual . . .* For descriptions of different initiation rituals of the Gbe-speaking area, see Verger, *Notas . . .*, 81–118; and Herskovits, *Dahomey . . .*, 2:111–26, 162–66, 178–90. I use the feminine to refer to the initiated person because women make up the majority of devotees in Candomblé and the vodun religion, but it is important to note that men may also be initiated as *vodunsis*.

36. Verger, *Notas . . .*, 82, 105.

37. *Gaiaku* Luiza, December 25, 1994, August 20, 1996.

38. *Gaiaku* Luiza, August 17, 2002; *Ogã* Boboso, September 7, 2002. However, *O Alabama* documents the case of a Bogum woman being initiated, "in the act of performing the *sapocan*, a ceremony that consists in *cutting the hair* and only being able to cross the threshold of the house *after six months*" (*O Alabama*, April 14, 1869, 1; emphasis added). Other reports from *O Alabama* (i.e., March 6, 1867, 2–3; December 24, 1870, 5; November 11, 1871, 4) rather close-mindedly describe aspects of the initiation in other Jeje terreiros, denouncing hygienic conditions, sexual exploitation, ill treatment, and even eventual deaths resulting from punishments.

39. *Gaiaku* Luiza, December 25, 1994; *Humbono* Vicente, May 4, 1999, May 16, 1901.

40. *Gaiaku* Luiza, December 25, 1994.

41. *Humbono* Vicente, November 13, 1999, October 20, 2000. Glélé, *Le Danxomé . . .*, 75; Hazoumé, *Le pacte. . . .* In Benin, *hunve*, literally "red deity," refers to a category of voduns represented by an *aciná* (a type of shrine) and called *atinmevodun*. This category includes the panther-voduns Ajahuto and Agasu, and others such as Loko, Massé, and so on.

42. *Gaiaku* Luiza, August 20, 1996; *Humbono* Vicente, November 29, 2000; Everaldo Duarte, April 21, 1999.

43. Binon-Cossard, "Contribution," 206.

44. In a similar ritual observed in Ouidah (in the temple of Avimanje, July–September, 1995), it was the priest who called out the names of the new *vodunsi* and not the vodun. The public presentation of the novices occurred in three ceremonies, each more than a month apart.

45. *Humbono* Vicente, November 29, 2000; Waldeloir Rego, December 31, 1995.

46. *O Alabama*, November 11, 1871, 4.

47. For a description of the *purchase of the iaôs* in 1942 in a Bahian Ketu house, see Herskovits, "The Panan . . . ," 133–40. See also Marques, *O feiticeiro . . .*, 109.

48. One year after initiation, a *vodunsi* may remove the *quelê*, a necklace tied around the neck symbolizing submission to the entity (*Gaiaku* Luiza, December 25, 1994).

49. For an analysis of the memory of slavery in religious ritual, see Parés, "Memories. . . ."

50. Carneiro, *Candomblés . . .*, 141. *Humbono* Vicente, August 22, 1999. *Ogo* is a stick in Yorubá. For further information on the *quitanda*, see Bastide, *Imagens . . .*, 61–62.

51. Binon-Cossard, "Contribution," 188, 207.

52. In 1961 Runhó gave the following sequence (the date being in parenthesis): Oxalá (January 1); Azana Odo (January 6); Sogbo (the following Sunday); Bessen (eight days later). During the middle of the week the *yabas* and other saints were celebrated: file

no. 1, CEAO, January 27, 1961. The 1973 calendar was Olissá (January 1); Azounoodor (January 7); Bafono Decá (January 10); Obessein (January 14); Ogun and Agangatolú (January 18); Loco (January 21); Sogbô (January 23); Tobosse (January 28); Badé (February 4); and Ojonsu (Azonsu) (February 11); J. de Carvalho (unidentified newspaper), December 31. The 2003 calendar was Olisá (January 1–5); Zonodor (January 7); Bessen (January 12); Loko (January 19); Ogun, Agangatolu, and Ague (January 26); Sogbo (January 29); Tobosi (February 2); Ibeji (February 9); and Ojonsu, Nana (February 16–18).

53. Among the vodun cults of the Gbe-speaking area, however, Legba does have devotees consecrated to him (*Legbasi*). For an analysis of this question in relation to Exu in Brazil, see Capone, *La quête . . .*, 81–87.

54. Peixoto, *Obra nova . . .*, 32. Pruneau de Pommegorge, who was in Ouidah from 1743 to 1765, gives the first reference to Legba, speaking of the "Priapus god" (*Description . . .*, 201). In 1804, the Dahomean king Adadozan writes of "my great God Leba" (Verger, *Os libertos . . .*, 106; Verger, *Fluxo . . .*, 273, 288). In 1845, d'Avezac mentions *Elegwa* in relation to the religion of the Ijebu ("Notice . . .," 84, qtd. in Verger, *Notas . . .*, 133–34). Bowen, in 1852, provides the first reference to *Esu*, in Abeokuta (*A Grammar . . .*, 16).

55. *O Alabama*, November 21, 1871.

56. *Humbono* Vicente, June 30, 1999, December 28, 1999, October 20, 2000.

57. Verger cites the *Ògún bèrèke* tree (*Delonix regia*, Leguminosae) among those in which the *iamis* perch ("Grandeza . . .," 71). Capone documents the orixá Oloque or Oloroquê, the patron deity of the Efon (*La quête . . .*, 126–27 and illustration no. 5).

58. For further details on the *padé*, see J. E. dos Santos, *Os nagô . . .*, 184–95; and Capone, *La quête . . .*, 76–79. For more information on the Oxoronga *iamis*, see Verger, "Grandeza . . .," 13–72; and Capone, *La quête . . .*, 78–81.

59. Verger, *Notas . . .*, 49, 553; Le Hérissé, *L'ancien . . .*, 274–77; Segurola, *Dictionnaire . . .*, 32.

60. Herskovits, *Dahomey . . .*, 1:208.

61. *Humbono* Vicente, December 28, 1999. Some consider Aizan to be a sick woman who takes care of the dead (*Gaiaku* Luiza, January 3, 2000).

62. I attended the ritual at Seja Hundé on December 25, 1999, and January 6, 2001, and at Huntoloji on January 20, 2001.

63. Hypolite Brice Sogbossi, personal communication, January 6, 2001.

64. The description of the *zandró* is based on observations at Seja Hundé (January 6, 1996; January 8, 1999; December 25, 1999; January 8, 2000; January 6, 2001) and at Huntoloji (January 23, 1999; January 30, 1999; January 20, 2001).

65. Many names were given me for this liquid: *degué, padé, amia, ifun,* and *eko* (the last is *acaçá* mixed with water). For the Efon nation, see Capone, *La quête . . .*, 77.

66. Phonetic versions freely transcribed from the songs of *Humbono* Vicente (interview, January 13, 1999) and from the *zandró* of the *boitá* at Huntoloji (January 30, 1999). The time-line of the *ferro* is "/x.xxx./" and matches the *sató* rhythm. At Seja Hundé I heard another variation, perhaps "/xxx.xx.xx./."

67. The song sequence at Huntoloji reveals some variation in its order; I also found some choreography not seen at Seja Hundé.

68. Segurola, *Dictionnaire . . .*, 626–27. I am grateful to Hypolite Brice Sogbossi for calling this to my attention.

69. At Huntoloji, devotees sometimes sing to Nanã before Sogbo, during the *yabas* (female deities) segment. Among the Jeje-Savalu at the Inlegedá Jigemin terreiro, the order is Ogun, Oxóssi (Agangatolu), Agué, Bessen, Azonsu, Sogbo, Oiá, Tobosi, Nanã, Oxalá.

70. The *hun do dji* or *e no do hun ji* (let's suspend drum) is the ritual segment in which the *huntó* (the head drummer) is asked to begin the drum beats, but the term, by extension, also designates the complex series of private rituals that precede the *zandró* or *dohué* (Basil Semasu, Abomey, August 11, 1995; Olivier Semasu, Ouidah, September 18, 1995).

71. Basil Semasu, Abomey, August 11, 1995.

72. Formerly the *boitá* was carried by Aguesi at Seja Hundé (Geninho, January 28, 2001). But the vodun Agué "always goes with Ogun."

73. I witnessed the *boitá* at Seja Hundé on January 9, 1999, and January 9, 2000, and at Huntoloji on January 31, 1999, and January 28, 2001.

74. Version transcribed from the *boitá* celebrated at Huntoloji on January 31, 1999. Variants of the first verse of this song are "hena hero eta kaio" and "hena heno eta va yo"; Huntoloji, January 28, 2001. Or even, "ena ero ita kaia" and "eno du vodun ita, eno beto esi": *Humbono* Vicente, February 4, 1999, April 28, 1999.

75. *Gaiaku* Luiza, in CEAO, *2º Encontro . . .*, 77, 78; *Humbono* Vicente, February 4, 1999.

76. Milton Moura, September 1, 2001.

77. *Gaiaku* Luiza, in CEAO, *2º Encontro . . .*, 80.

78. J. de Carvalho, "Nação jeje . . . ," 53. See also "Locose toma assento na cadeira de Ruinho," *A Tarde*, January 6, 1979; J. de Carvalho, "Mundo jeje comemora cinqüentenário de sua mãe-de-santo," *A Tarde*, July 26, 1988.

79. *Equede* Santa, Salvador, interview, 1981. Menininha was born on February 10, 1894 (D. F. da Silva, "A morte . . ."). The information on the name of Salaco comes from Vivaldo da Costa Lima, personal communication, August 10, 1999.

80. J. de Carvalho, "Nação jeje . . . ," 53.

81. Lody, *Ao som . . .*, 47; *Gaiaku* Luiza, February 17, 1998; Nenem de Mello, January 7, 2003.

82. *Humbono* Vicente, November 13, 1999.

83. Lima, "A família-de-santo . . . ," 21, 43. Everaldo Duarte also suggests a possible relation between Azonodo and Azoani, but he does not identify them (April 21, 1999).

84. Rego, "Mitos . . . ," 186. Segurola, *Dictionnaire . . .*, 84. Other, more questionable, interpretations associate Azonodo with a vodun related to heavenly bodies, or with Sogbo: *Ogã* Boboso, December 18, 1998; J. de Carvalho, "Nação jeje . . . ," 53.

85. Avimanjenon, Ouidah, November 24, 2001.

86. Everaldo Duarte, August 31, 2002.

87. "Mataram árvore africana adorada no terreiro Gêge," unidentified newspaper and date, 1978; J. de Carvalho, "Nação jeje . . . ," 54.

88. Lody, *Ao som . . .*, 47.

89. *Equede* Santa, Salvador, interview, 1981.

90. Everaldo Duarte, April 21, 1999.

91. *O Alabama*, November 24, 1871, 4.

92. For a more detailed study of this section's topic, see Parés, "O triângulo. . . ."

93. Semasusi, Ouidah, interview, October 4, 1995. Azilinon, Ouidah, interview, September 20, 1995.

94. For an analysis of the *bɔ̀* (or *gbo*) in the Gbe-speaking area, see Blier, *African . . .*, 2–4, and chap. 2.

95. Aguesi, August 10, 1996; *Gaiaku* Luiza, November 28, 1998, December 17, 1998. Some consider Kaia or Kaiala to be the Angola name for Iemanjá, indicating yet again the Jeje-Angola interpenetration.

96. Aguesi, August 10, 1996. On Azili in Haiti, see Gleason, "Report . . . ," 28; Métraux, *Le vaudou . . .*, 78, 97.

97. Querino, *Costumes . . .*, 37.

98. The description is based on the rituals performed at Huntoloji on February 2, 1999, and at Seja Hundé on January 12, 2000.

99. *O Alabama*, March 6, 1867; February 16, 1869, 2–3.

100. *O Alabama*, May 10, 1867; March 19, 1869, 2–3.

101. *Ogã* Boboso, September 25, 2000; Everaldo Duarte, August 30, 2003.

102. Francisco Viana, "Ritual da guerra fecha candomblés após o carnaval," *A Tarde*, February 17, 1973. Cacciatore presents two possible etymologies: (1) has departed (*lo*), is ready for war (*rogun*), or (2) festival (*olórò*) of war (*ogun*) (*Dicionário . . .*, 165).

103. *Gaiaku* Luiza, February 16, 1999, February 14, 1999, April 2, 2000; *Humbono* Vicente, February 19, 1999.

104. Segurola, *Dictionnaire . . .*, 200; Peixoto, *Obra nova . . .*, 18; Correia Lopes, "O pessoal . . . ," 47.

105. *Gaiaku* Luiza, August 20, 1996, June 22, 1999, June 25, 1999; *Humbono* Vicente, August 22, 1999.

BIBLIOGRAPHY

Abraham, R. C. *Dictionary of Modern Yoruba*. London: University of London Press, 1958.

Adoukonou, Barthélemy. *Jalons pour une théologie africaine: Éssai d'une herméneutique chrétienne du Vodun dahoméen*. Paris: Lethielleux, Le Sycomore, 1980.

Aguessy, Honorat. "Convergences religieuses dans les sociétés aja, éwé et yoruba sur la côte du Bénin." In *Peuples du Golfe du Bénin (Aja-Éwé)*, edited by François de Medeiros, 235–40. Paris: Karthala, 1984.

Ajayi, J. F. A. de. "Nineteenth-Century Origins of Nigerian Nationalism." *Journal of the Historical Society of Nigeria* 2 (1961): 196–211.

Akindélé, A., and Aguessy, C. "Contribution à l'étude de l'histoire de l'ancien royaume de Porto-Novo." *Mémoire de l'Institut Français d'Afrique Noire* 25. Dakar: IFAN, 1953.

Akinjogbin, I. A. *Dahomey and Its Neighbours, 1708–1818*. Cambridge: Cambridge University Press, 1967.

Albuquerque, Wlamyra Ribeiro de. "Esperanças de boaventuras: Construções da África e africanismos na Bahia (1887–1910)." *Estudos Afro-Asiáticos* 24, no. 2 (January 2002): 215–45.

Amaral, Braz do. "As tribos negras importadas. Estudo etnográfico, sua distribuição regional no Brasil." In *Estudos sobre a escravidão negra*, edited by Dantas Silva. Recife: Fundação Joaquim Nabuco, Massangana, 1988 (1915).

Anais do Arquivo Público da Bahia (AAPBa). "Livro de tutelas e inventários da Vila de São Francisco do Conde," no. 37 (n.d.).

———. "Devassa do levante de escravos ocorrido em Salvador em 1835," no. 38 (1968): 131–35; no. 40 (1971): 9–170; no. 53 (1996): 9–198; no. 54 (1996): 9–322.

Andrade, Maria José de Souza. *A mão-de-obra escrava em Salvador, 1811–1860*. Salvador: Corrupio, 1988 (1975).

Antonil, André João. *Cultura e opulência do Brasil por suas drogas e minas*. São Paulo, Rio de Janeiro, n.p., 1923 (1706).

Apter, Andrew. *Black Critics and Kings: The Hermeneutics of Power in Yoruba Society*. Chicago: University of Chicago Press, 1992.

———. "Notes on Orisha Cults in the Ekiti Yoruba Highlands." *Cahiers d'Études Africaines*, 138–39, XXXV-2-3 (1995): 369–401.

Asiwaju, A. I. "The Aja-Speaking Peoples in Nigeria: A Note on Their Origin, Settlement and Cultural Adaptation up to 1945." In *Peuples du Golfe du Bénin (Aja-Éwé)*, edited by François de Medeiros, 87–102. Paris: Karthala, 1984.

Atkins, John. *A Voyage to Guinea, Brazil, & the West Indies in His Majesty's Ships, the Swallow and Weymouth, Describing the Several Islands and Settlements*. London: Frank Cass, 1970 (1735).

Aufederheide, Patricia. "Order and Violence: Social Deviance and Social Control in Brazil, 1780–1840." Ph.D. diss., University of Minnesota, 1976.

Bancolé, Alexis, and Gilles Raoul Soglo. "Porto Novo et la traite négrière." In *Le Bénin et la Route de l'Esclave*. Cotonou: ONEPI, 1994.

Banton, Michael. *Racial and Ethnic Competition*. Cambridge: Cambridge University Press, 1983.

Barbosa, Manoel de Aquino. *Efemérides da Freguezia de Nossa Senhora da Conceição da Praia*. Salvador, n.p., 1970.

———. *Retalhos de um arquivo*. Salvador, n.p., 1972.

Barbot, Jean. *A Description of the Coasts of North and South Guinea; and of Ethiopia Inferior, Vulgarly Angola: Being a New and Accurate Account of the Western Maritime Countries of Africa*. London, n.p., 1732.

———. *Barbot on Guinea: the Writings of Jean Barbot on West Africa, 1678–1712*. 2 vols. Edited by Paul Hair, Adam Jones, and Robin Law. London: Hakluyt Society, 1992.

Barickman, B. J. *A Bahian Counterpoint: Sugar, Tobacco, Cassava and Slavery in the Recôncavo, 1780–1860*. Stanford, Calif.: Stanford University Press, 1998.

———. "Até a véspera: O trabalho escravo e a produção de açúcar nos engenhos do Recôncavo baiano (1850–1881)." *Afro-Ásia*, nos. 21–22 (1998–99): 177–238.

Barlei, Gaspari. *Res gestae Mauritii in Brasília*. Amsterdam, 1647 [or Barléus, Gaspar. *Rerum per Octennium in Brasilien*. Clèves, 1660, Portuguese translation by Ministry of Education and Health, Rio de Janeiro, 1940].

Barnes, Sandra T. *Africa's Ogun: Old World and New*. Bloomington: Indiana University Press, 1997 (1989).

Barth, Fredrik. "Grupos étnicos e suas fronteiras." In *Teorias da etnicidade*, edited by P. Poutignat and J. Streiff-Fenart, 187–227. São Paulo: Editora UNESP, 1997 [originally published as *Ethnic Groups and Boundaries: The Social Organization of Cultural Difference*. London: George Allen and Unwin, 1969].

Bastide, Roger. *Imagens do Nordeste místico em branco e preto*. Rio de Janeiro: Cruzeiro, 1945.

———. *Sociología de la religión*. Madrid: Jucar, 1986 [originally published as *Les religions africaines au Brésil*, 1960].

———. *Les Amériques noires: Les civilisations africaines dans le Nouveau Monde*. Paris: Payot, 1967.

Baudin, R. P. *Fetichism and Fetish Worshippers*. New York, n.p., 1885.

Bay, Edna G. *Wives of the Leopard: Gender, Politics and Culture in the Kingdom of Dahomey*. Charlottesville: University of Virginia Press, 1998.

Bergé, J. A. M. A. R. "Étude sur le Pays Mahi (1926–1928)." *Bulletin du Comité d'Études Historiques et Scientifiques de l'Afrique Occidentale Française* 11, no. 4 (October–December 1928).

Binon-Cossard, Gisèle. *La musique dans le Candomblé*. Paris: Ocora, 1967.

———. "Contribution à l'étude des candomblés au Brésil: Le candomblé angola." Ph.D. diss. Paris, 1979.

Bittremieux, Léo. *La société secrète des Bakhimba au Mayombe*. Bruxelles : Falk fils, 1936.

Blier, Suzanne Preston. *African Vodun: Arts, Psychology and Power*. Chicago: University of Chicago Press, 1995.

————. "The Path of the Leopard: Motherhood and Majesty in Early Danhomè." *Journal of African History*, 36 (1995).

Boddy, Janice. *Wombs and Alien Spirits: Women, Men and the Zar Cult in Northern Sudan*. Madison: University of Wisconsin Press, 1989.

Bolouvi, Lébéné Philippe. *Nouveau dictionnaire étymologique afro-brésilien: Afro-brasilérismes d'origine Éwé-Fon et Yoruba*. Lomé: Presses de l'Université du Bénin, 1994.

Borghero, Francesco. "Relation sur l'établissement des missions dans le vicariat apostolique du Dahomey." *Annales de la Propagation de la Foi* 36 (1964).

————. *Journal de Francesco Borghero, premier missionnaire du Dahomey, 1861–1865*. Paris: Karthala, 1997.

Bosman, William. *A New and Accurate Description of the Coast of Guinea*. London: Frank Cass, 1967 (1704).

Bouche, Abbé P. *La Côte des esclaves et le Dahomey*. Paris: Plon, Nourrit, 1885.

Bowen, T. J. *A Grammar and Dictionary of the Yoruba Language*. Washington, D.C.: Smithsonian Institution, 1858.

Bowser, Frederick P. *The African Slave in Colonial Peru, 1524–1650*. Stanford, Calif.: Stanford University Press, 1974.

Braga, Julio. *Na gamela do feitiço: Repressão e resistência nos candomblés da Bahia*. Salvador: Editora da Universidade Federal da Bahia, 1995.

Brásio, Antonio. *Monumenta missionaria africana*. 14 vols. 1st ser. Lisbon, n.p., 1952–85.

Burton, Richard. *Abeokuta and the Camaroons Mountains: An Exploration*. London: Tinsley Brothers, 1863.

————. *A Mission to Gelélé King of Dahome*. London: Routledge & Kegan Paul, 1966 (1864).

Butler, Kim. D. *Freedoms Given, Freedoms Won: Afro-Brazilians in Post-Abolition São Paulo and Salvador*. New Brunswick, N.J.: Rutgers University Press, 1998.

Cacciatore, Olga Gudolle. *Dicionário de cultos afro-brasileiros*. Rio de Janeiro: Forense Universitária,1977.

Campos, João da Silva. "Tradições bahianas." *Revista do Instituto Histórico e Geográfico*, no. 56 (1930).

————. "Procissões tradicionais da Bahia." *AAPBa*, no. 27 (1941): 252–518.

————. "Ligeiras notas sobre a vida íntima, costumes, e religião dos africanos na Bahia." *AAPBa*, no. 29 (1943 [1937]).

Capo, Hounkpati B. C. *Comparative Phonology of Gbe*. New York: Foris, 1991.

Capone, Stefania. *La quête de l'Afrique dans le Candomblé: Pouvoir et tradition au Brésil*. Paris: Karthala, 1999.

Caprara, Andréa. "Médico ferido: Omolu nos labirintos da doença." In *Antropologia da saúde: Traçando identidade e explorando fronteiras*, edited by Paulo César Alves and Miriam Cristina Rabelo. Rio de Janeiro: Relume-Dumará, 1998.

Carneiro, Edison. *Candomblés da Bahia*. Salvador: Ediouro, 1985 (1948).

————. *Religiões negras e Negros bantos*. Rio de Janeiro: Civilização Brasileira, 1991 (1937).

Carneiro da Cunha, Maria Manuela. "Etnicidade: Da cultura residual mas irredutível." *Revista de Cultura e Política* 1, no. 1 (1979): 35–39.

———. *Negros, estrangeiros: Os escravos libertos e sua volta à África.* São Paulo: Brasiliense, 1985.

Carvalho, Jehová de. "Nação jeje." In *Encontro de nações-de-candomblé,* 49–58. Salvador: Inamá, Centro de Estudos Afro-Orientais, 1984.

———. *Reinvenção do reino dos voduns.* Salvador: Littera, 1989–91.

Carvalho, José Murilo. *Teatro de sombras.* Rio de Janeiro: Editora da Universidade Federal do Rio de Janeiro, Relume-Dumará, 1996.

Castro, José Guilherme da Cunha, ed. *Miguel Santana.* Salvador: Editora da Universidade Federal da Bahia, 1996.

Castro, Yeda Pessoa de. "Língua e nação de candomblé." *África,* no. 4 (1981): 57–77.

———. *A presença cultural negro-africana no Brasil: Mito e realidade.* Salvador: Centro de Estudos Afro-Orientais, 1981.

———. *Falares africanos na Bahia (Um vocabulário afro-brasileiro).* Rio de Janeiro: Academia Brasileira das Letras, Topbooks, 2001.

———. *A língua mina-jeje no Brasil: Um falar africano em Ouro Preto do século XVIII.* Belo Horizonte: Fundação João Pinheiro, Secretaria de Estado da Cultura, 2002.

Castro, Yeda Pessoa de, and Guilherme A. de Souza Santos Castro. "Culturas africanas nas Américas: Um esboço de pesquisa conjunta da localização dos empréstimos." Paper presented at FESTAC, Lagos, 1977.

Centro de Estudos Afro-Orientais (CEAO). "Pesquisa sobre os candomblés de Salvador," directed by Vivaldo da Costa Lima (113 files). Salvador, CEAO, Universidade Federal da Bahia, 1960–69.

———. *2o Encontro de Nações de Candomblé (Salvador, 1995).* Salvador: Centro de Estudos Afro-Orientais, 1997.

Cohen, Abner, ed. *Urban Ethnicity.* London: Tavistock, 1974.

Cornevin, Robert. *Histoire du Dahomey.* Paris: Berger-Levrault, 1962.Correia Lopes, Edmundo. "O pessoal gêge." *Revista do Brasil,* 1940, 44–47.

———. "Exéquias no bogum do Salvador." *O Mundo Português,* no. 109 (1943): 559–67.

———. "Os trabalhos de Costa Peixoto e a língua evoe no Brasil." In António da Costa Peixoto, *Obra nova da língua geral de Mina.* Lisbon: Agência Geral das Colônias, 1945.

———. "A propósito de A Casa das Minas." *Atlântico: Revista Luso-Brasileira,* n.s., no. 5 (1948).

Costa, Ana de Lourdes Ribeiro da. "Ekabó: Trabalho escravo, condições de moradia e reordenamento urbano em Salvador no século XIX." M.A. thesis, Universidade Federal da Bahia, Salvador, 1989.

Costa e Silva, Alberto da. *A manilha e o libambo: A África e a escravidão de 1500 a 1700.* Rio de Janeiro: Nova Fronteira, Fundação Biblioteca Nacional, 2002.

Couto Ferraz, Aydano do. "Vestígios de um culto daomeano no Brasil." *Revista do Arquivo Municipal* (São Paulo), year 7, vol. 76 (May 1941): 271.

Craemer, Willy de, Jan Vansina, and Renée C. Fox. "Religious Movements in Central Africa: A Theoretical Study." *Comparative Studies in Society and History* 18, no. 4 (1976): 458–75.

Cuche, Denys. *A noção de cultura nas ciências sociais.* Bauru: Editora da Universidade do Sagrado Coração, 1999.

Curto, José C. "The Story of Nbena, 1817–1820: Unlawful Enslavement and the Concept of 'Original Freedom' in Angola." In *Trans-Atlantic Dimensions of Ethnicity in the African Diaspora*, edited by Paul E. Lovejoy and David V. Trotman, 44–64. London: Continuum, 2003.

d'Albeca, A. L. "Essai sur les langues jedji et mina parlées au Dahomey et dans les établissements." In *Les établissements français du Golfe de Bénin*. Paris: Librairie Militaire de L. Baudoin et Cie., 1889.

Dalzel, Archibald. *The History of Dahomy, an Inland Kingdom of Africa*. London: Frank Cass, 1967 (1793).

Dantas, Beatriz Góis. "Pureza e poder no mundo dos candomblés." In *Candomblé: Desvendando identidades (Novos estudos sobre a religião dos orixás)*, edited by Carlos Eugênio Marcondes de Moura, 121–28. São Paulo: EMW, 1987.

———. *Vovó nagô e papai branco: Usos e abusos da África no Brasil*. Rio de Janeiro: Graal, 1988 (1982).

Dapper, Olfert. *Naukeurie Beschrijvinge der Afrikaensche Gewesten*, 2nd ed. Amsterdam, n.p., 1676 (1668).

d'Avezac, M. "Notice sur le pays et le peuple des Yébous en Afrique." In *Mémoire de la Société d'Éthnologie*. Paris: Veuve Dondey-Dupré, 1845.

de Marees, Pieter. *Description and Historical Account of the Gold Kingdom of Guinea (1602)*. Translated and edited by Albert van Dantzig and Adam Jones. Oxford: Oxford University Press, 1988.

de Sandoval, Alonso. *Naturaleza, policia sagrada i profana, costumbres i ritos, disciplina i catechismo evangelico de todos Etiopes*. Seville, n.p., 1627.

Debret, Jean B. *Voyage pittoresque et historique au Brésil au séjour d'un artiste français au Brésil depuis 1816 jusqu'en 1834 inclusivement*. Paris: Firmin-Didot Frères, 1835.

Desribes, E. *L'Évangile au Dahomey et à la Côte des esclaves, ou Histoire des missions africaines de Lyon*. Clermont-Ferrand: Imprimerie Centrale, Meneboode, 1877.

Dias do Nascimento, Luiz Cláudio. *A Capela d'Ajuda já deu o sinal: Relações de poder e religiosidade em Cachoeira*. Cachoeira: Centro de Estudos Afro-Orientais, 1995.

———. *Candomblé e Irmandade da Boa Morte*. Cachoeira: Fundação Maria América da Cruz, 1999.

——— "Presença do Candomblé na Irmandade da Boa Morte." M.A. thesis, Universidade Federal da Bahia, Salvador, 2001.

Dissou, M. I. "Essai de reconnaissance et de détermination de l'origine des principales familles yoruba de Porto Novo à partir de leur 'Oriki.'" *Études Dahoméennes*, n.s., no. 13. Porto Novo: IRAD, 1969.

Drewal, Margaret Thompson. "Dancing for Ògún in Yorubaland and Brazil." In *Africa's Ogun: Old World and New*, edited by Sandra T. Barnes, 199–234. Bloomington: Indiana University Press, 1997.

Duarte, Everaldo. "O terreiro do Bogum e o Parque São Bartolomeu." In *Parque Metropolitano de Pirajá: História, natureza e cultura*, edited by Ana Luzia Menezes Formigli et al., 19–22. Salvador: Centro de Educação Ambiental São Bartolomeu, 1998.

Duncan, John. *Travels in Western Africa in 1845 and 1846*. 2 vols. London: Johnson Reprint; New York: Richard Bentley, 1967 (1847).

Dunglas, Édouard. "Contribution à l'histoire du Moyen Dahomey." *Études Dahoméennes*, nos. 19–21. Porto Novo: IRAD, 1957–1958.

Durkheim, Émile. *Les formes élémentaires de la vie religieuse.* Paris: Quadrige, PUF, 1998 (1960).

Eduardo, Otavio da Costa. *The Negro in Northern Brazil: A Study in Acculturation.* Seattle: University of Washington Press, 1966 (1948).

Ellis, Alfred B. *The Ewe-Speaking Peoples of the Slave Coast of West Africa.* London: Chapman & Hall, 1890.

———. *The Yoruba-Speaking Peoples of the Slave Coast of West Africa.* London: Chapman & Hall, 1894.

Eltis, David. "The Volume and Structure of the Transatlantic Slave Trade: A Reassessment." Paper presented at "Enslaving Connections: Africa and Brazil during the Era of the Slave Trade," York University, October 2000.

Eltis, David, Stephen D. Behendt, and David Richardson. "A participação dos países da Europa e das Américas no tráfico transatlântico de escravos: Novas evidências." *Afro-Ásia*, no. 24 (2000): 9–50.

Eltis, David, Stephen D. Behendt, David Richardson, and Herbert S. Klein, eds. *The Transatlantic Slave Trade: A Database on CD-ROM.* Cambridge: Cambridge University Press, 1999.

Eriksen, Thomas Hylland. *Ethnicity and Nationalism.* London: Pluto, 1993.

"Étude sur la région de Holli-Ketou." *Mémoire du Benin (Matériaux d'histoire)*, no. 2 (1993 [1936–38]): 11–26.

Falcon, R. P. Paul. "Religion du vodun." *Études Dahoméennes*, n.s., nos. 18–19. Porto Novo: IRAD, 1970.

Faria, Sara Oliveira. "Irmãos de cor, de caridade e de crença: A Irmandade do Rosário do Pelourinho na Bahia do século XIX." M.A. thesis, Universidade Federal da Bahia, Salvador, 1997.

Ferretti, Sérgio Figueiredo. *Querebentan de Zomadonu: Etnografia da Casa das Minas do Maranhão.* São Luís: Editora da Universidade Federal do Maranhão, 1996 (1985).

Figueira, Luiz. *Africa Bantu: Raças e tribos angola.* Lisbon, n.p., 1938.

Fio Agbonon II. *Histoire de Petit Popo et du royaume Guin.* Edited by N. L. Gayibor. Lomé: Université du Benin, 1984 (1934).

Forbes, Frederick E. *Dahomey and the Dahomans.* 2 vols. London: Longman, Brown, Green and Longmans, 1851.

Freyre, Gilberto. *Casa-grande e senzala.* Rio de Janeiro: Record, 1999 (1933).

Frézier, A. F. *Relation d'un voyage de la mer au sud des côtes du Chili, du Pérou et du Brésil, fait pendant les années 1712, 1713 et 1714.* Amsterdam, n.p., 1717.

Frobenius, Léo. *Mythologie de l'Atlantide.* Paris: Payot, 1949.

Gadmer, Frédéric. *Dahomey Mission: R. P. Aupiais–Frédéric Gadmer.* Boulogne: Archives de la Planète, Musée Albert Kahn, 1929–1930, Religion section, film.

Gavoy. "Note historique sur Ouidah par l'Administrateur Gavoy (1913)." *Études Dahoméennes*, no. 8. Porto Novo: IRAD, 1955 (1913).

Gayibor, Nicoué Lodjou. *Les peuples et royaumes du Golfe du Benin.* Lomé: Université du Bénin, 1986.

Geertz, Clifford. *Old Societies and New States: The Quest of Modernity in Asia and Africa*. Glencoe, Ill.: Free Press, 1963.

———. *A interpretação das culturas*. Rio de Janeiro: LTC, 1989.

Giles, Linda L. "Possession Cults on the Swahili Coast: A Re-examination of the Theories of Marginality." *Africa* 57, no. 2 (1987): 234–57.

Glazer, Nathan, and Daniel Patrick Moynihan. *Beyond the Melting Pot*. Cambridge, Mass.: Harvard University Press, MIT Press, 1963.

Gleason, Juthid. "Report from Savalu." *Attitude: The Dancers' Magazine*, Spring–Summer 1992.

Glélé, Maurice Ahanhanzo. *Le Danxomé: Du pouvoir Ajá à la nation Fon*. Cotonou: Nubia, 1974.

Graden, Dale. "'So Much Superstition among These People!' Candomblé and the Dilemmas of Afro-Brazilian Intellectuals, 1864–1871." In *Afro-Brazilian Culture and Politics*, edited by H. Kraay, 57–73. Armonk, N.Y.: M. E. Sharpe, 1998.

Guran, Milton. *Agudas: Os "brasileiros" do Benim*. Rio de Janeiro: Nova Fronteira, 1999.

Hansen, J. *Dahomey & pays limitrophes: Carte dressée d'après les plus récentes explorations, 1892*. http://www.axs-tech.com/demo/lumiere/.

Harding, Rachel Elizabeth. "Candomblé and the Alternative Spaces of Black Being in Nineteenth-Century Bahia, Brazil: A Study of Historical Context and Religious Meaning." Ph.D. diss., University of Colorado, 1997.

———. *A Refuge in Thunder: Candomblé and Alternative Spaces of Blackness*. Bloomington: Indiana University Press, 2000.

Hazoumé, Paul. *Le pacte de Sag au Dahomey*. Paris: Institut d'Ethnologie, 1937.

———. "L'âme du Dahoméen animiste révélée par sa religion." *Revue Présence Africaine*, nos. 14–15 (1957): 65–86.

Herskovits, Melville J. "African Gods and Catholic Saints in the New World Negro Belief." *American Anthropologist* 39, no. 4 (1937): 635–43.

———. *Dahomey, an Ancient West African Kingdom*. 2 vols. New York: J. J. Augustin, 1938.

———. *The Myth of the Negro Past*. New York: Harper Bros., 1941.

———. *Man and His Works: The Science of Cultural Anthropology*. New York: Knopf, 1948.

———. "The Panan, an Afro-Bahian Religious Rite of Transition." *Les Afro-Américains (Mémoire de l'Institut Français d'Afrique Noire)*, no. 27 (1952): 133–40.

Herskovits, Melville J, and Frances E. Herskovits. *Folk Music of Brazil: Afro-Bahian Religious Songs*. Archive of American Folk Song, Library of Congress, 1947, LP.

———. "An Outline of Dahomean Religious Belief." *Memoirs of the American Anthropological Association* 3, no. 41 (1933).

Higgs, David. "The Inquisition in Brazil in the 1790s." Lecture, University of Toronto, 1986.

Houseman, M., et al. "Notes sur la structure évolutive d'une ville historique." *Cahiers d'Études Africaines* 104, no. 26-4 (1986): 530–41.

Iroko, Félix A. *Mosaïques d'histoire béninoise*. Limousin: Corrèze Buissonnière, 1998.

Isert, Paul Erdman. *Voyage en Guinée et dans les îles Caraïbes en Amérique*. Edited by Nicoué Gayibor. Paris: Karthala, 1989 (1793).

Janzen, John M. *The Quest for Therapy: Medical Pluralism in Lower Zaire.* Berkeley: University of California Press, 1978.

———. *Ngoma (Discourses of Healing in Central and Southern Africa).* Berkeley: University of California Press, 1992.

Johnson, Samuel. *The History of the Yorubas.* Lagos: CSS Bookshops, 1976 (1921).

Jones, Adam. "Little Popo and Agoué at the End of the Atlantic Slave Trade: Glimpses from the Lawson Correspondence and Other Sources." In *Ports of the Slave Trade (Bights of Benin and Biafra),* edited by Robin Law and Silke Strickrodt, 122–34. University of Stirling, Centre of Commonwealth Studies, Occasional Paper no. 6, October 1999.

Karasch, Mary C. *A vida dos escravos no Rio de Janeiro, 1808–1850.* São Paulo: Companhia das Letras, 2000 (1987).

Karl, Emmanuel. *Traditions orales au Dahomey-Benin.* Niamey, Niger: Centre Régional de Documentation pour la Tradition Orale, 1974.

Kubik, Gerhard. *Theory of African Music,* vol. 1.Wilhelmshaven, Germany: Florian Noetzel Verly, 1994.

Labat, Jean-Baptiste. *Voyage du Chevalier des Marchais en Guinée, isles voisines et à Cayenne, fait en 1725, 1726 et 1727.* 4 vols. Paris: Chez Saugrain, Quay de Gesvres, à la Croix Blanche, 1730.

Labouret, Henri, and Rivet, Paul. *Le royaume d'Arda et son évangélisation au XVIIe siècle.* Paris: Travaux et Mémoires de l'Institut d'Ethnologie, 1929, 7. Facsimile edition of *Doctrina christiana; y explicación de sus misterios en nuestro idioma español, y en lengua arda. Consagrase, y dedicanla a la Concepcion Purisima de Maria Santissima Señora Nuestra los primeros misioneros de aquel reyno.* Madrid: Biblioteca San Isidro, 1658, opus 8, no. 47.523.

Laffitte, M. l'Abbé. *Le pays des nègres et la Côte des esclaves.* 3rd ed. Tours: Alfred Mame et Fils, 1881.

Landes, Ruth. "A Cult Matriarchate and Male Homosexuality." *Journal of Abnormal and Social Psychology* 35, no. 3 (1940): 386–97.

Lara, Silvia Hunold. "Linguagem, domínio senhorial e identidade étnica nas Minas Gerais de meados do século XVIII." In *Trânsitos coloniais: Diálogos críticos luso-brasileiros,* edited by Cristiana Bastos, Bela Feldman-Bianco, and Miguel Vale de Almeida, 205–25. Lisbon: Imprensa de Ciências Sociais, 2002.

Law, Robin. *The Oyo Empire, c. 1600–c. 1836: A West African Imperialism in the Era of the Atlantic Slave Trade.* Oxford: Clarendon, 1977.

———. *The Slave Coast of West Africa, 1550–1750: The Impact of the Atlantic Slave Trade on an African Society.* Oxford: Oxford University Press, 1991.

———. "The Atlantic Slave Trade and the Construction of African Ethnicity: The Case of the Yoruba." Unpublished ms., 1997.

———. "Ethnicity and the Slave Trade: 'Lucumi' and 'Nago' as Ethnonyms in West Africa." *History in Africa,* no. 24 (1997): 205–19.

———. *The Kingdom of Allada.* Leiden, the Netherlands: CNWS Research School, CNWS Publications, 1997.

———. "Francisco Felix de Souza in West Africa, 1800–1849." Paper presented at

"Enslaving Connections: Africa and Brazil during the Era of the Slave Trade," York University, October 12–15, 2000.

Law, Robin, ed. *Further Correspondence of the Royal African Company of England Relating to the "Slave Coast," 1681–1699: Selected Documents from Ms. Rawlinson C745–747 in the Bodleian Library*. Madison: African Studies Program, University of Wisconsin–Madison, 1992.

Le Hérissé, A. *L'ancien royaume du Dahomey: Moeurs, religion, histoire*. Paris: Emile Larose, 1911.

Lepine, Claude. "As metamorfoses de Sakpata, deus da varíola." In *Leopardo dos olhos de fogo: Escritos sobre a religião dos orixás VI*, edited by Carlos Eugênio Marcondes de Moura, 119–44. São Paulo: Ateliê, 1998.

Lewis, Ioan M. *Êxtase religioso: Um estudo antropológico da possessão por espírito e do xamanismo*. São Paulo: Perspectiva, 1977 (1971).

Lima, Vivaldo da Costa. "A família-de-santo nos candomblés jeje-nagôs da Bahia: Um estudo de relações intragrupais." M.A. thesis, Universidade Federal da Bahia, Salvador, 1977.

———. "Os obás de Xangô." *Afro-Ásia*, nos. 2–3 (June–December 1966): 5–36. [Republished in Carlos Eugênio Marcondes de Moura, ed., *Olóòrisá*. São Paulo: Agora, 1981.]

———. "O candomblé da Bahia na década de trinta." In *Cartas de Edison Carneiro a Artur Ramos*, edited by Vivaldo da Costa Lima and Waldir Freitas Oliveira, 37–74. São Paulo: Corrupio, 1987.

Lody, Raul. *Ao som do Adja*. Salvador: Departamento de Cultura da SMEC–Prefeitura Municipal de Salvador, 1975.

Lopez de Carvalho, Marcos Antônio. Document on Jeje Candomblé in Cachoeira. Unpublished ms., 1999.

———. *Gaiaku Luiza e a trajetória do Jeje-Mahi na Bahia*. Rio de Janeiro: Pallas, 2006.

Lühning, Angela E. "'Acabe com este santo, Pedrito vem aí . . .': Mito e realidade da perseguição policial ao candomblé baiano entre 1920 e 1942." *Revista USP*, no. 28 (December 1995–February 1996): 194–220.

———. "O compositor Mozart Camargo Guarnieri e o 2º Congresso Afro-Brasileiro em Salvador, 1937 (homenagem póstuma)." In *Ritmos em trânsito: Socioantropologia da música baiana*, edited by L. Sansone and J. Teles dos Santos, 59–72. São Paulo: Dynamis; Salvador: Programa A Cor da Bahia, 1998.

Maggie, Ivonne. *Guerra de orixá: Um estudo de ritual e conflito*. Rio de Janeiro: Jorge Zahar, 2001 (1975).

Maia, Rita, ed. *Projeto fundiário do Engenho Velho da Federação*. Salvador: Vice-Reitorado para Assuntos Comunitários–Universidade Católica de Salvador, n.d.

Malinowski, Bronislaw. *Magic, Science and Religion and Other Essays*. Long Grove, Ill.: Waveland, 1992 (1948).

Manning, Patrick. *Slavery, Colonialism and Economic Growth in Dahomey, 1640–1960*. Cambridge: Cambridge University Press, 1982.

Marques, Xavier. *O feiticeiro*. 3rd ed. São Paulo: GRD-INL, 1975.

Matory, J. Lorand. "Man in the 'City of Women': Transnationalism, Matriarchy, and the Rise of the Afro-Brazilian Candomblé." Unpublished ms. of *Black Atlantic Religion*, version of February 24, 1997.

———. "Afro-Atlantic Culture: On the Live Dialogue between Africa and the Americas." In *Africana: The Encyclopedia of the African and African American Experience*, edited by Kwame Anthony Appiah and Henry Louis Gates Jr., 36–44. New York: Basic Civitas, 1999.

———. "The English Professors of Brazil: On the Diasporic Roots of the Yoruba Nation." *Society for Comparative Study of Society and History* 41, no. 11 (1999): 72–103.

———. "Jeje: Repensando nações e transnacionalismo." *Mana*, no. 5 (April 1999): 57–80.

———. *Black Atlantic Religion: Tradition, Transnationalism and Matriarchy in the Afro-Brazilian Candomblé*. Princeton, N.J.: Princeton University Press, 2005.

Mattos, Wilson Roberto de. "Negros contra a ordem: Poder público, populações negras e territorialidade na cidade de Salvador (1871–1888)." Lecture, Universidade Federal da Bahia, 1999.

Mattoso, Kátia M. de Queirós. "A propósito de cartas de alforria: Bahia, 1779–1850." *Anais de História*, no. 4 (1972): 23–52.

———. *Bahia: A cidade do Salvador e seu mercado no século XIX*. São Paulo: Hucitec; Salvador: Secretaria Municipal de Educação e Cultura, 1978.

———. *Ser escravo no Brasil*. São Paulo: Brasiliense, 1982.

———. "Testamentos de escravos libertos na Bahia do século XIX." *Publicações do Centro de Estudos Baianos*, no. 85 (1979).

———. *Bahia século XIX: Uma província no Império*. Rio de Janeiro: Nova Fronteira, 1992.

Maupoil, Bernard. *La géomancie à l'ancienne Côte des esclaves*. Paris: Institut d'Ethnologie, 1988 (1946).

Mckenzie, P. R. "O culto aos òrìsà entre os yoruba: Algumas notas marginais relativas a sua cosmologia e seus conceitos de divindade." In *Candomblé: Desvendando identidades (Novos estudos sobre a religião dos orixás)*, edited by Carlos Eugênio Marcondes de Moura, 129–48. São Paulo: EMW, 1987.

Medeiros, François de. "Le couple aja-éwé en question: Note sur l'historiographie contemporaine en Afrique de l'Ouest." In *Peuples du Golfe du Bénin (Aja-Éwé)*, edited by François de Medeiros, 35–46. Paris: Karthala, 1984.

Mello e Souza, Laura de. *O diabo e a Terra de Santa Cruz*. São Paulo: Companhia das Letras, 1999 (1986).

Mello e Souza, Marina de. *Reis negros no Brasil escravista: História da festa de coroação de rei congo*. Belo Horizonte: Editora da Universidade Federal de Minas Gerais, 2002.

Mercier, Paul. "Notice sur le peuplement yoruba au Dahomey-Togo." *Études Dahoméennes*, no. 4. Porto Novo: IRAD, 1950.

Merlo, Christian. "Hiérarchie fétichiste de Ouidah." *Bulletin de l'IFAN* 2, nos. 1–2 (1940): 1–84.

Merlo, Christian, and Pierre Vidaud. "Dangbé et le peuplement houéda." In *Peuples du Golfe du Bénin (Aja-Éwé)*, edited by François de Medeiros, 269–304. Paris: Karthala, 1984.

Métraux, Alfred. *Le vaudou haïtien*. Paris: Gallimard, 1958.

Milton, Aristides A. *Ephemerides cachoeiranas*. Bahia: Typographia Bahiana, 1903.

Mintz, Sidney W., and Richard Price. *An Anthropological Approach to the Afro-American Past: A Caribbean Perspective*. Philadelphia: ISHI, 1976.

———. *The Birth of Afro-American Culture: An Anthropological Perspective*. Boston: Beacon, 1992.

Monteiro, Antônio. *Notas sobre negros malês na Bahia*. Salvador: Inamá, 1987.

Mota, Antonia da Silva, Kelcilene Rose Silva, and José Dervil Mantovani. *Cripto maranhenses e seu legado*. São Paulo: Siciliano, 2001.

Mott, Luiz. "Acotundá: Raízes setecentistas do sincretismo religioso afro-brasileiro." *Revista do Museu Paulista* 31, n.s. (1986): 124–47.

———. "A vida mística e erótica do escravo José Francisco Pereira, 1705–1736." *Tempo Brasileiro*, nos. 92–93 (January–June 1988): 85–104.

———. "O Calundu-Angola de Luzia Pinta: Sabará, 1739." *Revista do Instituto de Artes e Cultura*, no. 1 (December 1994): 73–82.

Mott, Luiz, and Marcelo Cerqueira, eds.*Candomblés da Bahia: Catálogo de 500 casas de culto afro-brasileiro de Salvador*. Salvador: Centro Baiano Anti-Aids, 1998.

———. *As religiões afro-brasileiras na luta contra a aids*. Salvador: Centro Baiano Anti-Aids, 1998.

Mouléro, Thomas. "Histoire et légendes des Djêkens." *Études Dahoméennes*, n.s., no. 3 (1964): 51–76.

Mulvey, Patricia. "The Black Lay Brotherhoods of Colonial Brazil." Ph.D. diss., Columbia University, 1976.

Nascimento, Ana Amelia Vieira. *Dez freguesias da cidade de Salvador: Aspectos sociais e urbanos do século XIX*. Salvador: Fundação Cultural do Estado da Bahia, 1986.

Norris, Robert. *Memoirs of the Reign of Bossa Ahádee, King of Dahomy, an Inland Country of Guiney, to Which Are Added the Author's Journey to Abomey, the Capital, and a Short Account of the African Slave Trade*. London: Frank Cass, 1968 (1789).

Oke, Finagnon Mathias. "Notice sur les villages lacustres du Dahomey." *Études Dahoméennes*, n.s., no. 13. Porto Novo: IRAD, 1969.

Oké, Raymond. "Les siècles obscurs du royaume Aja du Danxome." In *Peuples du Golfe du Bénin (Aja-Éwé)*, edited by François de Medeiros, 47–66. Paris: Karthala, 1984.

Oliveira, Maria Inês Cortes de. *O liberto: O seu mundo e os outros (Salvador, 1790–1890)*. Salvador: Corrupio, 1988.

———. "Retrouver une identité: Jeux sociaux des africains de Bahia vers 1790–1890." Ph.D. diss., Université Sorbonne–IV, 1992.

———. "Viver e morrer no meio dos seus: Nações e comunidades africanas na Bahia do século XIX." *Revista USP*, no. 28 (December 1995–February 1996): 175–93.

———. "Quem eram os 'negros da Guiné'? A origem dos africanos na Bahia." *Afro-Ásia*, nos. 19–20 (1997): 37–74.

Ortiz, Fernando. *Contrapunteo cubano del tabaco el azúcar (Advertencia de sus contrastes agrarios, económicos, históricos y sociales, su etnografía y su transculturación)*. Havana: Jesús Montero, 1940.

———. *Los bailes y el teatro de los negros en el folklore de Cuba*. Havana: Publicaciones del Ministerio de Educación, 1951.

———. *La africania de la música folklórica de Cuba.* Havana: Letras Cubanas, 1993 (1950).

Ossório, Uvaldo. *A ilha de Itaparica*, 2nd ed. Salvador: Artes Gráficas, 1953.

Ott, Carlos. "O negro bahiano." *Les Afro-Américains (Mémoire de l'Institut Français d'Afrique Noire)*, no. 27 (1952): 141–53.

———. "A Irmandade de Nossa Senhora do Rosário dos Pretos do Pelourinho." *Afro-Ásia*, nos. 6–7 (1968): 119–26.

Parés, Luis Nicolau. "The Jeje in the Bahian Candomblé and in the Tambor de Mina of Maranhão." In *Rethinking the African Diaspora: The Making of a Black Atlantic World in the Bight of Benin and Brazil*, edited by K. Mann and E. Bay, 91–115. London: Frank Cass, 2001.

———. "O triângulo das *tobosi* (Uma figura ritual no Benin, Maranhão e Bahia)." *Afro-Ásia*, nos. 25–26 (2001): 177–213.

———. "The Birth of the Yoruba Hegemony in Post-abolition Candomblé." *Journal de la Société des Américanistes* (2005): 139–59.

———. "The Nagôization Process in Bahian Candomblé." In *The Yoruba Diaspora in the Atlantic World*, edited by T. Falola and M. Childs, 185–208. Bloomington: Indiana University Press, 2005.

———. "O processo de crioulização no Recôncavo baiano (1750–1800)." *Afro-Ásia*, no. 33 (2005).

———. "Transformations of the Sea and Thunder Voduns in the Gbe-Speaking Area and in the Bahian Jeje Candomblé." In *Africa and the Americas: Interconnections during the Slave Trade*, edited by J. C. Curto and R. Soulodre–La France, 69–93. Trenton, N.J.: Africa World, 2005.

———. "Memories of Slavery in Religious Ritual: A Comparison between the Benin Vodun Cults and Bahian Candomblé." In *Activating the Past: History and Memory in the Black Atlantic World*, edited by Andrew Apter and Lauren Derby, 71–97. Cambridge: Cambridge Scholars, 2010.

Patterson, Orlando. *Slavery and Social Death: A Comparative Study*. Cambridge, Mass.: Harvard University Press, 1982.

Pazzi, Roberto. *Introduction à l'histoire de l'aire culturelle ajatado*. Lomé: Université du Benin, Institut National des Sciences Humaines, 1979.

———. "Aperçu sur l'implantation actuelle et les migrations anciennes des peuples de l'aire culturelle Aja-Tado." In *Peuples du Golfe du Bénin (Aja-Éwé)*, edited by François de Medeiros, 11–20. Paris: Karthala, 1984.

Peel, John David Yeadon. "A Comparative Analysis of Ogun in Precolonial Yorubaland." In *Africa's Ogun (Old World and New)*, edited by Sandra T. Barnes, 263–89. Bloomington: Indiana University Press, 1997.

———. *Religious Encounters and the Making of the Yoruba*. Bloomington: Indiana University Press, 2000.

Peixoto, António da Costa. *Obra nova da língua geral de Mina*. Manuscript of the Biblioteca Pública de Évora, published and presented by Luis Silveira in 1943. Lisbon: Agência Geral das Colónias, 1943–44 (1741).

Pereira, Duarte Pacheco. *Esmeraldo de situ orbis*. Lisbon: Imprensa Nacional, 1892 (1508).

Pereira, Nunes. *A Casa das Minas: Culto dos voduns jeje no Maranhão*. Petrópolis: Vozes, 1979 (1947).

Pérez, Jesús Guanche. "Contribución al estudio del poblamiento africano en Cuba." Unpublished ms. Havana, 1995.

Pierson, Donald. *Brancos e prêtos na Bahia: Estudo de contacto racial*. São Paulo: Nacional, 1971 (1942).

Pietz, William. "The Problem of the Fetish I." *Res: Anthropology and Aesthetics*, no. 9 (Spring 1985): 5–17.

———. "The Problem of the Fetish II: The Origin of the Fetish." *Res: Anthropology and Aesthetics*, no. 13 (Spring 1987): 23–45.

———. "The Problem of the Fetish IIIa: Bosman's Guinea and the Enlightenment Theory of Fetishism." *Res: Anthropology and Aesthetics*, no. 16 (Fall 1988): 106–23.

Pommegorge, Pruneau de. *Description de la Nigritie, par M. P. D. P., ancien conseiller au Conseil Souverain du Sénégal*. Amsterdam: Maradan, 1789.

Pondé, Maria do Carmo. "A Capelinha dos Quinze Mistérios e a devoção do rosário entre os pretos." *Anais do Arquivo Público da Bahia*, no. 29 (1943).

Prandi, Reginaldo. *Os candomblés de São Paulo (A velha magia na metrópole nova)*. São Paulo: Hucitec, Editora da Universidade de São Paulo, 1991.

Querino, Manuel. *Costumes africanos no Brasil*. Recife: Fundação Joaquim Nabuco, Massangana, 1988 (1938).

Ramos, Artur. *As culturas negras no Novo Mundo*. São Paulo: Nacional, INL, MEC, 1979 (1937).

———. Introduction to Manuel Nunes Pereira, *A Casa das Minas: Culto dos voduns Jeje no Maranhão*. Petrópolis: Vozes, 1979 (1947): 11–20.

———. *O negro brasileiro: Etnografia religiosa e psicanálise*. Recife: Fundação Joaquim Nabuco, Massangana, 1988 (1934).

Ratis e Silva, Pedro. "Exu-Obaluaiê e o arquétipo do médico ferido na transferência." In *Candomblé: Desvendando identidades (Novos estudos sobre a religião dos orixás)*, edited by Carlos Eugênio Marcondes de Moura. São Paulo: EMW, 1987.

Rego, Waldeloir. "Terras beneditinas." In *A Grande Salvador: Posse e uso da terra*. Salvador: Governo do Estado da Bahia, Secretaria de Saneamento e Desenvolvimento Urbano, 1978.

———. "Mitos e ritos africanos da Bahia." In Caribé, *Os deuses africanos no Candomblé da Bahia*. Salvador: Bigraf, 1993.

Reis, João José. "Nas malhas do poder escravista: A invasão do Candomblé do Accú na Bahia, 1829." *Religião e Sociedade* 13, no. 3 (1986): 108–27.

———. "Magia Jeje na Bahia: A invasão do calundu do asto de Cachoeira, 1785." *Revista Brasileira de História* 8, no. 16 (March–August 1988): 57–81, 233–49.

———. *A morte é uma festa*. São Paulo: Companhia das Letras, 1991.

———. "The Politics of Identity and Difference among Slaves and Freedmen in Nineteenth-Century Bahia." Paper presented at "The World the Diaspora Makes," Ann Arbor, Mich., 1992.

———. "Recôncavo rebelde: Revoltas escravas nos engenhos baianos." *Afro-Ásia*, no. 15 (1992): 100–126.

———. "Identidade e diversidade étnicas nas irmandades negras no tempo da escravidão." *Tempo* 2, no 3 (1997): 7–33.

———. "Candomblé in Nineteenth-Century Bahia: Priests, Followers, Clients." In *Rethinking the African Diaspora: The Making of a Black Atlantic World in the Bight of Benin and Brazil*, edited by Kristin Mann and Edna Bay, 116–34. London: Frank Cass, 2001.

———. "Tambores e temores: A festa negra na Bahia na primeira metade do século XIX." In *Carnavais e outras f(r)estas: Ensaios de história social da cultura*, edited by Maria Clementina Pereira Cunha, 101–55. Campinas: Editora da UNICAMP, CECULT, 2002.

———. *Rebelião escrava no Brasil: A história do levante dos malês em 1835.* 2nd ed. Revised and expanded. São Paulo: Companhia das Letras, 2003 (1986).

Reis, João José, and Eduardo Silva. *Conflito e negociação: A resistência negra no Brasil escravista.* São Paulo: Companhia das Letras, 1989.

Reis, Meire Lucia Alves dos. "A cor da notícia: Discursos sobre o negro na imprensa baiana. Do pós-abolição a 1937." M.A. thesis, Universidade Federal da Bahia, Salvador, 2000.

Rex, John. *Raça e etnia.* Lisbon: Estampa, 1988.

Rodrigues, Nina. *O animismo fetichista dos negros baianos.* Rio de Janeiro: Civilização Brasileira, 1935 (1896).

———. *Os africanos no Brasil.* São Paulo: Companhia Editora Nacional, 1977 (1906).

Roosens, Eugeen E. *Creating Ethnicity: The Process of Ethnogenesis.* London: Sage, 1989.

"Le royaume des Fittas." *Mémoire du Benin (Matériaux d'histoire)*, no. 2 (1993 [c. 1908]): 75–83.

Russell-Wood, A. J. R. "Aspectos da vida social das irmandades leigas da Bahia no século XVIII." In *O bicentenário de um monumento bahiano.* Salvador: n.p., 1971.

Sahlins, Marshall. *Ilhas de história.* Rio de Janeiro: Zahar, 1990.

Santos, Deoscóredes Maximiliano dos (mestre Didi). *História de um terreiro nagô: Crônica histórica.* São Paulo: Carthago & Forte, 1994.

Santos, Jocélio Teles dos. *O dono da terra (O caboclo nos candomblés da Bahia).* Salvador: Sarah Letras, 1995.

Santos, Juana Elbein dos. *Os Nàgo e a morte: Pàde, Àsésé e o culto Égun na Bahia.* Petrópolis: Vozes, 1986.

Santos, Manuel Victorino dos. "O mundo religioso do negro da Bahia." In *O negro no Brasil: Trabalhos apresentados ao 2o Congresso Afro-Brasileiro (Bahia)*, 343–47. Rio de Janeiro: Civilização Brasileira, 1940.

Santos, Maria Stella de Azevedo. *Meu tempo é agora.* São Paulo: Oduduwa, 1993.

Schwarcz, Lilia Moritz. *As barbas do imperador D. Pedro II: Um monarca nos trópicos.* São Paulo: Companhia das Letras, 1998.

Schwartz, Stuart B. "A manumissão dos escravos no Brasil colonial: Bahia, 1684–1745." *Anais de História*, no. 6 (1974): 71–114.

———. "Resistance and Accommodation in 18th-Century Brazil." *Hispanic American Historical Review* 57, no. 1 (February 1977): 69–81.

———. *Segredos internos: Engenhos e escravos na sociedade colonial.* São Paulo: Companhia das Letras, 1999 (1985).

Segurola, R. P. B. *Dictionnaire fon-français*. 2 vols. Cotonou: Procure de l'Archidiocèse, 1988 (1963).

Silva, Denise Ferreira da. "A morte de Mãe Menininha: Cooptação ou resistência?" *Comunicação do ISER*, no. 21, year 5 (1986).

Silva, Pedro Celestino da. "Datas e tradições cachoeiranas." *AAPBA*, no. 29, 1943 (1938).

Silva, Vagner Gonçalves da. *Orixás da metrópole*. Petrópolis: Vozes, 1995 (1992).

Silveira, Renato da. "Iyá Nassô Oká, Babá Axipá e Bomboxê Obitikô: Uma narrativa sobre a fundação do Candomblé da Barroquinha, o mais antigo terreiro baiano de Ketu." Unpublished ms., 1999. [An abridged version of this work was published as "Jeje-Nagô, Iorubá-Tapá, Aon Efan, Ijexá: Processo de constituição do candomblé da Barroquinha, 1764–1851." *Cultura Vozes*, no. 6, year 94, vol. 94 (2000): 80–100.]

Slenes, Robert W. "'Malungu Ngoma vem!' A África coberta e descoberta do [no] Brasil." *Revista USP*, no. 12 (December 1991–February 1992): 48–67.

———. *Na senzala uma flor: Esperanças e recordações na formação da família escrava— Brasil, Sudeste, século XIX*. Rio de Janeiro: Nova Fronteira, 1999.

Smith, Robert S. *Kingdoms of the Yoruba*. London: James Currey, 1988 (1969).

Snelgrave, William. *A New Account of Some Parts of Guinea and the Slave Trade*. London: Frank Cass, 1971 (1734).

Soares, Carlos Eugênio Líbano, and Flávio Gomes. "Gênero, 'nações' e trabalho urbano no Rio de Janeiro escravista, século XIX." Paper presented at seminar "Escravidão e Invenção da Liberdade," Universidade Federal da Bahia, 2004, 1–42.

Soares, Mariza de Carvalho. *Devotos da cor: Identidade étnica, religiosidade e escravidão no Rio de Janeiro, século XVIII*. Rio de Janeiro: Civilização Brasileira, 2000.

Sodré, Jaime, ed. *Música sacra do candomblé*. Salvador, 1990, CD-ROM.

Sodré, Muniz. *O terreiro e a cidade*. Petrópolis: Vozes, 1988.

Sogbossi, Hypolite Brice. "Mina-jeje em São Luis do Maranhão, Brasil: Contribuição ao estudo de uma tradição daomeana." M.A. thesis, Universidade Federal do Rio de Janeiro, 1999.

Soumonni, Elisée A. *Daomé e o mundo atlântico*. Rio de Janeiro: SEPHIS, CEAA, 2001.

———. "Dahomean Yorubaland." In *Yoruba Historiography*, edited by Toyin Falola, 65–74. Madison: University of Wisconsin, 1991.

Spieth, Jacob. *Die Religion der Eweer in Süd-Togo*. Göttingen: Vandenhoeck und Ruprecht, 1911.

Spiro, Melford E. "Religion Problems of Definition and Explanation." In *Culture and Human Nature: Theoretical Papers of Melford E. Spiro*, edited by B. Kilborne and L. L. Langness, 187–222. Chicago: University of Chicago Press, 1987.

Stoller, Paul. *Embodying Colonial Memories: Spirit Possession, Power and the Hauka in West Africa*. New York: Routledge, 1995.

Strickrodt, Silke. "Afro-Brazilians of the Western Slave Coast in the Nineteenth Century." In *Enslaving Connections, Changing Cultures of Africa and Brazil during the Era of the Slavery*, edited by José C. Curto and Paul E. Lovejoy, 213–44. Amherst, N.Y.: Humanity, 2004.

Thompson, E. P. *A formação da classe operária inglesa*. 3 vols. Rio de Janeiro: Paz e Terra, 1988 (1963).

Tidjani, A. Serpos. "Notes sur le mariage au Dahomey." *Études Dahoméennes*, no. 6. Porto Novo: IFAN, 1951.

Turner, Jerry Michael. "Les Brésiliens: The Impact of Former Brazilian Slaves upon Dahomey." Ph.D. diss., Boston University, 1975.

Turner, Victor Witter. *Schism and Continuity in an African Society*. Manchester: Manchester University Press, 1964.

———. *The Drums of Affliction: A Study of Religious Processes among the Ndembu of Zambia*. Oxford, U.K.: Clarendon, 1968.

———. *The Ritual Process: Structure and Anti-Structure*. Ithaca, N.Y.: Cornell Paperbacks, 1977.

van Dantzing, Albert. *Dutch Documents Relating to the Gold Coast and the Slave Coast (Coast of Guinea) 1680–1740 (Translations of Letters and Papers Collected in the Algemeen Rijks Archief, State Archives of the Netherlands at The Hague)*, 1971. Copy belonging to the Fundação Verger (Salvador).

van den Boogaart, Ernst, and Pieter Emmer. "The Dutch Participation in the Atlantic Slave Trade, 1569–1650." In *The Uncommon Market: Essays in the Economic History of the Atlantic Slave Trade*, edited by Henry A. Gemery and Jan S. Hogendorn, 353–75. New York: Academic, 1979.

Van Gennep, A. *Rites of Passage*. Chicago: University of Chicago Press, 1960 (1909).

Vansina, Jan. *Oral Tradition as History*. Madison: University of Wisconsin Press, 1985.

Vatin, Xavier. "Étude comparative de différentes nations de candomblé à Bahia, Brésil." Ph.D. diss., École des Hautes Études en Sciences Sociales, 2001.

Verger, Pierre. "The Yoruba High God: A Review of the Sources." *Odu*, no. 2 (1966): 19–40.

———. *Orixás*. Salvador: Corrupio, 1981.

———. *Fluxo e refluxo do tráfico de escravos entre o golfo do Benin e a Bahia de Todos os Santos*. São Paulo: Corrupio, 1987 (1968).

———. *Os libertos: Sete caminhos na liberdade de escravos da Bahia no século XIX*. São Paulo: Corrupio, 1992.

———. "Orixás da Bahia." In Carybé, *Os deuses africanos no candomblé da Bahia*. Salvador: Bigraf, 1993.

———. "Raisons de la survie des religions africaines au Brésil." In *Vodun*, 141–55. Paris: Présence Africaine, 1993 (1970).

———. "Grandeza e decadência do culto de Ìyàmi Òsòròngà (Minha Mãe Feiticeira) entre os Yorùbá." In *As senhoras do Pássaro da Noite*, edited by Carlos Eugênio Marcondes de Moura. São Paulo: Editora da Universidade de São Paulo, 1994.

———. *Notas sobre o culto aos orixás e voduns na Bahia de Todos os Santos, no Brasil, e na antiga Costa dos Escravos, na África*. Translated by Carlos Eugenio Marcondes de Moura. São Paulo: Editora da Universidade de São Paulo, 1999 (1957).

———. *Notícias da Bahia—1850*. Salvador: Corrupio, 1999 (1981).

Viana Filho, Luiz. *O negro na Bahia*. 2nd ed. São Paulo: Martins, MEC, 1976.

Videgla, Michel. "Le royaume de Porto Novo face à la politique abolitionniste des nations européennes de 1848 à 1882." In *Ports of the Slave Trade (Bights of Benin and Biafra)*, edited by Robin Law and Silke Strickrodt, 135–52. University of Stirling, Centre of Commonwealth Studies, Occasional Paper no. 6, October 1999.

Weber, Max. "The Social Psychology of the World Religions." In *From Max Weber: Essays in Sociology*, edited by H. H. Gerth and C. Wright Mills. New York: Oxford University Press, 1975 (1946).

———. *Economia e sociedade: Fundamentos de sociologia compreensiva*. Brasília: Editora Universidade de Brasília, 1994 (1972).

Wimberly, Fayette. "The African *Liberto* and the Bahian Lower Class: Social Integration in Nineteenth-Century Bahia, Brazil, 1870–1900." Ph.D. diss., University of California, Berkeley, 1988.

———. "The Expansion of Afro-Bahian Religious Practices in Nineteenth-Century Cachoeira." In *Afro-Brazilian Culture and Politics*, edited by H. Kraay, 74–89. Armonk, N.Y.: M. E. Sharpe, 1998.

Wimmer, Linda. "Ethnicity and Family Formation among Slaves of Tobacco Farms in the Bahian Recôncavo, 1698–1820." Paper presented at "Enslaving Connections Africa and Brazil during the Era of the Slave Trade," York University, October 2000.

Yai, Olabiyi Babalola. "From Vodun to Mahu: Monotheism and History in the Fon Cultural Area." In *L'invention religieuse en Afrique: Histoire et religion en Afrique Noire*, edited by Jean-Pierre Chrétien, 242–63. Paris: Karthala, 1992.

INDEX

164, 165, 166; initiation of, 139, 140, 159;
   initiations led by, 160–62, 171, 178; Seja
   Hundé terreiro and, 153, 154–55, 159–65,
   167, 329 (n. 1)
Agorensi title, 159, 237
Agoué (port city), 27, 33, 60, 65
Agué (vodun), 108, 116, 160, 161, 176, 187, 214,
   222, 224, 225, 241, 274
Agueda, *Sinhá*, 152
Aguerê (drum rhythm), 255
Aguesi (Eliza Gonzaga de Souza), 153, 155,
   159, 161, 167, 169, 170, 237; Seja Hundé ter-
   reiro leadership and, 160, 191–92, 283–84
Aguesi, Vivi. *See* Aguesi
Aguessy, Cyrille, 29, 107, 250
Aguessy, Honorat, 13, 14–15
Aguidavi (drum stick), 107, 252
Ahémé, Lake, 17, 25
Ahwan wa uli ye (the war is going to capture
   them) ritual, 261, 262
AIDS, 234
Ailton, *Ogã*, 280
Aizã. *See* Aizo language/people
Aizan/Ayizan (vodun), 214, 223, 267–70,
   348 (n. 61); rituals of, 266, 268–69
Aizo language/people, 7, 9, 13, 14, 15, 30, 217
Aïzo-Seto people, 215, 217, 220
Ajahuto (vodun in Allada), 241
Ajahuto (king of Allada), 11
Ajauntó (vodun), 241, 259, 347 (n. 41)
Ajayi, Ade, 121
Ajda people, 9, 17, 27, 28
Ájèji, 27
Ajonsu. *See* Azonsu
Ajuasse (*Mãe* Tança/Constança da Rocha
   Pires), 203
Ajuda fort, 29, 30, 31
Akan territory, 216, 340 (n. 21)
Akindélé, Adolphe, 29, 107, 250
Akinjogbin, I. A., 10, 16
Aklobè. *See* Akolombé
Ako, 50, 217
Akolombé (vodun), 219, 221, 226, 274
Akorombe (orixá), 161

Akotoquem (vodun), 160, 161, 169, 224
Akron, 28, 29
Akwamu people, 5
Ala (white cloth), 257, 278, 288
Alaketo candomblé, 115, 205, 319 (n. 75)
Aleijadinha candomblé, 152, 164
Aligbonon, 10, 302 (n. 23)
Allada (city), 5, 7, 217, 306 (n. 92); slaves
   from, 12, 20, 21, 27, 38
Allada (kingdom), 9, 10, 20, 22, 29, 30, 38;
   founding of, 11; slave trade and, 26, 27;
   vodun cults and, 70, 73, 216, 241, 269
Allada (Arda) language, 14, 303 (n. 33)
Almeida, Cecília Ovídia de, 162
Almeida Cardoso, Manoel de, 83
Altamira, Fazenda, 137
Altars, 81–83, 87, 92, 104, 107, 171; annual
   festival cycles and, 264, 271, 276, 277, 288;
   initiations and, 249, 258, 259. *See also*
   Animal sacrifices; *Pejis*; Ritual practices;
   Sacred trees
Alujá (drum rhythm), 255
Alvares, José Joaquim, 57
Amado, Jorge, 183, 185
Amalá (ritual food), 109, 251
Amalá of Xangô (festival), 203
Amâncio de Melo, *Ogã*. *See* Melo, Amâncio
   Ângelo de
Amaral, Braz do, 23
Amasi, 107, 278, 281
Amélia, Rita, 126
Amorim, Manoel Cirqueira de. *See* Portão,
   Nezinho do
Amulets, 70, 78, 81, 90
Anacleto, *Tio*, 151, 233, 327 (n. 98)
Anacleto do Capivari candomblé, 151, 152,
   170, 233, 327 (n. 98)
Anagô. *See* Nagô people of Africa
Anagonu. *See* Nagô people of Africa
Ancestor deities, 50, 158, 210, 237, 241, 259,
   266, 268, 269, 278
Andrade, Maria José de Souza, 43, 46
Aného, 15, 27, 31, 32, 33, 40. *See also* Petit-Popo
Anglo-Portuguese treaty of 1810, 40

consecrated objects (*fundamento*) and, 280; eighteenth century and, 32, 40; ethnic groups and, 7–13, 57; hierarchical titles and, 249, 250, 345 (n. 14); initiations and, 256, 259, 260, 261, 347 (n. 41); Legba and, 267, 348 (nn. 53–54); Sakpata/Omolu/Nanã Buruku triad of deities in, 230; sea voduns and, 216, 284; thunder voduns and, 157, 216–17, 340 (nn. 21–23); *zandró* ritual and, 271, 276. *See also* Dahomey; "Gbe-speaking area" of Africa; Mina Coast; Ouidah

Benin, Republic of, xii, 3, 6, 11, 188

"Benoi," 248, 345 (n. 5)

Bergé, J. A. M. A. R., 16, 157

Bernadinho, *Seu*, 169, 170, 330 (n. 33)

Bernardino, *Ogã* (Bernardino Ferreira dos Santos), 170, 190, 193

Bessem. *See* Bessen

Bessen (vodun), 281, 289; Bogum terreiro and, 177, 179, 182, 234; *boitá* ritual and, 277, 279; drumming and, 253, 254; family organization and, 214, 222, 223, 234–38; initiations and, 161, 177, 190, 193; as Jeje vodun, 152, 202, 204; ritual emblems of, 238, 344 (n. 82); Roça de Cima terreiro and, 154, 240; Seja Hundé terreiro and, 159, 161, 167, 168, 190, 192, 193, 194, 234, 240; shrines of, 278–79; *zandró* ritual and, 273, 274, 275, 276

Béta (*Bètà*) etymology, 201, 338 (n. 158). *See also* Poço Béta terreiro

Bigodeiro, Gregório, 178

Binon-Cossard, Gisèle, 237, 248, 260, 263

Bispo, Tomas de Aquino. *See* Caboco Acaçá, *Ogã*

Bi Tedô candomblé. *See* Oba Tedô candomblé

Blessings, 247–48, 272, 273, 275, 345 (nn. 4–5)

Blu people, 14

Boa Morte sisterhood, 61, 135, 144, 147, 159, 168, 171, 327 (n. 99)

Boboso, *Ogã* (Ambrósio Bispo Conceição), 135, 145, 169, 192, 193, 257, 323 (n. 31); Seja

Hundé terreiro and, 153, 154, 167–68, 170, 190, 321 (n. 2)

Bogum, etymology, 127, 156–57

Bogum terreiro, 114, 292–93, 331–32 (n. 53); 1860s and, 128–31, 172; into 1900s, 172–75; 1920s, inactivity of, 165, 166, 173, 174, 331 (n. 52); 1940s and, 173, 177–79; 1950s and, 172, 173, 179–80; 1960s to the present, 126, 173, 183–89, 193, 195–200, 207, 337 (nn. 144, 149); Africans vs. Creoles in, 131, 174; animal sacrifices and, 130, 131, 249–50; annual festival cycles and, 264, 265–66, 274, 347–48 (n. 52); area of, 126–27, 131–32, 195–200, 336 (n. 138); Aziri Tobosi ceremony and, 283; Azonodo feast, 280–82; Azonsu/Ajonsu and, 173, 177, 185, 189, 190, 191, 222, 233; Bessen and, 177, 179, 182, 234; *boitá* ritual and, 279; *caboclos* and, 243; deities and, 157–58, 222, 226, 227, 241; drumming and, 252; etymology of name of, 127, 156–58; *fechar o balaio* festival and, 287; funeral rites, 128–29, 130–31, 133, 185, 186, 323 (n. 35); hierarchical titles and, 249–50; initiations and, 118, 129–30, 133, 173–74, 176, 177–78, 181, 185, 186–87, 262, 332 (nn. 57, 64); Jeje liturgy and, 345 (n. 3); leadership of, 130, 133, 139, 172–73, 200, 321 (n. 2); Mawu-Lissá deity couple and, 235–36; Maria Romana Moreira and, 176–77, 178, 179–83, 333–34 (n. 87); neighboring candomblés and, 131–33, 195, 201, 206, 323 (n. 31); newspapers advertising and, 199–200; Nicinha leadership of, 133, 173, 178, 185–89, 197, 198, 243, 282; *ogãs* and *equedes*, 173, 178–79, 183, 187, 198, 333–34 (n. 87); origins of, 125–28, 321 (nn. 5, 7); Maria Emiliana da Piedade period and, 172, 173, 174–79, 198, 333 (n. 72); research on, xi, xvi–xvii, 124–25, 321 (nn. 1–2); Roça de Cima terreiro and, 139, 141–42, 144, 176; Runhó leadership and, 115, 125, 172, 173, 183–86, 195, 197, 252, 333 (n. 75); sacred trees and, 197, 280–82; Salvador cultural protection area and, 198–99; Seja Hundé terreiro

and, 175, 180, 182–83, 184–85, 332 (n. 54),
333 (n. 77); snake/serpent voduns and,
239–40; Sogbo family of voduns and, 234;
Valentina (Creole Bogum terreiro leader)
period and, 139, 155, 172–75, 176, 331 (n. 48)
Boitá ritual, 154, 164, 204, 241, 294; animal
sacrifices and, 265, 277; annual festival
cycles and, 234–35, 264, 266, 271, 280; ele-
ments of, 277–80, 349 (n. 74); *fundamento*,
279; *ogãs* and *equedes* and, 278; sacred
trees and, 257, 277, 278, 280
Bolouvi, Lébéné Philippe, 156, 157, 158
Bomfin, Martiniano Eliseu de, 122, 165
Bonfires, 257, 264–65, 288–89, 294
Borghero, Francesco, 217
Bosman, William, 70, 71, 72, 210, 216
Braga, Julio, 107
Branco, Joaquim Francisco Devodê, 122
Brandão, Cotia, 104
Bravum (drum rhythm), 238, 253, 254
Brazilianization, 65. *See also* Assimilation
Brito, Antônio de, 55
Brito, Edvaldo, 186, 197
Brotas parish, 91, 100, 103, 113, 126–27, 204,
317 (n. 39), 319 (n. 75), 322 (n. 12)
Burton, Richard, 217, 236
Buruku. *See* Nanã Buruku

Cabaça (gourd instrument), 251
Cabeça de Boi (ritual), 264, 279–80
Caboceers, 18, 31, 250, 303 (n. 48)
Caboclos/cabaclos, 156, 192, 242–43
Caboco Acaçá, *Ogã* (Tomas de Aquino
Bispo), 161, 162–63, 166, 169, 177, 179, 181,
329 (n. 13)
Cabras, 37, 41
Cachoeira, xi, 139; black elite of, 145–46,
147–50, 326 (n. 75); *calundus* and, 51, 57,
66, 82, 92, 134, 158; candomblés and, 321
(n. 2), 325 (n. 71); Catholic lay brotherhoods and, 54, 55, 56–57, 58, 77, 134, 159,
309–10 (n. 38); cholera epidemic, 1855,
145–46, 151; hierarchical titles in terreiros
in, 250, 346 (n. 16); Jeje terreiros and,
118, 133, 134–36, 142, 152–53, 234; Ketu

terreiros and, 171; Nagô candomblés and,
151–52, 327 (n. 100); slave population of,
35, 36, 39, 134; tobacco industry and, 134,
151. *See also* Roça de Cima terreiro; Seja
Hundé terreiro
Cactuses, 270
Cacunda de Yaya terreiro, 179, 180, 203, 338
(n. 162)
Cajá tree, 151
Calundu do Pasto, 51, 57, 66, 82, 134, 158
Calundus, xvi, 67; Catholic lay brotherhoods
and, 77; Jeje nation and, 134; repression/
tolerance and, 82–83, 90–92; as stage
in formation of Candomblé, 75–76, 88;
witchcraft (*feitiçaria*) and, 78–81, 313–14
(n. 29)
Calunduzeiro, 80–81
Camamu, Viscount de, 93, 127
Caminho Dois de Julho. *See* Caminho
Rio Vermelho
Caminho Rio Vermelho, 131, 195, 196, 322
(nn. 12, 23)
Campina de Boskejan (Boskeji) terreiro,
115, 116, 165
Campinas terreiro, 95, 101–2, 103, 104, 115, 116
Campo Grande terreiro, 114
Campos, João da Silva, 55, 59–60, 61, 135
Candomblé (religious institution): access to
land and, 104, 154, 195–200; Africanisms
and, xv, 111–12, 242, 328 (n. 112); Africanization and, 122–23, 194; as Afro-Brazilian
religious institution, xi, xiv, 84–86, 104,
194–95, 199, 301 (n. 1); *caboclos* and,
242–43; *calundus* as stage in formation
of, 75–76, 88; Catholic lay brotherhoods
influencing formation of, xiii–xiv, 75–77,
84–85, 98, 100; drumming and, 49, 67,
75, 251–55; ethnic groups and, xii, xiv, 49,
88–89, 291; freed Africans and formation
of, 45, 47, 89–90, 95, 144; "Gbe-speaking
area" of Africa, and formation of,
212–13, 339 (n. 14); initiations as central
characteristic of, 255–64, 347 (n. 35);
Jeje liturgy and terminology and, 244–46,
247; Jeje nation and voduns and, 15, 19, 45,

105, 106–18, 215, 221, 225, 239; Jeje nation influence on formation of, xi, xvi, xvii, xviii, 85, 106–18, 214; multi-nations and, 68–69, 205; multiple deities and, 104–5, 208–29, 235–36; Nagocentrism of study of, 207, 212–13; Nagô-Ketu influence on, 229, 231, 295–96; Nagô vs. Jeje nation influence on, 107, 118–23, 226; nation divisions and, 88–89, 110, 112–19; orixá cults and Gbe vodun cults and, 105–6; politics and, 102, 317 (n. 53); repression/tolerance 1920s–1930s, 165–66; research sources for study of, 87–88, 94–95, 314–15 (n. 1), 315 (n. 3), 316 (n. 22); ritual practices of, according to different nations, 112–19; slavery and, 88, 89–90, 95, 341–42 (n. 47); songs of, 242, 247; vodun cults and, 107–8, 110, 209–10, 262, 295, 296; women leaders in, 228. *See also* Ritual practices

Candomblés (congregations/terreiros): Africans vs. Creoles in, 94, 96, 98–100, 112, 116–17, 120, 121; annual festival cycles and, 135, 138, 141–42; Barroquinha, 61, 101, 105, 311 (n. 65); *calundus* and, 67, 75, 81, 83; defined, 301 (n. 1); *eguns* and, 129, 132, 133, 135, 250; Engenho Velho and, 93, 94, 102, 103, 116, 117, 127, 129, 130, 132; founding of first in Bahia, early nineteenth century, 61; Jeje nation and, 91–92, 99, 105, 107–9, 112–13, 119, 177, 319 (n. 71); kinship and, 163–64; leadership of, 95–98, 113, 316 (nn. 22, 27), 319 (n. 72); leadership terms, 108–9; multi-nations and, 68–69, 110–11, 152; multiple deities in, 104–5, 151–52, 208–9, 317–18 (n. 61); Nagô nation and, 105, 107, 108, 109–10, 112–14, 119–23, 151–52, 319 (nn. 71, 75), 327 (nn. 98–99); Nagô vs. Jeje nation mentions in *O Alabama* and, 106–10, 111, 318 (n. 63), 318–19 (n. 68), 319 (n. 69); nation divisions and, 68–69, 88–89, 312 (n. 6); police cases and, 87, 100–104, 118, 165, 208; political celebrations and, 102, 317 (n. 53); racial mixing and, 94–100, 316 (n. 27); runaway slaves and, 103, 317 (n. 55); of Salvador, 90,

100–101, 103–4, 106, 112–19, 132, 317 (n. 39), 317–18 (n. 61); social networks and, 164–65; tolerance/repression of, 90–94, 101–3; in urban spaces, 100–104, 195–200; white men and women and, 93, 95–96, 316 (n. 27); witchcraft (*feitiçaria*) and, 95, 102; women leaders in, 96–98, 226–27, 228, 316 (n. 30). *See also* Angola candomblés; Initiation; Ritual practices

Candomblés da Bahia (Carneiro), 177

Canga, Maria, 79

Canjica, 288, 289

Capivari, Anacleto do, 151, 152. *See also* Anacleto do Capivari candomblé

Capivari candomblé. *See* Anacleto do Capivari candomblé

Capo, Hounkpati B. C., xii, 12, 15

Capone, Stefania, 184

Caprara, Andrea, 234

Capuchins, 14, 303 (n. 33)

Caquende River, 136, 137

Caribé, 185

Carmo, Maria Ana do, 161, 170

Carneiro, Edison, 119, 200, 235, 238–39, 246, 251, 262; candomblé nations and, 68, 116, 177, 179, 201, 202, 205–6, 312 (n. 6); "Nagôization" and, 122–23; Second Afro-Brazilian Congress and, 165–66, 177

Carneiro da Cunha, Maria, xiii

Carneiro de Campos, José, 195

Carnival, 105, 203, 265, 266, 275, 286, 287

Carvalho, Antônio, 142

Carvalho, Antônio Teixeira de, 126, 322 (n. 11)

Carvalho, Jehová de, 117, 127–28, 153, 157, 186, 197, 222, 280, 281, 282

Carvalho, Kelba, 186

Casa Branca, 131, 179, 195, 197, 198. *See also* Engenho Velho district

Casa das Minas, 115, 163, 284, 286

Casa Estrela (House of the Star), 135, 138, 324 (n. 49)

Casinha/huncó (initiation room), 138, 256, 257

Castelnau, Francis, 34, 45

Castro, Manoel Figueiredo, 198

Castro, Martinho de Mello e, 67, 81

Hueda people, 9, 13, 15, 18, 21, 22, 25, 28, 30; sea and thunder voduns and, 19, 218, 220; snake/serpent voduns and, 237, 239

Huédo, 50

Huin (ritual name), 256, 260–61

Hula people, 9, 13, 14, 15, 25, 28, 30, 239, 304 (n. 57); sea and thunder voduns and, 5, 19, 215, 216, 218, 219, 220, 242

Humbono, 249, 250

Humbono Vicente do Matatu. *See* Vicente, *Humbono*

Hun, 14, 158, 249, 252, 346 (n. 20)

Hun ciò, 256

Huncó/casinha (initiation room), 256

Hundeva, 250

Hun do dji ritual, 275–76, 349 (n. 70)

Hun fínfòn, 256

Hungan, 249

Hunsó, 148, 179, 183, 189, 249

Hun su dide, 261

Huntó, 249, 252, 278

Huntoloji terreiro, 190, 207, 223, 237, 321 (n. 2), 335 (n. 117); Aizan ritual and, 266, 270; annual festival cycles and, 265, 266; drumming and, 252, 346–47 (n. 33); food offerings and, 284–85; *zandró* ritual and, 266, 274, 275, 276, 349 (n. 69)

Hwegbaja (king of Dahomey), 18, 30

Ialorixá, 115, 213

Iamoró, 268, 346 (n. 18)

Ianno, 51, 309 (n. 31)

Iansã (orixá), 222, 224, 274

Ia-Omi-Ni-Que, 203

Iaôs, 204, 276–77; as slave, 262–63

Ibejis (orixás), 105

Idassa. *See* Dassa people

Idjé people, 28, 29

Iemanjá (orixá), 152, 162, 203, 228, 253, 274, 284

Ifá, 108, 122, 145; divining system of, 79, 189. *See also* Cowry shells: divination using; Fa

Ifé people, 12, 18, 229

Igbí (drum rhythm), 255

Igbogila, 213, 339 (n. 14)

Ijexá-Nagô terreiros, 192, 252, 253

Ijexá nation, 179

Ilê Axé Jitolú terreiro, 203

Ilê Ayé Carnival group, 203

Ilê Ibece Alaketu Axé Ogun Megege terreiro, 171, 331 (n. 37)

Ilê Ibece Alaketu terreiro, 152, 332–33 (n. 67)

Ilê Ifé, 8, 9, 12, 230

Ilê Iyá Nassô candomblé, 101, 105, 118, 131, 195, 208, 209, 322 (n. 23)

Ilê Iyá Omin Axé Iyamassé. *See* Gantois terreiro

Ilê Maroialaje terreiro, 205

Ilê Ogun Anauegi Belé Ioman terreiro, 184

Ilê Omó Kétá Posú Bétá terreiro (House of the Children of Posú Bétá), 202–3

Initiation, 177–78, 203, 226–27, 283, 332 (n. 64); Bogum terreiro and, 118, 129–30, 133, 173–74, 176, 177–78, 181, 185, 186–87, 262, 332 (nn. 57, 64); as central characteristic of Candomblé, 255–64; coming out period, 257–58; death during, 129–30, 347 (n. 38); "Gbe-speaking area" of Africa and, 71, 72, 255, 261, 263, 347 (n. 44); gender of initiates and, 133, 181, 323 (n. 36), 347 (n. 35); hierarchical titles given to initiates and, 117, 118, 130, 160–61, 169, 186–87, 250, 256, 263, 329 (n. 5); *huncó/casinha* (initiation room), 138, 256, 257; Jeje terms for, 107, 109, 111; *kele* necklace, 162, 329 (n. 10); nation differences and, 68, 133, 263–64; "purchase of the *iaô/slave*" rituals, 261, 262–63; *quitanda* and, 262–63, 264; ritual clothing and, 257, 259, 260; ritual death and resurrection, 256, 257, 347 (n. 38); ritual names and, 256, 260–61, 347 (n. 44); Roça de Cima terreiro and, 138–40, 155, 160, 329 (n. 6); *sapocã (sarapocã)*, 129, 130; seclusion of initiate and, 95, 256, 257–58; Seja Hundé terreiro and, 154, 160–62, 178, 190–91, 192, 262, 329 (n. 6), 335 (nn. 118–19); shaving and, 191, 257, 259, 260, 266; *Sinhá Abalhe* and, 169–70, 171, 190, 330–31 (n. 34); social reintegration and, 260, 261, 262–63;

twentieth century and, 204–5, 206, 207.
See also Nagô-Ketu terreiros
Kinship, 49–50, 68, 99, 163–64, 193
Kola nuts, 109, 201, 270, 272, 278, 285
Koro koro (song), 274
Kpengla (king of Dahomey), 31, 39
Kplakpla mats, 276
Kpo (panther vodun), 28, 132, 161, 173, 180,
201, 221, 222, 233, 240, 241, 274
Kpole ritual, 258
Kposu. *See* Kpo
Kututo/Kutito, 171, 323 (n. 35)
Kwe Simba terreiro, 193, 241, 336 (n. 132)

Labat, Jean-Baptiste, 21, 26
Ladeira Manoel Bomfin street, 126, 127,
196–97
Laffitte, M. l'Abbé, 28
Lagos, 13, 31, 32, 33, 40, 113, 114, 121, 202
Lagosian Renaissance, 121
Laguidibá (ritual necklace), 234
Landes, Ruth, 97, 200
Leaf offerings, 83, 103, 109, 131, 271
Leal, Gilberto, 187, 198
Leba/Lebal (vodun), 108, 118, 267. *See also*
Legba
Legba (vodun), 108, 118, 133, 138, 222, 225,
235, 266–68, 269; in Africa, 267, 348
(nn. 53–54); rituals for, 223, 267–68,
270–71, 273, 293
Le Hérissé, A., 217, 218, 220, 236, 269
Lembá, Mariquinha, 179, 183
Lent, 105, 141, 265, 286, 287, 288
Lepine, Claude, 8, 74, 229, 234
Lewis, Ioan M., 70, 72
Lima, Vivaldo da Costa, 27, 68, 107, 122, 205,
312 (n. 4)
Lissá/Olissá (vodun), 14, 169, 214, 217, 231,
240, 265, 287, 288; name derived from
orisa (Nagô term), 14–15. *See also* Mawu-
Lissá pantheon
Livaldina terreiro, 200, 238
Lôcco tree. *See* Gameleira tree
Loco (vodun). *See* Loko
Loco tree. *See* Gameleira tree

Lody, Raul, 282
Logun Edé, 190, 191
Loko (vodun), 115, 116, 169, 170, 177, 192, 204,
222, 225, 233, 303 (n. 36); as tree god, 108,
117, 120, 151, 214, 221, 240–41
Lokosi, *Gamo* (Maria da Augusta Conceição
Marques), 160, 169, 190, 191, 192–93, 195
Lopes, José Clarião, 147
Lopez, Antônio, 143
Lopez de Carvalho, Marcos Antônio, 144,
164, 166, 190, 194, 207
Luanda Africans, 57. *See also* Angola nation
Lucaia River, 126, 131, 196
Lugar, Catherine, 35
Luiza, *Gaiaku* (Luiza Franquelina da
Rocha), 201, 204; Huntoloji terreiro and,
190, 207, 223, 321 (n. 2), 335 (n. 117); initia-
tion of, 178, 181, 332–33 (n. 67); initiations
by, 256–57, 258, 262; ritual practices and,
161, 248, 252, 273, 280, 289; Seja Hundé
terreiro and, 160, 162, 166, 178, 194; *Sinhá*
Abalhe and, 169, 171; vodun families and,
214, 223, 227, 237, 238, 242
Luizinha, 178, 333 (n. 68)
Lustral water, 272–73

Mabaças, 105, 108
Mãe d'Água, 105, 108, 114, 152
Mães d'água (water deities), 105, 108, 152
Mães-de-santo, 68, 115, 125, 139, 165, 173,
248–49
Mães-pequena, 160, 174, 175, 176, 178, 179, 180,
183, 189, 249
Magalhães, Maria Claudina, 176
Magno, Luís, 191, 204, 335 (n. 119)
Mahi-Agonlis people, 228
Mahi nation, 6, 16, 49, 51, 52, 65, 126, 155, 204,
248. *See also* Jeje-Mahi terreiros
Mahi people, 12, 328 (n. 112); Bogum
terreiro origins and, 157; etymology of,
16; migrations of, 16–17; prisoners in war
taken for slaves, 30, 38; river spirits and, 19,
228, 283; Sakpata and, 232; snake/serpent
vodun cults and, 237, 239, 240, 344 (nn. 85,
87); voduns and, 15, 19, 157, 230

Makii people, 51. *See also* Mahi nation

Malagueta pepper, 272, 273

Malaqué de Xangô, *Tia*, 152

Malê Revolt, 46, 62, 64, 65–66, 127–28, 157

Malinowski, Bronislaw, 69

Malungos, 49, 63

Mamãe/papai, 108, 114

Mandinga pouches, 78, 81, 89, 90. *See also* Amulets

Mané, *Papai*, 113

Manning, Patrick, 37

Maragogipe, 52, 134, 141, 153, 159, 171, 180, 204

Maranhão, 6, 24, 215, 221, 227, 251, 255, 261, 284, 286

Marees, Pieter de, 20

Mariwo palms, 278, 287

Marriage, 41–42, 54, 308 (n. 18)

Marx, Karl, 72

Mata, Silvanton da, 206

Mata Escura da Vasco da Gama, 179, 205, 238

Matatu. *See* Brotas parish

Matory, J. Lorand, 25, 106, 121, 200, 203, 207, 239

Matrilineality, 10, 14

Matta, Lídice da, 199

Mattos, Gregório de, 78

Mattos, Wilson Roberto de, 100

Mattoso, Kátia, 35, 44

Maupoil, Bernard, 73, 210

Mawu-Lissá pantheon, 73, 210, 211, 231, 235–36, 240, 241

Mckenzie, P. R., 212

Mejito, 248

Melandras, Isidoro, 142, 172

Mello, Zaildes Iracema de (*Doné* Naa Doji), 173, 186, 189

Mello e Souza, Laura de, 78, 79, 90–91

Melo, Amâncio Ângelo de, 172, 183, 187, 249–50

Melo, Gonçalo Alpiniano de, 183

Menez, Manuel, 201

Menezes, Vasco Fernandez César de, 29

Menininha, *Mãe*, of Gantois, 152, 179, 281, 349 (n. 79)

Mere Doji, 183, 334 (n. 94). *See also* Runhó, *Doné*

Merlo, Christian, 28, 29, 220

Mestizo, 37, 44, 96, 100, 119

Miguel, *Seu*. *See* Rocha, Miguel Rodrigues da

Milhazes, Albino José, 149, 153–54

"Mina blacks," 50–51

Mina Coast: Africans in Brazil returning to, 33, 60, 65, 121–22; Catholic lay brotherhoods and, 59, 60; "nations" and, 1; ritual practices from, xv–xvi, 82; slave trade and, 20–21, 22, 26, 29–31, 38, 40, 48; witchcraft (*feitiçaria*) and, 80, 81, 313–14 (n. 29). *See also* "Gbe-speaking area" of Africa

Mina-Gen people in Africa, 15

Mina nation, 2, 21, 42; African origins of, 7; candomblés and, 113; Catholic lay brotherhoods and, 55, 56, 57, 61, 311 (n. 64); eighteenth century and, 50–51; language/dialect from Africa and, 6, 7, 302 (n. 15); sixteenth century use of *Mina* name and, 4–6; slave population in Bahia and, 23–24, 38, 39, 41, 45, 54

Mina-Popo area, 27

Mina-Popo nation, 202

Minas Gerais, 6, 7, 23, 25, 79, 134, 181

Minona (vodun), 230, 231

Mintz, Sidney, xiv–xv, 70, 75

Missions Africaines de Lyon, 25

Mitogbodji (island), 17, 18

Moinho candomblé, 113–14

Mono River, 5, 9, 27, 217, 219, 221

Montaguère, Olivier, 31

Monteiro, Antonio, 127, 128, 156, 157

Montenegro, Jaime, 203

Monte Pio Society, 147–49

Moraes, José, 129, 142, 172

Mordoma, 56

Moreira, Edith, 169

Moreira, Maria Romana, 206, 333 (nn. 77, 82); *Sinhá* Abalhe and, 172, 181; Bogum terreiro and, 173, 176–77, 178, 179–83, 333–34 (n. 87); death of, 181–82, 183; initiation of, 139–40, 145; initiations and, 180, 181, 332–33 (n. 67); Seja Hundé terreiro and, 180, 184

Mott, Luiz, 80, 81

Motta, Maria de, 145, 146, 147, 326 (n. 80)

Moura, Belchior Rodrigues de, 145–46

Mulattoes, 36, 37, 53, 57, 58, 60, 96, 99

Muller, Wilhelm Johann, 5

Multideity cults: aggregation principle of voduns and, 209, 221–28, 229, 237; in Bahia, eighteenth century, 208; Candomblé formation and, 104–5, 208–29, 235–36; as "Creole" Brazilian process, 208–9; Dan and Bessen family of voduns and, 222–23, 224, 234–38; "Gbe-speaking area" of Africa and, xvi, 105, 209, 210–12, 213–17, 218–21, 227–28, 230–32, 236–37; Jeje terreiros and, 108, 151–52, 209–10, 214–17, 221–28, 233–34, 238–40, 245; leadership and, 213, 340 (n. 15); as New World creation, 212–13; vodun, in nineteenth-century Bahia, 104–5, 208, 213, 232–33, 340 (n. 15); Yoruba people and, 213–14

Mulungu tree, 233

Mundubi dance, 171, 254, 275, 346–47 (n. 33)

Mundubi family of voduns, 215, 221, 222, 223, 224, 227, 228, 237

Mundubi-Mahi voduns, 224, 225, 228

Mundubi nation, 19, 303 (n. 52), 303–4 (n. 54). *See also* Jeje-Mundubi nation

Music, 147–48, 179; Candomblé orchestra, 251–52, 272, 273. *See also* Dancing; Drumming; Songs

Musical Corporation of Nossa Senhora d'Ajuda, 147

Muslims. *See* Islam

Naa Doji, *Doné*, 189. *See also* Mello, Zaildes Iracema de

Naeté, 218, 221, 227, 341 (n. 46)

Nagô, Belchior, 62, 311 (n. 71)

Nagô, José, 46

Nagô-Ketu terreiros, 119, 122, 123, 131, 145, 152, 179, 204; aggregation principle of voduns and, 223–25, 229; animal sacrifices and, 276–77; annual festival cycles and, 265–66; blessings, asking for, 275; *caboclos* and, 242; Candomblé formation and, 229, 231, 295–96; deities and, 229–34, 267, 295; drumming and, 253, 255; hierarchical titles and, 249; initiations and, 261; *padé* ritual and, 268, 270; *xirê*, 234, 274, 275, 276–77

Nagô language. *See* Yoruba language

Nagô nation: African origins of, 3, 6, 12; African "purity" and, 200; in Bahia, eighteenth century, 37, 43, 44, 45, 57, 308 (n. 20); in Bahia, nineteenth century, 37, 43, 44, 46, 88, 309 (n. 22); Candomblé influence, end of nineteenth century, 107, 118–23, 226; candomblés and, 105, 107, 108, 109–10, 112–14, 151–52, 319 (nn. 71, 75), 327 (nn. 98–99); Catholic lay brotherhoods and, 53, 54, 60–61, 311 (nn. 58, 65); deities of, 108, 226, 266; Jeje nation and, xvii, 62–64; orixá cults and, 106, 118, 215, 222, 223, 224–25, 226; slave populations in Bahia and, 37, 39, 40, 41, 43, 44, 45–46, 88, 90; subnations of, 152, 292

Nagô people of Africa, 12, 13, 18; deities of, 14–15, 232, 241; ethnic groups and, 16–17; *Jeje* term and, 27, 28, 29; orixá cults and, 237; slaves to Bahia, 32, 63

Nagô terreiros, 180, 319 (n. 71), 320 (n. 88); blessings, asking for, 248, 345 (n. 4); Anacleto do Capivari, 151, 152, 170, 233, 327 (n. 98); deities of, 113–14, 118, 228, 293; vodun cults and, 231–32

Na Hwanjile, 210

Nanã (orixá), 108, 161, 201, 203, 204, 214, 225, 252, 253, 274

Nanã, Valentina, 169

Nanã Buruku (vodun), 229–34, 240

National Guard, 150

Nations: Bahian enslaved populations and, 36, 37, 44; defined, 1; formation in colonial Brazil, 2; shift of term from political to religious domain in Bahia, 68; subnations and, 292. *See also* Angola nation; Jeje nation; Mina nation; Mundubi nation; Nagô nation

Nazaré, Luís de, 79

nation and, 63; royal dynasties of, 11; slave trade and, 31, 32, 33, 34, 40, 46, 48; vodun cults and, 107, 213, 238, 241, 250

Portuguese: in Africa, 5, 9, 30, 40; Brazilian independence and, 46; Catholic lay brotherhoods in Bahia and, 55, 77–78; slave trade and, 20–24, 27, 29, 31, 32, 35, 305 (n. 64), 307 (n. 2); treaties with Dutch, eighteenth century, 22–23

Possession, 80, 97, 117, 131, 161, 176, 238; *caboclos* and, 242–43; drumming and, 253; importance of deity and, 226; non-possession and, 249, 250; speaking and, 261. See also *Vodunsis/vudunças*

Povo-de-santo, 192, 255, 293; Cachoeira and, 136, 141, 144; defined, 75; loss of knowledge and, 207, 225, 287; Salvador and, 127, 141, 152, 179, 200, 201. See also Candomblé (religious institution)

Povo de veia, 163

Povolide, Count of (Martinho de Mello e Castro), 67, 81

Pó Zerrem terreiro, 117, 131, 132–33, 170, 176, 179, 195, 227, 323 (n. 31)

Preto, 48, 50, 56, 60, 94, 96

Preto, Pássaro (Sátiro Humberto de Silva), 169–70

Price, Richard, xiv–xv, 70, 75

"Primeira semana de palestras: O povo malê e suas influências" (First Seminar on the Malê People and Their Influences), 188, 198

Primeiro Encontro de Nações de Candomblé (First Meeting of the Candomblé Nations), 280

Príncipe de Oliveira, Hermógenes, 195

Procópio, 179, 330 (n. 19)

Project Mapeamento de Monumentos Negros da Bahia (MAMNBA, Mapping of the Black Monuments of Bahia), 187, 197–98

Projeto Fundiário do Engenho Velho da Federação (Engenho Velho da Federação Agrarian Project), 126

Provenience groups and identities, 4. *See also* Ethnic identity/groups/ethnicity

Puppets, 78, 81, 92

Quebrado (drum rhythms), 254, 275, 346–47 (n. 33)

Quenquém (vodun), 222, 237

Querebentã de Zomadonu, 115. *See also* Casa das Minas

Querebetan, 115

Querino, Manuel, 240, 284

Queto nation. *See* Ketu terreiros

Quilombos, 66, 78, 90, 103, 126; in Cachoeira, before 1860, 135, 136, 146

Quinta das Beatas candomblé, 99, 102, 103, 114–15, 117, 208, 317–18 (n. 61)

Quinta das Devotas candomblé, 111

Quitanda das iaôs, 262–63, 264

Quixareme (African candomblé leader), 135

Rachel, "negress," 129, 130, 142, 172, 200, 325 (n. 60)

Rainbows, 235, 236, 237, 238, 239

Ramiro, Manoel, 176

Ramos, Artur, 116, 119, 123, 238

Rams, 109, 111, 276

Ratis e Silva, Pedro, 234

Recife, 2, 31, 67, 81

The Recôncavo. *See* Bahian Recôncavo

Recuada, 135, 147, 168, 172, 192, 326 (n. 80). *See also* Cachoeira

Régis, Olga Francisca, 115, 205

Rego, Waldeloir, 132, 156, 185

Reinado festivities, 49, 51

Reis, João José, 58, 87, 127, 209; *calundus* and, 82, 83; candomblés and, 91, 94, 96, 99; Nagô vs. Jeje nation mentions in *O Alabama* and, 106–7, 113; slave populations in Bahia and, 36, 43, 49; women leaders in candomblés and, 97, 98

Religion, definitions and models, 69–70, 313 (n. 8); "fortune-misfortune complex," 69, 75–76; practices of African origin in Brazil, eighteenth century, 74–83

Rio de Janeiro, 24, 166, 189, 191, 241; *calundus* and, 79, 91; Catholic lay brotherhoods and, 50–51, 61; Jeje-Mahi terreiros of, 207; *Jeje* term and, 25; Jeje terreiros and, 193–94, 336 (n. 132); Seja Hundé terreiro and, 192, 193; slavery and, 5–6, 76

Rio Vermelho region, 131, 132, 322 (nn. 12, 23)

Risério, Antônio, 199

Rita, Epifânio Santa, 167, 330 (n. 24)

Ritual death and resurrection, in initiation, 256, 257, 347 (n. 38)

Ritual practices: *Acará* (palm oil) ritual, 117; African roots of Brazilian, xv–xvi, 82, 290; for Aziri/Azili Tobosi, 228, 264, 283–86, 289; Azonodo feast, 264, 280–82, 289; blessings, asking for, 247–48, 272, 273, 275, 345 (nn. 4–5); boiling oil and, 117, 320 (n. 87); *Cabeça de Boi*, 264, 279–80; coal stepping, 117; consecrated objects (*fundamento*) used in, 277–78; cowry shell divination, 79, 176, 189, 335 (n. 117); *Decá*, 107, 140, 167, 263, 264, 295, 318 (n. 65), 332–33 (n. 67); defined, 70; in 1860s, 104, 107, 112–19; *Fa* divination system, 210, 303 (n. 38), 318–19 (n. 68), 345 (n. 14); Legba, Ogun Xoroque, and Aizan playing similar roles in, 223, 267–68, 270–71, 273, 293; Nagô-Ketu terreiros and, 229; *ossé* (shrine cleansing), 264, 265, 270; *padé* ritual, 264, 268, 270, 273, 293, 346 (n. 18); *panã* ritual, 263, 264, 295; private vs. public rituals, 264; red dye and, 233, 342–43 (n. 63); ritual colors and, 238, 270, 294; ritual objects and, 90, 92, 276, 317–18 (n. 61), 344 (n. 82); secrecy of, 90, 244–45, 314–15 (n. 1); social reintegration of initiates and, 260, 261, 262–63; spilling water on ground, 268, 273; straw skirts and, 233, 294, 342–43 (n. 63); terms for objects used in, Jeje vs. Nagô, 109–10, 318 (n. 67), 318–19 (n. 68); *vodun só gbo* (the vodun grabs the goat), 249; war ritual, 287–88, 350 (n. 102). *See also* Animal sacrifices; Annual festival cycles; *Boitá* ritual; Drumming; Food

offerings; Funeral rites; Initiation; Jeje terreiros; Witchcraft; *Zandró* ritual

Roça de Cima terreiro: area of, 136, 137, 324 (n. 47); *Sinhá* Abalhe and, 155, 166, 167, 171, 172; Bessen and, 240; Bogum terreiro and, 139, 141–42, 144, 176; ceasing to exist, 154–55, 328 (n. 110); initiations, 138–40, 155, 160, 329 (n. 6); leadership of, 137–38, 139, 140–44, 325 (n. 60); Ludovina Pessoa and, 136, 138, 140–44; Maria Romana Moreira and, 176, 180; Nagô terreiros and, 151–52; oral history and, 136, 139, 141, 147, 153; origins of, 136, 323 (n. 40); research on, 124, 321 (nn. 1–2); sacred trees and, 136–37, 232–33; Sakpata and, 232–33; Seja Hundé terreiro and, 124, 137, 138–39, 153, 154–55, 160

Roça de Ventura terreiro. *See* Seja Hundé terreiro

Rocha, Agenor Miranda, 189

Rocha, Eugenio Rodrigues da. *See* Geninho, Seu

Rocha, Luiza Franquelina da. *See* Luiza, Gaiaku

Rocha, Miguel Rodrigues da, 154, 161, 162, 163, 166

Rocha, Pedro de Alcantara (Pedrinho), 203

Rodrigues, Nina: Afro-Brazilian religious practices in Bahia and, 87, 99, 105–6, 114, 213, 238–39, 240, 251; Brazilian slave nations and, 5, 6; deities and, 225–26, 227, 233, 235, 236, 267; Jeje nation and, 26–27, 119, 120, 200, 246, 248–49; Nagô nation and, 120, 122, 200

Rodrigues da Costa, Theodozio, 31

Rolavo, Zé, 111

Romana. *See* Moreira, Maria Romana

Roman Catholic Church: African "paganism" and, 77–78, 314 (n. 35); annual festival cycles and, 105, 189, 209, 279, 286, 288–89, 294; assimilation and, 65; blessings, asking for, 247; Jeje annual festival cycles and, 265, 286, 288; Lent, 105, 141, 265, 286, 287, 288; Saint Bartholomew and,

Santos, Bernardino Ferreira dos (*Ogã Bernardino*), 170, 190, 193

Santos, Eugênia Ana dos (*Mãe* Aninha), 122

Santos, Hilda Dias dos, 203

Santos, José Magna Ferreira dos (Zé Careca), 170, 190

Santos, Juana Elbein dos, 123, 268

Santos, Maria Epifania dos. *See* Abalhe, Sinhá

Santos, Maria São Pedro dos, 170

Santos, Vicente Paulo dos. *See* Vicente, Humbono

São Benedito Brotherhood, 147

São Caetano district, 116, 203, 320 (n. 82)

São Félix, 151, 152, 233

São Francisco do Conde, 39, 80, 90, 134, 201

São Frei Pedro Gonsalves chapel, 59

São Luís, 115, 244, 286

São Miguel, 267

São Paulo, 193, 194, 336 (n. 133)

São Pedro Velho candomblé, 100

São Sebastião de Passé parish, 153

São Tomé, 20, 21, 42

Sapocã, 129, 130, 257, 347 (n. 38)

Sapoca, Anninha, 99

Saponan/Xapanan (orixá/vodun), 108, 226. *See also* Sakpata

Sarapoça. See Sapocã

Sardinha, Antonio, 24

Satô (drum rhythm), 253–54, 346 (n. 31)

Savalou/Sabaru, 16, 17, 18, 38, 51, 52, 157, 229, 231, 232

Savè, 9, 12, 229, 230

Savi, 21, 30, 70, 71

Schwartz, Stuart, 37, 38, 42

Sea voduns, 19, 71, 214–17, 218–22, 226, 284; aggregation principle of voduns and, 227–28

Segum. See Sirrum/segum

Segurola, R. P. B., 232, 249, 289

Seja Hundé terreiro, xi, xvi–xvii, 141, 292–93, 321 (n. 2); Abalhe period, 160, 165–72, 175, 177, 178, 179, 203, 330 (nn. 22, 24–25); aggregation principle of voduns and, 223, 224; Agorensi leadership of, 153, 154–55,

159–65, 167, 329 (n. 1); Aguesi leadership of, 160, 191–92, 283–84; animal sacrifices and, 276; annual festival cycles and, 265, 266; area of, 153–54, 327–28 (n. 107); Aziri Tobosi ceremony and, 283–84, 285; Azonsu and, 165, 214, 233; Bessen and, 159, 161, 167, 168, 190, 192, 193, 194, 234, 240; Bogum terreiro and, 175, 180, 182–83, 184–85, 332 (n. 54), 333 (n. 77); bonfire of Sogbo and, 289; collaborations with other terreiros and, 170–71, 203; dancing and, 226; devotees from Rio and São Paulo and, 193–94, 195, 336 (n. 133); drumming and, 252, 346–47 (n. 33); etymology of name of, 156–58; founding of, 172, 224; funeral rites, 165, 171, 191; golden age of, 164–65; hierarchical titles and, 249; inactivity, 1920s, 165, 166–67, 329–30 (n. 16), 330 (n. 22); initiations and, 154, 160–62, 178, 190–91, 192, 262, 329 (n. 6), 335 (nn. 118–19); kinship and, 163, 170; leadership of, 154–55, 160; Legba ritual, 270; Lokosi and, 160, 192–93; Ludovina Pessoa and, 153, 154, 155, 156, 224; nations practicing in, 155–56; 1960s to the present, 160, 189–95; *ogãs* and *equedes*, 161–62, 163, 170, 181, 193; Pararasi and, 160, 162, 169, 182, 184, 189–91, 193, 203; Rio de Janeiro and, 192, 193; Roça de Cima terreiro and, 124, 137, 138–39, 153, 154–55, 160; sea voduns and, 227; second golden age of, 167, 172; snake/serpent voduns and, 237, 238, 240

Senhora, *Mãe*, 122

Sé parish, 100, 101

Serra, Ordep, 187, 197–98

Setohum. See Hevioso

Shapana. *See* Sakpata

Shaving, 116, 191, 257, 259, 260, 266

Sheep, 276

Shrines. *See* Altars; *Pejis*

Sibeboran, 202–3, 338 (n. 161)

Sierra Leone, 121, 315 (n. 12)

Silva, Galdina (*Mãe* Baratinha), 145

Silva, João Duarte da, 62

Silva, Manuel da, 173, 175, 331 (n. 46)

Silva, Sátiro Humberto de (Pássaro Preto), 169–70

Silveira, Renato da, 64, 91

Sinhá Abalhe. *See* Abalhe, Sinhá

Sirrum/segum, 101, 109, 116, 128–29, 132, 185, 186, 191, 318–19 (n. 68). *See also* Funeral rites

Sisterhood of the Senhor do Martírios, 144

Sítio do Charema, 137

Slave revolts, 23–24, 98, 308 (n. 14), 323 (n. 37); in Cachoeria, 1820s and earlier, 136, 324 (n. 44); Hausa people and, 90; Itapuã rebellion, 90; Malê Revolt, 46, 62, 64, 65–66, 127–28, 157; religion and, 90

Slavery: African "nations" in Brazil and, 2–3, 4–7; assimilation and resistance, 64, 65; in Bahia, early nineteenth century, 32–33, 36–37, 307 (n. 5); in Bahia, early to late nineteenth century, 35; in Bahia, eighteenth century, 23–24, 37, 38–39, 308 (nn. 11, 20); Brazilian abolition of, 148–49, 152; Cachoeira population of, 35, 36, 39, 134; Candomblé formation and, xi, 75–76, 88, 89–90, 95, 341–42 (n. 47); depersonalization and, 47–48; ethnic groups and, 20, 38–39, 48, 308 (n. 12); first slave shipments to Brazil, 21, 304 (nn. 60–61); "Gbe-speaking area" of Africa and, 30–31; Jeje nation in Bahia, eighteenth century, characteristics, 41–43; *Jeje* term used in Bahia and, 24–25, 26, 305 (n. 72); manumission and, 143, 146; multi-deity cults and, 208–9; among peoples of Africa, 16, 21, 38; religious practices and, 67, 80, 88, 90, 91; runaway slaves, 103, 317 (n. 55); slave populations in Bahia, ethnic makeups, eighteenth century, 35–47; slave vs. free population and, 95, 316 (n. 24); use of term *African* in nineteenth century and, 46, 48; women leaders in candomblés and, 97–98; work activities and, 43

Slave trade, xii; to Bahia, early nineteenth century, 27, 32, 307 (n. 105); to Bahia, eighteenth century, 27, 32, 37; Brazilian abolition of, 33, 35–36, 46, 67, 88–89;

British abolition of, 32, 35, 40; cycles of, 20; Dutch in Africa and, 20–21, 22–23, 25–26, 27, 30; eighteenth century and, 25–26, 27, 29–31, 306 (n. 95); ethnic groups and, 3–6, 7–8, 19, 26–27, 33, 49, 88–89, 305 (n. 80); illegal period, 20, 33, 34; mid-nineteenth century, 35–36; nation, use of term in, 1, 2–3; overview of, prior to eighteenth century, 19–24; sugar production and, 38, 40–41; tobacco trade and, 23, 134, 323 (n. 37)

Smallpox, 74, 214, 230, 231; Sakpata and, 73, 222, 227, 232

Snake deities, 108. *See also* Bessen; Dan; Ophidian cults; Vodun pantheon

Snakes, 168–69

So (thunder god), 217, 218

Soares, Mariza de Carvalho, 4, 51

Soares de Sá, Julia, 114, 319 (n. 75), 322 (n. 23)

Sociedade Afro-Brasileira Fiéis de São Bartolomeu (Afro-Brazilian Society of the Faithful of Saint Bartholomew), 177, 187, 198, 335 (n. 109)

Sociedade Monte Pio dos Artistas Cacho-eiranos (Cachoeiran Mount Pio Artists' Society), 147

Sodré, Domingos Pereira (*Papai* Domingos), 113, 114

Sodré, Jaime, 187, 198

Sodré, Muniz, 100

Sogbo (vodun), 108, 115, 132, 133; Adan, 183, 201; animal sacrifices and, 276; bonfire of, 257, 264–65, 288–89, 294; Dan and, 222–23, 227; devotees consecrated to, 158, 161, 174, 282; rainbows and, 236; songs and, 274; vodun families and, 214, 218, 221, 225, 241, 338 (n. 158)

Sogbossi, Hypolite Brice, 28

Songs, 242, 247, 258, 270, 293; Aziri Tobosi ceremony and, 285; *boitá* ritual and, 278, 279, 349 (n. 74); initiations and, 259, 261; *zandró* ritual and, 271, 272, 273, 274, 285, 348 (n. 67)

Sonrai, 9

and, 208, 233; ethnic groups on Mina Coast and, 5, 19; multiple deities and, 212, 213; slave trade and, 20, 22, 23, 31; vodun cults and, 229, 230; voduns and, 217, 236, 269

Viagem, Zezinho da Boa, 192, 193–94

Viana, Francisco, 287

Viana Filho, Luiz, 20

Vicente, *Humbono* (Vicente do Matatu/ Vicente Paulo dos Santos), 140, 145, 182, 186, 192, 238, 289; *Sinhá* Abalhe and, 168, 169, 324 (n. 52); death of, 189; initiations and, 258, 259, 262; Jeje terreiros and, 132, 133, 237, 242, 296, 321 (n. 2); Maria Romana Moreira and, 139, 180, 181; Pararasi and, 190, 191; Roça de Cima vs. Bogum terreiros' founding, 141; Seja Hundé terreiro and, 158, 162, 165; Seja Hundé terreiro founding and, 153, 154; songs and, 207, 221

Vidal, *Tio*, 204–5

Vidaud, Pierre, 28, 29

Virgilio of Bessen, 161, 329 (n. 9)

Vitória, Dona, 204

Vitória parish, 126, 322 (n. 12)

Viva Deus terreiro, 152

Vodun, as term: *bogum* term and, 156; etymology of, 14; first use of, 14, 303 (n. 33), 316 (n. 14); geographic area in Africa for, 14–16; Jeje nation and, 15, 91–92, 316 (n. 13); linguistic analysis of, 107–8; religious meaning and, xi, xii. *See also* Vodun pantheon

Vodun cults: in Africa, 33, 70–74, 107; in Brazil, 72, 221; Cachoeira and, 134; Candomblé institution and, 107–8, 262; as central religious institutions, 70–72; *eguns* and incompatibility with, 133, 323 (n. 35); initiation into, 71, 72; Jeje nation and, 108; multideity cults, xvi, 208, 209–10; peripheral religious institutions and, 72–74; priests/priestesses, 71–72, 73; religious leaders coming and going from Africa and, 143–44; ritual practices and, 117, 246, 320 (n. 87); Sakpata and, 73–74;

smallpox and, 73, 74; Zo ordeal and, 117. *See also Vodunsis/vudunças*

Vodun pantheon, xi, xvii, 86, 108; aggregation principle of, 218, 220, 221–28; Aziri/Azili, 228, 264, 283–86, 293; Dadá, 145, 325–26 (n. 74); Dandagojí, 136–37, 138, 233, 324 (n. 45); earth pantheon, 210, 229–30, 269; female deities, 227, 228; hierarchies within, 210, 211–12, 218–19, 221; hunter voduns, 108, 176, 241–42, 344 (n. 92); Jeje, 115, 120, 214–17, 221–28; Mawu-Lissá and, 73, 210, 211, 231, 235–36, 240, 241; Nanã, 108, 161, 201, 203, 204, 214, 225, 252, 253, 274; panthers and, 132, 201, 221, 241, 342 (n. 62), 347 (n. 41); Parara, 160, 190, 233; rainbows and, 235, 236, 237, 238, 239; Sakpata/Omolu/ Nanã Buruku triad of, 229–34; sea voduns, 19, 214–17, 218–22, 226, 284; sky voduns, 210, 216, 231, 236; smallpox and, 73, 74, 214, 222, 225, 227, 230, 231; snake/serpent voduns, 158, 210, 214, 215, 225, 234–40, 281, 289, 343 (n. 78); thunder voduns, 19, 108, 158, 210, 214–17, 218–22, 328 (n. 122); tree voduns, 116, 151; voduns speaking and, 260–61; water voduns, 131–32, 151, 152, 242, 283–84; *Yabas*, 225; Zomadonu, 115. *See also* Agué; Averekete; Azonsu; Bessen; Dan; Hevioso; Legba; Ogun; Oxum; Sakpata; Sogbo

Vodunsis/vudunças, 71, 102, 117, 118, 147, 203, 255–64; *baiana* clothing and, 259; Bogum terreiro and, 173–74, 177–78, 184, 185, 186–87; *boitá* ritual and, 277, 278; *caboclos* and, 242–43; coming out period, 257–58; head shaving and cutting and, 259; hier- archical titles and, 109; men in Seja Hundé terreiro, 161–62, 193; Maria Emiliana da Piedade and, 177–78, 332 (n. 64); possession and, 256, 257, 260, 261, 275, 276–77, 279, 283, 284, 285, 289; ritual death and resurrection, 256, 257; ritual names and, 256, 260–61; Runhó and, 184, 185, 334 (nn. 100, 102); seclusion and, 92, 256, 257–58; Seja Hundé terreiro and, 160–62, 169–70, 190–91, 335 (nn. 118–19); as "slaves," 262, 347 (n. 48); social reintegration and,

260, 261; songs/dances/language of
vodun and, 259; speaking and, 260–61;
zandró ritual and, 272, 273–74, 275, 277
Vodunsis lè na sa gi, 261
Volta River, 5, 8, 11, 23, 221, 229
Voyage du Chevalier des Marchais en Guinée
(Labat), 21

Weber, Max, xiii, 52, 69
Weekly cycles, among African peoples, 14
West African towns and regions: Abeokuta,
16, 228, 305–6 (n. 84); Agoué, 27, 33, 60,
65; Aného, 15, 27, 31, 32, 33, 40; Apa, 21,
27, 29, 30, 31, 216; Ashanti region, 5, 229,
230, 231; Atakpamé area, 229, 231; Badagri,
13, 15, 27, 30, 31, 32, 40, 221, 232; Egbado
region, 3, 7, 12, 213, 228, 339 (n. 14); Grand-
Popo, 20, 30, 31; Hollidjè region, 12, 28, 213,
342 (n. 49); Ilê Ifé, 8, 9, 12, 230; Jakin, 21,
26, 29, 30, 31, 216, 220; Ké (Kétou), 9, 12,
28, 29, 61, 122, 205, 229, 230, 231; Ketonou,
31, 217, 219; Lagos, 13, 31, 32, 33, 40, 121,
202; Notsé, 11, 12, 246; Petit-Popo, 5, 6, 21,
22, 23, 219, 250; Savalou, 16, 17, 18, 51, 157,
229, 231, 232; Savè, 9, 12, 229, 230; Savi,
21, 30, 70, 71. *See also* Abomey; Allada
(city); Allada (kingdom); Benin, Gulf of;
Ouidah
Westermann, Diedrich, 11
White elite, 46, 134; African ethnic groups
and, 50; Cachoeira and, 147; *calundus*
tolerance/repression and, 90–92; living
arrangements of, 103
Wimberly, Fayette, 151
Witchcraft (*feitiçaria*), xvii, 63, 66; amulets
and charms and, 81–82; Bogum terreiro
and, 130; candomblés and, 95, 102;
healing, exorcism, and fortune telling,
79–80, 81, 85, 102, 113, 114, 313–14 (n. 29),
319 (n. 73); male sorcerers, 200; police
and, 82–83; Roça de Cima terreiro and,
144, 145; Roman Catholic Church and,
77–79; Seja Hundé terreiro and, 171
Women: candomblé leadership and, 96–98,
228, 316 (n. 30); Catholic lay brotherhoods

and, 54, 56, 57, 61, 168, 311 (n. 64); Catholic
sisterhoods, 61, 135, 144, 159, 168, 171; Creoles (*crioulos*) in candomblés, 116–17, 120;
founding candomblés and, 61; as initiates
in Jeje candomblés, 226–27; Jeje nation
in Bahia, eighteenth century, 41–42, 308
(n. 18); possession and, 97; as slaves for
tobacco plantations, 38, 41; *vodunsi*, 71–72.
See also Boa Morte sisterhood
World Conference on Orixá Tradition,
Second, 188

Xagulan, Oyesis, 188
Xangô, 108, 157, 223, 328 (nn. 119, 122), 340
(nn. 21, 23); bird associated with, 109;
celebration of, 203; Nagô terreiros and,
114, 192; Oyo kingdom and, 122, 220; Saint
Geronimo and, 183, 287; water cycle and,
236–37; wives of, 225, 227, 341 (n. 45);
Zé de Brechó and, 145
Xarene, *Tio* (African candomblé leader),
135, 136, 137, 139, 140, 180, 233
Xaxará, 181, 233
Xeré, 251
Xirê, 229, 234, 275, 276–77
Xògbónú, 29

Yabas, 215, 225, 226, 227
Yai, Olabiyi, 210
Yam festival, 282
Yehwe, 14, 15, 218–19
Yewa River, 15
Yivodo ritual, 283
Yoruba language, 3, 7, 63, 109, 110, 119, 121,
202, 231, 254; *Jeje* term and, 27, 29, 305–6
(n. 84)
Yoruba people, 16–17, 89, 211, 229, 230, 340
(n. 23); Adja people, contrasted with,
13–14; deities of, 14, 303 (n. 38); ethnic
groups of, 12, 302 (n. 26); identity in Brazil
and, 121; Idjé people and, 28; migrations
of, 8, 12; orixá cults, 14, 105, 208, 212, 213,
280, 340 (n. 16); Sakpata and, 232; slave
trade and, 29, 31. *See also* Nagô people of
Africa

Za people, 9

Zambi (supreme god), 240

Zandró ritual, 270, 271–77, 285, 294; baptism of the drums, 275–76; drumming and, 252, 254, 275–76, 349 (n. 70); Jeje-Mahi terreiros and, 204, 264, 266; Legba, Ogun Xoroque, and Aizan in, 268; Nagô part of ritual, 223–24, 234; ritual items used in, 272, 348 (n. 65)

Zan kpíkpé, 261

Zé Careca (José Magna Ferreira dos Santos), 170, 190

Zé de Brechó (José Maria Belchior), 136, 137, 139, 140, 154, 155, 162, 167, 180, 325 (n. 71), 328 (n. 110); *Sinhá* Abalhe and, 145, 155, 168, 330 (n. 27); origins and life of, 144–51, 326 (n. 76). *See also* Xarene, *Tio*

Zelim, 128–29, 142, 180, 188, 291

Zen-li, 83

Zerebetan (Kerebetan) terreiro, 115

Zerrem, 132

Zò, 157, 176, 328 (n. 119)

Zomadonu (vodun), 115

Zoogodô Bogum Malê Rundô. *See* Bogum terreiro

Zoogodô Bogum Malê Seja Hundé. *See* Seja Hundé terreiro

Zo Ogodo Dangara Seja Hundé. See Seja Hundé terreiro

Zoogodô term, 157–58

Zo ordeal, 117, 320 (n. 86)

Zou River, 12, 16, 18, 283

Zuntôno (Sinfrônio Eloi Pires), 203

www.ingramcontent.com/pod-product-compliance
Lightning Source LLC
Chambersburg PA
CBHW021806270326
41932CB00007B/79